AQA Science
Additional Science

Teacher's Book

New GCSE

Geoff Carr
Darren Forbes
Sam Holyman
Ruth Miller
Bev Cox
Niva Miles
Gavin Reeder
John Scottow
Series Editor
Lawrie Ryan

Nelson Thornes

Published in 2011 by:
Nelson Thornes Ltd
Delta Place
27 Bath Road
CHELTENHAM
GL53 7TH
United Kingdom

11 12 13 14 15 / 10 9 8 7 6 5 4 3 2 1

A catalogue record for this book is available from the British Library

ISBN 978 1 4085 0825 1

Cover photograph: Jack Peters/Getty Images (girls); Ruslan Gilmanshin/iStockphoto
(background)

Illustrations include artwork drawn by Tech-Set Ltd
Page make-up by Tech-Set Ltd

Printed and bound in Spain by GraphyCems

Additional Science

Contents

Welcome to AQA GCSE Science!

New AQA GCSE Science remains the only series to be endorsed and approved by AQA. This Teacher's Book is written and reviewed by experienced teachers who have worked closely with AQA on their specifications. This book is structured around the Student Book and offers guidance, advice, support for differentiation and lots of practical teaching ideas to give you what you need to teach the AQA specifications.

Learning objectives

These tell you what your students should know by the end of the lessons and relate to the learning objectives in the corresponding Student Book topic, although extra detail is provided for teachers.

Learning outcomes

These tell you what your students should be able to do to demonstrate that they have achieved against the learning objectives. These are differentiated where appropriate to provide suitable expectations for all your students. Higher Tier outcomes are labelled.

AQA Specification link-up: Biology B1.1

These open every spread so you can see the AQA specification references covered in your lessons, at a glance.

Lesson structure

This provides you with guidance and ideas for tackling topics in your lessons. There are short and long starter and plenary activities so you can decide how you structure your lesson. Explicit **support** and **extension** guidance is given for some starters and plenaries.

Support

These help you to give extra support to students who need it during the main part of your lesson.

Extend

These provide ideas for how to extend the learning for students aiming for higher grades.

Further teaching suggestions

These provide you with ideas for how you might extend the lesson or offer alternative activities. These may also include extra activities or suggestions for homework.

Summary answers

All answers to questions within the Student Book are found in the Teacher's Book.

Practical support

For every practical in the Student Book you will find this corresponding feature, which gives you a list of the equipment you will need to provide, safety references and additional teaching notes. There are also additional practicals given that are not found in the Student Book.

The following features are found in the Student Book, but you may find additional guidance to support them in the Teacher's Book:

 **Did you know ... ?**

 **How Science Works**

 **Maths skills**

Activity

How Science Works

There is a chapter dedicated to 'How Science Works' in the Student Book as well as embedded throughout topics and end of chapter questions. The teacher notes within this book give you detailed guidance on how to integrate 'How Science Works' into your teaching.

End of chapter pages

And at the end of each chapter you will find Summary answers and AQA Examination-style answers. You will also find;

Kerboodle resources **k**

Kerboodle is our online service that holds all of the electronic resources for the series. All of the resources that support the chapter that are provided on Kerboodle are listed in these boxes.

Where you see **k** in the Student Book, you will know that there is an electronic resource on Kerboodle to support that aspect.

Just log on to www.kerboodle.com to find out more.

AQA Practical suggestions

These list the suggested practicals from AQA that you need to be aware of. Support for these practicals can be found on Kerboodle, or are covered within the practical support section of the Teacher Book. The **k** indicates that there is a practical in Kerboodle. The ⚙ indicates that there is a 'How Science Works' worksheet in Kerboodle. The 📖 indicates that the practical is covered in this Teacher's Book.

Bump up your grades

These are written by AQA examiners giving advice on how students can pick up additional marks to improve their grades.

AQA Examiner's tip

These are written by AQA examiners giving advice on what students should remember for their exams and highlighting common errors.

B2 1.1 Animal and plant cells

Learning objectives

Students should learn:
- the functions of the different parts of animal and plant cells
- the differences between plant and animal and plant cells.

Learning outcomes

Most students should be able to:
- describe the structure of animal and plant cells
- describe the functions of the parts of animal and plant cells
- list the differences between animal and plant cells.

Some students should also be able to:
- describe the functions of the special structures in plant cells and algal cells.

Answers to in-text questions

a Nucleus, cytoplasm, cell membrane, mitochondria, ribosomes.

b Plant cells have a cell wall, chloroplasts and a permanent vacuole.

Support

- Give students an outline of a plant cell and an animal cell with labels to cut out and stick on.
- They could try making model cells using cardboard boxes and polythene bags. This could be a test of their ingenuity in finding different materials to represent the organelles. Run a competition, display the entries and award a small prize for the best one.

Extend

- Get students to find out more about how an electron microscope works and how it is used to look at cells. You can find some references in more advanced Biology texts such as *Tools, Techniques and Assessment in Biology*, Adds, Larkcom, Miller and Sutton (Nelson Advanced Science series).

Specification link-up: Biology B2.1

- Most human and animal cells have the following parts:
  - a *nucleus*, which controls the activities of the cell
  - cytoplasm, in which most of the chemical reactions take place
  - a cell membrane, which controls the passage of substances into and out of the cell
  - mitochondria, which is where most energy is released in respiration
  - ribosomes, which is where protein synthesis occurs. *[B2.1.1 a)]*
- Plant and algal cells also have a cell wall made of cellulose, which strengthens the cell. Plant cells often have:
  - chloroplasts, which absorb light energy to make food
  - a permanent vacuole filled with cell sap. *[B2.1.1 b)]*

Lesson structure

Starters

What does it do? – Write up a list of functions of parts of an animal cell on the board, splitting them up so that there is more than one function per part, e.g. 'controls activities' and 'contains chromosomes' for nucleus. Support students by providing a list of parts and asking them to match a part with a function. Extend students by giving them the functions and getting them to name the parts. Let them work through the list by themselves and then check each other's responses. *(5 minutes)*

Plant or animal? – Show a drawing or electron microscope image of a typical plant cell. (Search the internet for 'plant cell' images.) Students to say whether it is a plant or an animal cell, giving reasons. Get them to suggest labels for the parts and decide whether these are common features of cells or special to plant cells. *(10 minutes)*

Main

- This exercise is designed to show students that what they can see using a light microscope is limited, and that structures such as mitochondria and ribosomes are only visible using electron microscopy. The students could work in groups, each having light microscopes with slides of stained cheek cells, onion bulb inner epidermal cells and algal cells (a filamentous alga such as *Spirogyra* would be suitable) and a set of electron micrographs of plant and animal cells (there are plenty in A level text books). They could identify structures in both, and make a comparison of what they can observe from the slides and from the electron micrographs.

- If the magnification of the light microscope is given and the magnification of the electron micrographs known, they can work out how much bigger the latter are. Gather together and discuss the information, particularly with respect to the structures revealed by electron microscopy. Ask: 'Why do they all appear to have membranes around them?'

- Plant cells, such as rhubarb petiole epidermis or the inner epidermal cells from onion bulbs, are relatively easy to mount, stain and observe using light microscopes. In order for students to see cell structures, some staining is advisable. Filamentous algae are easy to find and easy to mount. They will not need staining. The procedure, (see 'Practical support') could be demonstrated to the students and they can then have a go at making their own slides and drawing and labelling some cells.

- Using safe, sterile procedures, students could make slides of their own cheek cells. (See 'Practical support'). Some cells could be drawn and labelled.

Plenaries

Our wonderful world – There are some excellent scanning electron micrographs (SEM) and transmission electron micrographs (TEM) of cells. Show a selection (from www.cellsalive.com) with a 'Guess what this is' attached to each one. This would help students appreciate the complexity of some structures. *(5 minutes)*

A question of size – A typical cell is $20\ \mu m$ wide ($0.002\,mm$). You will need to talk about scales and the relationship between millimetres and micrometres. Support students by giving them a sheet of the units of measurement involved and their relationship to one another. They can then calculate how many cells will fit across the page of their Student Book. Extend students by giving them extra examples to work out. *(10 minutes)*

Practical support

Looking at cells

Equipment and materials required

Light microscopes (at least one per group of two or three students), clean microscope slides and cover slips, onion bulbs or rhubarb petiole, scalpels, scissors and mounted needles, dilute iodine solution in dropping bottles (CLEAPSS Hazcard 54), tissues, eye protection.

Details

Cut an onion in half and remove the thin inner epidermis of the leaves with forceps. This can be cut up into small squares about 5 mm square. Place a square of epidermis on a slide, trying to get it as flat as possible, and then place a drop of dilute iodine solution on top to stain the cells. Place a cover slip over the top, lowering it carefully down so that air bubbles are not trapped. Place the slide under the low power of the microscope, focusing carefully. Then switch to high power and focus using the fine adjustment.

Safety: Follow CLEAPSS Hazcard 54B Iodine.

Cheek cells

Equipment and materials required

Light microscopes (at least one per group of two or three students), new cotton buds, clean microscope slides and cover slips, dilute methylene blue solution, disinfectant, or another approved way, for disposal of used cotton buds and slides.

Details

The inside of the cheek is gently scraped using a sterile cotton bud and the scrapings smeared on to the middle of a clean microscope slide. A drop of dilute methylene blue is added on top of the cells and covered with a cover slip. The slide can then be observed under the microscope. Some gentle pressure might be needed to spread the cells out, so that they are easier to see. When finished, place prepared slides and cotton buds in a container of freshly prepared sodium hypochlorite solution.

Safety: (See CLEAPSS Student Safety Sheet 3 and follow Society of Biology guidelines.) CLEAPSS Hazcard 89 Sodium chlorate(I) – corrosive.

Cells, tissues and organs

Animal and plant cells

B2 1.1 — Animal and plant cells Ⓚ

Learning objectives

- What do the different parts of your cells do?
- Are human cells the same as other animal cells?
- How do plant and algal cells differ from animal cells?

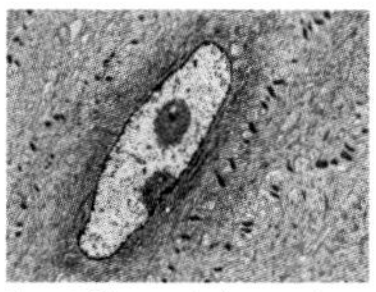

Figure 1 Diagrams of cells are much easier to understand than the real thing seen under a microscope. This picture shows a magnified animal cell.

The Earth is covered with a great variety of living things. However, they all have one thing in common – they are all made up of cells. Most cells are very small. You can only see them using a microscope.

The **light microscopes** in schools may magnify things several hundred times. Scientists have found out even more about cells using **electron microscopes**. These can magnify things more than a hundred thousand times!

Animal cells – structure and function

All cells have some features in common. We can see these clearly in animal cells. The cells of your body have these features, just like the cells of every other living thing.

- The **nucleus** – controls all the activities of the cell. It contains the genes on the chromosomes. They carry the instructions for making new cells or new organisms.
- The **cytoplasm** – a liquid gel in which most of the chemical reactions needed for life take place.
- The **cell membrane** – controls the passage of substances into and out of the cell.
- The **mitochondria** – structures in the cytoplasm where oxygen is used and most of the energy is released during respiration.
- **Ribosomes** – where protein synthesis takes place. All the proteins needed in the cell are made here.

Plant cells – structure and function

Plants are very different organisms from animals. They make their own food by photosynthesis. They stay in one place, and do not move their whole bodies about from one place to another.

Plant cells have all the features of a typical animal cell, but they also contain features that are needed for their very different way of life. Algae are simple aquatic organisms. They also make their own food and have many similar features to plant cells.

Examiner's tip

Remember that not all plant cells have chloroplasts. Don't confuse chloroplasts and chlorophyll.

All plant and algal cells have:

- a cell wall made of **cellulose** that strengthens the cell and gives it support.

Many (but not all) plant cells also have these other features:

- **Chloroplasts** are found in all the green parts of the plant. They are green because they contain the green substance **chlorophyll**. Chlorophyll absorbs light energy to make food by photosynthesis. Root cells do not have chloroplasts because they are underground and do not photosynthesise.
- A **permanent vacuole** is a space in the cytoplasm filled with cell sap. This is important for keeping the cells rigid to support the plant.

links

For more information on photosynthesis, look at B2 2.1 Photosynthesis.

a What are the main features found in all living cells?
b How do plant cells differ from animal cells?

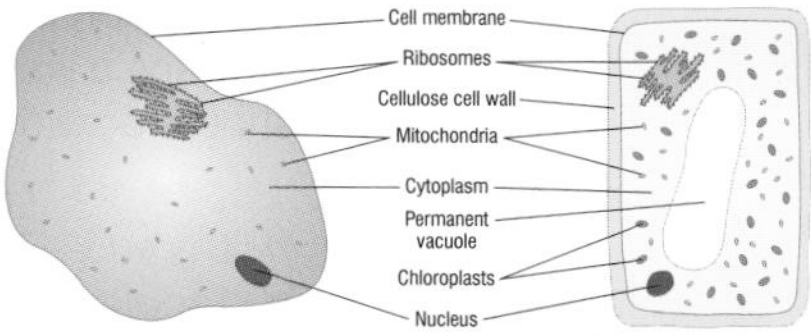

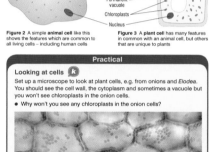

Figure 2 A simple **animal cell** like this shows the features which are common to all living cells – including human cells

Figure 3 A **plant cell** has many features in common with an animal cell, but others that are unique to plants

Labels: Cell membrane, Ribosomes, Cellulose cell wall, Mitochondria, Cytoplasm, Permanent vacuole, Chloroplasts, Nucleus

?? Did you know …?

Animal cells vary in size but we can only see most of them using a microscope. Eggs are the biggest animal cells. Unfertilised ostrich eggs are the biggest of all – they have a mass of around 1.35 kg!

Practical

Looking at cells Ⓚ

Set up a microscope to look at plant cells, e.g. from onions and *Elodea*. You should see the cell wall, the cytoplasm and sometimes a vacuole but you won't see chloroplasts in the onion cells.

- Why won't you see any chloroplasts in the onion cells?

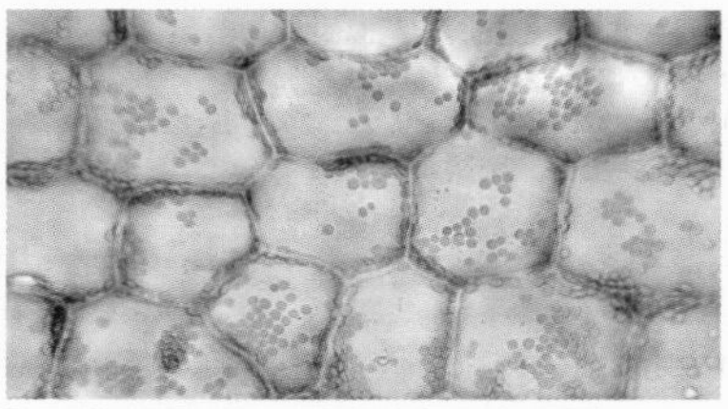

Figure 4 Microscopes can be used to look at the features of a plant cell

Examiner's tip

Practise labelling an animal cell and a plant cell. You need to know the functions of each part of a cell. For example, chloroplasts contain chlorophyll, which absorbs light energy for photosynthesis. Write the functions of the parts on the diagram.

Summary questions

1 a List the main structures you would expect to find in an animal cell.
   b You would find all the things we have in animal cells also in a plant or algal cell. There are three extra features that are found in plant cells but not animal cells. What are they?
   c What are the main functions of these three extra structures?

2 Why are the nucleus and the mitochondria so important in all cells?

3 Chloroplasts are found in many plant cells but not all of them. Give an example of plant cells without chloroplasts and explain why they have none.

Key points

- Most human cells are like most other animal cells and contain a nucleus, cytoplasm, cell membrane, mitochondria and ribosomes.
- Plant and algal cells contain all the structures seen in animal cells as well as a cell wall. Many plant cells also contain chloroplasts and a permanent vacuole filled with sap.

2 / 3

Further teaching suggestions

Observing cytoplasm

- Using rhubarb petiole or onion bulb epidermis will not show chloroplasts, so a demonstration of some moss leaf cells or leaves of a water plant such as *Elodea* which could be mounted in water and projected. The cells will be living and so it is possible that the streaming of the cytoplasm can be observed.

Computer simulations

- If you have access to computers, you could use them to model the relative size of different cells, organelles and molecules for students.

Summary answers

1 a nucleus, cytoplasm, cell membrane, mitochondria, ribosomes
   b Cell wall, chloroplasts, permanent vacuole.
   c Cell wall provides support and strengthening for the cell and the plant; chloroplasts for photosynthesis; permanent vacuole keeps the cells rigid to support the plant.

2 The nucleus controls all the activities of the cell and contains the instructions for making new cells or new organisms. Mitochondria are the site of aerobic respiration, so they produce energy for the cell.

3 Root cells in a plant do not have chloroplasts because they don't carry out photosynthesis – they are underground so have no light.

B2 1.2

Bacteria and yeast

AQA Specification link-up: Biology B2.1

- A bacterial cell consists of cytoplasm and a membrane surrounded by a cell wall; the genes are not in a distinct nucleus. [B2.1.1 c)]
- Yeast is a single-celled organism. Yeast cells have a nucleus, cytoplasm and a membrane surrounded by a cell wall. [B2.1.1 d)]

Learning objectives

Students should learn:

- the structure of a bacterial cell
- that the genes in a bacterial cell are not in a distinct nucleus
- the structure of a yeast cell.

Learning outcomes

Most students should be able to:

- describe the structure of a bacterial cell
- describe the structure of a yeast cell
- list the differences between bacterial and yeast cells.

Some students should also be able to:

- compare animal, plant and algal cells with bacteria and yeasts.

Lesson structure

Starters

What are bacteria really like? – Show a clip from the internet of an advert for bleach or a sterilising agent that has animations or cartoons of germs. How does this picture fit with reality? Are there any similarities between the pretend bacteria and real ones? *(5 minutes)*

Marmite – love it or hate it? – Bring out a jar of Marmite. Pass it around for students to smell. Ask if anyone knows what it is made from. Make the students write down a brief description of what yeast is, and what it does. Support students by prompting them to produce a limited description. Extend students by asking them about wild yeasts, they should provide detailed descriptions with a variety of examples. *(10 minutes)*

Main

- Produce a PowerPoint presentation or exposition to show the structure of a typical bacterium. Bring out the features which all bacterial cells have and then add in some features that may be found, relating these to their function (flagella, slime capsules). Create a list of questions for the students to fill in as you proceed through the exposition. Compare a bacterial cell with a plant and an animal cell and bring out the differences.

- Look at prepared slides of bacteria under the microscope. Students will not be able to see very much, so project some TEM and SEM images. Discuss how difficult it is to see structures and thus difficult to identify different bacteria. Simple classification is based on shape, but more detailed identification depends on their growth and biochemistry.

- Remind the students of previous work on pathogens. In addition, bring in the useful bacteria (for yoghurt, cheese making and antibiotic production). Link some pathogens with the diseases they cause.

- Set up a culture of yeast at the beginning of the lesson. Show some pictures of yeast cells and remind students that yeast is a fungus. Then let them make slides of the culture. Examine the culture at the end of the lesson when there should be some budding visible. Get students to make sketches of the budding process.

- If the yeast culture is active, there should be frothing. Bubble some of the gas given off through limewater and get the students to say what is going on. Link this in with the uses of yeast and the fact that it can respire aerobically and anaerobically.

Plenaries

Am I a yeast or a bacterium? – Prepare a series of statements about yeast and bacterial cells, such as 'I have a flagellum', 'I have a cell wall', 'I have a true nucleus' (some common features and some specific ones as well as sizes). Write these up as a numbered list on the board and get students to write 'Y', 'B' or 'Both' in their notebooks. Check the answers and get students to agree on the list of similarities and differences. *(5 minutes)*

Job lists – Show the students an imaginary 'To do' list for a teacher (you can put some humorous bits in). Write down two 'To do' list headings on the board: one for bacteria and one for yeasts. Ask for suggestions from the students – these should include both positive and negative aspects of the roles of these organisms. Support students by providing prompt cards which can be sorted into the respective job lists. Extend students by providing them with some background reading about the roles of bacteria and yeasts and get them to select more detail. *(10 minutes)*

Answers to in-text questions

- **a** Smaller, have genetic material but no nucleus, may have plasmids.
- **b** Bigger, have a nucleus.

Support

- Provide students with blank bacterial cells which they can add features to, as the activity proceeds.

Extend

- Get students to find out about ginger beer plants and how ginger beer can be made from simple ingredients.

Further teaching suggestions

Bread making demonstration
- Set up a demonstration of the use of yeast in bread making. Have dough with and without yeast added and take measurements of the rise in the dough. There are many variations of this investigation: varying the temperature, addition of vitamin C. Get students to think about the type of respiration that is going on.

Bacteria in the body
- Get students to think about the presence of bacteria in and on the body. Discuss the importance of bacteria in the gut – both good and bad ones.

Table of differences
- Build up a comprehensive table of differences between bacterial, yeast, animal, plant and algal cells.

Cells, tissues and organs

Bacteria and yeast

B2 1.2 Bacteria and yeast ⓚ

Learning objectives
- What are bacterial cells like?
- How are yeast cells different from bacterial, plant and animal cells?

Bacteria are single-celled living organisms that are much smaller than animal and plant cells. Most bacteria are less than 1 μm in length. You could fit hundreds of thousands of bacteria on to the full stop at the end of this sentence. You can't see individual bacteria without a powerful microscope.

When you culture bacteria on an agar plate you grow many millions of bacteria. This enables you to see the **bacterial colony** with your naked eye.

Cell membrane — Slime capsule — Cell wall — Plasmids
Cytoplasm —
Genetic material —
— Flagella
— 1 μm —

Figure 1 Bacteria come in a variety of shapes, but they all have the same basic structure

Bacterial cells

Each bacterium is a single cell. It is made up of cytoplasm surrounded by a membrane and a cell wall. Inside the bacterial cell is the **genetic material**. Unlike animal, plant and algal cells, the genes are not contained in a nucleus. The long strand of DNA (the bacterial chromosome) is usually circular and found free in the cytoplasm.

Many bacterial cells also contain **plasmids**, which are small circular bits of DNA. These carry extra genetic information. Bacteria may have a slime capsule around the outside of the cell wall. Some types of bacterium have at least one flagellum (plural: flagella), a long protein strand that lashes about. These bacteria use their flagella to move themselves around.

Although some bacteria cause disease, many are harmless. Some are actually really useful to us. We use them to make food like yoghurt and cheese. Others are used in sewage treatment and to make medicines.

a How are bacteria different from animal and plant cells?

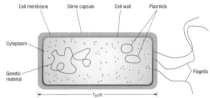

Figure 2 Bacteria come in several different shapes and sizes. This helps us to identify them under the microscope. *Streptococcus* causes sore throats and *E. coli* live in your gut.

Yeast

Another type of microorganism that is very useful to people is yeast. Yeasts are single-celled organisms. Each yeast cell has a nucleus containing the genetic material, cytoplasm, and a membrane surrounded by a cell wall.

The cells vary in size but most are about 3–4 μm. This makes them bigger than bacteria but still very small.

The main way in which yeasts reproduce is by **asexual budding**. This involves a new yeast cell growing out from the original cell to form a new separate yeast organism.

b How do yeast cells differ from bacterial cells?

Yeast cells are specialised to be able to survive for a long time even when there is very little oxygen available. When yeast cells have plenty of oxygen they use **aerobic respiration**. They use oxygen to break down sugar to provide energy for the cell. During this process they produce water and carbon dioxide as waste products.

However, when there isn't much oxygen, yeast can use **anaerobic respiration**. When yeast cells break down sugar in the absence of oxygen, they produce **ethanol** and carbon dioxide.

Ethanol is commonly referred to as alcohol. The anaerobic respiration of yeast is sometimes called **fermentation**.

We have used yeast for making bread and alcoholic drinks almost as far back as human records go. We know yeast was used to make bread in Egypt 6000 years ago. Not only that, some ancient wine found in Iran is over 7000 years old.

— Nucleus
— Cell wall
— Cytoplasm
— Cell membrane

Figure 3 Yeast cells – these microscopic organisms have been useful to us for centuries

?? Did you know ...?

In Ethiopia, natural yeast from the air is enough to make injera, the traditional bread. The dough is left for a couple of days before it is cooked for the yeast to produce carbon dioxide bubbles, which give injera its texture.

AQA Examiner's tip

Be clear about the similarities and differences between animal, plant, algal, bacterial and yeast cells.

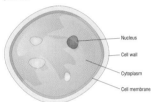

Figure 4 Brewers use the ethanol produced by yeast in their alcoholic drinks

Summary questions

1 Copy and complete using the words below:
 nucleus bacteria cell wall microorganism yeast plasmids
 .... and .... are both types of .... Bacterial cells do not contain a .... but often have .... Bacteria and yeast cells both have a ....

2 a What is unusual about the genetic material in bacterial cells?
 b Which are bigger, bacterial cells or yeast cells?
 c What are flagella and what are they used for?

3 Make a table to compare the structures in animal, plant and algal, bacterial and yeast cells.

Key points
- A bacterial cell consists of cytoplasm and a membrane surrounded by a cell wall. The genes are not in a distinct nucleus.
- Yeast is a single-celled organism. Each cell has a nucleus, cytoplasm and a membrane surrounded by a cell wall.

Summary answers

1 bacteria/yeast, yeast/bacteria, microorganism, nucleus, plasmids, cell wall

2 a It isn't contained in a nucleus and there are extra genes known as plasmids separate from the main genetic material.
 b Yeast cells.
 c Flagella are long protein strands found in some bacteria which are used for moving the bacteria about.

3
Feature	Animal cell	Plant or algal cell	Bacterial cell	Yeast cell
Cell membrane	yes	yes	yes	yes
Nucleus	yes	yes	no	yes
Plasmids	no	no	yes	no
Chloroplasts	no	yes	no	no
Cell wall	no	yes	yes	yes
Cytoplasm	yes	yes	yes	yes

B2 1.3 Specialised cells

Specification link-up: Biology B2.1

- Cells may be specialised to carry out a particular function. *[B2.1.1 e)]*
- Relate the structure of different types of cells to their function. *[B2.1]*
  Controlled Assessment: AS4.3 Collect primary and secondary data. *[AS4.3.1 a)]*, *[AS4.3.2 c) d)]*

Learning objectives

Students should learn:
- that cells may be specialised to carry out particular functions.

Learning outcomes

Most students should be able to:
- recognise different types of cells
- relate the structure of given types of cells to their functions in a tissue or an organ.

Some students should also be able to:
- relate the structure of unfamiliar cells to other functions in a tissue or organ.

Answers to in-text questions
a The middle section.
b To breakdown the outer layers of the egg.

Lesson structure

Starters

How big can cells be? – Show a goose egg, explaining that it is a single cell, and break it on to a plate. The students may be able to see the place where the embryo will develop (the germinal disc). Discuss with the students why it is so big and how it is specialised. If possible show an empty ostrich egg. *(5 minutes)*

Do you know what this is? – Project some images of specialised cells – do not label them but give each one a number. Support students by giving them a list of the names. Extend students by asking them to name the ones they know and have a guess at the ones they do not. Check the answers at the end. *(10 minutes)*

Main

- 'Observing specialised cells: Root hair cells'. This practical activity can be prepared a few days before the lesson (see 'Practical support' for full details). It can be set up as a demonstration or for groups of students. This exercise introduces some of the concepts of 'How Science Works', such as making single measurements, if the micrometer idea is used.
- Video footage of sperm cell activity is readily available. There are clips available which show fertilisation, emphasising the difference in sizes of egg cells and sperm and also the relative numbers.
- Prepared slides of rat testes could be available for students to look at, observing the different stages in sperm development. Prepare a worksheet with some drawings of different stages so that students can look for specific features and make labelled drawings of their own. This activity can link with the showing of the video.
- **How structure is related to function in animal cells** – Show students pictures of a range of different animal cells, to include blood cells, neurons, muscle cells, cells from glands (secretory cells), fat cells and gametes. Get the students to make a list of the cells, their special features and how each specialised cell differs from a generalised animal cell. Allow the students to make their notes individually and then go through the cells again, discussing the important points.
- **How structure is related to function in plant cells** – This could be presented in a similar manner to the above, using a range of plant cells, such as palisade cells, guard cells, root hair cells, lignified cells (fibres) and epidermal cells. Cells from the cortex of the stem or the root could be used as generalised plant cells.
- Students are required to be able to relate the structure of different types of cell to their functions in a tissue or an organ, so these exercises will give them a record for future reference and revision.

Plenaries

20 Questions – One student goes out of the room and the others decide which type of specialised cell they are. The student comes back in and asks the rest of the class questions about their specialisation to guess what they are. Repeat several times. *(5 minutes)*

What can I do and how can I do it? – Project images of the specialised cells mentioned/described in the text (fat cell, cone cell, root hair cell, sperm cell) but do not label them. Ask students to write down the function of each cell and to state a particular feature of each which is related to its function (for example, for the fat cell, storage of fat and little normal cytoplasm). Support students by giving them the names of the cells, then asking them to state a feature. Extend students by adding extra examples from the activities suggested in the main lesson. *(10 minutes)*

Support
- Use domino-style cards with specialised cells on one side and their special features on the other. Ask the students to play with these as dominoes. Alter the number of cards and the labelling according to ability.

Extend
- Suggest to students that they design a special cell found in an alien or undiscovered species. Ask them to give it an interesting, unusual or gruesome feature and make it scientifically feasible.

Practical support

Observing specialised cells – Root hair cells

Equipment and materials required
Cress seedlings with root hairs, forceps, cling film, blotting paper or filter paper, digital camera, binocular microscopes, Petri dishes, micrometer eyepiece, if available.

Details
A few days before the lesson, sow some cress seeds on damp blotting paper or filter paper in Petri dishes. Handle the seedlings by the cotyledons using forceps. When ready to use them, remove the lids and cover with cling film to keep the moisture levels high. Place the dishes under a binocular microscope and take digital photographs down the microscope. The photographs can then be stuck in the students' records. This can either be set up as a demonstration or groups of students could work together on the activity.

If a micrometer eyepiece is inserted in the microscope, the length of some of the root hairs can be measured. The measurements can either be left as eyepiece units (eu) or converted to millimetres if the eyepiece is calibrated. This exercise will reinforce the extent to which the root hairs are specialised for the increase of the SA (surface area) available for the uptake of water. Students should consider the following questions:

- How is this cell different in structure from a generalised plant cell?
- How does the difference in structure help it to carry out its function?

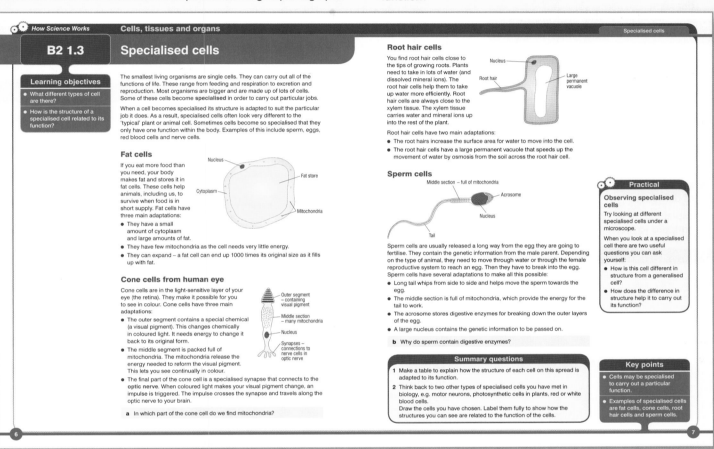

Further teaching suggestions

Fun with colour vision
- Students could have fun with their colour vision by staring at brightly coloured cardboard and then at white paper to perceive residual false colour images. Search the internet for 'flags' to illustrate such after-images. In the retina, there are three types of cone: sensitive to red, green or blue. When you stare at a particular colour for too long, these receptors get 'tired' or 'fatigued'. After looking at the flag with the strange colours, your receptors that are tired do not work as well. Therefore the information from all the different colour receptors is not in balance.

Single-celled organisms
- Show images of single-celled organisms as a contrast to specialised cells. Good examples to find on the internet are chlamydomonas, paramecium and amoeba, and then discuss how these organisms can carry out all the functions of life.

Am I colour-blind?
- Search the internet for 'colour-blind' to find tests you can use to investigate colour-blindness further.

Summary answers

1 **Fat cells:** not much cytoplasm so room for fat storage; ability to expand to store fat; few mitochondria as they do not need much energy, so do not waste space.

Cone cells from human eye: outer segment containing visual pigment; middle segment packed full of mitochondria; specialised nerve ending.

Root hair cells: no chloroplasts so no photosynthesis; root hair increases SA (surface area) for water uptake; vacuole to facilitate water movement; close to xylem tissue.

Sperm cells: tail for movement to egg; mitochondria to provide energy for movement; acrosome full of digestive enzymes to break down the outside layers of the egg cell; large nucleus full of genetic material.

2 [Any two cells chosen, appropriately labelled and annotated.]

B2 1.4

Diffusion

Learning objectives

Students should learn:

- that substances, such as oxygen, move in and out of cells by a process called diffusion
- the factors that affect the rate of diffusion.

Learning outcomes

Most students should be able to:

- define diffusion in cells
- list factors that affect the rate of diffusion
- describe how cells may be adapted to facilitate diffusion.

Some students should also be able to:

- explain the factors that affect the rate of diffusion
- explain in detail how cells may be adapted to facilitate diffusion.

Specification link-up: Biology B2.1

- Dissolved substances can move into and out of cells by diffusion. *[B2.1.2 a)]*
- Diffusion is the spreading of the particles of a gas, or of any substance in solution, resulting in a net movement from a region where they are of a higher concentration to a region with a lower concentration. The greater the difference in concentration, the faster the rate of diffusion. *[B2.1.2 b)]*
- Oxygen required for respiration passes through cell membranes by diffusion. *[B2.1.2 c)]*

    Controlled Assessment: AS4.3 Collect primary and secondary data. *[AS4.3.1 a)]*, *[AS4.3.2 c) d)]*

Lesson structure

Starters

Watching diffusion – In advance of the lesson set up a boiling tube of water with a few crystals of potassium permanganate in the bottom of the tube. Using a digital camera take shots of the tube every 20 minutes for several hours. Use these to create a PowerPoint slideshow, projecting the shots in sequence. Get the students to comment on what they think is happening and why. *(5 minutes)*

Human diffusion – Ask the students if they have ever been in a crowd coming out from a major football match or other event. Show a slide of a big crowd. Ask what happens to the concentration of people as they move away from the stadium. Draw an analogy to diffusion in particles in that they go from an area of high concentration to an area of low concentration. Support students by giving them this definition of diffusion and a broken sentence to reassemble. Extend students by asking them to sort the strengths and weaknesses of the analogy – where is it valid and where does it break down? *(10 minutes)*

Main

- It is possible to demonstrate and measure the rate of diffusion of ammonia along a glass tube using litmus paper (see 'Demonstration support' for full details). This shows that the ammonia diffuses along the tube from an area where it is in high concentration to a lower concentration. It is possible to work out the rate of diffusion. The overall time to diffuse 28 cm can be found and the individual times for the diffusion from one 2 cm mark to the next can be recorded. This gives several possibilities for discussion and calculation. It also introduces 'How Science Works' concepts.

Additional suggestions include:

- Comparing the rate of diffusion of the strong solution with that of a weaker solution by setting up an identical tube and timing the change in colour of the litmus squares.
- Measuring the diffusion of liquids. Cut wells into the agar gel dyed with universal indicator or hydrogencarbonate indicator. Add acid at various concentrations into the wells, allow a set time and then measure the extent of the colour change around each well. Alkali could be used as well as acid for different colour changes.
- There are some good internet-based animations illustrating diffusion. Make the point that the length of the diffusion pathway is also important hence thin layers on absorbent tissues.
- If you have access to computers, you could use them to model the process of diffusion for students.

Plenaries

Surface area to volume – Get students to fold up a sheet of A4 paper as small as they can get it, without tearing. Measure the dimensions and try to fit it into a matchbox. Relate this to diffusion rate. *(5 minutes)*

Defining diffusion – Give the students the key words of the topic and get them to write a definition of diffusion and the factors which affect the rate. Support students by providing a sentence or sentences into which they fit the key words. Extend students by asking them to include in their definition an explanation of how cells in living organisms are adapted to make diffusion more rapid. *(10 minutes)*

Support

- Provide students with figures and prepared grids on which to plot the results of the experiments.

Extend

- Ask students to consider how well single-celled organisms are adapted to facilitate diffusion. How big could they grow? Is there a limit?

Practical support

Demonstrating and measuring the rate of diffusion

Equipment and materials required

Glass tubes, 30 cm long and of diameter 20 mm should be marked using a felt tip pen at 2 cm intervals starting at 10 cm from one end, each tube requires two corks, one ordinary one and one which has had a core of cork taken out the cavity plugged with cotton wool, felt-tip pen, litmus paper, wire or glass rod, strong ammonia solution and a stopwatch.

Details

It is possible to demonstrate and measure the rate of diffusion of ammonia along a glass tube. Litmus paper is used to show the progress of the gas along the tube. Small squares of pink litmus paper are dipped into distilled water, shaken and placed inside each tube with a piece of wire or a glass rod. The pieces of litmus paper should be pushed into position and lined up with the markings on the outside of the tube. Saturate the cotton wool in the cork at one end with a strong ammonia solution, then place it in the end of the tube, start the clock or stopwatch and time how long it takes each piece of litmus paper to turn from pink to completely blue.

Safety: Care is needed when using the strong ammonia solution – eye protection should be worn. CLEAPSS Hazcard 5/6. Ventilating the laboratory.

Diffusion of glucose

Equipment and materials required

Visking tubing, beaker of water, glucose solution (Benedict's).

Details

The diffusion of glucose through a cell membrane can be demonstrated by placing a solution of glucose in Visking tubing and immersing the tubing in a beaker of water. The water is tested for glucose at the start of the experiment and then again after 20 minutes.

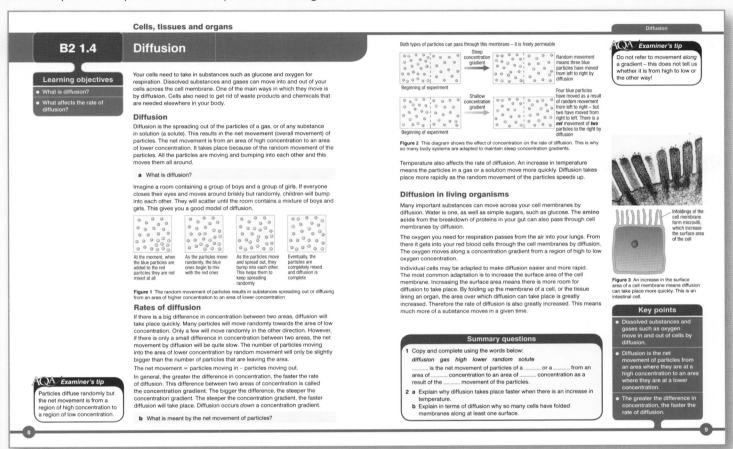

Further teaching suggestions

More diffusion in liquids

- Give students boiling tubes containing clear gelatine up to a marked level. They can then pour a thin layer of gelatine coloured with methylene blue on to the top, allow it to set and then pour on a quantity of clear gelatine equal to the volume in the bottom of the tube. (Levels could be marked for them.) The tubes should be left for a week and then the distribution of the blue colour recorded.

Two-way diffusion

- Pour some gelatine into a boiling tube and colour it with 10 drops of cresol red (it will go yellow). Mix thoroughly and allow to set. Pour a further layer of clear gelatine on top of the coloured layer. Allow this layer to set. Finally add about 5 cm³ of ammonia solution to the top of the tube and insert a bung. Leave the tube for about 4 days. The cresol red will diffuse into the clear gelatine and the ammonia will diffuse into the gelatine. This can be shown by the cresol red turning from yellow to red.

Answers to in-text questions

a The spreading out of the particles of a gas, or of any substance in solution.

b The difference between the numbers of particles moving in and those moving out of cells.

Summary answers

1 diffusion, gas/solute, solute/gas, high, lower, random

2 a The oxygen moves along a concentration gradient from a region of high to low oxygen concentration.

b Folded membranes provide an increased surface area so diffusion can take place more quickly.

B2 1.5 — Tissues and organs

Learning objectives

Students should learn:

- that a tissue is a group of cells with similar structure and function
- that organs are made of tissues.

Learning outcomes

Most students should be able to:

- define a tissue
- describe some plant and animal tissues
- understand that organs are made up of tissues working together to carry out a function.

Some students should also be able to:

- explain how organs are adapted for the exchange of materials.

AQA Specification link-up: Biology B2.2

- Large multicellular organisms develop systems for exchanging materials. During the development of a multicellular organism, cells differentiate so that they can perform different functions. [B2.2.1 a)]
- A tissue is a group of cells with similar structure and function. Examples of tissues include:
  - muscular tissue, which can contract to bring about movement
  - glandular tissue, which can produce substances such as enzymes and hormones
  - epithelial tissue, which covers some parts of the body. [B2.2.1 b)]
- Organs are made of tissues. One organ may contain several tissues. The stomach is an organ that contains:
  - muscular tissue, to churn the contents
  - glandular tissue, to produce digestive juices
  - epithelial tissue, to cover the outside and the inside of the stomach. [B2.2.1 c)]

Lesson structure

Starters

Sentences – Give the students the words 'cell', 'tissue', 'organ' and 'function'. They have to write down four simple sentences, one with each of these words in. The idea is to find out what they understand so far about the words. On completion, get some of the students to read out their sentences and discuss as a class. Support students by providing them with simple sentences which they have to complete, choosing the correct word. Extend students by asking them to compose an additional sentence containing all four words. *(5 minutes)*

Schools and cells – What jobs do the various members of the school team do? Make a list of who does what. Draw out that the various staff members can be seen as being parts of teams, each team with an overall function, e.g. the individual teaching staff are part of a department responsible for a subject, or in pastoral terms are part of looking after a year group or a house. Draw an analogy with cells. *(10 minutes)*

Main

- Levels of organisation – Label some toy building bricks of one colour 'Cell' and fit them together. On the back of the block formed stick a label 'Tissue'. Make some more 'Tissue' blocks from 'Cells' of other colours. Stick these together and label it 'Organ'. Have several of these and place them in a circle on the floor or the bench labelled 'Organ system'. Get the students to identify some organ systems and work back suggesting the organs, tissues and cells involved.

- Microscope work – look at slides of various individual cells and of tissues such as fat and muscle. Identify the similarities between the cells of a tissue.

- Use a torso model to gather the students around and identify various organs and then the systems to which they belong. Discuss the functions of the organs and the systems, particularly with respect to the exchange of materials. Create a worksheet for students to summarise the various systems and their relationship to one another.

- Show slides of a range of plant tissues e.g. palisade, mesophyll, spongy mesophyll, epidermis, parenchyma, xylem and phloem. Discuss their functions and how exchange of materials is achieved.

Plenaries

CTOS – Give the students a piece of scrap A4 with a blank side. Draw lines on to break it into four sections. Get them to write in big letters 'C', 'T', 'O' and 'S' on the paper and fold along the lines to make a little leaflet which can display each of the letters. Display or write on the board items which are a cell, a tissue, an organ or a system. The students have to fold their leaflet to the appropriate letter and hold it up. *(5 minutes)*

Matching game – Using a Java interactive exercise generation programme, such as the excellent one found at www.quia.com, draw out a list of various cells, tissues, organs and systems and write out definitions for them. Use Quia or similar to create digital flashcards with the name on one side and the definition on the other or alternatively a pairs-type matching game. Play this either as a class or if computers are available as a class IT exercise. Support students by restricting the number of cards and simplifying the definitions. Extend students by having a larger number of cards and making the definitions and links more challenging. *(10 minutes)*

Support

- Provide students with blank outlines of different cells and ask them to add structures and labels from their observations.

Extend

- Let students carry out a more detailed study of the exchange of materials in an organ system (e.g. excretory system, digestive system).

Further teaching suggestions

The circulatory system

- How necessary is the circulatory system? Review a range of animals from different phyla and consider how materials are circulated and exchanged. This links cells, tissues and organs as well as considering that increase in complexity depends on a good circulatory system.

Drawing analogies

- Show pictures of the pipes and console of a church organ, especially details of the writing on the voicing stops. Ask students to draw analogies between this type of organ and the biological meaning of the word 'organ'– similarities and differences?

Function and appearance

- Show the students some more plant tissues, e.g. water storage tissue, aerenchyma, modified epidermis, collenchymas. Ask the students if they could determine the function of the tissue from its appearance.

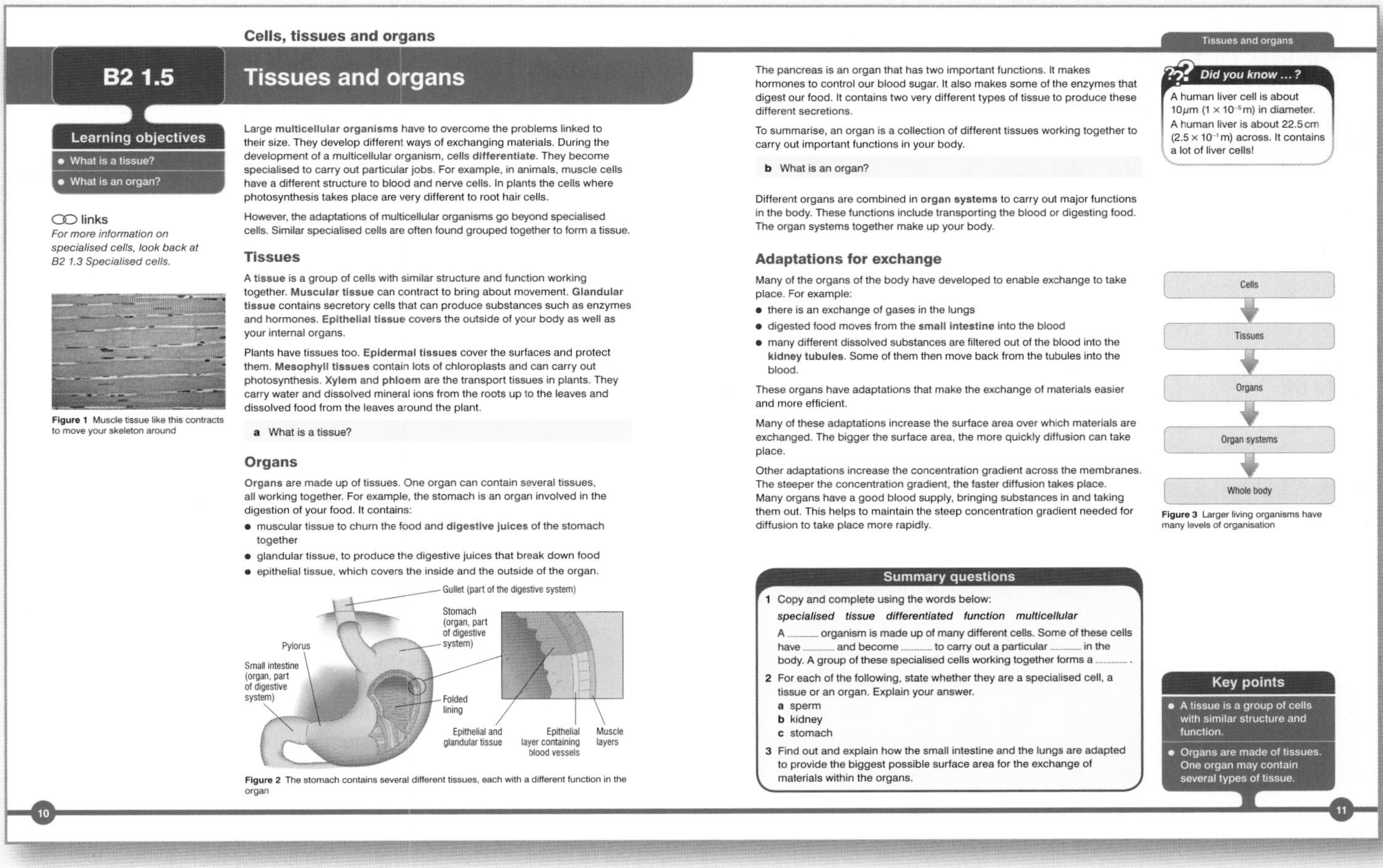

Cells, tissues and organs

B2 1.5   Tissues and organs

Learning objectives

- What is a tissue?
- What is an organ?

links

For more information on specialised cells, look back at B2 1.3 Specialised cells.

Large **multicellular organisms** have to overcome the problems linked to their size. They develop different ways of exchanging materials. During the development of a multicellular organism, cells **differentiate**. They become specialised to carry out particular jobs. For example, in animals, muscle cells have a different structure to blood and nerve cells. In plants the cells where photosynthesis takes place are very different to root hair cells.

However, the adaptations of multicellular organisms go beyond specialised cells. Similar specialised cells are often found grouped together to form a tissue.

Tissues

A tissue is a group of cells with similar structure and function working together. **Muscular tissue** can contract to bring about movement. **Glandular tissue** contains secretory cells that can produce substances such as enzymes and hormones. **Epithelial tissue** covers the outside of your body as well as your internal organs.

Plants have tissues too. **Epidermal tissues** cover the surfaces and protect them. **Mesophyll tissues** contain lots of chloroplasts and can carry out photosynthesis. **Xylem and phloem** are the transport tissues in plants. They carry water and dissolved mineral ions from the roots up to the leaves and dissolved food from the leaves around the plant.

Figure 1 Muscle tissue like this contracts to move your skeleton around

a What is a tissue?

Organs

Organs are made up of tissues. One organ can contain several tissues, all working together. For example, the stomach is an organ involved in the digestion of your food. It contains:

- muscular tissue to churn the food and **digestive juices** of the stomach together
- glandular tissue, to produce the digestive juices that break down food
- epithelial tissue, which covers the inside and the outside of the organ.

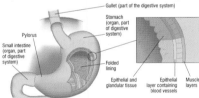

Figure 2 The stomach contains several different tissues, each with a different function in the organ

The pancreas is an organ that has two important functions. It makes hormones to control our blood sugar. It also makes some of the enzymes that digest our food. It contains two very different types of tissue to produce these different secretions.

To summarise, an organ is a collection of different tissues working together to carry out important functions in your body.

b What is an organ?

Different organs are combined in **organ systems** to carry out major functions in the body. These functions include transporting the blood or digesting food. The organ systems together make up your body.

Adaptations for exchange

Many of the organs of the body have developed to enable exchange to take place. For example:

- there is an exchange of gases in the lungs
- digested food moves from the **small intestine** into the blood
- many different dissolved substances are filtered out of the blood into the **kidney tubules**. Some of them then move back from the tubules into the blood.

These organs have adaptations that make the exchange of materials easier and more efficient.

Many of these adaptations increase the surface area over which materials are exchanged. The bigger the surface area, the more quickly diffusion can take place.

Other adaptations increase the concentration gradient across the membranes. The steeper the concentration gradient, the faster diffusion takes place. Many organs have a good blood supply, bringing substances in and taking them out. This helps to maintain the steep concentration gradient needed for diffusion to take place more rapidly.

Did you know …?

A human liver cell is about 10μm (1×10^{-5} m) in diameter. A human liver is about 22.5 cm (2.5×10^{-1} m) across. It contains a lot of liver cells!

Cells → Tissues → Organs → Organ systems → Whole body

Figure 3 Larger living organisms have many levels of organisation

Summary questions

1 Copy and complete using the words below:

specialised tissue differentiated function multicellular

A .... organism is made up of many different cells. Some of these cells have .... and become .... to carry out a particular .... in the body. A group of these specialised cells working together forms a ....

2 For each of the following, state whether they are a specialised cell, a tissue or an organ. Explain your answer.
   a sperm
   b kidney
   c stomach

3 Find out and explain how the small intestine and the lungs are adapted to provide the biggest possible surface area for the exchange of materials within the organs.

Key points

- A tissue is a group of cells with similar structure and function.
- Organs are made of tissues. One organ may contain several types of tissue.

10   11

Answers to in-text questions

a A tissue is a collection of cells of similar structure and function all working together.

b An organ is a collection of different tissues working together to carry out a specific function in the body.

Summary answers

1 multicellular, differentiated, specialised, function, tissue

2 **a** sperm – specialised cell – found individually.
  b kidney – organ – several tissues working together.
  c stomach – organ – several tissues working together.

3 **Small intestine** – villi and microvilli to increase SA (surface area) for the diffusion of dissolved food molecules from small intestine into the blood. Any other valid points.

Lungs – many alveoli to give large surface area for exchange of oxygen and carbon dioxide.

B2 1.6

Organs systems

AQA

Specification link-up: Biology B2.2

- Organ systems are groups of organs that perform a particular function. The digestive system is one example of a system in which humans and other mammals exchange substances with the environment. The digestive system includes:
  - glands, such as the pancreas and salivary glands, which produce digestive juices
  - the stomach and small intestine, where digestion occurs
  - the liver, which produces bile
  - the small intestine, where the absorption of soluble food occurs
  - the large intestine, where water is absorbed from the undigested food, producing faeces. *[B2.2.1 d)]*
- Plant organs include stems, roots and leaves. *[B2.2.2 a)]*
- Examples of plant tissues include:
  - epidermal tissues, which cover the plant
  - mesophyll, which carries out photosynthesis
  - xylem and phloem, which transport substances around the plant. *[B2.2.2 b)]*

Learning objectives

Students should learn:

- that organ systems are groups of organs that perform a particular function
- that the digestive system of a mammal is an example of a system in which substances are exchanged with the environment
- that plant organs include stems, roots and leaves.

Learning outcomes

Most students should be able to:

- define an organ system
- describe the digestive system as an example of an organ system
- describe the main organs of a plant, with the leaf in more detail.

Some students should also be able to:

- explain in detail how organs in an organ system work together.

Lesson structure

Starters

Down the hatch! – Ask a student what they last ate. Ask the class to describe as far as they know what will happen to the food as it goes through the student's body – which organs will it pass through and what will each one do to it? Read out some examples. *(5 minutes)*

Differentiation of cells – Ask students to visualise themselves getting younger and younger until they were back inside their mother's womb, as a single cell. Think of all the different jobs that all the cells in an adult body have to do. Write a command list to the cell telling it what functions we will need in the future from its offspring. Share the list with the rest of the class. Support students by using a writing frame to assist with the presentation of the command list. Extend students by expecting them to produce a more comprehensive list and by putting more detail into the job descriptions. *(10 minutes)*

Main

- Break the class into small groups. Give each one a dissecting board and a small weed in flower such as groundsel. Ask them to separate out the different parts of the plant (e.g. root system, shoot system, flower) and place them on a sheet of paper. Then stick them on with sticky tape and write next to each part what its name is and what its function is.
- They could also label the individual parts of each system, such as the leaves, leaf stalks, stem, etc. of the shoot system. Add to these labels the functions of the component parts.
- A video or DVD of science programmes giving a tour of the digestive system would be useful here.
- Provide the class with a set of large information sheets spaced out around the room, one per system, giving relevant facts regarding the component organs and how the system is put together, what its overall function is, how it interacts with other systems, etc. Provide the students with question sheets on each system which they can fill in as they go around. Have a marking session at the end, either peer, self, or collective as required.
- Comparison of plant and animal organs and organ systems – get students to list the characteristics of living organisms. Alongside each characteristic, get them to decide which organs and/or organ systems are involved in a plant and a mammal. Are there similar organs? Are there similar functions? Are there basic differences?

Plenaries

System hangman – Play a version of the traditional game by either using a whiteboard or an electronic projected version (many are freely available as downloads from the internet). To enhance competition, have small prizes available for winners. *(5 minutes)*

System card sort – Give the students several large cards of one colour with the names of systems on them. Give them also a pack of smaller cards of a different colour with the names of organs on. Their job is to sort the organs into the systems and place them on the correct pile. You can have the names of the relevant organs on the back of the system cards if the students won't cheat! Support students by limiting the number of cards and the complexity of the descriptions. Extend students by encouraging them to devise their own game to reinforce the ideas. You could also run the exercise again this time against the clock – see if they can beat their record! *(10 minutes)*

Support

- Provide students with pre-prepared labels for the plant organs and functions.

Extend

- Let students discover how the digestive systems of carnivores and herbivores are different from the human digestive system.

Cells, tissues and organs

B2 1.6 Organ systems

Learning objectives
- What are organ systems?
- What organs form the digestive system?
- What are plant organs?

Organ systems are groups of organs that all work together to perform a particular function. The way one organ functions often depends on others in the system. The human digestive system is a good example of an organ system.

The digestive system

The digestive system of humans and other mammals exchanges substances with the environment. The food you take in and eat is made up of large **insoluble molecules**. Your body cannot absorb and use these molecules. They need to be broken down or digested to form smaller, soluble molecules. These can then be absorbed and used by your cells. This process of digestion takes place in your **digestive system**.

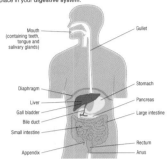

Figure 1 The main organs of the human digestive system

The digestive system is a **muscular tube** that squeezes your food through it. It starts at one end with your mouth, and finishes at the other with your anus. The digestive system contains many different organs. There are glands such as the pancreas and **salivary glands**. These glands make and release digestive juices containing enzymes to break down your food.

The stomach and the small intestine are the main organs where food is digested. Enzymes break down the large insoluble food molecules into smaller, soluble ones.

Your small intestine is also where the soluble food molecules are absorbed into your blood. Once there they get transported in the bloodstream around your body. The small intestine is adapted to have a very large surface area. This increases diffusion from the gut to the blood.

The muscular walls of the gut squeeze the undigested food onwards into your large intestine. This is where water is absorbed from the undigested food into your blood. The material left forms the faeces. Faeces are stored and then pass out of your body through the rectum and anus back into the environment.

a What is the digestive system and what does it do?

Plant organs

Animals are not the only organisms to have organs and organ systems – plants do too.

Plants have differentiated cells that form specialised tissues. These include mesophyll, xylem and phloem. Within the body of a plant, tissues such as these are arranged to form organs. Each organ carries out its own particular functions.

Plant organs include the leaves, stems and roots, each of which has a very specific job to do.

b What are the main organs in a plant?

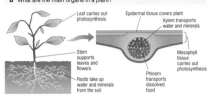

Figure 2 Plant organs and tissues

AQA Examiner's tip
Learn the sequence for multicellular organisms:
organism
↓
organ systems
↓
organs
↓
tissues
↓
cells

Summary questions

1 Match each of the following organs to its correct function.

A stem	i breaking down large insoluble molecules into smaller soluble molecules
B root	ii photosynthesising in plants
C small intestine for absorption	iii providing support in plants
D leaf	iv anchoring plants and obtaining water and minerals from soil

2 Explain the difference between organs and organ systems, giving two examples.

3 Using the human digestive system as an example, explain how the organs in an organ system rely on each other to function properly.

Key points
- Organ systems are groups of organs that perform a particular function.
- The digestive system in a mammal is an example of a system where substances are exchanged with the environment.
- Plant organs include stems, roots and leaves.

Further teaching suggestions

More organ systems
- Find videos or presentations of other organ systems, such as the respiratory system and the circulatory system in mammals.

Support systems
- Compare support systems in plants with support systems in animals.

Leaf systems
- Get the students to work out how many different functions are carried out by a leaf and how these link with the other systems in a plant.

Answers to in-text questions
a The digestive system is a system of organs all working together to bring about the digestion of your food.

b The main organs in a plant are the stems, roots and leaves.

Summary answers

1 A iii, B iv, C i, D ii.

2 An organ is a collection of several different tissues that work together to carry out a particular function in the body, e.g. heart pumps blood around the body, the stomach collects the food you eat and continues the digestive process (any two examples).

An organ system is a number of organs which work together to carry out a major function in the body, e.g. the digestive system which gradually breaks down insoluble food molecules into soluble molecules which can be taken into the blood stream, and then gets rid of the waste material (any two examples).

3 Each part of the digestive system relies on the parts before it, e.g. the stomach relies on the mouth, teeth and salivary glands to deliver chunks of chewed food, the small intestine depends on the stomach to continue the process of digestion and then on the enzymes made by the pancreas to help with the digestive process. The large intestine can only deal with the remains of the food which has already been digested in the small intestine and the soluble molecules absorbed into the blood. This leaves the waste material and lots of water, so the large intestine can absorb the water and remove faeces from the body.

Summary answers

1 a Nucleus, chloroplast, starch, cytoplasm, membrane, cell wall.

b Flagellum for moving around, eye spot for sensing light.

c Chlamydomonas is classified as a plant. It is a green alga – has chloroplasts and a cellulose cell wall.

2 a Correctly labelled diagrams.

b **i Palisade cell:** it carries out photosynthesis;

ii White blood cell: defending the body against pathogens/immune system/destroying/engulfing pathogens;

iii Sensory nerve cell: carrying nerve impulses.

c **i Palisade cell:** it has lots of chloroplasts to capture the light energy and enzymes needed for photosynthesis;

ii White blood cell: can flow and engulfs organisms, it doesn't produce antibodies;

iii Sensory nerve cell: sensory receptor to respond to changes, long axon to carry impulse long distances around body, synapse to pass impulse to other nerve cells, transmitter substance in the synapse to transfer impulse across gap.

3 a See B1.2 for correctly drawn bacterial cell and yeast cell.

b • Nucleus containing genetic material – the instructions for making a new cell and controlling the reactions in the cell.
• Cell membrane – controls the movement of substances into and out of the cell.
• Ribosomes – make proteins.
• Mitochondria – produce energy by cellular respiration.
• Cytoplasm – liquid gel in which the reactions of life take place.

4 a Diffusion is the net movement of particles of a gas or dissolved substance from an area of high concentration to an area of lower concentration.

b The blood spreads into the water by diffusion so the water turns red and it looks as if there is a lot more blood.

c Diffusion takes place more rapidly at higher temperatures because the particles have more energy and move more quickly. So on a warm, still day the scent molecules will travel faster from the area in the flower where they are at their highest concentration into the garden air, so you will smell them. On a cold still day, although the concentration gradient will be the same, the particles will be moving much more slowly so you are less likely to smell the flowers.

5 a The bigger the surface area (SA), the faster diffusion can take place across a boundary.

b **i** Individual cells have a folded cell membrane – microvilli – to increase the SA (surface area) available for diffusion.

ii Any sensible suggestions, e.g. body organs have folded epithelial linings, etc. to give a bigger SA (surface area) for diffusion.

6 a Epidermis, mesophyll, xylem, etc. – any three plant tissues.

b Stem – supports other areas of the plant, transports materials around the plant; roots – anchor plant in soil, uptake of water and mineral ions from the soil; leaves – photosynthesis.

c Xylem and phloem – because xylem brings water and minerals to all the cells from the roots, and phloem

---

Summary questions

1 *Chlamydomonas* is a single-celled organism that lives under water. It can move itself to the light to photosynthesise, and stores excess food as starch.

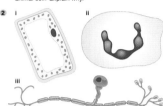

a What features does it have in common with most plant cells?

b What features are not like plant cells and what are they used for?

c Would you class *Chlamydomonas* as a plant cell or an animal cell? Explain why.

2
Each of these cells is specialised for a particular function in your body.

a Copy each of these diagrams and label the cells carefully. Carry out some research if necessary.

b Describe what you think is the function of each of these cells.

c Explain how the structure of the cell is related to its function.

3 a Draw and label a bacterial cell and a yeast cell.

b What are the common structures in all plant, algal and animal cells? Describe their functions.

4 a What is diffusion?

b If you cut your hand and then put it in a bowl of water, it looks as if there is a lot of blood. Explain why this happens.

c The scent of flowers in a garden is much more noticeable on a warm, still day than it is on a cold, s day. Explain this in terms of diffusion.

5 a What effect does surface area have on diffusion?

b Describe one way in which the following can be adapted to increase the surface area available for diffusion:
  i individual cells
  ii body organs.

6 Plants have specialised cells, tissues and organs just a animals do.

a Give three examples of plant tissues.

b What are the main plant organs and what do they de

c Which plant tissues are found in all of the main plan organs and why?

7 It is possible to separate the different parts of a cell us a centrifuge which spins around rather like a very fast spin dryer. They are used to separate structures that might be mixed together in a liquid. One of their uses i to separate the different parts of a cell.

The cells are first broken open so that the contents spill out into the liquid. The mixture is then put into the centrifuge. The centrifuge starts to spin slowly and a pellet forms at the bottom of the tube. This is removed The rest is put back into the centrifuge at a higher spe and the next pellet removed and so on.

Here are some results:

Centrifuge speed (rpm*)	Part of cell in pellet
3000	nuclei
10 000	mitochondria
12 000	ribosomes

*rpm = revolutions per minute

a From these observations can you suggest a link between the speed of the centrifuge and the size of the part of the cell found in the pellet?

b What apparatus would you need to test your suggestion?

c If your suggestion is correct, what results would you expect?

d What would be the easiest measurement to make to show the size of the mitochondria?

e Suggest how many mitochondria you might measur

f How would you calculate the mean for the measurements you have taken?

14

---

transports dissolved food (glucose, sugars) which all the cells need for energy from respiration.

7 a The slower the centrifuge spins, the larger the cell part found in the pellet. Or reverse argument.

b A microscope with attachment to measure, e.g. length.

c For the results you would expect the mean size of part of the cell in the pellet to be larger with slower centrifuge speed.

d Measure the length – because they are 'cigar-shaped'.

e As many as possible! But a minimum of 10.

f Add up all the measurements and divide by how many there are.

Kerboodle resources

Resources available for this chapter on Kerboodle are:

- Chapter map: Cells, tissues and organs
- Support: Cell A Vie (B2 1.1)
- Extension: Artificial life, but is it intelligent? (B2 1.1)
- Practical: Observation of cells under a microscope (B2 1.1)
- Bump up your grade: Hunt the answer – Cells (B2 1.3)
- Interactive activity: Cells
- Podcast: Cells, tissues and organs
- Test yourself: Cells, tissues and organs
- On your marks: Cells, tissues and organs
- Examination-style questions: Cells, tissues and organs
- Answers to examination-style questions: Cells, tissues and organs

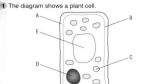

AQA Examination-style questions 🄺

1 The diagram shows a plant cell.

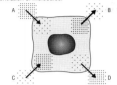

a Identify the structures listed. Choose the correct letter A, B, C, D or E for each structure.
  i nucleus   (1)
  ii chloroplast   (1)
  iii cell wall   (1)

b Animal cells are different from plant cells. Give the letters of the two parts that are also found in animal cells.   (2)

c What is a tissue?   (2)

2 The parts of plant cells have important functions. **List A** contains names of cell parts. **List B** lists some functions of cell parts.

Match each cell part to its correct function.

List A	List B
nucleus	controls entry of materials into cell
mitochondria	produce protein
chloroplasts	release energy
ribosomes	controls cell activities
	absorb light for photosynthesis

  (4)

3 Plant and animal organs contain tissues.

a Name one example of a plant tissue and describe its function.   (2)

b **i** Name one example of an animal tissue.   (1)
  ii Give an example of an organ where this tissue would be found.   (1)
  iii What is the function of the tissue you have named?   (1)

4 The diagram shows four ways in which molecules may move into and out of a cell. The dots show the concentration of molecules.

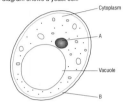

a Name the cell structure that controls the movement of materials into or out of cells.   (1)

b **i** Name the process illustrated by A and B.   (1)
  ii Explain the direction of the arrows in A and B.   (2)

5 The diagram shows a yeast cell.

a Identify the parts labelled A and B.   (2)

b The cytoplasm also contains mitochondria and ribosomes. What is the function of these structures?   (2)

c Suggest what is found in the vacuole.   (1)

6 *In this question you will be assessed on using good English, organising information clearly and using specialist terms where appropriate.*

The digestive system is a group of organs which changes food from insoluble into soluble molecules. Soluble molecules can be absorbed into the blood stream. Some food cannot be digested.

Describe the functions (jobs) of the organs in the digestive system.   (6)

15

AQA Practical suggestions

Practicals	AQA	🄺	📖	⚙️
Observation of cells under a microscope, e.g. sprouting mung beans to show root hair cells.	✓	✓	✓	
Computer simulations to model the relative size of different cells, organelles and molecules.	✓		✓	
Computer simulations to model the process of diffusion.	✓		✓	
Making model cells.	✓			
Diffusion of ammonium hydroxide in a glass tube using litmus as the indicator.	✓		✓	
Investigate how temperature affects the rate of diffusion of glucose through Visking tubing.	✓		✓	

AQA Examination-style answers

1 a **i** D   **ii** C   **iii** A   *(3 marks)*

  b B and D   *(2 marks)*

  c Group of cells – with similar function.   *(2 marks)*

2 Nucleus – controls cell activities.
Mitochondria – release energy.
Chloroplasts – absorb light for photosynthesis.
Ribosomes – produce protein.   *(4 marks)*

3 a Named plant tissue, e.g. epidermal/mesophyll/xylem/phloem.

    Function correctly linked to chosen tissue, covers surface/photosynthesis/transport.   *(2 marks)*

  b **i** Correctly named animal tissue, e.g. muscular/glandular/epithelial.   *(1 mark)*
      (Allow other relevant answer).

    ii Correct organ named, which contains named tissue, e.g. stomach.   *(1 mark)*

    iii Correct function for named tissue, e.g. contracts to cause movement/produces enzymes/lines organ.   *(1 mark)*

4 a (Cell) membrane.   *(1 mark)*

  b **i** diffusion   *(1 mark)*

    ii Molecules move from a region of higher concentration to a region of lower concentration.   *(2 marks)*

5 a A = nucleus, B = cell wall.   *(2 marks)*

  b Mitochondria – release energy/respiration.
    Ribosomes – produce protein.   *(2 marks)*

  c Solution/liquid/(cell) sap or description e.g. water and sugar.   *(1 mark)*

6 Marks awarded for this answer will be determined by the Quality of Written Communication (QWC) as well as the standard of the scientific response.

There is a clear, balanced and detailed description referring to most of the key organs in the digestive system and their functions. The answer shows almost faultless spelling, punctuation and grammar. It is coherent and in an organised, logical sequence. It contains a range of appropriate or relevant specialist terms used accurately.   *(5–6 marks)*

There is some description of at least three organs and their functions. There are some errors in spelling, punctuation and grammar. The answer has some structure and organisation. The use of specialist terms has been attempted, but not always accurately.   *(3–4 marks)*

There is a brief description of the functions of at least two organs, which has little clarity and detail. The spelling, punctuation and grammar are very weak. The answer is poorly organised with almost no specialist terms and/or their use demonstrating a general lack of understanding of their meaning.   *(1–2 marks)*

No relevant content.   *(0 marks)*

Examples of biology points made in the response:

- Glands produce digestive juices
- Salivary glands
- Pancreas
- Digestion occurs in the stomach and small intestine
- The liver produces bile
- The soluble food is absorbed in the small intestine
- Water is absorbed from the undigested food
- In the large intestine.

B2 2.1 Photosynthesis

Learning objectives

Students should learn:

- that light energy is absorbed by the chlorophyll in the chloroplasts of green plants and some algae
- that light energy is used by converting carbon dioxide and water into sugar
- that oxygen is released as a by-product.

Learning outcomes

Most students should be able to:

- summarise the process of photosynthesis in a word equation
- describe where the energy comes from and how it is absorbed
- describe experiments that show the raw materials needed and the resulting products.

Some students should also be able to:

- explain the build up of sugars into starch during photosynthesis.

Answers to in-text questions

a carbon dioxide + water $\xrightarrow{(+\ light\ energy)}$ glucose + oxygen

b The green substance that absorbs light energy in plants.

c Provides a large surface area for the light to fall on.

Support

- Provide students with the components of a word equation for photosynthesis. Ask them to assemble it in the correct order.

Extend

- Ask students to find out the actual structure of glucose and then use chemical symbols for the photosynthesis equation and balance it.

Specification link-up: Biology B2.3

- Photosynthesis is summarised by the equation:
  carbon dioxide + water $\xrightarrow{(+\ light\ energy)}$ glucose + oxygen. [B2.3.1 a)]
- During photosynthesis:
  - light energy is absorbed by a green substance called chlorophyll, which is found in chloroplasts in some plant cells
  - this energy is used by converting carbon dioxide and water into sugar (glucose)
  - oxygen is released as a by-product. [B2.3.1 b)]

  Controlled Assessment: AS4.3 Collect primary and secondary data [AS4.3.1 a)], [AS4.3.2 a)]; AS4.5 Analyse and interpret primary and secondary data. [AS4.5.4 a)]

Lesson structure

Starters

Why are leaves green? – Lead a discussion based on a concept cartoon-style talking head. Revise light reflection and absorbance. *(5 minutes)*

What will happen to my leaf? – During the growing season (or if you have plants in a greenhouse), give each student a spot label on which they can write their initials. Allow them to choose and label a young leaf. They should then measure the length of the leaf and record it. Back in the laboratory, ask them to predict what will happen to the leaf and explain why. Support students by prompting them to consider what the leaf needs in order to grow. Extend students by asking them to explain in detail all the processes involved. The leaves will need to be checked at intervals. *(10 minutes)*

Main

- Prepared microscope slides of transverse sections through leaves could be projected or viewed under the microscope, so that students can distinguish the different tissues within the leaf. Point out the palisade tissue, the vascular tissue and the stomata. Students could draw plans of the tissues to show where photosynthesis takes place (see 'Practical support').

- When carrying out experiments on photosynthesis, we can test for the products i.e. the presence of sugars or the evolution of oxygen. In most plants, the sugars are converted to starch (shown by the presence of starch grains in chloroplasts). The starch test can then be used on leaves to show that photosynthesis has occurred (see 'Practical support').

- The experiment to show that oxygen has been produced (see 'Practical support') can be done using water plants such as *Elodea canadensis* (Canadian pondweed). If students carry out and extend the experiment into an investigation, individually or in groups, several of the concepts of 'How Science Works' could be introduced. They can formulate a hypothesis, make predictions, draw conclusions and evaluate the validity of experimental design. Focus on one or two skills.

- The experiment on testing for starch to show that chlorophyll is necessary for photosynthesis can use variegated plants, such as a spider plant or geranium (see 'Practical support').

- In the 'Observing leaves' practical (see 'Practical support'), the adaptations of leaves for the process of photosynthesis are investigated.

Plenaries

Summary – Use a summary of photosynthesis with missing words. Support students by providing a list of the missing words from which they choose the appropriate one. Extend students by asking them to write their own summaries. They could be provided with a list of words that should be included. *(5 minutes)*

Prove it! – Write on the board, or project, a number of statements about photosynthesis. Then the students have to write out or discuss how we know each of the statements is true. *(10 minutes)*

Practical support

Producing oxygen
Equipment and materials required
Elodea canadensis (Canadian pondweed), glass funnel, beaker of water, test tube full of water, light conditions.

Details
This practical will show that oxygen has been produced using water plants such as *Elodea canadensis* (Canadian pondweed) which is readily available from garden centres. The water plant is placed under the wide part of an inverted glass funnel in a beaker of water. A test tube full of water is inverted and placed over the end of the funnel. The apparatus can be set up as described and kept illuminated for several hours, so that enough gas can be collected to be able to test it satisfactorily. If groups of students set up their own, it is unlikely to yield enough gas to test within a lesson.

Safety: Wash hands after contact with pond water.

Testing for starch
Equipment and materials required
Variegated plants, such as geranium, dilute iodine solution in dropping bottles, water baths to kill the leaves/make them more permeable/softer, ethanol for decolourising leaves/removing chlorophyll, white tiles or dishes to put the leaves in, forceps.

Details
The plants need to be kept in bright light for several hours. Keep one plant in the dark for two days to destarch it as a control. Each student can be given a leaf from an illuminated plant. A record should be made of the distribution of the green and white areas of the leaf, before testing for starch. Test for starch by dipping the leaf to be tested into boiling water for 15 seconds using forceps. Remove the leaf and place in a test tube of ethanol until the green colour is removed. Wash leaf in water and add dilute iodine solution. After carrying out the test, another drawing can be made showing the areas that remain brown and those that have been stained blue/black. Comparison of the two drawings will enable a conclusion to be drawn. Testing a leaf from the control plant will show that if there is no light, then no starch will be produced.

Safety: CLEAPSS Hazcard 54B Iodine. CLEAPSS Hazcard 40A Ethanol – highly flammable/harmful. Keep away from naked flames. Take care when handling hot water. Wear eye protection.

Observing leaves
Equipment and materials required
Prepared slides of sections through leaves and microscopes. Use whole leaves of different types.

Details
Slides should be projected or viewed under a microscope and students draw plans of the sections showing where the tissues are situated. Students should make drawings of whole leaves and label the parts, annotating each to indicate the adaptations for photosynthesis.

Safety: No special precautions needed.

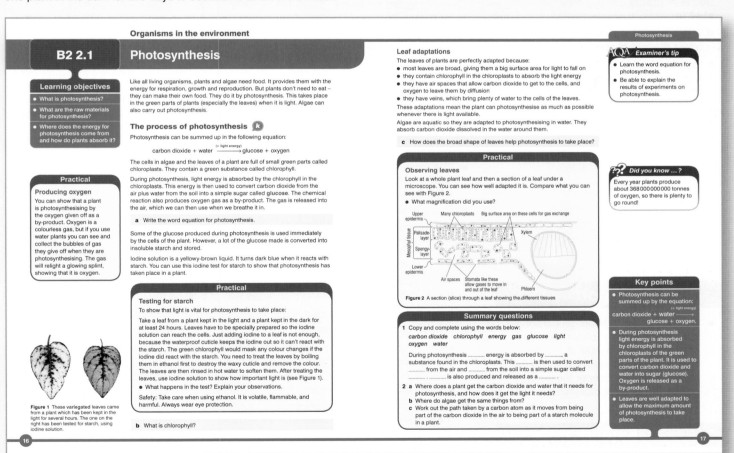

Summary answers

1 light, chlorophyll, energy, carbon dioxide, water, glucose, oxygen, gas

2 **a** CO₂ comes from the air; water from the soil; light energy from the sun/electric light.

   b Carbon dioxide and water from the water it lives in, light from Sun or electric light.

   c From the air into the air spaces in the leaf; into plant cells; into chloroplasts; joined with water to make glucose; converted to starch for storage.

B2 2.2 | Limiting factors

Learning objectives

Students should learn:

- that the rate of photosynthesis may be limited by low temperature and the shortage of carbon dioxide or light
- that these factors interact
- that if any of these factors are in short supply, the rate of photosynthesis is limited.

Learning outcomes

Most students should be able to:

- list the factors that limit the rate of photosynthesis
- describe how the factors interact
- describe how the environment in which plants grow can be artificially manipulated to grow more food.

Some students should also be able to:

- interpret data showing how the factors affect the rate of photosynthesis
- explain why the rate of photosynthesis is limited by low temperature, shortage of carbon dioxide or shortage of light.

Support

- Use pondweed in hydrogencarbonate indicator solution to show the effect of varying the light intensity on the rate of photosynthesis. Explain to the students that the deeper the purple colour, the more photosynthesis has occurred.

Extend

- Give students some cross sections of tree branches and, using hand lenses or binocular microscopes, ask: 'Why are there rings present? What do they represent? Why would they vary from year to year?' Expect the students to make links between growth rate, temperature and light intensity as limiting factors.

AQA Specification link-up: Biology B2.3

- The rate of photosynthesis may be limited by:
  - shortage of light
  - low temperature
  - shortage of carbon dioxide. *[B2.3.1 c)]*
- Light, temperature and the availability of carbon dioxide interact and in practice any one of them may be the factor that limits photosynthesis. *[B2.3.1 d)]*
- Interpret data showing how factors affect the rate of photosynthesis. *[B2.3]*
  Controlled Assessment: AS4.1 Plan practical ways to develop and test candidates' own scientific ideas. *[AS4.1.1 a) b) c)]*

Lesson structure

Starters

Oxygen production and light intensity – Show students the 'Producing oxygen' practical from the previous lesson. Support students by telling them that the rate of oxygen production varies with light intensity. Show them different graphs and ask them to choose which they think is the most likely and why. Extend students by asking them to draw a sketch graph of how the rate of oxygen production would vary with light intensity. Draw onto mini whiteboards. *(5 minutes)*

The limiting factors game – Have three sorts of counters (or small cards): one set labelled 'L' for suitable light level, another 'T' for suitable temperature and the third 'CO_2'. For each group of students, place some of each set of counters (or cards) into a bag so that they get a mixture of 'L', 'T' and 'CO_2'. The students are to take out a counter one at a time, placing them on a base line on paper or on the desk. The aim is to make sets of three counters side by side, at which point they can start on the next layer as they have grown. If they draw out a counter which they have already got in that layer, they put it back. The objective is to grow the 'plant' to as many levels as possible during a set time. Adjust each bag's contents so that some groups run out of 'L' counters first, some of 'T' counters and some of 'CO_2' ones. Discuss the results. *(10 minutes)*

Main

- The experiment 'How does the intensity of light affect the rate of photosynthesis' is easy to set up (see 'Practical support'). Students can work in groups and vary the light intensity by altering the distance of the lamp from the plant.

- This is a good experiment for developing 'How Science Works' concepts. A hypothesis can be formulated, predictions made, variables such as temperature controlled, measurements taken, results expressed as graphs, conclusions drawn and evaluation carried out. Choose which skills to actively teach. These might be the same for the whole group or use the opportunity to respond to areas of specific weakness identified in different groups.

- Results can be plotted as number of bubbles evolved, in a set time, against distance of the lamp from the plant. A more accurate way of plotting the results is to use light intensity, given by $\frac{1}{d^2}$ where d is the distance of the lamp from the plant.

- How does temperature affect the rate of photosynthesis? Show the students a graph of the effect of temperature on the rate of photosynthesis. Discuss the graph and get the students to think about the temperature fluctuations in a day. Discuss how the apparatus used to investigate the effect of different light intensity could be modified to investigate the effect of varying the temperature.

- How does carbon dioxide concentration affect the rate of photosynthesis? Project the graph of the effect of different concentrations of carbon dioxide on the rate of photosynthesis. Ask the students whether they think this is the most important limiting factor and why? Go on to discuss how carbon dioxide concentrations can be increased and what effect this could have on productivity.

Plenaries

Question loop – Students play a loop game on the factors limiting photosynthesis. *(5 minutes)*

Finish off the graph – Give the students some semi-completed graphs showing photosynthesis rates featuring various limiting factors to finish off and label. Support students by giving them completed graphs and asking them which factor is limiting under certain sets of circumstances, e.g. in a dense jungle, high up a mountain, etc. Extend students by asking them to say how the graphs could vary at different times of the year. *(10 minutes)*

Practical support

How does the intensity of light affect the rate of photosynthesis?

Equipment and materials required

Sprigs of *Elodea,* boiling tubes and test-tube racks, bench lamps, rulers, beakers, funnels, stopwatches or stop clocks, graph paper.

Details

Place some sprigs of *Elodea* in the mouth of a glass funnel and place the funnel in a beaker of water as shown in the diagram in the

Student Book. The level of the water should be above the funnel so that a test tube of water can be inverted over the opening of the funnel to collect the gas given off. Start with the light source close to the beaker (high light intensity) and either count the number of bubbles of gas given off in a set time (1 minute) or allow a set time and measure the volume of the gas in the test tube. Vary the distance of the lamp from the beaker, allow time for the plant to adjust and then take more readings.

Safety: Wash hands after contact with pond water. Dry hands before using mains electricity (lamps).

Organisms in the environment

Limiting factors

B2 2.2   Limiting factors

Learning objectives

- What factors limit the rate of photosynthesis in plants?
- How can we use what we know about limiting factors to grow more food?

AQA Examiner's tip

Make sure you can explain limiting factors.
Learn to interpret graphs that show the effect of limiting factors on photosynthesis.

You may have noticed that plants grow quickly in the summer, yet they hardly grow at all in the winter. Plants need certain things to grow quickly. They need light, warmth and carbon dioxide if they are going to photosynthesise as fast as they can.

Sometimes any one or more of these things can be in short supply. Then they may limit the amount of photosynthesis a plant can manage. This is why they are known as **limiting factors**.

a   Why do you think plants grow faster in the summer than in the winter?

Light

The most obvious factor affecting the rate of photosynthesis is light. If there is plenty of light, lots of photosynthesis can take place. If there is very little or no light, photosynthesis will stop. It doesn't matter what other conditions are like around the plant. For most plants, the brighter the light, the faster the rate of photosynthesis.

Practical

How does the intensity of light affect the rate of photosynthesis?

We can look at this experimentally (see Figure 1). At the start, the rate of photosynthesis goes up as the light intensity increases. This tells us that light intensity is a limiting factor.

When the light is moved away from this water plant, the rate of photosynthesis falls – shown by a slowing in the stream of oxygen bubbles being produced. If the light is moved closer (keeping the water temperature constant) the stream of bubbles becomes faster, showing an increased rate of photosynthesis.

However, we reach a point when no matter how bright the light, the rate of photosynthesis stays the same. At this point, light is no longer limiting the rate of photosynthesis. Something else has become the limiting factor.

The results can be plotted on a graph, which shows the effect of light intensity on the rate of photosynthesis.
- Why is light a limiting factor for photosynthesis?
- Name the **independent** and the **dependent** variables in this investigation.

Bubbles of oxygen-rich gas

Figure 1 Investigating the effect of light intensity on the rate of photosynthesis

Temperature

Temperature affects all chemical reactions, including photosynthesis. As the temperature rises, the rate of photosynthesis increases as the reaction speeds up. However, photosynthesis is controlled by enzymes. Most enzymes are destroyed (denatured) once the temperature rises to around 40–50°C. So if the temperature gets too high, the enzymes controlling photosynthesis are denatured. Therefore the rate of photosynthesis will fall (see Figure 2).

b   Why does temperature affect photosynthesis?

Carbon dioxide levels

Plants need carbon dioxide to make glucose. The atmosphere only contains about 0.04% carbon dioxide. This means that carbon dioxide levels often limit the rate of photosynthesis. Increasing the carbon dioxide levels will increase the rate of photosynthesis.

On a sunny day, carbon dioxide levels are the most common limiting factor for plants. The carbon dioxide levels around a plant tend to rise at night. That's because in the dark a plant respires but doesn't photosynthesise. Then, as the light and temperature levels increase in the morning, the carbon dioxide all gets used up.

However, in a science lab or greenhouse the levels of carbon dioxide can be increased artificially. This means they are no longer limiting. Then the rate of photosynthesis increases with the rise in carbon dioxide.

In a garden, woodland or field rather than a lab, light, temperature and carbon dioxide levels interact and any one of them might be the factor that limits photosynthesis.

Figure 2 The effect of increasing temperature on the rate of photosynthesis

Figure 3 This graph shows the effect of increasing carbon dioxide levels on the rate of photosynthesis at a given light level and temperature

Summary questions

1 a What is photosynthesis?
   b What are the three main limiting factors that affect the rate of photosynthesis in a plant?

2 a In each of these situations *one* factor in particular is most likely to be limiting photosynthesis. In *each* case listed below, suggest which factor this is and explain why the rate of photosynthesis is limited.
      i   a wheat field first thing in the morning
      ii   the same field later on in the day
      iii plants growing on a woodland floor in winter
      iv   plants growing on a woodland floor in summer.
   b Why is it impossible to be certain which factor is involved in each of these cases?

3 Look at the graph in Figure 1.
   a Explain what is happening between points A and B on the graph.
   b Explain what is happening between points B and C on the graph.
   c Look at Figure 2. Explain why it is a different shape to the other two graphs shown in Figures 1 and 3.

Key points

- The rate of photosynthesis may be limited by shortage of light, low temperature and shortage of carbon dioxide.
- We can manipulate the levels of light, temperature and carbon dioxide artificially to increase the rate of photosynthesis in food crops.

18   19

Further teaching suggestions

Under glass (choose one)

- Arrange a visit to a commercial glasshouse or encourage students to find out how conditions are controlled.
- Students could discuss the interactions of the factors and how they can be altered. Relate this to the production of glasshouse crops.

ICT link (choose one)

- Use a computer simulation where conditions for plant growth are varied, such as the one suggested above.
- Carry out a data-logging exercise, recording the temperature and light levels as they fluctuate throughout the day.

Answers to in-text questions

a It is warmer in summer and there is more light, so photosynthesis takes place more quickly making more food, so plants grow faster.

b Photosynthesis is a chemical reaction; temperature affects all chemical reactions. An increase in temperature speeds up the reactions as reacting particles collide more frequently and with more energy.

Summary answers

1 a The process by which plants use light energy trapped by chlorophyll to convert carbon dioxide and water into glucose (sugar).

   b Carbon dioxide, light and temperature.

2 a i   Light levels are low until sunrise, temperature falls overnight.
      ii Carbon dioxide will limit photosynthesis.
      iii Low light levels in winter, days are shorter, temperature colder.
      iv Trees will limit the light, temperature will be warm so carbon dioxide will be limiting.

   b Above 40–50°C the enzymes controlling photosynthesis are denatured so the rate of photosynthesis decreases.

3 a As light intensity increases, so does the rate of photosynthesis. This tells us that light intensity is a limiting factor.

   b An increase in light intensity has no effect on the rate of photosynthesis, so it is no longer a limiting factor; something else probably is.

   c Temperature acts as a normal limiting factor to begin with; increase in temperature increases the rate of photosynthesis. But above a certain temperature, the enzymes in the cells are destroyed so no photosynthesis can take place.

B2 2.3 — How plants use glucose

Specification link-up: Biology B2.3

- The glucose produced in photosynthesis may be converted into insoluble starch for storage. Plant cells use some of the glucose produced during photosynthesis for respiration. [B2.3.1 e)]
- Some glucose in plants and algae is used:
  - to produce fat or oil for storage
  - to produce cellulose, which strengthens the cell wall
  - to produce proteins. [B2.3.1 f)]
- To produce proteins, plants also use nitrate ions that are absorbed from the soil. [B2.3.1 g)]

Controlled Assessment: AS4.3 Collect primary and secondary data [AS4.3.1 a)]; AS4.5 Analyse and interpret primary and secondary data. [AS4.5.4 a)]

Learning objectives

Students should learn:

- that glucose is converted into starch for storage
- that some of the glucose produced in plants and algae is used for respiration and some is used to produce fat or oil for storage
- that cellulose and proteins are also produced.

Learning outcomes

Most students should be able to:

- describe how and where starch is stored in plants
- state that some of the glucose produced is used in respiration and some is used to produce fat and oil for storage
- state that some sugars can combine with nitrate ions and other mineral ions to form amino acids which can be built into proteins
- state that cellulose is also produced.

Some students should also be able to:

- explain that the energy released by plants in respiration is used to build smaller molecules into larger molecules
- describe how proteins and cellulose are produced.

Answers to in-text questions

a To provide energy for their cells.

b Starch.

Support

- Give students samples of glucose and corn starch. Tell them to stir the powders into two beakers of water. They should observe what happens and make comments on the solubility. Then ask them to filter the contents of both beakers and isolate and dry the corn starch.

Extend

- Ask students to find out about the differences in structure between starch and cellulose. Relate these differences to their functions within the plant.

Lesson structure

Starters

Showing that respiration has occurred – Issue all the students with drinking straws, and then give half of them boiling tubes containing a little fresh limewater in the bottom and the other half boiling tubes with a little hydrogencarbonate indicator solution in the bottom. Wearing eye protection, ask them to blow *gently* through the drinking straws into the solutions. They should note and compare colour changes, suggesting explanations. *(5 minutes)*

Make a starch molecule – Get the students to draw a chain of about 10 to 12 blank joined hexagons on a narrow strip of paper. Ask them to write 'glucose' inside each hexagon and then to turn the paper over and write 'starch' across the whole of the back. Get them to coil up the strip of paper into as tight a coil as they can and tell them that this represents a starch molecule in a cell. Ask them why they think glucose is converted to starch. What benefit does it have? Lead into how good a storage molecule it is. Support students by prompting them with simple questions about the nature of starch and how much more can be stored. Extend students by asking about the effects of starch and glucose on the water balance of the cells. *(10 minutes)*

Main

- There are many ways to show that a plant produces starch. The most straightforward is to use potted plants: some should be kept in the dark for 48 hours (so that they are destarched) and others kept in daylight conditions.
- Students could be provided with a list of instructions for the procedure, and then asked to test a leaf that has been kept in the light and one that has been kept in the dark.
- The destarched leaves are half-covered with foil or initials cut out of thin card or foil, kept in bright light for several hours and then tested for starch.
- Use the practical experiment 'Where is the starch stored?' (see 'Practical support').
- Roughly compare the starch content of fruits, such as apples, with potato tubers and some seeds. Choose some oily seeds and show by staining that they contain oils using a staining technique or by grinding them up and pressing out the oil.
- Give a PowerPoint presentation or exposition on algae. Introduce them as a group, showing a range of different types from freshwater examples and plankton to large seaweeds. Explain that they do not always look green but they all contain chlorophyll and can carry out photosynthesis. Get the students to say how the algae get the raw materials for the process, bringing in the need for minerals, and discuss the products.

Plenaries

Matching exercise – Write up a list of definitions and key words about photosynthesis, limiting factors and the use of glucose and ask students to match them up. *(5 minutes)*

From the air to a chip – In small groups, the students could produce a series of bullet points of the stages from carbon dioxide in the air to the starch in the chips on their plates. Support students by giving them the stages which they should put into the correct order. Extend students by getting them to add the stages from the starch in the chip back to the carbon dioxide in the air. Gather together the suggestions from all groups and build up the chain of events. *(10 minutes)*

Practical and demonstration support

Making starch

Equipment and materials required

Destarched and illuminated plants, water baths for killing leaves/making them permeable, ethanol to decolourise the leaves/remove chlorophyll, dilute iodine solution in dropping bottles, white tiles, forceps for handling leaves, eye protection.

Details

Remove the leaf to be tested and dip into boiling water for 15 seconds using the forceps. Remove the leaf from the water bath and place in a test tube of ethanol until the green colour is removed. Wash the leaf in water and spread it out on a white tile. Add dilute iodine solution and note the areas of the leaf which have stained blue-black and those that have remained brown.

Safety: Wear eye protection. CLEAPSS Hazcard 54B Iodine solution. CLEAPSS Hazcard 40A Ethanol – highly flammable/harmful. No naked flames.

Where is the starch stored?

Equipment and materials required

Microscopes, slides, cover slips, filter paper, a variety of plant parts (potato tubers, fruits, seeds, nuts, etc.), dilute iodine solution in dropping bottles, eye protection.

Details

The presence of large numbers of starch grains in potato tuber cells can be demonstrated by cutting thin slices of the tissue. Place the thin slices of tissues on microscope slides, cover with a drop of water and then with a cover slip. A drop of dilute iodine solution can be drawn through using filter paper. The starch grains will stain blue-black. In order to see the grains more clearly, it is advisable to draw some water through the slide to remove the surplus iodine solution.

The technique described above can be used on a variety of plant parts. Very thin sections of tissue from fruits, seeds, nuts and other plant organs can then be tested for the presence of starch grains.

Safety: Wear eye protection. CLEAPSS Hazcard 54B Iodine solution.

Organisms in the environment

B2 2.3   How plants use glucose

Learning objectives

- What do plants do with the glucose they make?
- How do plants store food?
- What other materials do plant and algal cells need to produce proteins?

AQA Examiner's tip

Two important points to remember:
- Plants respire 24 hours a day to release energy.
- Glucose is soluble in water, but starch is insoluble.

Figure 2 Algal cells contain a nucleus and chloroplasts so they can photosynthesise

Plants and algae make glucose when they photosynthesise. This glucose is vital for their survival. Some of the glucose produced during photosynthesis is used immediately by the cells. They use it for respiration to provide energy for cell functions such as growth and reproduction.

Figure 1 Worldwide, algae produce more oxygen and biomass by photosynthesis than plants do – but we often forget all about them

Using glucose

Plants cells and algal cells, like any other living thing, respire all the time. They use some of the glucose produced during photosynthesis as they respire. The glucose is broken down using oxygen to provide energy for the cells. Carbon dioxide and water are the waste products of the reaction.

The energy released in respiration is used to build up smaller molecules into bigger molecules. Some of the glucose is changed into starch for storage. Plants and algae also build up glucose into more complex carbohydrates like cellulose. They use this to strengthen the cell walls.

Plants use some of the glucose from photosynthesis to make amino acids. They do this by combining sugars with **nitrate ions** and other **mineral ions** from the soil. These amino acids are then built up into proteins to be used in the cells. This uses energy from respiration.

Algae also make amino acids. They do this by taking the nitrate ions and other materials they need from the water they live in.

Plants and algae also use glucose from photosynthesis and energy from respiration to build up fats and oils. These may be used in the cells as an energy store. They are sometimes used in the cell walls to make them stronger. In addition, plants often use fats or oils as an energy store in their seeds. They provide lots of energy for the new plant as it germinates.

Some algal cells are very rich in oils. They are even being considered as a possible source of biofuels for the future.

a Why do plants respire?

Starch for storage

Plants make food by photosynthesis in their leaves and other green parts. However, the food is needed all over the plant. It is moved around the plant in the phloem.

Plants convert some of the glucose produced in photosynthesis into starch to be stored. Glucose is soluble in water. If it were stored in plant cells it could affect the way water moves into and out of the cells. Lots of glucose stored in plant cells could affect the water balance of the whole plant.

Figure 3 Oilseed rape plants use energy from respiration and glucose from photosynthesis to produce oil to store in their seeds. We use this to make oil for cooking and as a source of biofuels.

Starch is insoluble in water. It will have no effect on the water balance of the plant. This means that plants can store large amounts of starch in their cells.

So, the main energy store in plants is starch and it is found all over a plant. It is stored in the cells of the leaves. The starch provides an energy store for when it is dark or when light levels are low.

Insoluble starch is also kept in special storage areas of a plant. Many plants produce **tubers** and bulbs. These help them to survive through the winter. They are full of stored starch. We often take advantage of these starch stores and eat them ourselves. Potatoes and onions are all full of starch to keep a plant going until spring comes again.

b What is the main storage substance in plants?

Summary questions

1 Copy and complete using the words below:
energy glucose growth photosynthesise respiration reproduction starch storage 24

Plants make .... when they .... Some of the glucose produced is used by the cells of the plant for ...., which goes on .... hours a day. It provides .... for cell functions, ... and .... Some glucose is converted to .... for ....

2 List as many ways as possible in which a plant uses the glucose produced by photosynthesis.

3 a Why is some of the glucose made by photosynthesis converted to starch to be stored in the plant?

   b Where might you find starch in a plant?

   c How could you show that a potato is a store of starch?

Practical

Making starch

The presence of starch in a leaf is evidence that photosynthesis has taken place. You can test for starch using the iodine test. See B2 2.1 Photosynthesis for details of how to treat the leaves so they will absorb the iodine. After this treatment, adding iodine will show you clearly if the leaf has been photosynthesising or not.

Figure 4 The leaf on the right has been kept in the dark. Its starch stores have been used for respiration or moved to other parts of the plant. The leaf on the left has been in the light and been able to photosynthesise. The glucose has been converted to starch, which is clearly visible when it reacts with iodine and turns blue-black.

Key points

- Plant and algal cells use the soluble glucose they produce during photosynthesis in several different ways:
  - for respiration
  - to convert into insoluble starch for storage
  - to produce fats or oils for storage
  - to produce fats, proteins or cellulose for use in the cells and cell walls.
- Plants and algal cells need other materials including nitrate ions to make the amino acids which make up proteins.

Further teaching suggestions

Formation, use and storage of glucose
- Students can produce a poster showing how glucose is produced, used and stored in the plant. This can either be done individually or in groups.

Respiring plants
- To demonstrate that plants respire, keep some *Elodea* in a boiling tube of hydrogencarbonate indicator. The boiling tube will need to have foil around it or be kept in the dark, so that photosynthesis does not occur. The cherry-red colour should turn yellow as it becomes more acidic due to the evolution of carbon dioxide. Compare with the starter activity that shows respiration in mammals has occurred.

Summary answers

1 glucose, photosynthesise, respiration, 24, energy, growth/reproduction, reproduction/growth, starch, storage

2 Respiration; energy for cell functions; growth; reproduction; building up smaller molecules into bigger molecules; converted into starch for storage; making cellulose; making amino acids; building up fats and oils for a food store in seeds.

3 a Glucose is soluble and would affect the movement of water into and out of the plant cells. Starch is insoluble and so does not disturb the water balance of the plant.

   b Leaves, stems, roots and storage organs.

   c [Any sensible suggestions involving a slice of potato and dilute iodine solution.]

B2 2.4

Making the most of photosynthesis

Learning objectives

Students should learn:

- that different factors affect the rate of photosynthesis
- that the environment in which plants are grown can be artificially manipulated.

Learning outcomes

Most students should be able to:

- describe the factors that affect the rate of photosynthesis
- describe some ways in which the environment in which plants are grown can be manipulated.

Some students should also be able to:

- evaluate the benefits of artificially manipulating the environment in which plants are grown.

Support

- Give each student some sunflower seeds to plant: one set in the school garden and another set indoors or in a glasshouse. They could compare the growth of the two sets. Each week (or more frequently) hold a strip of coloured paper 2–3 cm wide next to the plant and cut the paper off at the same height as the plant. Stick the strips on to a bar chart frame, using a different colour each time. Get them to state why there is a difference in the growth rate.

Extend

- Get students to research ways of manipulating the growth of plants, other than by manipulating the environment. Hint: using breeding techniques or genetic engineering to produce varieties of plants that grow well at lower temperatures.
- Get students to find out more about Tiberius and making their 'prophecies' cryptic.

AQA Specification link-up: Biology B2.3

- Evaluate the benefits of artificially manipulating the environment in which plants are grown. [B2.3]

  Controlled Assessment: AS4.1 Plan practical ways to develop and test candidates' own scientific ideas *[AS4.1.1 a) b) c)]*; AS4.3 Collect primary and secondary data *[AS4.3.1 a)]*; AS4.4 Select and process primary and secondary data *[AS4.4.2 a) b) c)]*; AS4.5 Analyse and interpret primary and secondary data. *[AS4.5.4 a)]*

Lesson structure

Starters

Mini-greenhouse – If available, set up a miniature greenhouse. Alternatively, use a transparent plastic container, such as a lemonade bottle cut in half. Rig up a data logger with a couple of temperature sensors, one placed inside and one outside. Shine a heat lamp at the 'greenhouse' and observe the temperature changes. Relate this to the Student Book and ask whether people would have managed to keep plants alive during the winter before greenhouses were invented. *(5 minutes)*

Farming indoors – Tell the students you are going to show them a photograph of a farm. Show the students a photograph of the outside of an ordinary looking terraced house. Assure them that it is a farm and ask them how this can be? Show them a newspaper article featuring a raid on a hydroponic cannabis cultivation factory within an ordinary house (these are frequent occurrences). Emphasise that this activity is illegal and can result in severe punishment. Ask the students to list the features of the environment that would have to be controlled. Support students by encouraging them to come up with simple suggestions, e.g. light, temperature, and plant 'food'. Extend students by getting them to give indications of ranges of these factors and specific nutrients for inclusion. *(10 minutes)*

Main

- Investigating the need for minerals. Provide each group of students with three specimens of tomato plants that have been given different nutrient treatments. Alternatively, provide large coloured photographs (laminated for future use). Ask the students to compare the three plants by describing their appearance, measuring the leaves and estimating root growth.
- Tell the students that the plants have been in the same conditions of light, temperature and carbon dioxide concentration. Ask students to examine and tabulate the differences. Apart from the obvious deficiency symptoms, they could measure leaves, height, etc. Lead a discussion and ask the students to draw conclusions.
- Produce a PowerPoint presentation or exposition on hydroponics to include basic principles and some information on the Nutrient Film Technique. If possible, show pictures of the set-up, including the ways in which all the conditions are monitored and controlled. Apart from optimum growing conditions for the growth of crops, get students to think about some of the other benefits of using this method of cultivation (e.g. cleaner crops, easier harvesting, pest control, etc.). Provide students with a set of questions (with the level adjusted to the ability of the class) and allow some time for discussion – put the process into the context of making the most of photosynthesis.
- Students could then set up their own experiment (see 'Practical support') with sets of plants using water culture (hydroponics). This is a good experiment for introducing the concepts of 'How Science Works'. Hypotheses can be formulated, predictions made, variables considered and controlled, and measurements taken.
- Ask students 'Where does the nitrate come from?' – Draw out the sequence of events from nitrogen in the air (remind the students of the percentage to the protein in plants). You can start with the nitrates in the soil as the centre of a spider diagram or flow chart. This can be accompanied by a modelling activity of 'Pass the N'.

Plenaries

Is it worth it? – Students to consider whether the cost of installing hydroponics systems to grow crops is worth it. Do the crops cost more? Do we need to produce crops out of season – strawberries in January? What are the cost and environmental implications of importing strawberries? *(5 minutes)*

Calling Tiberius – Refer to the Did you know …? feature on the first recorded greenhouse. Imagine that scientists have found a way of getting messages back to people in the past. To the recipient, this would of course be a message from the future. Write down a message to Tiberius Caesar, giving him a prophecy as to how his simple mica greenhouse will be improved in the future. Support students by giving them a writing frame or cloze passage to assist with the message to Tiberius. Extend students by getting them to add other information about scientific inventions which could help him. *(10 minutes)*

Practical support

Hydroponics

Equipment and materials required

Small flasks or bottles, culture solutions lacking magnesium and nitrate, an aquarium aerator, kitchen foil to cover flasks or bottles.

Details

Students could set up their own sets of plants using water culture (hydroponics). Broad bean or cereal seedlings could be used and grown in small flasks or bottles (root development can also be

observed in this way). The seedlings should all be at the same stage of growth, as the plants need to grow.

The cultures need to be aerated at intervals and the containers covered to prevent the growth of photosynthetic algae. It is possible to use duckweed in a water culture experiment. It has the advantage of growing more quickly and the growth can be assessed by the number of leaves produced. It will also show the deficiency symptoms.

Safety: No special precautions needed.

B2 2.4 — Making the most of photosynthesis

Learning objectives

- How can we control the environment in which plants are grown?
- What are the advantages and disadvantages of growing plants in an artificial environment?

The more a plant photosynthesises, the more biomass it makes and the faster it grows. It's not surprising that farmers want their plants to grow as fast and as big as possible. It helps them to make a profit.

In theory, if you give plants a warm environment with plenty of light, carbon dioxide and water, they should grow as fast as possible. Out in the fields it is almost impossible to influence any of these factors. However, people have found ways in which they can artificially control the environment of their plants.

The garden greenhouse

Lots of people have glass or perspex greenhouses in their gardens. Farmers use the same idea in huge plastic 'polytunnels'. They are used for growing crops ranging from tomatoes to strawberries and potatoes.

So how does a greenhouse affect the rate of photosynthesis? Within the glass or plastic structure the environment is much more controllable than outside. Most importantly, the atmosphere is warmer inside than out. This affects the rate of photosynthesis, speeding it up so plants grow faster. They will flower and fruit earlier and produce higher yields. We can also use greenhouses to grow fruit like peaches, lemons and oranges, which don't normally grow well outside in the UK.

?? Did you know ...?

The first recorded greenhouse was built in about 30AD for Tiberius Caesar, a Roman emperor who wanted to eat cucumbers out of season.

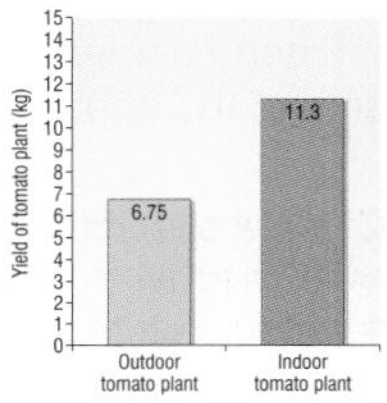

Figure 1 One piece of American research showed that the crop yield inside a greenhouse was almost double that of crops grown outdoors

Figure 2 Tomatoes certainly grow better in a greenhouse

a Why do plants grow faster in a greenhouse than outside?

Controlling a crop's environment

In a science lab you can change one factor at a time while keeping the others constant. Then you can judge how each one limits the rate of photosynthesis.

Outside, most plants are affected by a mixture of these factors. Early in the morning, light levels and temperature rise, carbon dioxide levels become limiting. On a bright, cold day, temperature might be the limiting factor. So there is a continuous interaction between the different factors.

Control through technology

Companies using big commercial greenhouses take advantage of what we know about limiting factors. They control the temperature and the levels of light and carbon dioxide. The levels are varied to get the fastest possible rates of photosynthesis. As a result the plants grow increasingly quickly.

The plants can even be grown in water with a perfect balance of mineral ions instead of soil, so nothing slows down their growth. This type of system is known as **hydroponics**.

The greenhouses are huge and conditions are controlled using computer software. It costs a lot of money but controlling the environment has many benefits. Turnover is fast, which means profits can be high. The crops are clean and unspoilt. There is no ploughing or preparing the land and in these systems crops can be grown where the land is poor.

b What are hydroponics?

It takes a lot of energy to keep conditions in the greenhouses just right – but fewer staff are needed. Monitoring systems and alarms are vital in case things go wrong, but for plants grown hydroponically, limiting factors are a thing of the past!

Figure 3 By controlling the temperature, light and carbon dioxide levels in a greenhouse like this you can produce the biggest possible crops – fast!

Activity

The National Farmer's Union (NFU) wants to produce a resource to explain to people how hydroponic farming works. Your job is to produce *either* a presentation *or* a poster series that can be sent out to schools around the country, explaining how it works and the biology behind the technology.

Key points

- Factors such as light levels, low temperature and carbon dioxide levels affect the rate of photosynthesis.
- The environment can be artificially controlled to make sure these factors do not limit growth, which has a number of benefits.

Summary questions

1 What are the main differences between a garden greenhouse and a hydroponics growing system?

2 What are the main benefits of artificially controlling the environment in which we grow our food plants?

Further teaching suggestions

Other mineral ions

- Water culture experiments could include plants grown in solutions deficient in other mineral ions such as iron, phosphate etc. There are water culture tablets available to make up the appropriate solutions.

What is in the fertilisers?

- Students to investigate the components of lawn fertiliser and Baby Bio and any other fertilisers, by looking at the boxes or containers. This will introduce the idea of commercial fertilisers not just containing one mineral ion, especially if the need for other mineral ions is demonstrated in the water culture experiments.

Answers to in-text questions

a The atmosphere is warmer which increases the rate of photosynthesis, so plants make more food and grow faster.

b Hydroponics is growing plants in water full of mineral ions providing an ideal environment for them to grow in.

Summary answers

1 **Garden greenhouse:** higher temperatures, plants not affected by wind, gardener can water with added food, etc.

  Hydroponics growing system: plants grown in mineral enriched water rather than soil, everything controlled including temperature, carbon dioxide levels and light levels.

2 By artificially manipulating the environment we can eliminate limiting factors and allow photosynthesis to take place at its maximum rate. This means plants grow as fast and as large as possible, maximising the profit we can make and allowing us to grow more crops in season and out of season.

B2 2.5

Organisms in their environment

Learning objectives

Students should learn:

- that the distribution of living organisms is affected by physical factors in the environment
- that the distribution of both plants and animals is affected by the interaction of the physical factors.

Learning outcomes

Most students should be able to:

- list the physical factors which affect the distribution of living organisms
- describe the effects of some of these factors on the distribution of plants and animals.

Some students should also be able to:

- explain in detail why some of the factors that influence the distribution of plants affect the distribution of animals.

Answers to in-text questions

a Low levels of nutrients mean plants like the Venus flytrap (which can capture prey and get nutrients from them) is at an advantage and can grow well. In a soil with plenty of nutrients such plants cannot compete with normal plants.

b Raised carbon dioxide levels affect distribution because plants are more vulnerable to insect attacks.

Support

- Provide students with a list of the features of woodlice and some information about their habitat, which they could link in to their write-up following the investigation of the distribution of the woodlice.

Extend

- Get students to consider abiotic factors such as altitude and aspect and find out how other abiotic factors are linked with these two.

Specification link-up: Biology B2.4

- Physical factors that may affect organisms are:
  - temperature
  - availability of nutrients
  - amount of light
  - availability of water
  - availability of oxygen and carbon dioxide. *[B2.4.1 a)]*

  Controlled Assessment: AS4.3 Collect primary and secondary data *[AS4.3.1 a)]*, *[AS4.3.2 a) b) c) d)]*; AS4.4 Select and process primary and secondary data. *[AS4.4.2 a) b) c)]*

Lesson structure

Starters

Match up – Show the students a number of plants and animals which are adapted to survive in particular environmental conditions, such as those mentioned in the text. Give them a list of the environmental conditions which the animals and plants are suited to and ask them to match the organism with the environment. Get them to either verbalise or write down the relationship between the environmental factor and the distribution of organisms. *(5 minutes)*

Factor list – Ask the students to write down as many measurable environmental factors as they can. Give them a time limit suitable for the ability of the class. To conclude, count up and read out the longest few lists. Support students by prompting. Extend students by encouraging them to include on their list, ranges of values and the name of the apparatus used to measure the factor. *(10 minutes)*

Main

- There is a wide range of wildlife films and DVDs available, many of which feature the interactions between organisms and their environments, often hostile ones. Seek out suitable video support material available in your school, view it in advance and prepare a set of questions to be answered while the students are watching the film. The video can either be periodically stopped, or the answers filled in at the end. Writing key words and phrases down on a board as they are covered in the film is helpful.

- Demonstrate the effect of light limitation by placing a bin or similar lightproof container upside down with some weight on it on grass during the growing season (informing the grounds staff is a good idea). Come back after a week, remove the bin and examine the changes. Get the students to explain why this response to low light levels will be useful to the plants (no chlorophyll needed as no light is present; is metabolically expensive to make so it is not made; plant goes yellow and uses the metabolites for extra growth instead, hence the straggly fast growth). Explain that removing the light makes the plant put everything it has at its disposal to get some leaf surface back into the light or it will die. Extend students by using the word 'etiolation' and link it to trees growing very straight when packed densely together.

- Measurement of specific abiotic factors (see practical on the use of maximum-minimum thermometers, rainfall gauges and oxygen meters described in B1.4). Introduce the students to the use of light meters and hygrometers to measure humidity. Other abiotic factors that can be measured are pH, wind speed and soil moisture. Demonstrate the apparatus and methods of measurement and provide the students with a list of instructions, telling them that they will need to use some of the methods in fieldwork investigations.

- Take the students into the school grounds and get them to try to find woodlice. Having a nature area is useful, as is a pile of rotting logs. If available, use light meters and hygrometers to assess the light and moisture conditions in which the woodlice live. Back in class, carry out a write-up linking their features to their distribution.

Plenaries

Flash cards – Make (or get the students to make) a set of flash cards with the name of an organism on one side and the environmental factor likely to limit its distribution on the other. Play in pairs, looking at the organism and trying to guess what is on the reverse side of each card in turn. Extend students by inverting the pack and getting them to guess the organism based on the environmental conditions. *(5 minutes)*

Just don't go there! – Get the students to consider organism distribution linked with environmental conditions by writing short, witty notes addressed to various creatures and plants advising them on places they should **not** go to, with reasons. Support students by reading them several examples to get them going. Extend students by encouraging them to apply their imagination and creativity to come up with more detailed and appropriate advice. *(10 minutes)*

Further teaching suggestions

Why do animals migrate?
- Ask the students this question and compile a list of their answers. What are the influencing factors? Discuss examples.

Plotting and interpreting data
- Students could be provided with data, such as temperature changes in a rock pool, oxygen levels in a stream near a sewage outfall or mean January temperatures over a 50-year span. They can be asked to plot the data and produce

reasoned explanations of the changes and how they could affect the distribution of organisms.

Hay infusions
- Set up hay infusions (place cut grass into pond water in a jar and cover loosely) and observe the effect of changes on the population of organisms over a period of time (wash hands after contact with pond water).

Organisms in the environment

B2 2.5

Organisms in their environment

Learning objectives
- What factors affect the distribution of organisms in their natural environment?
- Are animals as well as plants affected by physical factors?

In any habitat you will find different distributions of living organisms. These organisms form communities, with the different animals and plants often dependent on each other.

Factors affecting living organisms
A number of factors affect how living organisms are distributed in the environment. They include the following.

Temperature
You have seen that temperature is a limiting factor on photosynthesis and therefore growth in plants. In cold climates temperature is always a limiting factor. For example, Arctic plants are all small. This in turn affects the numbers of herbivores that can survive in the area.

?! Did you know ...?
Reindeer live in cold environments where most of the plants are small because temperature limits growth. They eat grass, moss and lichen. Reindeer travel thousands of miles as they feed. They cannot get enough food to survive in just one area.

Figure 1 Reindeer distribution depends on temperature, which affects the rate of photosynthesis and growth of their food

Nutrients
The level of mineral ions (e.g. nitrate ions) available has a big impact on the distribution of plants. Carnivorous plants such as Venus flytraps thrive where nitrate levels are very low because they can trap and digest animal prey. The nitrates they need are provided when they break down the animal protein. Most other plants struggle to grow in these areas with low levels of mineral ions.

Figure 2 The distribution of plants like these Venus flytraps depends heavily on nutrient levels

a How do nutrient levels affect the distribution of plants like the Venus fly trap?

Amount of light
Light limits photosynthesis, so it also affects the distribution of plants and animals. Some plants are adapted to living in low light levels. They may have more chlorophyll or bigger leaves. However, most plants need plenty of light to grow well.

The breeding cycles of many animal and plant species are linked to the day length. They only live and breed in regions where day length and light intensity are right for them.

Availability of water
The availability of water is important in the distribution of plants and animals in a desert. As a rule plants and animals are relatively rare in a desert. However, the distribution changes after it rains. A large number of plants grow, flower and set seeds very quickly while the water is available. These plants are eaten by many animals that move into the area to take advantage of them. If there is no water, there will be little or no life.

Availability of oxygen and carbon dioxide
The availability of oxygen has a big impact on water-living organisms. Some invertebrates can survive in water with very low oxygen levels. However, most fish need a high level of dissolved oxygen. The distribution of land organisms is not affected by oxygen levels as there is plenty of oxygen in the air and levels vary very little.

Carbon dioxide levels act as a limiting factor on photosynthesis and plant growth. They can also affect the distribution of organisms. For example, mosquitoes are attracted to the animals on whose blood they feed by high carbon dioxide levels. Plants are also more vulnerable to insect attacks in an area with high carbon dioxide levels.

b How do carbon dioxide levels affect the distribution of plants?

The physical factors that affect the distribution of living organisms do not work in isolation. They interact to create unique environments where different animals and plants can live.

?! Did you know ...?
Scientists thought that all organisms, apart from specialised microorganisms, needed oxygen to live. Then in 2010, multicellular organisms that do not need oxygen were discovered living deep under the Mediterranean seas. If more of these amazing organisms are found, our ideas of how oxygen affects the distribution of organisms will have to change.

Figure 3 One of the first known multicellular organisms that do not need oxygen to respire

Figure 4 Mosquitoes are attracted to us by the carbon dioxide we breathe out

Summary questions
1 What are the physical factors most likely to affect living organisms?
2 How do carnivorous plants survive in areas with very low levels of nitrate ions whilst other plants cannot grow there?
3 Explain how the limiting factors for photosynthesis – light, temperature and carbon dioxide levels – also affect the distribution of animals directly and indirectly.

Key points
- Physical factors that may affect the distribution of living organisms include:
  - temperature
  - nutrients
  - the amount of light
  - the availability of water
  - the availability oxygen and carbon dioxide.

Summary answers

1 Temperature, amount of light, level of nutrients, availability of water, oxygen and carbon dioxide.

2 Carnivorous plants capture and digest animals and use the nitrate ions produced as the animal proteins are broken down. Other plants rely on taking nitrate ions from the soil and there are not enough of them available for the plants to grow well.

3 Temperature affects animals directly because some animals are adapted to life in cold climates and others to hot climates. Animals are only found in appropriate temperatures and if the temperature of an area changes it can have a significant impact on the distribution of animals, e.g. bird distribution.

Carbon dioxide levels affect animals directly because some animals are attracted to the carbon dioxide produced by other animals, e.g. mosquitoes.

Light affects the distribution of animals because it often affects the breeding cycles of animals, and also how well they can see to hunt.

All three influence indirectly because of their affect on plant growth as limiting factors – and the distribution of plants has a major impact on the distribution of animals as a major food source.

B2 2.6

Measuring the distribution of organisms

AQA

Specification link-up: Biology B2.4

- Quantitative data on the distribution of organisms can be obtained by:
  - random sampling with quadrats
  - sampling along a transect. *[B2.4.1 b)]*
- Suggest reasons for the distribution of living organisms in a particular habitat. *[B2.4]*

Learning objectives

Students should learn that:

- how to measure the distribution of living organisms in their natural environment by means of random sampling using quadrats
- the meaning of the terms mean, median and mode
- how to count organisms along a transect.

Learning outcomes

Most students should be able to:

- describe the method of random sampling using quadrats
- calculate the mean and identify the mode and median from a set of data
- describe the use of a transect.

Some students should also be able to:

- explain the importance of collecting data by quantitative sampling.

Answers to in-text questions

a A quadrat is a frame used as a sample area when measuring distribution and population numbers of organisms (plants and animals).

Support

- Provide students with a very simple way of remembering the differences between mean, median and mode. For example: the mean is the sum of all the values divided by the number of values, the median is the middle of the range and the mode is the most frequently occurring value or number.

Extend

- Ask students to investigate quadrat size. Is the same size of quadrat ideal for counting all organisms? What size quadrat would you use to count the density of barnacles on a rock? What factors determine the size of quadrat used?

Lesson structure

Starter

Find a link – Ask students to look for situations in the school grounds where the distribution of organisms shows a change. Provide guidance, it may be useful to find an obvious place in advance, such as the density of vegetation changing under trees with less in the dark area and more in the bright, lichen distribution on tree trunks, etc. Get the students to come up with a hypothesis to test. Support students by giving them clear direct guidance to help them to find a change in distribution. Extend students by encouraging them to find a link by themselves and possibly a number of different links for group investigations. *(5 minutes)*

Main

- Use quadrats to survey the distribution of daisy and dandelion plants in a field. Select a suitable section of the school field (see 'Practical support').
- A much more scientific technique is to select the area to be studied and mark out a grid. Using random numbers, either from an internet-based random number generator or from a table of random numbers, select two numbers to provide the *x* and *y* co-ordinates of squares in which to take the samples. An alternative is to sample in a regular pattern, but to be unbiased, the pattern should be chosen before looking at the site. Students may need to be guided through the maths of scaling up the average to provide an estimate for the total.
- Sampling with quadrats in this way can be used to compare two areas. For example, the daisy population of one field could be compared with that of another field. The dandelion plants in a section of mown grass could be compared with those in a section of unmown grass or in well-worn areas of the playing field.
- A line transect can be used to find patterns of grass growth under trees. Use a reel of tape of the type used on sports fields, weighted down to avoid shifting. Decide which type of transect the students are going to use – recording all plants present in terms of distance covered on the line, point sampling at regular intervals, a belt transect of continuous quadrats along the line or an interrupted belt transect with regular gaps between the quadrats. Record the distance from the tree where the tree canopy stops. Measure the light levels, humidity and temperature associated with each quadrat. Soil samples can be taken from each quadrat area or as required. Get the students to label them as they collect them. Back in the laboratory, the soil could be tested for pH, moisture content and humus content. Take care over hygiene when handling soil as it can carry pathogens and parasites (e.g. *Toxocara canis*).
- Now students can process their data to calculate the distribution. A kite diagram can be used to provide a visual impression of the distribution along a transect line. The results of random sampling can be tabulated and density of plants per m² calculated. If a comparison is carried out, a bar chart could be used to show differences.
- Introduce the mean, median and mode. Check who knows the definitions already. Make sure the students have an understanding of these terms by providing them with more sets of practice data. They need to become familiar with the terms and their calculation before actually carrying out an investigation.

Plenary

Why bother? – Get the students to think of situations where scientists may want to record the distribution of a species. Discuss in small groups, write out a summary of ideas and report back to the whole class. Students could be supported by providing them with stimulus material to help them think of situations in which it would be valuable to have some distribution data. Students could be extended by asking them to recommend appropriate methods and sampling strategies as well as identifying where scientists may want to record distribution. *(10 minutes)*

Practical support

Surveying the distribution of daisies

Equipment and materials required
Half-metre square quadrats, measuring tapes, tape to lay out a transect line, data logger/light meter, hygrometer, thermometers, trowel and plastic bags for soil samples, universal indicator papers, oven for drying soil samples, balance.

Details
Use quadrats to survey the distribution of daisy and dandelion plants in a field. Select a suitable section of the school field. Show the students what daisy plants look like (large photographs and real specimens). Emphasise that they will be looking at the number of plants, not the number of flowers. Ensure that they can spot the leaves and track them back to the body of the plant. Get them to decide how they will count if a plant is in the quadrat (e.g. more than 50% or just presence?). The method suggested in the student book will provide a rough idea on the distribution. Rather than 1m² quadrats, a ball of paper can be dropped and four metre rulers placed around it. If using smaller quadrats remind the students to do the appropriate calculation to convert their findings to plants per m².

Safety: Do not allow the students to throw quadrats, especially not with eyes closed and/or after spinning! (Use of a small Frisbee can be a fun, safe alternative). Wash hands after contact with soil. Follow school guidelines for outside activities.

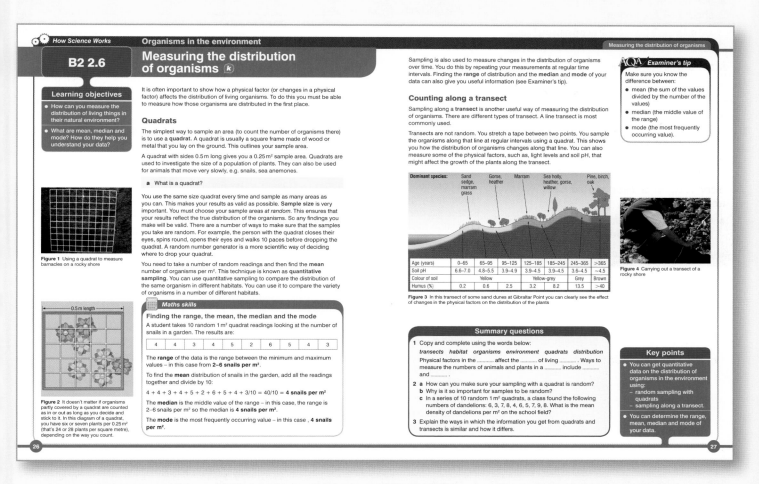

Figure 1 Using a quadrat to measure barnacles on a rocky shore

Figure 2 It doesn't matter if organisms partly covered by a quadrat are counted as in or out as long as you decide and stick to it. In this diagram of a quadrat, you have six or seven plants per 0.25 m² (that's 24 or 28 plants per square metre), depending on the way you count.

Figure 3 In this transect of some sand dunes at Gibraltar Point you can clearly see the effect of changes in the physical factors on the distribution of the plants

Figure 4 Carrying out a transect of a rocky shore

Summary answers

1. environment, distribution, organisms, habitat, quadrats/transects, transects/quadrats

2. a Spin round with eyes closed, keep eyes closed, walk a given number of paces and drop the quadrat, or any other sensible method.

   b To give a representative and unbiased sample.

   c $\frac{6 + 3 + 7 + 8 + 4 + 6 + 5 + 7 + 9 + 8}{10} = \frac{63}{10} = 6.3$

   so the mean density of dandelions is 6/m² if you count only whole plants or 6.3/m² if not.

3. Information similar – often use quadrats along the transect so using the same technique in different ways.

   Quadrats used for random measurements to get an overall picture of population or distribution of an organism or variety of organisms. Transect is a very specific study of a particular section of a habitat and measures zonal changes.

B2 2.7

How valid is the data?

Learning objectives

Students should learn:

- that appropriate sampling methods need to be used
- that sample size is related to reproducibility and validity
- that as many variables as possible should be controlled.

Learning outcomes

Most students should be able to:

- choose an appropriate sampling method
- explain that the sample size is important if the results are to be considered valid
- describe how some variables can be controlled.

Some students should also be able to:

- explain why it is difficult to control all the variables in fieldwork.

Specification link-up: Biology B2.4

- Evaluate methods used to collect environmental data, and consider the validity of the method and the reproducibility of the data as evidence for environmental change. *[B2.4]*

  Controlled Assessment: AS4.1 Plan practical ways to develop and test candidates' own scientific ideas. *[AS4.1.1 a) b) c)]*

Lesson structure

Starters

Valid and reproducible – Get the students to create and write down two sentences, one with the word 'valid' in it and one with the word 'reproducible'. Emphasise that we are after current understanding, drawing out what these words mean in general English usage, so the sentences can be about anything, not just scientific topics. Get volunteers to read theirs out and collect examples on the board. Come to a collective understanding. *(5 minutes)*

Right tool for the job – Give the students a number of scenarios where data is to be gathered. The complexity of these will depend on the ability of the class, but could include whether the population of a species of flat fish in the North Sea is declining or whether carbon dioxide levels are rising in the atmosphere. Get the students to suggest suitable data collection techniques and as a class discuss and critically evaluate them. Support students by giving clear prompts and clues pointing towards a straightforward example. Extend students by asking them to give more details and reasons for their choice of data collection methods and to say why they have dismissed alternatives. *(10 minutes)*

Main

- Go over the specific meanings of the terms 'valid' and 'reproducible' as outlined in the Student Book. 'Reproducible' as in if someone else did the same experiment they would get similar results, and 'valid' meaning it answers the question you are asking. Get the students to memorise the definitions. Get students to give examples of the opposites, where an investigation would not be able to be reproduced and where the data would not be valid.

- Discuss what is meant by variables. Identify some dependant, independent and controlled variables in experiments the students have already undertaken. Discuss the difficulty of controlling all the variables in biological situations and particularly fieldwork.

- Discuss the strength of evidence. Ask how the students could tell if a coin was biased and fell on heads more often than tails. Throw a coin a few times and analyse the results. You can find digital coin tossing on the internet, which can be projected if required. Get the class to throw a coin many more times and plot the ratio of heads to tails on a graph – the fluctuations will settle out eventually and it should become evident to the students that the more times you repeat an experiment, the stronger your evidence will be.

- Give the students a data set to analyse the trends. It could be the penguin data set from the Student Book or a more limited range for support level students. Whatever it is, a clear trend should be discernible. Get the students to plot graphs of the data, either manually or by using a spreadsheet tool. Excellent simple tools for data analysis, especially useful for less able students, exist such as 'Simple Data Handling' and 'FlexiData'. Project and share students' analyses.

Plenaries

Spot the blot – Give the students a version of a summary of the content covered in this spread. It should have a number of errors in it. The students are to identify these and to make a list of corrections. *(5 minutes)*

Simples? – It is easy to make mistakes in handling data. Read the penguins passage in the Student Book. Produce icons/symbols to represent each possible reason for reductions in the penguin population and write an advisory note to scientists studying the penguins encouraging them to be aware of all the possibilities. Support students by providing a range of symbols/icons from which the students can choose suitable ones; state what they represent and give a cloze passage for the advisory note. Extend students by getting them to produce their own icons without assistance and to envisage other potential problems, such as bioaccumulation of toxins, disease, and parasites, etc. *(10 minutes)*

Support

- Provide students with printed definitions of the words 'reproducible' and 'valid' that they can stick in their notebooks.

Extend

- Get students to review the pertussis (whooping cough) controversy in the light of what they have learnt about scientific method, the collection of data and controlling variables.

Further teaching suggestions

More fieldwork
- Some of the fieldwork suggestions mentioned in the previous spread could be carried out if time permits.

Planning
- If time is short, these investigations could be planned, the number of variables to be controlled and how this is to be managed described, the number and type of measurements needed could be stated and the best way of displaying the results indicated.

How Science Works   **Organisms in the environment**

B2 2.7   How valid is the data?

Learning objectives
- Will the method used answer the question that has been asked?
- Have all the variables been controlled?
- Does the size of your sample matter?

Environments are changing naturally all the time. But people also have an effect on the environment. This can be locally, e.g. dropping litter or building a new road, or on a worldwide scale with possible global warming and climate change. A change in the distribution of living organisms can be evidence of a change in the environment. However, if you want to use this type of data as evidence for environmental change it is important to use **reproducible** and **valid** methods to collect your results.

Reproducible, valid data

When you measure the distribution of living organisms you want your investigation to be reproducible and valid. In a reproducible investigation, other people can do the same investigation and get results that are very similar or the same as yours. And for the investigation to be valid it must answer the question you are asking. For example: What is the population density of snails in this garden?

One important factor is the size of your sample. If you do 10 quadrats, your data will not be as reproducible or as valid as if you carry out 100 quadrats.

Your method of sampling must be appropriate. If you want to measure the distribution of plants in an area, random quadrats work well. If you want to measure change in distribution over a range of habitats, a transect is a better technique to use.

If you are trying to measure change over time, you must be able to replicate your method every time you repeat your readings.

Changes in the distribution of a species are often used as evidence of environmental change. You must use a method of measuring that works regardless of who is collecting the data.

Controlling variables

When you are working in a lab you can control as many of the **variables** as possible. Then other scientists can carry out the investigation under the same conditions. This increases the likelihood that your results will be reproducible.

In fieldwork, it is not possible to control all the variables of the natural environment, but you can control some. For example, you can always measure at the same time of day. However, you cannot control the weather or the arrival of different organisms.

You must be clear about the problems of collecting data if you want to use them as evidence of environmental change.

A penguin case study

In the early 1980s Dee Boersma noticed that the numbers of penguins in a breeding colony in Argentina were falling. In 1987 she set up a research project making a transect of the colony with 47 permanent stakes, 100 metres apart.

Figure 1 If you are trying to find evidence of environmental change in an area as big as this, it is important to use a method that is as valid as possible

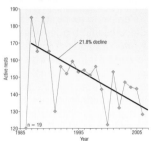
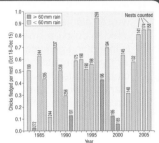

Figure 2 Patagonian penguins reflect environmental change in a very sensitive way. This graph shows clearly the effect of heavy rain on chick survival.

Every year Dee counted the active nests within a 100 m² circle around 19 of the stakes. She surveyed the remaining sites less regularly. However, Dee found the same pattern everywhere – numbers were falling.

What is causing these changes? Climate change seems to be significant:
- There have been several breeding seasons where unusually heavy rainfall has occurred. This has destroyed many nests and killed many chicks (see Figure 2).
- There have been changes in the numbers of small fish that the penguins eat. This is in response to changes in the water temperature. So there has been less food available in some years.

However, in biology things are rarely simple. The penguins are also affected by oil and waste from nearby shipping lanes. Around 20 000 penguins were killed by one major oil spill in 1991 alone. People catch the same small fish that the penguins feed on. Thousands of tourists visit the colony every year. They trample the area and cause stress to the birds.

Many factors, probably including climate change, are involved in the distribution changes of the penguins.

Figure 3 The penguin population at Punta Tombo fell by almost 22% between 1987 and 2006

Summary questions

1 What is meant by the terms: **a** reproducible and **b** valid, when you are talking about scientific data?
2 Look at Figure 2 and Figure 3 and the text above to help you answer this question.
  a When was the penguin population at Punta Tombo at its peak?
  b When was the population at its lowest? Suggest a reason for this.
  c How could Professor Boersma's data be used as evidence for environmental change?
3 Professor Boersma is widely respected in the scientific community. In what ways can you see that her data are both reproducible and valid?

Key points
- Different methods can be used to collect environmental data.
- Validity and reproducibility must be considered carefully as it is difficult to control variables in fieldwork.
- Sample size is an important factor in both reproducibility and validity of data.

Summary answers

1 a **Reproducible** – other people can do the same investigation and get results that are very similar or the same as yours.
  b **Valid** – it must answer the question you are asking.

2 a 1987 and 1989.
  b 2000 – heavy rain 2 years running which killed a lot of chicks.
  c Evidence shows increase in numbers of years with heavy rainfall – often linked to climate change and also change in sea temperatures with change in numbers of fish species – again often linked to climate change and changes in the ocean currents.

3 Data is reproducible because it has been carried out over many years on the same transect, on the same nests by different people every time. When a wider variety of nests are examined, the same pattern of results emerges. In a year of heavy rain there is a much lower level of chick survival.

Different groups of students were involved in different years and the results still follow the same pattern. So, in these ways, the results can be seen to be reproducible.

Results are valid because they answer the question, 'what is happening to the penguin population at Punta Tomobo', 'is the penguin population at Punta Tombo falling?' Or any of a number of other pertinent questions.

Summary answers

1 a carbon dioxide + water $\xrightarrow{\text{(+ light energy)}}$ glucose + oxygen

b Starch.

2 a Credit accurately drawn graphs, correctly labelled axes, etc.

b Plants in higher light intensity photosynthesise faster and therefore produce more food and grow well. Light will not limit them – CO_2 or temperature might. For plants in lower light, the light is a limiting factor on their growth.

3 a In the oceans, rivers, lakes and ponds of the world.

b Some glucose is used in respiration in much the same way as plants – the energy released in respiration is used to build up smaller molecules into bigger ones. Some of the glucose is converted into starch for storage. Plants also build up sugars into more complex carbohydrates like cellulose. They use this to make new plant cell walls. Some of the energy from respiration is used to combine sugars with other nutrients from the soil to make amino acids. These amino acids are then built up into proteins to be used in the cells. Energy from respiration is also used to build up fats and oils to make a food store. Any other sensible suggestions.

4 a Ideal growing conditions – warm, plenty of light, lots of water as it rains most days – the same conditions which enable tropical rain forests to grow so well; support rapid growth of oil palms.

b Made from the products of photosynthesis.

c To provide energy for the growing seedling when it germinates.

d Energy for respiration making cellulose, starch stores, making protein, etc.

5 a Hydroponic growing eliminates limiting factors, so more photosynthesis takes place.

b Rice, potatoes, tomatoes, peas and cucumbers because these are the crops where you get the biggest percentage increase in yield by growing hydroponically.

c Wheat and cabbage – relatively very small increase in yield from hydroponic growing.

d i Benefits: relatively easy and cheap, no specialist equipment needed, can use natural growing cycle. Any other valid points.

Problems: open to pests and weeds, weather can affect growth, limiting factors such as temperature and light levels mean plants don't get the maximum growth. Any other valid points.

ii Benefits: maximum growth, no limiting factors, relatively easy to control pests and weeds, can grow out of season, crops clean when harvested, not affected by changes in the weather, good working conditions inside. Any other valid points.

Problems: big set up costs, expensive to run, vulnerable to failings in technology.

Summary questions 🄺

1 a Write the word equation for photosynthesis.

b Much of the glucose made in photosynthesis is turned into an insoluble storage compound. What is this compound?

2 The figures in the table show the mean growth of two sets of oak seedlings. One set was grown in 85% full sunlight, the other set in only 35% full sunlight.

Year	Mean height of seedlings grown in 85% full sunlight (cm)	Mean height of seedlings grown in 35% full sunlight (cm)
2005	12	10
2006	16	12.5
2007	18	14
2008	21	17
2009	28	20
2010	35	21
2011	36	23

The figures in the table show the mean growth of two sets of oak seedlings. One set was grown in 85% full sunlight, the other set in only 35% full sunlight.

a Plot a graph to show the growth of both sets of oak seedlings.

b Using what you know about photosynthesis and limiting factors, explain the difference in the growth of the two sets of seedlings.

3 More of the biomass and oxygen produced by photosynthesis comes from algae than from plants.

a Where do you find most algae?

b How do algal cells use the products of photosynthesis?

4 Palm oil is made from the fruit of oil palms. Large areas of tropical rainforests have been destroyed to make space to plant these oil palms, which grow rapidly.

a Why do you think that oil palms grow rapidly in the conditions that support a tropical rainforest?

b Where does the oil in the oil palm fruit come from?

c What is it used for in the plant?

d How else is glucose used in the plant?

5 Here are the yields of some different plants grown in Bengal, India. The yields per acre when grown normally the field and when grown hydroponically are compared.

Name of crop	Hydroponic crop per acre (kg)	Ordinary soil crop per acre (kg)
wheat	3629	2540
rice	5443	408
potatoes	70760	8164
cabbage	8164	5896
peas	63503	11340
tomatoes	181437	9072
lettuce	9525	4080
cucumber	12700	3175

a Why are yields always higher when the crops are grown hydroponically?

b Which crops would it be most economically sensible to grow hydroponically? Explain your choice.

c Which crops would it be least sensible to grow hydroponically? Explain your choice.

d What are the benefits and problems of growing crop

i in their natural environment

ii in an artificially manipulated environment?

Kerboodle resources 🄺

Resources available for this chapter on Kerboodle are:

- Chapter map: Organisms in the environment
- How Science Works: Does the amount of light affect the rate of photosynthesis? (B2 2.1)
- Simulation: Limiting factors of photosynthesis (B2 2.2)
- Data Handling Skills: Limiting factors (B2 2.2)
- Bump up your grade: Limiting factors (B2 2.2)
- Extension: Limiting factors (B2 2.2)
- Practical: Photosynthesis experiments (B2 2.2)
- Support: Photosynthesis (B2 2.3)
- Maths skills: Calculating the mean (B2 2.2)
- How Science Works: Measuring the distribution of organisms (B2 2.6)
- Practical: Fieldwork (B2 2.6)
- Interactive activity: Photosynthesis
- Podcast: Photosynthesis
- Test yourself: Organisms in the environment
- On your marks: Organisms in the environment
- Examination-style questions: Organisms in the environment
- Answers to examination-style questions: Organisms in the environment

AQA Practical suggestions

Practicals	AQA	🄺	📖	⚙
Investigating the need for chlorophyll for photosynthesis with variegated leaves.	✓		✓	
Taking thin slices of potato and apple and adding iodine to observe under the microscope.	✓		✓	

AQA Examination-style questions 🄺

The picture shows a snail. Snails feed on plants.

Some students wanted to investigate the distribution of snails in the hedges on two sides of their school field. All the hedges were trimmed to a height of 1.5 metres. One side of the field was very open but the opposite side was shaded by trees. The students thought there would be more snails in the hedges on the open side because birds living in the trees would eat the snails. In the investigation they:

- measured a transect of 50 metres along the hedge on the open side of the field
- leaned a 1 m² quadrat against the hedge every 5 metres
- counted all the snails they could see in the quadrat
- recorded the data in a table
- repeated the investigation with the hedge that was shaded by trees.

a Choose the correct answer to complete each sentence.
  i The idea that birds in the trees eat the snails is a .... (1)
    conclusion   hypothesis   test
  ii A transect is a .... (1)
    line   square   triangle
  iii One thing that was controlled in this investigation was the .... (1)
    light intensity   number of trees   size of quadrat

b The data recorded by the students can be seen in the table.

	Number of snails									
Quadrat number	1	2	3	4	5	6	7	8	9	10
Open hedge	3	3	5	3	2	3	6	3	6	2
Hedge shaded by trees	2	3	4	3	5	2	1	4	1	5

Use the data to answer the questions. Choose the correct answer.

  i The mean for the number of snails in the open hedge is [3 / 3.6 / 5]. (1)
  ii The median for the number of snails in the shaded hedge is [2 / 3 / 4]. (1)
c One student said he didn't think the results would be valid. Suggest one reason why. (1)

2 A farmer has decided to grow strawberry plants in polytunnels, similar to the one shown in the diagram.

The tunnels are enclosed spaces with walls made of plastic sheeting. The farmer decides to set up several small polytunnels, as models, so he can work out the best conditions for the strawberry plants to grow. He needs help from a plant biologist who provides some data.

The data is shown in the graph.

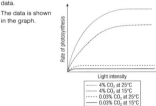

---- 4% CO₂ at 25°C
---- 4% CO₂ at 15°C
---- 0.03% CO₂ at 25°C
---- 0.03% CO₂ at 15°C

a In this question you will be assessed on using good English, organising information clearly and using specialist terms where appropriate.
  You are advising the farmer.
  Using all the information given, describe the factors the farmer should consider when building his model tunnels so he can calculate the optimal conditions for growing strawberry plants. (6)
b Biologists often use models in their research. Suggest one reason why. (1)

AQA, 2007

31

AQA Examination-style answers

1 a i hypothesis (1 mark)
    ii line (1 mark)
    iii size of quadrat (1 mark)
  b i 3.6 (1 mark)
    ii 3 (1 mark)

  c Any sensible suggestion relating to method of counting or uncontrolled variables. e.g. difficulty of counting inside the hedge/quadrat would miss all snails in top 0.5 metres/ hard to see snails under leaves/not all parts of the hedge are shaded on the shaded side of the field/birds might live in the hedges not just the trees/allow – snails might move about and be counted twice. (1 mark)

2 a There is a clear, balanced and detailed description referring to the data in the graph about light, temperature and carbon dioxide and how to set up a controlled experiment. The answer shows almost faultless spelling, punctuation and grammar. It is coherent and in an organised, logical sequence. It contains a range of appropriate or relevant specialist terms used accurately. (5–6 marks)

  There is some description of setting up a controlled experiment, including at least two variables. There are some errors in spelling, punctuation and grammar. The answer has some structure and organisation. The use of specialist terms has been attempted, but not always accurately. (3–4 marks)

  There is a brief description with reference to setting up several tunnels and mention of at least one variable, but little clarity and detail. The spelling, punctuation and grammar are very weak. The answer is poorly organised with almost no specialist terms and/or their use demonstrating a general lack of understanding of their meaning. (1–2 marks)

  No relevant content. (0 marks)

  Examples of biology points made in the response:
  - Use of term limiting factors
  - The more photosynthesis the more growth
  - Carbon dioxide optimum around 4%
  - Plants need water
  - Control of light intensity
  - Types of light
  - Temperature control/25°C
  - Idea that light changes with type of plastic/colour of plastic/thickness of plastic
  - Idea that might need heating/ventilation to control/ monitor temperature
  - Idea that need to contain the carbon dioxide/have a source of carbon dioxide gas.
  - Reference to having different sets of conditions in each model tunnel to be able to determine optimum/idea that might try slightly lower/higher temperature/carbon dioxide level to check cost effectiveness.

  b Any one from the following:
  - Possible to mimic large scale events/idea of/on a small scale.
  - Can be used to predict changes/changes in variables.
  - Allow a description e.g. predict the spread of disease/can predict the effect of a chemical on all bacteria using a safe organism/can use fast breeding organisms to mimic processes which occur slowly in others/can predict the effect of global warming on organisms in a locality. (1 mark)

Practicals	AQA	🄺	📖	⚙️
Investigate the effects of light, temperature and carbon dioxide levels, (using Cabomba, algal balls or leaf discs from brassicas) on the rate of photosynthesis.	✓	✓	✓	✓
Computer simulations to model the rate of photosynthesis in different conditions.	✓		✓	
The use of sensors to investigate the effect of carbon dioxide and light levels on the rate of photosynthesis and the release of oxygen.	✓		✓	
Investigative fieldwork involving sampling techniques and the use of quadrats and transects…	✓	✓	✓	✓
Analysing the measurement of specific abiotic factors in relation to the distribution of organisms.	✓		✓	
The study of hay infusions.	✓		✓	
The use of sensors to measure environmental conditions in a fieldwork context.	✓		✓	

B2 3.1

Proteins, catalysts and enzymes

Learning objectives

Students should learn:

- that protein molecules are made up of long chains of amino acids
- that proteins act as structural components, hormones, antibodies and catalysts
- that an enzyme is a biological catalyst
- how enzymes work.

Learning outcomes

Most students should be able to:

- describe how long chains of amino acids form protein molecules
- state the roles of proteins in the formation of muscles, hormones, antibodies and enzymes
- describe the structure and mode of action of an enzyme.

Some students should also be able to:

- explain in detail the concept of the active site of the enzyme.

Answers to in-text questions

a A building block of protein.

b A substance that speeds up a chemical reaction without being changed itself.

Support

- Use toy building blocks to represent large molecules, such as starch, proteins and fats. Label each one on one side with the name of the substrate ('starch', 'protein') then label the individual bricks with the name of the products ('sugars', 'amino acids'). Use plastic knives with the word 'Enzyme' on to cut up the blocks.

Extend

- Ask students to research the structure of proteins and use a length of Bunsen tubing to demonstrate the differences between the primary, secondary and tertiary structure. Different sequences of amino acids can be marked with a pen and the tubing can be coiled and twisted into a C shape to illustrate the active site.

AQA Specification link-up: Biology B2.5

- Protein molecules are made up of long chains of amino acids ... *[B2.5.1 a)]*
- Catalysts increase the rate of chemical reactions ... *[B2.5.1 b)]*
- The shape of an enzyme is vital for the enzyme's function ... *[B2.5.2 a)]*
- Different enzymes work best at different pH values. *[B2.5.2 b)]*

  Controlled Assessment: AS4.3 Collect primary and secondary data *[AS4.3.2 a) b) c) d) e) f)]*; AS4.4 Select and process primary and secondary data *[AS4.4.1 a) b)]*, *[AS4.4.2 b)]*; AS4.5 Analyse and interpret primary and secondary data. *[AS4.5.4 a)]*

Lesson structure

Starter

Biological stains – Bring in a cheap, clean white T-shirt and allow students to smear it with selected food and drink (tomato ketchup, mustard, egg). Discuss with the students how they could remove the stains and get the T-shirt clean. Show the students a box of biological washing powder and a box of non-biological washing powder and get them to say which one would be best to use with reasons. (Care needed if washing powders are handed around – some people can have sensitive skin). Support students by prompting as to the nature of the stains and how they could be broken down. Extend students by asking them to compare the contents of the two washing powders and to say what the enzymes are, breaking down, e.g. starches, proteins, fats. *(10 minutes)*

Main

Enzymes in action

- The experiment 'Breaking down hydrogen peroxide' shows the action of manganese(IV) oxide, an inorganic catalyst, and a piece of liver, which contains the enzyme catalase, on hydrogen peroxide.
- Use a PowerPoint presentation to build up a picture of how enzymes are composed of long chains of amino acids folded and coiled into special shapes. Introduce the concept of the active site, enzyme specificity, how they work and what they can do. Introduce them to the convention of naming enzymes – the '-ase' suffix for many – and give some examples. Provide students with a worksheet that they can fill in as the presentation proceeds.
- Catalase is present in living tissue. The more active the tissue, the greater the catalase activity (see Practical support 'Catalase in living tissues' for full details). The reactions can be described or they can be measured. (This links to 'How Science Works' – making observations and measurements.) If the experiment is to be a qualitative one, i.e. just a simple comparison of the activity by observation, then written descriptions or comparative statements can be made.
- It is possible to make this experiment more quantitative by using the same quantities of each tissue, and then measuring the activity when placed in the same volume of hydrogen peroxide. Simple heights of froth up the tube in a given time can be measured. A more accurate measurement is given by collecting the gas evolved in a given time. (This demonstrates many 'How Science Works' concepts.)
- There are many variations of the catalase experiments:
  – Investigate the volume of gas released when different quantities of fresh liver are used in the same volume of hydrogen peroxide, i.e. varying the amount of enzyme with a fixed quantity of substrate.
  – The converse of this is to use the same quantity of liver and vary the concentration of hydrogen peroxide used, i.e. varying the quantity of the substrate with a fixed quantity of enzyme.

Plenary

Find the substrate for the enzyme – Using thin card, make sets of 'enzymes' of different shapes and with differently shaped 'active sites', and a corresponding set of 'substrates' that fit into the enzymes' 'active sites'. (You could adapt very simple jigsaw pieces.) Support students by making the pieces very simple. Extend students by using more complex shapes and making the 'substrates' consist of two parts which fit together into the active site. Students need to find the 'enzyme' and 'substrate' that fit together. *(10 minutes)*

Practical support

Breaking down hydrogen peroxide
Equipment and materials required

Manganese(IV) oxide, fresh liver, tiles and knives for cutting, test tubes, hydrogen peroxide solution, eye protection, some method of collecting the gas given off (syringes/inverted test tubes, rulers if height of froth to be measured), water bath if liver is to be boiled and denatured.

Details

By adding hydrogen peroxide, students can compare the activity of the inorganic catalyst with cubes of fresh liver and liver in which the enzymes have been denatured by heating. The denatured liver shows that the enzyme is present in living tissue and is destroyed by heating. Include a test tube containing hydrogen peroxide as a control. An additional control using a piece of boiled and cooled liver would show that the enzyme from the living tissue can be denatured.

Safety: CLEAPSS Hazcard 33 – disposal of organic waste. CLEAPSS Hazcard 50 Hydrogen peroxide.

Catalase in living tissue
Equipment and materials required

Fresh liver, potato tuber tissue, apple, etc., tiles and knives for cutting, test tubes, hydrogen peroxide solution, eye protection, some method of measuring the gas given off (syringes/inverted test tubes or manometers; rulers if height of froth to be measured), stopwatches or stop clocks, water bath if tissues are to be boiled and denatured.

Details

Drop small cubes of different tissues, such as liver, muscle, apple and potato, into test tubes containing hydrogen peroxide (10 cm³ to 15 cm³ depending on the size of the tubes). If the experiment is to be qualitative, students should record their observations, make comparisons and write statements about the activity of the enzyme in the different tissues. If it is to be quantitative, then the same quantities of tissue and hydrogen peroxide should be used and measurements taken of the activity.

Safety: Wear eye protection, CLEAPSS Hazcard 50 Hydrogen peroxide. Take care with tubes, which can become hot.

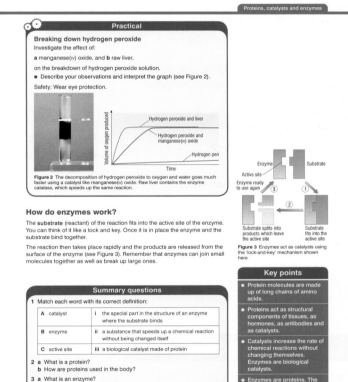

The reproduced textbook spread (pages 32–33) "B2 3.1 Proteins, catalysts and enzymes"

Further teaching suggestions

Catalase activity in plant tissues

- The different parts of a plant can be tested for catalase activity. Take equal quantities of leaf, stem and root tissue and test with hydrogen peroxide. Alternatively, use equal quantities of germinating and non-germinating seeds to show that the more active the tissue, the greater the catalase activity.

Computer simulations – modelling enzymes

- Use computer simulations of enzymes to model their action in varying conditions of pH, temperature and concentration.

Summary answers

1 A ii   B iii   C i

2 a A molecule made up of long chains of amino acids.
   b As structural components, as hormones, as antibodies and as catalysts (enzymes).

3 a A biological catalyst.
   b Protein/amino acid chains.
   c Substrate molecule/s arrive at the active site. They fit perfectly together, like a lock and key. The substrate molecules react and change shape. The products leave the active site. The enzyme is left unchanged and ready to catalyse the next reaction.

B2 3.2 Factors affecting enzyme action

Learning objectives

Students should learn:

- that enzymes are vital to all living cells
- that changes in temperature affect the rate at which enzymes work
- that different enzymes work best at different pH values.

Learning outcomes

Most students should be able to:

- describe experiments that show the effect of changes in temperature and pH on the rate of enzyme-controlled reactions
- describe how changes in temperature and pH affect enzyme action.

Some students should also be able to:

- explain in detail how changes in temperature and pH affect the active site of an enzyme.

Answers to in-text questions

a Enzymes in bacteria in the milk break down proteins that makes the milk go sour/bad. This happens faster in the sun as it is warmer.

b When an enzyme is denatured the shape of the active site is lost, so it does not work properly anymore.

Support

- Tell students that bits of milk need to be joined together by enzymes to make yoghurt. Make some yoghurt in a vacuum flask, a water bath or preferably a commercial yoghurt maker. Set up controls in the refrigerator and at room temperature. Prepare a work sheet with a results table for time taken for it to run through a funnel. Adjust the bore so that some yoghurt will very slowly flow through. Try it with boiled yoghurt (risk assessment).

Extend

- Get students to research some of the organisms that live in hot springs, very cold conditions and conditions of extreme pH.

AQA Specification link-up: Biology B2.5

- The shape of an enzyme is vital for the enzyme's function. High temperatures change the shape. *[B2.5.2 a)]*
- Different enzymes work best at different pH values. *[B2.5.2 b)]*

  Controlled Assessment: AS4.4 Select and process primary and secondary data *[AS4.4.2 a) b) c)]*; AS4.5 Analyse and interpret primary and secondary data. *[AS4.5.2 a) b) c)]*, *[AS4.5.3 a)]*

Lesson structure

Starters

What happens to milk when it goes off? – Show the students fresh and sour milk. If possible, have one that is really solid but careful risk assessment is necessary. Discuss what has happened to the milk and why putting milk in the refrigerator stops it going off. *(5 minutes)*

Denaturing eggs – Crack raw eggs (or get students to do this) into three beakers: one beaker at room temperature, one at a temperature where visible changes to the egg white just occur, and one at boiling point. Support students by asking them to describe the visible and textural changes to the egg white. Extend students by asking them to explain the changes that are happening to the shape of the protein. Are the changes irreversible? Introduce the concept of denaturation. *(10 minutes)*

Main

Investigating the effect of temperature on enzymes

- Students can use their own saliva to carry out this experiment on the action of amylase on starch (see Practical support 'Investigating the effect of temperature on enzymes').
- A graph can be plotted of the rate of disappearance of starch (1/time taken in seconds) against the temperature. Many concepts of 'How Science Works' can be developed in the investigative work, e.g. hypotheses are formulated, predictions are made, variables are controlled and conclusions drawn. Concentrate on one or two of these, e.g. drawing conclusions from the graph plotted.
- Other enzymes could be used for investigations into the effect of temperature. If the use of the students' saliva is not possible, commercial amylase could be used, but it is usually derived from fungi and can give odd results.
- If pepsin or trypsin (protein digesting enzymes) are used, the substrate to use is the white of hard-boiled eggs or an egg-white suspension made by adding 5 g of egg white to 500 cm^3 of very hot water and whisking briskly. The rate at which the egg-white suspension clears can be timed at the different temperatures. More 'How Science Works' concepts are introduced here too.

Investigating the effect of pH

- The effects of varying pH can also be investigated by modifying the experiments described above. Keep the temperature constant and vary the pH by using a range of buffer solutions.
- The effect of varying pH on catalase. Potato discs can be added to hydrogen peroxide and buffer solutions and the quantity of oxygen evolved in a set time can be measured at each pH. A graph can be plotted of volume of oxygen evolved against pH and the optimum pH for catalase determined.

Plenaries

What temperature do I work best at? – Discuss what might be the optimum temperature for the enzymes in the human body. What happens if we get a fever? Why do parents worry when you get too hot? Contrast our body temperature with that of other organisms – include some fish, reptiles and invertebrates. Do all enzymes have the same optimum temperature? *(5 minutes)*

Definitions – Write up a list of the key words and phrases used in this topic so far. Support students by providing a list of definitions which they need to match with the words. Extend students by asking them to write their own definitions and using them to compose a short passage which they could use as a revision card. *(10 minutes)*

Practical support

Investigating the effect of temperature on enzymes

Equipment and materials required

Test tubes and racks, water baths for different temperatures, 2% starch solution, fresh saliva, boiled saliva, iodine solution, white tiles, glass rods, eye protection.

Details

Each student will need at least 2 cm depth of saliva in a test tube. Test tubes should be set up containing equal volumes of saliva and starch solution, shaken and then placed into water baths at different temperatures. Drops of the mixtures are then tested at 30 second intervals for the presence or absence of starch by dipping a glass rod into the mixture and then into a drop of iodine solution on a white tile. Note the colour each time and record how long it takes for the starch to disappear at each temperature. A control could be set up using boiled saliva.

Safety: CLEAPSS Hazcard 54B Iodine solution. Dispose of saliva in disinfectant. CLEAPSS Hazcard 33 Enzymes.

Enzymes

B2 3.2 — Factors affecting enzyme action

Learning objectives

- How does increasing the temperature affect your enzymes?
- Why does a change in pH affect your enzymes?

A container of milk left at the back of your fridge for a week or two will be disgusting. The milk will go off as enzymes in bacteria break down the protein structure.

Leave your milk in the sun for a day and the same thing happens – but much faster. Temperature affects the rate at which chemical reactions take place even when they are controlled by biological catalysts.

Biological reactions are affected by the same factors as any other chemical reactions. Factors such as concentration, temperature and surface area all affect them. However, in living organisms an increase in temperature only works up to a certain point.

a Why does milk left in the sun go off quickly?

The effect of temperature on enzyme action 🇰

The reactions that take place in cells happen at relatively low temperatures. Like other reactions, the rate of enzyme-controlled reactions increases as the temperature increases.

However, this is only true up to temperatures of about 40 °C. After this the protein structure of the enzyme is affected by the high temperature. The long amino acid chains begin to unravel. As a result, the shape of the active site changes. We say the enzyme has been **denatured**. It can no longer act as a catalyst, so the rate of the reaction drops dramatically. Most human enzymes work best at 37 °C.

b What does it mean if an enzyme is denatured?

Practical

Investigating the effect of temperature on enzymes

You can show the effect of temperature on the rate of enzyme action using simple practical procedures.

The enzyme amylase (found in your saliva) breaks down starch into simple sugars. You can mix starch solution and amylase together and keep them at different temperatures. Then you test samples from each temperature with iodine solution at regular intervals.

- How does iodine solution show you if starch is present?
- Why do we test starch solution without any amylase added?
- What conclusion can you draw from the results?

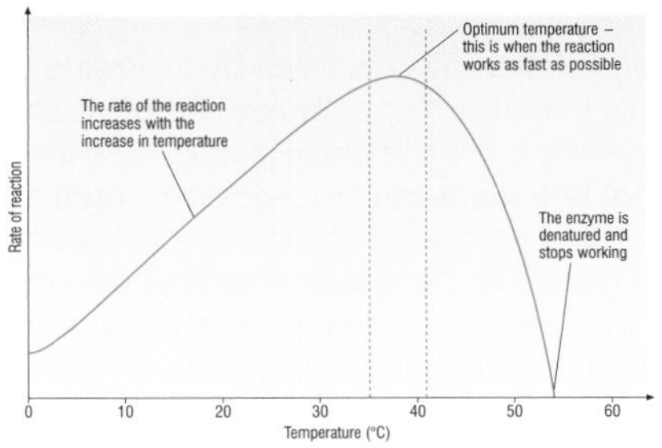

Figure 1 The rate of an enzyme-controlled reaction increases as the temperature rises – but only until the protein structure of the enzyme breaks down

Effect of pH on enzyme action 🇰

The shape of the active site of an enzyme comes from forces between the different parts of the protein molecule. These forces hold the folded chains in place. A change in the pH affects these forces. That's why it changes the shape of the molecule. As a result, the active site is lost, so the enzyme no longer acts as a catalyst.

Different enzymes have different pH levels at which they work best. A change in the pH can stop them working completely.

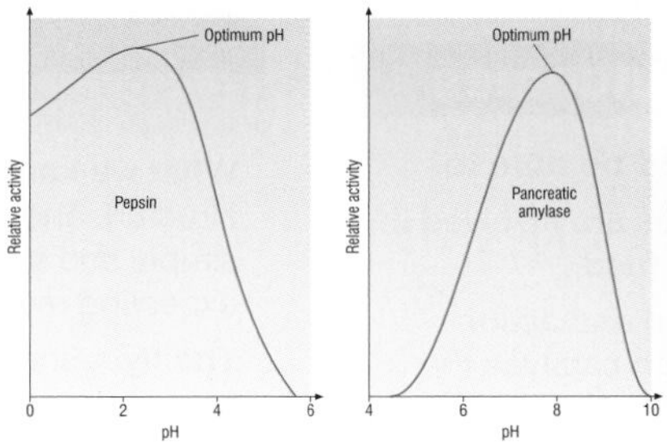

Figure 2 These two digestive enzymes need very different pH levels to work at their maximum rate. Pepsin is found in the stomach, along with hydrochloric acid, while pancreatic amylase is in the small intestine along with alkaline bile.

Without enzymes, none of the reactions in your body would happen fast enough to keep you alive. This is why it is so dangerous if your temperature goes too high when you are ill. Once your body temperature reaches about 41 °C, your enzymes start to be denatured and you will soon die.

Summary questions

1 Copy and complete using the words below:

active site   cells   denatured   enzyme   increase   protein
reactions   shape   temperatures   40 °C

The chemical .... that take place in living .... happen at relatively low .... The rate of these ....-controlled reactions .... with an increase in temperature. However, this is only true up to temperatures of about .... After this the .... structure of the enzyme is affected and the .... of the .... is changed. The enzyme has been ....

2 Look at Figure 2.
   a At which pH does pepsin work best?
   b At which pH does amylase work best?
   c What happens to the activity of the enzymes as the pH increases?
   d Explain why this change in activity happens.

?? Did you know ... ?

Not all enzymes work best at around 40 °C. Bacteria living in hot springs survive at temperatures up to 80 °C and higher. On the other hand, some bacteria that live in the very cold, deep seas have enzymes that work effectively at 0 °C and below.

Figure 3 The magical light display of a firefly is caused by the action of an enzyme called luciferase

AQA Examiner's tip

Enzymes aren't killed (they are molecules, not living things themselves) – use the term 'denatured'.

Key points

- Enzyme activity is affected by temperature and pH.
- High temperatures and the wrong pH can affect the shape of the active site of an enzyme and stop it working.

Further teaching suggestions

Luciferase

- Search the internet and show pictures of flashlight fish, luminous jellyfish, fungi and glow worms that all have this enzyme, which catalyses a reaction and releases energy as light. Some plants have the enzyme and glow green. Tell the true story of a pilot lost at sea from an aircraft carrier at night who navigated his way back and landed successfully after following the faint trail of light from phosphorescent algae, which glowed in the wake of the ship following its passage. Break a lightstick of the kind used by the armed forces, campers and at discos. Demonstrate the reaction of luciferase by mixing the appropriate chemicals *in vitro*. Students could do internet research on luciferase to see what else they can find out about this unique enzyme.

Extended experiments

- With the pH experiments, the introduction of a wider range of pH values could make the experiment more reliable. The quantities of alkali and acid could be varied and the pH ascertained by testing with pH papers or a pH sensor. Alternatively, make up solutions of known pH for use.

How to make sour cream

- Milk protein can be curdled by adding lemon juice to it. Demonstrate and discuss with the students what is happening. Link with the starter and link with the effects of temperature and pH together. Reinforce the idea of what causes the milk to go off or go sour.

Summary answers

1 reactions, cells, temperatures, enzyme, increase, 40 °C, protein, shape, active site, denatured

2 a About pH 2.
   b About pH 8.

c The activity levels fall fast.
d The increase in pH affects the shape of the active site of the enzyme, so it no longer bonds to the substrate. It is denatured and no longer catalyses the reaction.

B2 3.3

Enzymes in digestion

Learning objectives

Students should learn:

- that during digestion, the breakdown of large molecules into smaller molecules is catalysed by enzymes
- that these enzymes, which are produced by specialised cells in glands, pass out into the gut
- that the enzymes include amylases that catalyse the breakdown of starch, proteases that catalyse the breakdown of proteins and lipases that catalyse the breakdown of lipids.

Learning outcomes

Most students should be able to:

- explain how enzymes are involved in the digestion of our food
- describe the location and action of the enzymes which catalyse the breakdown of carbohydrates (starch), proteins and lipids.

Some students should also be able to:

- explain digestion in terms of the molecules involved.

Answers to in-text questions

a They work outside the cells of your body.
b Amylase.
c Proteases.
d Lipases.

Support

- Use flip cards with foods on one side and their components on the other. Some students might need a clue, such as starting letters or vowels. Alternatively, use an internet version for whiteboards, or individual computers such as those created through 'Quia' (use this as a search term).
- Play **floor dominoes.** Make up large 'domino' cards of food types, their components and the enzymes and allow the students to play in groups.

Extend

- Get students to research how cystic fibrosis affects the digestive system and the use of enzymes in its treatment.

AQA Specification link-up: Biology B2.5 and B2.6

- The chemical reactions inside cells are controlled by enzymes. *[B2.6.1 a)]*
- Some enzymes work outside the body cells … . *[B2.5.2 c)]*
- The enzyme amylase is produced in the salivary glands … . *[B2.5.2 d)]*
- Protease enzymes are produced by the stomach … . *[B2.5.2 e)]*
- Lipase enzymes are produced by the pancreas and small intestine … . *[B2.5.2 f)]*
- The stomach also produces hydrochloric acid. The enzymes … . *[B2.5.2 g)]*
- The liver produces bile, which is stored in the gall bladder … . *[B2.5.2 h)]*

    Controlled Assessment: AS4.5 Analyse and interpret primary and secondary data. *[AS4.5.2 a) b) c) d)], [AS4.5.3 a)], [AS4.5.4 d)]*

Lesson structure

Starters

What we know about enzymes so far, a quick quiz – Ask 10 questions on enzyme structure and factors affecting their action. Support students by making the questions simple and straightforward. Extend students by asking more difficult questions and expecting more detailed answers. *(5 minutes)*

The fly – Show photographs of a fly's mouthparts and talk through how they function, or how a spider sucks the juice out of its victims. (For a taster, search the internet for 'The Fly watch trailer'). *(10 minutes)*

Main

- Introduce the different types of digestive enzymes by reviewing the different components of the diet. Get the students to realise that complex carbohydrates, proteins and lipids have to be digested before they can be absorbed. Introduce the groups of digestive enzymes and what they do. Reference to carbohydrases, proteases and lipases, their substrates and their products is required. Project a diagram of the human digestive system and its associated glands and indicate where the different enzymes work in the gut. Also indicate on this diagram where the enzymes are produced as well as where they act. It could be helpful to provide the students with an outline of the digestive system, so that they can fill in the information for themselves.

- Making a model gut – each group of students will need two 15 cm lengths of dialysis (Visking) tubing to model the gut (see 'Practical support'). If desired, the experiments can be left for 24 hours at room temperature before testing.

- If there is not time for the students to carry out their own experiments, then a length of dialysis tubing can be filled with a mixture of 30% glucose solution and 3% starch solution and placed in a test tube of distilled water. If this is left for about 15 minutes, the water can be tested for starch and glucose.

- Some glucose should have diffused through the tubing into the water, but the starch should not. Tests for starch and glucose will confirm this. Note: This only demonstrates that glucose will pass through the tubing but starch will not; it does not show that the enzyme catalyses the breakdown of the starch.

- The model gut can be used to show the effect of changes in temperature and pH on the activity of saliva or amylase on starch. The tubing should be placed in boiling tubes, and samples of the water surrounding the tubing can be tested for starch and sugars at intervals to determine whether or not digestion has taken place.

- To investigate changes in temperature, the boiling tubes containing the enzyme-substrate mixtures in the tubing should be incubated in a range of temperatures from about 5 °C to 60 °C using water baths.

- To investigate the range of pH values, buffer solutions should be used, providing another opportunity to develop the investigative aspects of 'How Science Works', such as evaluation.

Plenary

Cryptic word search – Support students by giving them a wordsearch of the enzymes, substrates and products from the lesson. Extend students by getting them to write cryptic definitions of the words and using them to test each other. *(10 minutes)*

Practical support

Investigating digestion

Equipment and materials required

Visking or dialysis tubing, dropping pipettes, elastic bands, starch and enzyme solutions (the concentration of these solutions may need to be increased to give results in a single lesson), water baths, beakers, test tubes and racks, iodine solution, Benedict's solution.

Details

Each group of students will need two 15 cm lengths of dialysis (Visking) tubing, which has been soaked in water. Each piece should be knotted securely at one end. Using a dropping pipette, fill one length of the tubing with 3% starch solution and place it in a test tube. Fold the top of the tubing over the rim of the test tube and secure with an elastic band. Remove all traces of the starch solution from the outside of the tubing by filling the test tube with water and emptying it several times. Finally, fill the test tube with water and place it in a rack.

Repeat the procedure with the second length of tubing but add 5 cm³ saliva or amylase solutions to the starch solution, and shake before filling the dialysis tubing. The test tubes should be labelled A and B and placed in a water bath at 35 °C for 30 minutes. The water in the test tubes should then be tested for: starch, using iodine solution; sugars, using Benedict's solution.

Safety: CLEAPSS Hazcard 54B Iodine solution. CLEAPSS Hazcards 27C and 95A Benedict's solution – harmful. CLEAPSS Hazcard 33 Enzymes. Wear eye protection.

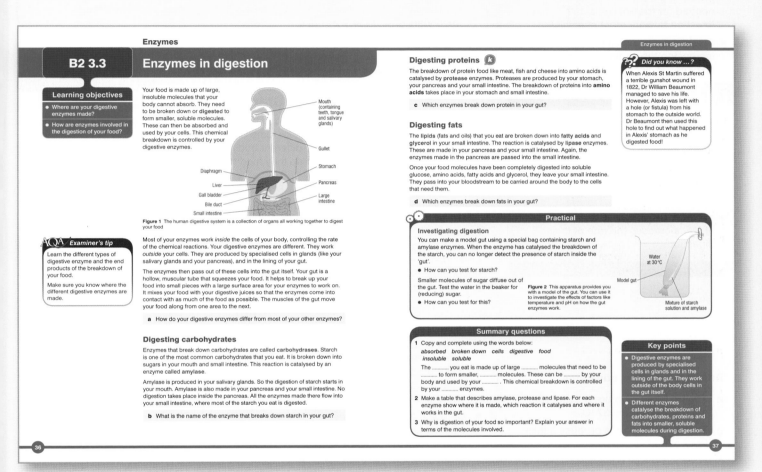

Enzymes

B2 3.3 Enzymes in digestion

Learning objectives
- Where are your digestive enzymes made?
- How are enzymes involved in the digestion of your food?

Your food is made up of large, insoluble molecules that your body cannot absorb. They need to be broken down or **digested** to form smaller, soluble molecules. These can then be absorbed and used by your cells. This chemical breakdown is controlled by your digestive enzymes.

Figure 1 The human digestive system is a collection of organs all working together to digest your food

Labels: Mouth (containing teeth, tongue and salivary glands); Gullet; Stomach; Pancreas; Large intestine; Small intestine; Bile duct; Gall bladder; Liver; Diaphragm

AQA Examiner's tip
Learn the different types of digestive enzyme and the end products of the breakdown of your food.
Make sure you know where the different digestive enzymes are made.

Most of your enzymes work *inside* the cells of your body, controlling the rate of the chemical reactions. Your digestive enzymes are different. They work *outside* your cells. They are produced by specialised cells in glands (like your salivary glands and your pancreas), and in the lining of your gut.

The enzymes then pass out of these cells into the gut itself. Your gut is a hollow, muscular tube that squeezes your food. It helps to break up your food into small pieces with a large surface area for your enzymes to work on. It mixes your food with your digestive juices so that the enzymes come into contact with as much of the food as possible. The muscles of the gut move your food along from one area to the next.

a How do your digestive enzymes differ from most of your other enzymes?

Digesting carbohydrates

Enzymes that break down carbohydrates are called **carbohydrases**. Starch is one of the most common carbohydrates that you eat. It is broken down into sugars in your mouth and small intestine. This reaction is catalysed by an enzyme called **amylase**.

Amylase is produced in your salivary glands. So the digestion of starch starts in your mouth. Amylase is also made in your pancreas and your small intestine. No digestion takes place inside the pancreas. All the enzymes made there flow into your small intestine, where most of the starch you eat is digested.

b What is the name of the enzyme that breaks down starch in your gut?

Digesting proteins

The breakdown of protein food like meat, fish and cheese into amino acids is catalysed by **protease** enzymes. Proteases are produced by your stomach, your pancreas and your small intestine. The breakdown of proteins into **amino acids** takes place in your stomach and small intestine.

c Which enzymes break down protein in your gut?

Digesting fats

The **lipids** (fats and oils) that you eat are broken down into **fatty acids** and **glycerol** in your small intestine. The reaction is catalysed by **lipase** enzymes. These are made in your pancreas and your small intestine. Again, the enzymes made in the pancreas are passed into the small intestine.

Once your food molecules have been completely digested into soluble glucose, amino acids, fatty acids and glycerol, they leave your small intestine. They pass into your bloodstream to be carried around the body to the cells that need them.

d Which enzymes break down fats in your gut?

Practical

Investigating digestion
You can make a model gut using a special bag containing starch and amylase enzymes. When the enzyme has catalysed the breakdown of the starch, you can no longer detect the presence of starch inside the 'gut'.
- How can you test for starch?

Smaller molecules of sugar diffuse out of the gut. Test the water in the beaker for (reducing) sugar.
- How can you test for this?

Figure 2 This apparatus provides you with a model of the gut. You can use it to investigate the effects of factors like temperature and pH on how the gut enzymes work.

Labels: Water at 30 °C; Model gut; Mixture of starch solution and amylase

Did you know …?

When Alexis St Martin suffered a terrible gunshot wound in 1822, Dr William Beaumont managed to save his life. However, Alexis was left with a hole (or fistula) from his stomach to the outside world. Dr Beaumont then used this hole to find out what happened in Alexis' stomach as he digested food!

Summary questions

1 Copy and complete using the words below:
absorbed broken down cells digestive food insoluble soluble

The .... you eat is made up of large .... molecules that need to be .... to form smaller, ... molecules. These can be .... by your body and used by your .... This chemical breakdown is controlled by your .... enzymes.

2 Make a table that describes amylase, protease and lipase. For each enzyme show where it is made, which reaction it catalyses and where it works in the gut.

3 Why is digestion of your food so important? Explain your answer in terms of the molecules involved.

Key points

- Digestive enzymes are produced by specialised cells in glands and in the lining of the gut. They work outside of the body cells in the gut itself.
- Different enzymes catalyse the breakdown of carbohydrates, proteins and fats into smaller, soluble molecules during digestion.

Summary answers

1 food, insoluble, broken down, soluble, absorbed, cells, digestive

2 Suitable table.

Enzyme	Where it is made	Reaction catalysed	Where it works
Amylase	Salivary glands, pancreas, small intestine	Starch → sugars/glucose	Mouth, small intestine
Protease	Stomach, pancreas, small intestine	Proteins → amino acids	Stomach, small intestine
Lipase	Pancreas, small intestine	Lipids → fatty acids and glycerol	Small intestine

3 Large insoluble molecules in food cannot be absorbed into the blood so have to be digested to form small insoluble molecules that can be absorbed.

B2 3.4

Speeding up digestion

AQA Specification link-up: Biology B2.5

- Some enzymes work outside the body cells ... . *[B2.5.2 c)]*
- The enzyme amylase is produced in the salivary glands ... . *[B2.5.2 d)]*
- Protease enzymes are produced by the stomach ... . *[B2.5.2 e)]*
- Lipase enzymes are produced by the pancreas and small intestine ... . *[B2.5.2 f)]*
- The stomach also produces hydrochloric acid. The ... . *[B2.5.2 g)]*
- The liver produces bile, which is stored in the gall bladder ... . *[B2.5.2 h)]*

Controlled Assessment: AS4.1 Plan practical ways to develop and test candidates' own scientific ideas *[AS4.1.1 a) b) c)]*; AS4.4 Select and process primary and secondary data. *[AS4.4.2 a) b) c)]*

Learning objectives

Students should learn:

- that the enzymes in the stomach work most effectively in the acid conditions resulting from the production of hydrochloric acid by the stomach
- that bile produced by the liver provides the alkaline conditions needed for the enzymes in the small intestine to work most effectively
- that bile also emulsifies the fats increasing the surface area for the enzymes to act upon.

Learning outcomes

Most students should be able to:

- describe how pH affects the enzymes in the different parts of the gut
- describe how bile emulsifies fats.

Some students should also be able to:

- explain in detail how the emulsification of fats increases the rate of their digestion.

Lesson structure

Starters

Effect of body temperature on digestion – Show a picture or footage of a reptile, such as a snake or a crocodile, eating a large lump of meat and show a picture of lions feeding. Ask: 'What consequences will their different body temperatures have on the rate at which they digest their meals? How often do they feed the reptiles in the zoo?' Students to make a list and compare. *(5 minutes)*

More about surface area – Get students to tell you what they know about SA (surface area) to volume ratio. Ask them to think about how this might be relevant to the process of digestion. Discuss the effect of the teeth and mastication on the break up of large masses of food in the mouth. Ask: 'What is the effect on digestion in the mouth? Does chewing affect digestion in the stomach?' Support students by reminding them of how SA (surface area) increases when the volume is decreased. Extend students by asking them to think about other examples of the importance of SA (surface area) in the process of digestion (e.g. chewing, absorption). *(10 minutes)*

Main

- The practical on 'Breaking down protein' described in the Student Book is easy to set up (see 'Practical support'). The experiment can be made more quantitative (introducing 'How Science Works'), by getting the students to formulate an hypothesis, make predictions, use stated volumes of enzyme and acid and weigh the pieces of meat used at the beginning and end of the experiment. A bar chart can be drawn showing the percentage change in mass.

- Compare the action of pepsin with the action of trypsin. Pepsin and trypsin work in different parts of the gut in different pH conditions. The experiment ('Effect of pH on enzyme action') described in 'B2 3.2 Factors affecting enzyme action' could be used here to show that pepsin works best in acid conditions and trypsin in alkaline conditions. If specific pH values are required, then the use of buffer solutions is recommended.

- Ask the students what the word 'emulsion' means (paint it on to a large sheet of paper – using emulsion paint). Bring in a salad, some vinegar and some olive oil. Get a student to pour some oil on top of the vinegar in a gas jar or similar vessel, shake vigorously and produce an emulsion. Students can do this themselves on a small scale in a boiling tube. Observe the globules formed and link to SA (surface area), then to speeding up digestion. Link the formation of an emulsion with the effect of bile salts.

- An experiment could be set up to demonstrate the effect of bile salts on the activity of lipase (see 'Practical support').

Answers to in-text questions

- **a** The body temperature is usually maintained around 37 °C.
- **b** The stomach glands produce a thick layer of mucus.
- **c** The food entering the small intestine from the stomach is acidic. The enzymes of the small intestine work best in alkaline conditions.

Support

- Get students to illustrate the formation of an emulsion.

Extend

- Get students to find out more about bile. What does it contain? How and where is it made?

Plenaries

Gallstones – Show some gallstones or photographs of gallstones. Discuss why gallstones occur and what might be the consequences. Get the students to write a letter to their doctor stating what problems they fear and asking advice. *(5 minutes)*

Colouring exercise: The pH in the gut – Give the students unlabelled diagrams of the digestive system and ask them to label them and colour in the different regions according to the different pH conditions that exist in the gut. Support students by giving them the list of different pH conditions. Extend students by getting them to work out the different regions and to add the names of the major enzymes present in each region. *(10 minutes)*

Practical support

Breaking down protein

Equipment and materials required

For each group:

At least three test tubes and a rack, small cubes of meat, 2% pepsin solution, 0.1 M solution of hydrochloric acid, water bath at 35 °C, balance, labels, filter papers, eye protection.

Details

Each group of students will require three test tubes and can set up their own experiment. Into one test tube, place about 20 cm³ of pepsin solution. Into a second tube place the same volume of hydrochloric acid and into a third tube place the same volume of a mixture of pepsin solution and hydrochloric acid. Cut three similar sized chunks of meat, weigh each one and place one piece into each of the three tubes, noting which piece of meat was placed into which tube. Leave for a few hours. An additional control tube could be added using boiled and cooled pepsin. If this done, it would be advisable to leave the experiment running for 24 hours. The pieces of meat should then be removed from the tubes, rinsed and dried on filter paper before reweighing.

Safety: Wear eye protection.

Demonstrating the effect of bile salts on the activity of lipase

Equipment and materials required

Two test tubes, 5 cm³ of milk, 7 cm³ sodium carbonate solution and 5 drops of phenolphthalein, washing up liquid, 2 cm³ of lipase.

Details

Set up two test tubes, each containing 5 cm³ of milk, 7 cm³ sodium carbonate solution and 5 drops of phenolphthalein. To one tube, add a drop of washing up liquid. Add 1 cm³ of lipase to each tube and stir each tube, timing how long it takes for the indicator to go from pink (alkaline) to colourless (acid) showing that the lipids in the milk have been broken down to fatty acids. The washing up liquid emulsifies the lipids and the reaction should therefore be quicker.

Safety: CLEAPSS Hazcard 33 Enzymes. Wear eye protection. Wash hands if reagents come into contact with the skin.

Enzymes

B2 3.4 — Speeding up digestion

Learning objectives

- Why does your stomach contain hydrochloric acid?
- What is bile and why is it so important in digestion?

links

For information on the sensitivity of enzymes to temperature and pH, look back at B2 3.2 Factors affecting enzyme action.

Your digestive system produces many enzymes that speed up the breakdown of the food you eat. As your body is kept at a fairly steady 37°C, your enzymes have an ideal temperature that allows them to work as fast as possible.

Keeping the pH in your gut at ideal levels isn't that easy because different enzymes work best at different pH levels. For example, the protease enzyme found in your stomach works best in acidic conditions.

On the other hand, the proteases made in your pancreas need alkaline conditions to work at their best

So, your body makes a variety of different chemicals that help to keep conditions ideal for your enzymes all the way through your gut.

a Why do your enzymes almost always have the right temperature to work at their best?

Changing pH in the gut

You have around 35 million glands in the lining of your stomach. These secrete protease enzymes to digest the protein you eat. The enzymes work best in an acid pH. So your stomach also produces a concentrated solution of hydrochloric acid from the same glands. In fact, your stomach produces around 3 litres of acid a day! This acid allows your stomach protease enzymes to work very effectively. It also kills most of the bacteria that you take in with your food.

Finally, your stomach also produces a thick layer of mucus. This coats your stomach walls and protects them from being digested by the acid and the enzymes.

b How does your stomach avoid digesting itself?

Practical

Breaking down protein

You can see the effect of acid on pepsin, the protease found in the stomach, quite simply. Set up three test tubes: one containing pepsin, one containing hydrochloric acid and one containing a mixture of the two. Keep them at body temperature in a water bath. Add a similar-sized chunk of meat to all three of them. Set up a webcam and watch for a few hours to see what happens.

- What conclusions can you make?

Figure 1 These test tubes show clearly the importance of protein-digesting enzymes and hydrochloric acid in your stomach. Meat was added to each tube at the same time.

After a few hours – depending on the size and type of the meal you have eaten – your food leaves your stomach. It moves on into your small intestine. Some of the enzymes that catalyse digestion in your small intestine are made in your pancreas. Some are also made in the small intestine itself. They all work best in an alkaline environment.

The acidic liquid coming from your stomach needs to become an alkaline mix in your small intestine. So how does it happen?

Your liver makes a greenish-yellow alkaline liquid called **bile**. Bile is stored in your gall bladder until it is needed.

As food comes into the small intestine from the stomach, bile is squirted onto it. The bile neutralises the acid from the stomach and then makes the semi-digested food alkaline. This provides the ideal conditions needed for the enzymes in the small intestine.

c Why does the food coming into your small intestine need neutralising?

Altering the surface area

It is very important for the enzymes of the gut to have the largest possible surface area of food to work on. This is not a problem with carbohydrates and proteins. However, the fats that you eat do not mix with all the watery liquids in your gut. They stay as large globules (like oil in water) that make it difficult for the lipase enzymes to act.

This is the second important function of the bile. It **emulsifies** the fats in your food. This means bile physically breaks up large drops of fat into smaller droplets. This provides a much bigger surface area for the lipase enzymes to act on. The larger surface area helps the lipase chemically break down the fats more quickly into fatty acids and glycerol.

?? Did you know …?

Sometimes gall stones block the gall bladder and bile duct. The stones can range from a few millimetres to several centimetres long and can cause terrible pain.

Figure 2 Gall stones

AQA Examiner's tip

Remember, food is not digested in the liver or the pancreas.

Bile is *not* an enzyme and it does *not* break down fat molecules.

Bile emulsifies fat droplets to increase the surface area, which in turn increases the rate of fat digestion by lipase.

Summary questions

1 Copy and complete using the words below:

alkaline   emulsifies   gall bladder   liver   neutralises   small intestine

Bile is an .... liquid produced by your .... It is stored in the .... and released onto food as it enters the .... It .... the acidic food from the stomach and makes it alkaline. It also .... fats.

2 Look at Figure 1.
  a In what conditions does the protease from the stomach work best?
  b How does your body create the right pH in the stomach for this enzyme?
  c In what conditions does the proteases in the small intestine work best?
  d How does your body create the right pH in the small intestine for this enzyme?

3 Draw a diagram to explain how bile produces a big surface area for lipase to work on and explain why this is important.

Key points

- The enzymes of the stomach work best in acid conditions.
- The enzymes made in the pancreas and the small intestine work best in alkaline conditions.
- Bile produced by the liver neutralises acid and emulsifies fats.

38

39

Further teaching suggestions

Estimating the rate of digestion

- Use small pieces of cooked sausage, 2% pepsin and 0.01M HCl in water baths at different temperatures to estimate the rate of digestion. Compare this with the cooked sausage in 2% trypsin and 0.1M NaOH. The concentration of both enzymes can be varied and the effect of specific pH values can be estimated with the use of buffer solutions.

Summary answers

1 alkaline, liver, gall bladder, small intestine, neutralises, emulsifies

2 a Acid
  b Hydrochloric acid is made in glands in the stomach.
  c Alkaline/alkali
  d The liver produces bile that is stored in the gall bladder and released when food comes into the small intestine.

3 [Marks for a good diagram showing a large fat droplet coated in bile splitting into many small fat droplets.] This produces a larger SA (surface area) so enzymes can get to many more fat molecules and so break them down more quickly.

B2 3.5

Making use of enzymes

Learning objectives

Students should learn:

- that enzymes from microorganisms have many uses in the home and in industry
- that proteases and lipases are used in the manufacture of biological detergents
- that proteases, carbohydrases and isomerase are used in food manufacture.

Learning outcomes

Most students should be able to:

- explain how biological detergents work
- describe some of the ways in which enzymes are used in the food industry.

Some students should also be able to:

- evaluate the advantages and disadvantages of using enzymes in home and in industry.

Answers to in-text questions

a It's a washing powder that contains enzymes, usually proteases and lipases.

b Enzymes in yeast turn sugar (glucose) into ethanol. They wouldn't work on starch.

Support

- Use name boards with a fold-over end. Write 'carbohydrate' on one and use the hinged fold-over to convert it into 'carbohydrase'. Have examples of all the enzymes required in the specification.

Extend

- Ask students to find out the differences in the structural formulae of glucose and fructose. They can try to work out why these sugars have different effects on the taste buds.

AQA Specification link-up: Biology B1.5

- Some microorganisms produce enzymes that pass out of the cells ... . [B2.5.2 i)]
- In industry, enzymes are used to bring about reactions ... . [B2.5.2 j)]

  Controlled Assessment: AS4.1 Plan practical ways to develop and test candidates' own scientific ideas. [AS4.1.1 a) b) c)]

Lesson structure

Starters

Taste tests – Fructose is now available in many supermarkets. You could make up separate solutions of fructose, sucrose and glucose of the same strength (e.g. 2 teaspoons in a beaker of water) and get the students to do a blind tasting scoring them for sweetness on a 5-point scale. Note: this must be done in hygienic conditions following risk assessment and not in a laboratory. *(5 minutes)*

Baby food for lunch? – Show the students some samples of baby food. Have disposable plastic spoons and be prepared for joking. Some pelican bibs will help to create the atmosphere. Ask: 'How does baby food differ from adult food? What did parents do before the commercially prepared baby foods were available?' Compile lists on the board and compare. Support students by prompting them to suggest how enzymes might be involved. Extend students by asking them to list the processes involved in the commercial production of baby food. *(10 minutes)*

Main

- Use agar plates containing starch, milk and mayonnaise (or salad cream or egg yolk) to demonstrate the activity of enzymes in biological detergents (see 'Practical support'). This activity can be used to compare different biological washing powders or liquids (the advantage of liquids is that volumes can be measured and dilutions made more easily). It can also be used to compare dishwasher detergents with clothes washing detergents and to discover whether the age of the detergent has any effect on its efficiency.

- All of these can be used to introduce many 'How Science Works' concepts. Predictions can be made, measurements made and recorded, variables controlled and conclusions drawn. It also gives students some scope for designing their own investigations.

- The experiment above can be modified to demonstrate that the proteases in a biological detergent can work at higher temperatures than trypsin from an animal source. Samples of both can be heated to temperatures of 30 °C, 40 °C, etc. and then placed in holes in milk agar plates. Use a separate plate for each enzyme or detergent tested and the number of holes should correspond to the number of different temperatures tested. The plates should then be treated as above and the clear areas measured and recorded. A graph can then be plotted of temperature against area of clear zone.

- The effect of biological detergent on egg albumin can be demonstrated by immersing cubes of egg white in a solution of a biological detergent. A solution of a biological washing powder is made by dissolving 3 g of powder in 30 cm³ of water. A cube of egg white is weighed and placed in this solution for 20 minutes, after which time it is removed, rinsed and dried. The effect of the washing powder can be assessed by reweighing.

- This investigation can be expanded to consider different variables. Comparisons can be made using different biological detergents. The strength of the detergent needed can be investigated and the optimum temperature found.

Plenary

Enzymes table – Give the students two minutes to write down as many advantages and disadvantages of using enzymes in commercial processes as they can. Gather together the suggestions and build up a table of advantages and disadvantages. Discuss how the disadvantages can be overcome. *(5 minutes)*

Practical support

Investigating biological washing powder

Equipment and materials required

Some biological detergent (either in powder or liquid form in order to make up different concentrations if needed – avoid contact with skin), egg white in chunks/cubes (or agar plates containing starch, milk, mayonnaise, salad cream or egg yolk), test tubes and racks, tissues for drying, iodine solution (CLEAPSS Hazcard 54B) balance for weighing, eye protection, protective gloves.

Details

A cork borer is used to remove cylinders of agar from the prepared plates. The number of cylinders removed depends on the number of detergents being tested. Into the holes, solutions of the detergents can be placed and the plates incubated at 25 °C for about 24 hours.

Iodine solution is poured over the starch-agar plate and left for 5 minutes before being poured away. The diameter of clear areas around the holes can be measured and recorded. It should be possible to measure clear areas around the holes on the milk-agar plates and the mayonnaise-agar plates.

Safety: Care when handling detergents. CLEAPSS Hazcard 54B Iodine solution. Eye protection and protective gloves needed.

Enzymes

B2 3.5 — Making use of enzymes

Learning objectives

- How do biological detergents work?
- How are enzymes used in the food industry?

Enzymes were first isolated from living cells in the 19th century. Ever since then, we have found more and more ways of using them in industry. Some microorganisms produce enzymes that pass out of the cells and are easy for us to use. In other cases we use the whole microorganism.

Enzymes in the home

In the past, people boiled and scrubbed their clothes to get them clean – by hand! Now we have washing machines and enzymes ready and waiting to digest the stains.

Many people use **biological detergents** to remove stains such as grass, sweat and food from their clothes. Biological washing powders contain proteases and lipases. These enzymes break down the proteins and fats in the stains. They help to give you a cleaner wash. Biological detergents work better than non-biological detergents at lower temperatures. This is because the enzymes work best at lower temperatures – they are denatured if the water is too hot. This means you use less electricity too.

a What is a biological washing powder?

Figure 1 Many people now have a dishwasher. Dishwasher detergents contain enzymes that digest cooked-on proteins like eggs, which are often hard to remove.

Practical

Investigating biological washing powder

Weigh a chunk of cooked egg white and leave it in a strong solution of biological washing powder.

- What do you think will happen to the egg white?
- How can you measure just how effective the protease enzymes are?
- How could you investigate the effect of surface area on enzyme action?

Enzymes in industry

Pure enzymes have many uses in industry.

Proteases are used to make baby foods. They 'predigest' some of the protein in the food. When babies first begin to eat solid foods they are not very good at digesting it. Treating the food with protease enzymes makes it easier for a baby's digestive system to cope with it. It is easier for them to get the amino acids they need from their food.

Carbohydrases are used to convert starch into sugar (glucose) syrup. We use huge quantities of sugar syrup in food production. You will see it on the ingredients labels on all sorts of foods.

Starch is made by plants like corn and it is very cheap. Using enzymes to convert this plant starch into sweet sugar provides a cheap source of sweetness for food manufacturers.

It is also important for the process of making fuel (ethanol) from plants.

b Why does starch need to be converted to sugar before it is used to make ethanol?

Figure 2 Learning to eat solid food isn't easy. Having some of it predigested by protease enzymes can make it easier to get the amino acids you need to grow.

Sometimes the glucose syrup made from starch is passed through another process that uses a different set of enzymes. The enzyme **isomerase** is used to change glucose syrup into fructose syrup.

Glucose and fructose contain exactly the same amount of energy (1700 kJ or 400 kcal per 100 g). However, fructose is much sweeter than glucose. Much smaller amounts are needed to make food taste sweet. Fructose is widely used in 'slimming' foods – the food tastes sweet but contains fewer calories.

The advantages and disadvantages of using enzymes

In industrial processes, many of the reactions need high temperatures and pressures to make them go fast enough to produce the products needed. This needs expensive equipment and requires a lot of energy.

Enzymes can solve industrial problems like these. They catalyse reactions at relatively low temperatures and normal pressures. Enzyme-based processes are therefore often fairly cheap to run.

One problem with enzymes is that they are denatured at high temperatures, so the temperature must be kept down (usually below 45 °C). The pH also needs to be kept within carefully controlled limits that suit the enzyme. It costs money to control these conditions.

Many enzymes are also expensive to produce. Whole microbes are relatively cheap, but need to be supplied with food and oxygen and their waste products removed. They use some of the substrate to grow more microbes. Pure enzymes use the substrate more efficiently, but they are also more expensive to produce.

Figure 3 Some people are always trying to lose weight. Enzyme technology is used to convert more and more glucose syrup into fructose syrup to make so-called 'slimming' foods.

AQA Examiner's tip

Remember that most enzyme names end in '-ase'.

Some enzymes used in industry work at quite high temperatures – so don't be put off if a graph shows an optimum temperature well above 45 °C!

Summary questions

1 List three enzymes and the ways in which we use them in the food industry.
2 Biological washing powders contain enzymes in tiny capsules. Explain why:
   a they are more effective than non-biological powders at lower temperatures
   b they are not more effective at high temperatures.
3 Make a table to show the advantages and disadvantages of using enzymes in industry.

Key points

- Some microorganisms produce enzymes that pass out of the cells and can be used in different ways.
- Biological detergents may contain proteases and lipases.
- Proteases, carbohydrases and isomerase are all used in the food industry.

Further teaching suggestions

How good are biological detergents?

Students could find out how many people use biological detergents in dishwashers and washing machines, and whether or not there are differences between them. Some preparatory work for the next lesson could be set as homework tasks here.

More about temperatures

There have been efforts made to persuade people to reduce the temperature at which they run their washing machine programmes. Discuss this with students and get them to suggest ways of finding out if the detergents work as well at lower temperatures as they do at higher temperatures.

Summary answers

1 Proteases: predigested baby food. Carbohydrases: convert starch to glucose syrup. Isomerase: converts glucose syrup to fructose syrup.

2 **a** The protease and lipase enzymes digest proteins and fats on the clothes, so the clothes get cleaner than detergent alone. The enzymes work best at lower temperatures. Detergent alone needs higher temperatures to work at its best, so biological detergents are much more effective at low temperatures.

   b At temperatures above about 45 °C, the enzymes may be denatured and so have no effect on cleaning.

3

Advantages	Disadvantages
Work at relatively low temperatures.	Denatured by high temperatures.
Work at relatively low pressures.	Sensitive to pH changes.
Efficient catalysts.	If whole organisms, need food, oxygen and waste products removed.
Processes often cheap to run.	Enzymes can be expensive to produce.

B2 3.6 High-tech enzymes

Learning objectives

Students should learn:

- that there are advantages and disadvantages to using enzymes at home and in industry
- that enzymes can be used as diagnostic tools in medicine and in the treatment of some diseases.

Learning outcomes

Most students should be able to:

- describe some of the advantages and disadvantages of using biological detergents
- describe some of the ways in which enzymes are used in medicine.

Some students should also be able to:

- evaluate the advantages and disadvantages of using enzymes in the home and in industry.

Support

- Provide students with the text and pictures with which to build up a poster on 'Enzymes in medicine'.

Extend

- Get students to find out more about unusual enzymes, such as bromelain and papain, and their uses in the food industry.

AQA Specification link-up: Biology B2.5

- Evaluate the advantages and disadvantages of using enzymes in the home and in industry. [B2.5]

  Controlled Assessment: AS4.1 Plan practical ways to develop and test candidates' own scientific ideas. [AS4.1.1 a) b) c)]

Lesson structure

Starters

A question of temperature – Some washing machine cycles can operate at temperatures as low as 30 °C. Ask: 'Is this always a good thing?' Draw up a balance sheet of advantages and disadvantages of the lowering of the temperature. Ask: 'Do the advantages outweigh the disadvantages? Would you wash your baby's dirty clothes in a low temperature wash?' *(5 minutes)*

Will it come out in the wash? – Get students to suggest stains they might get on their clothes and build up a list. Add a few of your own suggestions (such as tar, ballpoint pen, etc.). Then ask which ones will come out if the clothes are washed with a biological detergent. Support students by making the list fairly simple and reminding them about the enzymes in the detergent. Extend students by including some more unusual examples (chilli sauce!) and get them to identify the class of enzyme that would get rid of the stain. *(10 minutes)*

Main

- Clinistix and albustix can be used to test for the presence of glucose and protein in urine. Carry out a 'Tinkle test' experiment with fake urine doctored with glucose, protein, both and neither. Discuss the benefits of such tests compared with the standard methods of testing for glucose and protein in the lab (using Benedict's solution and the Biuret test). Discuss the value of the tests in making quick diagnoses and helping people with diabetes to control their condition.

- Discuss the problems of cystic fibrosis and the use of enzymes in its treatment. Tell students about the consequences of the blocking of the pancreatic duct. Ask the students what they think the consequences could be and how the problem could be overcome. Show the video *Sammi's story* (Channel 4 Television, 1995) if available or go to the cystic fibrosis website for more information about the treatment.

- Use the internet to research other uses of enzymes in medicine, such as streptokinase for heart attacks and a treatment for childhood leukaemia. Allow the students to carry out their own research or prepare a PowerPoint presentation with a worksheet for the students to complete.

- Carry out the poster activity 'Enzymes in medicine' recommended in the Student Book. It would be quite difficult to include masses of information on one poster so students could decide to make a series of posters about different uses of enzymes, along the lines of 'Did you know that … streptokinase is used to treat heart attacks?' etc. Use could be made of ICT in the design and production of the posters.

- Students could carry out the activity suggested in the Student Book and design an experiment to compare the effectiveness of a biological detergent with an ordinary detergent at 40 °C. Encourage students to think about the variables that need to be controlled and the way in which they are going to assess the results. They should be able to use the knowledge they have gained from setting up the enzyme experiments described in other spreads.

Plenaries

Enzyme anagrams round-up – Prepare anagrams of the enzymes mentioned in this chapter. Students could be supported by using the simpler, straightforward ones. Students could be extended by including more enzymes and/or leaving out the vowels. *(5 minutes)*

The perfect detergent – Students, in groups, could decide on the most favourable properties that a clothes-washing detergent should have and then give it a name and design a simple poster advertising its advantages. There should be good scientific reasons behind the claims made for its efficacy! Posters could be displayed around the classroom. *(10 minutes)*

B2 3.6   High-tech enzymes

Learning objectives

- What are the advantages and disadvantages of using enzymes in detergents?
- Can doctors use enzymes to help keep you healthy?

The pros and cons of biological detergents

For many people, biological washing powders have lots of benefits. Children can be messy eaters and their clothes get lots of mud and grass stains as well. Many of the stains that adults get on their clothes – sweat, food and drink – are biological too. So these enzyme-based washing powders are effective and therefore widely used.

Biological powders have another advantage. They are very effective at cleaning at low temperatures. Therefore they use a lot less electricity than non-biological detergents. That's good for the environment and cheaper for the consumer.

Figure 1 Biological detergents come in many different forms

Figure 2 The enzymes in biological detergents are held in tiny capsules – these are seen under an electron microscope

However, when biological detergent was first manufactured many factory staff developed allergies. They were reacting to enzyme dust in the air – proteins often trigger allergies. Some people using the powders were affected in the same way. But there was a solution – the enzymes were put in tiny capsules and then most of the allergy problems stopped.

Unfortunately, it got bad publicity, which some people still remember. However, research (based on 44 different studies) was published by the British Journal of Dermatology in 2008. This showed that biological detergents do not seem to be a major cause of skin problems.

Some people worry about all the enzymes going into our rivers and seas from biological detergents. The waste water from washing machines goes into the sewage system. Also, the low temperatures used to wash with biological detergents may not be as good at killing pathogens on the clothes.

Practical

Plan and carry out an investigation to compare the effectiveness of a biological detergent with a non-biological detergent at 40°C.

Enzymes and medicine

Some of the ways in which enzymes are used in medicine

TO DIAGNOSE DISEASE

If your liver is damaged or diseased, some of your liver enzymes may leak out into your bloodstream. If your symptoms suggest your liver isn't working properly, doctors can test your blood for these enzymes. This will tell them if your liver really is damaged.

TO DIAGNOSE AND CONTROL DISEASE

People who have diabetes have too much glucose in their blood. As a result, they also get glucose in their urine. One commonly used test for sugar in the urine relies on a colour change on a test strip. The test strip contains a chemical indicator and an enzyme. It is placed in a urine sample. The enzyme catalyses the breakdown of any glucose found in the urine. The strip changes colour if the products of this reaction are present. This shows that glucose was present in the original sample.

TO CURE DISEASE

- If your pancreas is damaged or diseased it cannot make enzymes. So, you have to take extra enzymes – particularly lipase – to allow you to digest your food. The enzymes are in special capsules to stop them being digested in your stomach.
- If you have a heart attack, an enzyme called streptokinase will be injected into your blood as soon as possible. It dissolves clots in the arteries of the heart wall and reduces the amount of damage done to your heart muscle.
- An enzyme is being used to treat a type of blood cancer in children. The cancer cells cannot make one particular amino acid. They need to take it from your body fluids. The enzyme speeds up the breakdown of this amino acid. The cancer cells cannot get any and they die. Your normal cells can make the amino acid so they are not affected.

Figure 3 Enzymes are vital in the human body, so it is not surprising that they are widely used in the world of medicine as well

Activity

Make a poster with the title 'Enzymes in medicine' which could be displayed on the walls of the science department to inform and interest students in KS3 and/or KS4. Use this material as a starting point and do some more research about the way enzymes are used, to help you make your poster as interesting as possible.

Key points

- Enzymes in detergents break down biological stains such as sweat. They work at low temperatures so use less electricity, which is cheaper and environmentally friendly. They originally caused problems with allergies, but this has been solved now. The lower-temperature washes are less good at killing pathogens; but higher temperatures can denature the enzymes.
- Enzymes can be produced industrially, both to diagnose and to treat disease.

Summary questions

1 Some people think that biological detergents are better for the environment than non-biological detergents. Why is this?

2 Write a short report in the use of one enzyme in industry or medicine. Explain things such as where the enzyme comes from, what it does, why it is an advantage to use it and what disadvantages there might be.

Further teaching suggestions

The differences between detergents

- Students could research the constituents of the biological detergents used in washing machines and those used in dishwashers. Are they different? Are the enzymes the same? Relate the different constituents to the functions of each detergent.

The ethics of using biological detergents

- Get students to consider the ethics of using biological detergents. Do they have effects on the environment? It could be interesting to compare the constituents and claims made for one brand range of cleaning products compared to other brands.

Summary answers

1 Enzymes work best at around 40°C therefore biological detergents are most effective in a cooler wash cycle. This uses less electricity and can therefore be argued to be ecologically more sound.

2 Students should provide information on where the enzyme comes from, what it does, why it is an advantage to use it, what disadvantages there are. Credit given for accuracy, interest and detail in the report.

Summary answers

1 a A vi   B iv   C ii   D i   E iii   F v

b Enzymes work by bringing reacting particles together and lowering the energy needed for them to react. Enzymes are large protein molecules with a hole or indentation known as the 'active site'. The substrate of the reaction fits into the active site of the enzyme like a lock and key. Once it is in place, the enzyme and substrate bind together. This is called the 'enzyme-substrate complex'. Then the reaction takes place rapidly and the products are released from the surface of the enzyme. [The use of diagrams would make this explanation very clear.]

2 a Smooth curve drawn through points and a good graph plot with suitable scale chosen, axes right way round, axes labelled correctly and accurately plotted points.

b Alkaline.

c This enzyme could be found in the small intestine, because it works in alkaline conditions. Other protein-digesting enzymes work in the stomach, but the conditions there are acidic.

3 a Well drawn graph.

b The reaction speeds up with the increase in temperature. Particles moving faster with more energy, so more likely to collide and react.

c A well drawn graph.

d Catalase.

e That it increases the rate up to about 40 °C and after that, the rate of the reaction decreases and eventually stops.

f Manganese(IV) oxide is a chemical and not adversely affected by temperature. Catalyse is an enzyme made of protein – as temperature goes up, the enzyme is denatured, the shape of the active site is lost and it can no longer catalyse the reaction.

g Carry out the test on temperatures around 40 °C to see which temperature took the shortest time.

Kerboodle resources

Resources available for this chapter on Kerboodle are:
- Chapter map: Enzymes
- Animation: Enzyme action (B2 3.1)
- How Science Works: Does temperature affect the speed of an enzyme reaction? (B2 3.2)
- Bump up your grade: Nearly everything about enzymes (B2 3.1)
- How Science Works: Lines of best fit and error bars (B2 3.2)
- Maths skills: Enzymes and rates (B2 3.5)
- Support: Enzyme memory (B2 3.5)
- Practical: Biological and non-biological washing powders (B2 3.5)
- Interactive activity: Enzymes
- Podcast: Enzymes
- Test yourself: Enzymes
- On your marks: Enzymes
- Examination-style questions: Enzymes
- Answers to examination-style questions: Enzymes

Summary questions

1 a Copy and complete the following sentences, matching each beginning with its correct ending.

A	A catalyst will speed up a reaction	i	.... could not occur without enzymes.
B	Living organisms make very efficient catalysts	ii	.... made of protein.
C	All enzymes are	iii	.... binds to the active site.
D	The reactions that keep you alive	iv	.... known as enzymes.
E	The substrate of an enzyme	v	.... a specific type of molecule.
F	Each type of enzyme affects	vi	.... but is not changed itself.

b Explain how an enzyme catalyses a reaction. Use diagrams if they make your explanation clearer.

2 The table gives some data about the relative activity levels of an enzyme at different pH levels.

pH	Relative activity
4	0
6	3
8	10
10	1

a Plot a graph of this data.

b Does this enzyme work best in an acid or an alkaline environment?

c This is a protein-digesting enzyme. Where in the gut do you think it might be found? Explain your answer.

3 The results in these tables come from a student who w investigating the breakdown of hydrogen peroxide usir manganese(IV) oxide and mashed raw potato.

Table 1 Manganese(IV) oxide

Temperature (°C)	Time taken (s)
20	106
30	51
40	26
50	12

Table 2 Raw mashed potato

Temperature (°C)	Time taken (s)
20	114
30	96
40	80
50	120
60	no reaction

a Draw a graph of the results using manganese(IV) oxide.

b What do these results tell you about the effect of temperature on a catalysed reaction? Explain your observation.

c Draw a graph of the results when raw mashed pota was added to the hydrogen peroxide.

d What is the name of the enzyme found in living cells that catalyses the breakdown of hydrogen peroxide

e What does this graph tell you about the effect of temperature on an enzyme-catalysed reaction?

f Why does temperature have this effect on the enzy catalysed reaction but not on the reaction catalysed by manganese(IV) oxide?

g How could you change the second investigation to find the temperature at which the enzyme works be

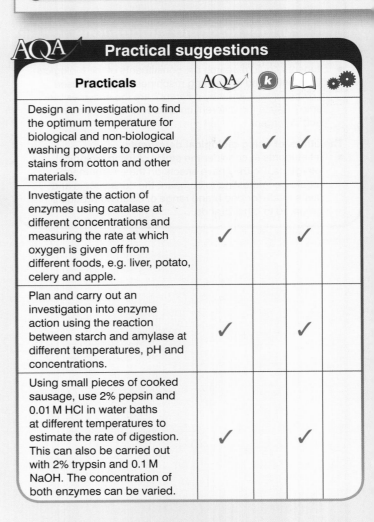

Practical suggestions

Practicals	AQA	k	📖	⚙
Design an investigation to find the optimum temperature for biological and non-biological washing powders to remove stains from cotton and other materials.	✓	✓	✓	
Investigate the action of enzymes using catalase at different concentrations and measuring the rate at which oxygen is given off from different foods, e.g. liver, potato, celery and apple.	✓		✓	
Plan and carry out an investigation into enzyme action using the reaction between starch and amylase at different temperatures, pH and concentrations.	✓		✓	
Using small pieces of cooked sausage, use 2% pepsin and 0.01 M HCl in water baths at different temperatures to estimate the rate of digestion. This can also be carried out with 2% trypsin and 0.1 M NaOH. The concentration of both enzymes can be varied.	✓		✓	

AQA Examination-style questions

Enzymes are chemicals produced in living cells.

a Copy and complete the following sentences, using some of the words below.

amylase bile catalysts fats lipase protease protein sugars

i Enzymes are described as biological .... (1)
ii Enzyme molecules are made of .... (1)
iii The enzyme that digests starch is called .... (1)
iv The substance that neutralises stomach acid is called .... (1)
v Glycerol is one of the products of the digestion of .... (1)

b An enzyme works well in pH 7.
i What happens to this enzyme when it is placed in an acid solution? (1)
ii Give **one** other factor that will affect the activity of the enzyme. (1)

c Explain what happens to starch when it is digested. (2)

AQA, 2002

Enzymes have many uses in the home and in industry.

a Which type of organisms are used to produce these enzymes?

Choose the correct answer from the following options:

mammals microorganisms plants (1)

b Babies may have difficulty digesting proteins in their food. Baby-food manufacturers use enzymes to 'pre-digest' the protein in baby food to overcome this difficulty.

Copy and complete the following sentences, using some of the words below.

amino acids amylases proteases sugars

i Proteins are 'pre-digested' using enzymes called .... (1)
ii This pre-digestion produces .... (1)

c A baby-food manufacturer uses enzyme **V** to predigest protein.
He tries four new enzymes, **W, X, Y** and **Z**, to see if he can reduce the time taken to predigest the protein. The graph shows the time taken for the enzymes to completely predigest the protein.
The manufacturer uses the same concentration of enzyme and the same mass of protein in each experiment.

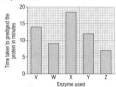

i How long did it take enzyme **V** to predigest the protein? (1)
ii Which enzyme would you advise the baby food manufacturer to use?
Choose the correct answer from the following options:

enzyme V enzyme W enzyme X enzyme Y enzyme Z

Give a reason for your answer. (2)
iii Give **two** factors which should be controlled in the baby-food manufacturer's investigations.
Choose the correct answer from the following options:

oxygen concentration temperature light intensity pH (2)

3 *In this question you will be assessed on using good English, organising information clearly and using specialist terms where appropriate.*

Describe the roles of the liver and pancreas in the digestion of fats. (6)

Practicals	AQA↗	ⓚ	📖	⚙
Using computer simulations of enzymes to model their action in varying conditions of pH, temperature and concentration.	✓		✓	

AQA Examination-style answers

1 a i catalysts *(1 mark)*
ii protein *(1 mark)*
iii amylase *(1 mark)*
iv bile *(1 mark)*
v fats *(1 mark)*

b i It is denatured/changes shape does not work as well. *(1 mark)*

ii Temperature *(allow concentration)*. *(1 mark)*

c Large molecules are broken down into small molecules. Starch is changed into sugar. *(2 marks)*

2 a Microorganisms. *(1 mark)*

b i proteases. *(1 mark)*
ii amino acids (both words). *(1 mark)*

c i 14 minutes *(1 mark)*
ii *mark independently*
enzyme Z
It takes the least time (to pre-digest protein)/works fastest.
Allow only 7 minutes/less time/faster
*(do **not** allow works best).* *(2 marks)*
iii temperature
pH *(2 marks)*

3 There is a clear, balanced and detailed description of the roles of both the liver and pancreas. The answer shows almost faultless spelling, punctuation and grammar. It is coherent and in an organised, logical sequence. It contains a range of appropriate or relevant specialist terms used accurately. *(5–6 marks)*

There is some description of the roles of both the liver and pancreas which lacks some details. There are some errors in spelling, punctuation and grammar. The answer has some structure and organisation. The use of specialist terms has been attempted, but not always accurately. *(3–4 marks)*

There is a brief description reference to the role of either the liver or pancreas. The spelling, punctuation and grammar are very weak. The answer is poorly organised with almost no specialist terms and/or their use demonstrating a general lack of understanding of their meaning. *(1–2 marks)*

No relevant content. *(0 marks)*

Examples of biology points made in the response:
- liver produces bile
- bile neutralises acid
- acid produced by stomach
- pancreas produces lipase
- lipase is an enzyme
- lipase works best in neutral/alkaline conditions
- lipase catalyses the breakdown of fat
- to fatty acids and glycerol
- allow reference to, or a description of emulsification.

B2 4.1

Aerobic respiration

Learning objectives

Students should learn:

- that during aerobic respiration, glucose and oxygen are used to release energy
- how carbon dioxide and water are released as waste products
- that most of the reactions in aerobic respiration occur inside mitochondria.

Learning outcomes

Most students should be able to:

- describe the raw materials and products of the process of respiration
- describe where the reactions take place in cells
- explain why more active cells, such as muscle cells, have greater numbers of mitochondria than less active cells.

Some students should also be able to:

- design experiments independently to show that oxygen is taken up and carbon dioxide is released during aerobic respiration.

Answers to in-text questions

a   It provides energy for all the functions of the cells.

b   The folded inner membranes provide a large surface for all the enzymes needed to control the reactions of respiration.

Support

- Get students to make model mitochondria from date boxes or washing liquid capsule boxes. They should line them with corrugated cardboard to represent the inner membrane. Fill with used batteries to indicate their role as energy carriers and display on a large poster.
- Give them cards with the components of the word equation for aerobic respiration and get them to assemble the equation.

Extend

- Give students a sheet on the theories of Alan Templeton and Rebecca Cann with regard to 'Mitochondrial Eve' and the origins of the human species. Ask them to summarise points for and against each theory.

AQA / Specification link-up: Biology B2.6

- The chemical reactions inside cells are controlled by enzymes. *[B2.6.1 a)]*
- During aerobic respiration (respiration that uses oxygen) chemical reactions occur that:
  - use glucose (a sugar) and oxygen
  - release energy. *[B2.6.1 b)]*
- Aerobic respiration takes place continuously in both plants and animals. *[B2.6.1 c)]*
- Most of the reactions in aerobic respiration take place inside mitochondria. *[B2.6.1 d)]*
- Aerobic respiration is summarised by the equation:

  glucose + oxygen → carbon dioxide + water (+ energy) *[B2.6.1 e)]*
- Energy that is released during respiration is used by the organism. The energy may be used:
  - to build larger molecules from smaller ones
  - in animals, to enable muscles to contract
  - in mammals and birds, to maintain a steady body temperature in colder surroundings
  - in plants, to build up sugars, nitrates and other nutrients into amino acids which are then built up into proteins. *[B2.6.1 f)]*

Controlled Assessment: AS4.3 Collect primary and secondary data *[AS4.3.2 a)]*; AS4.5 Analyse and interpret primary and secondary data. *[AS4.5.2 a)]*, *[AS4.5.4 a)]*

Lesson structure

Starters

Turning limewater cloudy – Draw crosses on the bottoms of test tubes with a chinagraph pencil. Half-fill each tube with limewater. Give each student a drinking straw (use bendy straws) and a tube of limewater and tell them to blow gently through the straw into the limewater until they can no longer see the cross on the bottom from the top. Eye protection must be worn. Ask: 'How long does it take? What is happening?' Go over the reaction and introduce respiration. *(5 minutes)*

Instant energy – Show glucose drink bottles, energy drinks and energy bars. Read or show their labels and read as a class (search an image bank for 'energy drink label'). Support students by giving them preprinted lists of sugar content and energy and ask to put the products in order of their highest sugar and energy content to the lowest. Extend students by asking them to study the contents and decide which would supply the most energy and which would supply energy the fastest, giving reasons. *(10 minutes)*

Main

- Provide a short, introductory PowerPoint presentation or exposition on the need for energy and the process of aerobic respiration. Build up the word equation, getting students to work out what the raw materials and the products are. Introduce mitochondria and show a diagram and electron micrograph images of mitochondria in cells. Provide the students with a worksheet containing an outline of a mitochondrion which they can complete.
- As a follow-up to the starter 'Turning limewater cloudy', a more refined piece of apparatus can be used to show that the air that is breathed in contains less carbon dioxide than air breathed out (see 'Practical support').
- Investigating respiration using a small mammal or plant (see 'Practical support'). All these experiments need controls, which should be discussed with the students (this relates to 'How Science Works'– validity of experimental design). In most cases, with the bell jar experiments, the removal of the living organism should be considered as a control.

Plenaries

How small can you get it? – Have a competition to see who can fold an A4 sheet of paper into the smallest volume. Ask: 'What is the best method?' Relate to surface area (SA) and cristae in mitochondria. *(5 minutes)*

What do I need energy for? – Ask students to write down as many uses for the energy released by respiration that they can think of. Build up a list on the board. Support students by providing prompts once they have completed their initial list. Extend students by ensuring their lists include references to cell activities and animals other than humans. *(10 minutes)*

Practical support

Composition of inhaled and exhaled air

Equipment and materials required

Test tubes half-full of limewater in racks, test tubes with 2-hole bungs, delivery tubes (one long, one short), rubber tubing, sterile mouth pieces, chinagraph pencil, drinking straws (bendy ones if possible or tubing and clips, eye protection.

Details

Arrange two tubes of limewater, tubing and clips, so that air can be drawn in through one tube containing limewater and breathed out through another tube containing limewater. After a few breaths, it can clearly be seen that the limewater in the two tubes differs in cloudiness.

 ## Investigating respiration using a small mammal or plant

Equipment and materials required

Limewater, soda lime in U-tube, small mammals in a bell jar, potted plant, earthworms, maggots or woodlice, black paper, tubing, air pump, 2 boiling tubes, bungs, delivery tubes, boiling tube rack, eye protection.

Details

A small mammal, or other small living animals, can be placed under a bell jar on a glass plate sealed with Vaseline. Emphasise to the students that the animal has fresh air drawn across it all the time, just with the carbon dioxide removed. Air is drawn through the apparatus, first passing through a U-tube of soda lime (to remove carbon dioxide and then through a tube of limewater (to show that carbon dioxide has been removed before entering the bell jar). After leaving the bell jar, the air is drawn through another tube of limewater to show that carbon dioxide is given off. Any small mammal is usually quite active and a result is achieved fairly quickly. Alternatively, other small animals, such as earthworms, woodlice or maggots can be used in such a demonstration/investigation.

It is possible to substitute a potted plant for the small mammal and to show that carbon dioxide is given off during respiration in plants. The pot and soil of the plant need to be enclosed in a polythene bag and the bell jar needs to be covered in black paper to exclude light. The apparatus should be left running for a couple of days.

● Ask: 'Why is the plant pot covered up? Why is light excluded?'

Safety: CLEAPSS Hazcard 18 Limewater – irritant. CLEAPSS Hazcard 91 Soda lime – corrosive.

Energy from respiration

B2 4.1 — Aerobic respiration ⓚ

Learning objectives

● What is aerobic respiration?
● Where in your cells does respiration take place?

Did you know … ?

The average energy needs of a teenage boy are 11 510 kJ of energy every day – but teenage girls only need 8830 kJ a day. This is partly because on average girls are smaller than boys, but also because boys have more muscle cells, which means more mitochondria demanding fuel for aerobic respiration.

One of the most important enzyme-controlled processes in living things is aerobic respiration. It takes place all the time in plant and animal cells.

Your digestive system, lungs and circulation all work to provide your cells with the glucose and oxygen they need for respiration.

During aerobic respiration, glucose reacts with oxygen. This reaction releases energy that your cells can use. This energy is vital for everything that goes on in your body.

Carbon dioxide and water are produced as waste products of the reaction. We call the process aerobic respiration because it uses oxygen from the air.

Aerobic respiration can be summed up by the equation:

glucose + oxygen → carbon dioxide + water (+ energy)

a Why is aerobic respiration so important?

Practical

Investigating respiration

Animals, plants and microorganisms all respire. It is possible to show that cellular respiration is taking place. You can either deprive a living organism of the things it needs to respire, or show that waste products are produced from the reaction.

Depriving a living thing of food and/or oxygen would kill it. This would be unethical. So we concentrate on the products of respiration. Carbon dioxide is the easiest to identify. We can also measure the energy released to the surroundings.

Limewater goes cloudy when carbon dioxide bubbles through it. The higher the concentration of carbon dioxide, the quicker the limewater goes cloudy. This gives us an easy way of showing that carbon dioxide has been produced. We can also look for a rise in temperature to show that energy is being released during respiration.

● Plan an ethical investigation into aerobic respiration in living organisms.

Mitochondria – the site of respiration

Aerobic respiration involves lots of chemical reactions. Each reaction is controlled by a different enzyme. Most of these reactions take place in the mitochondria of your cells.

Mitochondria are tiny rod-shaped parts (organelles) that are found in almost all plant and animal cells. They have a folded inner membrane. This provides a large surface area for the enzymes involved in aerobic respiration.

The number of mitochondria in a cell shows you how active the cell is.

b Why do mitochondria have folded inner membranes?

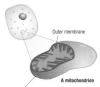

Outer membrane

A mitochondrion

Folded inner membrane gives a large surface area where the enzymes which release cellular respiration are found

Figure 1 Mitochondria are the powerhouses that provide energy for all the functions of your cells

Reasons for respiration

Respiration releases energy from the food we eat so that our cells can use it.

● Living cells need energy to carry out the basic functions of life. They build up large molecules from smaller ones to make new cell material. Much of the energy released in respiration is used for these 'building' activities (synthesis reactions). For example, in plants the sugars, nitrates and other nutrients are built up into amino acids. The amino acids are then built up into proteins.

● In animals, energy from respiration is used to make muscles contract. Muscles are working all the time in your body. Even when you sleep your heart beats, you breathe and your gut churns. All muscular activities use energy.

● Finally, mammals and birds keep their bodies at a constant temperature inside almost regardless of the temperature of their surroundings. So on cold days you will use energy to keep warm, while on hot days you use energy to sweat and keep your body cool.

Figure 2 When the weather is cold, birds like this robin use up a lot of energy from respiration just to keep warm. Giving them extra food supplies can mean the difference between life and death.

Summary questions

1 Copy and complete using the words below:

aerobic respiration mitochondria glucose waste products energy water

.... is released from .... in a reaction with oxygen by a process known as .... This takes place in the .... of the cells. Carbon dioxide and .... are formed as ....

2 Why do muscle cells have many mitochondria but fat cells very few?

3 You need a regular supply of food to provide energy for your cells. If you don't get enough to eat you become thin and stop growing. You don't want to move around and you start to feel cold.

a What are the three main uses of the energy released in your body during aerobic respiration?

b How does this explain the symptoms of starvation described above?

4 Suggest an experiment to show that: **a** oxygen is taken up, and **b** carbon dioxide is released, during aerobic respiration.

AQA Examiner's tip

Make sure you know the word equation for aerobic respiration. Remember that aerobic respiration takes place in the mitochondria.

Key points

● Aerobic respiration involves chemical reactions that use oxygen and sugar and release energy. The reaction is summed up as:
glucose + oxygen → carbon dioxide + water (+ energy)

● Most of the reactions in aerobic respiration take place inside the mitochondria.

● The energy released during respiration is used to build large molecules from smaller ones. This allows muscles to contract. In mammals and birds, it enables them to maintain a steady body temperature.

46 / 47

Summary answers

1 energy, glucose, aerobic respiration, mitochondria, water, waste products

2 Muscle cells are very active and need a lot of energy so they need large numbers of mitochondria to supply the energy. Fat cells use very little energy so need very few mitochondria.

3 **a** The main uses of energy in the body are for movement, building new molecules and heat generation.

b The symptoms of starvation are: people become very thin, stored energy is used up and growth stops, new proteins are not made and there is not enough energy or raw materials, people lack energy, as there is a lack of fuel for the mitochondria, people feel cold, as there is not enough fuel for the mitochondria to produce heat energy.

4 See practical box 'Investigating respiration' in the Student Book. Any sensible suggestions for practical investigations.

B2 4.2

The effect of exercise on the body

Learning objectives

Students should learn:

- that muscles need energy from respiration in order to contract
- that, during exercise, there is an increase in the blood flow to the muscles so more glucose and oxygen is supplied and carbon dioxide removed
- that glycogen provides a store of energy in the muscles.

Learning outcomes

Most students should be able to:

- describe how the body responds to the demands of exercise
- describe how glycogen is used in the body.

Some students should also be able to:

- interpret data on the use of oxygen/heart rate increase during exercise.
- relate the responses of the body to exercise and the ability of the muscles to contract efficiently.

Support

- Create and use jigsaw sheets of the human body and the changes which happen due to exercise. Blank jigsaw sheets can be bought or you can make your own. Support students by offering clues if necessary.

Extend

- Tell students that a young woman has been found dead in a field. No one knows her identity. Students could write a letter of advice from a pathologist telling the police what they can find out about her exercise habits and lifestyle from her corpse, to aid with her identification.
- Get them to calculate the percentage changes in the parameters measured in the table in the Student Book and to comment on the significance of these changes.

AQA Specification link-up: Biology B2.6

- Energy that is released during respiration is used by the organism. The energy may be used:
  - to build larger molecules from smaller ones
  - in animals, to enable muscles to contract
  - in mammals and birds, to maintain a steady body temperature in colder surroundings
  - in plants, to build up sugars, nitrates and other nutrients into amino acids which are then built up into proteins. [B2.6.1 f)]
- During exercise a number of changes take place:
  - the heart rate increases
  - the rate and depth of breathing increases
  - the arteries supplying the muscles dilate. [B2.6.1 g)]
- These changes increase the blood flow to the muscles and so increase the supply of sugar and oxygen and increase the rate of removal of carbon dioxide. [B2.6.1 h)]
- Muscles store glucose as glycogen, which can then be converted back to glucose for use during exercise. [B2.6.1 i)]
- Interpret the data relating to the effects of exercise on the human body. [B2.6]

  Controlled Assessment: AS4.1 Plan practical ways to develop and test candidates' own scientific ideas [AS4.1.1 a) b, c)]; AS4.3 Collect primary and secondary data [AS4.3.2 a) b)]; AS4.4 Select and process primary and secondary data [AS4.4.1 a) b)], [AS4.4.2 a) b) c)]; AS4.5 Analyse and interpret primary and secondary data. [AS4.5.4 a) c) d)]

Lesson structure

Starters

Cardiac muscle contraction – Show an MPEG file or a video clip of contracting heart muscle. Discuss what the energy source for this movement will be and the reaction involved. Support students by prompting and extend students by asking how the energy source gets to the muscle and what happens to the waste products. *(5 minutes)*

Exercise … how much do you get? – Show a clip from an old exercise video such as Mr Motivator, with some good 1980s clothes to have a laugh at. Also, show some footage of modern gym clubs. Carry out a quick survey to find out the health and exercise activities of the class members and their families. *(10 minutes)*

Main

- Investigate the effect of exercise on heart rate (see 'Practical support'). There are many variations on this investigation that can be carried out:
  - The intensity of the exercise can be varied.
  - The increase in breathing rate (number of breaths per minutes) can be investigated either separately from the pulse rate or in conjunction with it.
  - In addition to the performance of individuals, comparisons could be made between members of the class who exercise regularly and those who do not.
- This investigation can be used for teaching/assessing 'How Science Works': hypotheses can be formulated and predictions made, measurements taken and results tabulated, graphs produced and conclusions drawn, finishing with an evaluation. This can deliver the complete range of investigative requirements from which to choose a skill or skills to develop.
- Digital pulse monitors can be used and it is possible to use data loggers and get live read-out graphs that can be displayed through a projector.

Plenaries

Animal starch – Glycogen has been referred to as 'animal starch'. Ask students to compile two lists: one headed 'similarities to starch' and the other headed 'differences from starch'. Stress that it is not starch and that animals do not store starch. Support students by giving them a number of straightforward statements about the two molecules which they have to sort into the correct list. Extend students by encouraging them to include differences in structure, location and use. They could continue the task for homework. *(5 minutes)*

'Unfit' club – Imagine an 'Unfit' club, where the membership rules included the banning of exercise. Write down instructions for the club's Unfitness Enforcers, giving a list of telltale signs that would indicate the person being investigated has been exercising. Use imagination and illustration, being careful regarding the size sensitivity of some students. *(10 minutes)*

Practical support

Testing fitness
Equipment and materials required
The practical activities suggested in this spread do not require complex apparatus. The pulse and breathing rate investigations simply require stopwatches or stop-clocks. If a spirometer is used, then follow the instructions supplied with it.

Details
This is best carried out in pairs, so that students can record each other's pulse rates. Before starting, the students should decide on the level and period of exercise. The simplest investigation could concentrate on one level of exercise, such as walking on the spot for a set time. The resting pulse rate in beats per minute should be determined (count beats in 15 seconds and then multiply by 4). Show the students how to do this either using the radial artery on their wrists, using the carotid artery in the neck or a pulse rate monitor. Ideally, this should be done three times and a mean taken. The student then undertakes the exercise and the pulse rate recorded immediately and at set intervals, such as every minute afterwards, until the rate returns to normal. A graph can be plotted of heart/pulse rate against time. The students exchange roles.

Safety: Students should exercise sensibly.

Energy from respiration

B2 4.2
The effect of exercise on the body (k)

Learning objectives
- How does your body respond to the increased demands for oxygen during exercise?
- What is glycogen and how is it used in the body?

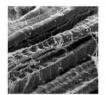

Figure 1 All the work done by the muscles is based on these special protein fibres, which contract when they work and relax afterwards

Your muscles use a lot of energy. They move you around and help support your body against gravity. Your heart is made of muscle and pumps blood around your body. The movement of food along your gut depends on muscles too.

Muscle tissue is made up of protein fibres. These contract when they are supplied with energy from respiration. Muscle fibres need a lot of energy to contract. They contain many mitochondria to carry out aerobic respiration and supply the energy needed.

Muscle fibres usually occur in big blocks or groups known as muscles, which contract to cause movement. They then relax, which allows other muscles to work.

Your muscles also store glucose as the carbohydrate **glycogen**. Glycogen can be converted rapidly back to glucose to use during exercise. The glucose is used in aerobic respiration to provide the energy to make your muscles contract:

glucose + oxygen → carbon dioxide + water (+ energy)

a What is aerobic respiration?

The response to exercise (k)
Even when you are not moving about your muscles use up a certain amount of oxygen and glucose. However, when you begin to exercise, many muscles start contracting faster and faster. As a result they need more glucose and oxygen to supply their energy needs. During exercise the muscles also produce increased amounts of carbon dioxide. This needs to be removed for muscles to keep working effectively.

b Why do you need more energy when you exercise?

So during exercise, when muscular activity increases, several changes take place in your body:
- Your heart rate increases and the arteries supplying blood to your muscles dilate (widen). These changes increase the blood flow to your exercising muscles. This in turn increases the supply of oxygen and glucose to the muscles. It also increases the rate that carbon dioxide is removed from the muscles.
- Your breathing rate increases and you breathe more deeply. So you breathe more often and also bring more air into your lungs each time you breathe in. More oxygen is brought into your body and picked up by your red blood cells. This oxygen is carried to your exercising muscles. It also means that more carbon dioxide can be removed from the blood in the lungs and breathed out.

c Why do you produce more carbon dioxide when you are exercising hard?

The benefits of exercise
Your heart and lungs benefit from regular exercise. Both the heart and the lungs become larger. They both develop a bigger and more efficient blood supply. This means they function as effectively as possible, whether you are exercising or not. Look at the table below.

Table 1 A comparison of heart and lung functions before and after getting fit

	Before getting fit	After getting fit
Amount of blood pumped out of the heart during each beat at rest (cm³)	64	80
Volume of the heart at rest (cm³)	120	140
Resting breathing rate at rest (breaths/min)	14	12
Resting pulse rate (beats/min)	72	63
Maximum lung volume (cm³)	1000	1200

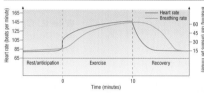

Figure 2 During exercise the heart rate and breathing rate increase to supply the muscles with what they need and remove the extra waste produced. The maximum rate to which you should push your heart is usually calculated as approximately 220 beats per minute minus your age. When you exercise, you should ideally get your heart rate into the range between 60 per cent and 90 per cent of your maximum.

Practical

Testing fitness
A good way of telling how fit you are is to measure your resting heart rate and breathing rate. The fitter you are, the lower they will be. Then see what happens when you exercise. The increase in your heart rate and breathing rate and how fast they return to normal is another way of finding out how fit you are – or aren't!

Summary questions
1 Using Figure 2, describe the effect of exercise on the heart rate and the breathing rate of a fit person and explain why these changes happen.
2 Plan an investigation into the fitness levels of your classmates. Describe how you might carry out this investigation and explain what you would expect the results to be.

AQA Examiner's tip
- Be clear about the difference between the rate and the depth of breathing.
- Be clear about the difference between the breathing rate and the rate of respiration.

Key points
- The energy that is released during respiration is used to enable muscles to contract.
- When you use your muscles you need more glucose and oxygen and produce more carbon dioxide.
- Body responses to exercise include:
  – an increase in heart rate, in breathing rate and in depth of breathing
  – glycogen stores in the muscle are converted to glucose for cellular respiration
  – the blood flow to the muscles increases.
- These act to increase the supply of glucose and oxygen to the muscle and remove more carbon dioxide.

48   49

Further teaching suggestions

Glycogen and its importance
- Introduce the structure of glycogen and its importance as a storage carbohydrate in the liver and the muscles. Link with its role in the maintenance of a steady level of glucose in the blood. Students can be reminded of the conversion of glucose to glycogen, stimulated by the release of insulin and the conversion of glycogen to glucose when the glucose levels in the blood decrease.

Answers to in-text questions
a Aerobic respiration is the complete breakdown of glucose using oxygen to release energy with carbon dioxide and water as waste products:

Glucose + oxygen → energy + carbon dioxide + water

b Your muscles are contracting harder for longer, so you need more energy.

c The muscles are contracting more, therefore using more energy. There is more aerobic respiration and more carbon dioxide produced. This is a waste product of the process.

Summary answers

1 **Heart rate:** increases before exercise starts as a result of anticipation. It rises rapidly, followed by a steady rise and then falls quite sharply as the exercise finishes. Increased heart rate supplies muscles with the extra blood they need to bring glucose/sugar and oxygen to the muscle fibres, and to remove the carbon dioxide which rapidly builds up.

Breathing rate: increases more slowly and evenly than the heart rate, but remains high for some time after exercise. To begin with, increased heart rate supplies enough oxygen, then the breathing rate needs to increase to meet demand. When exercise stops, breathing rate remains high until the oxygen debt is paid off.

2 [Mark depending on ideas presented when predicting results. Look for clear, sensible ideas, safe investigation, realistic expectations, appropriate methods of recording and analysing, awareness of weakness in investigation. Look also for clear understanding of independent, dependent and control variables].

B2 4.3 Anaerobic respiration

Learning objectives

Students should learn:

- that during long periods of vigorous activity, muscles respire anaerobically in order to obtain energy
- that less energy is released by anaerobic respiration than aerobic respiration [HT only]
- that during anaerobic respiration, incomplete breakdown of glucose results in the formation of lactic acid and the building up of an oxygen debt. [HT only]

Learning outcomes

Most students should be able to:

- explain why muscles respire anaerobically during vigorous exercise
- explain why less energy is released by anaerobic respiration [HT only]
- describe the oxygen debt and how it is repaid. [HT only]

Some students should also be able to:

- interpret data relating to the effects of exercise on the human body [HT only]
- explain the principle of oxygen debt and why speed of recovery from exercise is a measure of physical fitness. [HT only]

Answers to in-text questions

a Anaerobic respiration does not use oxygen; incomplete breakdown of glucose/sugars; lactic acid is the end product instead of carbon dioxide and water.

b The amount of oxygen needed to break down the lactic acid built up during a period of anaerobic respiration.

Support

- Make cards with the relevant words and symbols for students to compose equations for aerobic and anaerobic respiration.

Extend

- Ask students to research the differences between the different energy systems used by muscles. Get them to find out the differences in the training programmes of sprinters and marathon runners.

AQA Specification link-up: Biology B2.6

- During exercise, if insufficient oxygen is reaching the muscles, they use anaerobic respiration to obtain energy. [B2.6.2 a)]
- Anaerobic respiration is the incomplete breakdown of glucose and produces lactic acid. [B2.6.2 b)]
- As the breakdown of glucose is incomplete, much less energy is released than during aerobic respiration. Anaerobic respiration results in an oxygen debt that has to be repaid in order to oxidise lactic acid to carbon dioxide and water. [B2.6.2 c)] [HT only]
- If muscles are subjected to long periods of vigorous activity, they become fatigued, i.e. they stop contracting efficiently. One cause of muscle fatigue is the build up of lactic acid in the muscles. Blood flowing through the muscles removes the lactic acid. [B2.6.2 d)]

Controlled Assessment: AS4.1 Plan practical ways to develop and test candidates' own scientific ideas [SA4.1.1 a) b) c)]; AS4.3 Collect primary and secondary data [AS4.3.2 a) b)]; AS4.4 Select and process primary and secondary data. [AS4.4.1 a) b)], [AS4.4.2 a) b) c)]

Lesson structure

Starters

Wile E. Coyote and Road Runner – Show the students a video clip of Wile E. Coyote and Road Runner at the start of the episode 'Lickety Splat' – the first minute or so where Wile E. runs very hard and gets out of breath. This can be found on the internet. Draw out a thumbnail sketch of the graph you would expect of his breathing rate against time, labelling what is happening in each section. (5 minutes)

Sprinting! – Show a video of a 100 m sprint (from the Olympics or the World Championships), where the athletes are shown immediately before and afterwards. Get students to observe the behaviour of the athletes. Comment on breathing, whether they collapse, etc. Support students by asking questions such as: 'Are they breathing deeply? Can they talk?' Extend students by getting them to make their observations without prompting and expecting more detailed comments and reasons. (10 minutes)

Main

- Take the opportunity of clearing up the mistaken idea that it is lactic acid building up in muscles which makes them sore – this is not so! Lactate is actually used as a fuel by the mitochondria and makes no contribution to soreness/stiffness afterwards. Explain to extension level students that the actual reason for the acidification during exercise is the build up of H^+ ions which are released during the break down of ATP to $ADP + P_i$. They are produced so fast, they overcome the body's buffering mechanism and cause painful burning sensations.
- Practical on making lactic acid (see 'Practical support' for full details).
- There are variations on this investigation that can be discussed and students could be asked to design a standard test that everyone could do, and this could be used to determine whether muscle fatigue varied from person to person. For example, the same action could be carried out for a set time and a set recovery time allowed. Students could find out if they could continue longer doing that, rather than carrying out the investigation as first suggested.
- If the variation in breathing rate with activity was not used in the previous spread, it could be investigated here. (This relates to 'How Science Works'.) Again, it would be sensible for students to work in pairs, so that the record keeping is done by the partner, and then the roles can be reversed. In this case, it could be appropriate to vary the intensity of the exercise, starting with walking on the spot, then running on the spot and so on. Carry out the exercise for a set time and record breathing rates until they return to normal, before starting on a more vigorous exercise.

Plenaries

The long distance runner – Show video footage of a long-distance race, at the beginning, during and at the end. Students to observe the behaviour of the athletes and compare with the sprint shown as a starter. Ask: 'Do the athletes seem so out of breath? Or are they breathing as deeply?' Discuss why there are differences in behaviour. (5 minutes)

Energy yields – Anaerobic respiration in yeast cells produces alcohol. Show students that there is energy locked up in alcohol by igniting some in controlled conditions (could use it in a spirit lamp or similar). Link to the energy still in lactic acid. Get students to compare the energy yields of aerobic and anaerobic respiration. Support students by giving them the figures which they could represent in a simple way. Extend students by comparing the structures of glucose, lactic acid, alcohol and carbon dioxide, in terms of the numbers of C, H and O atoms in the molecules. (10 minutes)

Practical support

Making lactic acid

Equipment and materials required
Stopwatches, stop-clocks or a spirometer.

Details
Students should work in pairs and devise a simple repetitive action, such as stepping up and down on to a low bench, lifting a book from the bench to shoulder height or raising one arm and clenching and unclenching the fist twice a second. One student should perform the action as many times as they can before tiring, while the other student keeps a record of the number of actions and the time.

A period of recovery time is allowed – the student to decide when they are ready to resume the activity, but record the time. Ask: 'Can they do the same number of actions before tiring again? Are they performing the action at the same speed as before? Why does the student slow down?'

Safety: No student should feel under pressure to take part in any of the activities, particularly if they have any medical condition. If a spirometer is used, follow the instructions given in CLEAPSS Handbook CD-ROM section 14.5.

Energy from respiration

B2 4.3 — Anaerobic respiration

Anaerobic respiration

Learning objectives
- Why do muscles use anaerobic respiration to obtain energy?
- Why is less energy released by anaerobic respiration than aerobic respiration? [H]
- What is an oxygen debt? [H]

Your everyday muscle movements use energy released by aerobic respiration. However, when you exercise hard your muscle cells may become short of oxygen. Although you increase your heart and breathing rates, sometimes the blood cannot supply oxygen to the muscles fast enough. When this happens the muscle cells can still get energy from glucose. They use **anaerobic respiration**, which takes place without oxygen.

In anaerobic respiration the glucose is not broken down completely. It produces **lactic acid** instead of carbon dioxide and water.

If you are fit, your heart and lungs will be able to keep a good supply of oxygen going to your muscles while you exercise. If you are unfit, your muscles will run short of oxygen much sooner.

a How does anaerobic respiration differ from aerobic respiration?

Muscle fatigue k

Using your muscle fibres vigorously for a long time can make them become fatigued. This means they stop contracting efficiently. One cause of muscle fatigue is the build up of lactic acid. It is made by anaerobic respiration in the muscle cells. Blood flowing through the muscles removes the lactic acid.

Figure 1 Training hard is the simplest way to avoid anaerobic respiration. When you are fit you can get oxygen to your muscles and remove carbon dioxide more efficiently

Figure 2 Repeated movements can soon lead to anaerobic respiration in your muscles – particularly if you're not used to it

Anaerobic respiration is not as efficient as aerobic respiration. This is because the glucose molecules are not broken down completely. So far less energy is released than during aerobic respiration.

The end product of anaerobic respiration is lactic acid and this leads to the release of a small amount of energy, instead of the carbon dioxide and water plus lots of energy released by aerobic respiration.

Anaerobic respiration:

glucose → lactic acid (+ energy)

Oxygen debt

If you have been exercising hard, you often carry on puffing and panting for some time after you stop. The length of time you remain out of breath depends on how fit you are. But why do you keeping breathing faster and more deeply when you have stopped using your muscles?

The waste lactic acid you produce during anaerobic respiration is a problem. You cannot simply get rid of lactic acid by breathing it out as you can with carbon dioxide. As a result, when the exercise is over lactic acid has to be broken down to produce carbon dioxide and water. This needs oxygen.

The amount of oxygen needed to break down the lactic acid to carbon dioxide and water is known as the **oxygen debt**.

After a race, your heart rate and breathing rate stay high to supply the extra oxygen needed to pay off the oxygen debt. The bigger the debt (the larger the amount of lactic acid), the longer you will puff and pant!

Oxygen debt repayment:

lactic acid + oxygen → carbon dioxide + water

Figure 3 Everyone gets an oxygen debt if you exercise hard, but if you are fit you can pay it off faster

b What is an oxygen debt?

?? Did you know ...?
In a 100m sprint some athletes do not breathe at all. This means that the muscles use the oxygen taken in before the start of the race and then don't get any more oxygen until the race is over. Although the race only takes a few seconds, a tremendous amount of energy is used up so a big oxygen debt can develop, even though the athletes are very fit.

Practical

Making lactic acid

Carry out a single repetitive action such as stepping up and down or lifting a weight or a book from the bench to your shoulder time after time or even just clenching and unclenching your fist. You will soon feel the effect of a build up of lactic acid in your muscles.
- How can you tell when your muscles have started to respire anaerobically?

Summary questions

1 Define the following terms:
   aerobic respiration   anaerobic respiration   lactic acid

2 If you exercise very hard or for a long time, your muscles begin to ache and do not work so effectively. Explain why.

3 If you exercise very hard, you often puff and pant for some time after you stop. Explain what is happening. [H]

Key points
- If muscles work hard for a long time they become fatigued and don't contract efficiently. If they don't get enough oxygen they will respire anaerobically.
- Anaerobic respiration is respiration without oxygen. Glucose is incompletely broken down to form lactic acid.
- The anaerobic breakdown of glucose releases less energy than aerobic respiration.
- After exercise, oxygen is still needed to break down the lactic acid which has built up. The amount of oxygen needed is known as the oxygen debt. [H]

Further teaching suggestions

Review of aerobic and anaerobic respiration
- It could be useful to students to review both types of respiration by building up a table of the differences between aerobic and anaerobic respiration.

Measuring respiration in yeast
- Use carbon dioxide sensors to measure respiration in yeast.

Respiration in plants and microorganisms
- It could be instructive to students to consider respiration in other organisms. In microorganisms, for example, there are types that are strictly aerobic, strictly anaerobic and those that can respire aerobically if oxygen is present and anaerobically if oxygen is absent. Discuss the importance of these organisms and their possible locations.

Summary answers

1 **Aerobic respiration:** respiration using oxygen.

Anaerobic respiration: respiration that does not use oxygen and releases less energy than aerobic respiration.

Lactic acid: The chemical produced in animal cells during anaerobic respiration of glucose.

2 The muscles become fatigued. After a long period of exercise, your muscles become short of oxygen and switch from aerobic to anaerobic respiration, which is less efficient. The glucose molecules are not broken down completely, so less energy is released than during aerobic respiration. The end products of anaerobic respiration are lactic acid and a small amount of energy.

3 The waste lactic acid you produce during exercise as a result of anaerobic respiration has to be broken down to produce carbon dioxide and water. This needs oxygen, and the amount of oxygen needed to break down the lactic acid is known as the oxygen debt. Even though your leg muscles have stopped, your heart rate and breathing rate stay high to supply extra oxygen, until you have broken down all the lactic acid and paid off the oxygen debt.

Summary answers

1 a Award marks for standard of graphs, axes, etc.

b As the peas start to grow, they began to respire aerobically. As a result, a small amount of heat energy is produced so the temperature increased.

c Because the seeds were dry and not growing, so no respiration occurred or heat produced.

d As a control level.

e Any reasonable explanation, e.g. The important thing about flask C is that peas are dead so temperature for first five days remains at 20°C as they are not respiring. peas had gone mouldy and mould respiring so temperature goes up, anomaly: Sun on thermometer, poor reading, etc.

2 a [Credit will be given in the subsequent answers for extracting and using the information on the bar charts.]

b i Increased fitness means that the heart has a greater volume and pumps more blood at each beat. The heart therefore beats more slowly at rest.

ii Increased fitness affects the lungs by lowering the breathing rate.

3 a Both people are exercising hard. The fit person's breathing rate goes up more slowly, it doesn't go as high and it comes down faster than the unfit person.

b The breathing of the fit person doesn't need to increase immediately as their fit heart will simply pump more blood to the muscles. Their lungs will be larger than those of an unfit person so they will not need to breathe as quickly, and because they can keep their muscles better supplied with blood and oxygen, they will not fatigue as quickly. They won't build up such a large oxygen debt, so their breathing will return to normal faster.

c They could exercise more regularly and build up their own levels of fitness. Then their heart and lung capacity would increase and they would not get as breathless when they exercised.

4 a The complete breakdown of glucose using oxygen to produce carbon dioxide, water and energy.

b Aerobic respiration produces more energy to allow the muscles to contract more efficiently, so athletes want it to continue as long as possible before changing to less efficient anaerobic respiration.

c Red blood cells carry oxygen to the tissues, so if you have more red blood cells, you have more oxygen so aerobic respiration continues longer and muscles work more effectively.

d It increases the red blood cells in the body just before a performance and so allows more oxygen to be carried to the working muscles.

e They start anaerobic respiration where glucose is incompletely broken down to form lactic acid. Less energy is produced and the lactic acid can cause muscle fatigue.

f Any thoughtful opinion about the situation.

Summary questions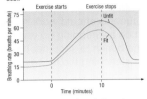

1 Edward and Jess wanted to investigate the process of cellular respiration. They set up three vacuum flasks. One contained live, soaked peas. One contained dry peas. One contained peas which had been soaked and then boiled. They took daily observations of the temperature in each flask for a week. The results are shown in the table.

Day	Room temperature (°C)	Temperature in flask A containing live, soaked peas (°C)	Temperature in flask B containing dry peas (°C)	Temperature in flask C containing soaked, boiled peas (°C)
1	20.0	20.0	20.0	20.0
2	20.0	20.5	20.0	20.0
3	20.0	21.0	20.0	20.0
4	20.0	21.5	20.0	20.0
5	20.0	22.0	20.0	20.0
6	20.0	22.2	20.0	20.5
7	20.0	22.5	20.0	21.0

a Plot a graph to show these results.

b Explain the results in flask A containing the live, soaked peas.

c Why were the results in flask B the same as the room temperature readings?

d Why did Edward and Jess record room temperature in the lab every day?

e How would you explain the results seen in flask C? Why is the temperature at 20°C for the first five days? Give two possible explanations why the temperature then increases.

2 It is often said that taking regular exercise and getting fit is good for your heart and your lungs.

	Before getting fit	After getting fit
Amount of blood pumped out of the heart during each beat (cm³)	64	80
Heart volume (cm³)	120	140
Breathing rate (breaths/ min)	14	12
Pulse rate (beats/min)	72	63

a The table shows the effect of getting fit on the heart and lungs of one person. Display this data in four bar charts.

b Use the information on your bar charts to explain exactly what effect increased fitness has on:
i your heart
ii your lungs.

3 Look at the graph that shows the difference between a fit and unfit person and the time taken to repay oxygen debt.

a Explain what is happening to both people.

b Why is the graph for the unfit person different from t graph for the fit person?

c What could the unfit person do to change their body responses to be more like those of the fit person?

4 Athletes want to be able to use their muscles aerobica for as long as possible when they compete. They train to develop their heart and lungs. Many athletes also train at altitude. There is less oxygen in the air so your body makes more red blood cells, which helps to avoi oxygen debt. Sometimes athletes remove some of the own blood, store it and then just before a competition transfuse it back into their system. This is called blood doping and it is illegal. Other athletes use hormones to stimulate the growth of extra red blood cells. This is al illegal.

a What is aerobic respiration?

b Why do athletes want to be able to use their muscle aerobically for as long as possible?

c How does developing more red blood cells by train at altitude help athletic performance?

d How does blood doping help performance?

e Explain in detail what happens to the muscles if the body cannot supply enough glucose and oxygen when they are working hard.

f It is legal to train at altitude but illegal to carry out blood doping or to take hormones that stimulate the development of red blood cells. What do you think about this situation?

52

Kerboodle resources

Resources available for this chapter on Kerboodle are:

- Chapter map: Energy from respiration
- Video: Exercise (B2 4.2)
- Support: Respiration (B2 4.2)
- How Science Works: The effect of exercise on the body (B2 4.2)
- Bump up your grade: Glucose-enriched drinks (B2 4.2)
- Practical: Measuring pulse rate before and after exercise (B2 4.2)
- How Science Works: How quickly do muscles fatigue? (B2 4.3)
- Extension: The cyanide deadline (B2 4.3)
- Interactive activity: Energy from respiration
- Podcast: Energy from respiration
- Test yourself: Energy from respiration
- On your marks: Energy from respiration
- Examination-style questions: Energy from respiration
- Answers to examination-style questions: Energy from respiration

AQA Examination-style questions ⓚ

① The diagram shows a group of muscle cells from the wall of the intestine.

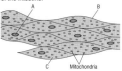

a Choose the correct words to name the structures labelled **A**, **B** and **C**.

cell membrane   cell wall   chloroplast   cytoplasm nucleus (3)

b Suggest **two** ways that these muscle cells are adapted to release a lot of energy? (2)

② Respiration is a chemical process.

a Where does respiration take place? Choose the correct answer.

chloroplasts   mitochondria   nuclei   ribosomes (1)

b Which food material is used in respiration? (1)

c Name the **two** waste materials that are produced in respiration. (2)

d Respiration is important in muscle contraction. Explain why. (2)

③ **a** Copy and complete the word equation for aerobic respiration.

oxygen + ... → water + ... (+ energy) (2)

b i Which substance is missing in anaerobic respiration? (1)

ii What is made during anaerobic respiration? (1)

iii Muscles get tired during anaerobic respiration. Explain why. (1)

④ An athlete started a fitness programme. He was advised to eat a diet containing 18 000 kJ per day.

a The athlete was told that 80% of this energy was needed to keep his body temperature at normal levels. Calculate the remaining number of kilojoules available to the athlete. Show your working. (2)

b The athlete decided to double his amount of exercise and assumed he should increase the number of kilojoules in his diet.
Using only the information available to the athlete, calculate the extra energy is he likely to need. (1)

c The energy supplied in the diet must be transferred to the muscles.
Explain in detail this process of energy transfer to the muscles. (4)

⑤ *In this question you will be assessed on using good English, organising information clearly and using specialist terms where appropriate.*

The bar charts show what happens in an athlete's muscles when running in two races of different distances.

The equations show two processes that occur in muscle cells.

aerobic respiration	glucose + oxygen → carbon dioxide + water
anaerobic respiration	glucose → lactic acid

Use all the information to explain what happens in the athlete's muscles when running in the two races. (6)

53

AQA Examination-style answers

1 a A nucleus
B (cell) membrane
C cytoplasm *(3 marks)*

b any **two** from
- (contain) mitochondria
- many (mitochondria)
- respiration (occurs in mitochondria) *(2 marks)*

2 a mitochondria *(1 mark)*

b glucose *(1 mark)*

c carbon dioxide and water *(either order)* *(2 marks)*

d energy is released which is then used for movement *(2 marks)*

3 a glucose, carbon dioxide *(2 marks)*

b i oxygen *(1 mark)*
ii lactic acid *(1 mark)*
iii less energy is released. This energy is needed for muscle contraction/movement *(1 mark)*

4 a 3600 *(2 marks)*
(If answer incorrect allocate 1 mark for working
$18\,000 - \dfrac{18\,000}{100} \times 80$)

b 21 600 *(1 mark)*

c respiration uses oxygen/is aerobic glucose/sugar is broken down in the mitochondria to release energy for muscle contraction. *(4 marks)*

5 There is a clear, balanced and detailed explanation about the differences between the two races in terms of aerobic and anaerobic respiration. The answer shows almost faultless spelling, punctuation and grammar. It is coherent and in an organised, logical sequence. It contains a range of appropriate or relevant specialist terms used accurately. *(5–6 marks)*

There is some attempt to explain the differences between the two races in terms of respiration. There are some errors in spelling, punctuation and grammar. The answer has some structure and organisation. The use of specialist terms has been attempted, but not always accurately. *(3–4 marks)*

There is a brief description of the differences between the two races. The spelling, punctuation and grammar are very weak. The answer is poorly organised with almost no specialist terms and/or their use demonstrating a general lack of understanding of their meaning. *(1–2 marks)*

No relevant content. *(0 marks)*

Examples of biology points made in the response:
- energy transferred faster in 100 m race
- carbon dioxide produced faster during 1500 m race/more
- carbon dioxide produced
- correct reference to twice/half as fast in either/both cases
- respiration during 100 m race (mainly) anaerobic
- respiration during 1500 m race (mainly) aerobic
- aerobic respiration produced carbon dioxide
- anaerobic respiration produced lactic acid.

AQA Practical suggestions

Practicals	AQA	ⓚ	📖	⚙
Investigating the rate of respiration in yeast using carbon dioxide sensors and dataloggers.	✓		✓	
Investigating the effect of exercise on pulse rate, either physically or using pulse sensors and data loggers.	✓	✓	✓	
Investigating the link between exercise and breathing rate with a breathing sensor.	✓		✓	
Investigating holding masses at arm's length and timing how long it takes the muscles to fatigue.	✓		✓	
Designing an investigation using force meters and dataloggers to find the relationship between the amount of force exerted by a muscle and muscle fatigue.	✓	✓	✓	

B2 5.1 Cell division and growth

Learning objectives

Students should learn:

- that mitosis results in the production of additional cells for growth, repair and replacement
- that before each cell division, the genetic information on the chromosomes is copied so that the new cells have the same genes as the parent cells
- that most animal cells differentiate at an early stage but most plant cells have the ability to differentiate throughout life.

Learning outcomes

Most students should be able to:

- understand that mitosis results in the production of new cells
- describe the process of mitosis
- describe how the cells produced by mitosis differentiate in plants and animals.

Some students should also be able to:

- explain why plants retain the ability to grow throughout their lives whereas cell division in mature animals is involved in repair and replacement of tissues.

Support

- Give a student two short pieces of modelling clay of one colour and two long ones of another colour. These are placed inside a ring of string representing the cell. Give the students balls of modelling clay and tell them to make copies of each and pass a set to two other students who do the same. Do this until the whole class has been involved and there are many copies inside string rings on the floor. This works well in a gym.

Extend

- Introduce students to the names of the stages of mitosis as an introduction to AS-level work.

Specification link-up: Biology B2.1

- In body cells, the chromosomes are normally found in pairs. Body cells divide by mitosis. [B2.7.1 a)]
- The chromosomes contain the genetic information. [B2.7.1 b)]
- When a body cell divides by mitosis:
  – copies of the genetic material are made
  – then the cell divides once to form two genetically identical body cells. [B2.7.1 c)]
- Mitosis occurs during growth or to produce replacement cells. [B2.7.1 d)]
- Body cells have two sets of chromosomes: sex cells (gametes) have only one set. [B2.7.1 e)]
- Most types of animal cells differentiate at an early stage, whereas many plant cells retain the ability to differentiate throughout life. In mature animals, cell division is mainly restricted to repair and replacement. [B2.7.1 j)]
- The cells of the offspring produced by asexual reproduction are produced by mitosis from the parental cells. They contain the same alleles as the parents. [B2.7.1 n)]

Controlled Assessment: AS4.4 Select and process primary and secondary data. [AS4.4.2 c)]

Lesson structure

Starters

Matching exercise – Give each student pieces of paper with 'cell', 'nucleus', 'chromosome', 'gene' and 'DNA' on them, plus definitions all muddled up. They have to join them correctly. *(5 minutes)*

Growth, repair or replacement? – Get students to write three headings in their notebooks: Growth, Repair and Replacement. Get them to think about where in their bodies cells are produced for growth, repair and replacement. They should write down the name of the organ or the region of the body where each might occur. Support students by prompting them with clues or by giving them a list of organs and sites to sort into the correct columns. Extend students by asking them to add the circumstances under which new cells are produced. Expect these students to recognise that some new growth takes place all the time (hair, fingernails) whereas growth in height does not. Discuss and lead students to the idea that the same genetic information needs to be passed on to the new cells and that the type of division producing these identical cells is mitosis. *(10 minutes)*

Main

- Observing mitosis – This can be done using prepared longitudinal sections of root tips, or the students can make their own root tip squashes. A number of different sources will give suitable root tips, although it is a good idea to choose something that does not have a large diploid number of chromosomes. Germinating broad bean or pea seeds work well, or the tips of roots produced from hyacinth or garlic bulbs suspended in water. (See 'Practical support').
- Students may require help mounting their root tips and in using microscopes. It may be useful to create a list for students with the details of the preparation on it. This could be accompanied by a series of diagrams or photographs showing stages so that they can have a go at identifying stages on their own slides. If a space is left beside each stage, then the students could make a sketch of what they can see on their slides. They do not need to know the names of the stages.
- Cloning a cauliflower – Students could try cloning for themselves (see 'Practical support').

Plenaries

Mitosis dominoes – In groups of four, play a dominoes-style game showing the stages of mitosis and a general description. No details, i.e. named stages, are required. *(5 minutes)*

Growing points – Using a small potted plant, remove all the leaves, so that the growing point (main bud and the buds in the axils of the leaves are left. Give the students a diagram of the plant with all the leaves pulled off. Support students by telling them where the growing points are, get them to mark them and then to draw in what they think the plant will look like in a couple of weeks. Extend students by asking them to indicate the positions of the growing points and then to draw in what they think will happen. Ask them to make a list of the different tissues that will be produced (reinforcing the idea that undifferentiated cells, similar to stem cells in animals, are produced and are capable of differentiating into the different tissues). Keep the plant in the lab and look at it when the time is up. *(10 minutes)*

Practical support

Observing mitosis

Equipment and materials required
Root tips of beans, peas, onions, garlic or other suitable material, dilute acetic orsein stain and dilute hydrochloric acid, watch glasses, heater/spirit lamp/hotplate, mounted needles, microscope slides and cover slips, blotting paper, microscopes.

Details
5 mm lengths of the root tips should be cut off and placed in a watch glass containing acetic orcein stain and hydrochloric acid. This should be warmed gently for 5 minutes. The tip is then placed on a microscope slide with a few drops of the stain, teased out with a pair of mounted needles and then covered with a cover slip. Cover with blotting paper and press gently to spread out the cells.

Safety: Care with the handling of stains and acids. Wear eye protection and wash hands if in contact with chemicals.

Cloning a cauliflower

Equipment and materials required
One of: a 3 mm tip of an 'eye' of a potato, a mini-floret from the floret of a cauliflower or a segment of carrot tap root treated with the plant growth regulator 2,4-D. Also bleach, sterilised water, agar, sterilised petri dishes

Details
Using sterile techniques, it is possible to grow clones of carrot, cauliflower or potato tissue on nutrient agar. Use a treated plant tissue (as above). The plant tissue should be sterilised in bleach, rinsed in four washes of sterilised water and then gently pressed into the agar in sterilised Petri dishes. The cultures should be loosely covered in cling film and kept incubated in a growth cabinet at about 25 °C in the light.

● Calluses should develop over the next few weeks and tiny plantlets should develop from buds. The cultures should be examined regularly and a photographic record kept.

Safety: Care with the handling of bleach and the plant growth regulator. Wear eye protection.

Simple inheritance in animals and plants

B2 5.1   Cell division and growth ⓚ

Learning objectives
● How are chromosomes arranged in body cells?
● What is mitosis?
● What is cell differentiation and how does it differ in animals and plants?

links
For more information on alleles, look at B2 5.5 Inheritance in action.

New cells are needed for an organism, or part of an organism, to grow. They are also needed to replace cells which become worn out and to repair damaged tissue. However, the new cells must have the same genetic information as the originals. Then they can do the same job.

Each of your cells has a nucleus containing the instructions for making both new cells and all the tissues and organs needed to make an entire new you. These instructions are carried in the form of genes.

A gene is a small packet of information that controls a characteristic or part of a characteristic, of your body. It is a section of DNA. Different forms of the same gene are known as **alleles**. The genes are grouped together on chromosomes. A chromosome may carry several hundred or even thousands of genes.

You have 46 chromosomes in the nucleus of your body cells. They are arranged in 23 pairs. One of each pair is inherited from your father and one from your mother. Your sex cells (gametes) have only one of each pair of chromosomes.

a Why are new cells needed?

Mitosis ⓚ
The cell division in normal body cells produces two identical cells and is called **mitosis**. As a result of mitosis all your body cells have the same chromosomes. This means they have the same genetic information.

In asexual reproduction, the cells of the offspring are produced by mitosis from the cells of their parent. This is why they contain exactly the same alleles as their parent with no genetic variation.

How does mitosis work? Before a cell divides it produces new copies of the chromosomes in the nucleus. Then the cell divides once to form two genetically identical cells.

In some parts of an animal or plant, cell division like this carries on rapidly all the time. Your skin is a good example. You constantly lose cells from the skin's surface, and make new cells to replace them. In fact about 300 million body cells die every minute so mitosis is very important.

This normal body cell has four chromosomes in two pairs.

As cell division starts, a copy of each chromosome is made.

The cell divides in two to form two daughter cells. Each daughter cell has a nucleus containing four chromosomes identical to the ones in the original parent cell.

Figure 1 Two identical cells are formed by the simple division that takes place during mitosis. For simplicity this cell is shown with only two pairs (not 23).

Practical
Observing mitosis
View a special preparation of a growing root tip under a microscope. You should be able to see the different stages of mitosis as they are taking place. Use Figure 2 for reference.
● Describe your observations of mitosis.

b What is mitosis?

Differentiation
In the early development of animal and plant embryos the cells are unspecialised. Each one of them (known as a **stem cell**) can become any type of cell that is needed.

In many animals, the cells become specialised very early in life. By the time a human baby is born most of its cells are specialised. They will all do a particular job, such as liver cells, skin cells or muscle cells. They have differentiated. Some of their genes have been switched on and others have been switched off.

This means that when, for example, a muscle cell divides by mitosis it can only form more muscle cells. So in a mature (adult) animal, cell division is mainly restricted. It is needed for the repair of damaged tissue and to replace worn out cells. This is because in most adult cells differentiation has already occurred. Specialised cells can divide by mitosis, but they only form the same sort of cell. Therefore growth stops once the animal is mature.

In contrast, most plant cells are able to differentiate all through their life. Undifferentiated cells are formed at active regions of the stems and roots. In these areas mitosis takes place almost continuously.

Plants keep growing all through their lives at these 'growing points'. The plant cells produced don't differentiate until they are in their final position in the plant. Even then the differentiation isn't permanent. You can move a plant cell from one part of a plant to another. There it can redifferentiate and become a completely different type of cell. You can't do that with animal cells – once a muscle cell, always a muscle cell.

We can produce huge numbers of identical plant clones from a tiny piece of leaf tissue. This is because in the right conditions, a plant cell will become unspecialised and undergo mitosis many times. Each of these undifferentiated cells will produce more cells by mitosis. Given different conditions, these will then differentiate to form a tiny new plant. The new plant will be identical to the original parent.

It is difficult to clone animals because animal cells differentiate permanently, early in embryo development. The cells can't change back. Animal clones can only be made by cloning embryos in one way or another, although adult cells can be used to make an embryo.

links
For information on cell differentiation, look back to B2 1.5 Tissues and organs.

Figure 2 The undifferentiated cells in this onion root tip are dividing rapidly. You can see mitosis taking place, with the chromosomes in different positions as the cells divide.

AQA Examiner's tip
Cells produced by mitosis are genetically identical.

Summary questions
1 Copy and complete the words below:
chromosomes genetic information genes growth mitosis nucleus replace

New cells are needed for .... and to .... worn out cells. The new cells must have the same .... in them as the originals. Each cell has a .... containing the .... grouped together on genes. The type of cell division that produces identical cells is known as ....

2 a Explain why the chromosome number must stay the same when the cells divide to make other normal body cells.
b Why is mitosis so important?

3 a What is differentiation?
b How does differentiation differ in animal and plant cells?
c How does this difference affect the cloning of plants and animals?

Key points
● In body cells, chromosomes are found in pairs.
● Body cells divide by mitosis to produce more identical cells for growth, repair and replacement, or in some cases asexual reproduction.
● Most types of animal cell differentiate at an early stage of development. Many plant cells can differentiate throughout their life.

Further teaching suggestions

Make a mitosis flick book
● Find or make some clear diagrams of the stages of mitosis. Copy on to a sheet for each student so that they can make their own 'flick book' by cutting up the pictures and assembling them in the correct order.

Make your own mitosis movie
● Using modelling clay to model the chromosomes and stop motion photography with a webcam, students can make their own animation of the process of mitosis.

Answers to in-text questions
a New cells are needed for growth, replacement and repair.
b Mitosis is cell division that takes place in the normal body cells and produces two identical cells containing exactly the same genes as their parents.

Summary answers
1 growth, replace, genetic information, nucleus, genes, chromosomes, mitosis

2 a Cells need to be replaced with identical cells to do the same job.
b Mitosis is important because cells die at the rate of 300 million per minute; cells are damaged; cells need to grow; in some organisms cells are needed for asexual reproduction.

3 a Differentiation is the process by which cells become specialised.
b In animals, it occurs during embryo development and is permanent. In plants, it occurs throughout life and can be reversed or changed.
c Plants can be cloned relatively easily. Differentiation can be reversed, mitosis is induced, conditions can be changed and more mitosis induced. The cells redifferentiate into new plant tissues. In animals, differentiation cannot be reversed, so clones cannot be made easily. In order to make clones, embryos have to be made.

B2 5.2 Cell division in sexual reproduction

Learning objectives

Students should learn:

- that cells which divide to form gametes undergo meiosis
- that gametes have a single set of genetic information, whereas body cells have two sets
- fertilisation results in the formation of a cell with new pairs of chromosomes, so sexual reproduction gives rise to variation
- how meiosis occurs. [HT only]

Learning outcomes

Most students should be able to:

- understand what happens during meiosis
- describe what happens to the number of chromosomes during fertilisation
- explain how sexual reproduction gives rise to variation.

Some students should also be able to:

- describe what happens to the chromosomes during the process of gamete formation. [HT only]

Support

- Write the word 'chromosomes' twice on the board, inside a ring to represent a cell. To model meiosis, get four students to copy the word 'chromosomes' once onto a piece of A4 and put each on the board inside a ring. To model fertilisation, cut two of these 'chromosomes' words out and stick them inside a single ring. To model mitosis, take both words, stick them onto a sheet and photocopy it repeatedly. (Bear in mind that how meiosis takes place is a concept required at Higher Tier level only).

Extend

- Get students to research the structure of chromosomes. They should find out what happens to them during the stages leading up to their becoming visible and the division.

AQA Specification link-up: Biology B2.7

- Cells in reproductive organs – testes and ovaries in humans – divide to form gametes. *[B2.7.1 f)]*
- The type of cell division in which a cell divides to form gametes is called meiosis. *[B2.7.1 g)]*
- When a cell divides to form gametes:
  - copies of the genetic information are made
  - then the cell divides twice to form four gametes, each with a single set of chromosomes. *[B2.7.1 h)]* **[HT only]**
- When gametes join at fertilisation, a single body cell with new pairs of chromosomes is formed. A new individual then develops by this cell repeatedly dividing by mitosis. *[B2.7.1 i)]*
- Sexual reproduction gives rise to variation because, when gametes fuse, one of each pair of alleles comes from each parent. *[B2.7.2 a)]*

Lesson structure

Starters

Introducing meiosis: a mnemonic for mitosis – Contrast meiosis with mitosis. Find a picture of some ghastly toes. (Search the internet for 'toes'.) Get the students to copy down and remember that 'Mitosis goes on in my toes' and toes are not sexy. Also introduce meiosis as the 'reduction' division, as it reduces the number of chromosomes. *(5 minutes)*

Naming the sex cells – Give the students an empty grid to stick in their books. They are to complete this with the names of the sex cells from animals and plants. Students could be supported by prompting or by providing a list which they can sort out into animals and plants. Students could be extended by getting them to find out and use the correct spellings i.e. 'spermatozoa' etc. and discussing where in animals and plants the sex cells are produced. *(10 minutes)*

Main

- A flow diagram of the events of meiosis can be built up, showing that there are similarities in that the chromosomes are copied, but that there are two divisions rather than one. The flow diagram can be adjusted to the ability of the group: simplify it for students that need support. It is probably best to concentrate on the formation of sperm to begin with (because four observable cells result from the division) and follow up with slides of testis showing stages in sperm development.

- Microscopic examination of testis slides – the best prepared slides are of rat or grasshopper testis squashes. Provide the students with a sheet of paper showing stages in the development of sperm that they are likely to be able to see on their slides. Extend students by producing a flow diagram to show the different stages of division. They may need help with their microscopes, as they will need to use high power if they are to see any chromosomes.

- Alternatively, sections of testis could be projected on to the board and students could identify the different cells with reasons for their choices. They should be able to see chromosomes at different stages and you could extend students by asking them to identify the stages.

- Microscopic examination of ovary slides – the slides could be projected and viewed by the class, or slides could be viewed using a microscope. There will be obvious differences in size of the sperm and egg. Extend students by explaining what happens during the meiotic divisions that produce ova, e.g. the formation of the polar bodies (and possible advantages of their formation).

- Model meiosis and the need for reduction by using model chromosomes. First without a reduction in number of the chromosomes, show how the number of chromosomes would go on increasing. Follow this with the reduction part of the division, so that gametes have half the number and the correct number is restored at fertilisation.

- Using modelling clay of different colours, it is possible to show how variation can occur during the process of meiosis. Students, in groups, could make models showing how the chromosomes separate, perhaps showing some exchange of genes (alleles), and then matching one set of gametes with another set, to represent the sperm and the ovum at fertilisation.

Plenaries

True or false? – Present students with statements about mitosis and meiosis. They are to write 'True' or 'False' on mini whiteboards. You could use the following statements:

Mitosis or meiosis? – Ask students to draw up a table of differences between mitosis and meiosis. Support students by giving them a list of simple statements about the two processes which they place in the correct column. Extend students by encouraging them to put as much detail as they can into their tables. *(10 minutes)*

Simple inheritance in animals and plants

B2 5.2 Cell division in sexual reproduction

Learning objectives

- What is meiosis?
- What happens to your chromosomes when your gametes are formed? [H]
- How does sexual reproduction give rise to variation?

Mitosis is taking place all the time, in tissues all over your body. But there is another type of cell division that takes place only in the reproductive organs of animals and plants. In humans this is the ovaries and the testes. **Meiosis** results in sex cells, called gametes, with only half the original number of chromosomes.

Meiosis

The female gametes or ova are made in the ovaries. The male gametes or sperm are made in the testes.

The gametes are formed by meiosis – cell division where the chromosome number is reduced by half. When a cell divides to form gametes, the chromosomes (the genetic information) are copied so there are four sets of chromosomes. The cell then divides twice in quick succession to form four gametes, each with a single set of chromosomes.

Each gamete that is produced is slightly different from all the others. They contain random mixtures of the original chromosomes pairs. This introduces variety.

a What are the names of the male and female gametes in animals? How do they differ from normal body cells?

?? Did you know ...?

The testes can produce around 400 million sperm by meiosis every 24 hours between them. Only one sperm is needed to fertilise an egg but each sperm needs to travel 100 000 times its own length to reach the ovum and less than one in a million make it!

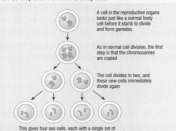

A cell in the reproductive organs looks just like a normal body cell before it starts to divide and form gametes

As in normal cell division, the first step is that the chromosomes are copied

The cell divides in two, and these new cells immediately divide again

This gives four sex cells, each with a single set of chromosomes – in this case two instead of the original four

Figure 1 The formation of sex cells in the ovaries and testes involves meiosis to halve the chromosome number. The original cell is shown with only two pairs of chromosomes to make it easier to follow what is happening.

b What type of cell division is needed to produce the gametes?

Fertilisation

More variety is added when fertilisation takes place. Each sex cell has a single set of chromosomes. When two sex cells join during fertilisation the single new cell formed has a full set of chromosomes. In humans, the egg cell (ovum) has 23 chromosomes and so does the sperm. When they join together they produce a single new body cell with the body human number of 46 chromosomes in 23 pairs.

The combination of genes on the chromosomes of every newly fertilised ovum is unique. Once fertilisation is complete, the unique new cell begins to divide by mitosis to form a new individual. This will continue long after the foetus is fully developed and the baby is born.

In fact about 80% of fertilised eggs never make it to become a live baby – about 50% never even implant into the lining of the womb.

Variation

The differences between asexual and sexual reproduction are reflected in the different types of cell division involved.

In asexual reproduction the offspring are produced as a result of mitosis from the parent cells. So they contain exactly the same chromosomes and the same genes as their parents. There is no variation in the genetic material.

In sexual reproduction the gametes are produced by meiosis in the sex organs of the parents. This introduces variety as each gamete is different. Then when the gametes fuse, one of each pair of chromosomes, and so one of each pair of genes, comes from each parent.

The combination of genes in the new pair of chromosomes will contain alleles from each parent. This also helps to produce variation in the characteristics of the offspring.

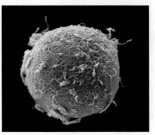

Figure 2 At the moment of fertilisation the chromosomes in the two gametes are combined. The new cell has a complete set of chromosomes, like any other body cell. This new cell will then grow and reproduce by mitosis to form a new individual.

AQA Examiner's tip

Learn to spell mitosis and meiosis.

Remember their meanings:
Mitosis – making identical **tw**o.
Meiosis – making **e**ggs (and sperm).

Key points

- Cells in the reproductive organs divide by meiosis to form the gametes (sex cells).
- Body cells have two sets of chromosomes; gametes have only one set.
- In meiosis the genetic material is copied and then the cell divides twice to form four gametes, each with a single set of chromosomes [H]
- Sexual reproduction gives rise to variety because genetic information from two parents is combined.

Summary questions

1 **a** How many pairs of chromosomes are there in a normal human body cell?
 b How many chromosomes are there in a human sperm cell?
 c How many chromosomes are there in a fertilised human egg cell?

2 Sexual reproduction results in variety. Explain how.

3 **a** What is the name of the special type of cell division that produces gametes from ordinary body cells? Describe what happens to the chromosomes in this process.
 b Where in your body would this type of cell division take place?
 c Why is this type of cell division so important in sexual reproduction? [H]

56 / 57

Further teaching suggestions

Differences between mitosis and meiosis

- Get students to make a leaflet or poster summarising the differences between mitosis and meiosis. They should make it memorable, perhaps using the 'non-sexy toes' statement.

Meiosis in plants

- Preparations of squashes of immature anthers from developing buds of lily show the stages of meiosis and chromosomes very clearly.

Answers to in-text questions

a Sperm, ova, half the number of chromosomes.

b Meiosis.

Summary answers

1 **a** 23 (pairs) **b** 23 **c** 46

2 As the gametes are formed, each gamete has a different combination of chromosomes and there is some exchange of genes. This introduces variation, as each gamete is different. In sexual reproduction, two unique gametes from two different people join together, so the combination of chromosomes and the mix of alleles on the chromosomes will be unique.

3 **a** Meiosis. After the chromosomes are copied, the cell divides twice quickly resulting in sex cells each with half the number of chromosomes.
 b In the reproductive organs/in the ovary or the testes.
 c Sexual reproduction involves the joining of gametes from mother and father. The chromosome number of the body cells needs to be halved to make the gametes, otherwise the number of chromosomes in the cell would just get bigger and bigger when gametes joined at fertilisation. Meiosis halves the chromosome number.

B2 5.3 Stem cells

Learning objectives

Students should learn:

- that stem cells are unspecialised cells found in human embryos and in some adult tissues such as the bone marrow
- how stem cells have the potential to differentiate into different types of specialised cells.

Learning outcomes

Most students should be able to:

- understand the special nature of stem cells
- describe the structure and location of stem cells in humans
- describe how stem cells have the potential to treat sick people.

Some students should also be able to:

- explain in detail the arguments for and against using stem cells from embryos.

Support

- Provide students with a pre-drawn diagram of a ball of cells and some labels of cells and organs. They can stick the labels around the stem cells to gain an understanding of these cells giving rise to all other types of cell.

Extend

- Begin by asking students to define for themselves when life starts. They can be given a list of criteria from contrasting organisations such as the Human Fertilisation and Embryology Authority and Pro-Life.

Specification link-up: Biology B2.7

- Most types of animal cells differentiate at an early stage whereas many plant cells retain the ability to differentiate throughout life. In mature animals, cell division is mainly restricted to repair and replacement. [B2.7.1 j)]
- Cells from human embryos and adult bone marrow, called stem cells, can be made to differentiate into many different types of cells, e.g. nerve cells. [B2.7.1 k)]
- Human stem cells have the ability to develop into any kind of human cell. [B2.7.1 l)]
- Treatment with stem cells may be able to help conditions such as paralysis. [B2.7.1 m)]
- Make informed judgements about the social and ethical issues concerning the use of stem cells from embryos in medical research and treatments. [B2.7]

Lesson structure

Starters

Stem cells salamander style – Search the internet for a clip called 'Building Body Parts: Saving lives, salamander style'. Make notes on the points covered in the clip and discuss with the class their opinions on the potential new technology. *(5 minutes)*

Gone! – Discuss what it would be like to have lost a limb. Be aware of any potential issues regarding family circumstances within the class. Get the students to spend a single minute silently concentrating on a specific limb of theirs. Start by concentrating on the feeling coming from the limb. If it is a leg, can they feel their socks? If an arm, can they feel the hairs on their forearm? Are they aware of the sensations coming from the front of their leg? The sole of the foot? Imagine life without it – what would they not be able to do? What would they miss? Link with ways of getting science to address the problem of lost limbs through stem cell research. Support students by helping them to empathise. Extend students by encouraging them to suggest how the problems encountered may be overcome. *(10 minutes)*

Main

- Some animals are able to regrow parts of their bodies. Show photographs from search engines of lizards regrowing their tails and starfish regrowing limbs. Lead into a discussion of injuries and how they heal. Allow students to discuss injuries that they have had and what happens to them (time limit will be needed!).
- Find photographs about therapeutic cloning. There are a number of good internet sites with lots of information on the use of stem cells. The important thing is to be aware of what is actually being done and what is hoped can be done in the future.
- Show photographs of different sources of stem cells. Search the internet for 'cell division blastocyst video' to show what happens after fertilisation. Otherwise, find a photograph of a ball of stem cells. After four divisions, the cells become increasingly specialised. Discuss what would happen to the cells if they were allowed to continue development. Other sources include umbilical cord blood (rich in blood stem cells), fetal germ cells (extracted from terminated pregnancies of 5–9 weeks), frozen embryos and adult stem cells from bone marrow.
- Initiate a debate on the pros and cons of the use of stem cells. Both arguments need to be put forward. The cons of stem cell research could be put to the students by a visiting speaker who will argue the case. Some internet sites provide a concise version of the sanctity of life (see www.justthefacts.org for some pre-birth information). The pros can also be summarised from internet sites. Some useful ones are given in the 'ICT link-up' in the 'Further teaching suggestions'.
- Use a summary sheet to state the main information and hold a snowball discussion where pairs of students brainstorm the concepts, then double up as fours and continue the process. The fours then gather into groups of eight in order to compare ideas and agree on a course of action (to endorse stem cell research or not). A spokesperson from each group of eight feeds back to the whole group.

Plenaries

Banking your baby's cord blood – It is now possible for the blood from the umbilical cord of a newborn baby to be collected and stored. Get the students to write a short paragraph explaining the benefits of this procedure to prospective parents. Select students to read out their efforts and discuss. *(5 minutes)*

Anagrams – Write up or project anagrams of the key words and terms from the lesson. Support students by giving them simpler words and terms. Extend students by omitting the vowels and asking them for definitions. *(10 minutes)*

Further teaching suggestions

Debate the use of prosthetic limbs at the Olympics
- Ask how the students would feel about competitors in the Olympic using prosthetic limbs which allow them to perform better than unaided humans. Encourage discussion.

ICT link-up
- There are a number of good internet sites that have useful information: New Scientist; Nature; Stem Cell Information; Christopher Reeve Foundation; Stem Cell Research Foundation. (See www.nature.com; www.stemcells.nih.gov; www.christopherreeve.org; www.newscientist.com; www.stemcellresearchfoundation. org.) If computers are available, set up a scavenger hunt style trail of internet sites to pull out the main bits of the pro and con arguments and details of the research carried

out. Ask students to find out about the original research and write a report of what was discovered. (See www. stemcellresearchfoundation.org.)

The meaning of 'totipotent', 'pluripotent' and 'multipotent'
- Get students to investigate the meaning of 'totipotent', 'pluripotent' and 'multipotent' when applied to stem cells. ['Totipotent' cells are found in very early embryos (for the first three or four divisions) and can differentiate into all types of cell. 'Pluripotent' stem cells are present in later embryos and can differentiate into any cell type. 'Multipotent' stem cells are found in adults as well as embryos and will only differentiate into certain cell types.] The Stem Cell Research Foundation has illustrations on its internet site.

Simple inheritance in animals and plants

B2 5.3 Stem cells

Learning objectives
- What is special about stem cells?
- How can we use stem cells to cure people?

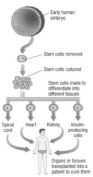

Figure 1 This shows how scientists hope embryonic stem cells might be formed into adult cells and used as human treatments in the future

The function of stem cells
An egg and sperm cell fuse to form a zygote, a single new cell. That cell divides and becomes a hollow ball of cells – the embryo. The inner cells of this ball are the stem cells. Stem cells differentiate to form the specialised cells of your body that make up your various tissues and organs. They will eventually produce every type of cell in your body.

Even when you are an adult, some of your stem cells remain. Your bone marrow is a good source of stem cells. Scientists now think there may be a tiny number of stem cells in most of the different tissues in your body. This includes your blood, brain, muscle and liver.

The stem cells can stay in the different tissues for many years. They are only needed if your tissues are injured or affected by disease. Then they start dividing to replace the different types of damaged cell.

a What are stem cells?

Using stem cells
Many people suffer and even die because parts of their body stop working properly. For example, spinal injuries can cause paralysis. That's because the spinal nerves do not repair themselves. Millions of people would benefit if we could replace damaged body cells.

In 1998, there was a breakthrough. Two American scientists managed to culture human embryonic stem cells. These were capable of forming other types of cell.

Scientists hope that the embryonic stem cells can be encouraged to grow into almost any different type of cell needed in the body. For example, scientists in the US have grown nerve cells from embryonic stem cells. In rats, these have been used to reconnect damaged spinal nerves. The rats regained some movement of their legs. In 2010 the first trials using nerve cells grown from embryonic stem cells in humans were carried out. The nerve cells were injected into the spinal cords of patients with new, severe spinal cord injuries. These first trials were to make sure that the technique is safe. The scientists and doctors hope it will not be long before they can use stem cells to help people who have been paralysed walk again.

We might also be able to grow whole new organs from embryonic stem cells. These organs could be used in transplant surgery. Conditions from infertility to dementia could eventually be treated using stem cells. Doctors in the UK hope to begin using embryonic stem cells to treat a common cause of blindness in 2011.

b What was the big scientific breakthrough by American scientists in 1998?

Problems with stem cells
Many embryonic stem cells come from aborted embryos. Others come from spare embryos in fertility treatment. This raises ethical issues. There are people, including many religious groups, who feel this is wrong. They question the use of a potential human being as a source of cells, even to cure others.

Some people feel that as the embryo cannot give permission, using it is a violation of its human rights. As well as this, progress with stem cells is slow. There is some concern that embryonic stem cells might cause cancer if they are used to treat sick people. This has certainly been seen in mice. Making stem cells is slow, difficult, expensive and hard to control.

c What is the biggest ethical concern with the use of embryonic stem cells?

The future of stem cell research
Scientists have found embryonic stem cells in the umbilical cord blood of newborn babies. These may help to overcome some of the ethical concerns.

Scientists are also finding ways of growing the adult stem cells found in bone marrow and some other tissues. So far they can only develop into a limited range of cell types. However, this is another possible way of avoiding the controversial use of embryonic tissue. Adult stem cells have been used successfully to treat some forms of heart disease and to grow some new organs such as tracheas (windpipes).

The area of stem cell research known as **therapeutic cloning** could be very useful. However, it is proving very difficult. It involves using cells from an adult to produce a cloned early embryo of themselves. This would provide a source of perfectly matched embryonic stem cells. In theory these could then be used to grow new organs for the original donor. The new organs would not be rejected by the body because they have been made from the body's own cells.

Most people remain excited by the possibilities of embryonic stem cell use in treating many diseases. At the moment, after years of relatively slow progress, hopes are high again that stem cells will change the future of medicine. We don't know how many of these hopes will be fulfilled; only time will tell.

Figure 2 For years, funding for stem cell research in the US was blocked by the government. In 2009 President Obama changed that ruling so US research could move forward. However, the battle continues in the courts.

Figure 3 In 2010 Ciaran Finn-Lynch was the first child to be given a life-saving new windpipe grown using his own stem cells

Summary questions
1 Copy and complete using the words below:
bone marrow differentiate embryos hollow inner stem cells
Unspecialised cells known as .... can .... (divide and change) into many different types of cell when they are needed. Human stem cells are found in .... and in adult .... The embryo forms a .... ball of cells and the .... cells of this ball are the stem cells.

2 a What are the advantages of using stem cells to treat diseases?
b What are the difficulties with stem cell research?
c How are scientists hoping to overcome the ethical objections to using embryonic stem cells in their research?

Key points
- Embryonic stem cells (from human embryos) and adult stem cells (from adult bone marrow) can be made to differentiate into many different types of cell.
- Stem cells have the potential to treat previously incurable conditions. We may be able to grow nerve cells or whole new organs for people who need them.

Answers to in-text questions
a Unspecialised cells that can differentiate to form many different types of specialised body cell.

b Culturing human embryonic stem cells.

c Some people think it is wrong to use a potential human being as a source of cells to help other people.

Summary answers
1 stem cells, differentiate, embryos, bone marrow, hollow, inner

2 **a** They can be used to make any type of adult cell to repair or replace damaged tissues, with no rejection issues.
b There are ethical objections and concerns over possible side effects.
c By using stem cells from umbilical blood, adult stem cells and therapeutic cloning.

B2 5.4

From Mendel to DNA

Learning objectives

Students should learn:

- about the work of Mendel and why its importance was not recognised until after his death
- why DNA fingerprinting is possible
- how specific proteins are made.

Learning outcomes

Most students should be able to:

- describe Mendel's discoveries
- recognise why Mendel's ideas were not accepted in his time
- describe how DNA fingerprinting is used to identify individuals.

Some students should also be able to:

- explain simply the structure of DNA
- explain how a gene codes for a specific protein. [HT only]

Answers to in-text questions

a Mendel became a monk because he was clever but poor and the only way to get an education if you were poor was to join the Church.

b He kept records and analysed his results.

Support

- Get students to use different coloured (yellow and green) dried peas, glue and a large sheet of paper to make a large poster showing Mendel's experiment as depicted in the Student Book.

Extend

- Ask students to draw up a plan for one of Mendel's experiments and calculate how long it took him to get his results. What precautions would he have to take? Did he use controls? Ask the students to apply some of the criteria needed when they design their own experiments. Would you do it the same way as he did it? What different techniques might you use?

Specification link-up: Biology B2.7

- Sexual reproduction gives rise to variation because when gametes fuse, one of each pair of alleles comes from each parent. *[B2.7.2 a)]*
- Some characteristics are controlled by a single gene. Each gene may have different forms called alleles. *[B2.7.2 c)]*
- An allele that controls the development of a characteristic when it is present on only one of the chromosomes is a dominant allele. *[B2.7.2 d)]*
- An allele that controls the development of characteristics only if the dominant allele is not present is a recessive allele. *[B2.7.2 e)]*
- Chromosomes are made up of large molecules of DNA (deoxyribo nucleic acid) which has a double helix structure. *[B2.7.2 f)]*
- A gene is a small section of DNA. *[B2.7.2 g)]*
- Each gene codes for a particular combination of amino acids which make a specific protein. *[B2.7.2 h)]* **[HT only]**
- Each person (apart from identical twins) has unique DNA. This can be used to identify individuals in a process known as DNA fingerprinting. *[B2.7.2 i)]*
- Explain why Mendel proposed the idea of separately inherited factors and why the importance of this discovery was not recognised until after his death. *[B2.7]*

Lesson structure

Starters

How did Mendel start? – Give the students a collection of dried peas to sort out into groups. Include smooth and wrinkled skins, yellow and green if possible. Ask them to predict what would happen if the peas were planted. Would you get peas identical to the ones you planted? Discuss. If students are interested, they could plant the peas and await the results. *(5 minutes)*

A model of DNA – If possible, have a model of DNA showing its structure with the different bases, the deoxyribose and the phosphate groups. Get the students to identify the component parts. Support students by providing labels of the component parts which they can stick on to the model. It could be useful to indicate here that a gene is a bit of DNA. Extend students by discussing the coding on a simple level. It could be helpful to provide students with a print-out of a DNA molecule which they can label and keep in their notebooks. *(10 minutes)*

Main

- Create/show a video or PowerPoint presentation on Mendel's life and work. There is plenty of information available and scope for introducing students to the demands of research (think about all those plants he grew and seeds he counted). Consider the characteristics that he investigated; introduce some of the easier terms, such as 'pure-breeding' and some of the simple ratios. Discuss his technique. (See www.mendelweb.org).
- 'Grow your own genetics experiment' (see 'Practical support').
- Prepare a PowerPoint presentation on genetic fingerprinting. The technique can be fairly simply explained (see NCBE publications or website for details) and then the implications discussed. Some examples of different uses can be given, e.g. forensic evidence, paternity issues. There are some good images available on the internet.

Plenaries

Press conference – Select a student who is prepared to be Mendel. Other students are to interview him about his work and why he did not get recognition at the time. The student can choose other members of the class to represent workers who followed up his discoveries. Differentiation by outcome: support level students will ask simpler questions and may need prompting. Students can be extended by asking 'Mendel' questions about what he thought the benefits of his work might be. *(5 minutes)*

Be a detective! – Present the students with some genetic evidence (some DNA from a murder weapon and three sets of genetic fingerprints). You could make it more complex by adding in some other forensic details, such as mud from the scene of the crime, bloodstains, etc. Let them work out who did the crime. Pick one group to present the solution with their reasons. Discuss the importance of genetic fingerprinting in solving crimes. Link with cases where someone has been wrongfully imprisoned for years until the DNA evidence showed them to be innocent. *(10 minutes)*

Practical support

Grow your own genetics experiment

Equipment and materials required
Sets of seeds from monohybrid genetic crosses can be obtained from suppliers, seed trays, compost.

Details
Plant seeds from monohybrid genetic crosses. When the seeds grow, it is possible to observe differences between the seedlings and make predictions about the genetic constitution of the parent plants. Tobacco (colour of cotyledons, hairiness of stem, colour of stem and leaf shape), tomato (leaf shape, hairiness of stem, colour of stem) and cucumber (bitterness of leaves) are all suitable for class use. The seeds are sown in seed trays, kept in light, airy conditions and watered every two or three days. They will be ready for scoring the characteristics after about 15 to 20 days. These seeds usually come provided with instructions and an explanation of the parental cross which produced them.

B2 5.4 — From Mendel to DNA

Learning objectives
- What did Mendel's experiments teach us about inheritance?
- What is DNA?
- How are specific proteins made in the body? [H]

Until about 150 years ago people had no idea how information was passed from one generation to the next. Today we can identify people by the genetic information in their cells.

Mendel's discoveries
Gregor Mendel was born in 1822 in Austrian Silesia. He was clever but poor, so he became a monk to get an education.

He worked in the monastery gardens and became fascinated by the peas growing there. He carried out some breeding experiments using peas. He used smooth peas, wrinkled peas, green peas and yellow peas for his work. Mendel cross-bred the peas and counted the different offspring carefully. He found that characteristics were inherited in clear and predictable patterns.

Mendel explained his results by suggesting there were separate units of inherited material. He realised that some characteristics were dominant over others and that they never mixed together. This was an amazing idea for the time.

a Why did Gregor Mendel become a monk?

Mendel kept records of everything he did, and analysed his results. This was almost unheard of in those days. Eventually in 1866 Mendel published his findings.

He had never seen chromosomes nor heard of genes. Yet he explained some of the basic laws of genetics using mathematical models in ways that we still use today.

Mendel was ahead of his time. As no one knew about genes or chromosomes, people simply didn't understand his theories. He died 20 years later with his ideas still ignored – but convinced that he was right.

b What was unusual about Mendel's scientific technique at the time?

Sixteen years after Mendel's death, his work was finally recognised. By 1900, people had seen chromosomes through a microscope. Other scientists discovered Mendel's papers and repeated his experiments. When they published their results, they gave Mendel the credit for what they observed.

From then on ideas about genetics developed rapidly. It was suggested that Mendel's units of inheritance might be carried on the chromosomes seen under the microscope. And so the science of genetics as we know it today was born.

DNA – the molecule of inheritance
The work of Gregor Mendel was just the start of our understanding of inheritance. Today, we know that our features are inherited on genes carried on the chromosomes found in the nuclei of our cells.

These chromosomes are made up of long molecules of a chemical known as DNA (deoxyribonucleic acid). This has a double helix structure. Your genes are small sections of this DNA. The DNA carries the instructions to make the proteins that form most of your cell structures. These proteins also include the enzymes that control your cell chemistry. This is how the relationship between the genes and the whole organism builds up. The genes make up the chromosomes in the nucleus of the cell. They control the proteins, which make up the different specialised cells that form tissues. These tissues then form organs and organ systems that make up the whole body.

The genetic code
The long strands of your DNA are made up of combinations of four different chemical bases (see Figure 2). These are grouped into threes and each group of three codes for an amino acid.

Each gene is made up of hundreds or thousands of these bases. The order of the bases controls the order in which the amino acids are put together so that they make a particular protein for use in your body cells. Each gene codes for a particular combination of amino acids, which make a specific protein.

A change or mutation in a single group of bases can be enough to change or disrupt the whole protein structure and the way it works.

A section of three bases like this codes for one amino acid

Figure 2 DNA codes for the amino acids that make up the proteins that make each individual

DNA fingerprinting
Unless you have an identical twin, your DNA is unique to you. Other members of your family will have strong similarities in their DNA. However, each individual has their own unique pattern. Only identical twins have the same DNA. That's because they have both developed from the same original cell.

The unique patterns in your DNA can be used to identify you. A technique known as 'DNA fingerprinting' can be applied to make the patterns known as DNA fingerprints.

These patterns are more similar between people who are related than between total strangers. They can be produced from very tiny samples of DNA from body fluids such as blood, saliva and semen.

The likelihood of two identical samples coming from different people (apart from identical twins) is millions to one. As a result, DNA fingerprinting is very useful in solving crimes. It can also be used to find the biological father of a child when there is doubt.

Did you know ... ?
The first time DNA fingerprinting was used to solve a crime, it identified Colin Pitchfork as the murderer of two teenage girls and cleared an innocent man of the same crimes.

Figure 3 A DNA fingerprint

Parents
Green peas × Yellow peas

Offspring (first generation)
All green peas

But when the offspring are bred ...
Green peas × Green peas

Offspring (second generation)
$\frac{3}{4}$ Green peas $\frac{1}{4}$ Yellow peas

Figure 1 Gregor Mendel, the father of modern genetics. His work was not recognised in his lifetime but now we know just how right he was!

Summary questions
1 **a** How did Mendel's experiments with peas convince him that there were distinct 'units of inheritance' that were not blended together in offspring?
  b Why didn't people accept his ideas?
  c The development of the microscope played an important part in helping to convince people that Mendel was right. How?
2 Two men claim to be the father of the same child. Explain how DNA fingerprinting could be used to find out which one is the real father.
3 Explain the saying 'One gene, one protein'. [H]

Key points
- Gregor Mendel was the first person to suggest separately inherited factors, which we now call genes.
- Chromosomes are made up of large molecules of DNA.
- A gene is a small section of DNA that codes for a particular combination of amino acids, which make a specific protein. [H]
- Everyone (except identical twins) has unique DNA that can be used to identify them using DNA fingerprinting.

Further teaching suggestions

Make your own model DNA
- Students could try to make their own model of a part of a DNA molecule, either from a kit or from materials to hand. (See internet site www.csiro.au and search for a 'DNA model template'.)

Did Mendel fiddle his results?
- There are several ways in which you could consider Mendel to be lucky. His choice of plants to work on, the characteristics he chose, the numbers he obtained – all these worked out well for him. Give students some of his results and let them work out the ratios. If there are any budding mathematicians in the group, ask if they can work out the probability of getting such good results. There are suggestions that he knew what he wanted to prove before he set up his experiments. Ask: 'What do you think?'

How to get enough DNA for a fingerprint
- Sometimes the quantity of DNA left at a crime scene is very small, but using PCR (the polymerase chain reaction), this can be increased. Find out how this works. Use a search engine and key in the words or go to the NCBE website for more information.

Summary answers

1 **a** He found that characteristics were inherited in clear and predictable patterns. He realised some characteristics were dominant over others and that they never mixed together.
  b No one could see the units of inheritance, so there was no proof of their existence. People were not used to studying careful records of results.
  c Once people could see chromosomes, a mechanism for Mendel's ideas of inheritance became possible.

2 The DNA fingerprint of the real father would have similarities to the DNA fingerprint of the child, whereas that of the other man would not.

3 A gene is made up of groups of three base pairs. Each group of three base pairs codes for a single amino acid. The order of the base pairs in the gene determines the sequence of the amino acids which are joined together to make a protein – so each gene codes for a unique protein.

B2 5.5

Inheritance in action

Learning objectives

Students should learn:

- that characteristics are controlled by genes which have different forms called alleles
- the difference between dominant alleles and recessive alleles
- how, in humans, the sex chromosomes determines whether you are female (XX) or male (XY).

Learning outcomes

Most students should be able to:

- explain how the inheritance of characteristics is controlled by dominant and recessive alleles
- explain how sex is determined in humans.

Some students should also be able to:

- use the terms homozygous, heterozygous, phenotype and genotype correctly [HT only]
- construct genetic diagrams. [HT only]

Support

- Play a card game using dominant and recessive cards for lobed ears, dimples and tongue rolling. Some students might be able to cope with the sex determination game in its simplest form.

Extend

- If the school has the facilities, students could try scoring the *Drosophila* crosses, particularly if the flies have been used for sixth-form classes.

AQA Specification link-up: Biology B2.7

- Interpret genetic diagrams, including family trees. [B2.7]
- Construct genetic diagrams of monohybrid crosses and predict the outcomes of monohybrid crosses and be able to use the terms homozygous, heterozygous, phenotype and genotype. [B2.7] [HT only]
- In human body cells, one of the 23 pairs of chromosomes carries the genes that determine sex. In females, the sex chromosomes are the same (XX); in males the sex chromosomes are different (XY). [B2.7.2 b)]
- Some characteristics are controlled by a single gene. Each gene may have different forms called alleles. [B2.7.2 c)]
- An allele that controls the development of a characteristic when it is present on only one of the chromosomes is a dominant allele. [B2.7.2 d)]
- An allele which controls the development of characteristics only if the dominant allele is not present is a recessive allele. [B2.7.2 e)]

Lesson structure

Starters

Can you? – Ask some of these: 'Can you roll your tongue? Can you taste quinine (the bitter tasting anti-malaria chemical present in Indian tonic water)? Do you have dimples? Do you have dangly ear lobes? Do you have straight thumbs or bendy thumbs?' Discuss some of these characteristics. Build up a list of positive and negatives on the board. Are there any discernible trends? *(5 minutes)*

Get the words right – Put up at the front of the room some word cards with the important terms from the spread on inheritance (e.g. allele, chromosome, dominant, recessive, Mendel, inheritance, etc.). Support students by giving them a numbered list of sentences to match with the terms. Extend students by asking them to compose sentences containing combinations of these words. Select from responses, noting key ideas. *(10 minutes)*

Main

- If students did not carry out the 'Grow your own genetics experiment' when studying the previous spread, it could be done here as an illustration of inheritance in action.

- Inherited conditions in humans are due to mutations of the DNA. The Human Genome Project has mapped all the human chromosomes. Prepare a PowerPoint presentation on this project, including references to why it was done, how it was done and how long it took. Discuss the implications. Information is available on The Wellcome Trust website and the Human Genome Project Information website.

- Sex determination game – prepare sets of sperm cards with either an X or a Y on the back and egg cards, all with X on the back. Working in pairs, the students are to turn one sperm card and one egg card over at a time. In a table, they note the sperm chromosome, the egg chromosome, the combination, the gender and give the baby a name. Run for about 5–7 minutes and then see who has the biggest family. Ask: 'Are there more boys than girls? What does this tell us about the ratio of the sexes?' How strong is your evidence? What would happen to the ratio if we did it thousands of times? Get the students to write an advice note on gender likelihood for prospective parents.

- Draw a Punnett square on the board with a number of different dominant and recessive alleles. Use some of the examples mentioned in the 'Can you?' starter. Get the students to fill in pre-printed frames to 'model' the crosses. Also give the students some examples of the crosses Mendel made with his peas to work out. It is recommended that the students get as much practice as possible in predicting the outcome of monohybrid crosses.

- Different coloured beads (or dyed haricot beans) can be used to model how different characteristics are inherited. Students could be given a characteristic, either a human one or one of Mendel's crosses, and carry out the exercise scoring the different combinations of alleles. They can relate the figures they obtain to the outcome predicted by a Punnett square.

Plenaries

Human karyotypes – Show students some pictures of sets of human chromosomes (karyotypes) where the chromosomes have not been matched into pairs. Can they identify the sex chromosomes and decide where the karotype is from a male or a female? Compare with karyotypes where the chromosomes are in pairs. When is this type of information helpful? *(5 minutes)*

Family trees – Draw on the board or project a family tree (or pedigree diagram) for tongue rolling, or another human single gene characteristic that is not sex-linked and that has not been used in the Student Book. Ask students to explain how the characteristic has been inherited. Support students by prompting them to trace the inheritance in a simple way. Extend students by getting them to describe the possible genotypes of the different members. *(10 minutes)*

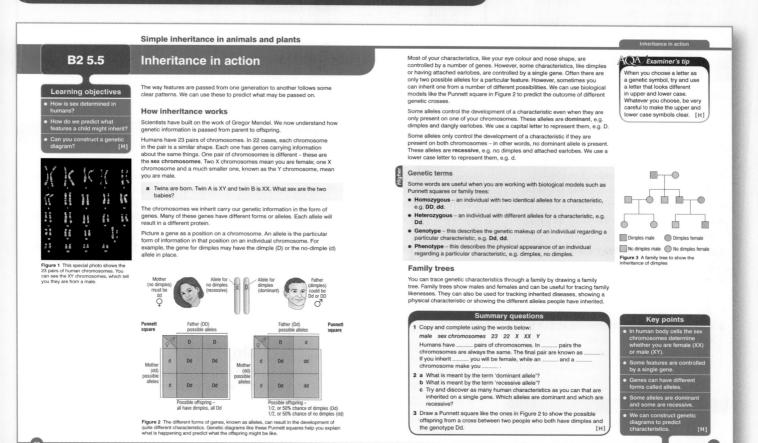

Further teaching suggestions

ICT link-up

- There are some excellent internet sites with genetics games that can be played online, e.g. the Canadian Museum of Nature website (www.nature.ca). Search for 'genome'.

Modify the sex determination game

- Using a symbol to represent a characteristic, such as tongue rolling, which can be stuck on the cards, the inheritance of a human characteristic (not a sex-linked one can be investigated at the same time. Just add another column to the table. It would be possible to model sex-linkage using this game, but it is beyond the specification.

Answers to in-text questions

a A is male and B is female.

Summary answers

1 23, 22, sex chromosomes, XX, X/Y, Y/X, male

2 a Dominant allele – an allele which controls the development of a characteristic even when it is present on only one of the chromosomes.

b Recessive allele – an allele which only controls the development of a characteristic if it is present on both chromosomes.

c Marks for each case where students identify correctly the single gene characteristic and the dominant and recessive alleles.

3 [Marks awarded for drawing a Punnett square correctly with the appropriate gametes.] DD, Dd, dD, dd is the one that doesn't have dimples; with dimples: 1 with no dimples.

B2 5.6 Inherited conditions in humans

Learning objectives

Students should learn:

- that some human disorders are inherited
- that some disorders are the result of the inheritance of a dominant allele (polydactyly), but others are the result of the inheritance of two recessive alleles (cystic fibrosis)
- that embryos can be screened for genetic disorders.

Learning outcomes

Most students should be able to:

- state that some human disorders may be inherited
- describe how genetic disorders caused by a dominant allele are inherited
- describe how a genetic disorder caused by a recessive allele must be inherited from both parents
- list some issues concerning embryo screening.

Some students should also be able to:

- draw genetic diagrams to show how genetic disorders are passed on [HT only]
- make informed judgements about the economic, social and ethical issues concerning embryo screening that they have studied or from information that is presented to them.

Support

- Provide students with large printed grids and cards with alleles on so that they could work out genetic crosses. They could work out the ratios and show them underneath.

Extend

- Suggest that students do some research on the frequency of particular alleles in populations. We are told that 1 person in 25 carries the allele for cystic fibrosis. Ask: 'How has this been calculated?' They could find out about the Hardy–Weinberg law and how it works. The law itself is fairly straightforward – students could work out how they can use it to inform people that the incidence of the alleles for certain conditions is quite high.

AQA Specification link-up: Biology B2.7

- Some disorders are inherited. *[B2.7.3 a)]*
- Polydactyly – having extra fingers or toes – is caused by a dominant allele of a gene and can therefore be passed on by only one parent who has the disorder. *[B2.7.3 b)]*
- Cystic fibrosis (a disorder of cell membranes) must be inherited from both parents. The parents may be carriers of the disorder without actually having the disorder themselves. It is caused by a recessive allele of a gene and can therefore be passed on by parents, neither of whom has the disorder. *[B2.7.3 c)]*
- Embryos can be screened for the alleles that cause these and other genetic disorders. *[B2.7.3 d)]*
- Construct genetic diagrams of monohybrid crosses and predict the outcomes of monohybrid crosses and be able to use the terms homozygous, heterozygous, phenotype and genotype. *[B2.7]* **[HT only]**

Lesson structure

Starters

Infectious or genetic or ...? – Read students a list of illnesses, including some infectious diseases and some genetic disorders. Students to respond by writing on 'Show me' boards whether a disease is infectious (writing I) or genetic (writing G). If they do not know then they should write a question mark. Draw up a list on the board in two columns. *(5 minutes)*

Interpreting pedigree diagrams – If the Family tree plenary was not done on the previous lesson, introduce a family tree or pedigree diagram for an invented 'condition' and get students to work out some of the offspring. Support students by prompting them and identifying the affected members and how they inherited the condition. They should be able to identify the carriers. Extend students by asking them to work out the way in which the alleles have been inherited. If time permits, use one condition caused by a dominant allele and one by a recessive allele. *(10 minutes)*

Main

- Polydactyly – Find and show images of polydactyly. The basic facts, symptoms and inheritability can be presented, together with some examples of polydactyly in other animals (cats, chickens, etc.).

- This could lead to a discussion on the condition and whether treatment is needed or desirable. If some images are shown where there is an extra thumb, then students could express their own feelings about how it should be treated. It is not a life-threatening condition, but students could think about whether or not genetic testing is a good idea.

- Cystic fibrosis – Useful internet sites can be found, including 'The Cystic Fibrosis Trust', the 'Cystic Fibrosis Foundation' (see www.cftrust.org.uk and www.cff.org), and the students could be asked to research different aspects of the disorder in groups and put together a lesson on the condition.

- One group could describe the disease and its symptoms, another the genetics of how it is inherited and a further group could review the different treatments. Ask: 'According to the statistics, 1 in 25 people carries the allele, so is it worth being screened for it?'

- Inherited or not? – It is difficult to know whether a particular disorder or condition is inherited or not. The only way to find out is to carry out pedigree analysis and go back through the generations if possible. Suggest to students that they think of a particular family trait and see if they can draw up a pedigree within their own family. It is probably better to choose a characteristic, such as dangly ear lobes or dimples, rather than a disorder unless a student has a particular interest.

Plenaries

Play the inheritance game – The sex determination game, from the previous spread, could be modified by adding a dominant or recessive genetic disorder sticker to some of the cards and to see what happens to the offspring. Allow 5 minutes for the game and then add up how many are affected offspring, how many are carriers and how many are unaffected by the disorder. *(5 minutes)*

Statistics or chance? – Much emphasis is put on the ratios of incidence of the condition, but it does not necessarily follow that it works like that. Ask: 'Why are there some families where there are no boys or no girls?' Every child of a person with polydactyly could inherit the disease. Students can try tossing a coin to see if they get equal numbers of heads and tails or if they get a run of heads. Ask students: What are the implications if it was your family? Get them to write down their thoughts. Support students by giving them a list of simple statements about the implications which they could put in order of importance. Extend students by getting them to express their thoughts coherently, backed up by scientific reasoning. *(10 minutes)*

Answers to in-text questions

a A genetic disorder is inherited from parents. An infectious disorder is caught from other people.

b Cystic fibrosis is caused by a recessive allele.

Simple inheritance in animals and plants

B2 5.6 Inherited conditions in humans

Learning objectives

- How are human genetic disorders inherited?
- How can we use a genetic diagram to predict whether a child will inherit a genetic disorder?
- Can you construct a genetic diagram to make predictions about the likelihood of inheriting a genetic disorder? **[H]**

Not all diseases are infectious. Sometimes diseases are the result of a problem in our genes and can be passed on from parent to child. They are known as **genetic or inherited disorders**.

We can use our knowledge of dominant and recessive alleles to work out the risk of inheriting a genetic disorder.

a How is an inherited disorder different from an infectious disease?

Polydactyly

Sometimes babies are born with extra fingers or toes. This is called polydactyly. The most common form of polydactyly is caused by a dominant allele. It can be inherited from one parent who has the condition. People often have their extra digit removed, but some live quite happily with them.

Higher If one of your parents has polydactyly and is heterozygous, you have a 50% chance of inheriting the disorder. That's because half of their gametes will contain the faulty allele. If they are homozygous, you will definitely have the condition.

Cystic fibrosis

Cystic fibrosis is a genetic disorder that affects many organs of the body, particularly the lungs and the pancreas. Over 8500 people in the UK have cystic fibrosis.

Organs become clogged up by thick, sticky mucus, which stops them working properly. The reproductive system is also affected, so many people with cystic fibrosis are infertile.

Treatment for cystic fibrosis includes physiotherapy and antibiotics. These help keep the lungs clear of mucus and infections. Enzymes are used to replace the ones the pancreas cannot produce and to thin the mucus.

However, although treatments are getting better all the time, there is still no cure.

Cystic fibrosis is caused by a recessive allele so it must be inherited from both parents. Children affected by cystic fibrosis are usually born to parents who do not suffer from the disorder. They have a dominant healthy allele, which means their bodies work normally. However, they also carry the recessive cystic fibrosis allele. Because it gives them no symptoms, they have no idea it is there. They are known as carriers.

In the UK, one person in 25 carries the cystic fibrosis allele. Most of them will never be aware of it. They only realise when they have children with a partner who also carries the allele. Then there is a 25% (one in four) chance that any child they have will be affected.

b You will only inherit cystic fibrosis if you get the cystic fibrosis allele from both parents. Why?

- ☐ Male with polydactyly
- ◯ Female with polydactyly
- ☐ Unaffected male
- ◯ Unaffected female

Figure 1 Polydactyly is passed through a family tree by a dominant allele

The genetic lottery

Higher When the genes from parents are combined, it is called a genetic cross. We can show this using a genetic diagram (see Figures 2 and 3). A genetic diagram shows us:

- the alleles for a characteristic carried by the parents (the genotype of the parents)
- the possible gametes which can be formed from these
- how these could combine to form the characteristic in their offspring. The genotype of the offspring allows you to work out the possible phenotypes too.

When looking at the possibility of inheriting genetic disorders, it is important to remember that every time an egg and a sperm fuse it is down to chance which alleles combine. So if two parents who are heterozygous for the cystic fibrosis allele have four children, there is a 25% chance (one in four) that each child might have the disorder.

But in fact all four children could have cystic fibrosis, or none of them might be affected. They might all be carriers, or none of them might inherit the faulty alleles at all. It's all down to chance!

		P	p	
	p	Pp	pp	50% chance polydactyly, PP or Pp, 50% chance normal pp
	p	Pp	pp	

Pp = Parent with polydactyly
pp = Normal parent

Figure 2 A genetic diagram for polydactyly

Both parents are carriers, so Cc

		C	c	
	C	CC	Cc	Genotype: 25% normal (CC) 50% carriers (Cc) 25% affected by cystic fibrosis (cc)
	c	Cc	cc	

Phenotype:
3/4, or 75% chance normal
1/4, or 25% chance cystic fibrosis

Figure 3 A genetic diagram for cystic fibrosis

Curing genetic diseases

So far we have no way of curing genetic disorders. Scientists hope that genetic engineering could be the answer. It should be possible to cut out faulty alleles and replace them with healthy ones. They have tried this in people affected by cystic fibrosis. Unfortunately, so far they have not managed to cure anyone.

Genetic tests are available that can show people if they carry the faulty allele. This allows them to make choices such as whether or not to have a family. It is possible to screen fetuses or embryos during pregnancy for the alleles which cause inherited disorders. You can also screen embryos before they are implanted in the mother during IVF treatment. These tests are very useful but raise many ethical issues.

Summary questions

1 **a** What is polydactyly?
   b Why can one parent with the allele for polydactyly pass the condition on to their children even though the other parent is not affected?
   c Look at the family tree in Figure 1. For each of the five people labelled A to E affected by polydactyly, give their possible alleles and explain your answers.

2 **a** Why are carriers of cystic fibrosis not affected by the disorder themselves?
   b Why must both of your parents be carriers of the allele for cystic fibrosis before you can inherit the disease?

3 A couple have a baby who has cystic fibrosis. Neither the couple, nor their parents, have any signs of the disorder.
   Draw genetic diagrams showing the possible genotypes of the grandparents and the parents to show how this could happen. **[H]**

Key points

- Some disorders are inherited.
- Polydactyly is caused by a dominant allele of a gene and can be inherited from only one parent.
- Cystic fibrosis is caused by a recessive allele of a gene and so must be inherited from both parents.
- You can use genetic diagrams to predict how genetic disorders might be inherited.
- You can construct genetic diagrams to predict the inheritance of genetic disease. **[H]**

64 / 65

Further teaching suggestions

Sex-linked genetic disorders

- The best-known sex-linked genetic disorders are haemophilia and colour blindness. Discuss the inheritance of conditions with genes located on the X chromosome. Draw up Punnett squares to show how the alleles are inherited and the probability of the disease occurring. It was suggested on the last spread that gifted and talented students did some research on haemophilia. This could be a good opportunity for them to present their findings.

AQA Examiner's tip

It is sensible for students to be able to use Punnett diagrams: it makes the interpretation of any genetic cross much easier. It could be a good idea to stress to students that they are dealing with ratios and probabilities. What happens in real life is not always the same!

Summary answers

1 **a** A genetic disorder which causes extra fingers or toes.
   b The faulty allele is dominant, so only one parent needs to have the allele and pass it on for the offspring to be affected.
   c A Pp only – as produced a child that was unaffected.
   B Pp – because mother must pass on a recessive allele to produce two unaffected children.
   C-E – could be PP or Pp as each parent has the genotype Pp.

2 **a** Carriers have a normal dominant allele, so their body works normally.
   b CF (cystic fibrosis) recessive – must inherit one from each parent to get the disease – but if parents had the disease themselves, they would almost certainly be infertile so parents must be carriers.

3 Genetic diagram based on Figure 3 in Student Book, showing how the cc (cystic fibrosis) arises.

B2 5.7

Stem cells and embryos – science and ethics

Learning objectives

Students should learn that:

- that there are social and ethical issues concerning the use of stem cells from embryos
- that there are economic, social and ethical issues concerning embryo screening
- to make informed judgements about these issues.

Learning outcomes

Most students should be able to:

- list some of the opinions for and against the use of stem cells in medical research and treatments
- describe the problems associated with the screening of embryos for genetic disorders.

Some students should also be able to:

- make informed judgements about the issues they have studied and from information presented to them.

AQA / Specification link-up: Biology B2.7

- Cells from human embryos and adult bone marrow called stem cells, can be made to differentiate into many different types of cells e.g. nerve cells. [B2.7.1 k)]
- Make informed judgements about the sort of social and ethical issues concerning the use of stem cells from embryos in medical research and treatments. [B2.7]
- Make informed judgements about the economic, social and ethical issues concerning embryo screening. [B2.7]

Lesson structure

Starters

In the beginning... – Get the students to think back through their lives and to their earliest memory. Share a few of these with the class. Ask did they actually exist before this memory? Engender a debate as to when they started – when they became themselves, possibly best phrased as getting them to think of a time when they were not themselves. Link this to the debate on whether a fertilised egg is a human being or not. *(5 minutes)*

Wished out of existence – Get the students to think of someone they know, either personally or know of through the media who has a disability of some description. Empathise with them. Ask the students to consider whether, if the parents had known that the child would be disabled, they would have allowed the child to be born (if they had been given the choice). Would they have tried for another baby instead? What factors would have influenced their decision? Support students by providing some examples of popular media figures who have some disability. Extend students by providing them with access to suitable sections from ethics text books on the subject. *(10 minutes)*

Main

- Carry out the stem cell dilemma activity ('Activity 1') from the Student Book. Several internet sites have been suggested as good sources of information about stem cell research. One of the ways in which the views of the target group can be discovered is by means of a questionnaire. The questions need to be phrased correctly to elicit the information. Students should ask whether or not the group they are questioning are aware of some of the pros and cons before asking for their opinions. Carefully designed questions should yield information and the results of such a questionnaire could form part of the display.

- Working in groups, get the students to produce display material as suggested, using the information for and against as starting points.

- The students can display the results of the original survey in a variety of different ways. They should be bold and innovative, making use of ICT. The subsequent survey and any changes of opinion can reveal how good their material was. Again, bold display of the data is needed. They might like to find out if their target group needed more information or whether it was pitched at the right level.

- Students could discuss the pros and cons of genetic screening using the material in the Student Book and from other sources. They may need to research more topics using the internet sites given previously.

- The activity suggested ('Activity 2') is a difficult one for some students to do without carrying out more research. It also requires a degree of confidence. Give students time to discuss their approach and suggest they work in small groups. Perhaps they could plan it like a film script or scenes from a TV documentary. The questions suggested could be expanded with some about the lives of the couple included. Ask: 'How demanding are their jobs? How have they coped with the child they already have?' If each group approached the activity from a slightly different perspective, then these role-play exercises could prove interesting to the class and provide them with a balanced view.

Support

- Ask simple questions, such as 'If you or someone you loved was ill, would you donate bone marrow, even if it hurt?'

Extend

- Get students to find out about different aspects of stem cell research which do not involve the use of embryos or foetal tissue.

Plenaries

Continuum – Ask students to place themselves, or a card with their name on it, along a line from two opposing viewpoints: for and against using embryonic stem cells. They could be asked to justify their position when challenged by their peers. *(5 minutes)*

Thank you for your bone marrow – Get students to write a postcard from hospital to the person who has just donated bone marrow to them. Support students by prompting or giving them some words and phrases to arrange. Extend students by getting them to explain how the donation will improve their life. Select some students to read out their messages. *(10 minutes)*

Further teaching suggestions

Counselling speaker
- If anyone knows a genetic counsellor, it might be a good opportunity to invite them in to the school to give a short talk and answer questions about the topic.

Bone marrow transplants
- Students could find information about bone marrow transplants. Information can be obtained from the Anthony Nolan Trust.

Identity transplants
- Explore how the students view the concept of identity transplants – will this ever be possible? Discuss the 2009 film *Avatar* and link with superstitious ideas about possession by demons. Discuss brain transplants and the possible future potential of memory transplants.

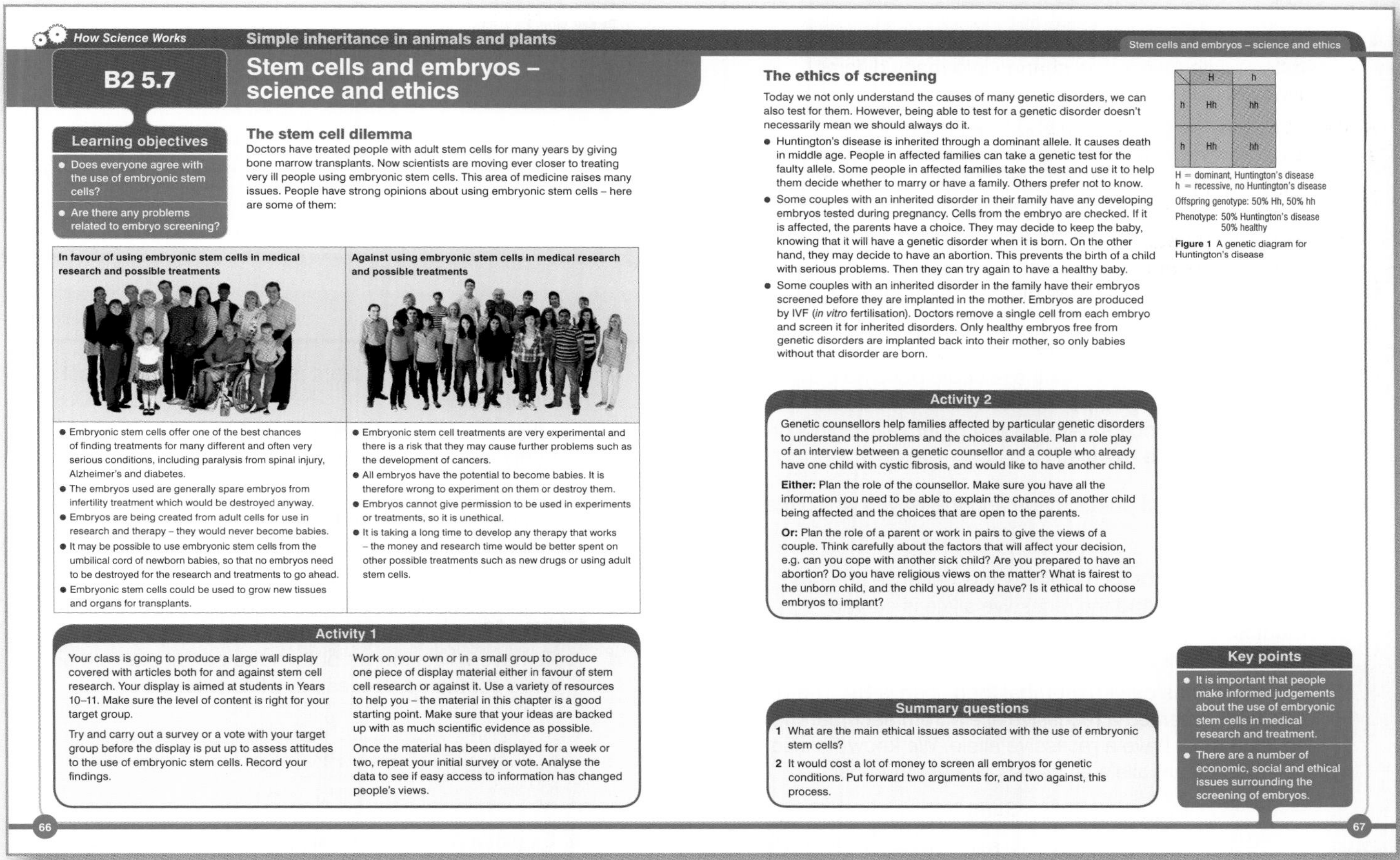

How Science Works   Simple inheritance in animals and plants   Stem cells and embryos – science and ethics

B2 5.7

Stem cells and embryos – science and ethics

Learning objectives
- Does everyone agree with the use of embryonic stem cells?
- Are there any problems related to embryo screening?

The stem cell dilemma
Doctors have treated people with adult stem cells for many years by giving bone marrow transplants. Now scientists are moving ever closer to treating very ill people using embryonic stem cells. This area of medicine raises many issues. People have strong opinions about using embryonic stem cells – here are some of them:

In favour of using embryonic stem cells in medical research and possible treatments	Against using embryonic stem cells in medical research and possible treatments

• Embryonic stem cells offer one of the best chances of finding treatments for many different and often very serious conditions, including paralysis from spinal injury, Alzheimer's and diabetes.	• Embryonic stem cell treatments are very experimental and there is a risk that they may cause further problems such as the development of cancers.
• The embryos used are generally spare embryos from infertility treatment which would be destroyed anyway.	• All embryos have the potential to become babies. It is therefore wrong to experiment on them or destroy them.
• Embryos are being created from adult cells for use in research and therapy – they would never become babies.	• Embryos cannot give permission to be used in experiments or treatments, so it is unethical.
• It may be possible to use embryonic stem cells from the umbilical cord of newborn babies, so that no embryos need to be destroyed for the research and treatments to go ahead.	• It is taking a long time to develop any therapy that works – the money and research time would be better spent on other possible treatments such as new drugs or using adult stem cells.
• Embryonic stem cells could be used to grow new tissues and organs for transplants.	

Activity 1
Your class is going to produce a large wall display covered with articles both for and against stem cell research. Your display is aimed at students in Years 10–11. Make sure the level of content is right for your target group.

Try and carry out a survey or a vote with your target group before the display is put up to assess attitudes to the use of embryonic stem cells. Record your findings.

Work on your own or in a small group to produce one piece of display material either in favour of stem cell research or against it. Use a variety of resources to help you – the material in this chapter is a good starting point. Make sure that your ideas are backed up with as much scientific evidence as possible.

Once the material has been displayed for a week or two, repeat your initial survey or vote. Analyse the data to see if easy access to information has changed people's views.

The ethics of screening
Today we not only understand the causes of many genetic disorders, we can also test for them. However, being able to test for a genetic disorder doesn't necessarily mean we should always do it.

- Huntington's disease is inherited through a dominant allele. It causes death in middle age. People in affected families can take a genetic test for the faulty allele. Some people in affected families take the test and use it to help them decide whether to marry or have a family. Others prefer not to know.
- Some couples with an inherited disorder in their family have any developing embryos tested during pregnancy. Cells from the embryo are checked. If it is affected, the parents have a choice. They may decide to keep the baby, knowing that it will have a genetic disorder when it is born. On the other hand, they may decide to have an abortion. This prevents the birth of a child with serious problems. Then they can try again to have a healthy baby.
- Some couples with an inherited disorder in the family have their embryos screened before they are implanted in the mother. Embryos are produced by IVF (*in vitro* fertilisation). Doctors remove a single cell from each embryo and screen it for inherited disorders. Only healthy embryos free from genetic disorders are implanted back into their mother, so only babies without that disorder are born.

Activity 2
Genetic counsellors help families affected by particular genetic disorders to understand the problems and the choices available. Plan a role play of an interview between a genetic counsellor and a couple who already have one child with cystic fibrosis, and would like to have another child.

Either: Plan the role of the counsellor. Make sure you have all the information you need to be able to explain the chances of another child being affected and the choices that are open to the parents.

Or: Plan the role of a parent or work in pairs to give the views of a couple. Think carefully about the factors that will affect your decision, e.g. can you cope with another sick child? Are you prepared to have an abortion? Do you have religious views on the matter? What is fairest to the unborn child, and the child you already have? Is it ethical to choose embryos to implant?

	H	h
h	Hh	hh
h	Hh	hh

H = dominant, Huntington's disease
h = recessive, no Huntington's disease

Offspring genotype: 50% Hh, 50% hh
Phenotype: 50% Huntington's disease
              50% healthy

Figure 1 A genetic diagram for Huntington's disease

Summary questions
1 What are the main ethical issues associated with the use of embryonic stem cells?
2 It would cost a lot of money to screen all embryos for genetic conditions. Put forward two arguments for, and two against, this process.

Key points
- It is important that people make informed judgements about the use of embryonic stem cells in medical research and treatment.
- There are a number of economic, social and ethical issues surrounding the screening of embryos.

Summary answers

1 The main ethical issue is the source of the stem cells – some people are completely against the use of embryos in this way, seeing them as potential human beings.

2 Any two arguments for and two against universal embryo screening.

Summary answers

1 a Mitosis is cell division that takes place in the normal body cells and produces genetically identical daughter cells.

b [Marks awarded for correct sequence of diagrams with suitable annotations.]

c All the divisions from the fertilised egg to the baby are mitosis. After birth, all the divisions for growth are mitosis, together with all the divisions involved in repair and replacement of damaged tissues.

2 Meiosis is a special form of cell division to produce gametes where the chromosome number is reduced by half. It takes place in the reproductive organs (the ovaries and testes).

3 a Meiosis is important because it halves the chromosome number of the cells, so that when two gametes fuse at fertilisation, the normal chromosome number is restored. It also allows variety to be introduced.

b [Marks awarded for correct sequence of diagrams with appropriate annotations.]

4 a Stem cells are unspecialised cells which can differentiate (divide and change into many different types of cell) when they are needed.

b They may be used to repair damaged body parts, e.g. grow new spinal nerves to cure paralysis; grow new organs for transplants; repair brains in demented patients. [Accept any other sensible suggestions.]

c **For:** They offer tremendous hope of new treatments; they remove the need for donors in transplants; they could cure paralysis, heart disease, dementia etc; can grow tissues to order.

Against: They use tissue from human embryos; it's wrong to use embryos, as these could become people; embryos cannot give permission; stem cells could develop into cancers. [Accept any other valid points on either side of the debate.]

5 [Give credit for valid points made and the way in which the letter is written.]

6 a Sami's alleles are **ss**. We know this because she has curved thumbs and the recessive allele is curved thumbs. She must have inherited two recessive alleles to have inherited the characteristic.

b If the baby has curved thumbs, then Josh is **Ss**. The baby has inherited a recessive allele from each parent, so Josh must have a recessive allele. We know he also has a dominant allele as he has straight thumbs.

Sami

Josh		s	s
	S	Ss	Ss
	s	ss	ss

c If the baby has straight thumbs, then Josh could be either Ss or SS. We know that the baby has inherited one recessive allele from mother, and we know that Josh has one dominant allele but we do not know if he has two dominant alleles.

Sami

Josh		s	s
	S	Ss	Ss
	S	Ss	Ss

Summary questions ⓚ

1 a What is mitosis?

b Explain, using diagrams, what takes place when a cell divides by mitosis.

c Mitosis is very important during the development of a baby from a fertilised egg. It is also important all through life. Why?

2 What is meiosis and where does it take place?

3 a Why is meiosis so important?

b Explain, using labelled diagrams, what takes place when a cell divides by meiosis. [H]

4 a What are stem cells?

b It is hoped that many different medical problems may be cured using stem cells. Explain how this might work.

c There are some ethical issues associated with the use of embryonic stem cells. Explain the arguments both for and against their use.

5 Hugo de Vries is one of the scientists who made the same discoveries as Mendel several years after Mendel's death. Write a letter from Hugo to one of his friends after he has found Mendel's writings. Explain what Mendel did, why no one took any notice of him and how the situation has changed so that you (Hugo) can come up with a clear explanation for the results of your own experiments. Explain your attitude to Mendel.

6 Whether you have a straight thumb or a curved one is decided by a single gene with two alleles. The allele for a straight thumb, S, is dominant to the curved allele, s. Use this information to help you answer these questions.

Josh has straight thumbs but Sami has curved thumbs. They are expecting a baby.

a We know exactly what Sami's thumb alleles are. What are they and how do you know?

b If the baby has curved thumbs, what does this tell you about Josh's thumb alleles? Draw and complete a Punnett square to show the genetics of your explanation.

c If the baby has straight thumbs, what does this tell us about Josh's thumb alleles? Draw and complete a Punnett square to show the genetics of your explanation. [H]

7 Amjid grew some purple flowering pea plants from seeds he had bought at the garden centre. He planted them in his garden.

Here are his results.

Seeds planted	247
Purple-flowered plants	242
White-flowered plants	1
Seeds not growing	4

a Is the white-flowered plant an anomaly? Why?

b Are the seeds that did not grow anomalies? Why?

c Suggest other investigations Amjid could carry out into the cause of the colour of the white-flowered plant.

Amjid was interested in these plants, so he collected the seed from some of the purple-flowered plants and used them in the garden the following year. He made careful note of what happened.

Here are his results:

Seeds planted	406
Purple-flowered plants	295
White-flowered plants	102
Seeds not growing	6

Amjid was slightly surprised. He did not expect to find that a third of his flowers would be white.

d i The purple allele (P) is dominant and the allele for white flowers (p) is recessive. Draw a genetic diagram that explains Amjid's numbers of purple and white flowers.

ii How accurate were Amjid's results compared with the expected ratio?

e How could Amjid have improved his method of growing the peas to make his results more valid? [H]

---

7 a Yes, the white flowered plant is an anomaly because it is not as expected.

b Yes, the seeds that did not grow are also anomalies probably due to the way they were grown or some genetic problem.

c As an anomaly, the white flowered plant should be investigated, e.g. to see if the colour was a result of a mutation or because of the particular conditions in which it was grown. He could breed from it, plant it in a different soil, etc.

d i To have white flowers both of the parent plants must have contained a recessive white allele so

	P	p
P	PP	Pp
p	Pp	pp

ii Expect a 3 : 1 ratio actual results 295 : 102 – very close.

e To improve his method of growing the peas to make his results more valid Amjid could have grown them under controlled conditions.

Kerboodle resources ⓚ

Resources available for this chapter on Kerboodle are:

- Chapter map: Simple inheritance in animals and plants
- Animation: Chromosomes (B2 5.1)
- Extension: Mitosis and cancer (B2 5.1)
- Bump up your grade: Mitosis or meiosis (B2 5.2)

Examination-style questions

Copy and complete the following sentences using the words or symbols below:

characteristics cytoplasm fitness genes nucleus proteins tissue

2 23 46 X XX XY Y

In the body cells of a boy there are .... chromosomes that are found in the .... The boy's cells can be identified as male by the .... chromosome. On all the chromosomes there are sections called .... that determine the .... of the boy.   (5)

The drawing shows some of the stages of reproduction in horses.

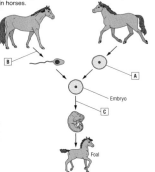

a i Name this type of reproduction   (1)
ii Name the type of cell labelled **A**.   (1)
b Name the type of cell division taking place at the stages labelled:
i B   (1)
ii C.   (1)
c How does the number of chromosomes in each cell of the embryo compare with the number of chromosomes in cell **A**?   (1)
d When the foal grows up it will look similar to its parents but it will **not** be identical to either parent.
i Explain why it will look similar to its parents.   (1)
ii Suggest **two** reasons why it will **not** be identical to either of its parents.   (2)
AQA, 2001

3 When an embryo is formed, the cells divide and start to differentiate. Some adult cells are still able to differentiate.
a What is meant by the term *differentiation*?   (1)
b What name do we give to cells which have not differentiated?   (1)
c Give an example of adult cells that can differentiate.   (1)
d Some of the embryo cells may be used in the future to treat conditions such as paralysis.
There are people who do not think we should use embryos in this way. What is an ethical reason for objecting to the use of embryos?   (1)

4 *In this question you will be assessed on using good English, organising information clearly and using specialist terms where appropriate.*

Doctors all over the world are investigating the use of stem cells to treat a wide variety of disorders.

Many doctors use adult stem cells but some use embryonic stem cells. There is evidence that adult stem cells do not cause cancer tumours if they are transferred soon after being removed from the body. Embryonic stem cells multiply very quickly and there is a risk of cancer developing after treatment with them.

Bone marrow cells are stem cells which continually replace your blood cells every day of your life.

Adult stem cells from bone marrow have been used successfully to treat leukaemia for over 40 years. Many patients with damage to the nervous system have reported improvements in movement following treatment with adult stem cells, but more research is needed before widespread use of the treatment.

One doctor said, 'It is safer to use adult stem cells. Using embryonic stem cells is not ethical.'

Using the information and your own knowledge explain the statement made by the doctor.   (6)

69

- Support: The gametes (B2 5.2)
- WebQuest: Stem cell research (B2 5.3)
- Viewpoints: Stem cell research (B2 5.3)
- Viewpoint: DNA Fingerprinting (B2 5.4)
- Animation: The inheritance of cystic fibrosis (B2 5.6)
- Interactive activity: Inheritance
- Podcast: Simple inheritance in animals and plants
- Test yourself: Simple inheritance in animals and plants
- On your marks: Simple inheritance in animals and plants
- Examination-style questions: Simple inheritance in animals and plants
- Answers to examination-style questions: Simple inheritance in animals and plants

Practical suggestions

Practicals	AQA	(k)	📖	⚙
Observation or preparation of root tip squashes to illustrate chromosomes and mitosis.	✓		✓	
Using genetic beads to model mitosis and meiosis and genetic crosses.	✓	✓	✓	
Making models of DNA.	✓		✓	
Extracting DNA from kiwi fruit.	✓	✓		

Examination-style answers

1 46   nucleus   Y   genes   characteristics   *(5 marks)*

2 a i sexual/sex   *(1 mark)*
ii egg/gamete/sex cell/ovum   *(reject* ovule)   *(1 mark)*
b i meiosis/reduction   *(1 mark)*
ii mitosis/somatic   *(1 mark)*
c twice as many *(reject answers based on 23/46 chromosomes)*   *(1 mark)*
d i information/genes/DNA passed from parents (chromosomes neutral)   *(1 mark)*
ii genes/genetic information/chromosomes from two parents
<u>alleles</u> may be different
environmental effect/named
may have been mutation
any two for 1 mark each   *(2 marks)*

3 a The cells change into other types of cell.   *(1 mark)*
b stem cells   *(1 mark)*
c bone marrow cells   *(1 mark)*
allow other types of adult stem cells – not umbilical cord cells
d It may lead to death of an embryo/An embryo cannot give consent.   *(1 mark)*
– allow other ethical reason – not religious reasons

4 There is a clear, balanced and detailed explanation about the differences between adult and embryonic stem cells and the uses and advantages of the adult stem cells. The answer shows almost faultless spelling, punctuation and grammar. It is coherent and in an organised, logical sequence. It contains a range of appropriate or relevant specialist terms used accurately.   *(5–6 marks)*

There is some attempt to explain the differences between adult and embryonic stem cells and the benefits of adult stem cells. There are some errors in spelling, punctuation and grammar. The answer has some structure and organisation. The use of specialist terms has been attempted, but not always accurately.   *(3–4 marks)*

There is a brief description of what stem cells do and some evidence of the uses of stem cells. The spelling, punctuation and grammar are very weak. The answer is poorly organised with almost no specialist terms and/or their use demonstrating a general lack of understanding of their meaning.   *(1–2 marks)*

No relevant content.   *(0 marks)*

Examples of biology points made in the response:
- Stem cells are able to change into other types of cell
- Stem cells can be removed from adults, e.g. bone marrow
- Embryonic stem cells are taken from early embryos before the cells have started to change into other cells
- This is unethical because the embryo is destroyed
- There is a risk of cancer with embryonic stem cells
- Adult stem cells have been used safely for 40 years
- To treat leukaemia/other named example
- Patients with nervous system disorders have shown improvements after treatment with adult stem cells
- Accept another relevant point which answers the doctor's statement.

B2 6.1 The origins of life on Earth

Learning objectives

Students should learn:

- the nature of fossils
- how fossils provide evidence for the existence of prehistoric plants and animals.

Learning outcomes

Most students should be able to:

- explain what a fossil is
- describe some of the ways in which fossils are formed
- suggest reasons why scientists cannot be certain about how life began on Earth.

Some students should also be able to:

- evaluate what can be learnt from the fossil record.

AQA Specification link-up: Biology B2.8

- Evidence for early forms of life comes from fossils. *[B2.8.1 a)]*
- Fossils are the 'remains' of organisms from many years ago, which are found in rocks. Fossils may be formed in various ways:
  - from the hard parts of animals that do not decay easily
  - from parts of organisms that have not decayed because one or more of the conditions needed for decay are absent
  - when parts of the organism are replaced by other materials as they decay
  - as preserved traces of organisms, e.g. footprints, burrows and rootlet traces. *[B2.8.1 b)]*
- Many early forms of life were soft-bodied, which means that they have left few traces behind. What traces there were have been mainly destroyed by geological activity. *[B2.8.1 c)]*
- Suggest reasons why scientists cannot be certain about how life began on Earth. *[B2.8]*

Lesson structure

Starters

Fossil five words – Get the students to explain their current understanding of what fossils are in five words. Read some examples out. Support students by placing some words to choose from on the board. Extend students by allowing them to create more five-word sentences – what they feel about fossils, what their importance is, etc. *(5 minutes)*

Fossil circus – Arrange a circus of numbered fossils or fossil pictures around the laboratory. Get students to look and make notes on what they might be. *(10 minutes)*

Main

- Create a PowerPoint presentation or exposition on the ways that fossils form, such as cast formation, impressions and ice fossils. Victims of Pompeii illustrate cast formation; mammoths are found in ice; dinosaurs left footprints and animal droppings fossilise over time. For pictures, search the internet using key words and especially look for Ardley Quarry in Oxfordshire for its dinosaur footprints. Provide the students with a worksheet that they can complete as the presentation proceeds.

- Give students a timeline exercise linking with the above. Using a long strip of paper (e.g. till roll), students should mark off the major evolutionary events for which there is evidence. An alternative to this is to use a clock face and discover that *Homo sapiens* evolved in the last few seconds before 12 midnight.

- Give students an outline account of some of the methods of dating fossils: layers in rocks and sediments, potassium-argon dating, radiocarbon dating and looking at fossils of other species that overlap. With some more recent human fossils, the presence of artefacts (tools or shaped stones) can give clues as to the age of a fossil.

- Try to get hold of some peat, look for plant remains and discuss their age (can be many thousands of years old).

- Show students pictures of reconstructions of large fossil dinosaurs (such as are on show in the Natural History Museum) and ask: Were these fossils found as complete skeletons? Show some pictures of how reconstruction of fossils takes place using bits of the original skeleton. Discuss how accurate these reconstructions are. How are scientists sure that what they build up is a true representation? Refer students to reconstruction that has been done with prehistoric human skulls.

Support

- Get students to make a fossil using modelling clay or plaster of Paris for a mould and molten stearic acid to pour in and set (take care with hot liquids). Alternatively, students could use a modelling clay mould and pour plaster of Paris into the impression of a shell.

Extend

- Set students the problem of finding out how long a representation of a timeline would need to be if the Earth is 4 600 000 000 years old and 100 years was represented by a millimetre. Ask: 'How many A4 sheets of paper would be needed, allowing 1 cm overlap for gluing?' [Do not try to make one – it is over 40 km!]

Plenaries

What makes a good fossil? – Lead a quick discussion on why some creatures became fossilised and others did not. Ask: 'Why are there few fossils of worms and other soft-bodied creatures?' *(5 minutes)*

Only half the story ... – Display a sentence with many of the letters missing, but enough left to see what it is saying. Ask the students to write their own completed version. Support students by leaving out fewer letters or giving them a list of the missing letters that they can insert in appropriate places. Extend students by leaving out more letters and some words. Read out and discuss. *(10 minutes)*

Maths skills

Introduce students to the idea of a scale. Remind them that 10^3 is a thousand, 10^6 is a million and 10^9 is a billion. Link this to evolutionary timescales, so that students have a clear idea of how sizeable they are.

Old and new species

B2 6.1

The origins of life on Earth ⓚ

Learning objectives

- What is the evidence for the origins of life on Earth?
- What are fossils?
- What can we learn from fossils?

There is no record of the origins of life on Earth. It is a puzzle that can never be completely solved. There is not much valid evidence for what happened – no one was there to see it! We don't even know exactly when life on Earth began. However, most scientists think it was somewhere between 3 to 4 billion years ago.

There are some interesting ideas and well-respected theories that explain most of what you can see around you. The biggest problem we have is finding the evidence to support the ideas.

a When do scientists think life on Earth began?

What can we learn from fossils?

Some of the best evidence we have about the history of life on Earth comes from **fossils**. Fossils are the remains of organisms from many thousands or millions of years ago that are found preserved in rocks, ice and other places. For example, fossils have revealed the world of the dinosaurs. These lizards dominated the Earth at one stage and died out millions of years before humans came to dominate the Earth.

Maths skills

Time scales for the evolution of life are big:

- A thousand years is 10^3 years.
- A million years is 10^6 years.
- A billion years is 10^9 years.

You have probably seen a fossil in a museum or on TV, or maybe even found one yourself. Fossils can be formed in a number of ways:

- They may be formed from the hard parts of an animal. These are the bits that do not decay easily, such as the bones, teeth, claws or shells.
- Another type of fossil is formed when an animal or plant does not decay after it has died. This happens when one or more of the conditions needed for decay are not there. This may be because there is little or no oxygen present. It could be because poisonous gases kill off the bacteria that cause decay. Sometimes the temperature is too low for decay to take place. Then the animals and plants are preserved in ice. These ice fossils are rare, but they give a clear insight into what an animal looked like. They can also tell us what an animal had been eating or the colour of a long-extinct flower. We can even extract the DNA and compare it to modern organisms.
- Many fossils are formed when harder parts of the animal or plant are replaced by other minerals. This takes place over long periods of time. These are the most common fossils (see Figure 3).
- Some of the fossils we find are not of actual animals or plants, but of traces they have left behind. Fossil footprints, burrows, rootlet traces and droppings are all formed. These help us to build up a picture of life on Earth long ago.

b Which is the most common type of fossil?

Figure 1 A fossil of *Tyrannosaurus rex*

An incomplete record

The fossil record is not complete for several reasons. Many of the very earliest forms of life were soft-bodied organisms. This means they have left little fossil trace. It is partly why there is so little valid evidence of how life began. There is no fossil record of the earliest life forms on Earth.

Most organisms that died did not become fossilised – the right conditions for fossil formation were rare. Also, many of the fossils that were formed in the rocks have been destroyed by geological activity. Huge amounts of rock have been broken down, worn away, buried or melted over the years. As this happens the fossil record is lost too. Finally, there are many fossils that are still to be found.

In spite of all these limitations, the fossils we have found can still give us a 'snapshot' of life millions of years ago.

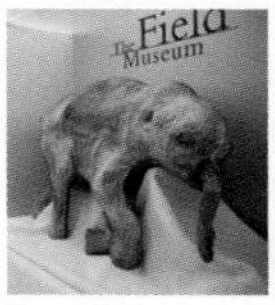

Figure 2 This baby mammoth was preserved in ice for at least 10 000 years. Examining this kind of evidence helps scientists check the accuracy of ideas based on fossil skeletons alone.

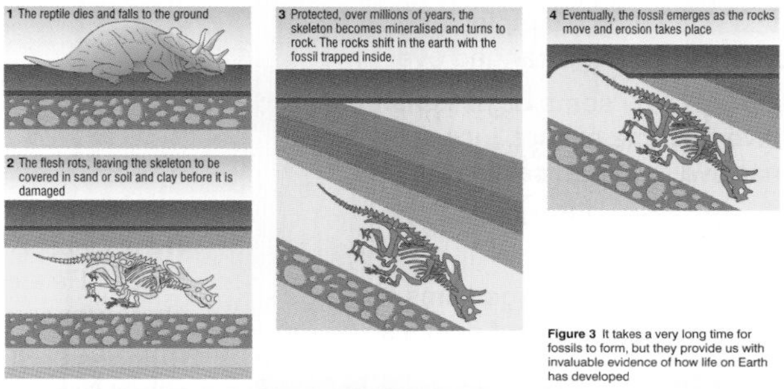

1 The reptile dies and falls to the ground

2 The flesh rots, leaving the skeleton to be covered in sand or soil and clay before it is damaged

3 Protected, over millions of years, the skeleton becomes mineralised and turns to rock. The rocks shift in the earth with the fossil trapped inside.

4 Eventually, the fossil emerges as the rocks move and erosion takes place

Figure 3 It takes a very long time for fossils to form, but they provide us with invaluable evidence of how life on Earth has developed

Summary questions

1 Copy and complete using the words below:

animal   decay   evidence   fossils   ice fossils   minerals   plant

One important piece of .... for how life has developed on Earth are .... The most common type are formed when parts of the .... or .... are replaced by .... as it decays. Some fossils are formed when an organism does not .... after it dies. An example is ...., which are very rare.

2 There are several theories about how life on Earth began.
   a Why is it impossible to know for sure?
   b Why are fossils such important evidence for the way life has developed?

3 How do ice fossils help scientists check the evidence provided by the main fossil record?

Key points

- Fossils are the remains of organisms from many years ago that are found in rocks.
- Fossils may be formed in different ways.
- Fossils give us information about organisms that lived millions of years ago.
- It is very difficult for scientists to know exactly how life on Earth began because there is little evidence that is valid.

Further teaching suggestions

Fossil formation conditions

- Many fossil plants were found in the coal seams. Try finding pictures of a few, and then link their presence in coal with why conditions were good for fossil formation. This ties in with the term 'fossil fuels'.

Go on a fossil hunt

- Fossils can be found in many unlikely places, such as on public buildings. These are usually as the fossil remains of invertebrates found in Portland stone and other natural building materials. A trip around some municipal buildings could reveal some evidence.

Find out more about the fossil hunters

- Charles Lyell and Arthur Holmes are mentioned in the answer to the timeline question. Who were they? How did they become interested in fossils and dating rocks? They could also look up Mary Anning and read of her pioneering fossil discoveries. There are good links with geology here for interested students. Why are there more fossils in some rocks than in others?

Construct a fossil?

- Provide the students with printed outlines of fossil bones or parts of a dinosaur skeleton that they can assemble. The activity can be made more realistic by only giving them some of the parts and allowing them to try and work out what animal the skeleton belonged to. The Natural History Museum Picture Library is a good source of material.

Answers to in-text questions

a Between 3 and 4 billion years ago.

b Fossils where the harder parts of living organisms are replaced by minerals over a long period of time.

Summary answers

1 evidence, fossils, animal/plant, plant/animal, minerals, decay, ice fossils

2 **a** No one was there to see it and there is no direct evidence for what happened.
   b They show us how plants and animals have changed over time, how many animals have appeared and that some no longer exist.

3 Scientists build up models of earlier animals from fossils (often from fragments) so they don't know exactly what they looked like. Ice fossils allow scientists to see exactly what the original animal looked like and its internal structures. Scientists can compare these with models built up from rock fossils and see how accurate they are; and so learn from this for future rock-based models.

B2 6.2 Exploring the fossil evidence

AQA
Specification link-up: Biology B2.8

- We can learn from fossils how much or how little different organisms have changed as life developed on Earth. [B2.8.1 d)]
- Extinction may be caused by:
  - changes to the environment over geological time
  - new predators
  - new diseases
  - new, more successful, competitors
  - a single catastrophic event, e.g. massive volcanic eruptions or collisions with asteroids
  - the cyclical nature of speciation. [B2.8.1 e)]

Learning objectives

Students should learn:

- how fossil evidence indicates the extent to which some organisms changed over time
- that mass extinction of organisms occurred in the past.

Learning outcomes

Most students should be able to:

- describe some examples of how much organisms have changed over time
- suggest why some organisms may have become extinct, including massive natural disasters.

Some students should also be able to:

- explain how living organisms can cause the extinction of species.

Support

- Give students a matching exercise where bits of evidence are placed in one column and the theories that they back up are in another – they have to join the evidence to the theory it supports.

Extend

- Ask students to find out the different methods of dating fossils. They could summarise their findings in a poster which can be displayed in the laboratory.

Lesson structure

Starters

Can you run on your toenails? – Sensitively find out who has got the longest fingernails in the class. Ask: 'Are they the strongest? Could you do press-ups resting on your middle finger?' Relate this to how a horse walks, and introduce equine foot development using photographs of ancient hooves. This leads to a discussion of fossil evidence. *(5 minutes)*

Guinness advert evolution – Search the internet for a clip of the Guinness 'Evolution' advert from 2006 where three men are traced back in time through reverse evolution until they are mud skippers not enjoying drinking mud. Ask the students to make a list of the things that have some validity in the advert and to spot any flaws with it. Support students by giving them a list of the organisms and getting them to place them in order. Extend students by asking for their ideas on how the advert would look if they extended the time travel sequence further back into the past. *(10 minutes)*

Main

- Following on from the 'Can you run on your toenails?' Starter activity, take the students through the evolution of the modern horse. Point out that this is not necessarily a direct line of evolution, that there could have been many other variations that died out and the evidence we have is probably incomplete.

- Another good example of a sequence of changes can be illustrated by the fossil evidence for human evolution from *Australopithecus* to *Homo sapiens*. Research the Natural History Museum website and the work of Professor Chris Stringer for more information. Discuss the position of the Neanderthals – one of our relatives that died out. Why?

- Two good examples of organisms that were thought to have been extinct and only known in the fossil record are the Wollemi pine *(Wollemia nobilis)* and the Coelacanth *(Latimeria chalumnae)*, both of which have been found alive unexpectedly. Students can compare pictures of real Wollemia pine and Coelacanth specimens with pictures of fossils, commenting on any similarities and differences.

Plenaries

An overactive pituitary gland? – It has been suggested that the demise of the dinosaurs was caused by them developing overactive pituitary glands resulting in the excessive growth of bones and cartilage. Get the students to think of reasons why bigger bones could be a disadvantage. Support students by providing them with a list of suggestions from which they could discuss and choose appropriate reasons. Extend students by asking them to explain their reasoning. *(5 minutes)*

The extinction game – Five players have cards saying 'Climate change', 'Meteorite', 'Predators', 'Disease' and 'Competition' with appropriate pictures. Another player represents a species trying to survive. The 'species' throws a dice and one of the 'extinction' players also throws a dice. If the numbers match, the species is extinct and the players swap places and continue. If the numbers are different, the species has survived, the player collects the combined score on the dice and plays against the next 'extinction' player, until they eventually become extinct. Play to a time limit. *(10 minutes)*

Old and new species

B2 6.2   Exploring the fossil evidence

Learning objectives

- How much have organisms changed over time?
- What is extinction?
- How do living organisms cause extinction?

links

For information on fossil records, look back at B2 6.1 The origins of life on Earth.

Using the fossil record

The fossil record helps us to understand how much organisms have changed since life developed on Earth. However, this understanding is often limited. Only small bits of skeletons or little bits of shells have been found. Luckily we have a very complete fossil record for a few animals, including the horse. These relatively complete fossil records can show us how some organisms have changed and developed over time.

Fossils also show us that not all animals have changed very much. For example, fossil sharks from millions of years ago look very like modern sharks. They evolved early into a form that was almost perfectly adapted for their environment and their way of life. Their environment has not changed much for millions of years so sharks have also remained the same.

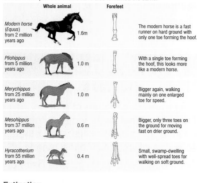

Whole animal		Forefeet	
Modern horse (Equus) from 2 million years ago	1.6m		The modern horse is a fast runner on hard ground with only one toe forming the hoof.
Pliohippus from 5 million years ago	1.0 m		With a single toe forming the hoof, this looks more like a modern horse.
Merychippus from 25 million years ago	1.0 m		Bigger again, walking mainly on one enlarged toe for speed.
Mesohippus from 37 million years ago	0.6 m		Bigger, only three toes on the ground for moving fast on drier ground.
Hyracotherium from 55 million years ago	0.4 m		Small, swamp-dwelling with well-spread toes for walking on soft ground.

Figure 1 The evolutionary history of the horse based on the fossil record

Extinction

Throughout the history of life on Earth, scientists estimate that about 4 billion different species have existed. Yet only a few million species of living organisms are alive today. The rest have become extinct. Extinction is the permanent loss of all the members of a species.

As conditions change, new species evolve that are better suited to survive the new conditions. The older species that cannot cope with the changes gradually die out. This is because they are not able to compete so well for food and other resources. This is how evolution takes place and the number of species on Earth slowly changes. Some of the species that have become extinct are lost forever or only exist in the fossil record. Others have left living relatives.

a What is extinction?
b How many species of living organisms are thought to have existed on Earth over the years?

There are many different causes of extinction. They always involve a change in the environment such as new predators, new diseases or new, more successful competitors.

The gradual change of the climate over millions of years has also caused changes in the species that are adapted for a particular area. This is still happening today.

Organisms that cause extinction

Living organisms can change an environment and cause extinction in several different ways:

- New predators can wipe out unsuspecting prey animals very quickly. This is because the prey animals do not have adaptations to avoid them. New predators may evolve, or an existing species might simply move into new territory. Sometimes this can be due to human intervention. People accidentally brought the brown tree snake from Australia to the island of Guam after World War II. This caused the rapid extinction of many bird species on Guam. They were being eaten by the snakes. The birds had no time to evolve a defence against this new predator.
- New diseases (caused by microorganisms) can bring a species to the point of extinction. They are most likely to cause extinctions on islands, where the whole population of an animal or plant are close together. The Australian Tasmanian devil is one example of this. These rare animals are dying from a new form of infectious cancer. It attacks and kills them very quickly.
- Finally, one species can cause another to become extinct by successful competition. New mutations can give one type of organism a real advantage over another. Sometimes new species are introduced into an environment by mistake. This means that a new, more successful competitor can take over from the original animal or plant and make it extinct. In Australia, the introduction of rabbits has caused severe problems. They eat so much and breed so fast that the other native Australian animals are dying out because they cannot compete.

Summary questions

1 Copy and complete using the words below:

climate competitors diseases Earth environment extinction predators species

.... is the permanent loss of all the members of a .... from the .... It may be caused by new ...., new .... or new, successful .... It can also be caused by changes in the .... or the ....

2 Look at the evolution of the horse shown in Figure 1. Explain how the fossil evidence of the legs helps us to understand what the animals were like and how they lived.

3 Explain how each of the following situations might cause a species of animal or plant to become extinct.
   a Mouse Island has a rare species of black-tailed mice. They are preyed on by hawks and owls, but there are no mammals that eat them. A new family bring their pregnant pet cat to the island.
   b English primroses have quite small leaves. Several people bring home packets of seeds from a European primrose, which has bigger leaves and flowers very early in the spring.

Did you know ...?

The Scottish island of North Uist has a similar problem to Guam. Hedgehogs were brought to the island to combat the problem of garden slugs. Unfortunately, the hedgehogs bred rapidly and are eating the eggs and chicks of the many rare sea birds that breed on the island. Now people are trying to kill or remove the hedgehogs to save the birds.

AQA Examiner's tip

Always mention a *change* when you suggest reasons for extinction.

Key points

- We can learn from fossils how much or how little organisms have changed as life has developed on Earth.
- Extinction may be caused by new predators, new diseases or new, more successful competitors.

Further teaching suggestions

Missing links

- Show pictures of the skeleton and reconstructions of *Archaeopteryx* and ask students whether they think it is a bird or a reptile. List the bird-like features and the reptilian features separately. Then consider the features of modern birds which are like reptiles. Discuss 'missing links' or 'transitional species' and their importance in the fossil record.

What if humans become extinct...?

- Ask the students what they think would happen if humans suddenly became extinct. Get them to think of reasons why this might happen. They could discuss this in small groups and then bring all the ideas together.

Fossil fraud

- Students can carry out an internet search for information about fake fossils and the difficulties of establishing that a specimen is genuine. This could include finding out about how fossils are dated.

'Piltdown Man' and other hoaxes

- Tell the story of 'Piltdown Man' and the two skulls that were first announced in 1912 and finally proved to be forgeries in 1953. Get students to consider how such forgeries could be made. Mention other 'mistakes' or misidentifications, such as 'Nebraska Man' and 'Archaeoraptor'.

Answers to in-text questions

a The permanent loss of all the members of a species from the face of the Earth.

b About 4 billion.

Summary answers

1 extinction, species, Earth, predators/competitors, competitors/predators, diseases, environment/climate, climate/environment

2 It shows us how tall they were, what their feet were like, what their jaws and teeth were like and the basic body shape. This in turn tells us how they might have lived, how fast they moved, what they ate; it also allows us to compare them to modern horses.

3 **a** The cat has kittens, the kittens breed and soon there are lots of cats. Cats catch black-tailed mice easily, the mice numbers fall until there are not enough to breed and mice become extinct. Knock-on effect on owls and hawks as part of their diet has gone – which in turn will affect other prey animals.

   b European primroses will make more food and have bigger leaves – however, set seeds which will germinate sooner will be too much competition for the English primrose and eventually it could become extinct.

B2 6.3

More about extinction

AQA Specification link-up: Biology B2.8

- Extinction may be caused by:
  - changes to the environment over geological time
  - new predators
  - new diseases
  - new, more successful competitors. [B2.8.1 e)]

Learning objectives

Students should learn:

- that environmental changes over geological time can cause extinction
- that mass extinctions of the past may have been caused by single catastrophic events.

Learning outcomes

Most students should be able to:

- explain what is meant by extinction
- describe some environmental changes that may have caused extinction
- suggest ways in which the extinction of the dinosaurs occurred.

Some students should also be able to:

- evaluate the theories for the extinction of the dinosaurs.

Lesson structure

Starters

Dead as a dodo – Search the internet for a picture of a dodo. Ask students to make a list, in rough, of as many types of extinct animal as they can in three minutes. Check who has the largest number and get the student to read the list. Ask others in the class to check and add. This leads into a discussion of what extinction means. (5 minutes)

What causes extinction? – Get the students to discuss in pairs or small groups the reasons why some species become extinct. Support students by giving prompts to help them identify ways in which animals may become extinct. Extend students by getting them to speculate on future causes of extinction and how they might be discussing this topic in 500 000 years time. (10 minutes)

Main

- Visit, for example, www.thedayaftertomorrowmovie.com to find information about global climatic changes. Highlight changes in temperature such as ice ages. Link, if possible, with the geological time scale discussed in B6.1 The origins of life on Earth and the evolution of different groups of organisms. Discuss the impact of these changes on the creatures around at the time. This can link up with the ideas of competition, survival of the fittest and natural selection.

- Much has been made of global warming altering our climate and the times at which plants flower, changing patterns of migration and growing different crops in different parts of the world. Ask: 'If our climate became warmer or colder, what animals and plants would be affected in Britain?'

- Show a video clip from the film *Deep Impact* of a simulated comet strike on Earth (search the web for 'Deep Impact trailer'). Make a model, using a light sensor attached to a data logger and a glass or plastic container containing some fine dust. Shine a light through and measure intensity before and after shaking up. Discuss the effects of the lack of light on life on Earth.

- Get the students to carry out an empathy exercise, imagining what it would have been like for the creatures living at the time of a comet strike or a global winter (if these theories are correct). Get them to write some creative prose or poetry to get across what it must have felt like being plunged into semi-darkness for months or years.

Plenaries

Greatest impact – Write up the words 'Climate change', 'Meteorite', 'Predators', 'Disease' and 'Competition', or use the cards from 'The extinction game'. Ask students to rank the words in order of importance. Choose some to explain their choices. (5 minutes)

Mass extinction storyboard – Establish the different theories of why there were mass extinctions at the end of the age of the dinosaurs. Get the students, in pairs or small groups, to come up with an illustrated storyboard to guide production of a film, telling students their age about the different theories. Support students by showing them an example. Extend students by getting them to add a theory of their own. These students should provide more imaginative and complex responses than supported students. (10 minutes)

Support

- Initiate a class discussion on alteration of the climate. Then ask students to draw a picture to represent the kinds of crops which might be grown and the types of animals that might be farmed in the UK if the climate became hotter.

Extend

- Ask students to come up with a way of evaluating the relative strengths and weaknesses of opposing ideas on the way in which mass extinctions came about. You could hold a discussion on peer review and the importance of public scrutiny of research published in scientific journals.

Old and new species

B2 6.3 More about extinction

Learning objectives

- How does environmental change over long time scales affect living organisms?
- What caused the mass extinctions of the past?

NOW	Approx. time years ago
50–70% species lost Dinosaurs died out	65 million
50% marine invertebrates lost 80% land quadrupeds lost	205 million
80–95% marine species lost	251 million
70% species lost	360–75 million
60% species lost	440 million
ORIGINS OF LIFE	3500 million years ago

Figure 2 The five main extinction events so far in the evolutionary history of the Earth

It isn't just changes in living organisms that bring about extinctions. The biggest influences on survival are changes in the environment.

Environmental changes

Throughout history, the climate and environment of the Earth has been changing. At times the Earth has been very hot. At other times, temperatures have fallen and the Earth has been in the grip of an Ice Age. These changes take place over millions and even billions of years.

Organisms that do well in the heat of a tropical climate won't do well in the icy conditions of an Ice Age. Many of them will become extinct through lack of food or being too cold to breed. However, species that cope well in cold climates will evolve and thrive by natural selection.

Changes to the climate or the environment have been the main cause of extinction throughout history. There have been five occasions during the history of the Earth when big climate changes have led to extinction on an enormous scale (see Figure 2).

Figure 1 The dinosaurs ruled the Earth for millions of years, but when the whole environment changed, they could not adapt and most of them died out. Mammals, which could control their own body temperature, had an advantage and became dominant.

a Why are Ice Ages often linked to extinctions?

Extinction on a large scale

Fossil evidence shows that at times there have been mass extinctions on a global scale. During these events many (or even most) of the species on Earth die out. This usually happens over a relatively short time period of several million years. Huge numbers of species disappear from the fossil record.

The evidence suggests that a single catastrophic event is often the cause of these mass extinctions. This could be a massive volcanic eruption or the collision of giant asteroids with the surface of the Earth.

b What is a mass extinction?

What destroyed the dinosaurs? [k]

The most recent mass extinction was when the dinosaurs became extinct around 65 million years ago. In 2010 an international team of scientists published a review of all the evidence put together over the last 20 years. They agreed that around 65 million years ago a giant asteroid collided with the Earth in Chicxulub in Mexico.

We can see a huge crater (180 km in diameter) there. Scientists have identified a layer of rock formed from crater debris in countries across the world. The further you move away from the crater, the thinner the layer of crater debris in the rock. Also, deep below the crater, scientists found lots of a mineral only formed when a rock is hit with a massive force such as an asteroid strike.

Figure 3 This layer of debris from the asteroid crater appears in rocks that are 65 million years old – the time the dinosaurs died out

The asteroid impact would have caused huge fires, earthquakes, landslides and tsunamis. Enormous amounts of material would have been blasted into the atmosphere. The accepted theory is that the dust in the atmosphere made everywhere almost dark. Plants struggled to survive and the drop in temperatures caused a global winter. Between 50–70% of all living species, including the dinosaurs, became extinct.

No sooner had this work been published than a group of UK scientists published different ideas and evidence. They suggest that the extinction of the dinosaurs started sooner (137 million years ago) and was much slower than previously thought.

Their idea is that the melting of the sea ice (caused by global warming) flooded the seas and oceans with very cold water. A drop in the sea temperature of about 9°C triggered the mass extinction. Their evidence is based on an unexpected change in fossils and minerals that they found in areas of Norway.

As you can see, building up a valid, evidence-based history of events so long ago is not easy to do. Events can always be interpreted in different ways.

AQA *Examiner's tip*

Remember that the time scales in forming new species and mass extinctions are huge.

Try to develop an understanding of time in millions and billions of years.

Summary questions

1 **a** Give four causes of extinction in species of living organisms.
  b Give two possible causes of mass extinction events.

2 Why do you think extinction is an important part of evolution?

3 **a** Summarise the evidence for a giant asteroid impact as the cause of the mass extinction event that resulted in the death of the dinosaurs.
  b Explain why scientists think that low light levels and low temperatures would have followed a massive asteroid strike. Why would these have caused mass extinctions?

Key points

- Extinction can be caused by environmental change over geological time.
- Mass extinctions may be caused by single catastrophic events such as volcanoes or asteroid strikes.

74

75

Further teaching suggestions

Is extinction still happening?

- Discuss present environmental changes and ask students how they think these changes may affect the extinction of some species. How may such extinctions be prevented?

The stupidity of the dodos ...

- Search the internet for 'Ice age Dodo' and mention how the film portrays them as being very stupid. Discuss how stupid the real birds were. Ask: 'What can you deduce from their appearance? Could they run fast?' A video on the extinction of the dodo is available from Channel 4 as part of the series *Extinct* (0870 1234 344): could be shown in addition. Draw out reasons as to why they may have appeared stupid to invading humans.

The quagga

- The quagga, a relative of the zebra, became extinct in the 1880s. In the 1990s, attempts were started to 'revive' the species. An internet search can be made to find out about how this works.

Answers to in-text questions

a Many species of plants and animals are not adapted to deal with the very cold conditions, lack of food, etc. and so die out.

b When many different species all become extinct over the same relatively short period of time.

Summary answers

1 **a** Any four sensible suggestions, e.g. new predators, new diseases, new, more successful competitors, environmental changes such as global warming, more rainfall, etc.
  b Any sensible suggestions, e.g. massive volcanic eruptions, collision of giant asteroids with the Earth.

2 Because without extinction unsuccessful species would not die out. There would be too much competition for resources. New species would find it difficult to evolve. Any thoughtful point.

3 **a** Evidence for giant asteroid strike – crater, layer of rock debris, mineral formed when massive force hits rocks. The age of the rocks suggest this happened immediately before the mass extinction of dinosaurs.
  b An asteroid impact would have blasted huge amounts of dust and debris into the atmosphere. It would have triggered huge fires, earthquakes, landslides that would generate smoke and dust. This would have greatly reduced the levels of light reaching the Earth. In turn, this would have stopped plants growing and caused very low temperatures. This global winter would have caused the extinction of up to 70% of all the species on the Earth, including the dinosaurs because of the lack of food and an inability to keep warm, etc.

B2 6.4

Isolation and the evolution of new species

Learning objectives

Students should learn that:

- that new species arise as a result of isolation
- that new species arise as a result of genetic variation and natural selection [HT only]
- that populations can be geographically isolated. [HT only]

Learning outcomes

Most students should be able to:

- describe the ways in which new species arise
- explain how some populations become isolated.

Some students should also be able to:

- explain that in isolated populations, alleles are selected which increase successful breeding [HT only]
- explain that speciation results when the isolated population becomes so different that interbreeding cannot take place. [HT only]

Answers to in-text questions

a The separation of two populations by geographical features.

b An organism which has evolved in one place only in geographical isolation.

Support

- Give students sets of diagrams to cut up, order in the correct sequence and stick into their books for each of the mechanisms of isolation. These should be checked for accuracy before sticking down.

Extend

- Get students to imagine a future global disaster where humans have been wiped out. Bearing in mind where our success as a species has come from, speculate as to how evolution may eventually fill the niche that we have up until now so dominantly occupied. Students could watch a clip from 'Planet of the Apes' as an introduction to this activity.

AQA Specification link-up: Biology B2.8

- New species arise as a result of:
  - isolation – two populations of a species become separated, e.g. geographically
  - genetic variation: each population has a wide range of alleles that control their characteristics [HT only]
  - natural selection – in each population, the alleles that control the characteristics which help the organism to survive are selected [HT only]
  - speciation – the populations become so different that successful interbreeding is no longer possible. [B2.8.1 f)] [HT only]

Lesson structure

Starters

Aussies only, please! – Get the students to make a list of animals that only exist in Australia. Have some photographs ready to project of the obvious ones but also quite a few other ones. Draw out that there are large numbers of species that exist in Australia and nowhere else. Ask the students to think of why this might be and to summarise their ideas in a sentence to be read out to the class. *(5 minutes)*

What we know so far... – Get the students to put down their own ideas on how they would define a species and how new species might arise. Give a strict, short time limit and don't allow discussion at this stage. Collect responses on the board as to the ideas that are pre-existent within the class and encourage discussion of these to see which have the most currency. Support students by providing some suggestions or a list to choose from to help them to get started. Extend students by getting them to provide suggestions that are quite sophisticated. *(10 minutes)*

Main

- **What is a species?** – It is important that students have an understanding of the term 'species' from the beginning of this topic, so a brief review of the characteristics of the taxon may be needed.

- One way to get across the idea of an ecological niche is to show a picture of an architectural niche, such as a slot in a wall where a statue might be placed. A niche is probably best looked at as an opportunity to make a living. Ask the students to think of ways in which people make a living – where do they get what they need to survive? Extend this idea to animals and plants – what opportunities do they have to make a living? Get the students to list some of these (plants making their own food, herbivores eating plants, carnivores eating animals, parasites, decomposers, etc.). Get specific with some extreme examples. Tell them about the Hawaiian cleaner wrasse, *Labroides phthirophagus* (search the internet for details). Get the students to realise that a mass extinction would open up lots of niches (and habitats) previously occupied by other species. These other species would otherwise have competed successfully, had they not become extinct. The openings given by the mass extinction provided opportunities for making a living that were rapidly filled by evolution driven by natural selection.

- Use PowerPoint and exposition to get across the idea of separation leading to evolution of differences that eventually prevent interbreeding between the separated populations. Use video footage, if available, and examples from real life, such as the species of freshwater fish (*Salvelinus sp.*) in the lakes of Switzerland, Scandinavia and Great Britain. Almost every lake has a different form due to the barriers between them.

Plenaries

Just the job! – Show the students pairs of examples of convergent evolution, e.g. sharp teeth in a variety of carnivores, tiger and thylacine, ostrich and dodo, basking shark and filter feeding whales, etc. Ask the students to set down reasons why such separate species could finish up with such similar features, link this to speciation [HT only] as the mechanism for change. *(5 minutes)*

Lost world – Using the Bosavi Crater expedition to Papua New Guinea as a stimulus, get the students to imagine that they have encountered a hidden valley within an isolated mountain range where species have been geographically isolated for millions of years. What sort of creatures might you encounter? Support students by providing them with some suggestions. You could show them a clip from *Valley of the Dinosaurs* or *The Land That Time Forgot*. Extend students by getting them to produce a wide range of examples, imaginatively constructed from an analysis of different ecological areas that could theoretically be occupied by the descendants of other species that have evolved to fit them. *(10 minutes)*

Old and new species

B2 6.4

Isolation and the evolution of new species

After a mass extinction, scientists have noticed that huge numbers of new species appear in the fossil record. This is evolution in action. Natural selection takes place and new organisms adapted to the different conditions evolve. But evolution is happening all the time. There is a natural cycle of new species appearing and others becoming extinct.

Learning objectives

- How do new species arise?
- How do populations become isolated?
- Do new species always form at the same rate?
- How does speciation take place in an isolated population? [H]

Isolation and evolution

You have already learnt about the role of genetic variation and natural selection in evolution. Any population of living organisms contains genetic variety. If one population becomes isolated from another, the conditions they are living in are likely to be different. This means that different characteristics will be selected for. The two populations might change so much over time that they cannot interbreed successfully. Then a new species evolves.

?? Did you know ...?

Sometimes the organisms are separated by **environmental isolation**. This is when the climate changes in one area where an organism lives but not in others. For example, if the climate becomes warmer in one area plants will flower at a different time of year. The breeding times of the plants and the animals linked with them will change and new species emerge.

How do populations become isolated?

The most common way is by **geographical isolation**. This is when two populations become physically isolated by a geographical feature. This might be a new mountain range, a new river or an area of land becoming an island.

There are some well-known examples of this. Australia separated from the other continents over 5 million years ago. That's when the Australian populations of marsupial mammals that carry their babies in pouches became geographically isolated.

As a result of natural selection, many different species of marsupials evolved. Organisms as varied as kangaroos and koala bears appeared. Across the rest of the world, competition resulted in the evolution of other mammals with more efficient reproductive systems. In Australia, marsupials remain dominant.

a What is geographical isolation?

Organisms in isolation

Organisms on islands are geographically isolated from the rest of the world. The closely related but very different species on the Galapagos Islands helped Darwin form his ideas about evolution.

When a species evolves in isolation and is found in only one place in the world, it is said to be **endemic** to that area. An area where scientists are finding many new endemic species is Borneo. It is one of the largest islands in the world. Borneo still contains huge areas of tropical rainforest.

Between 1994 and 2006 scientists discovered over 400 new species in the Borneo rainforest. There are more than 25 species of mammals found only on the island. All of these organisms have evolved through geographical isolation.

Figure 1 Both the marsupial koala and the eucalyptus tree have evolved in geographical isolation in Australia

Higher | Speciation 🅚

Any population will contain natural genetic variety. This means it will contain a wide range of alleles controlling its characteristics, that result from sexual reproduction and mutation. In each population, the alleles which are selected will control characteristics which help the organism to survive and breed successfully. This is natural selection. Sometimes part of a population becomes isolated with new environmental conditions. Alleles for characteristics that enable organisms to survive and breed successfully in the new conditions will be selected. These are likely to be different from the alleles that gave success in the original environment. As a result of the selection of these different alleles, the characteristic features of the isolated organisms will change. Eventually they can no longer interbreed with the original organisms and a new species forms. This is known as **speciation**.

This is what has happened on the island of Borneo, in Australia and on the Galapagos Islands. If conditions in these isolated places are changed or the habitat is lost, the species that have evolved to survive within it could easily become extinct.

b What is an endemic organism?

Geographical isolation may involve very large areas like Borneo or very small regions. Mount Bosavi is the crater of an extinct volcano in Papua New Guinea. It is only 4km wide and the walls of the crater are 1 km high. The animals and plants trapped within the crater have evolved in different ways to those outside.

Very few people have been inside the crater. During a 3-week expedition in 2009 scientists discovered around 40 new species. These included mammals, fish, birds, reptiles, amphibians, insects and plants. All of these species are the result of natural selection caused by the specialised environment of the isolated crater. They include an enormous 82 cm long rat that weighs 1.5 kg!

Figure 2 Orang-utans like these are just one example of the many endemic species that have evolved in isolation in Borneo

Figure 3 Mount Bosavi in Papua New Guinea – a small, geographically isolated environment where many new species have evolved

Key points

- New species arise when two populations become isolated.
- Populations become isolated when they are separated geographically, e.g. on islands.
- There are natural cycles linked to environmental change when species form and when species die out.
- In an isolated population alleles are selected that increase successful breeding in the new environment. [H]
- Speciation takes place when an isolated population becomes so different from the original population that successful interbreeding can no long take place. [H]

Summary questions

1 Copy and complete using the words below:
geographically interbreeding populations evolution species selection

When two .... become .... isolated .... may take place. Natural .... in each area means the populations become so different that successful .... can no longer take place. New .... have evolved.

2 **a** How might populations become isolated?
  b Why does this isolation lead to the evolution of new species?

3 Explain how genetic variation and natural selection result in the formation of new species in isolated populations. [H]

Further teaching suggestions

Geographical isolation animation

- Based on common diagrammatic ways of showing geographical isolation resulting in new species, get the students to create animated versions of the diagrams. They could show an original population being split in two by a barrier. The evolutionary pressures will be different on each side resulting in some characteristics being more favoured in one section of the population than the other. This should eventually result in two very different populations that cannot interbreed. Encourage the students to use imagination and humour in their animations.

The Red Queen hypothesis – is it true?

- The theory accounting for the rate at which speciation occurs was called the Red Queen hypothesis. New research on speciation from the University of Reading suggests that random events rather than natural selection are responsible for the formation of new species. Students could find out more about the hypothesis and Professor Mark Pagel's new theory.

Summary answers

1 populations, geographically, evolution, selection, interbreeding, species

2 **a** Geographically by the formation of mountains, rivers, continents breaking apart, etc.

  Environmentally – climate change in one area and not another or different types of change in different areas.

  b Natural selection means organisms best suited to a particular environment will be most likely to survive and breed. So in two different environments, different features will be selected for and the organisms will become more and more different until they cannot interbreed and new species have evolved.

3 All populations have natural genetic variation due to sexual reproduction and mutation. This results in a wide variety of alleles in the population. If part of the population becomes isolated and conditions are different from the original population, different alleles are likely to give an advantage. These alleles will be selected for, as the organisms which have them will be most likely to survive and reproduce successfully in the new environment. As a result the characteristics of the organism will change until eventually they can no longer interbreed with the original population and a new species has evolved.

Summary answers

1 a The remains of organisms from many years ago, often found in rocks. They can be formed in a number of different ways.

b **Fossil X:** The dinosaur dies and falls to the ground and the flesh rots away, leaving the skeleton. This is covered with sand, soil or clay before it is damaged. Protected under layers of soil and rocks for millions of years, the skeleton becomes mineralised and turns to rock. Eventually it comes to the surface as a result of earth movements and erosion.

Fossil Y: The animal died in conditions where decay could not take place. In this case, it was frozen immediately after death and preserved.

c Evidence of species which are now extinct, can be used to show links to modern species and relationships between different fossil species. Bone fossils show anatomical structures of organisms, size, etc. whilst ice fossils show appearance of animals in life, colours, can show food, etc. and give DNA for comparison with modern specimens. Limitations – not many fossils found; fossil record often incomplete; rarely find complete skeleton; skeletal fossils do not show what organisms actually looked like; few soft bodied fossils; few complete evolutionary sequences; most fossils do not yield DNA, etc. Any sensible points.

d Earliest organisms all soft bodied – do not form fossils so little or no fossil evidence of the earliest life forms.

2 a The loss of all members of a species in an area or on the Earth.

b Species extinction is the loss of an entire species. Mass extinction the loss of a large percentage of all the species alive on the Earth over a relatively short period of time.

c Evidence in the fossil record of huge number of species disappearing.

d Any two theories, e.g. asteroid strike, volcanic eruption, global temperature change due to carbon dioxide levels, etc. with examples of relevant evidence.

e Importance – they have lead to the evolution of many new species adapted to the new conditions to fill the available niches and so moved the development of life forward.

3 a Rhino/rhinoceros.

b Got bigger – size of skull increased a lot as measured by scale so whole animal must have got bigger as well. Animals became more armoured, so became more aggressive; ate more – jaws and teeth became a lot bigger and if the animals got larger would need to take in more food to support the body. Head carriage changed considerably – did the animal begin to charge opponents/enemies as head carriage dropped? Any other sensible points.

c Limited evidence as only have heads here. Don't have complete sequence to modern day etc. plus any valid points.

d Ideally whole body, certainly legs, pelvis, etc. to see how they moved, see what happened to the feet, see how tall they were, to see where they lived, etc. Fossil faeces to analyse diet. Ice fossil to see exactly what they looked like, what they ate, etc. Any sensible points.

Summary questions

1 Look at Figure 1 and answer the questions that follow.

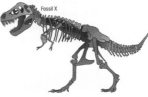

Fossil X

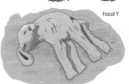

Fossil Y

Figure 1

a What is a fossil?

b Explain fully how fossil X and fossil Y were formed.

c How can fossils like these be used as evidence for the development of life on Earth and what are their limitations?

d Why are fossils of little use in helping us understand how life on Earth began?

2 a What is extinction?

b How does mass extinction differ from species extinction?

c What is the evidence for the occurrence of mass extinctions throughout the history of life on Earth?

d Suggest at least two theories about the possible causes of mass extinctions and explain the sort of evidence that is used to support these ideas.

e What important part have mass extinctions played in the evolution of life on Earth and why?

3

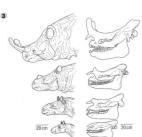

20 cm   20 cm

Figure 2

a This sequence of skulls comes from the fossil record of a group of animals known as perissodactyls. Suggest a possible living relative of these animals.

b How do you think these organisms changed as they evolved, based on the evidence of the diagram above?

c What are the limitations of this type of evidence?

d What other fossil remains would you want to see to understand more about the lives of these extinct organisms?

4 How does evolution take place?

5 Describe how evolution takes place in terms of speciation. Explain the roles of isolation and genetic variation in the process of speciation. Use as many examples and as much evidence as you can in your answer.

---

4 Students should demonstrate understanding of the importance of natural selection and changes in the environment as the driver of evolution. Answer should explain how changes in factors such as new predators etc. or new conditions mean some species die out and others evolve. Could include the idea of big changes and mass extinctions producing lots of new niches and organisms evolving to fill them. Look for good explanations and varied examples.

5 As answer to Question 4, but here the student should focus on the role of isolation – geographical or otherwise – as a reason for speciation to take place. Students should describe how organisms are unable to interbreed, natural genetic variety and how particular mutations become advantageous in isolated situations, leading to the formation of new species through natural selection. Look for good explanations and varied examples.

AQA Examination-style questions 🄺

The diagram shows a timeline for the evolution of some groups of animals. The earliest forms of the animals shown below the line for **Present day** are extinct.

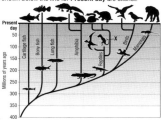

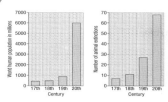

c Between 1900 and 1960 (20th century) 64 animals became extinct.
  i How many animals became extinct from 1960–2000? Show your working. (2)
  ii Suggest a reason for the difference in numbers between the beginning and the end of the 20th century. (2)

Use information from the diagram to answer these questions.

a Name the **four** groups of animals that developed legs. (1)

b Which group of animals shown in the diagram evolved first? (1)

c The animal labelled **X** has been extinct for over 50 million years.
How do scientists know that it once lived? (1)

d Copy and complete the sentence by choosing the correct words from below.
diseases enzymes hormones plants predators rocks
Animals may become extinct because of new .... and new .... (2)
AQA, 2003

2 a What is meant by the term 'extinction'? (2)
b The bar charts show the population of the world from the 17th to the 20th century and the number of animal extinctions that have taken place over the same period.
Use the information in the bar charts to answer the questions.
  i What was the world population in the 19th century? (1)
  ii How many animals became extinct in the 18th century? (1)
  iii What is the relationship between the population of humans and the number of animal extinctions? (2)

3 The diagram shows how the number of groups of animals has changed during the history of life on Earth.

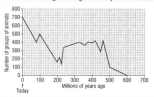

a i How long ago did the first living animals appear on Earth? Give your answer in millions of years. (1)
  ii How long did it take for the number of groups to rise to 400? Give your answer in millions of years. (1)
b i Calculate the proportion of groups that disappeared between 100 million years and 80 million years ago. Show your working. (2)
  ii Give **two** reasons why some groups of animals disappeared during the history of life on Earth (2)
AQA, 2008

4 *In this question you will be assessed on using good English, organising information clearly and using specialist terms where appropriate.*
Describe how new species may arise by isolation. [H] (6)

79

AQA Examination-style answers

1 a amphibia reptile birds mammals *(1 mark)*
  b cartilage fish *(1 mark)*
  c from fossils *(1 mark)*
  d diseases/predators *(2 marks)*

2 a **All** members of a species **die out**. *(2 marks)*
  b i 900 million (must have the units) *(1 mark)*
    ii 11 *(1 mark)*
    iii As the human population rises the number of extinctions rises. *(2 marks)*
  c i 4 [*if answer incorrect then 68-64 (1 mark)*] *(2 marks)*
    ii E.g. at the beginning of the century people using more land for housing etc.
    Loss of habitat; Industrialisation; Pollution
    E.g. at the end of the century more protected species (idea of) conservation of habitats/reintroduction. *(2 marks)*

3 a i 600 *(1 mark)*
    ii 135–140 millions of years *(1 mark)*
  b i 1/5 **or** 100/500 **or** 20%
    correct working shown but arithmetic error gains 1 mark *(2 marks)*
    ii any **two** from:
    • environmental change
    • new competitor
    • new disease
    • changing environmental conditions
    • new predator. *(2 marks)*

4 There is a clear, balanced and detailed explanation of speciation starting with isolation and ending with the inability to interbreed. The answer shows almost faultless spelling, punctuation and grammar. It is coherent and in an organised, logical sequence. It contains a range of appropriate or relevant specialist terms used accurately. *(5–6 marks)*

There is some attempt to explain speciation which shows an understanding of isolation. There are some errors in spelling, punctuation and grammar. The answer has some structure and organisation. The use of specialist terms has been attempted, but not always accurately. *(3–4 marks)*

There is a brief description of speciation. The spelling, punctuation and grammar are very weak. The answer is poorly organised with almost no specialist terms and/or their use demonstrating a general lack of understanding of their meaning. *(1–2 marks)*

No relevant content. *(0 marks)*

Examples of biology points made in the response:
• two populations of a species may become separated/idea of geographical separation
• populations have a wide range of alleles (allow genes)
• this leads to variation (of characteristics) in the population
• some characteristics may be beneficial
• organisms survive to breed
• if the populations stay separate/idea that separation may be for a long time
• they become too different
• can no longer interbreed.

Kerboodle resources 🄺

Resources available for this chapter on Kerboodle are:
• Chapter map: Old and new species
• Support: History of the Earth timeline (B2 6.1)
• Bump up your grade: Dead as a dodo (B2 6.2)
• Extension: A Madagascan mystery (B2 6.3)
• Interactive activity: How organisms change through time
• Podcast: Old and new species
• Test yourself: Old and new species
• On your marks: Old and new species
• Examination-style questions: Old and new species
• Answers to examination-style questions: Old and new species

AQA Examination-style answers

1 a i gene – chromosome – nucleus – cell *(1 mark)*
   ii controls the activity of the cell *(1 mark)*
   b i absorbs light *(1 mark)*
   ii oxygen *(1 mark)*

2 Fertilisation – A, Meiosis – C, Mitosis – B. *(3 marks)*

3 a i Stomach *(allow other correct organ which is part of the digestive tract)* *(1 mark)*
   ii Epithelial *(1 mark)*
   b Food materials are soluble. They diffuse from a region of high concentration (in the intestine) to a region of low concentration (in the blood) *(4 marks)*

4 a i 21.5–22 °C *and* 27–27.5 °C *(1 mark)*
   ii ideas of
   limiting factor/shortage of light/carbon dioxide/water/chlorophyll *(allow 1 for 'maximum/optimum rate of enzyme activity if no reference to limiting factors)* *(ignore denaturation)* *(2 marks)*
   b 21.5–22 °C
   (allow first figure from answer to i so that no 'double-penalty but only if this first answer is 20 or greater)
   Because this is the maximum rate of photosynthesis. It is at its highest and fastest
   (but related to flat part of curve)
   It is the most economical heating temperature (cheapest related to heating)
   (must relate to the temperature the candidate has given) *(3 marks)*

5 a i any **two** from:
   • structural components
   • hormones/named hormone
   • Antibodies *(allow antigens)* *(2 marks)*
   ii catalyst/speeds up a chemical reaction *(1 mark)*
   b protein changes shape/denatures *(2 marks)*
   c i amino acids *(1 mark)*
   ii Genes code for a particular combination (of amino acids/answer from **b**) *(1 mark)*

6 a i muscles (allow liver) *(1 mark)*
   ii (Normally) glycogen is turned to glucose and glucose is needed for the release of energy. *(2 marks)*
   b i female parent – Gg, male parent – Gg
   gametes correctly derived from parents
   offspring correctly derived from gametes *(4 marks)*
   ii $\frac{3}{4}$ or 3 out of 4 *(allow 3 : 1 or 75%, do not allow 1 : 3)* *(1 mark)*

7 There is a clear and detailed description of the changes which take place during exercise to ensure that the muscles receive enough oxygen and an explanation of anaerobic respiration. The answer shows almost faultless spelling, punctuation and grammar. It is coherent and in an organised, logical sequence. It contains a range of appropriate or relevant specialist terms used accurately. *(5–6 marks)*

There is a description of the changes which take place during exercise to ensure that the muscles receive enough oxygen and some explanation of anaerobic respiration. There are some errors in spelling, punctuation and grammar. The answer has some structure and organisation. The use of specialist terms has been attempted, but not always accurately. *(3–4 marks)*

1 a i Put the following structures into the correct order from the smallest to the largest. *(1)*
   cell chromosome gene nucleus
   smallest .... largest
   ii What is the function of the nucleus? *(1)*
   b Plant cells contain chloroplasts.
   i What is the role of chloroplasts in photosynthesis? *(1)*
   ii Name the gas produced in photosynthesis. *(1)*

2 The diagrams show three processes.
   Match the correct letter to the process.

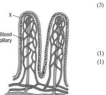

Process	Letter
Fertilisation	
Meiosis	
Mitosis	

A   B   C *(3)*

3 The diagram shows two villi in the small intestine of a healthy person.
The small intestine is an organ in the digestive system.
   a i Name another organ in the digestive system. *(1)*
   ii Name tissue X. *(1)*
   b The villi are surrounded by digested food materials which must enter the blood capillaries.
   Explain how these materials enter the blood. *(4)*

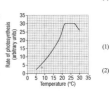

X
Blood capillary

AQA *Examiner's tip*
When reading graphs (see Q4)
Do not be put off by the term 'arbitrary units' just look at the numbers. Sometimes examiners use this term to avoid writing very complex numbers or unit names.

4 The graph shows the effect of temperature on photosynthesis.
   a i Between which temperatures is the rate of photosynthesis fastest?
   .... and .... °C *(1)*
   ii Suggest why the rate of photosynthesis stays the same between these two temperatures. *(2)*
   b A greenhouse owner wants to grow lettuces as quickly and cheaply as possible in winter.
   At what temperature should he keep his greenhouse in order to grow the lettuces as quickly and cheaply as possible? .... °C
   Explain your answer. *(3)*

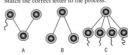

AQA *Examiner's tip*
Photosynthesis questions often ask about limiting factors.
If raising the temperature does not increase the rate of photosynthesis any further, some other factor must be preventing this. Ask yourself 'What do plants need for photosynthesis?'

There is a brief description of some of the changes which take place during exercise to ensure that the muscles receive enough oxygen and reference to why anaerobic respiration occurs. The spelling, punctuation and grammar are very weak. The answer is poorly organised with almost no specialist terms and/or their use demonstrating a general lack of understanding of their meaning. *(1–2 marks)*

No relevant content. *(0 marks)*

Examples of biology points used in the response:
• increased breathing rate
• increased depth of breathing
• increased heart rate/increased blood flow to muscles
• (if too little oxygen) anaerobic respiration
• production of lactic acid
• ref to oxygen debt. *(6 marks)*

5 The picture shows a model of a protein.

Some proteins are enzymes but proteins also have other functions.

a i Give two other functions of proteins.

1 ....

2 .... (2)

   ii What is the function of an enzyme? (1)

b This protein is normally found in neutral conditions. What would happen to the protein if it was placed in acid conditions? (2)

c When the model protein is put together the scientists use smaller molecules to make the specific shape.

   i Choose the correct answer to complete the sentence.

   amino acids   fatty acids   lactic acid

   The smaller molecules used to make the model protein are .... (1)

   ii Cells are able to put the smaller molecules together in the correct order.

   Explain how the cell does this. (1)

6 Some cattle are affected by an inherited condition called glycogen storage disease.

a i Where is glycogen stored? (1)

   ii Cattle with this disease become tired easily.

   Explain why. (2)

b Glycogen storage disease can be inherited by a calf whose parents do not have the disease.

   i Use the symbols G and g and a genetic diagram to explain how this is possible. (4)

   ii If the same parents have another calf, what is the probability that it will not have glycogen storage disease? (1)

7 *In this question you will be assessed on using good English, organising information clearly and using specialist terms where appropriate.*

Describe the changes which take place in the human body during exercise to ensure that the muscles receive enough oxygen and what happens if oxygen is in short supply. (6)

81

Bump up your grades

- Examiners are expected to challenge candidates at all levels with open prose style answers. Marks are also allocated for writing clearly, logically and using the correct scientific terms. So encourage candidates to plan their answers before writing.

Planning tips

- Writing a list of the key scientific terms before they start will not only be a memory aid but will allow them to think about the correct sequence of facts. They could number their words, rehearse the answer mentally, renumber the list if necessary, and then start to write.
- There is usually enough blank space below the answer lines for jotted notes.

Bump up your grades

When questions require candidates to evaluate information they will maximise their marks if they use the following three headings:

Advantages   Disadvantages   Conclusion

The conclusion should always be justified by referring back to the advantages and disadvantages.

Often candidates lose marks by giving several advantages and not mentioning at least one disadvantage which means they cannot make a reasoned conclusion. Other candidates start with a conclusion and can lose this mark if it is not linked into the rest of the answer.

AQA Examiner's comments

Photosynthesis questions often require an understanding of **limiting factors**. More able candidates usually have little difficulty in recognising what may be limiting the rate but weaker candidates often miss the point. Practising with computer models can help to develop an understanding of limiting factors.

AQA Examiner's tip

Use flash cards to link structure and function for plant and animal organs. Marks are lost because candidates know the word but cannot recognise the organ on a diagram.

Sticking post-it note labels on themselves can be a fun way to learn the positions of the major organs.

C2 1.1

Chemical bonding

Learning objectives

Students should learn:

- how elements can form compounds
- how elements in Group 1 bond with elements in Group 7.

Learning outcomes

Most students should be able to:

- state what a compound is
- name the two types of bonding present in compounds
- represent Cl^- and Na^+ using a diagram.

Some students should also be able to:

- explain why atoms bond
- explain and work out the charge on an ion
- explain the formation of ions when a Group 1 and Group 7 element react together.

Support

- Using A4 mini-whiteboards, encourage students to draw the electronic structure of simple atoms, including the number of protons and neutrons in the nucleus. Ask students to consider the outer shell electrons and whether the atom would lose or gain electrons. They should rub out or add in electrons in the correct places on their diagrams. Write the number of electrons gained or lost at the top right of the board. Then ask students to consider the charge: electrons add negative charge, so removing them leaves a positive charge.

Extend

- Ask students to consider molecular ions. Give students a diagram of an ionic compound, then students could label the ionic bond and the covalent bonds that it contains.

AQA Specification link-up: Chemistry C2.1

- Compounds are substances in which atoms of two or more elements are chemically combined. *[C2.1.1 a)]*
- Chemical bonding involves either transferring or sharing electrons in the highest occupied energy levels (shells) of atoms in order to achieve the electronic structure of a noble gas. *[C2.1.1 b)]*
- When atoms form chemical bonds by transferring electrons, they form ions. Atoms that lose electrons become positively charged ions. Atoms that gain electrons become negatively charged ions. Ions have the electronic structure of a noble gas (Group 0). *[C2.1.1 c)]*
- The elements in Group 1 of the periodic table, the alkali metals, all react with non-metal elements to form ionic compounds in which the metal ion has a single positive charge. *[C2.1.1 d)]*
- The elements in Group 7 of the periodic table, the halogens, all react with the alkali metals to form ionic compounds in which the halide ions have a single negative charge. *[C2.1.1 e)]*
- Write formulae for ionic compounds from given symbols and ionic charges. *[C2.1]*
- Represent the electronic structure of the ions in sodium chloride... *[C2.1]*

Lesson structure

Starters

Spider diagram – Ask students to think back to the work they completed in C1 about the fundamental ideas in chemistry. Ask students to work in small groups to make a spider diagram of the information about bonding that they can remember. You may wish to support students by giving them a few statements or diagrams to get them started. You could extend students by asking them to look at a different group's work and give feedback about statements that they think are not quite correct. *(5 minutes)*

Reflect and plan – Ask students to draw a table. The first column is what I know, the second column, what I want to know and the third column, what I **now** know. Explain to students that this chapter is about chemical bonding and in bullet points they should list all that they already know about bonding in the first column. In the second column, students should then write questions that they would like to be able to answer after studying this topic area. The final column should remain blank. When the whole of this chapter has been covered, students should review this, completing the final column of additional information that they have gained. *(10 minutes)*

Main

- Students may have seen the formation of sodium chloride in C1 1.4. Provide students with sodium chloride and ask them to note down its properties. They should be encouraged to contrast the properties of the compound with those of its constituent elements and reflect on the fact that a compound and its elements can have completely different properties.
- Students need to be able to understand ionic bonding and represent it as dot and cross diagrams. Ask students to use the Student Book to create a poster about ionic bonding. They should include at least two diagrams of ions, and one diagram of an ionic bond.
- Stress to students that ionic bonding involves electron transfer, but the actual ionic bonds arise from the electrostatic attraction between the oppositely charged ions formed as a result of electron transfer.

Plenaries

Match – Give students the names of ionic compounds and their formulae. Students should match them up. [e.g. copper sulfate – $CuSO_4$; aluminium chloride – $AlCl_3$; iron oxide – Fe_2O_3.] *(5 minutes)*

Classify – Give students a list of compounds and ask them to classify the bonding as ionic or covalent. You may wish to support students by highlighting the definition of each type of bonding given in C1.1.4. You could extend students by asking them to write the formula of each of the compounds. You could further extend students by asking them to draw diagrams of the compounds. [Sodium chloride (ionic, NaCl), carbon dioxide (covalent, CO_2), sulfur dioxide (covalent, SO_2), potassium bromide (ionic, KBr).] *(10 minutes)*

Further teaching suggestions

Models
- Students could look at and draw models of a salt crystal. They could label the ions.

Drawing and naming
- You could give students the electronic structure of different ions and then ask them to name them.

Dot and cross diagrams
- You could make a card sort of different ions with their symbol in the centre of the ionic diagram. Positive ions should be on the red card and negative ions on the blue card. The greater the charge, the darker the colour of the card. Students could then generate the dot and cross diagrams of a variety of ionic compounds, easily and quickly swapping ions to show the compounds.

Computer modelling
- You may wish to allow students to use computer modelling to simulate how electrons are shared between atoms to make molecules. You could extend students and allow them to make their own simulations using simple programs which will allow students to make their own flash animations.

Answers to in-text questions

a Mixing involves a physical change (easily reversed and no new substances are formed). Reacting involves a chemical change, which does involve making new substances.

b covalent

c ionic

Structure and bonding

C2 1.1   Chemical bonding (k)

Learning objectives
- How do elements form compounds?
- How do the elements in Group 1 bond with the elements in Group 7?

You already know that we can mix two substances together without either of them changing. For example, we can mix sand and salt together and then separate them again. No change will have taken place. But in chemical reactions the situation is very different.

When the atoms of two or more elements react they make a compound.

A compound contains two or more elements which are chemically combined.

The compound formed is different from the elements and we cannot get the elements back again easily. We can also react compounds together to form other compounds. However, the reaction of elements is easier to understand as a starting point.

a What is the difference between mixing two substances and reacting them?

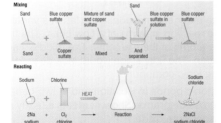

Figure 1 The difference between mixing and reacting. Separating mixtures is usually quite easy, but separating substances once they have reacted can be quite difficult. Why do atoms react?

When an atom has an arrangement of electrons like a noble gas in Group 0, it is stable and unreactive. However, most atoms do not have this **electronic structure**. When atoms react they take part in changes which give them a stable arrangement of electrons. They may do this by either:
- sharing electrons, which we call **covalent bonding**
- transferring electrons, which we call **ionic bonding**.

Losing electrons to form positive ions

In ionic bonding the atoms involved lose or gain electrons to form charged particles called ions. The ions have the electronic structure of a noble gas. So, for example, if sodium (2,8,1) loses one electron it is left with the stable electronic structure of neon (2,8).

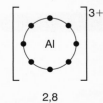

Figure 2 A positive sodium ion (Na⁺) is formed when a sodium atom loses an electron during ionic bonding

However, it is also left with one more **proton** in its **nucleus** than there are electrons around the nucleus. The proton has a positive charge so the sodium atom has now become a positively charged ion. The sodium ion has a single positive charge. We write the formula of a sodium ion as Na⁺. The electronic structure of the Na⁺ ion is 2,8. This is shown in Figure 2.

Gaining electrons to form negative ions

When non-metals react with metals, the non-metal atoms gain electrons to achieve a stable noble gas structure. Chlorine, for example, has the electronic structure 2,8,7. By gaining a single electron, it gets the stable electronic structure of argon (2,8,8).

In this case there is now one more electron than there are positive protons in the nucleus. So the chlorine atom becomes a negatively charged ion. This carries a single negative charge. We write the formula of the chloride ion as Cl⁻. Its electronic structure is 2,8,8. This is shown in Figure 3.

b When atoms join together by *sharing* electrons, what type of bond is formed?

c When ions join together as a result of *gaining* or *losing* electrons, what type of bond is this?

Representing ionic bonding

Metal atoms, which need to lose electrons, react with non-metal atoms, which need to gain electrons. So when sodium reacts with chlorine, each sodium atom loses an electron and each chlorine atom gains that electron. They both form stable ions. The electrostatic attraction between the oppositely charged Na⁺ ions and Cl⁻ ions is called ionic bonding.

We can show what happens in a diagram. The electrons of one atom are represented by dots, and the electrons of the other atom are represented by crosses. This is shown in Figure 4.

Figure 3 A negative chloride ion (Cl⁻) is formed when a chlorine atom gains an electron during ionic bonding

Figure 4 The formation of sodium chloride (NaCl) – an example of ion formation by transferring an electron

Summary questions

1 Copy and complete using the words below:
   covalent difficult compound gaining ionic losing new noble
   When two elements react together they make a .... substance called a .... It is .... to separate the elements after the reaction. Some atoms react by sharing electrons. We call this .... bonding. Other atoms react by .... or .... electrons. We call this .... bonding. When atoms react in this way they get the electronic structure of a .... gas.

2 Draw diagrams to show the ions that would be formed when the following atoms are involved in ionic bonding. For each one, state how many electrons have been lost or gained and show the charge on the ions formed.
   a aluminium (Al) b fluorine (F) c potassium (K) d oxygen (O)

Key points
- Elements react together to form compounds by gaining or losing electrons or by sharing electrons.
- The elements in Group 1 react with the elements in Group 7. As they react, atoms of Group 1 elements can each lose one electron to gain the stable electronic structure of a noble gas. This electron can be given to an atom from Group 7, which then also achieves the stable electronic structure of a noble gas.

82   83

Summary answers

1 new, compound, difficult, covalent, losing (gaining), gaining (losing), ionic, noble

2 **a** Al³⁺ ion, 3 electrons lost   **b** F⁻ ion, 1 electron gained   **c** K⁺ ion, 1 electron lost   **d** O²⁻ ion, 2 electrons gained

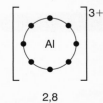
2,8

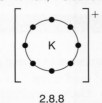
2,8

2,8,8

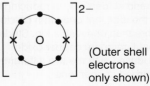
(Outer shell electrons only shown)
2,8

C2 1.2 Ionic bonding

Learning objectives

Students should learn:

- how ions are held together in a giant structure
- that elements which aren't in Groups 1 and 7 can also form ions.

Learning outcomes

Most students should be able to:

- describe ionic bonding in terms of electrostatic forces of attraction
- draw the dot and cross diagram for magnesium oxide and calcium chloride.

Some students should also be able to:

- describe in detail an ionic lattice
- apply their knowledge of ionic bonding to draw dot and cross diagrams for other ionic compounds.

??? Did you know ...?

Using X-rays, scientists have discovered that ionic lattices aren't perfect. There are sections where the ions aren't perfectly arranged, and if you tap the crystal it will break along cleavage planes.

Support

- Give students a sheet with dot and cross diagrams of a sodium ion, magnesium ion, calcium ion, oxide ion and two chloride ions. Encourage them to represent sodium chloride, magnesium oxide and calcium chloride by cutting out the ions and sticking them into the correct arrangement.

Extend

- Encourage students to research and discover the charges of transition metals and to find out different examples of ionic lattices involving these elements. You could further extend students by introducing them to the idea that one atom can form more than one stable ion. Students could compare copper oxide produced with the two differently charged copper ions.

AQA Specification link-up: Chemistry C2.1

- When atoms form chemical bonds by transferring electrons, they form ions. Atoms that lose electrons become positively charged ions. Atoms that gain electrons become negatively charged ions. Ions have the electronic structure of a noble gas (Group 0). [C2.1.1. c)]
- An ionic compound is a giant structure of ions. Ionic compounds are held together by strong electrostatic forces of attraction between oppositely charged ions. These forces act in all directions in the lattice and this is called ionic bonding. [C2.1.1 f)]
- Write formulae for ionic compounds from given symbols and ionic charges. [C2.1]
- Represent the electronic structure of the ions in ... magnesium oxide and calcium chloride. [C2.1]

Lesson structure

Starters

Define – Give students the following definitions and ask them to decide the key word that relates to each:

- A charged particle formed by an atom losing or gaining electrons. [Ion]
- All the atoms have the same number of protons. [Element]
- More than one type of atom chemically bonded together. [Compound]
- A chemical bond formed by transferring electrons. [Ionic bond]
- A section of the periodic table whose elements all form 1+ ions. [Group 1/Alkali metals] *(5 minutes)*

Guess the ion – Give the students a diagram of chlorine, sodium, calcium, oxygen and calcium ions. Encourage them to use the periodic table and the textbook to name each ion. You can support students by giving them the names of the ions and asking them to match them with the diagrams. You could extend students by asking them to suggest some ionic compounds that the ions could form. *(10 minutes)*

Main

- The students could make magnesium oxide in the lab in a variety of ways. Encourage students to represent the reaction in terms of a flow chart. The first stages should detail the structure of the atoms of the elements. The middle stages could show the observations of the reaction. The final stage would include a dot and cross diagram representing the resulting ionic compound.
- Often students consider ionic bonds in isolation and in two-dimensional particle diagrams or in dot and cross diagrams. Show students already made-up structures of calcium chloride and magnesium oxide.
- Students could then compare the structures to the actual substances (crystalline powders).
- Then, give students molecular model kits and ask them to generate a sodium chloride crystal. Use questions to encourage students to understand which part of the model represents ions and bonds and what the bonds are (electrostatic forces of attraction between oppositely charged ions).

Plenaries

Question – Split the class into four groups and give each team a different key term: 'ions', 'ionic bond', 'lattice', 'charge'. Each group should write a question which matches its answer. Students then share their questions with the rest of the class. *(5 minutes)*

AfL (Assessment for Learning) – Give students an examination question with a fictitious student answer. Encourage the students to work in small groups to mark the work. Then ask the class to say how many marks they would award the student. Reveal the actual mark. The questions could be selected from a Foundation or a Higher Tier paper and the groups of students could be selected accordingly. *(10 minutes)*

Answers to in-text questions

a giant lattice
b Electrostatic forces of attraction between oppositely charged ions.

Practical support

Burning magnesium

Equipment and materials required
Magnesium ribbon, magnesium powder, spatula, tongs, Bunsen burner and safety equipment, eye protection, blue plastic/glass.

Details
Students hold a small piece (< 1 cm) of magnesium ribbon in tongs. The metal should be held at the top of the blue gas cone in the Bunsen flame. As soon as it ignites, they need to remove it from the flame. This reaction produces a bright light that can blind if looked at directly, so either encourage the students to look past the reaction or through the special blue plastic.

Then ask the students to sprinkle about half a spatula of magnesium powder directly into the blue Bunsen flame and observe. As the surface area is greater, it will combust more quickly and produces a twinkling effect. Make sure that the students hold the Bunsen at an angle or the magnesium powder may fall down the Bunsen chimney and fuse the collar to the chimney.

Safety: CLEAPSS Hazcard 59A Magnesium ribbon, magnesium powder – highly flammable. During both of these reactions, eye protection must be worn. Magnesium oxide powder will aspirate, so it is advisable to complete this in a well-ventilated area, or demonstrate.

Structure and bonding

Ionic bonding

C2 1.2 — Ionic bonding ⓚ

Learning objectives
- How are ionic compounds held together?
- Which elements, other than those in Groups 1 and 7, form ions?

You have seen how positive and negative ions form during some reactions. Ionic compounds are usually formed when metals react with non-metals.

The ions formed are held next to each other by very strong forces of attraction between the oppositely charged ions. This electrostatic force of attraction, which acts in all directions, is called **ionic bonding**.

The ionic bonds between the charged particles result in an arrangement of ions that we call a **giant structure** (or a **giant lattice**). If we could stand among the ions they would seem to go on in all directions forever.

The force exerted by an ion on the other ions in the lattice acts equally in all directions. This is why the ions in a giant structure are held so strongly together.

The giant structure of ionic compounds is very regular. This is because the ions all pack together neatly, like marbles in a box.

a What name do we give to the arrangement of ions in an ionic compound?
b What holds the ions together in this structure?

- = Cl⁻
+ = Na⁺

Strong ionic bonds between oppositely charged ions

Figure 1 Part of the giant ionic lattice (3-D network) of sodium and chloride ions in sodium chloride

Sometimes the atoms reacting need to gain or lose two electrons to gain a stable noble gas structure. An example is when magnesium (2,8,2) reacts with oxygen (2,6). When these two elements react they form magnesium oxide (MgO). This is made up of magnesium ions with a double positive charge (Mg²⁺) and oxide ions with a double negative charge (O²⁻).

We can represent the atoms and ions involved in forming ionic bonds by **dot and cross diagrams**. In these diagrams we only show the electrons in the outermost shell of each atom or ion. This makes them quicker to draw than the diagrams on the previous page. Figure 2 on the next page shows an example.

2,8,2   2,6   2,8   **MgO**   2,8

Figure 2 When magnesium oxide (MgO) is formed, the reacting magnesium atoms lose two electrons and the oxygen atoms gain two electrons

Another example of an ionic compound is calcium chloride. Each calcium atom (2,8,8,2) needs to lose two electrons but each chlorine atom (2,8,7) needs to gain only one electron. This means that two chlorine atoms react with every one calcium atom to form calcium chloride. So the formula of calcium chloride is CaCl₂.

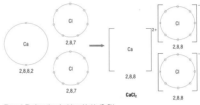

Figure 3 The formation of calcium chloride (CaCl₂)

Did you know …?
The structure of ionic lattices is investigated by passing X-rays through them.

Summary questions
1 a Copy and complete the table:

Atomic number	Atom	Electronic structure of atom	Ion	Electronic structure of ion
8	O			[2,8]²⁻
19		2,8,8,1	K⁺	
17	Cl		Cl⁻	
20		2,8,8,2		

b Explain why potassium chloride is KCl but potassium oxide is K₂O.
c Explain why calcium oxide is CaO but calcium chloride is CaCl₂.

2 Draw dot and cross diagrams to show how you would expect the following elements to form ions together:
a lithium and chlorine
b calcium and oxygen
c aluminium and fluorine.

Key points
- Ionic compounds are held together by strong forces of attraction between the oppositely charged ions. This is called ionic bonding.
- Besides the elements in Groups 1 and 7, other elements that can form ionic compounds include those from Groups 2 and 6.

Further teaching suggestions

Dot and cross diagrams
- Students could be encouraged to draw more complex dot and cross diagrams, e.g. for aluminium oxide. Encourage students to consider the arrangement of the ions, how the same charged ions would repel, therefore the positive and negatively charged ions alternate in all directions.
  Students could evaluate dot and cross diagrams as a means of representing ionic compounds, contrasting them with other methods of representing ionic compounds such as molecular model kits and computer models.
  Ask students to draw the dot and cross diagrams to represent sodium chloride, magnesium oxide and calcium chloride. To extend this activity, students could research and draw a diagram to represent the ionic lattice for each compound.

Iron wool and halogens
- You may wish to show students the reactions between iron wool and bromine, chlorine and iodine (see CLEAPSS 13.2.5). Follow CLEAPSS precautions.

Summary answers

1 a

Atomic number	Atom	Electronic structure of atom	Ion	Electronic structure of ion
8	O	2,6	O²⁻	[2,8]²⁻
19	K	2,8,8,1	K⁺	[2,8,8]⁺
17	Cl	2,8,7	Cl⁻	[2,8,8]⁻
20	Ca	2,8,8,2	Ca²⁺	[2,8,8]²⁺

b K forms K⁺ and Cl forms Cl⁻. Therefore one type of each ion is needed to make the compound electrically neutral. But O forms O²⁻, so two K⁺ are needed.

c Ca forms Ca²⁺ and O forms O²⁻. Therefore one type of each ion is needed to make the compound electrically neutral. But Cl forms Cl⁻, so two Cl⁻ are needed.

2 Students should show dot and cross diagrams for the three reactions **a**, **b** and **c**. These diagrams should use the same structure as the examples given in the Student Book. Lithium chloride should show one ion of lithium (Li⁺) and one chloride ion (Cl⁻). Calcium oxide should show one ion of calcium (Ca²⁺) and one oxygen ion (O²⁻). Aluminium chloride should show one ion of aluminium (Al³⁺) and three chloride ions (Cl⁻).

C2 1.3 Formulae of ionic compounds

Learning objectives

Students should learn that:

- how to write the formula of an ionic compound when its ions are given.

Learning outcomes

Most students should be able to:

- determine the formula of simple ionic compounds when the ions are given.

Some students should also be able to:

- determine the formula of ionic compounds that include brackets in the formula, when the ions are given.

Support

- Some students may struggle with this concept. Focus only on simple ions and you may wish to introduce a method for generating the formula without understanding why the subscript numbers are different. Students should write the symbols of the elements with the compound metal first and then the non-metal. They then add the charges of each ion. Ignore the + or − and cross the number down from the metal to the subscript position of the non-metal and vice versa. If there are any 1s, rewrite the formula without them, and cancel the subscripts down if this is possible.

Extend

- It is interesting that there are many examples of negative ions that consist of a group of atoms, but very few examples of positive ions with more than one. Extend students by asking them to find out examples of ions containing more than one atom, other than those listed in the Student Book.

AQA **Specification link-up: Chemistry C2.1**

- Write formulae for ionic compounds from given symbols and ionic charges. [C2.1]

Lesson structure

Starters

Draw that ion – Give students mini-whiteboards, pens and erasers. Ask them to draw the electronic structure of atoms or ions limited to the first 20 elements in the periodic table. Only ask them to draw one structure at a time, then the students show the answer to you and you can give instant feedback and encouragement. Support students by allowing them to look back in their notes, use the Student Book or even peek at other students' answers. You could extend students by asking them to write the shorthand notation for each of the electronic structures as well as the diagram. (5 minutes)

Count the atoms – Give the students a selection of different ionic compounds and ask them to count the atoms that they contain. [e.g. CuO – 2 atoms, $CuSO_4$ – 6 atoms, $(NH_4)_2SO_4$ – 15 atoms.] (5 minutes)

Main

- Explain to students that, when you touch an ionic compound, you do not get an electric shock. [The number of positive charges is the same as the number of negative charges.]

- Students should be quite familiar with sodium chloride and this is a good starting point. Ask students to suggest the type of bonding present [ionic] and how they know [it is a compound made of a metal and a non-metal]. Then ask for a volunteer to come to the board and write the symbol and charge of a sodium ion (Na^+). Ask a second volunteer to do the same for chlorine (Cl^-). Ask students to suggest how many chloride ions you would need for every sodium ion, reiterating that the charges have to balance. Students should recognise that there is a one-to-one ratio and therefore the formula is NaCl.

- Ask students to write the formulae of potassium chloride [KCl], sodium bromide [NaBr] and lithium iodide [LiI], as all of these compounds also have a one-to-one ratio of ions. Circulate around the classroom, making the students answer directly in their book and helping where necessary. You could extend students by giving them examples of ions also in a one-to-one relationship but with charges greater than 1, e.g. calcium sulfide [CaS].

- Use the same questioning technique to build up the formula for calcium chloride. Again ask students to generate the formulae for the following compounds: magnesium bromide [$MgBr_2$] barium iodide [BaI_2]. Extend students by asking them to generate the formula of sodium oxide [Na_2O]. Once again, circulate around the room giving instant feedback and help where necessary.

- Ask students to generate five names of ionic compounds (using a metal reacted with a non-metal). You could extend students by encouraging them to use ions that contain more than one atom as well. They can then swap their lists with their neighbours and write the formulae for the names that have been written down. Students then swap the paper back. The authors of the name consider the formulae written and award a score out of five to their partners. Students may wish to discuss their marking. Clarification from the teacher may be needed in some cases.

Plenaries

Sort it out – Give the students a selection of formulae and compound names. Students should then write the name and the correct formula. (5 minutes)

Objective question – Ask the students to answer the question posed in the objective. Students could be supported by being given a selection of correct answers, each more scientific than the last. They have to choose which one makes the most sense to them and copy it out. Students could be extended by being asked to include a worked example in their answer. (10 minutes)

Further teaching suggestions

Table

- You could ask students to write a table of ions, where they write the name of the ion, formula, electronic structure and an example of a compound that contains that ion.

Jigsaw puzzle

- You could create a jigsaw puzzle where students have to match the name of the ionic compound with its formula. Only one tessellation would give the correct shape and this makes the activity very easy to assess and allows students to have a lot of practice at recognising and generating formulae.

Structure and bonding

Formulae of ionic compounds

C2 1.3 Formulae of ionic compounds ⓚ

Learning objectives

- How can we write the formula of an ionic compound, given its ions?

In this chapter we have seen how three different ionic compounds are formed. You should understand how atoms turn to ions when sodium chloride, magnesium oxide and calcium chloride are formed from their elements.

The overall charge on any ionic compound is zero. The compounds are neutral. Therefore we do not have to draw dot and cross diagrams to work out each ionic formula. As long as we know or are given the charge on the ions in a compound we can work out its formula.

a What is the overall charge on an ionic compound?

If we look at the three examples above, we can see how the charges on the ions in a compound cancel out:

Ionic compound	Ratio of ions in compound	Formula of compound
sodium chloride	$Na^+ : Cl^-$ 1 : 1	NaCl
magnesium oxide	$Mg^{2+} : O^{2-}$ 1 : 1	MgO
calcium chloride	$Ca^{2+} : Cl^-$ 1 : 2	$CaCl_2$

b What is the formula of magnesium chloride?

We can work out the formula of some ions given a copy of the periodic table. Remember that in your exams you will have a Data Sheet which includes a periodic table and a table showing the charges of common ions.

Groups of metals

- The atoms of Group 1 elements form 1+ ions, e.g. Li^+.
- The atoms of Group 2 elements form 2+ ions, e.g. Ca^{2+}.

Groups of non-metals

- The atoms of Group 7 elements form 1− ions, e.g. F^-.
- The atoms of Group 6 elements form 2− ions, e.g. S^{2-}.

The names of compounds of transition metals contain the charge on their ions in brackets in roman numerals. This is because they can form ions carrying different sizes of positive charge. For example, iron can form 2+ and 3+ ions. So the name iron(III) oxide tells us that the iron is present as Fe^{3+} ions in this compound.

c What is the formula of lithium sulfide?
d What is the formula of iron(III) oxide?

?? Did you know ...?

Common salt is sodium chloride. In just 58.5 g of salt there are over 600 000 000 000 000 000 000 000 ions of Na^+ and the same number of Cl^- ions.

More complicated ions

Some ions are made up of more than one element. When you studied limestone, you learned that the formula of calcium carbonate is $CaCO_3$. It contains calcium ions, Ca^{2+}, and carbonate ions, CO_3^{2-}. The carbonate ions contain carbon and oxygen. However, the rule about cancelling out charges still applies as in one-element ions. Calcium carbonate is $CaCO_3$ as the 2+ and 2− ions in the ionic compound cancel out in the ratio 1 : 1.

Two-element ions you might come across are shown in the table below:

Name of ion	Formula of ion	Example of compound
hydroxide	OH^-	calcium hydroxide, $Ca(OH)_2$
nitrate	NO_3^-	magnesium nitrate, $Mg(NO_3)_2$
carbonate	CO_3^{2-}	sodium carbonate, Na_2CO_3
sulfate	SO_4^{2-}	calcium sulfate, $CaSO_4$

Notice how the formula of a compound containing a two-element ion sometimes contains brackets. To write calcium hydroxide as $CaOH_2$ would be misleading. It would tell us the ratio of Ca : O : H ions was 1 : 1 : 2. However, as there are twice as many hydroxide ions as calcium ions, the ratio should be 1 : 2 : 2. This is why we write the formula as $Ca(OH)_2$.

e What is the formula of calcium nitrate?

Figure 1 Haematite is an ore of iron. It is mined (as here) and used as a source of iron(III) oxide for the blast furnace in the extraction of iron.

Summary questions

1 Using the charges on the ions given on this spread, give the formula of:
   a calcium oxide
   b lithium oxide
   c magnesium chloride

2 Draw a table with K^+, Mg^{2+} and Fe^{3+} down the side and Br^-, OH^-, NO_3^- and SO_4^{2-} across the top. Then fill in the formula of the compound in each cell of the table.

3 a The formula of strontium nitrate is $Sr(NO_3)_2$. What is the charge on a strontium ion?
   b The formula of aluminium sulfate is $Al_2(SO_4)_3$. What is the charge on an aluminium ion?

AQA Examiner's tip

When naming compounds we use the ending –ide for simple non-metal ions such as oxide or sulfide. However, we use –ate for ions that include oxygen, such as sulfate, nitrate and carbonate.

AQA Examiner's tip

You do not have to learn the charges on ions – they are on the data sheet.

Think of each symbol as a single atom and the formula of each ion as a single ion. Small numbers multiply only the symbol they follow.

Brackets are needed when there is more than one type of atom in the ion being multiplied.

Key points

- The charges on the ions in an ionic compound always cancel each other out.
- The formula of an ionic compound shows the ratio of ions present in the compound.
- Sometimes we need brackets to show the ratio of ions in a compound, e.g. magnesium hydroxide, $Mg(OH)_2$.

86

87

Answers to in-text questions

a 0

b $MgCl_2$

c Li_2S

d Fe_2O_3

e $Ca(NO_3)_2$

Summary answers

1 **a** CaO   **b** Li_2O **c** $MgCl_2$

2

	Br^-	OH^-	NO_3^-	SO_4^{2-}
K^+	KBr	KOH	KNO_3	K_2SO_4
Mg^{2+}	$MgBr_2$	$Mg(OH)_2$	$Mg(NO_3)_2$	$MgSO_4$
Fe^{3+}	$FeBr_3$	$Fe(OH)_3$	$Fe(NO_3)_3$	$Fe_2(SO_4)_3$

3 **a** 2+   **b** 3+

C2 1.4

Covalent bonding

Learning objectives

Students should learn:

- how a covalent bond is formed
- the types of substance that have covalent bonds.

Learning outcomes

Most students should be able to:

- state a simple definition for a covalent bond
- draw a dot and cross diagram for simple covalent bonds (hydrogen, chlorine, hydrogen chloride, water)
- name an element that has a giant covalent structure (carbon, diamond).

Some students should also be able to:

- explain the formation of a covalent bond
- draw dot and cross diagrams for more complex covalent substances (methane, ammonia and oxygen)
- explain the bonding in a giant covalent structure and give an example, e.g. silicon oxide.

Answers to in-text questions

a covalent
b A giant covalent structure (macromolecule).

Support

- Some students will need additional support to understand fully how to generate dot and cross diagrams. To help students understand how to draw these diagrams, give them the electronic structures of key atoms (hydrogen, chlorine) using overhead transparencies. Then ask them to arrange the images so that each atom has a noble gas structure, by overlapping one image on to another. When they have the correct arrangement of electrons, they can copy the diagram into their books. This process can be demonstrated on an overhead projector in front of the class.

Extend

- You could extend students by asking them to represent molecular ions using dot and cross diagrams.

AQA Specification link-up: Chemistry C2.1

- When atoms share pairs of electrons, they form covalent bonds. These bonds between atoms are strong. Some covalently bonded substances consist of simple molecules such as H_2, Cl_2, O_2, HCl, H_2O, NH_3 and CH_4. Others have giant covalent structures (macromolecules), such as diamond and silicon dioxide. [C2.1.1 g)]
- Represent the covalent bonds in molecules such as water, ammonia, hydrogen, hydrogen chloride, methane and oxygen, and in giant structures such as diamond and silicon dioxide ... . [C2.1]

Lesson structure

Starters

Card sort – Give the students separate cards with images (just coloured circles and dot and cross diagrams) and words on them: 'compound', 'element', 'molecule', 'mixture', 'ionic bond', 'ion'. Students should then try to match the image with the key term. *(5 minutes)*

Demonstration – Ignite a small hydrogen balloon to get the attention of the class and generate excitement. The hydrogen will explode as it reacts with the oxygen in the air to make water (steam). Encourage the students to write a word equation for this reaction. You could support students by giving them the names of the chemicals and they have to select which are the reactants and which are the products. Students could be extended by being asked to write a balanced symbol equation. *(10 minutes)*

Main

- Students need to be able to draw dot and cross diagrams for certain molecules and some students should be able to explain how and why they are formed. Ask for volunteers to draw the electronic structure of hydrogen on the board.
- Then ask the students how many electrons it needs to obtain a noble gas structure [one]. Explain how and why hydrogen atoms make diatomic molecules.
- Ask the students to draw the dot and cross diagram of a chlorine molecule and explain, in no more than two sentences, why chlorine forms a diatomic molecule.
- Demonstrate how hydrogen and chlorine atoms bond to form hydrogen chloride. Then ask students to draw the other dot and cross diagrams for the appropriate molecules.
- Most substances that form covalent bonds make discrete molecules. However, students need to be aware of some macromolecules, e.g. carbon and silicon oxide.
- Give students molecular model kits and ask them to make models of different molecules. Then focus on carbon, and ask them to make a carbon molecule using only single bonds – hopefully the students will find that the structure is never-ending.
- Explain to students that this is an example of a macromolecule and that it, too, is made of covalent bonds. This links with C2 2.3.

Plenaries

Ionic/covalent – Give the students a piece of paper. Ask them to write in large letters 'ionic bonding' and 'covalent bonding', one on each side of the paper. Then read out the following substances, and the students should hold up the side of the paper that shows which type of bonding is present:

- Methane [Covalent]
- Sodium chloride [Ionic]
- Oxygen [Covalent]
- Water [Covalent]
- Magnesium oxide [Ionic]
- Carbon [Covalent]
- Silicon oxide [Covalent]
- Ammonia [Covalent]
- Calcium chloride [Ionic]
- Hydrogen chloride [Covalent]

You could support students by putting the definitions and one example of ionic and covalent bonding on the board for them to refer to. You could extend students by asking them to generate the formula for each of these compounds. *(5 minutes)*

Model – Split the class into teams and give each team a different covalent compound to represent. The students in each team should represent atoms and their hands and feet can make up to four bonds (e.g. C in methane). Each team should 'act out' its molecule and explain it to the class. *(10 minutes)*

Practical support

Burning hydrogen

Equipment and materials required
Small rubber balloon, string, hydrogen gas cylinder (pressurised gas), metre rule, splint, tape, matches.

Details
Fill a rubber balloon with hydrogen from a gas cylinder. Tie the balloon with a piece of string onto a tap or 1 kg mass, so that it is clear of any flammable materials, students and the ceiling.

Then light a splint taped to the end of a metre rule. Hold the lighted splint onto the stretched part of the rubber.

Safety: The demonstrator should wear eye protection and be aware that hot rubber can fly from the balloon. CLEAPSS Hazcard 48 Hydrogen – flammable. Soap bubbles filled with hydrogen are an alternative here.

Further teaching suggestions

Allotropes
● Students could define the term 'allotrope' and look up other allotropes of carbon [fullerenes]. This links with C2 2.3.

Naming
● You could ask students to suggest the names of other covalent compounds and try to draw dot and cross diagrams of them.

Comparing representations
● Students could evaluate the use of dot and cross diagrams to represent covalent compounds, comparing this representation with molecular model kits, space-saving diagrams, computer models and ball-and-stick diagrams.

Gases in air
● You could ask students to use dot and cross diagrams to show the gases in the air. This reinforces the work on bonding (as argon has a full outer shell of electrons and is therefore a monatomic gas) and nitrogen is a useful extension as this molecule contains a triple bond.

Computer modelling
● You may wish to allow students to use computer modelling to simulate how electrons are shared between atoms to make molecules. You could extend students and allow them to make their own simulations using simple programmes that would allow students to make their own flash animations.

Structure and bonding

C2 1.4 Covalent bonding ⓚ

Learning objectives
● How are covalent bonds formed?
● What types of substance have covalent bonds?

Reactions between metals and non-metals usually result in ionic bonding. However, many, many compounds are formed in a very different way. When non-metals react together their atoms share pairs of electrons to form molecules. We call this **covalent bonding**.

Simple molecules ⓚ

The atoms of non-metals generally need to gain electrons to achieve stable outer energy levels. When they react together neither atom can give away electrons. So they get the electronic structure of a noble gas by sharing electrons. The atoms in the molecules are then held together by the shared pairs of electrons. We call these strong bonds between the atoms covalent bonds.

a What is the bond called when two atoms share a pair of electrons?

Figure 1 Most of the molecules in substances which make up living things are held together by covalent bonds between non-metal atoms

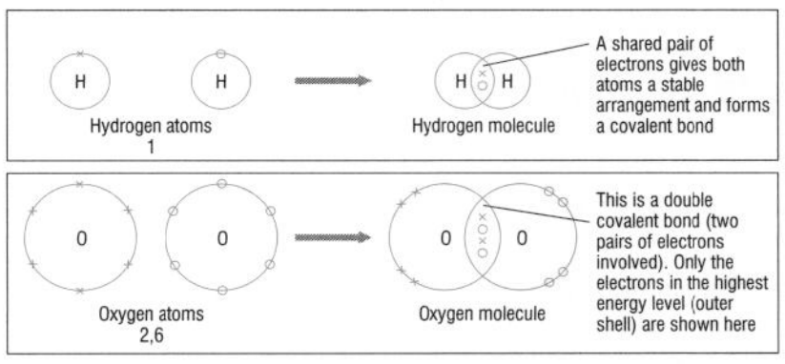

Hydrogen chloride HCl

Water H₂O

Methane CH₄

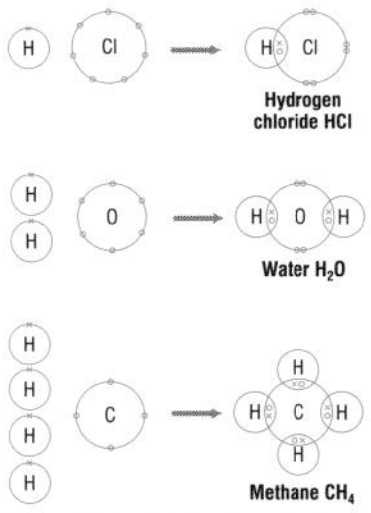

Figure 3 The principles of covalent bonding remain the same however many atoms are involved

Figure 2 Atoms of hydrogen and oxygen join together to form stable molecules. The atoms in H₂ and O₂ molecules are held together by strong covalent bonds.

A shared pair of electrons gives both atoms a stable arrangement and forms a covalent bond

Hydrogen atoms → Hydrogen molecule

This is a double covalent bond (two pairs of electrons involved). Only the electrons in the highest energy level (outer shell) are shown here

Oxygen atoms 2,6 → Oxygen molecule

Sometimes in covalent bonding each atom brings the same number of electrons to share. But this is not always the case. Sometimes the atoms of one element will need several electrons, while the other atom only needs one more electron for each atom to get a stable arrangement. In this case, more atoms become involved in forming the molecule.

We can represent the covalent bonds in substances such as water, ammonia and methane in a number of ways. Each way represents the same thing. The method chosen depends on what we want to show.

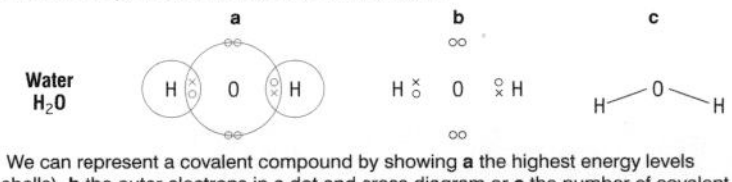

Water H₂O

Figure 4 We can represent a covalent compound by showing **a** the highest energy levels (or outer shells), **b** the outer electrons in a dot and cross diagram or **c** the number of covalent bonds

Giant covalent structures

Many substances containing covalent bonds consist of small molecules, for example, H₂O. However, some covalently bonded substances are very different. They have giant structures where huge numbers of atoms are held together by a network of covalent bonds. These are sometimes referred to as macromolecules.

Diamond has a giant covalent structure. In diamond, each carbon atom forms four covalent bonds with its neighbours. This results in a rigid giant covalent lattice.

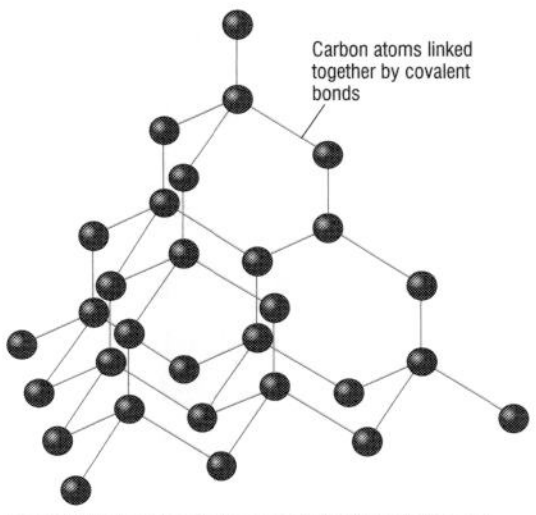

Carbon atoms linked together by covalent bonds

Figure 5 Part of the giant covalent structure of diamond

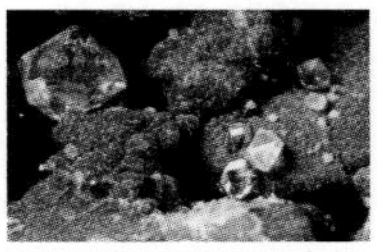

Silicon dioxide (silica) is another substance with a giant covalent structure.

b What do we call the structure of a substance held together by a network of covalent bonds?

Figure 6 Diamonds owe their hardness to the way the carbon atoms are arranged in a giant covalent structure

Summary questions

1 Copy and complete using the words below:
covalent   giant   molecules   macromolecules   shared

When non-metal atoms react together they make .... bonds. The atoms in these bonds are held together by .... electrons. Most substances held together by covalent bonds consist of ...., but some have .... covalent structures, sometimes called ....

2 Draw diagrams, showing all the electrons, to represent the covalent bonding between the following atoms.
  a two hydrogen atoms
  b two chlorine atoms
  c a hydrogen atom and a fluorine atom

3 Draw dot and cross diagrams to show the covalent bonds when:
  a a nitrogen atom bonds with three hydrogen atoms
  b a carbon atom bonds with two oxygen atoms.

Key points
● Covalent bonds are formed when atoms share pairs of electrons.
● Many substances containing covalent bonds consist of simple molecules, but some have giant covalent structures.

88 | 89

Summary answers

1 covalent, shared, molecules, giant, macromolecules

2 a

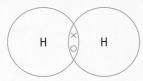

b

c

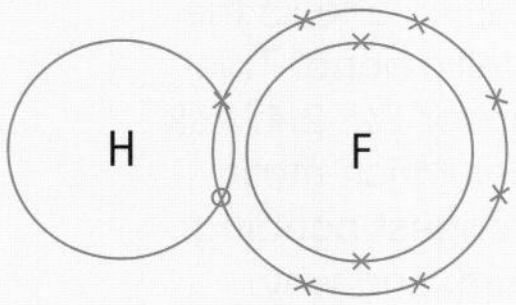

3 a

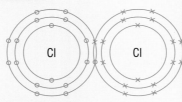

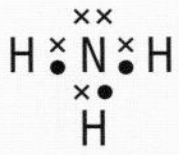

b

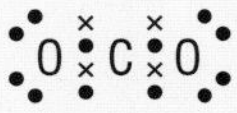

C2 1.5 Metals

AQA Specification link-up: Chemistry C2.1

Learning objectives

Students should learn:
- how atoms in metals are arranged
- what holds metal atoms (ions) together. [HT only]

Learning outcomes

Most students should be able to:
- list examples of elements that have a giant metallic structure
- describe the bonding in metals. [HT only]

Some students should also be able to:
- explain metallic bonding and structures in words and a labelled diagram, including delocalised electrons. [HT only]

Specification link-up: Chemistry C2.1
- Metals consist of giant structures of atoms arranged in a regular pattern. *[C2.1.1 h)]*
- The electrons in the highest occupied energy levels (outer shell) of metal atoms are delocalised and so free to move through the whole structure. This corresponds to a structure of positive ions with electrons between the ions holding them together by strong electrostatic attractions. *[C2.1.1 i)]* **[HT only]**
- Represent the bonding in metals … . *[C2.1]* **[HT only]**

Lesson structure

Starters

Odd one out – List the following metals: nickel, cobalt, iron and steel. Ask students to look at the list and decide which metal doesn't fit the pattern and why. [Steel is the odd one out as it is an alloy, whereas nickel, cobalt and iron are elements.] *(5 minutes)*

5, 4, 3, 2, 1 – Ask students to write a list of: five metal symbols, four metal properties, three magnetic elements, two metals used in jewellery and one metal that is a liquid at room temperature. Build up a class list on the board through questions and answers. You could support students by displaying a periodic table that has a colour-coded key to show the metals, non-metals and the state of each element at room temperature. You could extend students by asking them to define a metal. *(10 minutes)*

Main

- Metals are made up of grains, which can be seen using microscopes. Show students images of the grains and grain boundaries. The grains order themselves in metals and form crystals.
- Students can grow their own metal crystals by completing a solution displacement reaction. You could encourage students to record the metal crystal in the form of a diagram in their book.
- Visible metal crystals can be found in a variety of structures in and around the school site. Students could go out and about in small teams, armed with digital cameras to find examples. When students return to the class, they could display the photographs to the rest of the class.
- Discuss the nature of metallic bonding with Higher Tier students. **[HT only]**

Plenaries

Label – Give the students an unlabelled diagram of a metal structure (as shown in the specification). Ask the students to label the diagram as fully as possible. You could support students by making this a 'cut-and-stick' activity. You could extend them by asking them to evaluate this model and suggest its advantages and disadvantages. *(5 minutes)*

Explain and define – Ask students to explain metallic bonding to their neighbours. Then each pair should try to distil its explanation into a concise definition. Encourage a few couples to share and evaluate their definitions. *(10 minutes)* **[HT only]**

Answers to in-text questions

a The metal atoms (or ions) are arranged in a regular pattern.

b The outermost electrons.

Support

- Students could make a three-dimensional model of a metallic structure using art materials, e.g. polystyrene balls, string, paint and a shoe box.

Extend

- Ask students to consider how the charge on the metal ion affects the strength of the metallic bond. This is good preparation for C2. 2.4. Ask students to consider which metal would have the strongest bonding: sodium or aluminium, and why. [Al (aluminium), as it has more delocalised electrons.]

Practical support

Growing silver crystals

Equipment and materials required
Boiling tube, boiling tube rack, copper wire, silver nitrate solution less than 0.4 M, eye protection.

Details
- Wrap the copper wire into a spring shape and put it into a boiling tube. Wear eye protection. Add silver nitrate solution to the boiling tube so that it is about half full.
- Leave the solution to allow displacement to occur. It would be best if the experiment were left until next lesson and reviewed as a Starter.

Safety: CLEAPSS Hazcard 87 Silver nitrate solution – irritant.

Survey of metallic crystals

Equipment and materials required
Clipboards, digital camera, stationery.

Details
- Split the class into small groups. Take the students to an example of a metal crystal, e.g. a galvanised dustbin on the school site.
- Give the students a time limit (10 minutes) to find further examples of metal crystals around the school. They should record, in a table, the photograph number, the place where the crystal was found and the item on which it was found.

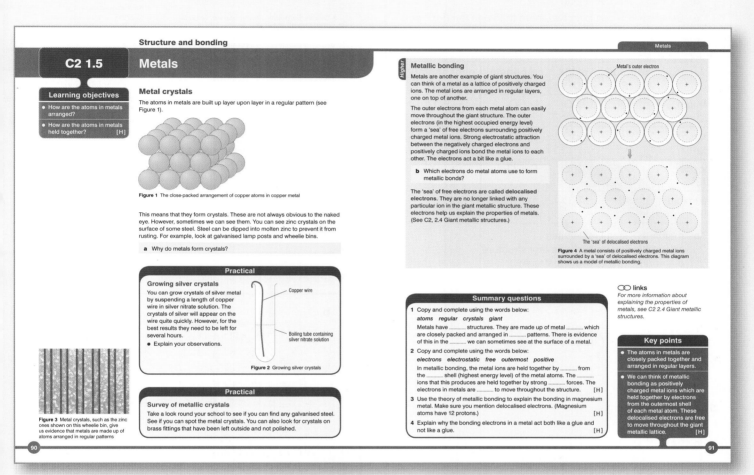

Structure and bonding

C2 1.5 — Metals

Metals

Learning objectives
- How are the atoms in metals arranged?
- How are the atoms in metals held together? [H]

Metal crystals
The atoms in metals are built up layer upon layer in a regular pattern (see Figure 1).

Figure 1 The close-packed arrangement of copper atoms in copper metal

This means that they form crystals. These are not always obvious to the naked eye. However, sometimes we can see them. You can see zinc crystals on the surface of some steel. Steel can be dipped into molten zinc to prevent it from rusting. For example, look at galvanised lamp posts and wheelie bins.

a Why do metals form crystals?

Practical
Growing silver crystals
You can grow crystals of silver metal by suspending a length of copper wire in silver nitrate solution. The crystals of silver will appear on the wire quite quickly. However, for the best results they need to be left for several hours.
- Explain your observations.

Copper wire

Boiling tube containing silver nitrate solution

Figure 2 Growing silver crystals

Figure 3 Metal crystals, such as the zinc ones shown on this wheelie bin, give us evidence that metals are made up of atoms arranged in regular patterns

Practical
Survey of metallic crystals
Take a look round your school to see if you can find any galvanised steel. See if you can spot the metal crystals. You can also look for crystals on brass fittings that have been left outside and not polished.

Metallic bonding
Metals are another example of giant structures. You can think of a metal as a lattice of positively charged ions. The metal ions are arranged in regular layers, one on top of another.

The outer electrons from each metal atom can easily move throughout the giant structure. The outer electrons (in the highest occupied energy level) form a 'sea' of free electrons surrounding positively charged metal ions. Strong electrostatic attraction between the negatively charged electrons and positively charged ions bond the metal ions to each other. The electrons act a bit like a glue.

b Which electrons do metal atoms use to form metallic bonds?

The 'sea' of free electrons are called **delocalised electrons**. They are no longer linked with any particular ion in the giant metallic structure. These electrons help us explain the properties of metals. (See C2, 2.4 Giant metallic structures.)

Metal's outer electron

The 'sea' of delocalised electrons

Figure 4 A metal consists of positively charged metal ions surrounded by a 'sea' of delocalised electrons. This diagram shows us a model of metallic bonding.

Summary questions
1 Copy and complete using the words below:
atoms regular crystals giant
Metals have .... structures. They are made up of metal .... which are closely packed and arranged in .... patterns. There is evidence of this in the .... we can sometimes see at the surface of a metal.

2 Copy and complete using the words below:
electrons electrostatic free outermost positive
In metallic bonding, the metal ions are held together by .... from the .... shell (highest energy level) of the metal atoms. The .... ions that this produces are held together by strong .... forces. The electrons in metals are .... to move throughout the structure. [H]

3 Use the theory of metallic bonding to explain the bonding in magnesium metal. Make sure you mention delocalised electrons. (Magnesium atoms have 12 protons.) [H]

4 Explain why the bonding electrons in a metal act both like a glue and not like a glue. [H]

links
For more information about explaining the properties of metals, see C2 2.4 Giant metallic structures.

Key points
- The atoms in metals are closely packed together and arranged in regular layers.
- We can think of metallic bonding as positively charged metal ions which are held together by electrons from the outermost shell of each metal atom. These delocalised electrons are free to move throughout the giant metallic lattice. [H]

Further teaching suggestions

Electrolysis
- Students could electrolyse copper sulfate solution in order to grow copper crystals or grow lead crystals from zinc foil suspended in lead nitrate solution.
  Safety: CLEAPSS Hazcard 27C Copper sulfate – harmful. CLEAPSS Hazcard 57A Lead nitrate – toxic.

Crystal models
- If the school has any examples, students could be shown different metal crystals and metal structural models.

Images
- Digital images taken by students or from the internet could be used by the students to create a PowerPoint display about metal crystals and where you can find them. They could then present them to their classmates.

Summary answers

1 giant, atoms, regular, crystals

2 electrons, outermost, positive, electrostatic, free

3 Each magnesium atom donates its two outermost electrons into the delocalised 'sea' of electrons. The electrostatic force of attraction between the negatively charged delocalised electrons and the positively charged metal ions hold the ions in position in the giant structure.

4 Like glue – because they hold the atoms together. Unlike glue – because atoms can still move/flow past each other when force is applied. The electrons can also move freely through the structure.

Summary answers

1 Compound – A substance made up of different types of atom/elements chemically bonded together.
Ionic bonding – The electrostatic force of attraction between oppositely charged ions.
Covalent bond – A pair of electrons shared between two atoms.

2 a iron(II) chloride, potassium oxide, lead bromide, silver nitrate.

  b These compounds all contain metals and non-metals.

  c covalent bonding

  d i H_2S **ii** $FeCl_2$

  e Because iron can form two/more than one ion (Fe^{2+} and Fe^{3+}).

3

	fluoride, F^-	oxide, O^{2-}	carbonate, CO_3^{2-}	phosphate(V), PO_4^{3-}
lithium, Li^+	LiF	Li_2O	Li_2CO_3	Li_3PO_4
barium, Ba^{2+}	BaF_2	BaO	$BaCO_3$	$Ba_3(PO_4)_2$
copper, Cu^{2+}	CuF_2	CuO	$CuCO_3$	$Cu_3(PO_4)_2$
aluminium, Al^{3+}	AlF_3	Al_2O_3	$Al_2(CO_3)_3$	$AlPO_4$

4 a methane – small molecules
    silicon dioxide – giant covalent structure
    diamond – giant covalent structure
    ammonia – small molecules

  b For ammonia (NH_3)   And/or

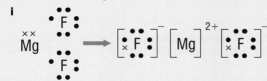

5 a A (magnesium)

  b Group 7.

  c i

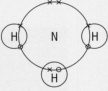

    where C (carbon) = Q

    ii covalent bonding

  d i

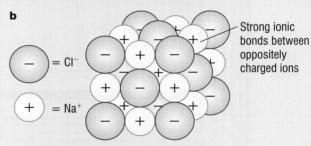

    where Mg = A and F = C

    ii ionic bonding

    iii MgF_2

6 a Atoms held together by sharing a pair of electrons to form a covalent bond, joining two F atoms together.

    F —— F

    Sharing electrons produces attractive force

Summary questions

1 Define the following terms:
  compound
  ionic bonding
  covalent bond

2 a Which of the following substances will have ionic bonding?
  hydrogen sulfide copper phosphorus(v) oxide
  iron(ii) chloride potassium oxide lead bromide
  silver nitrate

  b Explain how you decided on your answers in part **a**.

  c What type of bonding will the remaining substances in the list have?

  d What is the formula of:
    i hydrogen sulfide
    ii iron(ii) chloride.

  e Why does iron(ii) chloride have roman numerals in its name?

3 Copy and complete the following table with the formula of each compound formed.
(The first one is done for you).

	fluoride, F^-	oxide, O^{2-}	carbonate, CO_3^{2-}	phosphate(V), PO_4^{3-}
lithium, Li^+	LiF			
barium, Ba^{2+}				
copper, Cu^{2+}				
aluminium, Al^{3+}				

4 a Which of the following substances are made up of small molecules and which have a giant covalent structure?
  methane, CH_4
  silicon dioxide, SiO_2
  diamond, C
  ammonia, NH_3

  b Draw a dot and cross diagram to show the bonding in ammonia.

5 The diagrams show the arrangement of electrons in energy levels in three atoms.
(The letters are NOT the chemical symbols.)

a Which atom belongs to Group 2 of the periodic table?

b To which group does atom R belong?

c i Atom Q bonds with four atoms of hydrogen. Draw a dot and cross diagram to show the compound that is formed.
  ii What do we call the type of bonding between the atom of Q and the hydrogen atoms?

d i Draw dot and cross diagrams to show how atoms bonds with R atoms.
  ii What do we call the type of bonding in the compound formed by P and R?
  iii What is the formula of the compound formed by and R?

6 Describe, with diagrams, how the particles are held together in the following substances:
  a a molecule of fluorine (F_2).
  b a salt crystal (NaCl).

7 Draw a diagram which shows how the atoms in carbon dioxide, O=C=O, bond to each other.

---

b

Strong ionic bonds between oppositely charged ions

  — = Cl^-

  + = Na^+

Allow a 2-D single layer of the ionic lattice showing oppositely charged ions next to each other with suitable labelling.

7

O⦂⦂C⦂⦂O (dot and cross diagram)

End of chapter questions

End of chapter questions

AQA Examination-style questions 🄺

Use a periodic table and a table of charges on ions to help you to answer these questions.

1 Choose a word from the list to complete each sentence.
a When metals react with non-metals electrons are .... (1)

combined shared transferred

b When non-metal elements combine their atoms are held together by .... bonds. (1)

covalent ionic metallic

2 Choose a description from the list for each of the substances.

giant covalent giant ionic metal simple molecule

a ammonia, NH_3 c lithium, Li
b diamond, C   d sodium oxide, Na_2O (4)

3 Choose a number from the list to complete each sentence.

0 1 2 3 4 6 7

a The elements in Group .... in the periodic table all form ions with a charge of 1+. (1)
b The elements in Group .... in the periodic table all form ions with a charge of 2−. (1)
c The elements in Group 4 in the periodic table all form .... covalent bonds. (1)
d The aluminium ion has a charge of .... + (1)

4 a Choose the correct formula from the list for iron(III) chloride.

$FeCl$ Fe_2Cl $FeCl_3$ Fe_3Cl_3 (1)

b Choose the formula from the list for each of these ionic compounds.

NaS $NaSO_4$ $Na(SO_4)_2$ Na_2S NaS_2 Na_2SO_4

i sodium sulfide (1)
ii sodium sulfate (1)

5 Calcium hydroxide, $Ca(OH)_2$, is an ionic compound. Which of these ions in the list are the ions in calcium hydroxide?

Ca^+ Ca^{2+} Ca^{4+} OH^- OH_2^- OH^{2-} (2)

6 Sodium reacts with chlorine. The reaction forms sodium chloride.
a Use words from the list to answer the questions.

compound element hydrocarbon mixture

Which word best describes:
i sodium (1)
ii sodium chloride? (1)

b When sodium reacts with chlorine the sodium atoms change into sodium ions. The diagrams represent a sodium atom and a sodium ion.

Sodium atom (Na)   Sodium ion (Na⁺)

Use the diagrams to help you explain how a sodium atom turns into a sodium ion. (2)

c i The diagram below represents a chlorine atom. When chlorine reacts with sodium the chlorine forms negative chloride ions.
Copy and complete the diagram below to show how the outer electrons are arranged in a chloride ion (Cl^-). (1)

ii Chloride ions are strongly attracted to sodium ions in sodium chloride.
Explain why. (1)
AQA, 2010

7 Chlorine can form compounds with ionic or covalent bonds.
a Potassium chloride, KCl, has ionic bonds. Draw dot and cross diagrams to show what happens to potassium atoms and chlorine atoms when they react to form potassium chloride. You only need to show the outer electrons in your diagrams. (4)

b Hydrogen chloride, HCl, has covalent bonds. Draw a dot and cross diagram to show the bonding in hydrogen chloride. (2)

8 Sodium metal is a giant structure of sodium atoms.

Explain how the atoms are held together in sodium metal. [H] (3)

93

Examination-style answers

AQA Examination-style answers

1 a transferred   *(1 mark)*
  b covalent   *(1 mark)*

2 a simple molecule   *(1 mark)*
  b giant covalent   *(1 mark)*
  c metal   *(1 mark)*
  d giant ionic   *(1 mark)*

3 a 1   *(1 mark)*
  b 6   *(1 mark)*
  c 4   *(1 mark)*
  d 3   *(1 mark)*

4 a $FeCl_3$ *(1 mark)*
  b i Na_2S *(1 mark)*
    ii Na_2SO_4 *(1 mark)*

5 Ca^{2+}, OH^- *(2 marks)*

6 a i element   *(1 mark)*
    ii compound   *(1 mark)*
  b It loses an electron.   *(2 marks)*
  c i Right-hand diagram with seven crosses and one dot in outermost shell (allow diagram with all crosses). *(1 mark)*
    ii Oppositely charged ions attract each other. *(1 mark)*

7 a Each correctly drawn part of the diagram should be answered one mark.
  ● Correctly drawn potassium atom (one electron in outer shell).
  ● Correctly drawn chlorine atom (seven electrons in outer shell).
  ● Correctly drawn potassium ion: no electron in outer shell (*accept eight electrons in outer shell*) and brackets with + charge top right.
  ● Correctly drawn chloride ion: eight electrons in outer shell and brackets with − charge top right.
                                                     (4 marks)

  b For example, H atom: circle with a single dot, Cl atom: circle with seven crosses overlapping H circle so that a dot and cross are shared or alternative with no circles. Must be one electron different from seven others and a shared pair including that electron clearly shown for two marks. One mark for a shared pair of electrons, or eight electrons all with the same symbol. *(2 marks)*

8 Electrons in the highest (occupied) energy level/outer shell are delocalised/free (to move), leaving or surrounding positive ions (in regular lattice/arrangement), electrons attract/hold together the positive ions. *(3 marks)*

Kerboodle resources

Kerboodle resources 🄺

Resources available for this chapter on Kerboodle are:
● Chapter map: Structure and bonding
● Video: Medicinal chemist
● Support: Making sense of ions (C2 1.1)
● Animation: Ionic bonding (C2 1.2)
● Maths skills: Ionic formula (C2 1.3)
● Extension: What's the formula? (C2 1.3)
● Animation: Overview of covalent bonding (C2 1.4)
● Bump up your grade: Covalent bonding (C2 1.4)
● Interactive activity: Structure and bonding
● Revision podcast: Different types of bonding (C2 1.2–3, 1.5)
● Test yourself: Structure and bonding
● On your marks: Structure and bonding
● Examination-style questions: Structure and bonding
● Answers to examination-style questions: Structure and bonding

---

Practical suggestions

AQA Practical suggestions

Practicals	AQA	🄺	📖	⚙
Molecular modelling.	✓		✓	
Modelling electron transfer and electron sharing using computer simulations.	✓		✓	
Group 1 and Group 7 reactions, e.g. sodium with chlorine.	✓		✓	
The reactions of bromine, chlorine and iodine with iron wool.	✓		✓	
Growing metal crystals by displacement reactions using metals and salts.	✓		✓	
Modelling metal structures using polyspheres and bubble rafts.	✓		✓	

C2 2.1 Giant ionic structures

AQA Specification link-up: Chemistry C2.2

- Ionic compounds have regular structures (giant ionic lattices) in which there are strong electrostatic forces in all directions between oppositely charged ions. These compounds have high melting points and high boiling points because of the large amounts of energy needed to break the many strong bonds. *[C2.2.2 a)]*
- When melted or dissolved in water, ionic compounds conduct electricity because the ions are free to move and carry the current. *[C2.2.2 b)]*
- Suggest the type of structure of a substance given its properties. *[C2.2]*

Learning objectives

Students should learn:

- why ionic compounds are solids at room temperature and have high melting points
- why ionic compounds conduct electricity when they are molten or are dissolved in water.

Learning outcomes

Most students should be able to:

- state that ionic compounds have high melting points and are solid at room temperature
- describe how ionic compounds can conduct electricity when they are molten or dissolved in water.

Some students should also be able to:

- explain in detail why ionic compounds have high melting points
- explain in detail why ionic compounds can conduct electricity when molten or in solution.

Answers to in-text questions

a attractive electrostatic forces
b Because of the strong attractive electrostatic forces holding the oppositely charged ions together and the large number of ionic bonds in the crystal lattice.
c Because the ions are free to move.

Support

- You may find it easier if, in the experiment, you focus only on sodium chloride. This is a chemical that students experience every day and is safe to use. You could also provide students with the results table, so they just have to fill it in.

Extend

- Students could investigate more properties of ionic compounds (see 'Practical support'). You could encourage them to explain other physical properties of ionic compounds, e.g. symmetry of crystals, cleavage and hardness, in terms of the structure of the ionic lattice.

Lesson structure

Starters

List – Ask students to make a list of as many ionic substances as they can. Through question and answer, build up a list of them on the board and ask the students what they all have in common, other than that they have the same bonding. [All will be compounds and most examples given will probably consist of a metal bonded to a non-metal]. *(5 minutes)*

Anagrams – Give the students the set of anagrams below on the board. They should work out the key word in each case and then define it. You could support students by giving them the key words and definitions, so that they match them up. You could extend students by asking them to give examples of each of the key words.

- noi [Ion – a charged particle made when an atom loses or gains electrons].
- ttalcei [Lattice – a 3D arrangement of particles in a giant structure].
- conii dobn [Ionic bond – the electrostatic force of attraction between oppositely charged ions]. *(10 minutes)*

Main

- There are many examples of ionic compounds in everyday life, but students rarely consider the properties of these substances. Encourage them to investigate the properties of sodium chloride and potassium chloride. Students should first design a table to record information about the appearance, hardness, melting point and conductivity in different states. As it will be near impossible to melt these substances using a Bunsen burner, encourage students to use reference material to find their melting and boiling points.
- Students can then complete the practical detailed in the Student Book, in which they use a simple series circuit to explore the conductivity of ionic compounds when solid and dissolved. Once students have completed the experiment, they can work in groups and use the model of ionic bonding to explain their observations. Ask each group to feed back its ideas to the whole class and distil out a conclusion that all students could record in their notes.
- Give the students four same-coloured index cards. On one side, they should write a key physical property [high melting point, soluble in water and conducts in a solution or a liquid]. Then, on the reverse of each card, they should explain that property using key scientific terms and at least one labelled diagram.
- The fourth card should be a title card about ionic bonding. Ask the students to punch holes in the cards and the front of their exercise books. Using a piece of string the cards could be secured to the book and removed to add other revision cards about bonding. (You could also give other sets of coloured cards to the students for them to make notes about covalent and metallic bonding. They could add these to the set about ionic bonds.)

Plenaries

Summary – Split the class into three groups. Ask each team to explain why ionic compounds have certain physical properties. [Soluble in water, high melting point, conduct electricity when molten or dissolved, etc.] *(5 minutes)*

AfL (Assessment for Learning) – Give students an examination question about the properties of ionic compounds. Time the students (about 1 minute per mark). Then ask them to swap their answers with a partner, and give out mark schemes. Encourage the students to mark the work as it is presented (no discussions about 'what they really meant'). Then swap the papers back and you could collect in the marks. To differentiate this activity, use Foundation paper or Higher Tier past paper questions, depending on the tier of entry for each group of students. *(10 minutes)*

Practical support

Testing conductivity

Equipment and materials required

Sodium chloride, potassium chloride, two carbon electrodes, lab pack, two crocodile clips, three wires, lamp, beaker, wash bottle with water, glass rod, eye protection.

Details

Students put some sodium chloride/potassium chloride crystals into a beaker (to about a depth of 1 cm). Then submerge the electrodes and connect them to a lamp and power supply. Then turn on the power and make observations. Then add water from the wash bottle (half fill the beaker) and observe. Encourage the students to swirl the beaker to help the ionic compound dissolve.

- The lamp does not light at first but does once the salt dissolves.
- The ions are stuck in position within the giant lattice. However, as the sodium chloride dissolves in water, ions become free to move, carrying a charge between the electrodes, the lamp lights up.

Safety: Please note that this electrolysis will produce a small amount of chlorine gas. It should therefore be completed in a well-ventilated area. Be aware of students with respiratory problems (e.g. asthma) as the gas can aggravate them.

Other properties of ionic compounds

Equipment and materials required

Sodium chloride, potassium chloride, hand lens, mounted needle, spatula, two boiling tubes, boiling tube rack, boiling tube holder, beaker, glass rod, Bunsen burner and safety equipment, eye protection.

Details

Students to investigate the following:

Appearance – Students to look at the crystal through a hand lens and draw a diagram of the crystal.

Hardness – Students to try to scratch the surface with a mounted needle, and view the area using the hand lens.

Melting point – Students to put about half a spatula of the compound into a boiling tube and then hold it just above the blue gas cone in a roaring Bunsen flame. The tube should be at an angle, not pointing at any faces. Eye protection should be worn. The students should keep the compound in the flame until they have decided if it has a high or low melting point – the compounds are unlikely to melt. Then they place the boiling tube on a flameproof mat to cool.

Solubility – Students to half fill a beaker with warm water from the tap, then add a few crystals and swirl or stir with a glass rod.

Structure and properties

Giant ionic structures

C2 2.1 — Giant ionic structures

Learning objectives

- Why do ionic compounds have high melting points?
- Why do ionic compounds conduct electricity when we melt them or dissolve them in water?

We have already seen that an ionic compound consists of a giant structure of ions arranged in a lattice. The attractive electrostatic forces between the oppositely charged ions act in all directions and are very strong. This holds the ions in the lattice together very tightly.

a What type of force holds the ions together in an ionic compound?

Strong electrostatic forces of attraction called ionic bonds

Figure 1 The attractive forces between the oppositely charged ions in an ionic compound are very strong. The regular arrangement of ions in the giant lattice enables ionic compounds to form crystals.

AQA Examiner's tip

Remember that every ionic compound has a giant structure. The oppositely charged ions in these structures are held together by strong electrostatic forces of attraction. These act in all directions.

It takes a lot of energy to break up a giant ionic lattice. There are lots of strong ionic bonds to break. To separate the ions we have to overcome all those electrostatic forces of attraction. This means that ionic compounds have high melting points and boiling points. Look at the graph in Figure 2.

b Why do ionic compounds have high melting points and boiling points?

Once we have supplied enough energy to separate the ions from the lattice, they are free to move around. That's when the ionic solid melts and becomes a liquid. The ions are free to move anywhere in this liquid. Therefore they can carry their electrical charge through the molten liquid. A solid ionic compound cannot conduct electricity. That's because its ions are held in a fixed position in the lattice. They cannot move around. They can only vibrate 'on the spot' when solid.

Figure 2 The many strong forces of attraction in a lattice of ions mean that ionic compounds have high melting points and boiling points

Bulb lights as current flows

Moving ions carry the electrical charge through the molten potassium chloride

Molten potassium chloride

Figure 3 Because the ions are free to move, a molten ionic compound can conduct electricity

Many ionic compounds will dissolve in water. When we dissolve an ionic compound in water, the lattice is split up by the water molecules. Then the ions are free to move around in the solution formed. Just as molten ionic compounds will conduct electricity, solutions of ionic compounds will also conduct electricity. The ions are able to move to an oppositely charged electrode dipped in the solution (See Figure 3).

c Why can ionic compounds conduct electricity when they are molten or dissolved in water?

Ionic solid	Molten ionic compound	Ionic compound in solution
Ions are fixed in a lattice. They vibrate but cannot move around – it does not conduct electricity.	High temperature provides enough energy to overcome the many strong attractive forces between ions. Ions are free to move around within the molten compound – it does conduct electricity.	Water molecules separate ions from the lattice. Ions are free to move around within the solution – it does conduct electricity.

Practical

Testing conductivity (k)

Using a circuit as shown in Figure 3, dip a pair of electrodes into a 1 cm depth of sodium chloride crystals. What happens?

Now slowly add water.

- What happens to the bulb?

Repeat the experiment using potassium chloride.

- Explain your observations.

Summary questions

1 Copy and complete using the words below:

attraction conduct high lattice molten move oppositely solution

Ionic compounds have .... melting points and boiling points because of the many strong electrostatic forces of .... between .... charged ions in the giant .... Ionic compounds will .... electricity when .... or in .... because the ions are able to .... freely around in the liquids.

2 Why is seawater a better conductor of electricity than water from a freshwater lake?

Key points

- It takes a lot of energy to break the many strong ionic bonds which hold a giant ionic lattice together. So ionic compounds have high melting points. They are all solids at room temperature.
- Ionic compounds will conduct electricity when we melt them or dissolve them in water. That's because their ions can then move freely around and can carry charge through the liquid.

Further teaching suggestions

Explain a use

- Students could choose an ionic compound and explain why it is used for a specific purpose. For example, sodium fluoride is used in drinking water. Fluoride has been found to make teeth stronger and sodium fluoride dissolves easily into the drinking water supply. Students could then make 'top-trump' style fact cards and these could be used to make a colourful display in the classroom.

Summary answers

1 high, attraction, oppositely, lattice, conduct, molten, solution, move

2 Because it contains dissolved salt (ions).

C2 2.2

Simple molecules

AQA

Specification link-up: Chemistry C2.2

- Substances that consist of simple molecules are gases, liquids or solids that have relatively low melting points and boiling points. [C2.2.1a)]
- Substances that consist of simple molecules have only weak forces between the molecules (intermolecular forces). It is these intermolecular forces that are overcome, not the covalent bonds, when the substance melts or boils. [C2.2.1b)] **[HT only]**
- Substances that consist of simple molecules do not conduct electricity because the molecules do not have an overall electric charge. [C2.2.1c)]
- Suggest the type of structure of a substance given its properties. [C2.2]

Learning objectives

Students should learn:

- the properties of substances made up of simple molecules
- why simple molecular substances have low melting and boiling points **[HT only]**
- that substances made up of simple molecules do not conduct electricity.

Learning outcomes

Most students should be able to:

- recognise substances made up of simple molecules
- list examples of substances made up of simple molecules
- state the physical properties of substances made up of simple molecules
- state why substances made up of simple molecules do not conduct electricity.

Some students should also be able to:

- explain why substances made up of simple molecules have low melting and boiling points. **[HT only]**

Lesson structure

Starters

Crosswords – Create a crossword in which the answers are key words that will be needed in the lesson: 'molecule', 'electron', 'covalent', 'bond', 'compound', 'element', 'dot and cross'. There are some useful free websites such as www.discoveryschool.com where bespoke puzzles can be made quickly. *(5 minutes)*

Models – Split the class into small groups. Show the dot and cross diagram of hydrogen, then instruct the groups to make a model (using a molecular model kit) of this diagram and hold it in the air so that you can easily check. Then repeat with the other simple molecules that the students should know: hydrogen chloride, water, oxygen, ammonia and methane. Support students by supplying them with cards with diagrams of the molecules to make. Students then hold up the relevant model. Extend students by asking them to generate dot and cross diagrams themselves. *(10 minutes)*

Main

- Students often find it difficult to make connections between pieces of information. A mind map can be a very useful tool to help them make links within a topic.
- Split the students into groups of about four, and give them a felt pen each, some sticky-tac, a piece of sugar paper and a pack of A6 word cards. You should make these cards in advance, including key words for this topic: 'atom', 'electron', 'bond', 'covalent', 'melting point', 'boiling point', 'intermolecular forces', 'insulator', 'molecule', 'solid', 'liquid', 'gas'.
- The students should stick two key words on to the page: one should be the start of the sentence, the other the end. They should draw an arrow in the correct direction linking the words, then on the arrow write the middle section of the sentence. There is no limit to the number of arrows that can be drawn to and from each.
- Students come into contact with many covalent compounds in everyday life, but they have probably not considered their properties. Give them a selection of covalently bonded compounds, e.g. water, ethanol, iodine, sulfur.
- Ask them to discuss, in groups, any similarities in appearance [dull]. Then they could determine the physical properties of this group of substances experimentally.
- If it is not possible to complete the practical, students could use data books to obtain melting point, boiling point and conductivity information.

Support

- Give students the properties of some simple molecular compounds and a few 'red herrings' that are not the properties. Students could then list the properties of simple molecular compounds in their notes.

Extend

- Students could observe the sublimation of iodine. Put some iodine crystals into a conical flask and seal with a bung. Then heat the flask with running warm water and the iodine will sublime. Then run the flask under cold water and the iodine will solidify again. Ask the students to explain what is happening in terms of intermolecular forces.
  Safety: Be aware of broken glass (if the flask is dropped) and do not allow the students to touch iodine as it will stain their skin.

Plenaries

Stand by – Ask for a volunteer to stand in the centre of the classroom. The volunteer should make a statement about simple covalent molecules (either his or her own idea or read from prepared statement cards). The rest of the class decide how much they agree with this statement. The more they agree, the closer they should stand to the person who spoke. *(5 minutes)*

Summarise – Ask the students to summarise the physical properties of simple molecular compounds and give brief reasons for them in a bullet-point format. *(10 minutes)*

Practical support

Conductivity

Equipment and materials required

Beaker, water, carbon electrodes, lamp, power pack, wires, ethanol CLEAPSS Hazcard 40A – highly/flammable/harmful, solid wax pieces.

Details

Half-fill a beaker with water and put in the carbon electrodes. Set up a simple series circuit with a lamp and power pack, to see if the liquid conducts. Repeat the experiment with ethanol and solid wax pieces.

Safety: Keep ethanol away from any naked flames.

Melting and boiling points

Equipment and materials required

Boiling tubes, boiling-tube rack, boiling-tube holder, Bunsen burner and safety equipment, thermometer, water, wax, eye protection.

Details

Ask students to predict whether covalent compounds have low or high melting/boiling points and why they think this. Get the students to prepare a results table.

They need to put a small piece of wax into a boiling tube and heat it in a blue flame, noting the temperature at which the wax begins to melt. They then put about a 1 cm depth of water into a boiling tube and heat in a blue Bunsen flame, noting the temperature of boiling.

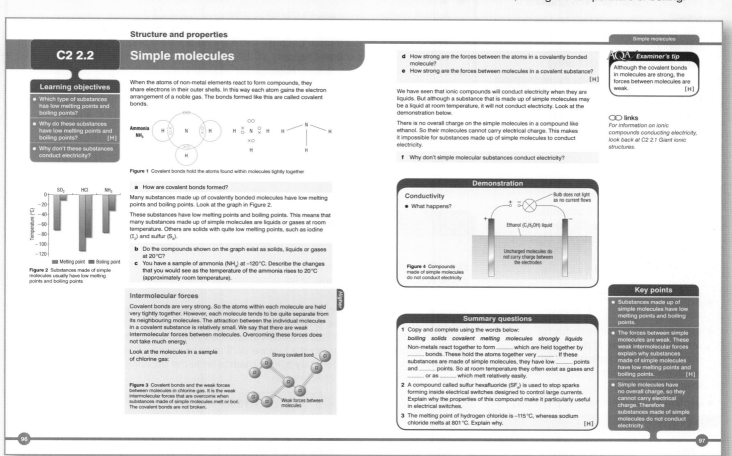

Further teaching suggestions

Displaying data

- Information from data books including databases such as the CD-ROM *RSC Data Book* could be used to get melting point/boiling point/conductivity information. The data for a particular group of covalent compounds could be collected and students could represent the data in a bar chart format.

Ice and water

- Students could find out how the intermolecular forces between water molecules make ice less dense than liquid water.

Answers to in-text questions

a By sharing pairs of electrons.

b gases

c It would be a solid to start with but at about −80 °C, it would melt into a liquid. Then at about −35 °C, it would boil to form ammonia gas. At 20 °C, it remains a gas.

d very strong

e Weak (compared with the forces between atoms held together by a covalent bond).

f The molecules have no overall electric charge to carry the electric current.

Summary answers

1 molecules, covalent, strongly, melting (boiling), boiling (melting), liquids, solids

2 It is a (simple) molecular substance so it doesn't conduct electricity.

3 In sodium chloride, to separate the oppositely charged sodium and chloride ions requires a lot of energy to overcome the strong electrostatic forces of attraction operating in every direction. In hydrogen chloride, there are only weak forces of attraction between individual HCl molecules, so they require far less energy to separate them. (No covalent bonds are broken in the process of melting.)

C2 2.3

Giant covalent structures

Learning objectives

Students should learn that:

- some of the physical properties of substances with giant covalent structures
- why diamond is hard and graphite is slippery
- why graphite conducts electricity [HT only]
- what fullerenes are. [HT only]

Learning outcomes

Most students should be able to:

- list examples of substances with giant covalent structures
- recognise giant covalent structures
- state the physical properties of graphite and diamond
- explain some physical properties of diamond and graphite, such as melting point and hardness, in terms of their structures.

Some students should also be able to:

- explain in detail what a giant covalent structure is
- explain why graphite conducts electricity in terms of delocalised electrons and its softness in terms of weak intermolecular forces between layers [HT only]
- explain what a fullerene is. [HT only]

Support

- Give students diagrams of the structures of diamond and graphite. On a separate sheet include the labels for the diagram and encourage the students to annotate their work.

Extend

- Ask students to find out other examples of giant covalent structures, e.g. silicon dioxide and fullerenes. They should find out and draw a diagram of the structure and annotate the diagram to explain its properties in terms of the structure.

AQA / Specification link-up: Chemistry C2.2

- Atoms that share electrons can also form giant structures or macromolecules. Diamond and graphite (forms of carbon) and silicon dioxide (silica) are examples of giant covalent structures (lattices) of atoms. All the atoms in these structures are linked to other atoms by strong covalent bonds and so they have very high melting points. [C2.2.3 a)]
- In diamond, each carbon atom forms four covalent bonds with other carbon atoms in a giant covalent structure, so diamond is very hard. [C2.2.3 b)]
- In graphite, each carbon atom bonds to three others, forming layers. The layers are free to slide over each other because there are no covalent bonds between the layers and so graphite is soft and slippery. [C2.2.3 c)]
- In graphite, one electron from each carbon atom is delocalised. These delocalised electrons allow graphite to conduct heat and electricity. [C2.2.3 d)] [HT only]
- Carbon can also form fullerenes with different numbers of carbon atoms. Fullerenes can be used for drug delivery into the body, in lubricants, as catalysts, and in nanotubes for reinforcing materials, e.g. in tennis rackets. [C2.2.3 e)] [HT only]
- Relate the properties of substances to their uses. [C2.2]
- Suggest the type of structure of a substance given its properties. [C2.2]

Lesson structure

Starters

List – Show students different images of diamonds – in the raw state, in jewellery and on a saw or drill. Ask the students to list different uses of diamonds and then ask for a few suggestions. *(5 minutes)*

Word search – Give students a word search about covalent bonding; however do not include the list of words. Encourage students to think about the topic and use the double-page spread in the Student Book to work out which words they should be finding. Support students by using only the key words that have been written in bold in the Student Book. Extend students by asking them to write the definitions for each of the words in the word search. *(10 minutes)*

Main

- Although graphite and diamond are both carbon, they have completely different structures. Give students some graphite to handle (this may be a bit messy!) and if it is possible, samples of diamonds to study. You may wish to allow students to investigate the melting point and solubility as detailed in practical support for C2.2 Simple molecules. Brainstorm the different properties of each of these materials, but explain they are the same element.

- Foundation candidates need to recognise and describe a macromolecule limited to silicon dioxide, carbon and diamond. Higher Tier students also need to be able to explain the properties of diamond, graphite and fullerenes based on their structures and give some uses of fullerenes.

- Ask students to make a poster to contrast the properties of these two substances and explain them in terms of their structures.

- Students could use the Student Book for information to create an A-map about giant covalent structures. They should select three colours. In the centre of the page, in one colour only, they should write the key phrase 'Giant covalent structures' and draw a small image that might help them to remember this. This colour is then not used again. The second colour is then used to create four long, wavy lines. Following the contour of the line, the student should write 'formation', 'graphite', 'diamond' and 'fullerene' on separate lines, each including an image. Each idea is then added to, with a third colour, again with wavy lines. Each line again should contain key words or phrases to summarise that branch of thought, and include an image to help the student remember. Encourage the students to complete one branch before moving to the next.

Plenaries

Explain – Split the students into pairs, and give them a pack of cards with key terms on it: 'graphite', 'diamond', 'silicon dioxide', 'delocalised electrons' [**HT only**], 'lattice'. The cards should be face down in front of the group. Each student in turn should take a card and try to explain the key term, but the guesser must draw a labelled diagram to match the key term. *(5 minutes)*

Models – Show the students molecular models of diamond and graphite. Ask them to list the similarities and differences. Ask for a volunteer to write them on the board. Then, through questions and answers, build up bullet points on the board. Support students by giving them a list of different statements, and they have to decide which is a similarity and which a difference. Volunteers could come to the board and write the statements into a table. Extend students by including different fullerene structures, e.g. buckminsterfullerene and nanotubes. [**HT only**] *(10 minutes)*

Answers to in-text questions

a giant covalent (lattice)

b High melting and boiling points, hard, insoluble in water.

c delocalised (free) electrons

Structure and properties

Giant covalent structures

C2 2.3 Giant covalent structures ⓚ

Learning objectives

- How do substances with giant covalent structures behave?
- Why is diamond hard and graphite slippery?
- Why can graphite conduct electricity? [H]
- What are fullerenes? [H]

AQA Examiner's tip

Giant covalent structures are held together by covalent bonds throughout the lattice.

Figure 2 Hard, shiny and transparent – diamonds make beautiful jewellery

⁇ Did you know …?

Diamond is the hardest natural substance that we know. Artificial diamonds can be made by heating pure carbon to very high temperatures under enormous pressures. 'Industrial diamonds' made like this are used in the drill bits oil companies use when drilling for oil.

Most covalently bonded substances are made up of individual molecules. However, a few form very different structures. These do not have a relatively small number of atoms in simple molecules. They form huge networks of atoms held together by covalent bonds. We call these **giant covalent structures**. They are sometimes called **macromolecules**.

Substances such as diamond, graphite and silicon dioxide (silica) have giant covalent structures.

Figure 1 The structures of diamond and silicon dioxide (silica) continue in all directions

Diamond   Silicon dioxide (SiO₂)

All the atoms in these giant lattices are held in position by strong covalent bonds. Both diamond and silicon dioxide are examples. This gives them some very special properties. They are very hard, have high melting and boiling points, and are insoluble in water. Diamond is exceptionally hard. All its carbon atoms each form four strong covalent bonds.

a What do we call the structures which contain many millions of atoms joined together by a network of covalent bonds?

b What kind of physical properties do these substances have?

We don't always find carbon as diamonds. Another form is graphite (well known for its use in pencil 'lead'). In graphite, carbon atoms are only bonded to three other carbon atoms. They form hexagons which are arranged in giant layers. There are no covalent bonds between the layers. So the layers can slide over each other easily. It's a bit like playing cards sliding off a pack of cards. This makes graphite a soft material that feels slippery.

Figure 3 The giant structure of graphite. When you write with a pencil, some layers of carbon atoms slide off the 'lead' and are left on the paper.

Graphite

Bonding in graphite

There are only relatively weak intermolecular forces between the layers in graphite, so they can slide over each other quite easily. The carbon atoms in graphite's layers are arranged in hexagons. So each carbon atom forms three strong covalent bonds (see Figure 3). Carbon atoms have four electrons in their outer shell available for bonding. This leaves one spare outer electron on each carbon atom.

This electron is free to move along the layers of carbon atoms. We call the free electrons found in graphite **delocalised electrons**. They behave rather like the electrons in a metallic structure.

These free electrons allow graphite to conduct electricity. Diamond – and most other covalent substances – cannot conduct electricity.

c What type of electrons enable graphite to conduct electricity?

Fullerenes

Apart from diamond and graphite, there are other different structures that carbon atoms can form. In these structures the carbon atoms join together to make large cages which can have all sorts of shapes. Chemists have made shapes looking like balls, onions, tubes, doughnuts, corkscrews and cones! They are all built up of hexagonal rings of carbon atoms.

Chemists discovered carbon's ability to behave like this in 1985. We call the large carbon molecules containing these cage-like structures fullerenes. Scientists can now place other molecules inside these carbon cages. This has exciting possibilities, including the delivery of drugs to specific parts of the body. They are sure to become very important in nanoscience applications, for example as catalysts and lubricants.

Figure 4 The first fullerene to be discovered contained 60 carbon atoms, but chemists can now make giant fullerenes which contain many thousands of carbon atoms

⊙⊙ links
For information about delocalised electrons, look back at C2 1.5 Metals.

⊙⊙ links
For more information on nanoscience, see C2 2.6 Nanoscience.

Key points

- Some covalently bonded substances have giant structures. These substances have high melting points and boiling points.

- Graphite contains giant layers of covalently bonded carbon atoms. However, there are no covalent bonds between the layers. This means they can slide over each other, making graphite soft and slippery. The atoms in diamond have a different structure and cannot slide like this. So diamond is a very hard substance.

- Graphite can conduct electricity because of the delocalised electrons along its layers. [H]

- As well as diamond and graphite, carbon also exists as fullerenes which can form large cage-like structures based on hexagonal rings of carbon atoms. [H]

Summary questions

1 Copy and complete using the words below:
atoms boiling carbon hard high covalent layers slide soft
Giant covalent structures contain many .... joined by covalent bonds. They have .... melting points and .... points. Diamond is a very .... substance because the .... atoms in it are held strongly to each other. However, graphite is .... because there are .... of atoms which can .... over each other. They can do this because there are no .... bonds between its layers.

2 Graphite is sometimes used to reduce the friction between two surfaces that are rubbing together. How does it do this?

3 Explain in detail why graphite can conduct electricity but diamond cannot. [H]

98   99

Further teaching suggestions

The hardness of pencils

- Graphite is used in pencil leads. Encourage students to research how the different levels of hardness (e.g. H and HB) are achieved.

Developments in carbon

- Fullerenes are a new and exciting class of carbon allotropes. Students could research into their discovery and development and create a timeline. This could include names of important scientists who work in their field of research, and diagrams of the macromolecules.
  Students could find a use for graphite and explain which property makes it suitable for this use.
  Life Gem is a company that offers to cremate pets and humans in a special way, which turns them into diamonds. Encourage students to use the internet to look up this idea. However, be sensitive to the emotional development of students in your class especially if they are recently bereaved.

Sand

- Sand is mainly silicon dioxide and has a macrostructure. You may wish to give students some samples of sand and allow them to investigate the properties using the same equipment as in 'Practical support' 'C2.2 Simple molecules'.

Summary answers

1 atoms, high, boiling, hard, carbon, soft, layers, slide, covalent

2 The graphite is used to coat the two surfaces. As they rub together, the layers of atoms in the graphite slip over each other, reducing the friction.

3 Graphite can conduct electricity because of the delocalised (free) electrons in its structure. These arise because each carbon is only bonded to three other carbon atoms. This leaves one electron to become delocalised. However, in diamond, all four outer electrons on each carbon atom are used in covalent bonding, so there are no delocalised electrons.

C2 2.4

Giant metallic structures

Learning objectives

Students should learn:

- why metals can be bent and shaped
- why alloys are harder than pure metals
- why metals can conduct electricity and energy/heat [HT only]
- the shape of memory alloys.

Learning outcomes

Most students should be able to:

- state the physical properties of metals
- suggest which property of a metal makes it suitable for a specific job
- state a definition of an alloy
- explain why metals can be bent into different shapes
- explain what a shape memory alloy is and give an example.

Some students should also be able to:

- explain why metals conduct electricity and energy in terms of delocalised electrons in their structures. [HT only]

Answers to in-text questions

a The layers of atoms can slide over each other when force is applied.

b By delocalised electrons from the outer energy levels of the metal atoms.

c Through the delocalised electrons, which are able to move through the giant metallic lattice.

Support

- Give students a diagram of the structure of a metal crystal and statements that can be used to annotate the diagram to explain the model. Extend students by giving them information about the properties of metals, explaining these in terms of the structure. Students can then complete a 'cut-and-stick' activity to label the diagram fully.

Extend

- Ask students to find out some other models of metallic structure such as molecular models and computer modelling. Students can then evaluate the different models. They should notice that different models are more appropriate for explaining certain properties of metals.

AQA Specification link-up: Chemistry C2.2

- Metals conduct heat and electricity because of the delocalised electrons in their structures. *[C2.2.4 a)]* **[HT only]**
- The layers of atoms in metals are able to slide over each other and so metals can be bent and shaped. *[C2.2.4 b)]*
- Alloys are usually made from two or more different metals. The different sized atoms of the metals distort the layers in the structure, making it more difficult for them to slide over each other and so make alloys harder than pure metals. *[C2.2.4 c)]*
- Shape memory alloys can return to their original shape after being deformed, e.g. Nitinol used in dental braces. *[C2.2.4 d)]*
- Relate the properties of substances to their uses. *[C2.2]*
- Suggest the type of structure of a substance given its properties. *[C2.2]*

Lesson structure

Starters

Smart demonstration – Obtain a comedy spoon from a joke shop. These are made from a shape memory alloy. When you submerge them into warm water, they change from looking like 'normal' teaspoons to twisted spoons. Demonstrate this action in a glass beaker of warm water, asking a student to stir. When the spoon has become twisted, ask the students to try to explain what has happened. *(5 minutes)*

Flash boards – Give the students A4 whiteboards (or laminated paper), a washable pen and eraser. Ask them to draw an electronic diagram of a metal of their choice and then hold their answers up to you [these should be dot and cross diagrams]. Support students by encouraging them to use their Student Books to help them or to look at other people's answers and the teacher's response. They can then draw a diagram of a metal structure in a solid (linking back to the particle model in KS3). Extend students by asking them to merge the two diagrams to form a model of metallic bonding [**HT only**] (as shown in the Student Book, C2 1.5 Metals). *(10 minutes)*

Main

- Metals are used in everyday life but often students do not consider which properties make them useful for certain jobs. Give the students adverts or catalogues to look through. Ask them to pick items that use metals and cut them out. They could then make a poster using these items, explaining which part is metal. Students could explain the useful property in terms of metallic bonding. It is important that each poster contains an example of a metal being ductile, a metal being malleable and a shape-memory alloy. Higher Tier students should also include an example of a metal conducting heat and a metal conducting electricity.

- Metal properties can be modelled in a variety of ways such as using equal-sized polystyrene balls, built up layer by layer. Show the students any pre-made molecular models that the school may have. Soap bubbles can be used to represent metal atoms and show ductility and malleability. Adding a different-sized bubble models an alloy.

- Higher Tier students should then explain their results relating the model to metallic bonding.

Plenary

'Circle of truth' – This is an interactive, self-marking exercise designed to be used on an interactive whiteboard. To create this activity, open board-specific interactive whiteboard software, or PowerPoint. Firstly, in a text box, type in the title 'Which are properties of metals?' In a small font size, and in separate text boxes, write wrong answers, e.g. 'dull', 'brittle' and 'insulator'. Then draw a circle. You may wish to add the text 'circle of truth' and group the objects. This circle should hide the previously written text, i.e. the wrong answers. Then, in separate text boxes write the correct answers: 'can be drawn out into wires', 'can be hammered into shapes', 'conductor of electricity', 'conductor of energy' and 'high melting point'. To use this activity, ask the students for volunteers to come to the board and suggest an answer to the question [Which are the properties of metals?]. They should then drag the circle to their answer. If they are correct, the answer is still visible; if it is incorrect, then the circle will cover the answer. You can make the questions easier to support students or include higher level concepts to extend students (using Bloom's taxonomy to determine the level of questioning). *(5 minutes)*

Practical support

Blowing bubbles

Equipment and materials required
Petri dish, pointed end of a dropping pipette, dropping pipette, soap solution, rubber tubing to connect to gas tap.

Details
Students should blow similar-sized bubbles into the Petri dish using the pipette. They observe and then blow different sized bubbles using a normal dropping pipette and observe.

You may wish to set up a flexicam or digital camera and connect to a digital projector or a TV. Then focus on the 'bubble raft' experiment. Using the image you can then explain how this experiment relates to the structure of metals.

Safety: Take care when using gas to make bubbles, it is flammable.

Structure and properties

C2 2.4 Giant metallic structures ⓚ

Learning objectives
- Why can we bend and shape metals?
- Why are alloys harder than pure metals?
- Why do metals allow electricity and energy pass through them? [H]
- What are shape memory alloys?

Figure 1 Drawing copper out into wires depends on being able to make the layers of metal atoms slide easily over each other

Iron

Alloy

Figure 2 The atoms in pure iron are arranged in layers which can easily slide over each other. In alloys the layers cannot slide so easily because atoms of other elements change the regular structure.

We can hammer and bend metals into different shapes, and draw them out into wires. This is because the layers of atoms in a pure metal are able to slide easily over each other.

The atoms in a pure metal, such as iron, are held together in giant metallic structures. The atoms are arranged in closely-packed layers. Because of this regular arrangement, the atoms can slide over one another quite easily. This is why pure iron is soft and easily shaped.

a Why can metals be bent, shaped and pulled out into wires when forces are applied? [H]

Alloys are usually mixtures of metals. However, most steels contain iron with controlled amounts of carbon, a non-metal, mixed in its structure. So there are different sizes of atoms in an alloy. This makes it more difficult for the layers in the metal's giant structure to slide over each other. So alloys are harder than the pure metals used to make them. This is shown in Figure 2.

Practical

Making models of metals

Tube connected to gas tap
Fine-pointed tube
Plastic container with soap solution
A regular arrangement of bubble 'atoms'

We can make a model of the structure of a metal by blowing small bubbles on the surface of soap solution to represent atoms.

- Why are models useful in science?

A larger bubble 'atom' has a big effect on the arrangement around it

Metal cooking utensils are used all over the world, because metals are good conductors of heat. Wherever we generate electricity, it passes through metal wires to where it is needed. That's because metals are also good conductors of electricity.

Explaining the properties of metals

The positive ions in a metal's giant structure are held together by a sea of delocalised electrons. These electrons are a bit like 'glue'. Their negative charge between the positively charged ions holds the ions in position.

However, unlike glue, the electrons are able to move throughout the whole giant lattice. Because they can move around and hold the metal ions together at the same time, the delocalised electrons enable the lattice to distort. When struck, the metal atoms can slip past one another without breaking up the metal's structure.

b How are metal atoms held together?

Metals are good conductors of heat and electricity because the delocalised electrons can flow through the giant metallic lattice. The electrical current and heat are transferred quickly through the metal by the free electrons.

c Why do metals conduct electricity and heat so well?

Shape memory alloys

Some alloys have a very special property. Like all metals they can be bent (or **deformed**) into different shapes. The difference comes when you heat them up. They then return to their original shape all by themselves.

We call these metals **shape memory alloys**, which describes the way they behave. They seem to 'remember' their original shape!

We can use the properties of shape memory alloys in many ways, for example in health care. Doctors treating a badly broken bone can use alloys to hold the bones in place while they heal. They cool the alloy before it is wrapped around the broken bone. When it heats up again the alloy goes back to its original shape. This pulls the bones together and holds them while they heal.

Dentists have also made braces to pull teeth into the right position using this technique.

Figure 3 Metals are essential in our lives – the delocalised electrons mean that they are good conductors of both energy and electricity

∞ links
For more about the bonding in metals, look back at C2 1.5 Metals.

Figure 4 This dental brace pulls the teeth into the right position as it warms up. It is made of a shape memory alloy called nitinol. It is an alloy of nickel and titanium.

Summary questions

1 Copy and complete using the words below:
delocalised electricity energy heat shape slide
The positively charged .... in metals are held together by .... electrons. These also allow the layers to .... over each other so that the metal's .... can be changed. They also allow the metal to conduct .... and .... [H]

2 **a** Use your knowledge of metal structures to explain how adding larger metal atoms to a metallic lattice can make the metal harder.
b What is a shape memory alloy?

3 Explain how a dental brace made out of nitinol is more effective than a brace made out of a traditional alloy.

4 Explain why metals are good conductors of heat and electricity. [H]

Key points
- We can bend and shape metals because the layers of atoms (or ions) in a giant metallic structure can slide over each other.
- Delocalised electrons in metals enable electricity and heat to pass through the metal easily. [H]
- If a shape memory alloy is deformed, it can return to its original shape on heating.

Further teaching suggestions

Arrangement of atoms
- Metal atoms stack in different layers, e.g. ABAB or ABCABC. Encourage students to find out different atom arrangements in different metals. You may want to use polystyrene balls or computer animations to show how the atoms can slide over each other.

Using metals
- Some metals are more useful for certain jobs, but substitutes are used, e.g. silver is the best metal electrical conductor, but it degrades easily, so other metals, e.g. gold, are used in satellites. Ask students to find other interesting uses and facts about metals.

Smart materials
- Students could find out what a smart material is. They could then find out examples of shape memory alloys, and list their properties and some of their uses. Making metal crystals: You may wish to make metal crystals as detailed in C2 1.5 'Bonding in metals'.

Testing metals
- You may wish to allow students to test the properties of metals. Give them samples of metals such as metal wires (without insulation), metal rods and metal sheets. The Design and Technology department may have some off-cuts that could be used. Encourage students to look at the metal using a hand lens. Flex the material and use a simple series circuit to test conductivity. You can use data tables to find other information such as melting point, boiling point and tensile strength. Students could work in groups to make a sugar paper poster displaying their results in a variety of different forms such as chart, graphs, tables and prose.

Summary answers

1 ions, delocalised, slide, shape, energy (electricity), electricity (energy)

2 **a** This helps to stop the layers of metal atoms sliding over each other.
b A metal which (when it gets deformed) will return to its original shape on heating.

3 The brace made out of shape memory metal can be designed to fit easily, then more pressure can be applied once warmed up in the mouth. A traditional metal would need more adjustments by a dentist to have the same effect.

4 The delocalised electrons in their structures carry the charge through a metal when it conducts electricity, and the energy through it when it conducts heat.

C2 2.5

The properties of polymers

Learning objectives

Students should learn:
- that the properties of polymers depend on their monomers
- that changing reaction conditions changes the polymers that are made
- the properties of the two classes of polymers (thermosetting and thermosoftening).

Learning outcomes

Most students should be able to:
- state that the monomers used to make a polymer will affect its properties
- give an example of a polymer whose properties differ when it is formed in different conditions
- explain why a given polymer is fit for a purpose
- recall a definition of thermosetting and thermosoftening polymers and give an example of each
- explain how cross linking in thermosetting plastics stops them from melting.

Some students should also be able to:
- explain how changing the reaction conditions changes the properties of the polymer
- explain how the intermolecular forces between the polymer molecules in thermosoftening plastics affect their properties. [HT only]

Answers to in-text questions

a In a tangled web.
b LD – low density; HD – high density.

Support

- Give students two polymers – one thermosetting and one thermosoftening – to complete the practicals.

Extend

- Ask students how intermolecular forces affect the properties of a polymer. Students could be given different examples of polymers, showing part of their structural formulae (some branched chain, some with cross links, some with different functional groups). Then give students a property, e.g. melting point, and ask them to order the structures from low to high melting point, and use the structures to suggest why they have chosen that order.

AQA Specification link-up: Chemistry C2.2

- The properties of polymers depend on what they are made from and the conditions under which they are made. For example, low density (LD) and high density (HD) poly(ethene) are produced using different catalysts and reaction conditions. *[C2.2.5 a)]*
- Thermosoftening polymers consist of individual, tangled polymer chains. Thermosetting polymers consist of polymer chains with cross-links between them so that they do not melt when they are heated. *[C2.2.5 b)]*
- Suggest the type of structure of a substance given its properties. *[C2.2]*
  Controlled Assessment: AS4.3 Collect primary and secondary data. *[AS4.3.1 a)]*

Lesson structure

Starters

Define – Ask the students to use the Student Book to find out what the two groups of polymers are and what property is used to distinguish between them. [Thermosoftening polymers can be reheated to become pliable and can be remoulded, whereas thermosetting polymers will eventually char.] *(5 minutes)*

Card sort – Give the students a pack of cards that has sets of information about poly(ethene), nylon, PVC and PTFE. The cards should be sorted into sets of three for each polymer. These would consist of the structural formula of the monomer, the structural formula of the polymer, and the final card would have the name of the polymer classified into thermosoftening/thermosetting and a use. Students could then arrange the cards into a table and copy it into their book. You could support students by only giving them the cards for polyethene and nylon (both of these are covered in this double-page spread). You could extend them by giving them the properties of each polymer, and they have to suggest a use. This activity links well with C1 5.2 'Making polymers from alkenes'. *(10 minutes)*

Main

- Students could be given a sample of a thermosetting and a thermosoftening polymer and compare their properties during heating in a fume cupboard. They could also try to remould the thermosoftening polymer. Results could then be recorded as a cartoon strip, drawing images to represent different stages of the practical. Below each image, the students could be encouraged to explain the observations in terms of intermolecular forces of attraction.

- Students could experiment with the consistency of slime made with PVA glue (poly(ethenol)). The polymer strands are H-bond cross linked with borate groups. This cross linking is not permanent and most of the space in the gel is taken up with water molecules. This makes it a pliable polymer. Adding different amounts of borax changes the number of cross links. The more there are, the stiffer the polymer. Ask the students to design and conduct an experiment to find out the effect of adding different amounts of borax to PVA glue. This relates to the Controlled Assessment [AS4.3.1] in which students are required to use data to develop hypotheses.

Plenaries

Classify – Give the students a number of examples of plastic items and ask them to sort them into thermosoftening or thermosetting. For example, *thermosoftening*: a chocolate box tray, nylon clothes, student's toys, plastic beakers; *thermosetting*: epoxy resin glues, electrical equipment, pan handles. Support students by writing a definition of thermosoftening and thermosetting on the board so that students can easily refer to them. Extend students by asking them to explain why it is important that the polymer is thermosetting/thermosoftening for that particular function. *(5 minutes)*

Guess the word – Separate the class into groups of six and give out a pack of cards. Each card should be like name cards for a party with one of the following key words written on: 'thermosoftening, thermosetting, poly(ethene), LD, HD, polymer, monomer'. The students should not look at the card that they have been given, but secure it so that it faces the rest of their group. They must then ask questions, to which the others can only answer 'yes/no' in order to guess their key word. *(10 minutes)*

Practical support

Making a polymer

Equipment and materials required

A 100 cm³ measuring cylinder, 250 cm³ beaker, dropping pipettes, hot plate, stirring rod, 4 g PVA glue, 4 g borax (toxic), eye protection, (food colouring).

Details

Before the lesson, make up a solution of borax, with 100 cm³ of warm water in a beaker in a fume cupboard with the fan off. The solution may need to be warmed for it to fully dissolve. Put 100 cm³ of water into the 250 cm³ beaker and heat gently. Add 4 g of PVA slowly, while stirring. The mixture must not boil. When all the PVA has dissolved, remove it from the heat, and add a few drops of the borax solution and stir. If too much borax is added, the polymer will be brittle, if not enough is added the slime will be runny. Food colourings can be added to make slime of different colours. This should be done before the borax is added. In time, the slime will dry out. Students can handle the slime, but should wash their hands afterwards, and eye protection should be worn throughout.

Safety: Students should wear eye protection when using borax solution. CLEAPSS Hazcard 14 Borax – toxic.

Heating different plastics

Equipment and materials required

Samples of a thermosoftening and thermosetting plastic (flammable and toxic fumes may be released), tin lid, tripod, Bunsen burner and safety equipment, glass rod, eye protection.

Details

Set up the Bunsen burner in a fume cupboard. Put a sample of each plastic on the same tin lid, and position it over the Bunsen burner on a tripod. Heat gently, and observe any changes. Then, as the thermosoftening plastic becomes pliable, touch it with a glass rod and gently pull away, drawing a thread of remoulded plastic. Then heat more strongly, and the thermoset should begin to combust. (Be aware that asthmatics may be affected by any fumes that escape.)

Structure and properties

C2 2.5 The properties of polymers

Learning objectives

- Do the properties of polymers depend on the monomers we use?
- Can changing reaction conditions modify the polymers that are made?
- What are thermosetting and thermosoftening polymers?

As you know, we can make **polymers** from chemicals made from crude oil. Small molecules called monomers join together to make much bigger molecules called polymers. As the monomers join together they produce a tangled web of very long chain molecules. Poly(ethene) is an example.

The properties of a polymer depend on:

- the monomers used to make it, and
- the conditions we choose to carry out the reaction.

a How are polymer chains arranged in poly(ethene)?

Different monomers

The polymer chains in nylon are made from two different monomers. One monomer has acidic groups at each end. The other has basic groups at each end. The polymer they make is very different from the polymer chains made from hydrocarbon monomers, such as ethene. So the monomers used make a big difference to the properties of the polymer made. (See Figures 1 and 2.)

Different reaction conditions

There are two types of poly(ethene). One is called high density (HD) and the other low density (LD) poly(ethene). Both are made from ethene monomers but they are formed under different conditions.

Polymer chains

LD poly(ethene) or LDPE   HD poly(ethene) or HDPE

Figure 3 The branched chains of LD poly(ethene) cannot pack as tightly together as the straighter chains in HD poly(ethene), giving them different properties

Using very high pressures and a trace of oxygen, ethene forms LD poly(ethene). The polymer chains are branched and they can't pack closely together.

Using a catalyst at 50 °C and a slightly raised pressure, ethene makes HD poly(ethene). This is made up of straighter poly(ethene) molecules. They can pack more closely together than branched chains. The HD poly(ethene) has a higher softening temperature and is stronger than LD poly(ethene).

b What do 'LD' and 'HD' stand for in the names of the two types of poly(ethene)?

Figure 1 The forces between the molecules in poly(ethene) are relatively weak as there are no strong covalent bonds (cross links) between the molecules. This means that this plastic softens fairly easily when heated.

Figure 2 Nylon is very much stronger than poly(ethene). This climber's life depends on nylon's high-tensile strength. Nylon can withstand large forces without snapping.

Thermosoftening and thermosetting polymers

We can classify polymers by looking at what happens to them when they are heated. Some will soften quite easily. They will reset when they cool down. These are called **thermosoftening polymers**. They are made up of individual polymer chains that are tangled together.

Other polymers do not melt when we heat them. These are called **thermosetting polymers**. These have strong covalent bonds forming 'cross links' between their polymer chains. (See Figure 4.)

The tangled web of polymer chains are relatively easy to separate

Chains fixed together by strong covalent bonds – this is called **cross linking**

Thermosoftening polymer   Thermosetting polymer

Figure 4 Extensive cross linking by covalent bonds between polymer chains makes a thermosetting plastic that is heat-resistant and rigid

Bonding in polymers

The atoms in polymer chains are held together by very strong covalent bonds. This is true for all plastics. But the size of the forces *between* polymer molecules in different plastics can be very different.

In thermosoftening polymers the forces between the polymer chains are weak. When we heat the polymer, these weak intermolecular forces are broken. The polymer becomes soft. When the polymer cools down, the intermolecular forces bring the polymer molecules back together. Then the polymer hardens again. This type of polymer can be remoulded.

However, thermosetting polymers are different. Their monomers make covalent bonds between the polymer chains when they are first heated in order to shape them. These covalent bonds are strong, and they stop the polymer from softening. The covalent 'cross links' between chains do not allow them to separate. Even if heated strongly, the polymer will still not soften. Eventually, the polymer will char at high enough temperatures.

Summary questions

1 Copy and complete using the words below:
   covalent thermosetting tangled cross links
   The polymer chains in thermosoftening polymers form a .... web. The polymer softens at relatively low temperatures. Other polymers have strong .... bonds between their chains which form .... We call these .... polymers.

2 Why do we use thermosetting polymers to make plastic kettles?

3 Polymer A starts to soften at 100 °C while polymer B softens at 50 °C. Polymer C resists heat but eventually starts to char if heated to very high temperatures.
   Explain this using ideas about intermolecular forces. [H]

Practical

Modifying a polymer k

Take some PVA glue ...   ... add a few drops of borax solution

Warm solution of PVA glue

Stir well for about 2 minutes

Slime

The glue becomes slimy because the borax makes the long polymer chains in the glue link together to form a jelly-like substance.

- How could you investigate if the properties of slime depend on how much borax you add?

Figure 5 Electrical sockets are made out of thermosetting plastics. If the plug or wires get hot, the socket will not soften.

Key points

- Monomers affect the properties of the polymers that they produce.
- Changing reaction conditions can also change the properties of the polymer that is produced.
- Thermosoftening polymers will soften or melt easily when heated. Thermosetting polymers will not soften but will eventually char if heated very strongly.

Further teaching suggestions

Flow chart

- You could ask students to create a flow chart to explain how poly(ethene) is made. The flow chart should have one starting point as one type of monomer is used. However, it should branch to show how HDPE and LDPE are made. You could link back to C1 4.2 Fractional distillation and C1 5.1 Cracking to show where the ethene comes from.

Nylon rope trick

- You may wish to complete the nylon rope trick, see Royal Society of Chemistry Classic Experiments.

Poly(ethene)

- Poly(ethene) can be high density (HD) or low density (LD). Each structure has different properties and so different uses. The type of poly(ethene) can be distinguished by comparing whether the sample floats or sinks in 50 : 50 water and ethanol mixture, with LD floating and HD sinking. You may wish to give students a selection of different colours of poly(ethene) pellets or small pieces of the materials and ask them to classify it using this method. It is better to use pellets or small pieces rather than sheets to avoid surface tension effects.

Summary answers

1 tangled, covalent, crosslinks, thermosetting

2 They need to be heated to 100 °C (and possibly above in the case of electrical faults) without melting.

3 Polymer A has stronger intermolecular forces than polymer B. Polymer C has stronger forces than both A and B between its polymer chains. It has covalent cross links between its polymer chains.

C2 2.6

Nanoscience

Learning objectives

Students should learn:
- what nanoscience is
- the potential benefits and risks of nanoscience.

Learning outcomes

Most students should be able to:
- recall a definition of nanoscience
- list advantages and disadvantages of nanoscience.

Some students should also be able to:
- evaluate the benefits and drawbacks of using nanotechnology.

Specification link-up: Chemistry C2.2

- Nanoscience refers to structures that are 1–100 nm in size, of the order of a few hundred atoms. Nanoparticles show different properties to the same materials in bulk and have a high surface area to volume ratio, which may lead to the development of new computers, new catalysts, new coatings, highly selective sensors, stronger and lighter construction materials, and new cosmetics such as sun tan creams and deodorants. [C2.2.6 a)]
- Relate the properties of substances to their uses. [C2.2]
- Evaluate developments and applications of new materials, e.g. nanomaterials, fullerenes and shape memory materials. [C2.2]

Lesson structure

Starters

Show and tell – Place various products that use nanotechnology in a tray, e.g. sun cream, some sticking plasters, self-cleaning glass. Ask students to work in small groups and suggest the connection between the products. Then reveal to the students that these are all examples of the use of nanotechnology. (5 minutes)

Definition – Ask students to use the textbook to find the definitions of nanoscience [the science of really tiny things], nanometer [1×10^{-9} m] and nanoparticles [a particle between 1 and 100 nm]. Support students by giving them both the key words and definitions so that they match them up. Extend students by asking them to definition the key words in prose and a labelled diagram. (10 minutes)

Main

- Split the class into two groups. Explain to the students that they are going to have a debate on the motion 'Nanotechnology should be banned.' Ask half of the class to prepare the 'for' debate and the other half 'against'. You may wish to give group members particular roles to help them work effectively as a team, e.g. speaker, researcher, information recorder or leader. Move around the class and help the students prepare their arguments. You may wish to have a number of resources about nanotechnology around the room open at the right page. Bring the class together and chair the debate.

- Nanotechnology is a very new science. Ask students to research the subject area using secondary sources of information and then make a radio news report. You could record the best news reports as an MP3 file and use them on the virtual learning platform as a revision file.

Plenaries

Key points – Pick famous people (either in the wider world or the school community) and put their names into a bag. Ask for volunteers to come to pick out a name. They should then read the key points in character. (5 minutes)

What do you think? – Ask students to raise their hands if they are 'for' or 'against' nanotechnology. Support students by asking them to work as a class to make a summary table on the board of advantages and disadvantages of nanotechnology. This will distil out the main points before students commit themselves to their decision. Extend students by reading fictitious viewpoints, e.g. Mrs Smith, who has arthritis, thinks that self-cleaning glass is a miracle as she can't easily wash her windows. Ask students to reflect on their thoughts and suggest whether these comments change their minds and why. (10 minutes)

Support

- Give students a table with two columns: 'Advantages' and 'Disadvantages'. They could then be given statements and they sort the statements to help them consider the two sides of the argument.

Extend

- Ask students to find out about developments in the field of nanotechnology. Ask them to consider whether this research should be publicly funded or whether it should be funded through industry only.

Further teaching suggestions

Library
- Your school's library may have cut out newspaper articles about issues such as nanotechnology. You could complete a room swap to the library and use its resources to help students research.

Reflection
- At the start of the lesson, ask students to say or write down whether they think nanotechnology should be banned and why. Then allow them to research the subject, making a list of current and predicted uses. Then ask students to reanswer the question and say whether their minds have been changed and why.

Contrast table
- Students could prepare a table of advantages and disadvantages of nanotechnology. Split the class in half, and ask half of the class to stand in a circle facing outwards. Ask the rest of the class to make a circle around the first group of students, facing inwards. So each student is in a pair. Ask the inner circle to talk for one minute positively about nanotechnology. Then ask the outer circle to talk one minute only negatively about nanotechnology. Ask the students on the outer circle to move one place to the right. Then ask the inner circle students to tell the outer students their thoughts on nanotechnology for one minute and the outer circle does the same for one minute. This activity involves students developing their listening skills and reasoning skills.

Structure and properties

C2 2.6 — Nanoscience

Learning objectives
- What is nanoscience?
- What are the potential benefits and risks associated with nanoscience?

?? Did you know ...?

You can get about a million nanometres across a pin-head, and a human hair is about 80000 nm wide.

Nanoscience is a new and exciting area of science. 'Nano' is a prefix like 'milli' or 'mega'. While 'milli' means 'one-thousandth', 'nano' means 'one thousand-millionth'.

1 nanometre (1 nm) = 1×10^{-9} metres (= 0.000000001 m or a billionth of a metre)

So nanoscience is the science of really tiny things. We are dealing with structures that are just a few hundred atoms in size or even smaller (between 1 and 100 nm in size).

We now know that materials behave very differently at a very tiny scale. Nanoparticles are so tiny that they have a huge surface area for a small volume of material. When we arrange atoms and molecules on a nanoscale, their properties can be truly remarkable.

a How many nanometres make up 1 millimetre?

Nanoscience at work

Here are some uses of nanoscience.
- Glass can be coated with titanium oxide nanoparticles. Sunshine triggers a chemical reaction which breaks down dirt which lands on the window. When it rains the water spreads evenly over the surface of the glass, washing off the broken down dirt.
- Titanium oxide and zinc oxide nanoparticles are also used in modern sun-screens. Scientists can coat nanoparticles of the metal oxide with a coating of silica. The thickness of the silica coating can be adjusted at an atomic level. These coated nanoparticles seem more effective at blocking the Sun's rays than conventional UV absorbers.
- The cosmetics industry is one of the biggest users of this new technology. The nanoparticles in face creams are absorbed deeper into the skin. They are also used in sun tan creams and deodorants.

The delivery of active ingredients in cosmetics can also be applied to medicines. The latest techniques being developed use nanocages of gold to deliver drugs where they need to go in the body. Researchers have found that the tiny gold particles can be injected and absorbed by tumours. Tumours have thin, leaky blood vessels with holes large enough for the gold nanoparticles to pass into. However, they can't get into healthy blood vessels.

When a laser is directed at the tumour the gold nanoparticles absorb energy and warm up. The temperature of the tumour increases enough to change the properties of its proteins but barely warms the surrounding tissue. This destroys the tumour cells without damaging healthy cells.

There is potential to use the gold nanocages to carry cancer-fighting drugs to the tumour at the same time. The carbon nanocages we met in C2 2.3 can also be used to deliver drugs in the body. Incredibly strong, yet light, nanotubes are already being used to reinforce materials (see Figure 3). The new materials are finding uses in sport, such as making very strong but light tennis racquets.

Figure 1 Nanoparticles will save many people from damaged skin and cancers caused by too much UV light

Figure 2 Nanoparticles in cosmetic products can work deeper in the skin

Silver nanoparticles are antibacterial. They also act against viruses and fungi. They are used in sprays to clean operating theatres in hospitals.

Future developments?

Nanotubes are now being developed that can be used as nanowires. This will make it possible to construct incredibly small electronic circuits. Nanotubes can be used to make highly sensitive selective sensors. For example, nanotube sensors have been made that can detect tiny traces of a gas present in the breath of asthmatics before an attack. This will let patients monitor and treat their own condition without having to visit hospital to use expensive machines.

Nanowires would also help to make computers with vastly improved memory capacities and speeds.

Scientists in the US Army are developing nanotech suits – thin, or even spray-on, uniforms which are flexible and tough enough to withstand bullets and blasts. The uniforms would receive aerial views of the battlefield from satellites, transmitted directly to the soldier's brain. There would also be a built-in air conditioning system to keep the body temperature normal. Inside the suit there would be a full range of nanobiosensors that could send medical data back to a medical team.

Possible risks

The large surface area of nanoparticles would make them very effective as catalysts. However, their large surface area also makes them dangerous. If a spark is made by accident, they may cause a violent explosion.

If nanoparticles are used more and more there is also going to be more risk of them finding their way into the air around us. Breathing in tiny particles could damage the lungs. Nanoparticles could enter the bloodstream this way, or from their use in cosmetics, with unpredictable effects. More research needs to be done to find out their effects on health and the environment.

b Why would nanoparticles make very efficient catalysts?

Figure 3 Nanocages can carry drugs inside them and nanotubes can reinforce materials

Activity

Whenever we are faced with a possible development in science there are two possible questions – what *can* we do? And what *should* we do? Look at the ideas about the uses of nanoscience and its future development here. Choose one idea and ask yourself 'what *can* we do and what *should* we do?' Present your answers to the rest of your group

Summary questions

1 What do we mean by 'nanoscience'?

2 In his book *Engines of Creation* K. Eric Drexler speculates that one day we may invent a nanomachine that can reproduce itself. Then the world could be overrun by so-called 'grey goo'. Some people are so worried they have called for a halt in nanoscience research. What are your views?

Key points
- Nanoscience is the study of small particles that are between 1 and 100 nanometres in size.
- Nanoparticles behave differently from the materials they are made from on a large scale.
- New developments in nanoscience are very exciting but will need more research into possible issues that might arise from their increased use.

Answers to in-text questions

a A million.

b They have a very large surface area.

Summary answers

1 The science of the very tiny – studying structures between 1 and 100 nm in size.

2 Students present points for and against in a balanced argument, then draw their own conclusion.

Summary answers

1 a D   **b** A   **c** B   **d** C

2 a Table showing:
Giant covalent: graphite, silicon dioxide.
Giant ionic: magnesium oxide, lithium chloride.
Simple molecular: ammonia, hydrogen bromide.
Giant metallic: cobalt, manganese.

b Ammonia, hydrogen bromide.

c Graphite – it conducts electricity even though it is a giant covalent compound, because the structure contains delocalised electrons.

3 **Example of an advantage** – it can be restored to its original shape if the frame is accidently damaged.
Example of a disadvantage – it will be more expensive than a conventional frame.

4 The ionic compound is sealed in a container with two electrodes and placed in the reactor. It is connected into an electrical warning circuit. If the temperature reaches 800 °C in the reactor the compound will melt, conducting electricity and activating the alarm.

5 Metals and graphite conduct electricity because both contain delocalised (free) electrons that can flow and carry an electric current. Layers of atoms in graphite are held together only weakly by these delocalised electrons, so the layers are able to slide easily over each other, making graphite soft. Although layers of atoms can slide over each other in metals, this does not happen so easily and metals are therefore hard.

6 a i Very small or smaller (not 'small' alone) or a few atoms thick or in range 1 to 100 nm
    ii Sensible idea of passing through smaller gaps, e.g. skin/pores/cells or more easily absorbed.

b Any two from: good at absorbing UV light/radiation, spread more easily, cover better, save money or use less, transparent, less chance of getting skin cancer or stops skin cancer.

c toxic (to cells or specific cells), allow harm/damage/kill cells

---

Structure and properties: C2 2.1–C2 2.6

Summary questions 🄚

1 Match the sentence halves together:

a	Ionic compounds have	A	.... conduct electricity when molten or in solution.
b	Ionic compounds	B	.... held together by strong electrostatic forces.
c	The oppositely charged ions in an ionic compound are	C	.... a giant lattice of ions.
d	Ionic compounds are made of	D	.... high melting points.

2 The table contains data about some different substances:

Substance	Melting point (°C)	Boiling point (°C)	Electrical conductor
cobalt	1495	2870	Good
ammonia	−78	−33	Poor
magnesium oxide	2852	3600	solid – poor liquid – good
manganese	1244	1962	Good
lithium chloride	605	1340	solid – poor liquid – good
silicon dioxide	1610	2230	Poor
hydrogen bromide	−88	−67	Poor
graphite	3652	4827	Good

a Make a table with the following headings:
Giant covalent, Giant ionic, Simple molecules, Giant metallic.
Now write the name of each substance above in the correct column.

b Which substances are gases at 20 °C?

c One of these substances behaves in a slightly different way than its structure suggests. Why?

3 One use of shape memory alloys is to make spectacle frames. Write down **one** advantage and **one** disadvantage of using a shape memory alloy like this.

4 A certain ionic compound melts at exactly 800 °C. A chemical company wants to design a device to activate a warning light and buzzer when the temperature in a chemical reactor rises above 800 °C. Suggest how this ionic compound could be used in an alarm.

5 'Both graphite and metals can conduct electricity – but graphite is soft while metals are not.' Use your knowledge of the different structures of graphite and metals to explain this statement.

6 Read the article about the use of nanoparticles in sun creams.

Sun creams

Many sun creams use nanoparticles. These sun creams are very good at absorbing radiation, especially ultraviolet radiation. Owing to the particle size, the sun creams spread more easily, cover better and save money because you use less. The new sun creams are also transparent, unlike traditional sun creams which are white. The use of nanoparticles is so successful that they are now used in more than 300 sun cream products.

Some sun creams contain nanoparticles of titanium oxide. Normal-sized particles of titanium oxide are safe to put on the skin.

It is thought that nanoparticles can pass through the skin and travel around the body more easily than normal-sized particles. It is also thought that nanoparticles might be toxic to some types of cell, such as skin, bone, brain and liver cells.

a i How is the size of nanoparticles different from normal-sized particles of titanium oxide?
    ii Suggest how the size of nanoparticles might help them to enter the body more easily.

b Give **two** advantages of using nanoparticles in sun creams.

c Why might nanoparticles be dangerous inside the body?

AQA, 2

Practical suggestions

Practicals	AQA	🄚	📖	⚙
Demonstration of heating sulfur and pouring it into cold water to produce plastic sulfur.	✓		✓	
Investigating the properties of ionic compounds, e.g. NaCl: – melting point, conductivity, solubility, use of hand lens to study crystal structure.	✓	✓	✓	
Investigating the properties of covalent compounds: – simple molecules, e.g. wax, methane, hexane – macromolecules, e.g. SiO₂ (sand).	✓	✓	✓	
Investigating the properties of graphite.	✓		✓	
Demonstrations involving shape memory alloys.	✓		✓	
Investigating the properties of metals and alloys: – melting point and conductivity, hardness, tensile strength, flexibility – using models, for example using expanded polystyrene spheres or computer animations to show how layers of atoms slide – making metal crystals by displacement reactions, e.g. copper wire in silver nitrate solution.	✓		✓	
Distinguishing between LD and HD poly(ethene) using 50 : 50 ethanol : water.	✓		✓	
Making slime using different concentrations of poly(ethenol) and borax solutions.	✓		✓	
Investigating the effect of heat on polymers to find which are thermosoftening or thermosetting.	✓		✓	

AQA Examination-style questions

Match each of the substances in the table with a description from the list.

giant covalent   ionic   metal   simple molecule

Substance	Formula	Melting point (°C)	Boiling point (°C)	Does it conduct electricity when liquid?
a	C	3550	4830	No
b	Co	1768	3142	Yes
c	CH₄	−182	−164	No
d	CaCl₂	1055	1873	Yes

(4)

Copper can be hammered into shape. The structure of copper metal can be represented as shown:

a Explain why copper can be hammered into shape. (1)

b Copper can be mixed with zinc to make the alloy called brass. Brass is much harder than copper. Explain why. (2)

c Copper can be mixed with zinc and aluminium to make a shape memory alloy. What is a shape memory alloy? (2)

Choose a word from the list to complete each sentence.

different   identical   smart   thermosoftening   thermosetting

The polymers low-density poly(ethene) (LDPE) and high-density poly(ethene) (HDPE) are made from monomers that are .... The polymers are produced using catalysts and reaction conditions that are .... LDPE melts at 120°C and HDPE melts at 130°C and they have no cross links between the polymer chains so they are both .... polymers. (3)

Chloroethene, C₂H₃Cl, can be polymerised to poly(chloroethene).

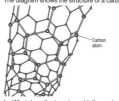

a Explain in terms of its structure why chloroethene is a gas at room temperature. (2)

b Explain in terms of its structure why poly(chloroethene) is a thermosoftening polymer. (2)
[H]

5 The picture shows a copper kettle being heated on a camping stove.

Copper kettle

Camping stove

a In this question you will be assessed on using good English, organising information clearly and using specialist terms where appropriate.

Copper is a good material for making a kettle because it has a high melting point.

Explain why copper, like many other metals, has a high melting point.

You should describe the structure and bonding of a metal in your answer. (6)

b An aeroplane contains many miles of electrical wiring made from copper. This adds to the mass of the aeroplane.

It has been suggested that the electrical wiring made from copper could be replaced by lighter carbon nanotubes.

The diagram shows the structure of a carbon nanotube.

Carbon atom

i What does the term 'nano' tell you about the carbon nanotubes? (1)

ii Like graphite, each carbon atom is joined to three other carbon atoms. Explain why the carbon nanotube can conduct electricity. (2)

AQA, 2010

107

AQA Examination-style answers

1 a giant covalent (1 mark)
  b metal (1 mark)
  c simple molecule (1 mark)
  d ionic (1 mark)

2 a Layers of atoms can slide/move over each other. (1 mark)
  b Zinc atoms are a different size from copper atoms they disrupt the structure, making it more difficult/less able to slide/move. (2 marks)
  c It returns to its original shape, after being deformed or when the temperature changes or when it is heated. (2 marks)

3 identical, different, thermosoftening (3 marks)

4 a Simple molecules or small molecules, weak intermolecular forces or weak attractions between molecules. Therefore it has a low boiling point. (2 marks)
  b There are no bonds/cross-links between polymer molecules or there are weak intermolecular forces/attractions between (polymer) molecules, these weak forces are overcome when the polymer is heated and so it softens/melts. (2 marks)

5 a Marks awarded for this answer will be determined by the Quality of Written Communication (QWC) as well as the standard of the scientific response.

There is a clear and detailed scientific description of why copper has a high melting point including details of the structure and bonding in a metal. The answer shows almost faultless spelling, punctuation and grammar. It is coherent and in an organised, logical sequence. It contains a range of appropriate and relevant specialist terms used accurately. (5–6 marks)

The answer has some structure and the use of specialist terms has been attempted, but not always accurately. There may be some errors in spelling, punctuation and grammar. There is a scientific description. There are some errors in spelling, punctuation and grammar. The answer has some structure and organisation. The use of specialist terms has been attempted, but not always accurately. (3–4 marks)

There is a brief description of the structure of a metal. The spelling, punctuation and grammar are very weak. The answer is poorly organised with almost no specialist terms and/or their use demonstrating a general lack of understanding of their meaning. (1 mark)

No relevant content. (0 marks)

Examples of chemistry points made in the response:
• giant structure/lattice atoms arranged in a regular pattern or in layers
• sea of electrons or delocalised electrons or free electrons
• awareness that outer shell/highest energy level electrons are involved
• positive ions
• (electrostatic) attractions/bonds between electrons and positive ions
• bonds/attractions (between atoms or ions and electrons) are strong
• a lot of energy/heat is needed to break these bonds/attractions.

  b i The tubes are very small (not 'small' on is own), or a few atoms across, or they are 1–100 nm across. (1 mark)
    ii Three electrons in carbon's outer shell are used in bonding, which leaves one electron free to move around or delocalise and carry current or charge. (2 marks)

107

Kerboodle resources

Resources available for this chapter on Kerboodle are:
• Chapter map: Structure and properties
• How Science Works: It's all about the ions (C2 2.1)
• Practical: How does the structure of a substance influence its properties? (C2 2.3)
• Support: Bonds and properties (C2 2.4)
• Extension: Bonds and properties (C2 2.4)
• Bump up your grade: Bonds and properties (C2 2.4)
• How Science Works: In the slime (C2 2.5)
• Webquest: Nanotechnology (C2 2.6)
• Viewpoint: Is small better? (C2 2.6)
• Interactive activity: Structure and properties
• Revision podcast: Giant covalent structures of carbon
• Test yourself: Structure and properties
• On your marks: Structure and properties
• Examination-style questions: Structure and properties
• Answers to examination-style questions: Structure and properties

C2 3.1

The mass of atoms

Learning objectives

Students should learn:

- what atomic number and mass number mean
- the relative masses of subatomic particles
- what isotopes are.

Learning outcomes

Most students should be able to:

- define atomic number and mass number
- use the periodic table to get atomic numbers and mass numbers for any atom and work out the number of each subatomic particle that an atom has
- state a definition of isotopes.

Some students should also be able to:

- compare the physical and chemical properties of isotopes of an element.

Support

- Some students will struggle with the vocabulary used in this topic area. Write a list of key words on to the board so they can use these throughout the lesson. You may wish to further support them by also having the definitions next to each word.

Extend

- Ask students to draw the structure of the two chlorine isotopes (^{35}Cl and ^{37}Cl). They could then try to explain why the relative atomic mass of chlorine is 35.5.

AQA Specification link-up: Chemistry C2.3

- Atoms can be represented as shown in this example:

  Mass number   23

                  Na

  Atomic number   11   [C2.3.1 a)]
- The relative masses of protons, neutrons and electrons ... . [C2.3.1 b)]
- The total number of protons and neutrons in an atom is called its mass number. [C2.3.1 c)]
- Atoms of the same element can have different numbers of neutrons; these atoms are called isotopes of that element. [C2.3.1 d)]

Lesson structure

Starters

True or false – If students agree with these statements they should show a thumbs up sign. If they disagree, their thumbs should point downwards, and if they don't know their thumbs should be horizontal.

- Atoms are charged particles. [False]
- Atoms contain charged particles. [True]
- Electrons are found in energy levels or shells. [True]
- Electrons have a negative charge. [True]
- Protons are in the nucleus of an atom. [True]
- Neutrons are found in shells around the nucleus. [False]

Support students by putting a labelled diagram of the atom on the board for them to refer to. Extend students by asking them to reword the false statements, so that they are true. *(5 minutes)*

Definitions – Give the students the definitions on the board. Students should match each definition with a key word:

- A positive particle in an atom's nucleus. [Proton]
- A neutral particle with a relative mass of 1. [Neutron]
- The subatomic particle that is found in energy levels. [Electron]
- The number of protons in an atom. [Atomic number or Proton number]
- The number of protons and neutrons in an atom. [Mass number]

Students could then be asked to draw a diagram of an atom and label it to demonstrate all these key terms. *(10 minutes)*

Main

- The structure of the atom can be summarised in a spider diagram. Encourage the students to include information about atomic number, mass number, subatomic particles. Students first met the terms 'mass number' and 'atomic number', as well as the structure of the atom in C1 Chapter 1.
- Later in the lesson, this spider diagram could be extended to include isotopes and uses of isotopes.
- Students could be asked to include a key in their diagram. For example, use specific colours for key terms: red – proton, green – neutron, blue – electron, orange – atom, purple – isotope.
- Students need to be able to use the periodic table to work out the number of each subatomic particle in an atom. With a question and answer session, draw out how the periodic table can be used to supply information about an atom.
- Show the students how to calculate the number of each subatomic particle using mass number and proton number.
- Then ask the students to design a table to record the number of each subatomic particle in the first 20 elements. Then ask them to complete their table.
- Introduce the students to isotopes with the examples given in the Student Book.

Plenaries

Association – Split the class into pairs. Students should face their partners. All students on the right should start first, saying a word or phrase about the lesson. Then the next person says another fact/key word based on the lesson. The activity swaps between partners until all the facts are exhausted. If a student hesitates or repeats previous statements, then they have lost the association game. *(5 minutes)*

Think – On the board, write the symbol for carbon-12 and carbon-14 isotopes. Ask the students to use the periodic table and their knowledge of isotopes to list all the similarities between the atoms and all their differences. [Similarities – same number and arrangement of electrons, same number of protons in the nucleus, same chemical properties, same atomic number. Differences – different number of neutrons in the nucleus, different mass numbers, different physical properties.] You could support students by using hydrogen isotopes and having the structure, including the subatomic particles of the three isotopes on the board. Extend students by asking them to draw the structures of the isotopes of carbon. They could be asked to find out about the third isotope of carbon: carbon-13 and also draw this structure. *(10 minutes)*

Answers to in-text questions

a Number of protons.

b Mass of proton = mass of neutron.

c Mass of electron is much less than the mass of a proton or neutron.

d Number of neutrons = mass number minus atomic number.

e Isotopes are atoms of the same element with different numbers of neutrons (or words to that effect).

f Tritium, ^3_1H.

Further teaching suggestions

Isotope article
- Students could use the internet to research some uses of isotopes, e.g. in medicine. Students could then use this information to make a magazine article for use in a teenage science magazine.

Heavy water
- Students could research 'heavy water', D_2O, and how its properties differ from normal water. Students should find out

that isotopes have the same chemical properties because they have the same number and arrangement of electrons, but different physical properties because their masses are different.

Isotope pairs
- Students could find an example of an isotope pair. Ask them to write down the symbols, with their proton and mass numbers and state the numbers of subatomic particles in the atoms of each isotope.

How much?

C2 3.1

The mass of atoms Ⓚ

Learning objectives
- What is an atom's atomic number and mass number?
- What are the relative masses of protons, neutrons and electrons?
- What are isotopes?

⁇ Did you know …?

It would take 1836 electrons to have the same mass as a single proton.

As you know, an atom consists of a nucleus containing positively charged protons, together with neutrons which have no charge. The negatively charged electrons are arranged in energy levels (shells) around the nucleus.

Every atom has the same number of electrons orbiting its nucleus as it has protons in its nucleus. The number of protons in an atom is called its **atomic number**.

The mass of a proton and a **neutron** is the same. This means that the relative mass of a neutron compared with a proton is 1. Electrons are much, much lighter than protons and neutrons. Because of this, the mass of an atom is concentrated in its nucleus. We can ignore the tiny mass of the electrons when we work out the relative mass of an atom.

Type of subatomic particle	Relative mass
Proton	1
Neutron	1
Electron	very small

a What is the atomic number of an atom?
b How does the mass of a proton compare with the mass of a neutron?
c How does the mass of an electron compare with the mass of a neutron or proton?

Mass number

Almost all of the mass of an atom is in its nucleus. This is because the mass of the electrons is so tiny. We call the total number of protons and neutrons in an atom its **mass number**.

We can show the atomic number and mass number of an atom like this:

Mass number → $^{12}_{6}C$ (carbon) $^{23}_{11}Na$ (sodium)

Atomic number

We can work out the number of neutrons in the nucleus of an atom by subtracting its atomic number from its mass number:

number of neutrons = mass number – atomic number

For the two examples above, carbon has 6 protons and a mass number of 12.

So the number of neutrons in a carbon atom is (12 − 6) = 6.

Sodium has an atomic number of 11 and the mass number is 23.

So a sodium atom has (23 − 11) = 12 neutrons. In its nucleus there are 11 protons and 12 neutrons.

d How do we calculate the number of neutrons in an atom?

○ Proton Number of protons gives atomic number
○ Neutron Number of protons plus number of neutrons gives mass number

Figure 1 An atom of carbon

Isotopes

Atoms of the same element always have the same number of protons. However, they can have different numbers of neutrons.

We give the name **isotopes** to atoms of the same element with different numbers of neutrons.

Isotopes always have the same atomic number but different mass numbers. For example, carbon has two common isotopes, $^{12}_{6}C$ (carbon-12) and $^{14}_{6}C$ (carbon-14). The carbon-12 isotope has 6 protons and 6 neutrons in the nucleus. The carbon-14 isotope has 6 protons and 8 neutrons.

Sometimes the extra neutrons make the nucleus unstable, so it is radioactive. However, not all isotopes are radioactive – they are simply atoms of the same element that have different masses.

e What are isotopes?

Samples of different isotopes of an element have different *physical* properties. For example, they have a different density and they may or may not be radioactive. However, they always have the same *chemical* properties. That's because their reactions depend on their electronic structure. As their atoms will have the same number of electrons, the electronic structure will be same for all isotopes of an element.

For example, hydrogen has three isotopes: hydrogen, deuterium and tritium (see Figure 2). Each has a different mass and tritium is radioactive. However, they can all react with oxygen to make water.

f Which isotope of hydrogen is heaviest?

Figure 2 The isotopes of hydrogen – they have identical chemical properties but different physical properties

^1_1H Hydrogen

^2_1H Deuterium

^3_1H Tritium

Summary questions

1 Copy and complete using the words below:
electrons isotopes protons mass atomic one
The number of protons in an atom is called its .... number. The relative mass of a neutron compared with a proton is .... Compared with protons and neutrons .... have almost no mass. The total number of .... and neutrons in an atom is called its .... number. Atoms of an element which have different numbers of neutrons are called ....

2 a State how many protons there would be in the nucleus of each of the following elements:
  a i ^9_4Be ii $^{16}_{8}O$ iii $^{22}_{10}Ne$ iv $^{31}_{15}P$ v $^{79}_{35}Br$.
  b State how many neutrons each atom in part a has.

3 a How do the physical properties of isotopes of the same element vary?
  b Why do isotopes of the same element have identical chemical properties?

Key points

- The relative mass of protons and neutrons is 1.
- The atomic number of an atom is its number of protons (which equals its number of electrons).
- The mass number of an atom is the total number of protons and neutrons in its nucleus.
- Isotopes are atoms of the same element with different numbers of neutrons.

Summary answers

1 atomic, one, electrons, protons, mass, isotopes

2 a i 4 ii 8 iii 10 iv 15 v 35
   b i 5 ii 8 iii 12 iv 16 v 44

3 a The atoms have a different mass/different density and they may be radioactive.
   b They have identical electronic structures which governs their reactivity.

C2 3.2

Masses of atoms and moles

Learning objectives

Students should learn:

- that the masses of atoms can be compared by their relative atomic masses
- that carbon-12 is used as a standard to measure relative atomic masses [HT only]
- that the relative formula mass of compounds can be calculated.

Learning outcomes

Most students should be able to:

- give a definition of relative formula mass
- calculate relative formula mass if the formula and the relative atomic mass are given
- state what a mole is.

Some students should also be able to:

- give a full definition of relative atomic mass. [HT only]

Support

- Provide students with a precut-out cube template that is also ready scored. To help further, add some information already on it, for example the titles or prose with missing words.

Extend

- Ask students to work out the formulae of compounds (either by using the Student Book or using dot and cross diagrams). Then encourage them to use the periodic table to get the A_r before working out the M_r.

AQA — Specification link-up: Chemistry C2.3

- The relative atomic mass of an element (A_r) compares the mass of atoms of the element with the ^{12}C isotope. It is an average value for the isotopes of the element. *[C2.3.1 e)]* **[HT only]**
- The relative formula mass (M_r) of a compound is the sum of the relative atomic masses of the atoms in the numbers shown in the formula. *[C2.3.1 f)]*
- The relative formula mass of a substance, in grams, is known as one mole of that substance. *[C2.3.1g)]*

Lesson structure

Starters

Demonstration – Have a mole of different elements premeasured in sealed containers, e.g. 12 g of carbon, 24 g of magnesium. Allow the students to handle different samples. Explain to these students that all these examples have something in common – but what? Encourage the students to use the Student Book and discuss in small groups how these samples relate to each other. They should realise that these are all examples of moles. Then ask students to raise their hands if they can tell you the mass of, e.g. 1 mole of carbon (and hold up the sample), etc. Repeat for all the samples that you have. *(5 minutes)*

Word search – Give the students a word search for the key words that they will be using in the lesson: 'relative', 'atomic', 'mass', 'formula', 'mole', 'atom'. Instead of just asking the students to find the words, give clues. Support students by giving them both the clues and the key words. They can then match them up before finding the key words in the word search. Extend students by asking them to write a definition for each of the key words. *(10 minutes)*

Main

- Higher Tier students should understand that the masses of atoms are compared to $\frac{1}{12}$ of the mass of a carbon-12 isotope. It is also worth noting that many periodic tables give the mass number of the most common isotope rather than the relative atomic mass based on natural proportions of different isotopes.
- Students need to be able to obtain A_r from the periodic table or a data book and calculate M_r. Give the students a set of cards showing the symbols of different elements (single atoms and molecules) and compound formulas. Write numbers that represent A_r or M_r on separate cards.
- Students should complete calculations and match the formula with its A_r and M_r. They should also decide if the number represents A_r or M_r. This could be made into a competition, by splitting the class into small teams.
- Students need to be able to define the key terms: 'relative atomic mass' [HT only for full definition including the use of carbon-12 as a standard], 'relative formula mass' and 'moles'.
- Give the students a template of a cube. They should write definitions of relative atomic mass, moles and relative formula mass on three faces. They should include a worked example of calculations relating to this topic on each of the remaining faces, using lots of colours. Then they cut out the template and score the lines to create sharp folds and stick the cube together.

Plenaries

Difference – Ask the students to explain the difference between the symbols A_r and Ar. Choose a volunteer to explain to the class. [Ar is the symbol for the element argon, A_r is the shorthand notation for relative atomic mass]. *(5 minutes)*

In the bag – Put the key words: 'relative atomic mass', 'relative formula mass' and 'mole' into a colourful bag. Ask for three volunteers to come to the front and remove a word in turns. After they have removed their word, they should show the class the word and explain what it means. You should interject with a question-and-answer session to help rectify any misconceptions. Support students by giving them a list of definitions on the board: the student chooses a word and then looks at the definition, picking the one they think the word matches. Extend students by listing words under the key word that they cannot use in their explanation. *(10 minutes)*

Further teaching suggestions

Relative formula mass

- Give students a set of timed questions to calculate relative formula masses of different substances. You could use some past paper questions that are laminated with the mark scheme on the back. Students can then use dry-wipe pens and erasers to complete the question and mark their own answers within a time limit set by the teacher (approximately 1 minute per mark and one-third of this time to mark their answers).

Mole day

- Celebrate Mole Day: there are lots of resources on www.moleday.org.

Calculations

- Ask students to work out the mass of a mole of the following:
  - Oxygen atoms [16 g]
  - Oxygen molecules [32 g]
  - Water molecules [18 g]

Encourage the students to show their working.

AQA Examiner's tip

When talking about moles of elements, be careful to specify moles of atoms or moles of molecules. For compounds, it is more complicated. Explain that a mole of a compound is related to its formula. If it is molecular, it will contain one mole of molecules. However, if it is ionic it does not consist of molecules, and it does not contain one mole of particles. For example, one mole of magnesium chloride, $MgCl_2$, contains one mole of magnesium ions and two moles of chloride ions (three moles of particles).

C2 3.2   Masses of atoms and moles

Learning objectives

- How can we compare the masses of atoms?
- What is the relative atomic mass of an element?   [H]
- How can we calculate the relative formula mass of a compound from the elements it is made of?

Balanced symbol equations show us how many atoms of reactants we need to make the products. But when we actually carry out a reaction we really need to know how much to use in grams or cm³.

For example, look at the equation:

$$Mg + 2HCl \rightarrow MgCl_2 + H_2$$

The symbol equation tells us that we need twice as many hydrogen and chlorine atoms as magnesium atoms. However, this doesn't mean that the mass of HCl will be twice the mass of Mg. This is because atoms of different elements have different masses.

To make symbol equations useful in the lab or factory we need to know more about the mass of atoms.

  a Why don't symbol equations tell us directly what mass of each reactant to use in a chemical reaction?

Relative atomic masses

The mass of a single atom is so tiny that it would not be practical to use it in experiments or calculations. So instead of working with the real masses of atoms we just focus on the relative masses of different elements. We call these relative atomic masses (A_r).

Relative atomic mass

We use an atom of carbon-12 ($^{12}_{6}C$) as a standard atom. We give this a 'mass' of exactly 12 units, because it has 6 protons and 6 neutrons. We then compare the masses of atoms of all the other elements with this standard carbon atom. For example, hydrogen has a relative atomic mass of 1 as most of its atoms have a mass that is one-twelfth of a $^{12}_{6}C$ atom.

The relative atomic mass of an element is usually the same as, or similar to, the mass number of its most common isotope. The A_r takes into account the proportions of any isotopes of the element found naturally. So it is an *average* mass compared with the standard carbon atom. (This is why chlorine has a relative atomic mass of 35.5, although we could never have half a proton or neutron in an atom.)

  b Which atom do we use as a standard to compare relative masses of elements?

He = 4   C = 12   Mg = 24   C = 12

Figure 1 The relative mass of $^{12}_{6}C$ atom is 12. Compared with this, the A_r of helium is 4 and the A_r of magnesium is 24.

Relative formula masses

We can use the A_r of the various elements to work out the **relative formula mass** (M_r) of compounds. This is true whether the compounds are made up of molecules or collections of ions. A simple example is a substance like sodium chloride. We know that the A_r of sodium is 23 and the A_r of chlorine is **35.5**. So the relative formula mass of sodium chloride (NaCl) is:

$$23 + 35.5 = \mathbf{58.5}$$
$$A_r: Na \quad A_r: Cl \quad M_r: NaCl$$

Another example is water. Water is made up of hydrogen and oxygen. The A_r of hydrogen is 1, and the A_r of oxygen is 16. Water has the formula H_2O. It contains two hydrogen atoms for every one oxygen, so the M_r is:

$$(1 \times 2) + 16 = \mathbf{18}$$
$$A_r: H \times 2 \quad A_r: O \quad M_r: H_2O$$

  c What is the relative formula mass of hydrogen sulfide, H_2S? (A_r values: H = 1, S = 32)

We can use the same approach with relatively complicated molecules like sulfuric acid, H_2SO_4. Hydrogen has a A_r of 1, the A_r of sulfur is 32 and the A_r of oxygen 16. This means that the M_r of sulfuric acid is:

$$(1 \times 2) + 32 + (16 \times 4) = 2 + 32 + 64 = \mathbf{98}$$

Moles

Saying or writing 'relative atomic mass in grams' or 'relative formula mass in grams' is rather clumsy. So chemists have a shorthand word for it: a **mole**.

They say that the relative atomic mass in grams of carbon (i.e. 12 g of carbon) is a mole of carbon atoms. One mole is simply the relative atomic mass or relative formula mass of any substance expressed in grams. A mole of any substance always contains the same number of atoms, molecules or ions. This is a huge number (6.02×10^{23}).

??? Did you know ...?

If you had as many soft drink cans as there are atoms in a mole they would cover the surface of the Earth to a depth of 200 miles!

AQA Examiner's tip

You don't have to remember the number 6.02×10^{23} or the relative atomic masses of elements. But practise calculating the mass of one mole of different substances from their formula and the relative atomic masses that you are given.

Summary questions

1 Copy and complete using the words below:

   atom   elements   formula   relative

   The mass of an individual .... is so small that we use .... values when comparing them. We calculate the relative .... mass of a compound by adding up the relative atomic masses of its .... in the ratio given by its formula.

2 The equation for the reaction of calcium and fluorine is:

$$Ca + F_2 \rightarrow CaF_2$$

  a How many moles of fluorine molecules react with one mole of calcium atoms?

  b What is the relative formula mass of CaF_2? (A_r values: Ca = 40, F = 19)

3 The relative atomic mass of helium is 4, and that of sulfur is 32. How many times heavier is a sulfur atom than a helium atom?

4 Define the term 'relative atomic mass' of an element.   [H]

Key points

- We compare the masses of atoms by measuring them relative to atoms of carbon-12.   [H]
- We work out the relative formula mass of a compound by adding up the relative atomic masses of the elements in it, in the ratio shown by its formula.
- One mole of any substance is its relative formula mass, in grams.

Answers to in-text questions

  a The atoms of different elements have different masses.

  b $^{12}_{6}C$/carbon-12

  c 34

Summary answers

1 atom, relative, formula, elements

2 a 1

   b 78

3 Eight times heavier.

4 The relative atomic mass of an element (A_r) is a comparison of the mass of atoms of the element with the ^{12}C isotope, taking into account the proportions of its naturally occurring isotopes.

C2 3.3

Percentages and formulae

Learning objectives

Students should learn that:

- how to calculate the percentage of an element in a compound from its formula
- how to calculate the empirical formula of a compound from its percentage composition. **[HT only]**

Learning outcomes

Most students should be able to:

- calculate the percentage composition of an element in a compound.

Some students should also be able to:

- calculate the empirical formula of a compound if the percentage composition of the elements is given. **[HT only]**

AQA Specification link-up: Chemistry C2.3

- The percentage of an element in a compound can be calculated from the relative mass of the element in the formula and the relative formula mass of the compound. *[C2.3.3 a)]*
- The empirical formula of a compound can be calculated from the masses or percentages of the elements in a compound. *[C2.3.3 b)]* **[HT only]**

Lesson structure

Starters

Measurement – Show the students different mass values on balances. Ask them to note the values shown to the nearest two decimal places. Read out the answers and ask the students to put up their hands if they got them all right, one wrong, two wrong, etc. Approach students who have been having difficulty and help them to see why they recorded the wrong answer. Support students by a worked example on the board to help them truncate data. Extend students by showing them different methods of measuring mass (bathroom scales, kitchen scales, top pan balance, accurate level balance) and using these to measure the mass of the same item. Ask students to comment on reliability and accuracy of the results and to suggest why truncation is useful. *(5 minutes)*

Concept cartoon – Show the students a concept cartoon to highlight the conservation of mass theory. Ask them to discuss the cartoon in small groups. Then feed back to the rest of the class. Address any misconceptions at this stage. *(10 minutes)*

Main

- Calculations often involve a set order of steps. Choose an example question to calculate the percentage composition of an element and write out each step onto separate cards.
- Encourage the students to order the cards and copy out the worked example correctly. Then give the students other examples to work out themselves.
- The same idea can be repeated with Higher Tier students, but for generating a formula of a compound from percentage composition data can be used instead. **[HT only]**
- Give the students two flash cards. On one side of the first card they should write how to calculate the percentage composition of an element in a compound. On the reverse, they should make up some questions of their own.
- Higher Tier students should write how to generate the formula on one side of the second card, and some questions on the reverse. **[HT only]**
- The students can then work out the answers and write them upside down on their revision card.
- In pairs, students swap their revision cards, tackle each other's questions and check their answers. They should be encouraged to feed back any problems that they are having to their partner.
- Higher Tier students could experimentally determine the formula of magnesium oxide. This requires them to be able to read a balance accurately to two decimal places. They should design their own results table and show all their working to generate the formula from their experimental data. They should calculate the mass of magnesium used (mass of initially full crucible minus mass of empty crucible). Then they should calculate the mass of oxygen in the compound (mass of crucible after heating minus mass of initially full crucible). **[HT only]**
- Once the mass of each element in the compound is known, the formula can be calculated as detailed in the Student Book. **[HT only]**

Plenaries

Calculation – Ask the students to calculate the percentage composition of each element in ammonia. They should recall the formula of ammonia from previous work. [N = 82 per cent; H = 18 per cent.] Support students by giving them the formula of ammonia and the A_r for H and N. Extend students by asking them to calculate the mass of nitrogen in 25 g of ammonia. [20.5 g.] *(5 minutes)*

On the spot – Ask for a volunteer to stand at the front of the class, and give the other students scrap paper. Read out questions to the volunteer, who should give an answer. The other students then write numbers and hold them up to show how strongly they agree with the answer. (If they strongly disagree they hold up 1; if they strongly agree they hold up 10, for example.) You could reveal the true answer. *(10 minutes)*

Support

- Some students will struggle with calculations. These students will benefit from having a worked example that they can refer to with the steps explicitly shown. Thought processes could be written in prose as reminders. Provide a writing frame that follows the worked example can also help to formalise the working.

Extend

- Give students more complex empirical formula questions to attempt, e.g. P_2O_5.

Practical support

Determining the formula of magnesium oxide

Equipment and materials required

Small strips of magnesium ribbon (less than 2 cm length), ceramic crucibles and lids, Bunsen burner and safety equipment, tongs, pipeclay triangle, tripod, accurate balance, eye protection.

Details

Students should note the mass of the crucible and lid. They should twist the magnesium ribbon into a coil shape and put it into the crucible. They should note the new mass of the crucible, put it onto the pipeclay triangle and heat it strongly in a blue Bunsen flame, lifting the lid gently and occasionally to boost the oxygen flow. They must not lift the lid up high, as some of the product will be lost as white smoke. When the lid is lifted and there is no white light, then the reaction is complete. Then they turn off the Bunsen and allow the crucible to cool, noting the mass of the crucible at the end of the reaction. **[HT only]**

Safety: Eye protection should be worn throughout the reaction and students should be warned that the crucible will retain heat for a surprising amount of time and may crack. CLEAPSS Hazcard 59 – Magnesium ribbon.

How much?

C2 3.3 — Percentages and formulae

Learning objectives

- How can we calculate the percentage of an element in a compound from its formula?
- How can we calculate the empirical formula of a compound from its percentage composition? [H]

Figure 1 A small difference in the amount of metal in an ore might not seem very much. However, when millions of tonnes of ore are extracted and processed each year, it all adds up!

Maths skills

To calculate the percentage of an element in a compound:

- Write down the formula of the compound.
- Using the A_r values from your data sheet, work out the M_r of the compound. Write down the mass of each element making up the compound as you work it out.
- Write the mass of the element you are investigating as a fraction of the M_r.
- Find the percentage by multiplying your fraction by 100.

We can use the formula mass of a compound to calculate the percentage mass of each element in it. It's not just in GCSE Chemistry books that calculations like this are done! Mining companies decide whether to exploit mineral finds using calculations like these.

Working out the percentage of an element in a compound [k]

Worked example 1

What percentage of the mass of magnesium oxide is actually magnesium?

Solution

We need to know the formula of magnesium oxide: MgO.

The A_r of magnesium is 24 and the A_r of oxygen is 16.

Adding these together gives us the relative formula mass is (M_r), of MgO
24 + 16 = 40

So in 40 g of magnesium oxide, 24 g is actually magnesium.

The fraction of magnesium in the MgO is:

$$\frac{\text{mass of magnesium}}{\text{total mass of compound}} = \frac{24}{40}$$

so the percentage of magnesium in the compound is:

$$\frac{24}{40} \times 100\% = \mathbf{60\%}$$

Worked example 2

A pure white powder is found at the scene of a crime. It could be strychnine, a deadly poison with the formula $C_{21}H_{22}N_2O_2$; but is it?

When a chemist analyses the powder, she finds that 83% of its mass is carbon. What is the percentage mass of carbon in strychnine? Is this the same as the white powder?

Solution

Given the A_r values: C = 12, H = 1, N = 14, O = 16, the formula mass (M_r) of strychnine is:

$(12 \times 21) + (1 \times 22) + (14 \times 2) + (16 \times 2) = 252 + 22 + 28 + 32 = 334$

The percentage mass of carbon in strychnine is therefore:

$$\frac{252}{334} \times 100 = \mathbf{75.4\%}$$

This is **not** the same as the percentage mass of carbon in the white powder – so the white powder is not strychnine.

a What is the percentage mass of hydrogen in ammonia, NH_3? (A_r values: N = 14, H = 1)

Working out the empirical formula of a compound from its percentage composition [k]

We can find the percentage of each element in a compound by experiments. Then we can work out the simplest ratio of each type of atom in the compound. We call this simplest (whole-number) ratio its empirical formula.

This is sometimes the same as the actual number of atoms in one molecule (which we call the molecular formula) – but not always. For example, the empirical formula of water is H_2O, which is also its molecular formula. However, hydrogen peroxide has the empirical formula HO, but its molecular formula is H_2O_2.

Worked example

A hydrocarbon contains 75% carbon and 25% hydrogen by mass. What is its empirical formula? (A_r values: C = 12, H = 1)

Solution

Imagine we have 100 g of the compound. Then 75 g is carbon and 25 g hydrogen.

Work out the number of moles by dividing the mass of each element by its relative atomic mass:

$$\text{For carbon: } \frac{75}{12} = 6.25 \text{ moles of carbon atoms}$$

For hydrogen: $\frac{25}{1} = 25$ moles of hydrogen atoms

So this tells us that 6.25 moles of carbon atoms are combined with 25 moles of hydrogen atoms.

This means that the ratio is 6.25 (C) : 25 (H).

So the simplest whole number ratio is 1 : 4 (by dividing both numbers by the smallest number in the ratio)

In other words each carbon atom is combined with 4 times as many hydrogen atoms.

So the empirical formula is **CH₄**.

b A compound contains 40% sulfur and 60% oxygen. What is its empirical formula? (A_r values: S = 32, O = 16)

c 5.4 g of aluminium react exactly with 4.8 g of oxygen. What is the empirical formula of the compound formed? (A_r values: Al = 27, O = 16)

Maths skills

To work out the formula from percentage masses:

- Change the percentages given to the masses of each element in 100 g of compound.
- Change the masses to moles of atoms by dividing the masses by the A_r values. This tells you how many moles of each different element are present.
- This tells you the ratio of atoms of the different elements in the compound.
- Then the *simplest* whole-number ratio gives you the empirical formula of the compound. [H]

Summary questions

1 Copy and complete using the words below:

compound   dividing   hundred   formula

The percentage of an element in a .... is calculated by .... the mass of the element in the compound by the relative .... mass of the compound and then multiplying the result by one ....

2 Ammonium nitrate (NH_4NO_3) is used as a fertiliser. What is the percentage mass of nitrogen in it? (A_r values: H = 1, N = 14, O = 16)

3 22.55% of the mass of a sample of phosphorus chloride is phosphorus. What is the empirical formula of this phosphorus chloride? (A_r values: P = 31, Cl = 35.5) [H]

Key points

- The relative atomic masses of the elements in a compound and its formula can be used to work out its percentage composition.
- We can calculate empirical formulae given the masses or percentage composition of elements present. [H]

Further teaching suggestions

Water of crystallisation

- Students could try to calculate the water of crystallisation in certain formulae, e.g. $CuSO_4 \cdot 5H_2O$.

Percentage of oxygen

- Ask students to calculate the highest proportion of oxygen in the following formulae. Encourage the students to calculate the percentage composition and to show their working.
  - CO [57 per cent O]
  - C_2H_5OH [35 per cent O]
  - CH_3COOH [53 per cent O]

Role play

- Before the lesson begins, select five famous people and write their names on a piece of paper and attach them to the underside of five chairs in the class. Then ask students to check under their chairs; if they have a famous person, they should read out the key point in the style of the famous person to the rest of the class.

Copper oxide

- You can reduce copper oxide by passing methane over it. This experiment may take up to an hour and details can be found at www.practicalchemistry.org by searching for copper(II) oxide. You can then use experimental data to determine the formula of the compound. **[HT only]**

Answers to in-text questions

a 17.6%

b SO_3

c Al_2O_3

Summary answers

1 compound, dividing, formula, hundred

2 35%

3 PCl_3

C2 3.4

Equations and calculations

Learning objectives

Students should learn:

- that balanced symbol equations show the relative numbers of molecules of reactants and products in a reaction [HT only]
- that balanced symbol equations can be used to calculate the masses of reactants and products. [HT only]

Learning outcomes

Most students should be able to:

- interpret how many moles of reactants/products are shown in a balanced symbol equation [HT only]
- balance symbol equations [HT only]
- use a balanced symbol equation to calculate the mass of reactants or products. [HT only]

Support

- Some students will find the calculations difficult. Give them half-finished calculations, where they need to add numbers into the working out to generate the answers. Peer mentoring could also be used, where the students are split into pairs, with Higher Tier students supporting Foundation Tier students.

Extend

- Give students more complex symbol equations to complete calculations. Include data that would encourage students to truncate answers.

AQA **Specification link-up: Chemistry C2.3**

- The masses of reactants and products can be calculated from balanced symbol equations. *[C2.3.3 c)]* **[HT only]**

Lesson structure

Starters

Multiple-choice – Give each student three coloured flashcards, e.g. blue, green and red. Then create a few multiple-choice questions, one per slide on PowerPoint, with three answers, each written in a different colour to match the flash cards. This could also be achieved using Word or whiteboard software. Then show each question in turn and the students hold up the card that represents the answer they think is correct. *(5 minutes)*

Chemical equations – Ask the students to complete the following chemical equations:

1. $Mg + [O_2] \rightarrow 2MgO$
2. $CH_4 + O_2 \rightarrow [CO_2] + 2H_2O$
3. $Zn + CuSO_4 \rightarrow [Cu] + [ZnSO_4]$
4. $[NaOH] + HCl \rightarrow NaCl + H_2O$

Then students could turn these into balanced symbol equations. Support students by giving them the missing words. To extend this activity, you could ask the students to say what type of reaction each of the above represents [1 oxidation; 2 combustion/oxidation; 3 displacement; 4 neutralisation]. *(10 minutes)*

Main

- Students may have been introduced to balancing symbol equations in Key Stage 3 and will have covered it during their studies of C1. You may wish to return to the familiar equation for the oxidation of hydrogen, which is often used to demonstrate balancing equations. Advance students by explaining that the numbers that are used to balance the equation can be thought of as a ratio. Therefore two molecules of hydrogen will react with one molecule of oxygen to make two molecules of water. However, as this is a ratio, we can also say that two moles of hydrogen will react with one mole of oxygen to make two moles of water. You may then wish to work through the calculation example given in the Student Book for the reaction between hydrogen and chlorine.

- Students need to be able to work out the masses of different substances in balanced symbol equations. Create a card loop by drawing a rectangle 10 cm by 15 cm. Draw a dotted line to make a square 10 cm by 10 cm. In the square, write out questions that involve balancing equations and calculating reacting masses. Then, in the 5 cm by 10 cm rectangle, write an answer (not one that matches the question on the card). Ensure that the questions match answers on other cards so that a loop is made. Give the question loop set to small groups of students and allow them to complete the card sort. Then encourage the students to pick two of the questions and answers to copy into their book, but show their working out stage by stage (as demonstrated in the Student Book).

- Split the class into pairs, and on separate pieces of paper write enough calculation questions for one per group. Give out the questions and allow the students to start to answer for 3 minutes (timed using a stopwatch). Then ask the students to hand the paper to another group. Give the next group 3 minutes to correct the previous work and then continue with the answer. Repeat this a number of times until there has been enough time for the answers to be completed. Then return the paper back to the 'owners' where they should copy up the question and the full answer.

Plenaries

Reflection – Ask students to think about the objectives for today's lesson. Ask them to consider if they have been met, and discuss this in small groups. Ask a few groups to feed back to the rest of the class, explaining how they know that they have met the objectives. *(5 minutes)*

AfL (Assessment for Learning) – Give students some calculations but, instead of tackling the questions, encourage them to create the mark scheme. Ask the students to work in small groups discussing the questions and devising the marking points, and include alternative answers that could still be given credit, and those that definitely should not be awarded marks. This activity can be differentiated by using questions from the tier of entry students are being entered for. *(10 minutes)*

Further teaching suggestions

State symbols
- Students could include state symbols in more complex balanced symbol equations.

Scaling up
- Students may attempt industrial-sized calculations (involving tonnes). This would involve them multiplying up the masses of the different components.

Calculating key points
- Ask the students to copy out the key points, then encourage them to illustrate each of the key points by using a worked example of a calculation.

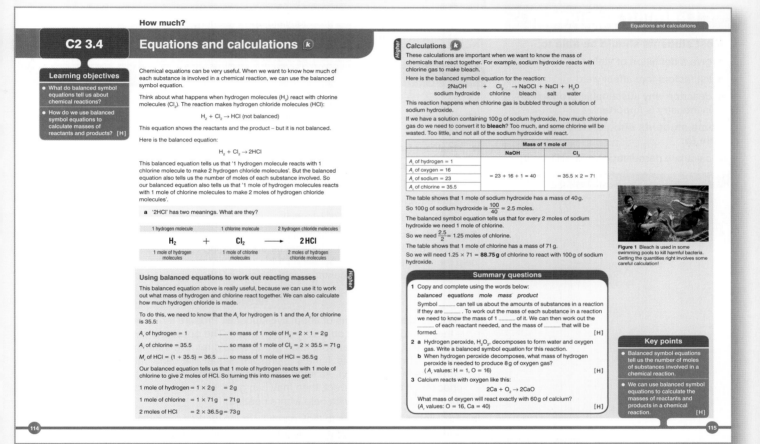

How much?

C2 3.4

Equations and calculations 🄺

Learning objectives

- What do balanced symbol equations tell us about chemical reactions?
- How do we use balanced symbol equations to calculate masses of reactants and products? [H]

Chemical equations can be very useful. When we want to know how much of each substance is involved in a chemical reaction, we can use the balanced symbol equation.

Think about what happens when hydrogen molecules (H_2) react with chlorine molecules (Cl_2). The reaction makes hydrogen chloride molecules (HCl):

$$H_2 + Cl_2 \rightarrow HCl \text{ (not balanced)}$$

This equation shows the reactants and the product – but it is not balanced.

Here is the balanced equation:

$$H_2 + Cl_2 \rightarrow 2HCl$$

This balanced equation tells us that '1 hydrogen molecule reacts with 1 chlorine molecule to make 2 hydrogen chloride molecules'. But the balanced equation also tells us the number of moles of each substance involved. So our balanced equation also tells us that '1 mole of hydrogen molecules reacts with 1 mole of chlorine molecules to make 2 moles of hydrogen chloride molecules'.

a '2HCl' has two meanings. What are they?

1 hydrogen molecule		1 chlorine molecule		2 hydrogen chloride molecules
H_2	+	Cl_2	⟶	$2HCl$
1 mole of hydrogen molecules		1 mole of chlorine molecules		2 moles of hydrogen chloride molecules

Using balanced equations to work out reacting masses

This balanced equation above is really useful, because we can use it to work out what mass of hydrogen and chlorine react together. We can also calculate how much hydrogen chloride is made.

To do this, we need to know that the A_r for hydrogen is 1 and the A_r for chlorine is 35.5:

A_r of hydrogen = 1   .... so mass of 1 mole of H_2 = $2 \times 1 = 2$ g

A_r of chlorine = 35.5   .... so mass of 1 mole of Cl_2 = $2 \times 35.5 = 71$ g

M_r of HCl = (1 + 35.5) = 36.5   .... so mass of 1 mole of HCl = 36.5 g

Our balanced equation tells us that 1 mole of hydrogen reacts with 1 mole of chlorine to give 2 moles of HCl. So turning this into masses we get:

1 mole of hydrogen = 1×2 g   = 2 g

1 mole of chlorine = 1×71 g = 71 g

2 moles of HCl   = 2×36.5 g = 73 g

Higher

Calculations 🄺

These calculations are important when we want to know the mass of chemicals that react together. For example, sodium hydroxide reacts with chlorine gas to make bleach.

Here is the balanced symbol equation for the reaction:

$$2NaOH + Cl_2 \rightarrow NaOCl + NaCl + H_2O$$
sodium hydroxide   chlorine   bleach   salt   water

This reaction happens when chlorine gas is bubbled through a solution of sodium hydroxide.

If we have a solution containing 100 g of sodium hydroxide, how much chlorine gas do we need to convert it to **bleach**? Too much, and some chlorine will be wasted. Too little, and not all of the sodium hydroxide will react.

	Mass of 1 mole of	
	NaOH	**Cl_2**
A_r of hydrogen = 1		
A_r of oxygen = 16	= 23 + 16 + 1 = 40	= 35.5 × 2 = 71
A_r of sodium = 23		
A_r of chlorine = 35.5		

The table shows that 1 mole of sodium hydroxide has a mass of 40 g.

So 100 g of sodium hydroxide is $\frac{100}{40}$ = 2.5 moles.

The balanced symbol equation tells us that for every 2 moles of sodium hydroxide we need 1 mole of chlorine.

So we need $\frac{2.5}{2}$ = 1.25 moles of chlorine.

The table shows that 1 mole of chlorine has a mass of 71 g.

So we will need 1.25 × 71 = **88.75 g** of chlorine to react with 100 g of sodium hydroxide.

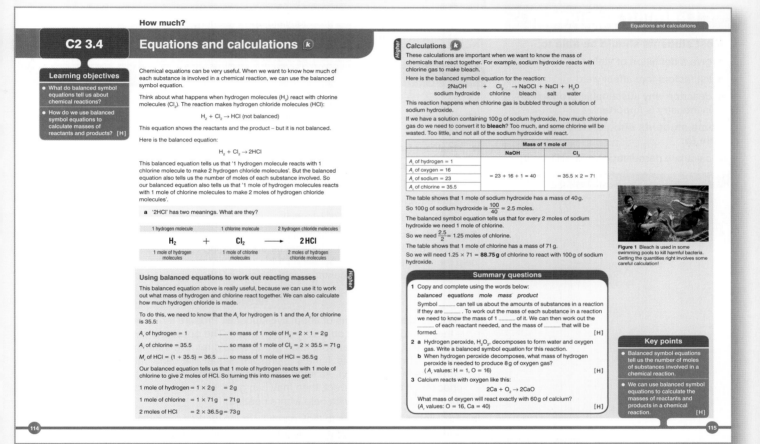

Figure 1 Bleach is used in some swimming pools to kill harmful bacteria. Getting the quantities right involves some careful calculation!

Summary questions

1 Copy and complete using the words below:

balanced equations mole mass product

Symbol .... can tell us about the amounts of substances in a reaction if they are .... To work out the mass of each substance in a reaction we need to know the mass of 1 .... of it. We can then work out the .... of each reactant needed, and the mass of .... that will be formed.   [H]

2 **a** Hydrogen peroxide, H_2O_2, decomposes to form water and oxygen gas. Write a balanced symbol equation for this reaction.   [H]
   b When hydrogen peroxide decomposes, what mass of hydrogen peroxide is needed to produce 8 g of oxygen gas? (A_r values: H = 1, O = 16)   [H]

3 Calcium reacts with oxygen like this:

$$2Ca + O_2 \rightarrow 2CaO$$

What mass of oxygen will react exactly with 60 g of calcium? (A_r values: O = 16, Ca = 40)   [H]

Key points

- Balanced symbol equations tell us the number of moles of substances involved in a chemical reaction.
- We can use balanced symbol equations to calculate the masses of reactants and products in a chemical reaction.   [H]

Answers to in-text questions

a '2 hydrogen chloride molecules' and '2 moles of hydrogen chloride molecules'.

Summary answers

1 equations, balanced, mole, mass, product

2 **a** $2H_2O_2 \rightarrow 2H_2O + O_2$
   b 17 g

3 24 g

C2 3.5 | The yield of a chemical reaction

Learning objectives

Students should learn:

- that the amount of product made can be expressed as a yield
- how to calculate percentage yield [HT only]
- that it is important to maximise yield in industrial processes and reduce the waste of energy.

Learning outcomes

Most students should be able to:

- give a definition of yield
- list factors that affect yield
- describe why sustainable production in industry is important.

Some students should also be able to:

- calculate percentage yield. [HT only]

Support

- Use a flow chart to show the steps that cause yield to be reduced in a chemical process. The different steps in the flowchart, such as transferring glassware etc., could be given to the students. They could then cut them out and stick them in the correct order into a predrawn flow chart outline.

Extend

- Ask students to complete yield equations that require manipulation of units, e.g. data given in tonnes or kg.

AQA Specification link-up: Chemistry C2.3

- Even though no atoms are gained or lost in a chemical reaction, it is not always possible to obtain the calculated amount of a product because:
  - the reaction may not go to completion because it is reversible
  - some of the product may be lost when it is separated from the reaction mixture
  - some of the reactants may react in ways different from the expected reaction. [C2.3.3 d)]
- The amount of a product obtained is known as the yield. When compared with the maximum theoretical amount as a percentage, it is called the percentage yield. [C2.3.3 e)]
- Evaluate sustainable development issues relating the starting materials of an industrial process to the product yield and the energy requirements of the reactions involved. [C2.3]

Lesson structure

Starters

Mirror words – Ask the students to work out these key words, which will be used in the lesson:

- stnatcaer [reactants]
- stcudorp [products]
- dleiy [yield]
- egatnecrep [percentage]
- noitaluclac [calculation] *(5 minutes)*

Definition – Ask the students to explain what a yield is. If they are a Higher Tier, ask how it can be calculated. Support students by encouraging them to use the Student Book to help them. Extend students by asking them to look at the worked example and find the actual, theoretical and percentage yields (including the units). *(10 minutes)*

Main

- Split the class into teams of about five students. Prepare ten questions for each group – they could be written on colour-coded paper. The questions should be face-down on a front desk. A volunteer from each group should retrieve their first question and take it back to his or her table. If the students are Higher Tier candidates, the team should complete the calculation. As soon as they have an answer, they take it to you to be checked. If they are correct, then they can get their next question. If they are incorrect, they should try again, with help where needed.
- Ask Higher Tier students to look carefully at the worked example for calculating the percentage yield. Ask them to draw two flow charts to show the steps of how to complete these calculations. Then give the students a number of questions they can answer using their flow charts to help them.
- Discuss the importance of sustainable production. Students can then list the advantages.

Plenaries

Steps – Write a question on the board that involves the calculation of a yield (an example could be used from the Student Book). Put each separate number or mathematical procedure on to separate sheets of A3 paper and arrange them on the floor in the wrong order. Ask for a volunteer to stand on the starting number and move on to the next sheet physically, showing the order of the calculation. Encourage the students to describe how they would do the calculation as they stand on the different pieces of paper. Support students by asking them to work in small groups to order the steps. Extend students by having parts of the equation missing. Students should therefore not only order the steps but also complete them. *(5 minutes)* [HT only]

What's the question? – Give students an answer such as yield, mass lost, 100 per cent yield, reversible reaction, etc. Encourage them to work in small groups to generate questions that match the answer given. You could support students by listing questions on the board: they could then choose the question that best fits their answer. For Higher Tier students, you could include answers to calculations of percentage yield. *(10 minutes)*

Further teaching suggestions

Theoretical and actual yields

- Students could be encouraged to reflect on the quantities of actual yield (what you make) compared with theoretical yield (maximum amount that you can make). In reality, no reaction ever produces the theoretical yield. Ask the students to think about why this is so. Note their ideas on a spider diagram in their books. Then ask them to contribute to an exhaustive diagram on the board – they should amend their own to ensure all the points are included and are correct.

Advert

- Students could make an advert for an industrial magazine, encouraging businesses to adopt more sustainable production. Students could then use the school's marking policy to assess each other's work. The author could make changes for homework based on the feedback from the AfL.

Measuring yield

- You may wish to allow students to complete the experiment of burning magnesium in a crucible as detailed in practical support 3.3 'Percentages and formulae'. Students know the mass of the magnesium that they started with. They can convert this into moles. Using the balanced symbol equation to determine that the ratio of magnesium to magnesium oxide is 1 : 1, students will then know the maximum number of moles of magnesium oxide that they could make and therefore work out the theoretical yield. Students could then measure the actual yield and Higher Tier students could calculate the percentage yield. A similar experiment can also be completed using iron wool.

How much?

C2 3.5 The yield of a chemical reaction

Learning objectives

- What do we mean by the yield of a chemical reaction and what factors affect it?
- How do we calculate the percentage yield of a chemical reaction? [H]
- Why is it important to achieve a high yield in industry and to waste as little energy as possible?

links

For information about using balanced symbol equations to predict reacting masses, look back to C2 3.4 Equations and calculations.

Many of the substances that we use every day have to be made from other chemicals. This may involve using complex chemical reactions. Examples include food colourings, flavourings and preservatives, the ink in your pen or printer, and the artificial fibres in your clothes. All of these are made using chemical reactions.

Imagine a reaction: A + 2B → C

If we need 1000kg of C, we can work out how much A and B we need. All we need to know is the relative formula masses of A, B and C and the balanced symbol equation.

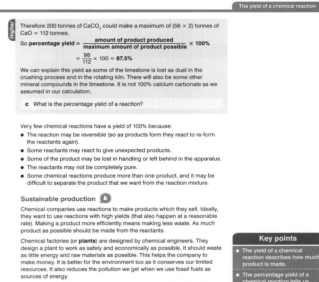

A + 2B → C
(reactants) (product)

a How many moles of B are needed to react with each mole of A in this reaction?
b How many moles of C will this make?

If we carry out the reaction, it is unlikely that we will get as much of C as we worked out. This is because our calculations assumed that all of A and B would be turned into C. We call the amount of product that a chemical reaction produces its yield.

It is useful to think about reactions in terms of their percentage yield. This compares the amount of product that the reaction really produces with the maximum amount that it could possibly produce.

$$\text{Percentage yield} = \frac{\text{amount of product produced}}{\text{maxmimum amount of product possible}} \times 100\%$$

Calculating percentage yield

An industrial example

Limestone is made mainly of calcium carbonate. Crushed lumps of limestone are heated in a rotating lime kiln. The calcium carbonate decomposes to make calcium oxide, and carbon dioxide gas is given off. A company processes 200 tonnes of limestone a day. It collects 98 tonnes of calcium oxide, the useful product. What is the percentage yield of the kiln, assuming limestone contains only calcium carbonate?

(A_r values: Ca = 40, C = 12, O = 16)

$$\text{calcium carbonate} \rightarrow \text{calcium oxide} + \text{carbon dioxide}$$
$$CaCO_3 \rightarrow CaO + CO_2$$

Work out the relative formula masses of $CaCO_3$ and CaO.

M_r of $CaCO_3$ = 40 + 12 + (16 × 3) = 100
M_r of CaO = 40 + 16 = 56

So the balanced symbol equation tells us that:

100 tonnes of $CaCO_3$ could make 56 tonnes of CaO, assuming a 100% yield.

Higher

Therefore 200 tonnes of $CaCO_3$ could make a maximum of (56 × 2) tonnes of CaO = 112 tonnes.

So **percentage yield** = $\dfrac{\text{amount of product produced}}{\text{maximum amount of product possible}} \times 100\%$

$= \dfrac{98}{112} \times 100 = \mathbf{87.5\%}$

We can explain this yield as some of the limestone is lost as dust in the crushing process and in the rotating kiln. There will also be some other mineral compounds in the limestone. It is not 100% calcium carbonate as we assumed in our calculation.

c What is the percentage yield of a reaction?

Very few chemical reactions have a yield of 100% because:

- The reaction may be reversible (so as products form they react to re-form the reactants again).
- Some reactants may react to give unexpected products.
- Some of the product may be lost in handling or left behind in the apparatus.
- The reactants may not be completely pure.
- Some chemical reactions produce more than one product, and it may be difficult to separate the product that we want from the reaction mixture.

Sustainable production

Chemical companies use reactions to make products which they sell. Ideally, they want to use reactions with high yields (that also happen at a reasonable rate). Making a product more efficiently means making less waste. As much product as possible should be made from the reactants.

Chemical factories (or **plants**) are designed by chemical engineers. They design a plant to work as safely and economically as possible. It should waste as little energy and raw materials as possible. This helps the company to make money. It is better for the environment too as it conserves our limited resources. It also reduces the pollution we get when we use fossil fuels as sources of energy.

Summary questions

1 Copy and complete using the words below:
high maximum percentage product waste yield
The amount of .... made in a chemical reaction is called its ....
The .... yield tells us the amount of product that is made compared to the .... amount that could be made. Reactions with .... yields are important because they result in less ....

2 Explain why it is good for the environment if industry finds ways to make products using high yield reactions and processes that waste as little energy as possible.

3 If the percentage yield for a reaction is 100%, 60 g of reactant A would make 80 g of product C. How much of reactant A is needed to make 80 g of product C if the percentage yield of the reaction is only 75%? [H]

Key points

- The yield of a chemical reaction describes how much product is made.
- The percentage yield of a chemical reaction tells us how much product is made compared with the maximum amount that could be made (100%).
- Factors affecting the yield of a chemical reaction include product being left behind in the apparatus and difficulty separating the products from the reaction mixture.
- It is important to maximise yield and minimise energy wasted to conserve the Earth's limited resources and reduce pollution.

116 | 117

Answers to in-text questions

a 2

b 1

c (amount of product made ÷ amount of product possible) × 100 per cent

Summary answers

1 product, yield, percentage, maximum, high, waste

2 It will conserve the Earth's limited resources and reduce pollution caused by waste products.

3 80 g

C2 3.6

Reversible reactions

Learning objectives

Students should learn:

- that reactions can be reversible
- how reversible reactions can be represented.

Learning outcomes

Most students should be able to:

- define a reversible reaction
- recognise a reversible reaction from its word or symbol equation.

Some students should also be able to:

- explain what a reversible reaction is, giving an example.

Answers to in-text questions

a The reaction goes in the forward direction only.

b The reaction is reversible.

c Both the red (ALit)/(Lit⁻) and blue forms of litmus are present; so mixed together in solution they look purple.

Support

- You could take the reactants and products in a reversible reaction to form a flow chart to explain the term 'reversible reaction'. This could be made into a 'cut-and-stick' activity which would generate a cycle.

Extend

- Ask students to find examples of reversible reactions that they benefit from in everyday life, e.g. oxygen binding to haemoglobin in their blood.

AQA / Specification link-up: Chemistry C2.3

- In some chemical reactions, the products of the reaction can react to produce the original reactants. Such reactions are called reversible reactions and are represented:

$$A + B \rightleftharpoons C + D$$

For example: ammonium chloride $\rightleftharpoons$ ammonia + hydrogen chloride. [C2.3.3 f)]

Lesson structure

Starters

Card sort – Create a card sort for the students to match the key words with their definitions. Put the cards into envelopes and give each pair of students a set to sort out on their desk. Then ask students to pick three new words and write them in their book, including the definition.

Reactants – starting substances in a chemical reaction.
Products – substances left at the end of a chemical reaction.
Reversible reaction – where the reactants make the products and the products make the reactants.
Indicators – chemicals that react with acids and alkalis to make different-coloured compounds.
Chemical reaction – a change in which a new substance is made.

Support students by encouraging them to use the Student Book to help them. Extend students by encouraging them to use the Student Book to give examples of each of the key words. *(5 minutes)*

Reflection – Ask students to draw a table with three columns headed 'What I already know', 'What I want to know', 'What I know now'. Encourage the students to look at the title of the page and the objectives. Then ask them to fill in the first column with facts they already know about the topic, presented as bullet points. Then ask them to think of questions that they think they need to have answered by the end of the lesson and note these in the second column. *(10 minutes)*

Main

- Students will be familiar with the use of indicators from their work on acids and alkalis at Key Stage 3. The colour changes produced by indicators are reversible reactions. Students could find out (experimentally or using secondary resources) the colour changes of different indicators in acidic/neutral/alkaline solutions.
- Heating ammonium chloride causes thermal decomposition to form ammonia and hydrogen chloride. This reaction can be completed experimentally in the lab by heating ammonium chloride in a boiling tube with a loosely fitted plug of mineral wool, then relating this to reversible reactions. Encourage the students to focus their attention on the cool part of the boiling tube. Ask them to explain in the form of a flow chart what is happening in the boiling tube.

Plenaries

True or false – On separate sheets of sugar paper, write the words 'true' and 'false'. Then stick them on opposite sides of the classroom. Read out the statements below. Students should stand next to the wall to represent their answer. If they don't know, they should stand in the centre of the room.

- A double-headed arrow in an equation shows that it is a non-reversible reaction. [False]
- In a reversible reaction, reactants make products and products make reactants. [True]
- All chemical reactions are reversible. [False]
- Indictors react with acids but not with alkalis. [False]
- The decomposition of ammonium chloride is a reversible reaction. [True]

Support students by giving them statements on a card and they discuss them in small groups before the movement commences. Extend students by asking them to rephrase the incorrect statements so that they are correct. *(5 minutes)*

Reflection – Ask students to review their starter table ('Reflection') and use a different colour pen/pencil to correct any misconceptions from the start of the lesson. Then ask the students to answer the questions they posed. If they can't, encourage them to talk in small groups, consult the Student Book and, if necessary, ask you. Finally, students should record, in bullet-point format, any other facts that they have picked up during the lesson, in the last column. *(10 minutes)*

Practical support

Litmus

Equipment and materials required
A test tube, test tube holder, red or blue litmus solution, 1.0 mol/dm^3 hydrochloric acid, 0.04 mol/dm^3 sodium hydroxide, 2 × dropping pipettes, eye protection.

Details
Put a few drops of litmus indicator into a test tube. Add a few drops of acid and observe. Add a few drops of alkali and observe. Repeat to demonstrate the reversible reaction.

Safety: CLEAPSS Hazcard 47A Hydrochloric acid – corrosive. CLEAPSS Hazcard 31 Sodium hydroxide – corrosive. Both solutions at the concentrations used are low hazard, but eye protection should be worn throughout the experiment.

Heating ammonium chloride

Equipment and materials required
A boiling tube, boiling tube holder, Bunsen burner and safety equipment, mineral wool, spatula, ammonium chloride, eye protection.

Details
Put about half a spatula of ammonium chloride into a boiling tube and insert a mineral wool plug at the top. Gently heat in a Bunsen flame.

Safety: Eye protection should be worn at all times. As acidic hydrogen chloride gas and alkaline ammonia gas are produced, the mineral plug must be used and the reaction should be carried out in a well-ventilated room. CLEAPSS Hazcard 9A Ammonium chloride – harmful.

Heating copper sulfate

Equipment and materials required
A boiling tube, boiling tube holder, Bunsen burner and safety equipment, spatula, hydrated copper sulfate, wash bottle, eye protection.

Details
Put about half a spatula of hydrated copper sulfate into a boiling tube and heat gently on a Bunsen flame until the colour change to white is complete. Remove from the heat and allow the boiling tube to cool. Then add a few drops of water and observe.

Link
This reaction will be studied in the next chapter in terms of the energy changes involved in reversible reactions.

Safety: Be careful to allow the boiling tube to cool before adding water as the glass could crack. Eye protection should be worn throughout this experiment. CLEAPSS Hazcard 27C Copper sulfate – harmful.

How much?

C2 3.6 Reversible reactions

Learning objectives
- What is a reversible reaction?
- How can we represent reversible reactions?

In all the reactions we have looked at so far the reactants react and form products. We show this by using an arrow pointing *from* the reactants *to* the products:

$$A + B \rightarrow C + D$$
reactants   products

But in some reactions the products can react together to make the original reactants again. We call this a **reversible reaction**.

A reversible reaction can go in both directions so we use two arrows in the equation. One arrow points in the forwards direction and one backwards:

$$A + B \rightleftharpoons C + D$$

a What does a single arrow in a chemical equation mean?
b What does a double arrow in a chemical equation mean?

Examples of reversible reactions

Have you ever tried to neutralise an alkaline solution with an acid? It is very difficult to get a solution which is exactly neutral. You can use an indicator to tell when just the right amount of acid has been added. Indicators react in acids to form a coloured compound. They also react in alkalis to form a differently coloured compound.

Litmus is a complex molecule. We will represent it as HLit (where H is hydrogen). HLit turns into the Lit$^-$ ion by losing an H$^+$ ion. Lit$^-$ is blue. If you then add more acid, blue Lit$^-$ changes back to red HLit and so on.

$$HLit \rightleftharpoons H^+ + Lit^-$$
Red litmus   Blue litmus

c Why does a neutral solution look purple with litmus solution?

> **Practical**
>
> **Changing colours**
> Use litmus solution, dilute hydrochloric acid and sodium hydroxide solution to show the reversible reaction described above.
> ● Explain the changes you see when adding acid and alkali to litmus.

When we heat ammonium chloride another reversible reaction takes place.

> **Practical**
>
> **Heating ammonium chloride**
> Gently heat a small amount of ammonium chloride in a test tube with a mineral wool plug. Use test tube holders or clamp the test tube at an angle. Make sure you warm the bottom of the tube.
> ● What do you see happen inside the test tube?
>
> **Safety:** Wear eye protection for both practicals.

Figure 1 Indicators undergo reversible reactions, changing colour to show us whether solutions are acidic or alkaline

Ammonium chloride breaks down on heating. It forms ammonia gas and hydrogen chloride gas. This is an example of thermal decomposition:

$$\text{ammonium chloride} \xrightarrow{\text{heat}} \text{ammonia} + \text{hydrogen chloride}$$
$$NH_4Cl \longrightarrow NH_3 + HCl$$

The two gases rise up the test tube. When they cool down near the mouth of the tube they react with each other. The gases re-form ammonium chloride again. The white solid forms on the inside of the glass:

$$\text{ammonia} + \text{hydrogen chloride} \rightarrow \text{ammonium chloride}$$
$$NH_3 + HCl \rightarrow NH_4Cl$$

We can show the reversible reactions as:

$$\text{ammonium chloride} \rightleftharpoons \text{ammonia} + \text{hydrogen chloride}$$
$$NH_4Cl \rightleftharpoons NH_3 + HCl$$

Figure 2 An example of a reversible reaction:
ammonium chloride $\rightleftharpoons$ ammonia + hydrogen chloride
$NH_4Cl \rightleftharpoons NH_3 + HCl$

> **Summary questions**
>
> 1 What do we mean by 'a *reversible* chemical reaction'?
>
> 2 Phenolphthalein is an indicator. It is colourless in acid and pure water but is pink-purple in alkali. In a demonstration a teacher started with a beaker containing a mixture of water and phenolphthalein. In two other beakers she had different volumes of acid and alkali. The acid and alkali had the same concentration.
>
> She then poured the mixture into the beaker containing 2 cm^3 of sodium hydroxide solution. Finally she poured the mixture into a third beaker with 5 cm^3 of hydrochloric acid in it.
>
> Describe what you would observe happen in the demonstration.
>
> 3 We can represent the phenolphthalein indicator as HPhe. Assuming it behaves like litmus, write a symbol equation to show its reversible reaction in acid and alkali. Show the colour of HPhe and Phe$^-$ under their formulae in your equation.

> **Key points**
> ● In a reversible reaction the products of the reaction can react to make the original reactants.
> ● We can show a reversible reaction using the $\rightleftharpoons$ sign.

Further teaching suggestions

Breathalyser
● Chromate ions undergo a reversible reaction with dichromate ions. These substances were used in the first breathalysers. Encourage students to discover the chemical reactions that occurred in these early testers.

Other reversible reactions
● You may wish to demonstrate 'blue bottle' reaction as detailed in 'RSC Classic Chemistry Experiments no. 83', or the oscillating reaction also from the 'RSC Classic Chemistry Experiments, no. 140'. You could also add alkali and acid successively to a small beaker with bromine water, or alternatively with potassium dichromate(VI) solution, to observe the reversible colour changes. Check CLEAPSS Hazcards.

Summary answers

1 The products can react to produce the original reactants.

2 The mixture turns pink-purple when added to sodium hydroxide solution and then turns back to colourless when added to the hydrochloric acid solution.

3   HPhe $\rightleftharpoons$ H$^+$ + Phe$^-$
    colourless   pink-purple

Analysing substances

Learning objectives

Students should learn:

- how to detect and identify artificial food colourings
- that there are advantages of using instrumental analysis.

Learning outcomes

Most students should be able to:

- describe an experiment to separate coloured additives
- list advantages of modern analysis techniques.

Some students should also be able to:

- explain in detail how coloured food additives can be detected and identified using paper chromatography.

Support

- You could use a simpler method of creating a chromatogram. An easier way to generate a chromatogram is to give the students a disk of filter paper. Ask them to use a paintbrush to put a sample of a food colouring into the centre. Then cut a wick (a wedge shape towards the centre). Balance the paper over a beaker with water in it. The wick must be submerged. The colours will then separate into rings.

Extend

- Encourage students to find out more about the stationary and mobile phases in paper chromatography and use them to give a more detailed explanation of chromatography.

AQA Specification link-up: Chemistry C2.3

- Chemical analysis can be used to identify additives in foods. Artificial colours can be detected and identified by paper chromatography. *[C2.3.2 b)]*
- Elements and compounds can be detected and identified using instrumental methods. Instrumental methods are accurate, sensitive and rapid and are particularly useful when the amount of a sample is very small. *[C2.3.2 a)]*

  Controlled Assessment: AS4.5 Analyse and interpret primary and secondary data. *[AS4.5.4 c) d)]*

Lesson structure

Starters

Original additive – Show students a picture of some spices and salt fish. Ask students to suggest their connection [food additives]. Spices are used to improve the taste, colour and smell of a food and salt can act as a preservative. Ask students to suggest any examples of modern-day additives that would not have been available 200 years ago (e.g. MSG). *(5 minutes)*

Dominoes – Give the students a card sort with the key words: 'preserve, food additive, solvent, chromatography' written on. Each card should also have a definition. Students should work in pairs to match the ends up, as in a domino game. *(10 minutes)*

Main

- Food colourings are often added to food to make them more appealing. Colours can be added to sweets and savoury foods. Students can complete chromatography experiments of different food colourings. Then the chromatograms could be stuck into their book and conclusions drawn from their results. Students can evaluate the reproducibility, repeatability and validity of the experiment as a means of detecting and identifying artificial colourings.

- If chromatography is being used to identify additives, then it is essential for the conditions to be the same. This allows test chromatograms to be compared with standard ones. You may wish to allow students to make 'standard' chromatograms for food colourings, then analyse a mystery food colouring (prepared in advance by mixing some of the food colouring available to the students) to determine which food colourings are present.

- Chromatography can be completed using a variety of different materials such as TLC plates. You may be able to make chromatograms using different stationary phases and solvents.

- Explain to students that using instruments for analysis has advantages and disadvantages. Give the students the six statements as detailed in the bullet points featured in the Student Book. Students should cut out and stick each statement into a table with two columns, headed 'Advantages' and 'Disadvantages' respectively. Support students by encouraging them to use their Student Book to help them. To extend students, ask them to consider why it has taken time to develop instrumental analysis [it is dependent on technological development].

Plenaries

AfL (Assessment for Learning) – Ask students to compare chromatograms produced – which group produced the best one for analysis purposes? Take a class vote on the best chromatogram and why. *(5 minutes)*

Explain – Ask the students to explain how chromatography works. Then pick three students randomly from the register to read their explanations. Reward the best explanation. Support students by giving them statements in the wrong order to explain chromatography. Extend students by suggesting other applications for chromatography. *(10 minutes)*

Practical support

Detecting dyes in food colourings

Equipment and materials required

Different food colourings, capillary tubes, boiling tube, boiling tube rack, ruler, pencil, strips of chromatography paper that fits into the boiling tube.

Details

Draw a pencil line 2 cm from the bottom of the chromatography paper. Draw three pencil crosses on the base line, an equal distance apart. Dip a clean capillary tube into a food colouring. The colour will suck into the tube. Gently dot one of the crosses, trying to add only a small amount of colouring. Repeat with two further colours on the remaining crosses. Put a small amount of water in the boiling tube (about 1 cm deep). Lower the chromatography paper into the tube and place in the rack. Leave the chromatogram to develop, until the solvent line is past the last separated colour. Try not to move the chromatograms while they develop or it will not be easy to compare them.

Students will see which colourings were pure substances and which were mixtures of dyes, and can list the component colours in any mixtures.

C2 3.7 — Analysing substances

Learning objectives

- What are food additives and how can we identify them?
- How can we detect artificial food colourings?
- What are the advantages of instrumental methods of analysis?

For hundreds of years we have added salt to food to preserve it. Nowadays, food technologists develop ways to improve the quality of foods. They also analyse foods to ensure they meet legal safety standards.

We call a substance that is added to food to extend its shelf life or to improve its taste or appearance a food additive. Additives that have been approved for use in Europe are given E numbers. The E numbers are like a code to identify the additives. For example, E102 is a yellow food colouring called tartrazine.

a What is a food additive?

Detecting additives

Scientists have many instruments that they can use to identify unknown compounds, including food additives. Many of these are more sensitive, automated versions of techniques we use in school labs.

One technique that is used to identify food additives is paper chromatography. It works because some compounds in a mixture dissolve better than others in particular solvents. Their solubility determines how far they travel across the paper.

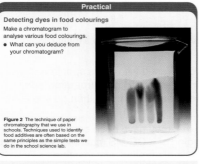

Figure 1 Modern foods contain a variety of additives to improve their taste or appearance, and to make them keep longer

Figure 3 A few years ago a batch of red food colouring was found to be contaminated with a chemical suspected of causing cancer. This dye had found its way into hundreds of processed foods. All of these had had to be removed from the shelves of our supermarkets and destroyed.

Practical

Detecting dyes in food colourings

Make a chromatogram to analyse various food colourings.

- What can you deduce from your chromatogram?

Figure 2 The technique of paper chromatography that we use in schools. Techniques used to identify food additives are often based on the same principles as the simple tests we do in the school science lab.

b What happens to the food colourings when you make a paper chromatogram?

Once the compounds in a food have been separated using chromatography, they can be identified. We can compare the chromatogram with others obtained from known substances. For this we must use the same solvent at the same temperature.

Instrumental methods

Many industries need rapid and accurate methods for analysing their products. They use modern instrumental analysis for this task.

Instrumental techniques are also important in fighting pollution. Careful monitoring of the environment using sensitive instruments is now common. This type of analysis is also used all the time in health care.

Modern instrumental methods have a number of benefits over older methods:

- they are highly accurate and sensitive
- they are quicker
- they enable very small samples to be analysed.

Against this, the main disadvantages of using instrumental methods are that the equipment:

- is usually very expensive
- takes special training to use
- gives results that can often be interpreted only by comparison with data from known substances.

c What do you think has aided the development of instrumental methods of chemical analysis?
d Why are these methods important?

Figure 4 Compared with the methods of 50 years ago, modern instrumental methods of analysis are quick, accurate and sensitive – three big advantages. They also need far fewer people to carry out the analysis than traditional laboratory analysis.

links

For more information on the instruments used by chemists to analyse substances, see C2 3.8 Instrumental analysis.

AQA Examiner's tip

Although simpler to use than bench chemistry methods, instrumental methods still need trained technicians to operate them.

Summary questions

1 Copy and complete using the words below:

    additives   paper   analyse   identify

Food scientists can .... different foods to see what .... have been used. For example, food colourings can be detected by .... chromatography. They can use results from known compounds to positively .... them.

2 **a** Carry out a survey of some processed foods. Identify some examples of food additives and explain why they have been used.
   b Describe how we can separate the dyes in a food colouring and identify them.

3 What are the main advantages and disadvantages of using instrumental analysis compared with traditional practical methods?

Key points

- Additives may be added to food in order to improve its appearance, taste and how long it will keep (its shelf life).
- Food scientists can analyse foods to identify additives, e.g. by using paper chromatography.
- Modern instrumental techniques provide fast, accurate and sensitive ways of analysing chemical substances.

Further teaching suggestions

Sweet chromatography

- Students could investigate the dye in sweets. Different coloured sweets could be put into dimple dishes. Students wet a paintbrush to remove the dye and complete a chromatogram.

Packaging

- Ask students to choose their favourite convenience food (could be a sweet or frozen pizza, etc.). They should bring in the packaging from home, or you can use online supermarkets to pull up the ingredients lists. Encourage them to list all the additives in that food, concentrating on food colourings.

Natural additives

- A lot of people are now very concerned about food additives but do not realise that many of them are naturally occurring chemicals such as pectin (E440), which is found in fruit. Split the class into half and give each group a different task. Ask half of the students to design and make a leaflet to be put in doctors' surgeries to explain that food additives aren't necessarily harmful. The remaining students should design a leaflet warning people about additives in their food and their effects.

Answers to in-text questions

a A substance that is added to food to make it keep longer or to improve its taste or appearance.

b Each dye separates into spots of pure colour.

c The development of technologies such as electronics and computing.

d These methods are highly accurate, quick and can be used with very small quantities of materials.

Summary answers

1 analyse, additives, paper, identify

2 **a** Examples of additives in some packaged food and why they have been added.
   b Description of using chromatography then comparing the chromatogram with chromatograms of known substances (or using an instrument, such as a mass spectrometer, to identify each substance separated – see C2 3.8 'Instrumental analysis').

3 **Advantages:** speed, sensitivity, ability to analyse small samples.
   Disadvantages: use expensive equipment, training is needed.

C2 3.8

Instrumental analysis

Learning objectives

Students should learn:

- that gas chromatography can be used to separate compounds
- that mass spectrometers can be combined with gas chromatography to identify the components in a mixture.

Learning outcomes

Most students should be able to:

- describe the use of gas chromatography linked with mass spectrometry to identify what is in a mixture.

Some students should also be able to:

- explain in detail the technique of gas chromatography – mass spectrometry
- explain how mass spectrometry is used to determine relative molecular masses. [HT only]

AQA Specification link-up: Chemistry C2.3

- Elements and compounds can be detected and identified using instrumental methods. Instrumental methods are accurate, sensitive and rapid and are particularly useful when the amount of a sample is very small. [C2.3.2 a)]
- Gas chromatography linked to mass spectroscopy (GC-MS) is an example of an instrumental method: gas chromatography allows the separation of a mixture of compounds. The time taken for a substance to travel through the column can be used to help identify the substance. The output from the gas chromatography column can be linked to a mass spectrometer, which can be used to identify the substances leaving the end of the column ... . [C2.3.2 c)]
- ... The mass spectrometer can also give the relative molecular mass of each of the substances separated in the column. [C2.3.2 c)] [HT only]

Lesson structure

Starter

Think – Show students an image of a science lab 100 years ago and *a modern* science laboratory. Ask students to think about why instrumental analysis has only recently developed. Allow students to discuss their ideas as a class. *(5 minutes)*

Main

- Instrumental analysis is very precise. It gives similar readings every time the same sample is analysed.
- Gas chromatography is often used with mass spectrometry. A sample made of a mixture of chemicals is injected into a gas chromatography machine in order to separate the mixture. The separate samples then go into a mass spectrometer for identification.
- Ask students to imagine that they have been commissioned to write an instruction leaflet to be in the packaging of a GC-MS machine. You could show some example leaflets such as those that are supplied with toasters or TVs. Students should include a schematic diagram of how the machine works. They could create a flow chart to detail the stages involved in separation and identification.
- Ask students to work in pairs to compare their leaflets. Students should comment on the science content, choice of language, activity and presentation, giving a mark out of 10 for each of these aspects. Then they can award an overall mark out of 40. They could make amendments as homework.

Plenaries

Persuade – Ask students to work in small groups, and imagine that they are research chemists who have made a new fertiliser. Each group should make a persuasive argument for a board of directors on why they should finance the use of instrumental analysis technique rather than using traditional laboratory techniques. Support students by giving them some statements that could provoke discussion. Extend students by asking some of them to role play the board of directors and encourage them to be biased against using the techniques. *(5 minutes)*

Paper round – Give each student a piece of A4 paper. Students should work in groups of six. Ask them to write an example of instrumental analysis at the top of the paper, then fold the paper over and pass to the student at the right. Then ask the next person to write, on the folded paper from another student, one new fact that they have learned. Again fold over the paper and pass it to the right. Ask the students to continue to fold over and pass the paper after writing a revised fact, an advantage of instrumental analysis, a disadvantage of instrumental analysis and one use of mass spectrometry. After the sixth paper move, ask each student to unfold the paper and read what has been written. If time allows, ask a few students to share the work from their paper. Examination technique can be highlighted from this exercise, as some students should have answered in sentences, whereas others may have used key words that might be ambiguous. *(10 minutes)*

Support

- Refer to chromatography as detailed in C2 3.7 Analysing substances as a scaffold to understanding gas chromatography (GC).

Extend

- Give students simple mass spectra and a list of compounds. They could then try to match the compound to the spectra. N.B. Students do not need to know about fragmentation patterns.

Further teaching suggestions

Mass spectra
- Students could be shown a spectra from mass spectrometry.

Lab visit
- A trip to a local university might be organised to see spectrometers in action.

Newspaper report
- Students could imagine that they are reporters in a newspaper in the past. They should write a news article documenting the discovery of mass spectroscopy and its uses. Students could use the internet to find out the date for such an article and people that may have given relevant quotes.

Web search
- Information about modern instrumental analysis can be found in www.sep.org.uk. Search for 'forensic chemistry'.

Videos
- The Royal Society of Chemistry has videos detailing different modern instrumental analysis techniques including mass spectrometry, as part of their Spectroscopy for Schools and Colleges.

Posters
- Show students chemical posters such as ones given free to schools from the RSC. Ask students to create a poster, which includes the key points.

Food scares
- In recent years, there have been a number of food scares involving additives, e.g. Sudan 1 dye. Students could look into these using the internet (e.g. search newspaper websites for 'food scare') and newspaper clippings kept in the school library. They could look at the economic and social effect of scares such as this and the impact on the British food industry.

How much?

C2 3.8 — Instrumental analysis

Learning objectives
- How can we use gas chromatography to separate compounds in a sample mixture?
- How can we use a mass spectrometer to identify the compounds in the sample?

Analysing mixtures

Samples to be analysed are often mixtures of different compounds. So the first step is to separate the compounds. Then they can be identified using one of the many instrumental techniques available. Chemists have developed a technique called gas chromatography–mass spectrometry (GC–MS) to do this task.

- Firstly, they use **gas chromatography** to separate compounds that are easily vaporised.
- Then the separated compounds pass into another instrument – the **mass spectrometer**, which can identify each of them. The mass spectrometer is useful for identifying both elements and compounds. The pattern of peaks it produces identifies the sample.

Gas chromatography

This separation technique is similar to paper chromatography. However, instead of a solvent moving over paper, it has a gas moving through a column packed with a solid.

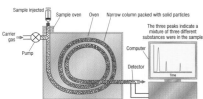

Figure 1 This is the apparatus used in gas chromatography. The solid in the column can be coated in a liquid and is sometimes then known as gas–liquid chromatography.

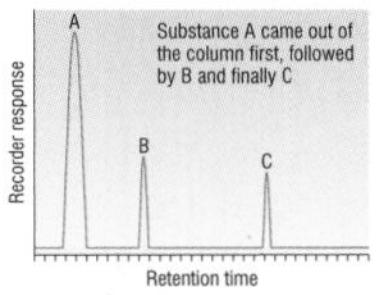

- First of all, the sample mixture is vaporised.
- A 'carrier' gas moves the vapour through the coiled column.
- The compounds in the sample have different attractions to the material in the column. The compounds with stronger attractions will take longer to get through the column. We say that they have a longer **retention time**.
- The compounds with weak attractions to the material in the column leave it first. They have shorter retention times.

The separated compounds can be recorded on a chart as they leave the column. Look at Figure 2 to see a gas chromatograph.

We can identify the unknown substances in the sample by comparing the chromatograph with the results for known substances. The analysis must have taken place in exactly the same conditions to compare retention times.

Figure 2 This is a gas chromatograph of a mixture of three different substances. There was more of substance A than B or C in the sample mixture.

(Figure 2: Recorder response vs Retention time — Substance A came out of the column first, followed by B and finally C)

Mass spectrometry

To ensure that we identify the unknown substances the gas chromatography apparatus can be attached directly to a **mass spectrometer**. This identifies substances very quickly and accurately and can detect very small quantities in the sample.

Measuring relative molecular masses

A mass spectrometer also provides an accurate way of measuring the relative molecular (formula) mass of a compound. The peak with the largest mass corresponds to an ion with just one electron removed. As you know, the mass of an electron is so small that it can be ignored when we look at the mass of atoms. This peak is called the **molecular ion peak**. It is always found as the last peak on the right as you look at a mass spectrum. The molecular ion peak of the substance analysed in Figure 3 is at 45. So the substance has a relative molecular mass of 45.

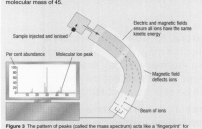

Figure 3 The pattern of peaks (called the mass spectrum) acts like a 'fingerprint' for unknown compounds. The pattern is quickly matched against a database of known compounds stored on computer.
NB You don't need to remember the details of how a mass spectrometer works.

Summary questions

1 Copy and complete using the words below:

   chromatography   database   mass   mixture   fingerprint

   Separating a .... of compounds can be carried out by gas .... Identifying compounds once they have been separated then uses techniques like .... spectrometry. The pattern of peaks is like a .... for each unknown compound. It is matched against known compounds on a computer ....

2 Describe how a mass spectrometer can be used to find the relative molecular mass of a compound.   [H]

Key points
- Compounds in a mixture can be separated using gas chromatography.
- Once separated, compounds can be identified using a mass spectrometer.
- The mass spectrometer can be used to find the relative molecular mass of a compound from its molecular ion peak.   [H]

Summary answers

1 mixture, chromatography, mass, fingerprint, database

2 Look to the far right of the mass spectrum to find the molecular ion peak (the peak with the highest relative mass). This gives you the relative molecular mass of the substance under analysis.

Summary answers

1 a B   **b** A   **c** D   **d** C

2 a 18 g
  b 16 g
  c 87 g
  d 102 g
  e 138 g
  f 158 g
  g 89 g

3 a 1   **c** 0.25   **e** 0.01
  b 3   **d** 0.2   **f** 0.05

4 a 75%
  b 8 g

5 $AlBr_3$

6 95%

7 a A reaction that can go in either direction, i.e. products → reactants as well as reactants → products.
  b An 'ordinary' reaction is normally regarded as going in one direction only, i.e. the 'forward' direction.
  c $C_2H_4 + H_2O \rightleftharpoons C_2H_5OH$

8 a 1
  b 98 kg
  c 96%
  d Any two valid reasons, for example a reaction is reversible or a reaction may not go to completion; loss/escape of product (from any stage); reactants may react in unexpected ways; sulfur/reactant may be impure; the catalyst might not be at the correct temperature.
  e Any two valid reasons, e.g. to conserve resources/sulfur; to conserve energy used in the process; to reduce energy needed for transporting sulfur; to reduce pollution/acid rain/loss of sulfur dioxide/trioxide.

Summary questions

1 Match up the parts of the sentences:

a	Neutrons have a relative mass of …	A	… negligible mass compared to protons and neutrons.
b	Electrons have …	B	… 1 compared to protons.
c	Protons have a relative mass of …	C	… found in its nucleus.
d	Nearly all of an atom's mass is …	D	… 1 compared to neutrons.

2 Calculate the mass of 1 mole of each of the following compounds:
  a H_2O
  b CH_4
  c MnO_2
  d Al_2O_3
  e K_2CO_3
  f $KMnO_4$
  g $Mn(OH)_2$
  (A_r values: C = 12, O = 16, Al = 27, H = 1, Ca = 40, K = 39, Mn = 55)

3 How many moles of:
  a Ag atoms are there in 108 g of silver,
  b P atoms are there in 93 g of phosphorus,
  c Ag atoms are there in 27 g of silver,
  d P atoms are there in 6.2 g of phosphorus,
  e Fe atoms are there in 0.56 g of iron,
  f P_4 molecules are there in 6.2 g of phosphorus?
  (A_r values: Ag = 108, P = 31, Fe = 56)

4 a The chemical formula of methane is CH_4. Use the relative atomic masses in question 2 to work out the percentage by mass of carbon in methane.
  b In 32 g of methane, work out the mass of hydrogen present in the compound.

5 When aluminium reacts with bromine, 4.05 g of aluminium reacts with 36.0 g of bromine. What is the empirical formula of aluminium bromide?
  (A_r values: Al = 27, Br = 80)

6 In a lime kiln, calcium carbonate is decomposed to calcium oxide:
  $CaCO_3 \rightarrow CaO + CO_2$
  50.0 tonnes of calcium carbonate gave 26.6 tonnes of calcium oxide. Calculate the percentage yield for the process.
  (A_r values: Ca = 40, O = 16, C = 12)

7 a What is a reversible reaction?
  b How does a reversible reaction differ from an 'ordinary' reaction?
  c Ethene (C_2H_4) reacting with steam (H_2O) to form ethanol (C_2H_5OH) is a reversible reaction. Write the balanced symbol equation for this reaction.

8 Sulfur is mined in Poland and is brought to Britain in ships. The sulfur is used to make sulfuric acid. Sulfur is burned in air to produce sulfur dioxide. Sulfur dioxide and air are passed over a heated catalyst to produce sulfur trioxide. Water is added to sulfur trioxide to produce sulfuric acid. The reactions are:
  $S + O_2 \rightleftharpoons SO_2$
  $2SO_2 + O_2 \rightleftharpoons 2SO_3$
  $SO_3 + H_2O \rightarrow H_2SO_4$
  Relative atomic masses: H = 1; O = 16; S = 32
  a How many moles of sulfuric acid are produced from one mole of sulfur?
  b Calculate the maximum mass of sulfuric acid that can be produced from 32 kg of sulfur.
  c In an industrial process the mass of sulfuric acid that was produced from 32 kg of sulfur was 94.08 kg. Use your answer to part b to calculate the percentage yield of this process.
  d Suggest two reasons why the yield of the industrial process was less than the maximum yield.
  e Give two reasons why the industrial process should produce a yield that is as close to the maximum yield as possible.

124

Practical suggestions

AQA

Practicals	AQA	k	📖	⚙
Investigating food colours using paper chromatography.	✓		✓	
Working out the empirical formulae of copper oxide and magnesium oxide.	✓		✓	
Calculating yields, for example magnesium burning to produce magnesium oxide or wire wool burning to produce iron oxide.	✓	✓	✓	
There are opportunities in this section to build in the idea of instrumentation precision, e.g. for the collection of gases, the use of boiling tubes, gas jars or gas syringes.	✓		✓	
Copper sulfate – hydration/dehydration.	✓		✓	
Heating ammonium chloride in a test tube.	✓		✓	
Adding alkali and acid alternately to bromine water or to potassium chromate solution	✓		✓	
'Blue bottle' reaction (RSC Classic Chemistry Experiments no. 83).	✓		✓	
Oscillating reaction (RSC Classic Chemistry Experiments no.140).	✓		✓	

Left side: End of chapter questions

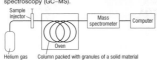

AQA Examination-style questions (k)

a An atom of phosphorus can be represented as:

31
P
15

  i What is the number of protons in this atom of phosphorus? (1)
  ii What is the number of neutrons in this atom of phosphorus? (1)
  iii What are the number of electrons in this atom of phosphorus? (1)

b A different atom of phosphorus can be represented as:

32
P
15

  i What are these two atoms of phosphorus known as? (1)
  ii Give one way in which these two atoms of phosphorus are different. (1)

Toothpastes often contain fluoride ions to help protect teeth from attack by bacteria.

Some toothpastes contain tin(II) fluoride.

This compound has the formula SnF_2.

a Calculate the relative formula mass (M_r) of SnF_2.
(Relative atomic masses: F = 19; Sn = 119) (2)

b Calculate the percentage by mass of fluorine in SnF_2. (2)

c A tube of toothpaste contains 1.2 g of SnF_2. Calculate the mass of fluorine in this tube of toothpaste. (1)

AQA, 2008

The diagram shows what happens when ammonium chloride is heated.

White solid
Test tube
Mineral wool plug
HEAT
Ammonium chloride

The reaction that takes place is:

$NH_4Cl(s) \rightleftharpoons NH_3(g) + HCl(g)$

a What does $\rightleftharpoons$ in the equation mean? (1)

b Explain why the white solid appears near the top of the test tube. (2)

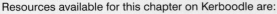

4 The diagram shows the main parts of an instrumental method called gas chromatography linked to mass spectroscopy (GC–MS).

Sample injector
Mass spectrometer
Computer
Helium gas
Oven
Column packed with granules of a solid material

This method separates a mixture of compounds and then helps to identify each of the compounds in the mixture.

a In which part of the apparatus:
  i is the mixture separated? (1)
  ii is the relative molecular mass of each of the compounds in the mixture measured? (1)
  iii are the results of the experiment recorded? (1)

b **i** Athletes sometimes take drugs because the drugs improve their performance. One of these drugs is ephedrine.
Ephedrine has the formula:
$C_{10}H_{15}NO$
What relative molecular mass (M_r) would be recorded by GC–MS if ephedrine was present in a blood sample taken from an athlete?
Show clearly how you work out your answer.
(Relative atomic masses: H = 1; C = 12; N = 14; O = 16.) (2)
  ii Another drug is amphetamine, which has the formula: $C_9H_{13}N$
The relative molecular mass (M_r) of amphetamine is 135.
Calculate the percentage by mass of nitrogen in amphetamine. (Relative atomic mass: N = 14.) (2)

c Athletes are regularly tested for drugs at international athletics events. An instrumental method such as GC–MS is better than methods such as titration. Suggest why. (2)

AQA, 2010

5 A chemist thought a liquid hydrocarbon was hexane, C_6H_{14}.
Relative atomic masses: H = 1; C = 12

a Calculate the percentage of carbon in hexane. (2)

b The chemist analysed the liquid hydrocarbon and found that it contained 85.7% carbon. Calculate the empirical formula of the hydrocarbon based on this result. You must show your working to gain full marks. (4)

c Was the liquid hydrocarbon hexane? Explain your answer. [H] (1)

125

Kerboodle resources (k)

Resources available for this chapter on Kerboodle are:

- Chapter map: How much?
- Support: All about atoms (C2 3.1)
- How Science Works: You need the right formula (C2 3.3)
- Bump up your grade: Chemical calculations (C2 3.3)
- Maths skills: Equations and calculations (C2 3.4)
- Extension: How much? (C2 3.4)
- Viewpoint: Making chemistry better (C2 3.5)
- Practical: Calculating the percentage yield of a reaction (C2 3.5)
- Interactive activity: How much?
- Revision podcast: Mass and atoms
- Test yourself: How much?
- On your marks: How much?
- Examination-style questions: How much?
- Answers to examination-style questions: How much?

Right side: Examination-style answers

AQA Examination-style answers

1 a **i** 15 *(1 mark)*
    ii 16 *(1 mark)*
    iii 15 *(1 mark)*

  b **i** isotopes *(1 mark)*
    ii One from: different mass (numbers), (number of) neutrons, total number of (subatomic) particles, (physical) properties *(but do not allow chemical properties)*. *(1 mark)*

2 a Give two marks for 157. If answer is incorrect either 2 × 19 + 119 or 119 + 19 = 138 gains one mark. *(2 marks)*

  b Give two marks for 24.2 (accept answers in the range 24 to 24.2038). If the answer is incorrect, 25 or 38/157 × 100 or 19/157 × 100 = 12 to 12.1 or 19/138 × 100 gains one mark (allow error carried forward from part **a** so 38/**a** × 100 gains two marks if calculated correctly). *(2 marks)*

  c 0.29 (accept answers in the range 0.28 to 0.3 and allow error carried forward from part **b**) *(1 mark)*

3 a Reversible (reaction). *(Accept reaction goes both ways)*. *(1 mark)*

  b Heating: causes (thermal) decomposition or forward reaction and so produces gases (ammonia gas *and* hydrogen chloride gas or NH_3 and HCl). The gases are cooled near the top of the test tube, which causes the reverse reaction and so solid ammonium chloride is formed. *(2 marks)*

4 a **i** the column *(1 mark)*
    ii the mass spectrometer *(1 mark)*
    iii the computer *(1 mark)*

  b **i** Give two marks for 165. If the answer is incorrect then evidence of correct working gains one mark, e.g 10 × 12 + 15 + 14 + 16. *(2 marks)*
    ii Give two marks for 10.37%. If the answer is incorrect, then evidence of correct working gains one mark. $\frac{14}{135} \times 100\% = 10.37\%$ *(2 marks)*

  c Two from: faster, more accurate, detects smaller amounts. *(2 marks)*

5 a Give two marks for 83.7 (per cent). *(Accept answers in the range 83.72 to 84.)* If the answer is incorrect, evidence of correct working gains one mark, e.g. 6 × 12/(6 × 12 + 14) × 100. *(2 marks)*

  b Give one mark for each correct step: one mark for mass of hydrogen – (100 g of hydrocarbon contains 85.7 g C and 14.3 g H); one mark for dividing masses by correct A_r – 85.7/12 and 14.3/1; one mark for correct proportions – 7.14... and 14.3 or simplified ratio 1:2; 1 mark for correct empirical formula CH_2. *(4 marks)*

  c Accept 'no' with a valid explanation – e.g. because the empirical formula is different/that of an alkene or it gives C_6H_{12} for six carbon atoms or it is not an alkane or because the percentage of carbon is different and compounds have fixed proportions (of elements). *Accept the answer that one cannot be sure if there is a valid explanation*, e.g. because of experimental error or only one result or one needs to confirm the result or to repeat the test. *Do not accept yes.* *(1 mark)*

C2 4.1

How fast?

Students should learn:
- that chemical reactions can happen at different rates
- how the rate of a chemical reaction can be calculated.

Learning outcomes

Most students should be able to:
- state a definition of the rate of reaction
- list ways of finding the rate
- suggest a method for finding the rate in a specified reaction.

Some students should also be able to:
- explain in detail why a particular method of finding the rate is suitable for a specified reaction.

Answers to in-text questions

a How fast the reactants are turned into products.

b In order to understand (and control) how fast chemicals are made. Economics require speedy reactions to cut production and energy costs.

Summary answers

1 reactants, products, rate, slope, time

2 **a** Graphs for **i** and **ii** are shaped like those in the second and first practicals respectively in the Student Book.

b The steeper the graph, the faster the rate of the reaction.

Support

- Some students find graph paper confusing. Therefore supply these students with squared paper, with the scales already drawn on. Once the students have plotted their graph, you could supply these statements (in the wrong order) for students to copy on to their graph.
  - Start of reaction.
  - Fast rate of reaction.
  - Slow rate of reaction.
  - End of reaction.

Extend

- Ask students to calculate the gradient at different points of the graph and actually give a value for the rate of reaction.

AQA Specification link-up: Chemistry C2.4

- The rate of a chemical reaction can be found by measuring the amount of a reactant used or the amount of product formed over time:

$$\text{Rate of reaction} = \frac{\text{amount of reactant used}}{\text{time}}$$

$$\text{Rate of reaction} = \frac{\text{amount of product formed}}{\text{time}} \quad [C2.4.1\ a)]$$

- Interpret graphs showing the amount of product formed (or reactant used up) with time, in terms of the rate of the reaction. [C2.4]

  Controlled Assessment: AS4.3 Collect primary and secondary data. [AS4.3.2 b) c)]; AS4.5 Analyse and interpret primary and secondary data. [AS4.5.2 b) d)]

Lesson structure

Starters

Fast or slow – Give each student a piece of paper with 'fast' on one side and 'slow' on the other. Then show them different images of chemical reactions, e.g. rusting, baking a cake, cooking an egg, magnesium reacting with acid and neutralisation. They should look at each image, decide if the rate is fast or slow and hold up the card to demonstrate their answer. Images could be shown using a data projector or PowerPoint slides. *(5 minutes)*

Cut and stick – Explain to students what 'rate of reaction' is. Then give the students different magazines and catalogues. Their task is to cut out an example of a reaction with a fast rate and a slow rate. They then compare their findings with a small group of students, and they choose the best from their selection. Students could then make a class montage on sugar paper. You could support students by giving them some examples of fast and slow reactions that they could find in the magazines. You could extend students by encouraging them to represent the reactions as a word or symbol equation. *(10 minutes)*

Main

- In many chemical reactions that we use to study rate, a gas is made. Students should produce a graph so that they can interpret information about a reaction. Using the reaction between magnesium and acid, ask students to plot a graph to show the production of hydrogen over two minutes. Then ask them to annotate their graph to explain the shape. They should include information that explains why the graph starts at $0\ cm^3$ of gas and they should explain the shape of the graph.

- The reaction between hydrochloric acid and sodium thiosulfate is the classic example used to highlight how light can be used to determine the rate of reaction. Students could complete this experiment themselves and reflect on the technique. Alternatively, this could be completed as a class demonstration. Draw the black cross on an overhead transparency and put it onto an overhead projector. Choose a student to be in charge of the stopwatch. Then put the reaction vessel on to the cross and ask students to raise their hands when they think the cross has gone. When most of the hands are raised, stop the watch and note the time.

- Compare this with using a light sensor and data logger. A plot of the light intensity could be made. Use this as an opportunity to teach about the 'Controlled Assessment' concepts of reliability, accuracy, and experimental error. The disappearing cross experiment relies on a person deciding when the cross disappears and this introduces errors, which data logging can help to address.

- There are also opportunities here to show students how to make measurements using sensors (e.g. carbon dioxide, oxygen, pH, gas pressure and temperature) to investigate reaction rates.

- After the students have watched the demonstration of the reaction between magnesium and acid, allow them to experiment with the different methods for measuring rate of reaction detailed in 'Practical support'. They will need a supply of the hydrochloric acid and magnesium strips (and eye protection). The aim of this activity is for the students to decide the most informative method. [They should realise that the balances available are not sensitive enough (need higher resolution), there is no precipitate formed, so the disappearing cross is useless, but collection of gas is the most accurate if a gas syringe is used.] You may wish to use a pH probe to monitor the reactions. You may wish to extend students further by giving them a selection of equipment to measure the volume of gas such as a gas syringe, a water trough and a measuring cylinder or burette. Again, encourage students to evaluate the different methods and decide which would be the most accurate [gas syringe].

Plenaries

Graph interpretation – Show students a graph of the rate of a particular reaction. Ask them to interpret the graph and explain the shape of the curve. Support students by giving them graphs on squared paper and with simple numbers. Extend students by using more complex scales and data points that involve decimals. *(5 minutes)*

Card sort – Make a set of eight cards: four with diagrams showing how the rate of reaction can be found (mass change, gas collection by displacement in a measuring cylinder, gas collection in a gas syringe, disappearing cross) and four with examples of reactions that can be measured using these techniques (magnesium + acid, calcium carbonate + acid, sodium thiosulfate + acid, hydrogen peroxide + manganese dioxide). Ask the students to match the methods with reactions. Encourage them to discuss their work in small groups, then feed back to the class in a question-and-answer session. [Note: Only the sodium thiosulfate reaction can be measured using the disappearing cross. *(10 minutes)*

Further teaching suggestions

Spider diagram
- Collision theory is a fundamental concept that underpins the whole of this chapter. Students could start a spider diagram using the key points from this spread. At the end of each lesson during this chapter, encourage students to add the new key points to their diagram.

Practical support

Measuring the mass of a reaction mixture
Equipment and materials required
Marble chips, 1 mol/dm³ hydrochloric acid (CLEAPSS Hazcard 47A), 250 cm³ conical flask, top-pan balance, cotton wool, stopwatch, measuring cylinder, eye protection.

Measuring the volume of gas given off
Equipment and materials required
Marble chips, 1 mol/dm³ hydrochloric acid (CLEAPSS Hazcard 47A), 250 cm³ conical flask, bung fitted with delivery tube, about 50 cm length of rubber tubing, 100 cm³ gas syringe (ensure syringe plunger is free moving), gas syringe holder, boss, stand, stopwatch, measuring cylinder, eye protection.

Measuring the light transmitted through a solution
Equipment and materials required
Two measuring cylinders, stopwatch, paper with large cross in the centre, conical flask, beaker, 0.2 mol/dm³ sodium thiosulfate, 0.2 mol/dm³ hydrochloric acid (irritant), eye protection (chemical splashproof goggles).

Safety: During this experiment, sulfur dioxide is produced which is toxic and can trigger asthmatic attacks. Therefore this should be completed in a well-ventilated room. Once the reaction is complete, the mixture should be disposed of following CLEAPSS guidelines in Hazcard 95C. CLEAPSS Hazcard 97 Sulfur dioxide – toxic.

Demonstration of the reaction between magnesium and acid
Equipment and materials required
Hydrochloric acid (1 mol/dm³) (CLEAPSS Hazcard 47A), strips of 1 cm magnesium ribbon (CLEAPSS Hazcard 59A), test tube, eye protection.

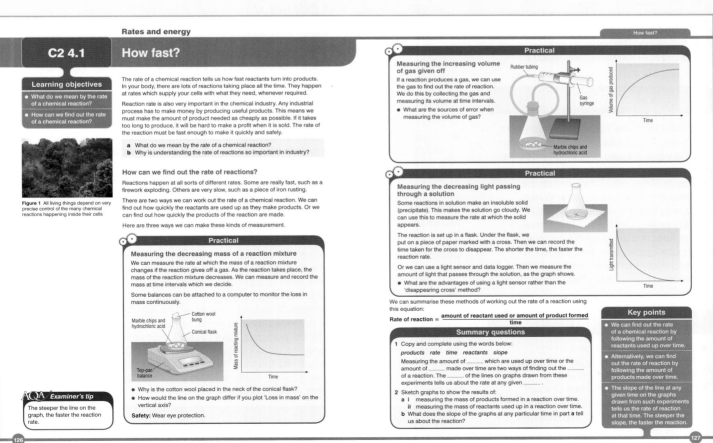

C2 4.2 Collision theory and surface area

Learning objectives

Students should learn:
- that different factors affect the rate of reaction
- what collision theory is
- how collision theory can be used to explain the effect of surface area on the rate of reaction.

Learning outcomes

Most students should be able to:
- list the factors that affect the rate of reaction
- recall a definition of collision theory
- describe how surface area affects the rate of reaction.

Some students should also be able to:
- explain in detail collision theory
- apply collision theory to explain in detail how surface area affects the rate of reaction.

Answers to in-text questions

a The particles must collide with sufficient energy for a reaction to occur.

b The activation energy.

c The same mass of small pieces of wood.

d Increasing the surface area increases the rate of the reaction.

Support

- Some students will have difficulty with isolating variables. You could provide the variables and give these students suggested measurements on separate cards. They could then match the values with the variables and use this in their experiment. To add to this activity, the variable that must be kept constant could be written in one colour, and the independent and dependent variables could be in another colour. Ask the students what the colour code means.

Extend

- Ask students to suggest which collisions would not cause a reaction (those with insufficient energy, incorrect orientation, two product particles or a reactant and a product colliding). Students could illustrate these factors as particle diagrams.

AQA Specification link-up: Chemistry C2.4

- Chemical reactions can only occur when reacting particles collide with each other and with sufficient energy. The minimum amount of energy particles must have to react is called the activation energy. *[C2.4.1 b)]*
- Increasing the surface area of solid reactants increases the frequency of collisions and so increases the rate of reaction. *[C2.4.1 f)]*
- Interpret graphs showing the amount of product formed (or reactant used up) with time, in terms of the rate of the reaction.

Controlled Assessment: AS4.2 Assess and manage risks when carrying out practical work. *[AS4.2.1 a) b)]*; AS4.3 Collect primary and secondary data. *[AS4.3.2 a)]*; AS4.4 Select and process primary and secondary data. *[AS4.4.2 c)]*

Lesson structure

Starters

Labelling – Give students a diagram of the equipment used to monitor the rate of the reaction of marble (calcium carbonate) with acid, when mass loss is being measured. Ask them to label the equipment. Support students by giving them the labels and completing the activity as a 'cut-and-stick' exercise. Extend students by explaining how this equipment could be used to monitor rate of reaction. *(5 minutes)*

Thinking – Ask students to work in pairs and list ways of monitoring the rate of reaction between an acid and a metal [mass loss, gas production]. Then ask students for ways in which this reaction could be speeded up [heat the acid, increase the surface area of the metal, increase the concentration of the acid]. *(10 minutes)*

Main

- Magnesium is often found as ribbon or in powdered form in schools. Show the students samples of each. Ask them to predict which would have the faster rate of reaction and why (using collision theory to explain). In their prediction, they should include a word equation (balanced symbol equation for Higher Tier students) to represent the reaction and what observations they would expect. They could then complete a risk assessment for the experiment, carry it out (once checked) and see if their prediction was correct.

- Marble chips come in a variety of sizes but each size is within a range. Show the students samples of different marble chips. Explain that they are going to investigate the mass lost during this experiment in order to decide how the surface area affects the rate. Encourage students to consider what the variables are in the experiment [time, temperature, concentration and volume of acid, mass of marble].

- Students should then decide on the appropriate values of each and detail which variables should be control variables. The investigation should then be completed and a conclusion written using collision theory. This provides an excellent opportunity to cover the investigative aspects of the Controlled Assessment.

Plenaries

Summarise – Ask the students to make a bullet-point list of facts about collision theory. *(5 minutes)*

Demonstration – For this demo you will need an iron nail, iron wool, iron filings, tongs, a heat-proof mat, a Bunsen burner, spatula, eye protection. Show students the iron nail, iron wool and iron filings. Ask them what reaction will happen when the iron is put in the flame and ask for a volunteer to write the word equation on the board [iron + oxygen → iron oxide]. You could extend students by asking them to write a balanced symbol equation $[4]Fe + [3]O_2 \rightarrow [2]Fe_2O_3$. Ask the students to predict which will combust most quickly and why. Support students by encouraging them to use the Student Book and think about the work that they have completed in the main part of the lesson. Demonstrate each type of iron in the flame: hold the nail into the blue flame using tongs; then hold a small piece of iron wool into the flame using tongs; finally sprinkle a few iron filings from a spatula into the flame. Wear eye protection. *(10 minutes)*

Practical support

Which burns faster – ribbon or powder?
Equipment and materials required

Bunsen burner and safety equipment, 2 cm length of magnesium ribbon (CLEAPSS Hazcard 59A), magnesium powder (highly flammable), spatula, tongs, stopwatch, eye protection.

Details

Hold the end of the magnesium ribbon with tongs. Put the tip of the ribbon in the top of the blue gas cone. As soon as the ribbon ignites, remove it from the flame and observe. Then sprinkle about half a spatula of magnesium powder directly into the blue flame (held at an angle).

Safety: Eye protection should be worn throughout this practical. Magnesium oxide powder will be made and may enter the air; this could irritate airways and therefore the reaction should be completed in a well-ventilated room. When magnesium ribbon burns, a very bright white light is produced. This can blind if people look at it

directly. Therefore encourage students to look past the reaction or alternatively use special blue glass/plastic to mute the light.

Investigating surface area
Equipment and materials required

Conical flask, 1 mol/dm^3 dilute hydrochloric acid (CLEAPSS Hazcard 47A), cotton wool, top-pan balance, marble chips of different sizes, measuring cylinder, stopwatch, eye protection.

Details

Wash and dry the marble chips (to remove the powder from the surface). Measure out about 1 g of marble chips of a certain size into a conical flask. Eye protection should be worn at this point. Add 25 cm^3 of acid and put in the cotton wool plug. Put the reaction vessel on to the top-pan balance and observe the mass change over time. Repeat the experiment with different sized marble chips.

Control variables are: concentration of acid, volume of acid, mass of marble, temperature.

Safety: Eye protection should be worn.

Rates and energy

C2 4.2 Collision theory and surface area

Learning objectives
- What affects the rate of a chemical reaction?
- What is collision theory?
- How does collision theory explain the effect of surface area on reaction rate?

In everyday life we control the rates of chemical reactions. People often do it without knowing! For example, cooking cakes in an oven or revving up a car engine. In chemistry we need to know what affects the rate of reactions. We also need to explain why each factor affects the rate of a reaction.

There are four main factors which affect the rate of chemical reactions:
- temperature
- surface area
- concentration of solutions or pressure of gases
- presence of a catalyst.

Reactions can only take place when the particles (atoms, ions or molecules) of reactants come together. But the reacting particles don't just have to bump into each other. They also need enough energy to react when they collide. This is known as **collision theory**.

The smallest amount of energy that particles must have before they can react is called the **activation energy**.

So reactions are more likely to happen between reactant particles if we:
- increase the chance of reacting particles colliding with each other
- increase the energy that they have when they collide.

If we increase the chance of particles reacting, we will also increase the rate of reaction.

a What must happen before two particles have a chance of reacting?
b Particles must have a minimum amount of energy to be able to react. What is this energy called?

Figure 1 There is no doubt that the chemicals in these fireworks have reacted. But how can we explain what happens in a chemical reaction?

Surface area and reaction rate

Imagine lighting a campfire. You don't pile large logs together and try to set them alight. You use small pieces of wood to begin with. Doing this increases the surface area of the wood. This means there is more wood exposed to react with oxygen in the air.

When a solid reacts in a solution, the size of the pieces of solid affects the rate of the reaction. The particles inside a large lump of solid are not in contact with the solution, so they can't react. The particles inside the solid have to wait for the particles on the surface to react first.

In smaller lumps, or in a powder, each tiny piece of solid is surrounded by solution. More particles are exposed to attack. This means that reactions can take place much more quickly.

c Which has the larger surface area – a log or the same mass of small pieces of wood?
d How does the surface area of a solid affect its rate of reaction?

Figure 2 Cooking – an excellent example of controlling reaction rates!

Practical

Which burns faster?

Make sure you have a heatproof mat under the Bunsen burner and you must wear eye protection.

Try igniting a 2 cm length of magnesium ribbon and time how long it takes to burn.

Take a small spatula tip of magnesium powder and sprinkle it into the Bunsen flame.
- What safety precautions should you take in this experiment?
- Explain your observations.

Practical

Investigating the effect of surface area

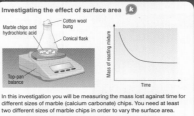

Marble chips and hydrochloric acid
Cotton wool bung
Conical flask
Top-pan balance

In this investigation you will be measuring the mass lost against time for different sizes of marble (calcium carbonate) chips. You need at least two different sizes of marble chips in order to vary the surface area.
- What variables should you control to make this a fair test?
- Why does this method of finding out the rate of reaction work?
- Use the data collected to draw a graph. Explain what the graph shows. (A data logger would help to plot a graph of the results.)

Safety: Wear eye protection.

AQA Examiner's tip

Particles collide all the time, but only some collisions lead to reactions.
Increasing the number of collisions in a certain time and the energy of collisions produces faster rates.
Larger surface area does not result in collisions with more energy but does increase the frequency of collisions.

Key points
- Particles must collide, with a certain amount of energy, before they can react.
- The minimum amount of energy that particles must have in order to react is called the activation energy.
- The rate of a chemical reaction increases if the surface area of any solid reactants is increased. This increases the frequency of collisions between reacting particles.

Summary questions

1 Copy and complete using the words below:
energy activation collide frequently minimum
Particles can react with each other only when they _____ with sufficient _____. Reaction rates increase when collisions are more energetic and/or happen more _____. The _____ amount of energy needed for particles to react is known as the _____ energy.

2 Draw a diagram to explain why it is easier to light a fire using small pieces of wood rather than large logs.

3 Why do you digest your food more quickly if you chew it well before you swallow it?

Further teaching suggestions

Evaluation
- Students could complete an evaluation about the calcium carbonate and acid reaction. For example, the problems that they might have found are: 'The same mass of marble in each experiment could not be achieved because of natural variation in the marble', 'Mass was lost before the reaction vessel was put on the balance', 'The balances aren't sensitive enough to get enough information to draw graphs.' Students could then consider ways to change the method, to try to reduce these problems and ultimately the errors in the experiment.

Bath bomb
- A bath bomb is mainly a metal carbonate and an acid. When they are put into water a neutralisation reaction happens. As the two reactants dissolve, they can collide and react. Ask students to explain why a bath bomb takes a long time to react with water, but if it is crumbled up, it reacts more quickly. You could even make a bath bomb in the lesson and investigate how the surface area of the bath bomb affects the rate at which it reacts.

Summary answers

1 collide, energy, frequently, minimum, activation

2 Students should draw a diagram clearly explaining/showing that cutting a solid into smaller pieces increases its surface area.

3 Because you have increased the food's surface area for reaction with digesting chemicals.

C2 4.3

The effect of temperature

Learning objectives

Students should learn that:

- that increasing the temperature affects the rate of reactions
- how collision theory can be used to explain how temperature affects rate of reaction.

Learning outcomes

Most students should be able to:

- describe how increasing the temperature affects the rate of reactions
- state two reasons why increasing the temperature increases the rate.

Some students should also be able to:

- use collision theory to explain in detail how and why increasing the temperature changes the rate of reaction.

Support

- Some students will have difficulty in understanding the link between rate of reaction and temperature. Using a familiar situation can help students to understand abstract concepts more easily. Link temperature and rate of reaction with dissolving sugar into tea. Ask students to predict which cup of tea will dissolve sugar the quickest. This physical change could be demonstrated or carried out by the students. Each group from the class could put its results from the thiosulfate experiment into spreadsheet. This could then be used to calculate a class mean quickly and plot a graph of these results.

Extend

- Students could consider the effect of temperature on a reaction where the particles are in a solid state. As the particles are only vibrating, not moving, there will be no increase or decrease in frequency of collisions as temperature is changed. However, the solids would need to be mixed for the reactant particles to come into contact with each other. They would then need an input of energy to overcome the activation energy.

AQA Specification link-up: Chemistry C2.4

- Increasing the temperature increases the speed of the reacting particles so that they collide more frequently and more energetically. This increases the rate of reaction. *[C2.4.1 c)]*
- Interpret graphs showing the amount of product formed (or reactant used up) with time, in terms of the rate of the reaction. *[C2.4]*

Controlled Assessment: AS4.1 Plan practical ways to develop and test candidates own scientific ideas. *[AS4.1.1 c)]*; AS4.3 Collect primary and secondary data. *[AS4.3.2 b) c)]*; AS4.5 Analyse and interpret primary and secondary data. *[AS4.5.2 b) d)]*

Lesson structure

Starters

Pictionary – Create packs of cards with these statements on: 'increase temperature', 'collision', 'particle', 'reactant', 'product', 'rate', 'chemical reaction'. Split the students into pairs and give them a pack of cards. Ask them to take it in turns to pick up the card and draw a picture (with no text, symbols or numbers) to get their partner to say the statement or word. *(5 minutes)*

What is in the bag? – In a bag, put in key words on separate pieces of paper: 'collision theory', 'temperature', 'particles', 'collision', 'rate', 'activation energy'. Then ask for a volunteer to come to the front and remove a key word. They can then explain what that words means. Allow students who have difficulty to go back to their seat and look through the Student Book, then talk to neighbours; invite them back at the end of the Starter. Extend students by asking them to use the word correctly in a sentence. In total, ask five volunteers to explain each of the words in turn. *(10 minutes)*

Main

- Students could experimentally determine the effect of temperature on rate of reaction by using the sodium thiosulfate reaction. As a class, decide on five temperatures that will be used – the maximum temperature should be 50 °C to minimise any sulfur dioxide liberated. In small groups each temperature is completed once, but then three groups (or the whole class) could pool their results and take a mean, making the results more reliable.
- Students could plot a graph, drawing a line of best fit. They should then use their graph and their knowledge of collision theory to draw a conclusion. This provides an opportunity to cover the investigative aspects of the Controlled Assessment.
- Ask students to draw a cartoon to show the effect of heating up a reaction in terms of its rate. Students could be encouraged to personify the particles and make a fun depiction of the reaction. To help them, the cartoon framework could be given with statements to include in a box below their images, to explain what is happening.
- Ensure that students understand the two reasons why increasing the temperature increases the rate of reaction. Some students will quote the increased frequency of collisions but fail to mention the greater proportion of collisions with energy greater than the activation energy in examination questions.

Plenaries

Spot the mistake – Ask students to spot the error in the following sentence: 'When temperature is dropped, particles have more energy but move around less and so the rate of reaction stays the same.' [When temperature is dropped, the particles have less energy and the rate of reaction will decrease.] *(5 minutes)*

Sentences – In small groups ask the students to finish the following sentence:

'As you heat up a reaction ...'

After a few minutes ask the groups to read out their finished sentences. Then choose the most scientific sentence and give that group a prize. Support students by giving them a selection of endings for the sentence – some correct, some incorrect and some more scientific than others. Encourage students to select which ending they want to use from the list. Extend students by asking them to draw a labelled diagram to illustrate their sentence. *(10 minutes)*

Practical support

Reacting magnesium and hydrochloric acid at different temperatures

Equipment and materials required

Ice bath, test tube rack, hot water bath, 1 mol/dm^3 hydrochloric acid (CLEAPSS Hazcard 47A), 1 cm magnesium strips (CLEAPSS Hazcard 59A), calcium carbonate, two measuring cylinders, six test tubes, thermometer, eye protection.

Details

Wearing eye protection, measure out 2 cm^3 of acid into each test tube, put two test tubes in an ice bath, two in a test tube rack and two in a hot-water bath. Allow the test tubes to rest in the water/ice baths for about 5 minutes to reach the appropriate temperature. Students can check the temperature of the acid using the thermometer. Add one strip of magnesium to each of the different temperatures of acid. Allow the students to observe the reaction and comment on the rate at different temperatures, encouraging them to decide how they are determining the rate [amount of bubbles produced]. Keep the lab well ventilated.

Repeat the reaction with one marble chip (calcium carbonate) in each test tube.

The effect of temperature on rate of reaction

Equipment and materials required

Two measuring cylinders, stopwatch, paper with large cross in the centre, conical flask, 0.2 mol/dm^3 sodium thiosulfate, 0.2 mol/dm^3 hydrochloric acid, ice bath, water bath/hot plate, thermometer, eye protection (chemical splashproof goggles).

Details

Measure 10 cm^3 of acid (eye protection should be worn) and 10 cm^3 of sodium thiosulfate in separate clean measuring cylinders and reduce or increase the temperatures of these solutions using ice baths/water baths/hot plates. Choose temperatures that are easy to attain, e.g. 10 °C, 20 °C, 30 °C, 40 °C, 50 °C (maximum). At least five experiments need to be completed to draw a line graph. Place the conical flask on the centre of the large cross; first add the sodium thiosulfate to the beaker. Then add the acid and start the stopwatch and swirl to mix the solutions. Stop the clock when the cross disappears and note the time. You may wish to use a light sensor.

Safety: This experiment produces sulfur dioxide, which is toxic and can trigger asthmatic attacks. Therefore this practical should be completed in a well-ventilated room. Once the reaction is complete, follow CLEAPSS guidelines in Hazcard 95C for correct disposal.

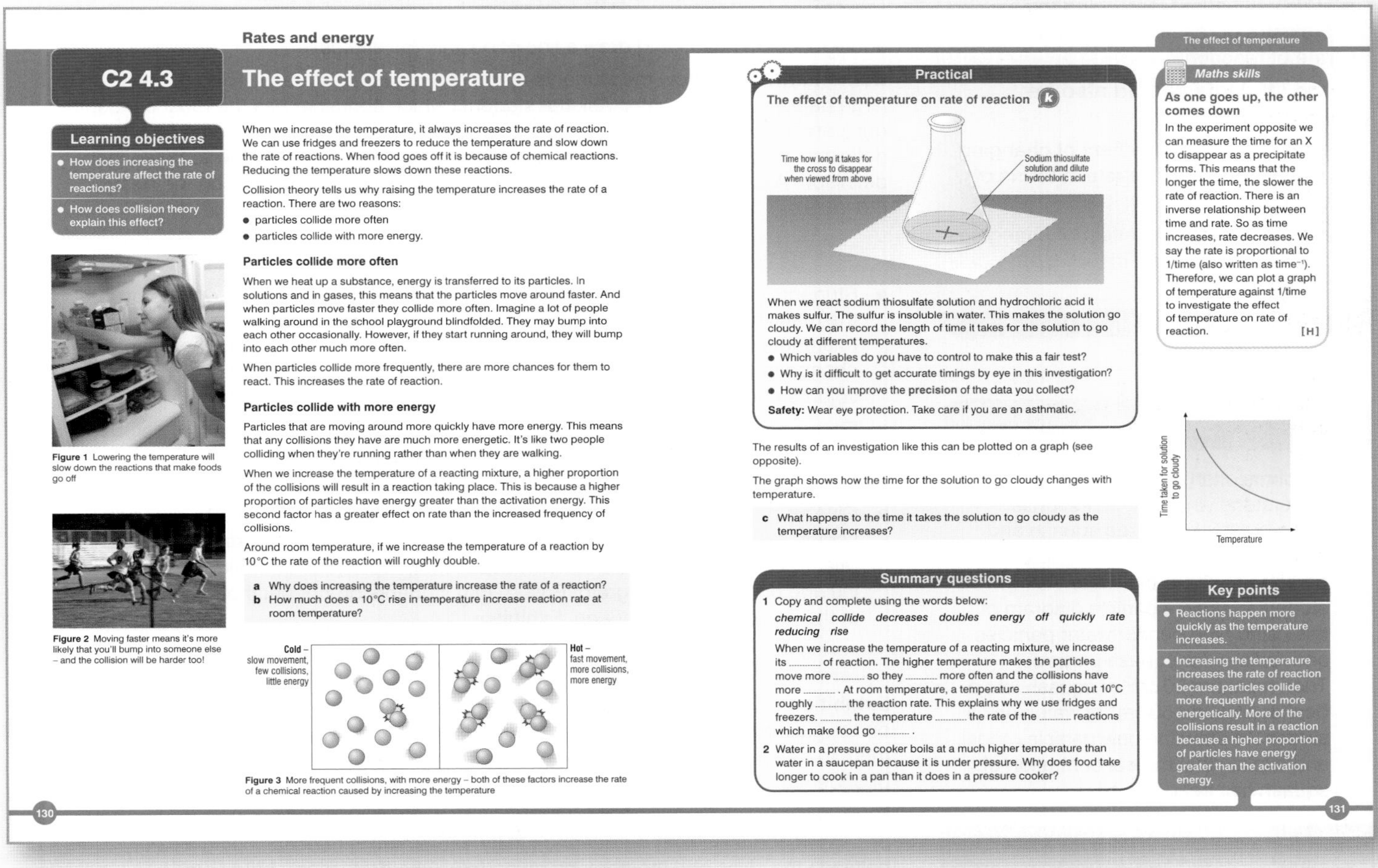

Rates and energy

C2 4.3 The effect of temperature

Learning objectives

- How does increasing the temperature affect the rate of reactions?
- How does collision theory explain this effect?

When we increase the temperature, it always increases the rate of reaction. We can use fridges and freezers to reduce the temperature and slow down the rate of reactions. When food goes off it is because of chemical reactions. Reducing the temperature slows down these reactions.

Collision theory tells us why raising the temperature increases the rate of a reaction. There are two reasons:

- particles collide more often
- particles collide with more energy.

Particles collide more often

When we heat up a substance, energy is transferred to its particles. In solutions and in gases, this means that the particles move around faster. And when particles move faster they collide more often. Imagine a lot of people walking around in the school playground blindfolded. They may bump into each other occasionally. However, if they start running around, they will bump into each other much more often.

When particles collide more frequently, there are more chances for them to react. This increases the rate of reaction.

Particles collide with more energy

Particles that are moving around more quickly have more energy. This means that any collisions they have are much more energetic. It's like two people colliding when they're running rather than when they are walking.

When we increase the temperature of a reacting mixture, a higher proportion of the collisions will result in a reaction taking place. This is because a higher proportion of particles have energy greater than the activation energy. This second factor has a greater effect on rate than the increased frequency of collisions.

Around room temperature, if we increase the temperature of a reaction by 10 °C the rate of the reaction will roughly double.

a Why does increasing the temperature increase the rate of a reaction?
b How much does a 10 °C rise in temperature increase reaction rate at room temperature?

Figure 1 Lowering the temperature will slow down the reactions that make foods go off

Figure 2 Moving faster means it's more likely that you'll bump into someone else – and the collision will be harder too!

Cold – slow movement, few collisions, little energy
Hot – fast movement, more collisions, more energy

Figure 3 More frequent collisions, with more energy – both of these factors increase the rate of a chemical reaction caused by increasing the temperature

130

The effect of temperature

Practical

The effect of temperature on rate of reaction

Time how long it takes for the cross to disappear when viewed from above
Sodium thiosulfate solution and dilute hydrochloric acid

When we react sodium thiosulfate solution and hydrochloric acid it makes sulfur. The sulfur is insoluble in water. This makes the solution go cloudy. We can record the length of time it takes for the solution to go cloudy at different temperatures.

- Which variables do you have to control to make this a fair test?
- Why is it difficult to get accurate timings by eye in this investigation?
- How can you improve the **precision** of the data you collect?

Safety: Wear eye protection. Take care if you are an asthmatic.

The results of an investigation like this can be plotted on a graph (see opposite).

The graph shows how the time for the solution to go cloudy changes with temperature.

c What happens to the time it takes the solution to go cloudy as the temperature increases?

Maths skills

As one goes up, the other comes down

In the experiment opposite we can measure the time for an X to disappear as a precipitate forms. This means that the longer the time, the slower the rate of reaction. There is an inverse relationship between time and rate. So as time increases, rate decreases. We say the rate is proportional to 1/time (also written as time^{-1}). Therefore, we can plot a graph of temperature against 1/time to investigate the effect of temperature on rate of reaction. [H]

Time taken for solution to go cloudy
Temperature

Summary questions

1 Copy and complete using the words below:

chemical collide decreases doubles energy off quickly rate reducing rise

When we increase the temperature of a reacting mixture, we increase its .... of reaction. The higher temperature makes the particles move more .... so they .... more often and the collisions have more .... At room temperature, a temperature .... of about 10°C roughly .... the reaction rate. This explains why we use fridges and freezers. .... the temperature .... the rate of the .... reactions which make food go ....

2 Water in a pressure cooker boils at a much higher temperature than water in a saucepan because it is under pressure. Why does food take longer to cook in a pan than it does in a pressure cooker?

Key points

- Reactions happen more quickly as the temperature increases.
- Increasing the temperature increases the rate of reaction because particles collide more frequently and more energetically. More of the collisions result in a reaction because a higher proportion of particles have energy greater than the activation energy.

131

Answers to in-text questions

a The particles collide more often and, when they do, they have more energy. So in a given time there are more collisions that have at least the activation energy required for the reaction.

b The rate roughly doubles.

c The time decreases.

Summary answers

1 rate, quickly, collide, energy, rise, doubles, reducing, decreases, chemical, off

2 It is at a higher temperature in the pressure cooker. This speeds up the chemical reactions that make food cook. The steam particles move around more quickly with greater energy when under pressure. This increases the collision frequency with food substances.

C2 4.4

The effect of concentration or pressure

AQA / Specification link-up: Chemistry C2.4

- Increasing the pressure of reacting gases increases the frequency of collisions and so increases the rate of reaction. [C2.4.1 d)]
- Increasing the concentration of reactants in solutions increases the frequency of collisions and so increases the rate of reaction. [C2.4.1 e)]
- Interpret graphs showing the amount of product formed (or reactant used up) with time, in terms of the rate of the reaction.
  Controlled Assessment: AS4.3 Collect primary and secondary data. [AS4.3.2 a)]; AS4.5 Analyse and interpret primary and secondary data. [AS4.5.3 a), AS4.5.4 a)]

Learning objectives

Students should learn that:

- that increasing the concentration of reactants in solutions increases the rate of reaction
- that changing the pressure of reacting gases changes the rate of reaction.

Learning outcomes

Most students should be able to:

- state what effect increasing the concentration of reactants in solutions has on the rate of reaction
- describe what we mean by gas pressure
- state what effect increasing the pressure of reacting gases has on the rate of reaction.

Some students should also be able to:

- explain in detail the effect of changing concentration on the rate in terms of collision theory
- explain in detail the effect of changing pressure on the rate in terms of collision theory.

Support

- Students often find it difficult to understand what concentration is. Get a bottle of coloured squash and explain that there are lots of coloured particles mixed in the water. Ask a student to draw a particle diagram of this using blue pen for water particles and red pen for squash particles. Then measure 50 cm³ of squash into a beaker and add 50 cm³ of water. Ask a student to draw the new particle model, and explain that the concentration of squash has been halved.

Extend

- Ask students to explain the effects of changing pressure on the rate of reaction for a chemical change with gaseous reactants [an increase in pressure increases the amount of gaseous reactants in a given volume/ space, making collisions more likely and rate of reaction increases]. You could extend students further to explain the effects of changing pressure on a chemical change that has no reactants in the gaseous state [no change].

Lesson structure

Starters

Graph – Give students an unfinished concentration–time graph with two curved lines to show reactants and products. Ask students to complete the axis labels (including units) and briefly explain the shape of the two curves. Support students by giving them the missing labels to add to the graph. Extend students by asking them to plot a few additional data points and draw a line of best fit. *(5 minutes)*

Demonstration – Show the students a bottle of undiluted squash. Then put half into a large beaker and add water. Ask the students which container has the most concentrated drink and how they know. Then ask the students to work in pairs to come up with a definition of concentration. Ask each pair to come to the board and write down their definition. Ask the whole class to consider the definitions and decide on the best. *(10 minutes)*

Main

- Students can experimentally determine the effect of concentration on rate by observing the reaction between marble chips and acid. At this point, moles have been introduced to students but not calculations in terms of moles per unit volume. Therefore, to change the concentration, the volume of the acid should be diluted with water but the volume of the mixture should remain constant, so that the experiment is fair.
- Encourage the students to plot all the curves on the same axis. Then ask students to explain their results using collision theory. (This offers another excellent opportunity to cover any investigative aspect of the Controlled Assessment.)
- Give students an A4 sheet of paper and ask them to split in it half. On one side they should explain how concentration affects rate and on the other how pressure affects rate. In each section they should define the key word (concentration/pressure) and include one labelled diagram. Ensure that students do not put their name on the front of the poster. (See Plenary on 'Exhibition'.)

Plenaries

Exhibition – Get all the students' posters from the main part of the lesson. Lay them out on the side benches and give each a number. Arrange students in small groups and ask them to rate each poster out of 10 in terms of presentation, accuracy of science and ease of understanding. *(5 minutes)*

Demonstration – For this demonstration, iron wool, tongs, deflagration spoon, a gas jar of oxygen and a Bunsen burner and safety equipment is needed. Using a safety screen between the class and the demonstration (plus eye protection), hold some iron wool into a blue Bunsen flame using tongs. Then put some iron wool on a deflagration spoon and heat it until it is glowing in the top of a blue gas cone. Then quickly put the wool into a gas jar of oxygen. Ask students, in small groups, to explain which reaction was more vigorous and why. Then choose a few students to feedback into the class. *(10 minutes)*

Answers to in-text questions

a There are more particles in the same volume, making collisions more likely.

b The higher acid concentration (green line) shows the fastest reaction because the line is steepest initially (or it finished reacting first).

Practical support

Investigating the effect of concentration on rate of reaction

Equipment and materials required

Marble chips, 1 mol/dm³ hydrochloric acid (CLEAPSS Hazcard 47A), 250 cm³ conical flask, top-pan balance, cotton wool, stopwatch, measuring cylinder, eye protection.

Details

Put about five marble chips into the bottom of a conical flask. Measure out 25 cm³ of acid (wear eye protection), and put it into the conical flask. Put a piece of cotton wool in the neck. Quickly place it on the balance and take a reading, start the stopwatch. Measure the mass of the conical flask every 10 s for 2 min. You may wish to monitor this reaction by sealing the container and using a carbon dioxide probe or gas pressure probe and data logger. Repeat for different concentrations.

Safety: Use a loose seal to prevent a build-up of pressure in the glass vessel.

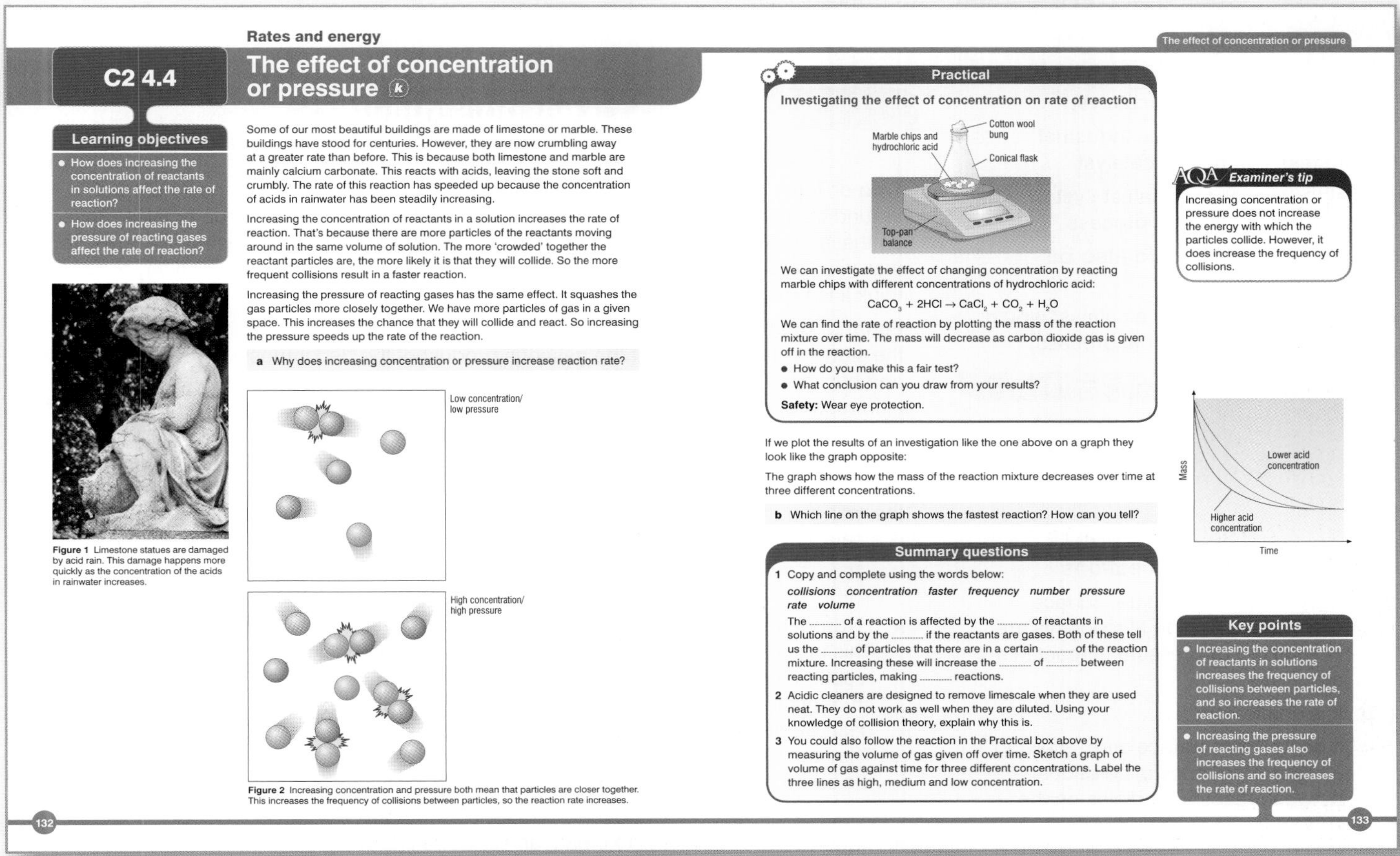

Rates and energy

The effect of concentration or pressure

C2 4.4 The effect of concentration or pressure (k)

Learning objectives

- How does increasing the concentration of reactants in solutions affect the rate of reaction?
- How does increasing the pressure of reacting gases affect the rate of reaction?

Some of our most beautiful buildings are made of limestone or marble. These buildings have stood for centuries. However, they are now crumbling away at a greater rate than before. This is because both limestone and marble are mainly calcium carbonate. This reacts with acids, leaving the stone soft and crumbly. The rate of this reaction has speeded up because the concentration of acids in rainwater has been steadily increasing.

Increasing the concentration of reactants in a solution increases the rate of reaction. That's because there are more particles of the reactants moving around in the same volume of solution. The more 'crowded' together the reactant particles are, the more likely it is that they will collide. So the more frequent collisions result in a faster reaction.

Increasing the pressure of reacting gases has the same effect. It squashes the gas particles more closely together. We have more particles of gas in a given space. This increases the chance that they will collide and react. So increasing the pressure speeds up the rate of the reaction.

a Why does increasing concentration or pressure increase reaction rate?

Low concentration/low pressure

High concentration/high pressure

Figure 1 Limestone statues are damaged by acid rain. This damage happens more quickly as the concentration of the acids in rainwater increases.

Figure 2 Increasing concentration and pressure both mean that particles are closer together. This increases the frequency of collisions between particles, so the reaction rate increases.

Practical

Investigating the effect of concentration on rate of reaction

Marble chips and hydrochloric acid — Cotton wool bung — Conical flask — Top-pan balance

We can investigate the effect of changing concentration by reacting marble chips with different concentrations of hydrochloric acid:

$$CaCO_3 + 2HCl \rightarrow CaCl_2 + CO_2 + H_2O$$

We can find the rate of the reaction by plotting the mass of the reaction mixture over time. The mass will decrease as carbon dioxide gas is given off in the reaction.

- How do you make this a fair test?
- What conclusion can you draw from your results?

Safety: Wear eye protection.

If we plot the results of an investigation like the one above on a graph they look like the graph opposite:

The graph shows how the mass of the reaction mixture decreases over time at three different concentrations.

b Which line on the graph shows the fastest reaction? How can you tell?

Summary questions

1 Copy and complete using the words below:

collisions concentration faster frequency number pressure rate volume

The .... of a reaction is affected by the .... of reactants in solutions and by the .... if the reactants are gases. Both of these tell us the .... of particles that there are in a certain .... of the reaction mixture. Increasing these will increase the .... of .... between reacting particles, making .... reactions.

2 Acidic cleaners are designed to remove limescale when they are used neat. They do not work as well when they are diluted. Using your knowledge of collision theory, explain why this is.

3 You could also follow the reaction in the Practical box above by measuring the volume of gas given off over time. Sketch a graph of volume of gas against time for three different concentrations. Label the three lines as high, medium and low concentration.

AQA Examiner's tip

Increasing concentration or pressure does not increase the energy with which the particles collide. However, it does increase the frequency of collisions.

Mass / Lower acid concentration / Higher acid concentration / Time

Key points

- Increasing the concentration of reactants in solutions increases the frequency of collisions between particles, and so increases the rate of reaction.
- Increasing the pressure of reacting gases also increases the frequency of collisions and so increases the rate of reaction.

Further teaching suggestions

Why only gases?

- Ask students to explain why changing the pressure of a reaction mixture only affects a reaction with one or more reactants in the gaseous phase.

Calculate the gradient

- Once the graph of the production of gas has been drawn, students could be shown how to calculate a numerical value for rate. The graph should be a curve. They choose a particular time and draw a tangent at this point on the curve. Then they work out the gradient (change in vertical value/change in horizontal value) and this is the rate measured in units that refer to volume of gas/time.

Moles per decimetre cubed

- Introduce the idea that concentration is measured in moles per decimetre cubed (mol/dm³). Ask about the relative concentrations of a 0.25 and a 2.0 mol/dm³ solution and ask students to explain the difference in terms of particles.

Sodium thiosulfate reaction

- You may wish to investigate how the concentration of sodium thiosulfate affects its reaction with hydrochloric acid. See www.chemistryteachers.org and search for 'sodium thiosulfate'.

Summary answers

1 rate, concentration, pressure, number, volume, frequency, collisions, faster

2 There are more particles in the acid to collide with limescale particles when the cleaner is more concentrated, so increasing the rate of reaction.

3 Graph with vertical axis labelled 'Volume of gas' and horizontal axis labelled 'Time'. Three curved lines rising at different gradients, gradually levelling off. The steepest curve labelled 'high concentration' and the shallowest labelled 'low concentration'.

C2 4.5

The effect of catalysts

AQA
Specification link-up: Chemistry C2.4

- Catalysts change the rate of chemical reactions but are not used up during the reaction. Different reactions need different catalysts. [C2.4.1 g)]
- Catalysts are important in increasing the rates of chemical reactions used in industrial processes to reduce costs. [C2.4.1 h)]

Controlled Assessment: AS4.4 Select and process primary and secondary data. [AS4.4.2 c)]

Learning objectives

Students should learn:

- what a catalyst is
- how catalysts affect the rate of reactions.

Learning outcomes

Most students should be able to:

- give a definition of a catalyst
- give an example of an industrial process that uses a catalyst
- list the reasons why a catalyst may be used in an industrial process.

Some students should also be able to:

- explain in detail why a catalyst would be used in an industrial process.

Answers to in-text questions

a Increasing temperature, surface area, concentration (if reactants are in solution) or pressure (if reactants are gases).

b It is unaffected.

c It has greater surface area, allowing a higher frequency of collisions between reacting particles on the surface.

Support

- You could support students in drawing the graph by giving them the labelled axis with the scales already written on to it. Encourage students to use a different colour for each catalyst that they consider for the decomposition of hydrogen peroxide.

Extend

- Ask students to discover some other examples of chemical reactions and the catalysts that they can use. You could also ask students to discover about inhibitors (catalysts that are used to slow down the rate of reaction or negative catalysts – e.g. in petrol).

Lesson structure

Starters

True or false – Give each student a statement about catalysts. Then they must walk around the room and ask three people if they think the statement is true or false. Based on these answers, the student should decide whether the statement is true or false. You may wish to ask each student to read his or her statement to the class and say if they think it is true or false. Then you give feedback. *(5 minutes)*

Foam of death – Write the formula of hydrogen peroxide (H_2O_2) on the board and ask the students to predict what the gaseous product of the decomposition reaction could be and how it could be tested [oxygen, which is tested with a glowing splint; they will often incorrectly suggest hydrogen, which 'pops' with a lighted splint]. See 'Practical support'. You could support students by using a periodic table and asking for volunteers to suggest the elements that the compound contains. As an extension, when the foam has dried slightly, allow students to come up to the foam and relight a glowing splint. Explain that the manganese(IV) oxide was not used up in the reaction, but increased the rate and this is a catalyst. *(10 minutes)*

Main

- Hydrogen peroxide is unstable in sunlight and will decompose into oxygen and water. This process is relatively slow, but a number of catalysts can be used to speed up this reaction: chopped raw potato; chopped fresh liver; manganese(IV) oxide. Encourage students to investigate gas production using the different catalysts to decide the best. Students should consider the dependent, independent and control variables. They should take a set of results for each catalyst and draw all the lines of best fit on the same graph, giving more coverage of the investigative aspects of the Controlled Assessment.

- Encourage the students to create an eight-line poem, where the first letters of each line spell 'catalyst'. Then choose some students to read their poem to the rest of the class.

Plenaries

Txt – Ask students to write a text message to summarise what they have learnt today. You could support students by giving them the text message and ask them to rewrite it in standard English. Students could be extended by being asked to include an example of a chemical reaction that can be affected by a catalyst. *(5 minutes)*

AfL (Assessment for Learning) – To continue 'the poem' activity from the main part of the lesson, ask students to swap their poem with a partner. If students feel that there is some incorrect science, they should amend the work in pencil. Once they have worked on the poem, it should be returned to its owner who should then review any comments that have been made. *(10 minutes)*

Summary answers

1 increases, used, remains, reaction

2 This increases their surface area.

3 The catalyst is not used up in the reaction.

Practical support

Foam of death

Equipment and materials required
Hydrogen peroxide (100 vol.) (CLEAPSS Hazcard 50 – corrosive), 1000 cm³ measuring cylinder, washing-up bowl, washing-up liquid, manganese(IV) oxide (harmful), spatula, cobalt chloride paper, splints, eye protection and gloves.

Details
Stand a 1000 cm³ measuring cylinder in a washing-up bowl. Add a good dash of washing-up liquid, and about 100 cm³ of 100 vol. H_2O_2. Add a spatula of manganese(IV) oxide and allow the students to observe.

Safety: Wear eye protection and be aware of skin burns. CLEAPSS Hazcard 60 Manganese(IV) oxide – harmful; 25 Cobalt chloride – toxic and harmful.

Investigating catalysis
Equipment and materials required
Stand, boss, gas syringe holder, gas syringe, 10 vol. hydrogen peroxide (irritant), manganese(IV) oxide (harmful), potato, liver,

white tile, knife, stopwatch, conical flask, bung, delivery tube, about a 25 cm length of rubber tube, measuring cylinder, spatula, eye protection.

Details
Measure out 25 cm³ of hydrogen peroxide and put it into the conical flask, eye protection should be worn. Finely chop some raw potato and put it into the flask. Quickly connect the bung to the gas syringe and note the volume of gas produced every 10 s for 2 min. Repeat with chopped liver, and repeat with a spatula of manganese(IV) oxide. Other transition metal oxides can also be investigated. You may wish to monitor this reaction by sealing the container and using a carbon dioxide probe or gas pressure probe and data logger.

Safety: Be aware of irritation caused by the hydrogen peroxide. Wash the affected area under cold water and it should dissipate. Make sure the syringe plunger is free moving. Make sure the seal is loose to avoid the glass container exploding. CLEAPSS Hazcard 60 Manganese(IV) oxide – harmful.

Rates and energy

C2 4.5 The effect of catalysts ⓚ

The effect of catalysts

Learning objectives
- What is a catalyst?
- How do catalysts affect the rate of reactions?

Sometimes a reaction might only work if we use very high temperatures or pressures. This can cost industry a lot of money. However, we can speed up some reactions by using **catalysts**.

a Apart from using a catalyst, how can we speed up a reaction?

A catalyst is a substance which increases the rate of a reaction. However, it is not changed chemically itself at the end of the reaction.

A catalyst is not used up in the reaction. So it can be used over and over again.

We need different catalysts for different reactions. Many of the catalysts we use in industry involve transition metals. For example, iron is used to make ammonia. Platinum is used to make nitric acid.

b How is a catalyst affected by a chemical reaction?

Figure 1 Catalysts are all around us, in the natural world and in industry. The catalysts in living things are called enzymes. Our planet would be very different without catalysts.

Figure 2 The transition metals platinum and palladium are used in the catalytic converters in cars

We normally use catalysts in the form of powders, pellets or fine gauzes. This gives them the biggest possible surface area.

c Why is a catalyst in the form of pellets more effective than a whole lump of the catalyst?

Not only does a catalyst speed up a reaction, but it does not get used up in the reaction. We can use a tiny amount of catalyst to speed up a reaction over and over again.

Practical

Investigating catalysis ⓚ

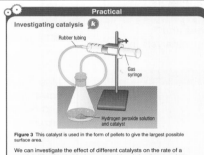

Figure 3 This catalyst is used in the form of pellets to give the largest possible surface area.

We can investigate the effect of different catalysts on the rate of a reaction. We will look at hydrogen peroxide solution decomposing:

$$2H_2O_2 \rightarrow 2H_2O + O_2$$

The reaction produces oxygen gas. We can collect this in a gas syringe using the apparatus shown above.

We can investigate the effect of many different substances on the rate of this reaction. Examples include manganese(IV) oxide and potassium iodide.

- State the independent variable in this investigation.

A table of the time taken to produce a certain volume of oxygen can then tell us which catalyst makes the reaction go fastest.

- What type of graph would you use to show the results of your investigation? Why?

Safety: Wear eye protection.

Summary questions

1 Copy and complete using the words below:
remains   increases   reaction   used
A catalyst .... the rate of a chemical reaction. However, it is not .... up and .... the same chemically after the ....

2 Solid catalysts used in chemical processes are often shaped as tiny beads or cylinders with holes through them. Why are they made in these shapes?

3 Why is the number of moles of catalyst needed to speed up a chemical reaction very small compared with the number of moles of reactants?

Did you know ... ?
The catalysts used in chemical plants eventually become 'poisoned' so that they don't work any more. This happens because impurities in the reaction mixture combine with the catalyst and stop it working properly.

AQA Examiner's tip
Catalysts change only the rate of reactions. They do not change the products.

Key points
- A catalyst speeds up the rate of a chemical reaction.
- A catalyst is not used up during a chemical reaction.
- Different catalysts are needed for different reactions.

134 / 135

Further teaching suggestions

Equations
- Encourage students to represent the reactions studied as balanced symbol equations. However, ensure that the condition of the reaction (including the catalyst) is listed on the arrow.

Hydrogen peroxide storage
- Ask students to consider why hydrogen peroxide is kept in a brown or black bottle away from light. [Light activates decomposition into water and oxygen.]

Questions and answers
- Give students a sheet of A4 paper and ask them to fold it in half (portrait). They should create five questions on the left-hand side about catalysts, using the Student Book for inspiration. Then they should write the answers on the right-hand side.

C2 4.6

Catalysts in action

AQA

Specification link-up: Chemistry C2.4

- Catalysts are important in increasing the rates of chemical reactions used in industrial processes to reduce costs. [C2.4.1 h)]
- Explain and evaluate the development, advantages and disadvantages of using catalysts in industrial processes. [C2.4]

Learning objectives

Students should learn:

- why catalysts are used in so many industrial processes
- how new catalysts are developed and the reason why there are so many different catalysts
- why there are disadvantages of using catalysts in industry.

Learning outcomes

Most students should be able to:

- state some advantages and disadvantages of using catalysts.
- explain why there are so many catalysts.

Some students should also be able to:

- evaluate the advantages and disadvantages of using catalysts in industry.

Lesson structure

Starters

Enzymes – Show students a photograph of a stomach, washing powder, washing-up liquid, and carpet cleaner. Ask students to make the link between the pictures [they all use enzymes]. Support students by giving them the word 'enzyme' as an anagram to help them get the connection. Extend students by asking them to give a definition of an enzyme [biological catalyst]. *(5 minutes)*

Catalytic converter – Get an old catalytic converter (from a scrapyard) and have it cut into slices (maybe in the Technology Department). Clean out the deposits, then show the slices (they look like a honeycomb) to the students. The students should be encouraged to discuss in small groups what this could be used for. Ask each group to feed back their thoughts and then share with the students that it is a catalytic converter used on a car exhaust to remove pollutant gases. *(10 minutes)*

Main

- Most industrial reactions use catalysts to reduce production costs. However, there are some disadvantages of using catalysts. Ask students to draw a table of advantages and disadvantages of using transition metals and their compounds, as well as enzymes. Extend students by asking them to underline the environmental statements in green, social statements in orange and economic statements in black.

- Catalysts are being developed all the time. Students could use secondary research such as books in the school library or the internet to find out current developments in catalysts. Key words would include: zeolites, fullerenes and nanochemistry. Students could then work in groups to make a 3-minute presentation about what they have found out.

Plenaries

Definitions – Ask students to use the Student Book to define the following key terms: catalyst [a chemical that changes the rate of reaction without being used up, e.g. manganese(IV) oxide used in the decomposition of hydrogen peroxide], enzyme [biological catalyst, e.g. lipase], transition metals [metals found in the central block of the periodic table and are often toxic, e.g. chromium]. Support students by giving them the words and the definitions so that they just match them up. Extend students by asking them to give an example for each. *(5 minutes)*

Press conference – Each group could give its presentation to the rest of the class. One student from each group in the audience should then pose a question to the presenters based on what they have seen and heard. The group should then answer the questions. *(10 minutes)*

Support

- Give students a flow chart with missing information to explain how new catalysts are researched, designed and made. You may wish to give the missing information to the students so that they can complete the activity as a 'cut-and-stick' activity.

Extend

- Ask students to research industrial processes and the catalysts that they use, e.g. the contact process to make sulfuric acid, which uses vanadium(V) oxide.

Further teaching suggestions

Debate
- Students could hold a debate about whether the use of catalysts is a good or bad idea for industrial processes.

Enzymes in industry
- Students could research to find out how enzymes are made (often by genetically modifying microorganisms) and consider the environmental, social and economic impact of this industry.

Questions and answers
- Students could copy out the objective questions and use the Student Book to answer them fully.

C2 4.6   Catalysts in action

Learning objectives
- Why are catalysts used in so many industrial processes?
- How are new catalysts developed and why are there so many different catalysts?
- What are the disadvantages of using catalysts in industry?

Catalysts are often very expensive precious metals. Gold, platinum and palladium are all costly but are the most effective catalysts for particular reactions. But it is often cheaper to use a catalyst than to pay for the extra energy needed without one. To get the same rate of reaction without a catalyst would require higher temperatures and/or pressures.

So catalysts save money and help the environment. That's because using high temperatures and pressures often involves burning fossil fuels. So operating at lower temperatures and pressures conserves these non-renewable resources. It also stops more carbon dioxide entering the atmosphere.

a Why do catalysts save a chemical company money?

However, many of the catalysts used in industry are transition metals or their compounds. These are often toxic. If they escape into the environment, they build up inside living things. Eventually they poison them. For example, the platinum and palladium used in catalytic converters slowly escape from car exhausts.

So chemists are working to develop new catalysts that are harmless to the environment. The search for the ideal catalyst is often a bit like trial and error. Each reaction is unique. Once a catalyst is found it might be improved by adding small amounts of other chemicals to it. All this takes a lot of time to investigate. However, the research is guided by knowledge of similar catalysed reactions. This knowledge is growing all the time.

Figure 1 Chinese scientists have recently developed a new catalyst for making biodiesel from vegetable oils. It's made from shrimp shells, and is cheaper and more efficient than conventional catalysts. The process that uses the new catalyst also causes less pollution.

Future development
Chemists have developed new techniques to look at reactions. They can now follow the reactions that happen on the surface of the metals in a catalytic converter. These are very fast reactions lasting only a fraction of a second. Knowing how the reactions take place will help them to design new catalysts.

Nanoparticles are also at the cutting edge of work on new catalysts. Scientists can arrange atoms into the best shapes for catalysing a particular reaction they have studied. A small mass of these catalysts has a huge surface area. This has raised hopes that fuel cells will one day take over from petrol and diesel to run cars.

○○ links
For information about nanoparticles, look back to C2 2.6 Nanoscience.

Catalysts in medicine
The catalysts used in making new drugs also contain precious metal compounds. The metal is bonded to an organic molecule. But now chemists can make these catalysts without the metal. The metal was needed to make a stable compound. However, research has resulted in a breakthrough which will mean much cheaper catalysts. There is also no risk of contaminating the drug made with a toxic transition metal.

b Why could it be unsafe to use compounds of transition metals to catalyse reactions to make drugs?

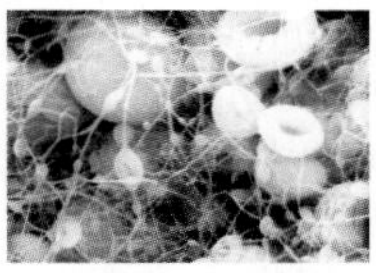

Enzymes
Enzymes are the very efficient catalysts found in living things. For years we've been using enzymes to help clean our clothes. Biological washing powders contain enzymes that help to 'break apart' stain molecules such as proteins at low temperatures. The low temperature washes save energy.

Low-temperature enzyme reactions are the basis of the biotechnology industry. Enzymes are soluble so would have to be separated from the products they make. However, scientists can bind them to a solid. The solution of reactants flows over the solid. No time or money has to be wasted separating out the enzymes to use again. The process can run continuously.

Figure 2 Scientists are developing long nanowires of platinum to use as catalysts in fuel cells. This photo is from an electron microscope. The wires are 1/50 000th of the width of a human hair. The breakthrough has been made in making them over a centimetre in length.

Summary questions
1 Give two ways in which catalysts are beneficial to the chemical industry.
2 What are the disadvantages of using transition metals or their compounds as catalysts?
3 Do some research to find out four industrial processes that make products using catalysts. Write a word equation for each reaction and name the catalyst used.

Key points
- Catalysts are used whenever possible in industry to increase rate of reaction and reduce energy costs.
- Traditional catalysts are often transition metals or their compounds, which can be toxic and harm the environment if they escape.
- Modern catalysts are being developed in industry which result in less waste and are safer for the environment.

Answers to in-text questions

a They save energy costs by allowing reactions to be conducted at lower temperatures or pressures.

b Drugs might be toxic if contaminated with transition metal compounds.

Summary answers

1 For example: they reduce energy costs and speed up the rate of production.

2 They can be toxic, so are harmful to living things if they escape into the environment. Some can be expensive.

3 For example:
Haber process, iron: nitrogen + hydrogen $\rightleftharpoons$ ammonia
Contact process, vanadium(v) oxide: sulfur dioxide + oxygen $\rightleftharpoons$ sulfur trioxide
Hydrogenation of oils, nickel: unsaturated oil + hydrogen $\rightarrow$ more saturated oil/fat
Making nitric acid, platinum/rhodium: ammonia + oxygen $\rightleftharpoons$ nitrogen(ii) oxide + water

C2 4.7

Exothermic and endothermic reactions

Learning objectives

Students should learn that:

- that energy changes are involved in chemical reactions
- what is meant by exothermic and endothermic reactions
- that energy changes in a chemical reaction can be measured.

Learning outcomes

Most students should be able to:

- state a definition of exothermic and endothermic reactions
- list one example of an exothermic reaction and one of an endothermic reaction
- recognise an endothermic or an exothermic reaction when data are given
- describe how energy change in a reaction can be monitored.

Some students should also be able to:

- explain in detail the difference between exothermic and endothermic reactions.

Answers to in-text questions

a exothermic
b endothermic
c Respiration/oxidation; combustion/burning; neutralisation (or other reaction releasing energy).
d Thermal decomposition, photosynthesis (or other reaction that absorbs energy).

Support

- Give students information to incorporate into their posters about exothermic and endothermic reactions. However, they would need to decide which poster the information is referring to before copying it into their work.

Extend

- Introduce the idea that exothermic and endothermic reactions are usually monitored by temperature changes and these indicate that energy is given out or taken in. Encourage students to consider other ways of monitoring a reaction for energy change (e.g. light or temperature sensor).

AQA Specification link-up: Chemistry C2.5

- When chemical reactions occur, energy is transferred to or from the surroundings. [C2.5.1 a)]
- An exothermic reaction is one that transfers energy to the surroundings. Examples of exothermic reactions include combustion, many oxidation reactions and neutralisation. Everyday uses … . [C2.5.1 b)]
- An endothermic reaction is one that takes in energy from the surroundings. Endothermic reactions include thermal decompositions. Some sports … . [C2.5.1 c)]
  Controlled Assessment: AS4.5 Analyse and interpret primary and secondary data. [AS4.5.4 d)]

Lesson structure

Starters

Sherbet – Give students a sherbet sweet before they enter the room. Ask students to detail what their observations are as they eat it. Then, using questions and answers, get feedback from the students and ask them if they think the reaction is chemical or physical and exothermic or endothermic. Support students by having these words already defined on the board for them to refer to. Extend students by telling them the reactants for this reaction (citric acid and sodium hydrogencarbonate), and ask them to write a word equation for this reaction and classify the reaction [citric acid + sodium hydrogencarbonate → sodium citrate + carbon dioxide + water, neutralisation]. *(5 minutes)*

Cut and stick – Give students photographs of different exothermic or endothermic processes, such as a fire burning, a sports cold pack being used and a match burning. They first need to make themselves aware of the definitions of 'exothermic' and 'endothermic'. They could then cut up the pictures and arrange them in a table to detail the energy changes shown in the reactions. *(10 minutes)*

Main

- The energy changes of a reaction can be recorded using a coffee-cup calorimeter. Explain to the students that most reactions show their energy change by getting hotter or colder and that the reaction needs to be insulated to prevent energy loss to the surroundings.
- Then ask students to complete the displacement reaction between zinc powder and copper sulfate solution. Students should design their own results table and record their results in order to draw a graph. They should be reminded that the scales do not have to start at zero (and the *y*-axis will probably start at about 15 °C). Students may struggle in drawing the line of best fit for this reaction; you could show them how to do this on the board. There are many whole investigations that this can be developed into to extend the Controlled Assessment concepts already covered. Consider concentrating on evaluating methodology in terms of the reproducibility and repeatability of the evidence generated.
- Give the students an A5 sheet of blue paper. They should write a definition of 'endothermic' on it and include examples of endothermic reactions. A similar poster could then be created for exothermic reactions on red paper.

Plenaries

Exo-/endothermic – Give the students a blue card with the word 'endothermic' written on, and a red card with the word 'exothermic' printed on. Then read out these reactions and ask the students to decide if they are exo- or endothermic, displaying the card to represent their answer:

- Thermal decomposition of marble. [Endothermic]
- Combustion of methane. [Exothermic]
- Neutralisation of hydrochloric acid and sodium hydroxide. [Exothermic]
- Rusting of an iron nail. [Exothermic]
- Thermal decomposition of copper carbonate. [Endothermic]

Support students by giving them the definitions on the board with an example to refer to. Extend students by asking them to complete balanced symbol equations for the reactions. You could demonstrate these reactions, show photographs or a video via a digital projector. *(5 minutes)*

Demonstration – Use a data logger to plot the temperature changes in a neutralisation reaction. Display the temperature graph using a digital projector. In small groups, students should decide whether the reaction is exothermic or endothermic and say how they could tell. Choose a few students to feed back to the class. *(10 minutes)*

Practical support

Investigating energy changes

Equipment and materials required

Polystyrene coffee cup, polystyrene lid with two holes in, a mercury thermometer (0–50 °C), 1 mol/dm³ copper sulfate solution (harmful), zinc powder (highly flammable), spatula, balance, measuring cylinder, stopwatch, stirrer, eye protection.

Details

Wear eye protection and measure 25 cm³ of copper sulfate solution into the coffee cup. Measure the temperature every 30 s for 5 min. Then add 1 g of zinc to the cup and quickly put on the lid and stir constantly. Take the temperature every 10 s for 10 min.

Safety: Make students aware that they are using a mercury thermometer for accuracy but that this involves a risk and they should be careful not to leave it by the edge of the bench. You should be aware of where the mercury spillage kit is and how to use it. CLEAPSS Hazcard 27C Copper sulfate – harmful; 107 Zinc powder – highly flammable.

Demonstration of neutralisation reaction

Equipment and materials required

Burette, measuring cylinder, burette holder, stand, 1 mol/dm³ sodium hydroxide (corrosive), 1 mol/dm³ hydrochloric acid, universal indicator (highly flammable), magnetic stirrer, conical flask, magnetic stirrer bar, temperature probe, interface, computer, digital projector, white tile, filter funnel, eye protection (chemical splashproof goggles).

Details

Measure 25 cm³ of sodium hydroxide into a conical flask and add a few drops of indicator. Place the flask on to the magnetic stirrer and add the bar. Fill the burette with hydrochloric acid using the filter funnel. Position the burette over the conical flask and add the temperature probe to the flask, taking care that it doesn't hit the stirrer. Set the graph to take data for about 2 min and begin stirring. Start the data collection. Turn on the flow of acid to the flask and observe.

This activity can be extended by adding a pH probe and comparing the temperature rise with the pH of the solution.

Safety: CLEAPSS Hazcard 91 Sodium hydroxide – corrosive; 47A Hydrochloric acid – corrosive; 32 Universal indicator – highly flammable/harmful.

Rates and energy

Exothermic and endothermic reactions

C2 4.7

Exothermic and endothermic reactions

Learning objectives

- How is energy involved in chemical reactions?
- How can we measure the energy transferred in a chemical reaction?

Whenever chemical reactions take place, energy is involved. That's because energy is always transferred as chemical bonds are broken and new ones are made.

Some reactions transfer energy **from** the reacting chemicals **to** their surroundings. We call these **exothermic** reactions. The energy transferred from the reacting chemicals often heats up the surroundings. This means that we can measure a rise in temperature as the reaction happens.

Some reactions transfer energy **from** the surroundings **to** the reacting chemicals. We call these **endothermic** reactions. As they take in energy from their surroundings, these reactions cause a drop in temperature as they happen.

a What do we call a reaction that releases energy to its surroundings?
b What do we call a reaction that absorbs energy from its surroundings?

Exothermic reactions

Fuels burning are an obvious example of exothermic reactions. For example, when methane (in natural gas) burns it gets oxidised and releases energy.

Respiration is a very special kind of oxidation. It involves reacting sugar with oxygen inside the cells of every living thing. The reaction produces water and carbon dioxide as waste products. Respiration is another exothermic reaction.

Neutralisation reactions between acids and alkalis are also exothermic. We can easily measure the rise in temperature using simple apparatus (see the practical on the next page).

c Give two examples of exothermic reactions.

Figure 1 When a fuel burns in oxygen, energy is transferred to the surroundings. We usually don't need a thermometer to know that there is a temperature change!

Figure 2 All warm-blooded animals rely on exothermic reactions to keep their body temperatures steady

Endothermic reactions

Endothermic reactions are much less common than exothermic ones.

Thermal decomposition reactions are endothermic. An example is the decomposition of calcium carbonate. When heated it forms calcium oxide and carbon dioxide. This reaction only takes place if we keep heating the calcium carbonate strongly. It takes in a great deal of energy from the surroundings.

d Give an example of an endothermic reaction.

Figure 3 When we eat sherbet we can feel an endothermic reaction. Sherbet dissolving in the water in your mouth takes in energy. It provides a slight cooling effect.

Practical

Investigating energy changes 🔑

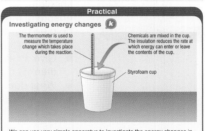

The thermometer is used to measure the temperature change which takes place during the reaction.

Chemicals are mixed in the cup. The insulation reduces the rate at which energy can enter or leave the contents of the cup.

Styrofoam cup

We can use very simple apparatus to investigate the energy changes in reactions. Often we don't need to use anything more complicated than a styrofoam cup and a thermometer.

● State two ways in which you could make the data you collect more accurate.

AQA Examiner's tip

Remember that exothermic reactions involve energy EXiting (leaving) the reacting chemicals, so the surroundings get hotter.

In endothermic reactions energy moves INTO (sounds like 'endo'!) the reacting chemicals, so the surroundings get colder.

Summary questions

1 Copy and complete using the words below:
endothermic exothermic changes neutralisation oxidation decomposition

Chemical reactions involve energy .... When a reaction releases energy we say that it is an .... reaction. Two important examples of this type of reaction are .... and .... When a reaction takes in energy we say that it is an .... reaction. An important example of this type of reaction is thermal ....

2 Potassium chloride dissolving in water is an endothermic process. What would you expect to observe when potassium chloride dissolves in a test tube of water?

Key points

- Energy may be transferred to or from the reacting substances in a chemical reaction.
- A reaction in which energy is transferred from the reacting substances to their surroundings is called an exothermic reaction.
- A reaction in which energy is transferred to the reacting substances from their surroundings is called an endothermic reaction.

138   139

Further teaching suggestions

Poster

- Ask the students to imagine that they work for a marketing company. They are to make a poster to encourage students to think about science in their everyday lives (such as the RSC posters 'Scientists don't always wear white coats'). Their poster should include all the key points.

Other reactions

- Students could use temperature probes, data loggers or thermometers to monitor the temperature change of a variety of exothermic or endothermic changes and classify them. Reactions include dissolving ammonium nitrate, citric acid and sodium hydrogencarbonate and adding ammonium nitrate to barium hydroxide.

Summary answers

1 changes, exothermic, neutralisation/oxidation (either order), endothermic, decomposition

2 The test tube would feel colder/temperature of the solution would fall.

C2 4.8

Energy and reversible reactions

Learning objectives

Students should learn:

- what happens in the energy transfers in reversible reactions.

Learning outcomes

Most students should be able to:

- recognise that if the forward reaction is exothermic, the reverse reaction will be endothermic
- recognise that if the forward reaction is endothermic, the reverse reaction will be exothermic
- recognise that the same amount of energy is taken in or released in either direction.

Some students should also be able to:

- explain why the same amount of energy is taken in or released in either direction.

Answers to in-text questions

a Amount of energy released in one direction is the same as the amount of energy absorbed in the other direction.

b water

c It absorbs water from the air.

d released

Support

- Give students the word equation for the reversible dehydration of hydrated copper sulfate. Ask them to annotate the equation to explain the observations and what the equation shows. You could support them further by giving them the labels and making this a 'cut-and-stick' exercise.

Extend

- Ask students to discover other examples of energy changes in reversible reactions.

AQA Specification link-up: Chemistry C2.5

- If a reversible reaction is exothermic in one direction, it is endothermic in the opposite direction. The same amount of energy is transferred in each case. For example:

endothermic

hydrated copper sulfate (blue) $\rightleftharpoons$ anhydrous copper sulfate (white) + water

exothermic   [C2.5.1 d)]

Lesson structure

Starters

Reversible reaction – Show students a solution of potassium dichromate(VI), $K_2Cr_2O_7$ (oxidising/very toxic), in a beaker, then add sodium hydroxide solution. Explain that the solution changes colour from orange to yellow as potassium chromate(VI), K_2CrO_4, forms, then restore the orange colour by adding dilute hydrochloric acid. Add the alkali and acid again to show that the reactions are reversible. Ask the students to write equations to represent the reactions. Support students by giving them a list of compounds present so they can write the word equations. Extend students by asking them to write the balanced symbol equations. *(5 minutes)*

Questions – Give each student an A4 whiteboard (or laminated sheet of paper), a washable pen and eraser. Then ask them the following series of questions. The students should note down their answers and show you for immediate assessment. If students are unsure of the answer, they could refer to the Student Book or wait for other students to hold up their answer and then use these responses to inform their answer.

- What is the symbol to show a reversible reaction? [$\rightleftharpoons$]
- Give an example of a reversible reaction. [Hydration of anhydrous copper sulfate, thermal decomposition of ammonium chloride.]
- What does 'exothermic' mean? [Energy is given out in the reaction.]
- What happens to the temperature in an endothermic reaction? [Temperature decreases.] *(10 minutes)*

Main

- The students can experimentally complete the reversible reaction of hydration/ dehydration of copper sulfate. Before the experiment is completed, encourage the students to think about how they will record their results (table, diagram, flow chart, paragraphs, bullet points, etc.).

- Once the practical is complete, show the exemplar work to the rest of the class and explain why it is a good way to record the results. You may wish to set up a flexi-cam or video camera. This can be used to show exemplar work quickly and easily to the rest of the class.

- Ask students to imagine that a top publisher has commissioned them to create a GCSE science revision book. Show students a selection of revision materials and ask them to discuss in groups what they like and dislike about the material.

- Explain that they have an A4-page spread in such a book to explain energy and reversible reactions. They must include a worked examination question and an extra question for the reader to attempt, with the answers upside-down on the page. Students could work in small teams to complete this, allowing them to distribute the tasks as they desire.

Plenaries

Objectives – Ask students to try to answer the questions posed by the objectives. *(5 minutes)*

Crossword – Create a crossword with the answers taken from this double-page spread (words could include: 'reversible', 'endothermic', 'exothermic', 'energy', 'hydrated', 'water'). There are many free sites on the internet that can be used to create your own crossword. Then ask students to complete the crossword. Students could be supported by being given both the words and the clues, so they match them up. *(10 minutes)*

Practical support

Energy changes in a reversible reaction

Equipment and materials required

Hydrated copper sulfate (CLEAPSS Hazcard 27C – harmful), spatula, Bunsen burner and safety equipment, dropping pipette, water, boiling tube, boiling-tube holder, eye protection.

Details

Eye protection should be worn throughout this practical. Put a spatula of copper sulfate crystals into a boiling tube. Using the boiling-tube holder, hold the boiling tube just above the blue flame of the Bunsen burner. The tube should be held at an angle and pointing away from people's faces. Do not overheat. Once the visible change is complete, allow the tube to cool. Add a few drops of water. Be aware that water added directly to the boiling tube may crack it.

Demonstration of making cobalt chloride paper

Equipment and materials required

Filter paper, cobalt chloride (toxic), $50\,cm^3$ beaker, stirring rod, wash bottle and water and a spatula, Bunsen burner, (desiccator), tweezers.

Details

Add half a spatula of cobalt chloride crystals to the beaker. Add water and stir until the crystals dissolves. Soak some filter paper in the solution. Take care drying the paper, using a yellow Bunsen flame. The paper will become blue (dehydrated), add water and it will become pink (hydrated).

Explain that the paper should be kept in a desiccator because the air contains water and will turn the paper pink. A desiccator could be shown to the students and they could research how it works.

Safety: Wear chemical splashproof eye protection. Keep cobalt chloride off skin (avoid handling papers with fingers). Wash hands after use. (See CLEAPSS Hazcard 25.)

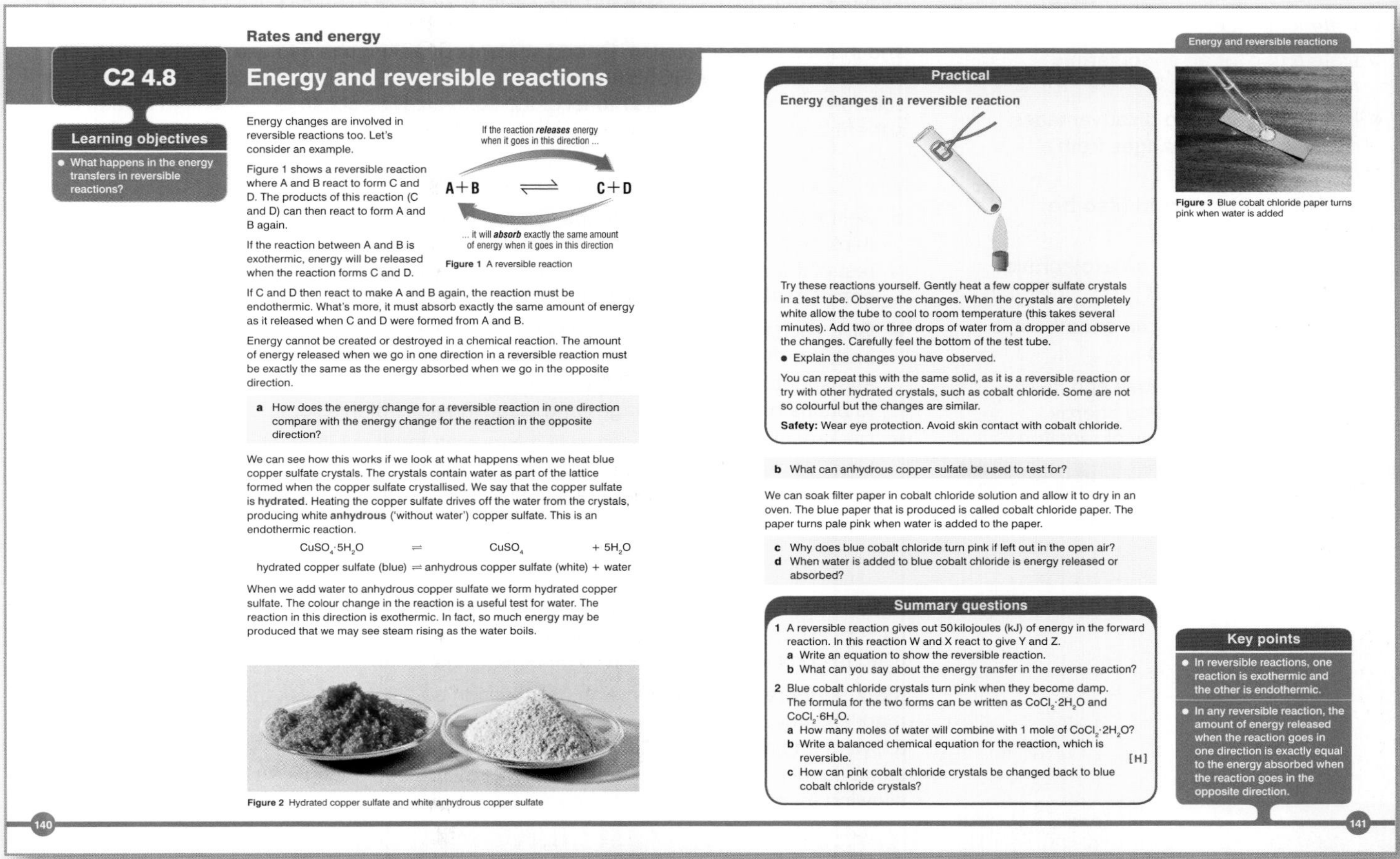

C2 4.8 Energy and reversible reactions

Learning objectives

- What happens in the energy transfers in reversible reactions?

Energy changes are involved in reversible reactions too. Let's consider an example.

Figure 1 shows a reversible reaction where A and B react to form C and D. The products of this reaction (C and D) can then react to form A and B again.

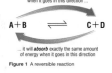

If the reaction *releases* energy when it goes in this direction ...

$$A + B \rightleftharpoons C + D$$

... it will *absorb* exactly the same amount of energy when it goes in this direction

Figure 1 A reversible reaction

If the reaction between A and B is exothermic, energy will be released when the reaction forms C and D.

If C and D then react to make A and B again, the reaction must be endothermic. What's more, it must absorb exactly the same amount of energy as it released when C and D were formed from A and B.

Energy cannot be created or destroyed in a chemical reaction. The amount of energy released when we go in one direction in a reversible reaction must be exactly the same as the energy absorbed when we go in the opposite direction.

a How does the energy change for a reversible reaction in one direction compare with the energy change for the reaction in the opposite direction?

We can see how this works if we look at what happens when we heat blue copper sulfate crystals. The crystals contain water as part of the lattice formed when the copper sulfate crystallised. We say that the copper sulfate is **hydrated**. Heating the copper sulfate drives off the water from the crystals, producing white **anhydrous** ('without water') copper sulfate. This is an endothermic reaction.

$$CuSO_4 \cdot 5H_2O \rightleftharpoons CuSO_4 + 5H_2O$$
hydrated copper sulfate (blue) $\rightleftharpoons$ anhydrous copper sulfate (white) + water

When we add water to anhydrous copper sulfate we form hydrated copper sulfate. The colour change in the reaction is a useful test for water. The reaction in this direction is exothermic. In fact, so much energy may be produced that we may see steam rising as the water boils.

Figure 2 Hydrated copper sulfate and white anhydrous copper sulfate

Practical

Energy changes in a reversible reaction

Try these reactions yourself. Gently heat a few copper sulfate crystals in a test tube. Observe the changes. When the crystals are completely white allow the tube to cool to room temperature (this takes several minutes). Add two or three drops of water from a dropper and observe the changes. Carefully feel the bottom of the test tube.

- Explain the changes you have observed.

You can repeat this with the same solid, as it is a reversible reaction or try with other hydrated crystals, such as cobalt chloride. Some are not so colourful but the changes are similar.

Safety: Wear eye protection. Avoid skin contact with cobalt chloride.

b What can anhydrous copper sulfate be used to test for?

We can soak filter paper in cobalt chloride solution and allow it to dry in an oven. The blue paper that is produced is called cobalt chloride paper. The paper turns pale pink when water is added to the paper.

c Why does blue cobalt chloride turn pink if left out in the open air?
d When water is added to blue cobalt chloride is energy released or absorbed?

Figure 3 Blue cobalt chloride paper turns pink when water is added

Summary questions

1 A reversible reaction gives out 50 kilojoules (kJ) of energy in the forward reaction. In this reaction W and X react to give Y and Z.
 a Write an equation to show the reversible reaction.
 b What can you say about the energy transfer in the reverse reaction?

2 Blue cobalt chloride crystals turn pink when they become damp. The formula for the two forms can be written as $CoCl_2 \cdot 2H_2O$ and $CoCl_2 \cdot 6H_2O$.
 a How many moles of water will combine with 1 mole of $CoCl_2 \cdot 2H_2O$?
 b Write a balanced chemical equation for the reaction, which is reversible. [H]
 c How can pink cobalt chloride crystals be changed back to blue cobalt chloride crystals?

Key points

- In reversible reactions, one reaction is exothermic and the other is endothermic.
- In any reversible reaction, the amount of energy released when the reaction goes in one direction is exactly equal to the energy absorbed when the reaction goes in the opposite direction.

Further teaching suggestions

Making cobalt chloride paper

- Cobalt chloride is usually made into paper for use in practicals to test for water. This can be shown to the students. See 'Practical support'.

Flash cards

- Encourage the students to copy out the key points on to flash cards. They can then create a bank of the key points on separate cards to use for revision.

Summary answers

1 a $W + X \rightleftharpoons Y + Z$
 b 50 kJ of energy is absorbed.

2 a 4
 b $CoCl_2 \cdot 2H_2O + 4H_2O \rightleftharpoons CoCl_2 \cdot 6H_2O$
 c Heat them (gently) to drive off the water.

C2 4.9

Using energy transfers from reactions

- Evaluate everyday uses of exothermic and endothermic reactions. [C2.5]

Learning objectives

Students should learn that:

- how the energy from exothermic reactions can be used
- how the cooling effect from endothermic reactions can be used
- that there are advantages and disadvantages of using energy changes in a chemical reaction.

Learning outcomes

Most students should be able to:

- state a use for an exothermic reaction
- state a use for an endothermic reaction
- list advantages and disadvantages of using energy changes from a chemical reaction.

Some students should also be able to:

- explain in detail how an exothermic reaction can be used
- explain in detail how an endothermic reaction can be used
- evaluate the advantages and disadvantages of using energy changes from a chemical reaction.

Lesson structure

Starters

Hand warmers – Give each group a hand warmer and ask them to pop the metal clip inside and observe. Ask students to share their observations with the whole class. *(5 minutes)*

Sports packs – Ask for a volunteer and give him or her a cooling sports pack. Allow the volunteer to break the inner bag and mix the chemicals. Encourage the student to describe what he or she is doing and observing. Allow the cool pack to be passed around the class. Explain to students that the change is between ammonium nitrate and water and that it creates a solution. Extend students by asking them to use their Key Stage 3 knowledge as well as GCSE knowledge to identify the solute, solvent and name of solution and draw a particle model of the solution. [The solute is ammonium nitrate, the solvent is water and the solution is ammonium nitrate mixed with water.] *(10 minutes)*

Main

- Split the class into small groups. Give each group a self-heating can and ask them to think about how it could be self-heating. Ask groups to feed back their ideas to the rest of the class. Show students one example of a used self-heating can cut open – complete this using appropriate protective clothing as the chemicals are hazardous.
- Give each table of students a different commercial product that uses an exothermic or endothermic reaction. Ask the students to classify the reaction type that has been used and suggest some chemicals that would produce the desired effect. Then ask students to brainstorm the advantages and disadvantages of this commercial use.
- Demonstrate the crystallisation of a supersaturated solution (see 'Practical support'). Link this demonstration with the 'Hand warmers' Starter. Explain to students that this is a physical change and ask them to suggest how they could easily reverse it [reheat the crystals].

Plenaries

Other uses of exothermic/endothermic reactions – Ask students to brainstorm other uses of exothermic or endothermic reactions – e.g. combustion is an exothermic reaction used to cook food. Encourage volunteers to share their ideas. *(5 minutes)*

Mark scheme – Give students an examination question and ask them to create the mark scheme rather than answer the question. Students should consider all acceptable answers and also answers that would not be worthy of credit. Use a question from the same tier of entry as the students in the class. You could further support students by allowing them to work in small groups. *(10 minutes)*

Support

- You can support students by giving them the advantages and disadvantages of using chemical reactions to generate an energy change. Students could then use these to generate a table to list the advantages and disadvantages for specific products such as the self-heating can.

Extend

- You can extend students by asking them to write balanced symbol equations for some of the chemical reactions that they have studied in this double-page spread.

Practical support

Demonstration: crystallisation of a supersaturated solution

Equipment and materials required
700 g sodium ethanoate, 50 cm³ of hot water, 250 cm³ glass conical flask, a crystal of sodium ethanoate, tweezers, magnetic hot plate, magnetic stirrer bar, eye protection.

Details
Eye protection should be worn throughout this practical. Put 50 cm³ of hot water into the conical flask. Add 700 g of sodium ethanoate and a magnetic stirrer bar. Stir on a warm hot plate until all the solid has dissolved. Remove the flask from the heat and allow it to cool to room temperature. Avoid 'shocking' – for example, violently moving it – or continued stirring of the liquid or it will start to crystallise at once. Seed the solution with one crystal and see how it solidifies, releasing the heat of crystallisation – an exothermic physical change.

You could alternatively demonstrate crystallisation by pouring the hot solution into a Petri dish on an overhead projector, and seeding the crystals there.

Safety: Refer to CLEAPSS Hazcard 38A.

Rates and energy

C2 4.9 — Using energy transfers from reactions

Using energy transfers from reactions

Learning objectives
- How can we use the energy from exothermic reactions?
- How can we use the cooling effect of endothermic reactions?
- What are the advantages and disadvantages of using exothermic and endothermic reactions in the uses described?

Practical

Crystallisation of a supersaturated solution

Dissolve 700 g of sodium ethanoate in 50 cm³ of hot water in a conical flask. Then let the solution cool to room temperature. Now add a small crystal of sodium ethanoate.

- What do you see happen? What does the outside of the flask feel like?

Figure 1 Here is a hand warmer based on the recrystallisation of sodium ethanoate

Warming up

Chemical hand and body warmers can be very useful. These products use exothermic reactions to warm you up. People can take hand warmers to places they know will get very cold. For example, spectators at outdoor sporting events in winter can warm their hands up. People usually use the body warmers to help ease aches and pains.

Some hand warmers can only be used once. An example of this type uses the oxidation of iron to release energy. Iron turns into hydrated iron(III) oxide in an exothermic reaction. The reaction is similar to rusting. Sodium chloride (common salt) is used as a catalyst. This type of hand warmer is disposable. It can be used only once but it lasts for hours.

Other hand warmers can be reused many times. These are based on the formation of crystals from solutions of a salt. The salt used is often sodium ethanoate. A supersaturated solution is prepared. We do this by dissolving as much of the salt as possible in hot water. The solution is then allowed to cool.

A small metal disc in the plastic pack is used to start the exothermic change. When you press this a few times small particles of metal are scraped off. These 'seed' (or start off) the crystallisation. The crystals spread throughout the solution, giving off energy. They work for about 30 minutes.

To reuse the warmer, you simply put the solid pack into boiling water to re-dissolve the crystals. When cool, the pack is ready to activate again.

a Common salt is used as a *catalyst* in some disposable hand warmers. What does this mean?

Exothermic reactions are also used in self-heating cans (see Figure 2). The reaction used to release the energy is usually:

$$calcium\ oxide + water \rightarrow calcium\ hydroxide$$

You press a button in the base of the can. This breaks a seal and lets the water and calcium oxide mix. Coffee is available in these self-heating cans.

Development took years and cost millions of pounds. Even then, over a third of the can was taken up with the reactants to release energy. Also, in some early versions, the temperature of the coffee did not rise high enough in cold conditions.

b Which solid is usually used in the base of self-heating coffee cans?

Activity

Hot food

Mountaineers and explorers can take 'self-heating' foods with them on their journeys. One uses the energy released when calcium oxide reacts with water to heat the food.

Design a self-heating, disposable food container for stew.
- Draw a labelled diagram of your container and explain how it works.
- What are the safety issues involved in using your product?

Cooling down

Endothermic processes can be used to cool things down. For example, chemical cold packs usually contain ammonium nitrate and water. When ammonium nitrate dissolves it takes in energy from its surroundings, making them colder. These cold packs are used as emergency treatment for sports injuries. The coldness reduces swelling and numbs pain.

The ammonium nitrate and water (sometimes as a gel) are kept separate in the pack. When squeezed or struck the bag inside the water pack breaks releasing ammonium nitrate. The instant cold packs work for about 20 minutes.

They can only be used once but are ideal where there is no ice available to treat a knock or strain.

The same endothermic change can also be used to chill cans of drinks.

Figure 2 Development of this self-heating can in the USA took about 10 years. The pink circle on the can turns white when the coffee is hot enough. This takes 6–8 minutes.

Figure 3 Instant cold packs can be applied as soon as an injury occurs to minimise damage to the sportsperson

Summary questions

1 a Describe how a disposable hand warmer works.
b Describe how a re-usable hand warmer works.
c Give an advantage and a disadvantage of each type of hand warmer.
d Name one use of an exothermic reaction in the food industry.

2 a Give two uses of endothermic changes.
b Which endothermic change is often used in cold packs?

Key points
- Exothermic changes can be used in hand warmers and self-heating cans. Crystallisation of a supersaturated solution is used in reusable hand warmers. However, disposable, one-off warmers can give off heat for longer.
- Endothermic changes can be used in instant cold packs for sports injuries.

Further teaching suggestions

Design hot and cold packs
- Ask students to design their own sports cold pack and hot packs. They should create a detailed diagram including the chemicals that would be contained within it.

Reuse the hand warmer
- Allow students to boil the hand warmer and then reuse it.

Answers to in-text questions

a The sodium chloride speeds up the reaction but remains unchanged at the end of the reaction.

b calcium oxide

Summary answers

1 a Iron is oxidised to give out energy. Iron turns into hydrated iron(III) oxide in an exothermic reaction. Sodium chloride is used as a catalyst.

b A supersaturated solution is made to crystallise by pressing a small metal disc. The crystals spread throughout the solution, giving off energy. The crystals are re-dissolved in hot water to use the warmer again.

c The disposable hand warmer lasts longer when activated than the reusable warmer. However, it can only be used once. The opposite applies to the re-usable hand warmers.

d Self-heating cans.

2 a To treat injuries with cold packs; to chill drinks in cans.

b Ammonium nitrate dissolving in water.

Summary answers

1 a A and C

b A

c B

d B

2 a Measure volume of gas or mass of reaction mixture over time.

b i Three of: increase concentration of acid; increase surface area of magnesium; increase temperature of reaction mixture; add a catalyst.

ii Increasing concentration/surface area increases number of collisions between reactants; increasing temperature increases number of collisions between reactants and the energy possessed by reacting particles; catalyst lowers activation energy.

3 a The mass of gas produced at each minute is the difference between the initial mass of the reaction flask and reactants (at the start of the reaction) minus the mass at each minute.

b

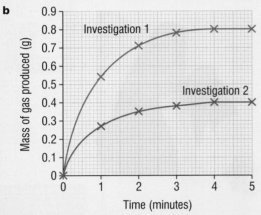

c The rate is less than in investigation 1.

d Half the mass of investigation 1.

e Investigation 2 uses acid with twice the concentration of that in investigation 1 (rate and volume of gas double), with at least enough marble chips to react fully with the acid in each case.

4 [Students should describe a way in which the temperature change can be measured when known amounts of sherbet dissolve in water.]

5 a and **b**

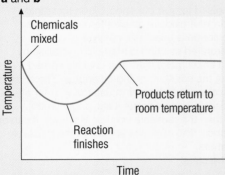

6 a The higher the temperature, the more quickly the cross will disappear.

b Wear eye protection or do not heat solution above 50 °C or dispose of solutions in fume cupboard.

Summary questions

1 Select from A, B and C to show how the rate of each reaction, **a** to **d**, could be measured.

a	Gas evolved from reaction mixture	A	Measure mass
b	Mass of reaction mixture changes	B	Measure light transmitted
c	Precipitate produced	C	Measure volume
d	Colour of solution changes		

2 A student carried out a reaction in which she dropped a piece of magnesium ribbon in sulfuric acid with a concentration of 0.5 mol/dm³.

a Suggest **one** way in which the student could measure the rate of this reaction.

b i Suggest **three** ways in which the student could increase the rate of this reaction.

ii Explain how each of these methods changes the rate of the reaction.

3 The following results show what happened when two students investigated the reaction of some marble chips with acid.

Time (minutes)	Investigation 1 Mass of gas produced (g)	Investigation 2 Mass of gas produced (g)
0	0.00	0.00
1	0.54	0.27
2	0.71	0.35
3	0.78	0.38
4	0.80	0.40
5	0.80	0.40

a The students were investigating the effect of concentration on rate of reaction. How did the students get the data for their table above?

b Plot a graph of these results with time on the x-axis.

c After one minute, how does the rate of the reaction in Investigation 2 compare with the rate of reaction in Investigation 1?

d How does the final mass of gas produced in Investigation 2 compare with that produced in Investigation 1?

e From the results, what can you say about the concentration of the acids in Investigations 1 and 2?

4 'When sherbet sweets dissolve in your mouth this is an endothermic process.' Devise an experiment to test your statement. Use words and diagrams to describe clearly what you would do.

5 Two chemicals are mixed and react endothermically. When the reaction has finished, the reaction mixture is allowed to stand until it has returned to its starting temperature.

a Sketch a graph of temperature (y-axis) against time (x-axis) to show how the temperature of the reaction mixture changes.

b Label the graph clearly and explain what is happening wherever you have shown the temperature is changing.

6 This student's account of an investigation into the effect of temperature on the rate of a reaction was found on the internet:

I investigated the effect of temperature on the rate of a reaction. The reaction was between sodium thiosulfate and hydrochloric acid. I set up my apparatus as in the diagram.

The cross was put under the flask. I heated the sodium thiosulfate to the temperature I wanted and then added the hydrochloric acid to the flask. I immediately started the watch and timed how long it took for the cross to disappear.

My results are below.

Temperature of the sodium thiosulfate	Time taken for the cross to disappear
15	110
30	40
45	21

My conclusion is that the reaction goes faster the higher the temperature.

a Suggest a suitable prediction for this investigation.

b Describe one safety feature that is not mentioned in the method.

c Suggest some ways in which this method could be improved. For each suggestion, say why it is an improvement.

d Suggest how the table of results could be improved.

e Despite all of the problems with this investigation, is the conclusion appropriate? Explain your answer.

c Ways in which the method could have been improved include:

- There should have been more temperatures chosen, so that the pattern could have been seen in the results.
- The range could have been wider, so that the effect of higher and lower temperatures could have been noted.
- The volume and concentration of the two reactants should be known, to make sure that the method is valid.
- The hydrochloric acid should have been heated to the desired temperature as well, to ensure that the reaction took place at the stated temperature.
- Data logging could have been used to detect the end point. It is difficult to tell accurately when the cross disappears.
- The solutions should be continually stirred, to ensure validity.
- A water bath should have been used to control the temperature.

The results would have been more valid if repeated values of time had been taken at each temperature and the mean values calculated.

d Include units in the table.

e It is not possible to tell because the evidence is not repeatable and reproducible. (Also accept an answer that indicates that the conclusion is appropriate because there are large differences between the results at different temperatures – assuming the timings were taken in seconds.)

End of chapter questions

AQA Examination-style questions

A glue is made by mixing together two liquids.

a When the liquids are mixed an exothermic reaction takes place. Complete the sentence below using a word or phrase from the list.

decrease   increase   stay the same

During the reaction the temperature of the mixture will .... (1)

b The time taken for the glue to set at different temperatures is given in the table below.

Temperature (°C)	Time taken for the glue to set
20	3 days
60	6 hours
90	1 hour

Complete the sentences below using words or phrases from the list.

decreases   increases   stays the same

i When the temperature is increased the time taken for the glue to set .... (1)

ii When the temperature is increased the rate of the setting reaction .... (1)

c Which **two** of the following are reasons why an increase in temperature affects the rate of reaction?

It gives the particles more energy.

It increases the concentration of the particles.

It increases the surface area of the particles.

It makes the particles move faster. (2)

AQA, 2009

Instant cold packs are used to treat sports injuries.

One type of cold pack has a plastic bag containing water. Inside this bag is a smaller bag containing ammonium nitrate.

The outer bag is squeezed so that the inner bag bursts. The pack is shaken and quickly gets very cold as the ammonium nitrate dissolves in the water.

a Explain why the pack gets cold. (2)

b Suggest and explain why the pack is shaken after the inner bag has burst. (2)

AQA, 2008

3 A student reacted small pieces of zinc with dilute acid to make hydrogen gas. The graph shows how the volume of hydrogen gas produced changed with time.

a Describe, as fully as you can, how the rate of this reaction changes with time. (2)

b The student wanted to make the reaction go faster. Which suggestion would make the reaction go faster?

Use bigger pieces of the same total mass of zinc.

Use more of the dilute acid.

Use zinc powder. (1)

c The student decided to increase the concentration of the acid. Explain, in terms of particles, why increasing the concentration of the acid increases the rate of reaction. (2)

d The student increased the temperature of the reaction by 10 °C. The student found that the reaction went twice as fast. Explain, as fully as you can, why an increase in temperature increases the rate of the reaction. (3)

AQA, 2008

4 Platinum is used as a catalyst in many industrial processes. Platinum is a very expensive metal. The catalysts often contain only about 1% platinum dispersed on an inert support such as aluminium oxide to give a surface area of about 200 m² per gram. Cobalt catalysts with nanosized particles have been developed as an alternative to platinum catalysts for use in some industrial processes.

a Suggest two reasons why platinum is used as a catalyst, even though it is very expensive. (2)

b Explain, in terms of particles, why catalysts like platinum should have a very large surface area. (2)

c Suggest an economic reason and an environmental reason why cobalt catalysts have been developed as alternatives to platinum catalysts. (2)

d Suggest **three** reasons why the use of catalysts is important in industrial processes. (3)

AQA Examination-style answers

1 a increase *(1 mark)*

b i decreases *(1 mark)*

ii increases *(1 mark)*

c It gives the particles more energy. It makes the particles move faster. *(2 marks)*

2 a The bag gets cold because heat is taken in from the surroundings. *(2 marks)*

b Two from: mix/spread (the ammonium nitrate and water), so the whole bag gets cold; dissolve faster; get cold faster; particles collide more or more collisions, *(allow increase rate or quicker reaction).* *(2 marks)*

3 a Two from: rate is high at the start *(allow fast at the start)*, decreases with time until it becomes zero. *(2 marks)*

b Use zinc powder. *(1 mark)*

c More particles in given volume or particles closer together/more crowded; particles collide more frequently or more often. *(2 marks)*

d The speed of particles increases and so there are more frequent collisions and the collisions are more energetic, therefore more particles have the activation energy or minimum energy to react. *(3 marks)*

4 a Two from: not used up in reaction or does not need replacing very often; only a small amount is needed or very effective; catalyses many reactions. *(2 marks)*

b There is a greater surface area of catalyst/metal and so particles of reactants collide with the surface (of catalyst/metal) more frequently. *(2 marks)*

c Economic: low(er) cost of cobalt (relative to platinum). Environmental: sensible suggestion, e.g. cobalt (may be) less toxic/harmful (to living things); cobalt mining causes less damage (because there is a higher percentage of cobalt in ores). *(2 marks)*

d Three from: increases rate of reaction; more product in less time; reduces costs; less energy needed; less fossil fuel needed (for energy/heating/pressure); smaller workforce. *(3 marks)*

AQA Practical suggestions

Practicals	AQA	k	📖	⚙
Designing and carrying out investigations into factors that affect the rate of reaction …	✓	✓	✓	
Investigating temperature changes of neutralisations and displacement reactions, e.g. zinc and copper sulfate.	✓	✓	✓	
Investigating temperature changes when dissolving ammonium nitrate, or reacting citric acid and sodium hydrogencarbonate.	✓		✓	
Adding ammonium nitrate to barium hydroxide.	✓		✓	
Demonstration of the addition of concentrated sulfuric acid to sugar.	✓		✓	
Demonstration of the reaction between iodine and aluminium after activation by a drop of water.	✓		✓	
Demonstration of the screaming jelly baby.	✓		✓	
Demonstration of the thermite reaction, i.e. aluminium mixed with iron(III) oxide.	✓		✓	
Investigation of hand warmers, self-warming cans, sports injury packs.	✓		✓	

Kerboodle resources (k)

Resources available for this chapter on Kerboodle are:

- Chapter map: Rates and energy
- Practical: The effect of surface area on reaction rate (C2 4.2)
- Practical: The effect of temperature on reaction rate (C2 4.3)
- Simulation: How can I change the rate of a reaction? (C2 4.2–4.4)
- Data handling skills: Effect of concentration on reaction rate (C2 4.4)
- Support: Changing the rate (C2 4.4)
- Bump up your grade: Changing the rate (C2 4.4)
- Practical: The effect of concentration on reaction rates (C2 4.4)
- How Science Works: The state of the rates (C2 4.4)
- Extension: How do catalysts work? (C2 4.5)
- Practical: The effect of catalysts reaction rate (C2 4.5)
- Webquest: Catalytic nanoparticles (C2 4.6)
- Practical: Exothermic and endothermic reactions (C2 4.7)
- Interactive activity: Rates and energy
- Revision podcast: Collision theory
- Test yourself: Rates and energy
- On your marks: Rates and energy
- Examination-style questions: Rates and energy
- Answers to examination-style questions: Rates and energy

C2 5.1 Acids and alkalis

Learning objectives

Students should learn:

- why solutions are acidic or alkaline
- what bases and alkalis are
- how acidity or alkalinity can be measured.

Learning outcomes

Most students should be able to:

- list some properties of acids and alkalis
- explain in terms of ions what acids and alkalis are
- give an example of an acid, an alkali and a base
- state the ions formed by acids and alkalis in solution
- recognise whether a solution is acidic or alkaline if the pH is given.

Some students should also be able to:

- explain the differences and similarities between alkalis and bases.

Answers to in-text questions

a Any soluble hydroxide, e.g. sodium hydroxide.
b A base is a substance that can neutralise acids.
c H^+ ions/hydrogen ions
d OH^- ions/hydroxide ions
e The substance is a solid.

Support

- Students may need support during the practical. The method to test the alkalinity of different household chemicals could be given to these students in labelled diagrams but in the wrong order. They could sort out the steps before completing the practical.

Extend

- Students will be familiar with the use of indicators to classify chemicals as acid, alkali or neutral from KS3. Encourage students to suggest how electricity can be used to measure pH. Encourage them to think about the ions in solution.

Specification link-up: Chemistry C2.6

- The state symbols in equations are (s), (l), (g) and (aq). *[C2.6.1 a]*
- Metal oxides and hydroxides are bases. Soluble hydroxides are called alkalis. *[C2.6.2 a]*
- Hydrogen ions, H^+ (aq), make solutions acidic and hydroxide ions, OH^- (aq), make solutions alkaline. The pH scale is a measure of the acidity or alkalinity of a solution. *[C2.6.2 d]*

  Controlled Assessment: AS4.1 Plan practical ways to develop and test candidates own scientific ideas. *[AS4.1.1 b) c)]*

Lesson structure

Starters

Table – Ask students to draw a three-column table, with titles: 'acid', 'base', 'neutral'. They should then list as many things about each category as they can, including examples. Then draw a similar table on the board, and ask each student in turn to write a piece of information into the table. Support students by giving them statements that they sort. Extend students by asking them to include a fourth column for alkalis. *(5 minutes)*

Think – Ask students to work in pairs to brainstorm everything that they can remember from KS3 about acids, alkalis and the pH scale. Feedback ideas from the class. *(10 minutes)*

Main

- It is important that students are clear about the definitions and some common examples of acids, alkalis and neutral substances. You may wish to supply students with a tray of examples containing acids (oranges, vinegar, a sealed bottle of water labelled as hydrochloric acid), alkalis (soap, washing powder, a sealed bottle of water labelled as sodium hydroxide) and neutral chemicals (two sealed bottles of water, one labelled 'water' and the other labelled 'alcohol', a sealed bottle of brine labelled 'sodium chloride solution'). Ask students to sort them into acids, alkalis and neutral chemicals and try to come up with a bullet-point definition for each key word.

- If you have not already introduced state symbols to students, it is important that you do so now. You could give students a simple activity in which the state symbols are listed in the left-hand column of a table and the name of the states are listed in the right-hand column. Students can then use a rule to match the state symbol with its state.

- Students could test a variety of solutions using universal indicator to find out their pH. Encourage them to design their own results table for the experiment. Point out to students that the independent variable (chemical) should be in the first column and the dependent variable (pH) in the second column (Controlled Assessment AS4.4.2 a). Then ask them to draw conclusions from their results. They should realise that some everyday acids can be eaten, whereas most alkalis are cleaning products.

- Students could design and carry out their own investigation to determine the alkalinity of different household cleaning products. Encourage students to work in pairs to plan their experiment. They could use a variety of methods, including universal indicator, digital pH probes or data loggers. This could lead to a useful discussion of the Controlled Assessment idea that technology such as data logging may provide a better means of obtaining data, and explaining why a particular technology is the most appropriate. The concept of accuracy in measurements (Controlled Assessment AS4.3.2 c) could also be included.

Plenaries

5, 4, 3, 2, 1 – Ask students to list the names of five everyday acids, four lab-based bases, three properties of acids, two properties of alkalis and one example of a neutral chemical. Support students by asking them to work in small teams. They could show you their answers on A4 whiteboards for instant feedback and praise. Extend students by encouraging them to use correct chemical formulae for their answers where possible. *(5–10 minutes)*

Review – Show students the table that the class made. Ask them to look carefully and consider any mistakes. Discuss the mistakes and make amendments. Then ask students to copy out three facts from the table and add a new fact that they have learned from the lesson into their notes. *(10 minutes)*

Practical support

Testing pH of various chemicals

Equipment and materials required
Dimple tiles, a beaker of water, dropping pipettes, samples of acids (irritants/harmful), alkalis (irritants/harmful), neutral chemicals and buffer solutions (irritants/harmful), universal indicator solution (highly flammable/harmful), universal indicator paper, scissors.

Details
Wear eye protection throughout the practical and wash hands in cold water if any of the solutions touch the skin. Be aware that universal indicator will stain the skin for about three days.
Put a few drops of each type of solution in separate dimples. Add either a few drops of universal indicator solution or a small square of universal indicator paper. Compare the colour of the paper or solution with the given colour chart (each brand of universal indicator will change to a different colour at each pH value, so it is important to compare with the appropriate chart). Put the dropping pipette into a beaker of water when finished.

Safety: Wear eye protection.

Investigating household cleaning products

Equipment and materials required
Different cleaning products (irritant/harmful), beakers, stirring rods, pH probes, pH data logger and equipment, universal indicator (highly flammable/harmful), dropping pipette, dimple tile, eye protection.

Details
Wear eye protection and put a small amount of cleaning product on a dimple tile. Add a few drops of water if the product is a solid. Then add universal indictor and compare with the colour chart. Alternatively, put the cleaning product into a beaker and submerge the calibrated pH probe (either digital or data logger) and note the reading.

Safety: If the cleaning product touches the skin, wash well with cold water. Be aware that some cleaning products may be 'corrosive' and 'toxic' – avoid these.

Salts and electrolysis

C2 5.1 — Acids and alkalis

Acids and alkalis

Learning objectives
- Why are solutions acidic or alkaline?
- What are bases and alkalis?
- How do we measure acidity?

Acids and bases are an important part of our understanding of chemistry. They play an important part inside us and all other living things.

What are acids and bases?
When we dissolve a substance in water we make an **aqueous solution**. The solution may be acidic, alkaline or neutral. That depends on which substance we have dissolved.

- Soluble hydroxides are called **alkalis**. Their solutions are alkaline. An example is sodium hydroxide solution.
- **Bases**, which include alkalis, are substances that can neutralise **acids**. Metal oxides and metal hydroxides are bases. Examples include iron oxide and copper hydroxide.
- Acids include citric acid, sulfuric acid and ethanoic acid. All acids taste very sour, although many acids are far too dangerous to put in your mouth. Ethanoic acid (in vinegar) and citric acid (in citrus fruit and fizzy drinks) are acids which we regularly eat.
- Pure water is **neutral**.

  a Name an alkali.
  b What is a base?

One acid that we use in science labs is hydrochloric acid. This is formed when the gas hydrogen chloride (HCl) dissolves in water:

$$HCl(g) \xrightarrow{water} H^+(aq) + Cl^-(aq)$$

All acids form H^+ ions when we add them to water. It is these H^+ ions that make a solution acidic. Hydrogen chloride also forms chloride ions (Cl⁻). The '(aq)' in the equation above is called a **state symbol**. It shows that the ions are in an 'aqueous solution'. In other words, they are dissolved in water.

  c What ions do all acids form when we add them to water?

Because alkalis are bases which dissolve in water, they are the bases we often use in experiments. Sodium hydroxide solution is often found in school labs. We get sodium hydroxide solution when we dissolve solid sodium hydroxide in water:

$$NaOH(s) \xrightarrow{water} Na^+(aq) + OH^-(aq)$$

All alkalis form hydroxide ions (OH⁻) when we add them to water. It is these hydroxide ions that make a solution alkaline.

  d What ions do all alkalis form when we add them to water?
  e What does the state symbol '(s)' stand for?

Figure 1 Acids and bases are all around us, in many of the things we buy at the shops, in our schools and factories – and in our bodies too

Measuring acidity or alkalinity
Indicators are substances which change colour when we add them to acids and alkalis. Litmus paper is a well-known indicator, but there are many more.
We use the pH scale to show how acidic or alkaline a solution is. The scale runs from 0 (most acidic) to 14 (most alkaline). We can use **universal indicator (UI)** to find the pH of a solution. It is a very special indicator made from a number of dyes. It turns a range of colours as the pH changes. Anything in the middle of the pH scale (pH 7) is neutral, neither acid nor alkali.

Practical

Which is the most alkaline product?
Compare the alkalinity of various cleaning products.

You can test washing-up liquids, shampoos, soaps, hand-washing liquids, washing powders/liquids and dishwasher powders/tablets.

You could use a pH sensor and data logger to collect your data.

- What are the advantages of using a pH sensor instead of universal indicator solution or paper?

Safety: Wear eye protection.

Maths skills
We can use the mathematical symbols ' > ' (read as 'is greater than') and ' < ' ('is less than') when interpreting pH values.
We can say:
pH < 7 indicates an acidic solution.
i.e. pH values less than 7 are acidic.

pH > 7 indicates an alkaline solution.
i.e. pH values greater than 7 are alkaline.

	Universal indicator solution		
pH 0			Very acidic
1		Hydrochloric acid	
2		Lemon juice	
3		Orange juice / Vinegar	
4			
5		Black coffee	Slightly acidic
6		Rainwater	
7		Pure water	Neutral
8		Seawater / Baking soda	
9		Milk of magnesia / Soap	Slightly alkaline
10			
11		Washing soda	
12			
13		Oven cleaner	
14		Sodium hydroxide	Very alkaline

Figure 2 The pH scale tells us how acidic or alkaline a solution is

Summary questions

1 Match the halves of the sentences together:

a	A base that is soluble in water	A	.... a pH of exactly 7.
b	Pure water is neutral with	B	.... form OH⁻ ions when they dissolve in water.
c	Acids are substances that	C	.... is called an alkali.
d	Alkalis are substances that	D	.... is acidic.
e	Indicators are substances that	E	.... form H⁺ ions when they dissolve in water.
f	A solution with a pH less than 7	F	.... change colour when we add them to acids and alkalis.

2 How could you use universal indicator paper as a way of distinguishing between pure water, sodium hydroxide solution and citric acid solution?

Key points
- Acids are substances which produce H⁺ ions when we add them to water.
- Bases are substances that will neutralise acids.
- An alkali is a soluble hydroxide. Alkalis produce OH⁻ ions when we add them to water.
- We can use the pH scale to show how acidic or alkaline a solution is.

146   147

Further teaching suggestions

Homemade indicator
- Ask students to find out how to make an indicator at home and write a bullet-pointed method on how to make it, e.g. using elderberries, cranberries or red cabbage.

Interactive pH scale
- Make a coloured universal indicator pH scale on interactive whiteboard software or PowerPoint. Invite the students to label weak/strong acid/alkali and neutral chemicals. Then show images of different things, e.g. stomach acid, then drag and drop the images on to the pH scale.

Other indicators
- Ask students to research and find out different indicators that can be used to test for acids and bases.

Summary answers

1 a C   b A   c E   d B   e F   f D

2 The paper would turn green in water (neutral), blue/purple in sodium hydroxide solution (strong alkali) and red/orange in citric acid solution (weak acid).

C2 5.2 Making salts from metals or bases

Learning objectives

Students should learn:

- the products of the reaction between acids and metals
- the products of the reaction between acids and bases
- that salts can be made using neutralisation.

Learning outcomes

Most students should be able to:

- state a definition of neutralisation
- state the general word equation when a metal reacts with an acid
- state the general word equation when an acid reacts with a base
- name the salt formed if the acid and alkali are given
- write the ionic equation for neutralisation.

Some students should also be able to:

- construct balanced symbol equations including state symbols.

Answers to in-text questions

a A salt and hydrogen.
b The substance is a gas.
c A salt and water.
d zinc sulfate
e The substance is a liquid.

Support

- Some students may find it difficult to represent chemical reactions in equations. Provide these students with a skeleton structure of the equations. Then each additional piece of information could be made into a card. Each card should have a separate chemical and then the students try to create the equations, using sticky-tac to secure the cards.

Extend

- Show students how to generate the ionic equation for neutralisation from first principles. They could then use the method to check other examples and prove that the same ionic equation is always generated.

Specification link-up: Chemistry C2.6

- The state symbols in equations are (s), (l), (g) and (aq). [C2.6.1 a]
- Soluble salts can be made from acids by reacting them with:
  - metals – not all metals are suitable; some are too reactive and others are not reactive enough
  - insoluble bases – the base is added to the acid until no more will react and the excess solid is filtered off ... [C2.6.1 b]
- Salt solutions can be crystallised to produce solid salts. [C2.6.1 c]
- The particular salt produced in any reaction between an acid and a base or alkali depends on:
  - the acid used (hydrochloric acid produces chlorides, nitric acid produces nitrates, sulfuric acid produces sulfates)
  - the metal in the base or alkali. [C2.6.2 b]

Lesson structure

Starters

Table – Ask students to complete the following table:

Name of acid	Name in salt	Example
Hydrochloric	[Chloride]	[e.g. Sodium chloride]
[Nitric]	Nitrate	[e.g. Copper nitrate]
Sulfuric	Sulfate	[e.g. Calcium sulfate]

Show the incomplete table on the board and ask different students to fill in the missing data. Support students by giving them the missing words for them to slot into the table. Extend students by asking them to write the formulae of the ions and compounds. *(5 minutes)*

Neutralisation experiment – Ask students to complete a neutralisation reaction between an acid and alkali in pairs. The first group to get exactly green is the winner. You might wish to use a pH probe and data logger so that students could chart the change in pH during their experiment. *(10 minutes)*

Main

- The word 'salt' is used in everyday life to mean sodium chloride. However, this is actually a chemical classification.
- Ask students to suggest names of acids that they have used in their school science lessons. You should write these formulae on the board. Ask the students to suggest what they all have in common [they all contain hydrogen]. Remind students that the H^+ ion is released when an acid is put into water. Then explain that the hydrogen ion can be swapped for a metal. Ask a student to name any metal and choose an acid and write the metal salt it would produce. Repeat this a few times with the other acids written on the board. Explain to students that when the hydrogen ion has been swapped for the metal ion, a new substance is made and this is known as a salt. Encourage students to write their own definition of a salt into their notes and give the name and formula of two metals salts of their choice.
- At KS3, most students will have had experience of neutralisation with an acid and an alkali. However, they may not have used an insoluble base before. Show the students some copper(II) oxide (harmful) and allow them to try to dissolve it in water. Then allow students to prepare copper sulfate crystals (harmful) using the method in the Student Book. Encourage the students to write up the method in a brief bullet-pointed format and summarise the reaction in a general word equation.
- Give each student three index cards. These can be made out of three different coloured pieces of card about A6 in size. Punch all the cards in the top right-hand corner hole. On the front of each card the student should write a general word equation. Then on the reverse a specific example, including a method and an equation for the reaction. After a few lessons when all of the cards have been completed, they can be joined together with a treasury tag or a piece of string. These can then be tied to their notes and used for revision for examination.

Plenary

Chemical equations – Ask students to complete the following equations (they get progressively more difficult). Time the students for 5 minutes and assure them that it doesn't matter how far they get.

- acid + alkali → [salt] + [water]
- [acid] + [metal] → metal salt + hydrogen
- acid + base → [salt] + [water]
- [sodium hydroxide] + [nitric acid] → sodium nitrate + water
- sulfuric acid + zinc → [zinc sulfate] + hydrogen
- [2HCl(aq)] + [Ca(s)] → CaCl$_2$ [(aq)] + H$_2$ [(g)]

When the notes are marked it will give an idea of the level that each student is working at. *(10 minutes)*

Summary answers

1 neutralisation, salt, water, metals, hydrogen

2 a Copper is not reactive enough to react with acid.

   b Potassium is too reactive and would explode on contact with acid.

   c Heat the solution in an evaporating basin on a water bath until the point of crystallisation. Then leave the liquid for a few days to allow the remainder of the water to evaporate off and the crystals to form.

Practical support

Preparing copper sulfate crystals

Equipment and materials required

Copper oxide (harmful), 1 mol/dm^3 sulfuric acid (irritant), stirring rod, beaker (100 cm^3), Bunsen burner, tripod, gauze, filter funnel, filter paper, conical flask, evaporating basin, beaker (250 cm^3), spatula, measuring cylinder, conical flask, eye protection.

Details

Add a spatula of copper oxide to a beaker, then add 25 cm^3 of sulfuric acid. Stir the reaction mixture well and note any observations. Warm the mixture gently on a tripod and gauze. Do not allow to boil. Let the mixture containing excess black copper oxide cool down. Fold the filter paper and put into the funnel in the neck of a conical flask. Filter the mixture. Collect the filtrate and put the solution into an evaporating basin. Heat it on a water bath until the point of crystallisation, then leave the liquid in a warm place for a few days to allow the crystals to form.

Safety: Eye protection should be worn throughout this practical. This reaction makes copper sulfate, which is harmful. CLEAPSS Hazcard 27C Copper sulfate – harmful; 98A Sulfuric acid–irritant.

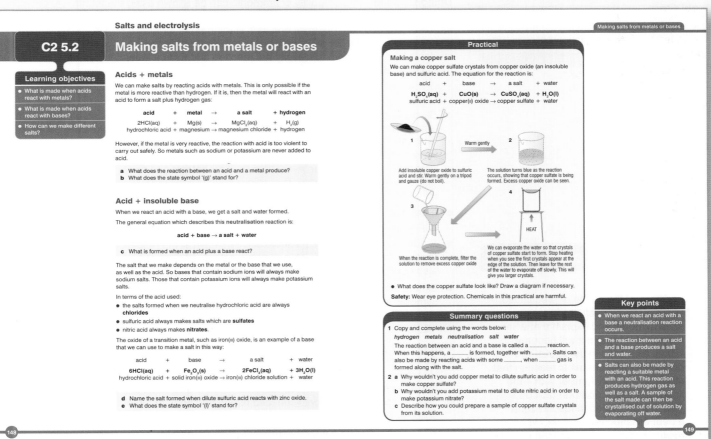

Further teaching suggestions

Calculations
- Higher Tier students could complete mole calculations on the balanced symbol equations.

Uses of neutralisation
- Students could find three uses for a neutralisation reaction (e.g. antacids, reduction of acidity of soils, to remove harmful gases from factory emissions).

Complete the table
- Ask students to draw a table where they list common acids in the first column, then the name of a base or metal in the second column and the third column should be the name of the salt. Support students by giving them the table with some missing information so they just need to complete one piece of information per row.

C2 5.3 Making salts from solutions

Learning objectives

Students should learn that:

- how salts can be made from an acid and alkali
- how insoluble salts can be made
- how unwanted ions can be removed from solutions.

Learning outcomes

Most students should be able to:

- record a method to make soluble salts
- record a method to make insoluble salts
- state what a precipitation reaction is and what they can be used for
- suggest a method for making a named salt.

Some students should also be able to:

- explain in detail what precipitation is in terms of the ions involved.

AQA Specification link-up: Chemistry C2.6

- Soluble salts can be made from acids by reacting them with: …
  - alkalis – an indicator can be used to show when the acid and alkali have completely reacted to produce a salt solution. [C2.6.1 b)]
- Insoluble salts can be made by mixing appropriate solutions of ions so that a precipitate is formed. Precipitation can be used to remove unwanted ions from solutions, for example in treating water for drinking or in treating effluent. [C2.6.1 d)]
- Ammonia dissolves in water to produce an alkaline solution. It is used to produce ammonium salts. Ammonium salts are important as fertilisers. [C2.6.2 c)]
- In neutralisation reactions, hydrogen ions react with hydroxide ions to produce water. This reaction can be represented by the equation:

$$H^+ (aq) + OH^- (aq) + H_2O (l) \qquad [C2.6.2 e)]$$

- Select an appropriate method for making a salt, given appropriate information. [C2.6]

Lesson structure

Starters

Definitions – Ask students to define the terms 'soluble' and 'insoluble'. Then ask them to write two sentences, each using one of the key words. *(5 minutes)*

Demonstration – The solubility of ammonia can be shown using the fountain experiment (see RSC Classic Chemistry demonstrations and CLEAPSS Handbook). Show the students and use their observations as a starting point for discussing solubility. Support students by having a list of prompt words to help them focus their observations. Extend students by asking them to classify the reaction and write a balanced symbol equation for this [$NH_3 + H_2O \rightarrow NH_4OH$, hydrolysis]. *(10 minutes)*

Main

- Students could make a flow chart to show how ammonia solution can be used to make ammonium nitrate. Students should consider that the ammonia solution is an alkali and undergoes a neutralisation reaction with nitric acid to make ammonium nitrate. They should include word equations in their flow chart. You could also encourage students to use a red pen every time they are referring to acids, a blue one for bases and a green one for neutral. This colour code will reinforce previous work on the pH scale and universal indicator.

- Extend students by asking them to find out the industrial conditions for this process and write a balanced symbol equation, including state symbols.

- Students could make an insoluble salt as shown in the Student Book. Encourage them to record this in a step-by-step method including an equipment list. The students could also generate the word equation for the reaction.

- Extend students by encouraging them to write a balanced symbol equation with state symbols for the reaction.

Plenaries

Method – Ask students to explain briefly how they would make one of the following salts:
- Sodium chloride. [Neutralisation between sodium hydroxide and hydrochloric acid. Use indicator to find the quantities needed. Repeat without indicator, then evaporate the water to the point of crystallisation and leave it to finish crystallising.]
- Lead iodide. [Reaction between lead nitrate and sodium iodide. Filter and collect the solid, wash it with distilled water and dry it.] *(5 minutes)*

Word search – Create a word search, but students need to answer questions to determine the words that they need to find:
- A method for removing pollutants from water. [Precipitation]
- When a solute will dissolve into a solvent, it is described as … [soluble]
- Chalk is described as this because it will not dissolve in water. [Insoluble]
- A chemical with a pH < 7 [Acid]
- A soluble base. [Alkali]
- The name of the chemical reaction between a hydrogen ion and hydroxide ion. [Neutralisation]

Support students by giving them both the word and clue. Encourage them to match the clue with the key word and then find the word in the word search. *(10 minutes)*

Support

- Some students may find it difficult to understand the cause of precipitation. You may find it useful to focus on state symbols and explain that when the salt is insoluble it will become visible as a solid in the liquid. You could refer to a chemical reaction that students are very familiar with – the limewater test for carbon dioxide. This is a precipitation reaction and a neutralisation reaction (between acidic carbon dioxide and the calcium hydroxide alkali). The cloudy parts are solid calcium carbonate.

Extend

- Ask students to find some other examples of precipitation reactions and to write balanced symbol equations for these reactions, including the state symbols.

Practical support

Making an insoluble salt

Equipment and materials required
Lead nitrate solution (toxic) (0.01 mol/dm³), potassium iodide solution, beaker, measuring cylinder, conical flask, filter funnel, filter paper, distilled water, eye protection.

Details
Measure 10 cm³ of potassium iodide and 5 cm³ of lead nitrate into a small beaker. Gently shake, and then filter the mixture and wash through with distilled water. Scrape the solid on to some fresh filter paper and allow it to dry. This is the insoluble salt.

Safety: Chemical splashproof eye protection should be worn throughout, and hands should be thoroughly washed after the experiment has been completed. Pregnant women should be aware that lead salts can affect unborn children. CLEAPSS Hazcard 57A – toxic. Dispose of waste following CLEAPSS guidelines.

Salts and electrolysis

C2 5.3 — Making salts from solutions (k)

Learning objectives
- How can we make salts from an acid and an alkali?
- How can we make insoluble salts?
- How can we remove unwanted ions from solutions?

There are two other important ways of making salts from solutions.
- We can react an acid and an alkali together to form a soluble salt.
- We can make an *insoluble* salt by reacting solutions of two soluble salts together.

Acid + alkali

When an acid reacts with an alkali, a neutralisation reaction takes place.

Hydrochloric acid reacting with sodium hydroxide solution is an example:

$$acid + alkali \rightarrow a\ salt + water$$
$$HCl(aq) + NaOH(aq) \rightarrow NaCl(aq) + H_2O(l)$$
hydrochloric acid + sodium hydroxide solution → sodium chloride + water

We can think about neutralisation in terms of $H^+(aq)$ ions reacting with $OH^-(aq)$ ions. They react to form water:

$$H^+(aq) + OH^-(aq) \rightarrow H_2O(l)$$

When we react an acid with an alkali we need to know when the acid and alkali have completely reacted. We can use an indicator for this.

We can make ammonium salts, as well as metal salts, by reacting an acid with an alkali. Ammonia reacts with water to form a weakly alkaline solution:

$$NH_3(aq) + H_2O(l) \rightleftharpoons NH_4^+(aq) + OH^-(aq)$$

Ammonia solution reacts with an acid (for example, nitric acid):

$$acid + ammonia\ solution \rightarrow an\ ammonium\ salt + water$$
$$HNO_3(aq) + NH_4^+(aq) + OH^-(aq) \rightarrow NH_4NO_3(aq) + H_2O(l)$$
nitric acid + ammonia solution → ammonium nitrate + water

Ammonium nitrate contains a high proportion of nitrogen, and it is very soluble in water. This makes it ideal as a source of nitrogen for plants to take up through their roots. It replaces the nitrogen taken up from the soil by plants as they grow.

Ammonium salts are made by adding ammonia solution to an acid until there is a small excess of ammonia. We can detect the excess ammonia by using universal indicator. We then crystallise the ammonium salt from its solution. The excess ammonia evaporates off.

a Write down a general equation for the reaction between an acid and an alkali.
b Name a salt which is used as a fertiliser to provide crops with nitrogen.

Making insoluble salts

We can sometimes make salts by combining two solutions that contain different soluble salts. When the soluble salts react to make an insoluble salt, we call the reaction a precipitation reaction. That's because the insoluble solid formed is called a **precipitate**.

Figure 1 Ammonium nitrate is used as a fertiliser

$$Pb(NO_3)_2(aq) + 2KI(aq) \rightarrow PbI_2(s) + 2KNO_3(aq)$$
lead nitrate solution + potassium iodide solution → lead iodide precipitate + potassium nitrate solution

Each of the reactant solutions contains one of the ions of the insoluble salt. In this case, they are lead ions in lead nitrate and iodide ions in potassium iodide. Lead iodide forms a yellow precipitate that we can filter off from the solution.

Practical

Making an insoluble salt

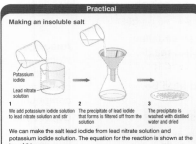

Potassium iodide
Lead nitrate solution

1 We add potassium iodide solution to lead nitrate solution and stir
2 The precipitate of lead iodide that forms is filtered off from the solution
3 The precipitate is washed with distilled water and dried

We can make the salt lead iodide from lead nitrate solution and potassium iodide solution. The equation for the reaction is shown at the top of this page.

- Why is the precipitate of lead iodide washed with distilled water?

Using precipitation

We use precipitation reactions to remove pollutants from the wastewater from factories. The effluent must be treated before it is discharged into rivers and the sea.

Precipitation is used in the removal of metal ions from industrial wastewater. By raising the pH of the water, we can make insoluble metal hydroxides precipitate out. This produces a sludge which we can easily remove from the solution.

The cleaned-up water can then be discharged safely into a river or the sea.

Precipitation can be also used to remove unwanted ions from drinking water.

Figure 2 Water treatment plants use chemical treatments to precipitate out metal compounds which can then be removed by filtering the solution

Summary questions

1 Copy and complete using the words below:
acid alkali insoluble metal polluted precipitation solid neutralisation soluble water indicator
We can make salts by reacting an .... with an .... This makes the salt and .... and is called a .... reaction. We need an .... to tell us when the reaction is complete. We can also make .... salts by reacting two .... salts together. We call this a .... reaction because the salt is formed as a .... This type of reaction is also important when we want to remove .... ions from .... water.

2 Write word equations and a brief method to show how to make the following salts:
a potassium nitrate (a soluble salt)
b silver chloride (an insoluble salt). Hint: all nitrates are soluble in water.

Key points
- An indicator is needed when a soluble salt is prepared by reacting an alkali with an acid.
- Insoluble salts can be made by reacting two solutions to produce a precipitate.
- Precipitation is an important way of removing some metal ions from industrial wastewater.

Further teaching suggestions

Role play
- Students could act out a precipitation reaction, where each student represents an ion.

Calculations
- Mole calculations could be completed from balanced symbol equations.

Solubility curves
- Students could test the solubility of salts at different temperatures and plot solubility curves (see 'Practical support'). Secondary data could be obtained to compare the solubility of different chemicals, e.g. from RSC Data book or search the internet for 'solubility data'.

Other reactions
- You may wish to allow students to make a different insoluble salt. One example is barium sulfate, prepared by mixing solutions of barium chloride and sodium sulfate (see www.practicalchemistry.org and search for 'insoluble salt').

Answers to in-text questions

a acid + alkali → salt + water
b ammonium nitrate/ammonium sulfate

Summary answers

1 acid (alkali), alkali (acid), water, neutralisation, indicator, insoluble, soluble, precipitation, solid, metal, polluted

2 a nitric acid + potassium hydroxide → potassium nitrate + water

Use an indictor to find how much of each solution is required. Repeat with the correct quantities. Evaporate the solution to the point of crystallisation and then leave it for the rest of the water to evaporate off to get crystals of potassium nitrate.

b silver nitrate + a soluble chloride, e.g. sodium chloride → silver chloride + e.g. sodium nitrate

Filter off the silver chloride precipitate, wash with distilled water and leave (or warm in an oven) to dry.

C2 5.4

Electrolysis

Learning objectives

Students should learn that:

- what electrolysis is
- which types of substance can be electrolysed
- the products of electrolysis.

Learning outcomes

Most students should be able to:

- state a definition for electrolysis
- recognise which compounds will undergo electrolysis
- add state symbols to an equation
- predict the products of molten electrolysis.

Some students should also be able to:

- explain how electrolysis occurs
- summarise electrolysis in balanced symbol equations.

Answers to in-text questions

a Using an electric current to break down a substance.

b electrolyte

c negative electrode

d positive electrode

Support

- Give students the parts of the flow chart for the decomposition of lead bromide but in the wrong order. The students can then cut them up and stick them into their own diagram in their notes.

Extend

- Ask students to find out what materials could be used to make electrodes, e.g. carbon, and to list the benefits and drawbacks of using them.

AQA **Specification link-up: Chemistry C2.7**

- When an ionic substance is melted or dissolved in water, the ions are free to move about within the liquid or solution. *[C2.7.1 a)]*
- Passing an electric current through ionic substances that are molten, for example lead bromide, or in solution breaks them down into elements. This process is called electrolysis and the substance that is broken down is called the electrolyte. *[C2.7.1 b)]*
- During electrolysis, positively charged ions move to the negative electrode, and negatively charged ions move to the positive electrode. *[C2.7.1 c)]*

Lesson structure

Starters

Anagram – As a title write: 'cysistrollee'. Explain to the students that they are going to study this topic, but the letters are jumbled up. Encourage them to find out the word [electrolysis] and write this as the title. Support students by giving them the first letter of the word. Extend students by asking them to write a brief definition [splitting up a compound using electricity]. *(5 minutes)*

Observations – Show the students an ampoule of bromine, and samples of lead and lead bromide in sealed containers. Ask students to work in pairs to make a list of everything they know about these chemicals and encourage them to use the periodic table and list the masses etc. Draw a three-column table on the board, each headed with a different one of the chemicals and ask each pair for pieces of information to fill in the table. Then ask the students how lead and bromine could be made from lead bromide. *(10 minutes)*

Main

- A classic demonstration is electrolysis of molten lead bromide. This is chosen as it is an ionic solid with a relatively low melting point. The reaction produces lead and bromine and therefore should be completed in a fume cupboard. Demonstrate the experiment and use questions and answers to extract observations from the students. Then ask them to draw a diagrammatic flow chart, including a symbol equation to represent the demonstration.

- Often it is difficult for students to see a demonstration in a fume cupboard. If the reaction can be filmed beforehand, it could be shown to students. Alternatively set up a flexicam or a camcorder connected to a TV or digital projector to show the demonstration magnified in real time.

- Students could complete their own electrolysis experiment. However, as a molten liquid is hazardous to use, they must use a solution instead. To prevent any confusion due to water producing oxygen or hydrogen, copper chloride solution should be used. Students could be given a set of questions to consider as they complete the reaction to channel their thoughts.

Plenaries

Definitions – Ask students to define the key words: 'electrolysis', 'electrolyte', 'decompose', 'electrode' in their books. Support students by giving them the definitions and the key words and they have to match them up. Extend students by asking them to define the term, then use it correctly in a sentence. *(5 minutes)*

Taboo – Create a set of cards with the key words: 'electricity', 'electrolysis', 'electrolyte', 'electrode', 'decompose'. Below each key word list three further words that would aid in explaining the main word. These will be the 'taboo' words. Give the pack of cards to groups of three. Each student should take it in turns to pick a card and try to explain the main word, without using the taboo words. The person who managed to explain the most words (without using any taboo words) is the winner. *(10 minutes)*

Practical support

Demonstration of the electrolysis of lead bromide

Equipment and materials required

Ceramic evaporating basin, lead bromide (CLEAPSS Hazcard 57 – toxic), spatula, tongs, Bunsen burner and safety equipment, tongs, two carbon electrodes, lamp, three wires, two crocodile clips, low voltage power supply (0–12 V), fume cupboard, tripod, pipe-clay triangle, eye protection, protective gloves.

Details

Half-fill the evaporating basin with lead bromide and submerge the ends of the electrodes. Connect the electrodes into the circuit involving the lamp and the power supply. Put the evaporating basin on the pipe-clay triangle above the Bunsen burner. Ignite the Bunsen burner and heat the lead bromide strongly, turn on the power supply and observe. Once the lamp is on, the electricity is flowing. This will only occur when the ions are free to move, i.e. the lead bromide is molten. Point out the vapour (CLEAPSS Hazcard 15 Bromine – toxic/corrosive). The molten salt is at a higher temperature than the boiling point of bromine, so the bromine is released as a gas not as a liquid, which is its state at room temperature. The molten lead collects at the bottom of the basin. Switch off the Bunsen and use the tongs to tip the molten lead on to the flameproof mat to show the students.

Safety: Chemical splashproof eye protection should be worn during this demonstration and it should be completed in a fume cupboard. Pregnant women should not use lead bromide. Anhydrous zinc chloride (CLEAPSS Hazcard 108A – corrosive) melts at a lower temperature than lead bromide, so can be used as an alternative.

Electrolysis of copper chloride solution

Equipment and materials required

A beaker, two carbon electrodes, lamp, three wires, two crocodile clips, low-voltage power supply (0–12 V), 1 mol/dm³ copper chloride solution (CLEAPSS Hazcard 27A – harmful), eye protection.

Details

Half-fill the beaker with copper chloride solution and immerse the tips of the electrodes. Connect the electrodes in a simple circuit with the low-voltage power supply and lamp. Start the current and observe. Chlorine (toxic) should be smelt at the positive electrode, do not smell directly at source, and copper should be deposited at the negative electrode. As soon as the observations are complete, the low-voltage power supply should be switched off.

Safety: Chemical splashproof eye protection should be worn throughout the practical. This experiment should be completed in a well ventilated room as the chlorine could irritate asthmatics. CLEAPSS Hazcard 22A Chlorine – toxic.

Salts and electrolysis

C2 5.4

Electrolysis (k)

Learning objectives

- What is electrolysis?
- What types of substance can we electrolyse?
- What is made when we electrolyse substances?

Figure 1 The first person to explain electrolysis was Michael Faraday. He worked on this and many other problems in science nearly 200 years ago.

Did you know ...?

Electrolysis is also a way of getting rid of unwanted body hair. A small electric current is passed through the base of each individual hair to be removed. The hair is destroyed through chemical changes caused by the electric current, which destroy the cells that make the hair grow.

The word **electrolysis** means 'splitting up using electricity'. In electrolysis we use an electric current to break down an ionic substance. We call the substance that is broken down by electrolysis the **electrolyte**.

a What is electrolysis?
b What do we call the substance broken down by electrolysis?

To set up an electrical circuit for electrolysis, we have two electrodes which dip into the electrolyte. The electrodes are conducting rods. One of these is connected to the positive terminal of a power supply. The other electrode is connected to the negative terminal.

The electrodes are often made of an unreactive (or **inert**) substance. This is often graphite or sometimes platinum. This is so the electrodes do not react with the electrolyte or the products made in electrolysis.

During electrolysis, positively charged ions move to the negative electrode. At the same time, the negative ions move to the positive electrode.

When the ions reach the electrodes they lose their charge and become elements. Gases may be given off or metals deposited at the electrodes. This depends on the compound used and whether it is molten or dissolved in water.

Demonstration

The electrolysis of molten lead bromide

- This demonstration needs a fume cupboard because bromine is toxic and corrosive.
- When does the bulb light up?

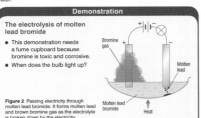

Figure 2 Passing electricity through molten lead bromide. It forms molten lead and brown bromine gas as the electrolyte is broken down by the electricity.

Figure 2 above shows how electricity breaks down lead bromide into lead and bromine:

lead bromide → lead + bromine
$PbBr_2(l) \rightarrow Pb(l) + Br_2(g)$

Lead bromide is an ionic substance. Ionic substances do not conduct electricity when they are solid. But once we melt them, the ions are free to move and carry their charge towards the electrodes.

The positive lead ions (Pb^{2+}) move towards the negative electrode. At the same time, the negatively charged bromide ions (Br^-) move towards the positive electrode.

Notice the state symbols in the equation. They tell us that the lead bromide and the lead are both at the temperature in the dish. The '(l)' stands for 'liquid'. The bromine is given off as a gas, shown as '(g)'.

c Which electrode do positive ions move towards during electrolysis?
d Which electrode do negative ions move towards during electrolysis?

Electrolysis of solutions

Many ionic substances have very high melting points. This can make electrolysis very difficult. But some ionic substances dissolve in water. When this happens, the ions also become free to move around.

However, when electrolysing solutions it is more difficult to predict what will be formed. This is because water also forms ions. So the products at each electrode are not always exactly what we expect.

When we electrolyse a solution of copper bromide, copper ions (Cu^{2+}) move to the negative electrode. The bromide ions (Br^-) move to the positive electrode. Copper bromide is split into its elements at the electrodes (see Figure 3):

copper bromide → copper + bromine
$CuBr_2(aq) \rightarrow Cu(s) + Br_2(aq)$

In this case the state symbols in the equation tell us that the copper bromide is dissolved in water. This is shown as '(aq)'. The copper is formed as a solid, shown as '(s)'. The bromine formed remains dissolved in the water – '(aq)'.

Covalent compounds cannot usually be electrolysed unless they react in water to form ions, e.g. acids in water.

links

For more information about the effect of water in electrolysis, see C2 5.5 Changes at the electrodes and C2 5.7 Electrolysis of brine.

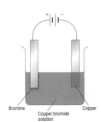

Figure 3 If we dissolve copper bromide in water, we can decompose it by electrolysis. Copper metal is formed at the negative electrode. Brown bromine appears in solution around the positive electrode.

Summary questions

1 Copy and complete using the words below:
   ions molten move solution
   For the current to flow in electrolysis, the .... must be able to .... between the electrodes. This can only happen if the substance is in .... or if it is ....

2 Predict the products formed at each electrode when the following compounds are melted and then electrolysed:
   a zinc iodide
   b lithium bromide
   c iron(III) fluoride.

3 Solid ionic substances do not conduct electricity. Using words and diagrams explain why they conduct electricity when molten or in solution.

Key points

- Electrolysis breaks down a substance using electricity.
- Ionic compounds can only be electrolysed when they are molten or in solution. That's because their ions are then free to move to the electrodes.
- In electrolysis, positive ions move to the negative electrode while negative ions move to the positive electrode.

152 / 153

Further teaching suggestions

Simulation

- Show students a simulation of the reaction detailing the particles.

Hoffman voltameter

- You may wish to demonstrate the electrolysis of water using a Hoffman voltameter – see CLEAPSS 11.4.2. A microscale version of this experiment that students can do is found at www.chemistryteachers.org – search for 'electrolysis of water'.

Summary answers

1 ions, move, solution, molten

2 a Zinc at −; iodine at +.
   b Lithium at −; bromine at +.
   c Iron at −; fluorine at +.

3 [Words/diagrams explain how ions carry charge.] If ions are not free to move (as they are not in a solid because they are held in position by strong electrostatic forces), no current can flow in the circuit.

C2 5.5

Changes at the electrodes

Specification link-up: Chemistry C2.7

- At the negative electrode, positively charged ions gain electrons (reduction) and at the positive electrode, negatively charged ions lose electrons (oxidation). *[C2.7.1 e)]*
- If there is a mixture of ions, the products formed depend on the reactivity of the elements involved. *[C2.7.1 f)]*
- Reactions at electrodes can be represented by half equations, for example:

$$2Cl^- \rightarrow Cl_2 + 2e^-$$

or

$$2Cl^- - 2e^- \rightarrow Cl_2. \quad \text{[C2.7.1 g)]} \text{ [HT only]}$$

- Predict the products of electrolysing solutions of ions. *[C2.7]*

Learning objectives

Students should learn:

- what happens to the ions during electrolysis
- that electrolysis can be represented in half-equations **[HT only]**
- that water affects electrolysis
- how to predict the products of electrolysis.

Learning outcomes

Most students should be able to:

- describe the transfer of electrons at the electrodes
- recognise oxidation and reduction at electrodes
- predict the products of electrolysis.

Some students should also be able to:

- explain in detail the transfer of electrons in electrolysis
- construct half equations **[HT only]**
- explain how water affects the products of electrolysis.

Answers to in-text questions

a Electron(s) are transferred from the ion to the electrode (electron loss).

b Electron(s) are transferred to the ion from the electrode (electron gain).

Support

- Some students may find it difficult to understand why oxygen or hydrogen can sometimes be produced. Use questions and answers to lead students through all of the particles that are in the electrolyte (water, metal ions, etc.). Then explain that water can split into H^+ and OH^-, which are present in low concentration. Explain that it is these ions that give rise to the oxygen or hydrogen.

Extend

- Give students the reactivity series and refer to the order of discharge of negatively charged ions. Students could then use these to explain how you can predict the chemicals that are discharged at each electrode.

Lesson structure

Starters

Card sort – Give the key words (oxidation, reduction and redox) and their definitions on separate cards. Students should sort the cards to match the key words with their definitions. Support students by encouraging them to complete the exercise in small groups. Extend students by asking them to represent each of these key words as symbol or ionic equations. *(5 minutes)*

Poem – Encourage the students to create a little poem or saying to help them remember that oxidation is the loss of electrons, which happens at the positive electrode, and that reduction is the gain of electrons, which occurs at the negative electrode. The best one could then be copied by all the students into their notes. *(10 minutes)*

Main

- Show the students a sample of potassium chloride and ask them to predict the products of electrolysing it when molten. Encourage a student to write the balanced symbol equation on the board. Now ask pairs of students to predict the products of electrolysing a solution of potassium chloride. Ask each pair their thoughts and why they came to this idea. Then allow the students to complete the experiment to find out it they were correct. Encourage students to note their work in the form of a fully labelled diagram, including half equations and brief notes to explain where the hydrogen comes from. (Note that half equations are Higher Tier only.)

- Students could act out an electrolysis experiment. They could wear black bibs and make a line to represent the electrodes and wires in the circuit. Polystyrene balls could be used as electrons, two students could stand by a bucket of balls – one student giving them out and one putting them into the bucket (this represents the power source). Different-coloured bibs (red for positively charged ions, blue for negatively charged ions) could be used to represent the solution. The circuit could then 'run' under your instructions. Students could use the play to describe what happens in terms of particles at the electrodes.

- Take digital photographs of the electrolysis play. These could then be used in the classroom to remind students of the play. If a photograph is displayed on an interactive whiteboard, then annotations could be added in front of the class.

Plenaries

Half equations – Ask students to complete the half equations as detailed in Question 2 of the summary questions. Then encourage the students to create a further example of a half equation of their choice. **[HT only]** *(5 minutes)*

What am I? – On sticky labels write the following words: 'redox', 'reduction', 'oxidation', 'reduced', 'oxidised', 'half equation'. Split the students into teams of six and give each a word and ask them to stick it on their forehead (but they should not know what their word is). Each student then takes it in turns to ask his or her group questions, to which the team can only respond with 'yes' or 'no'. The aim is for each student to guess their word. Support students by giving them a set of statements to prompt their questions to the other team members. Extend students by asking them to write a balanced symbol equation or ionic equation to illustrate each word. *(10 minutes)*

Practical support

Electrolysis of potassium chloride solution

Equipment and materials required

Beaker, two carbon electrodes, lamp, three wires, two crocodile clips, low-voltage power supply (0–12 V), saturated solution of potassium chloride, test tube, splint, eye protection.

Details

Half-fill the beaker with potassium chloride solution and immerse the tips of the electrodes. Connect the electrodes in a series circuit with the power supply and lamp. Start the current and observe:

(CLEAPSS Hazcard 22A Chlorine – toxic) should be smelt at the anode, and bubbles (CLEAPSS Hazcard 48 Hydrogen – extremely flammable) should be observed at the cathode. As soon as the observations are complete, the power supply should be switched off. The hydrogen could be collected in a test tube under displacement, and tested with a lighted splint.

Safety: Chemical splashproof eye protection should be worn throughout the practical. This experiment should be completed in a well-ventilated room as the chlorine could irritate asthmatics. Do not smell the chlorine directly at its source.

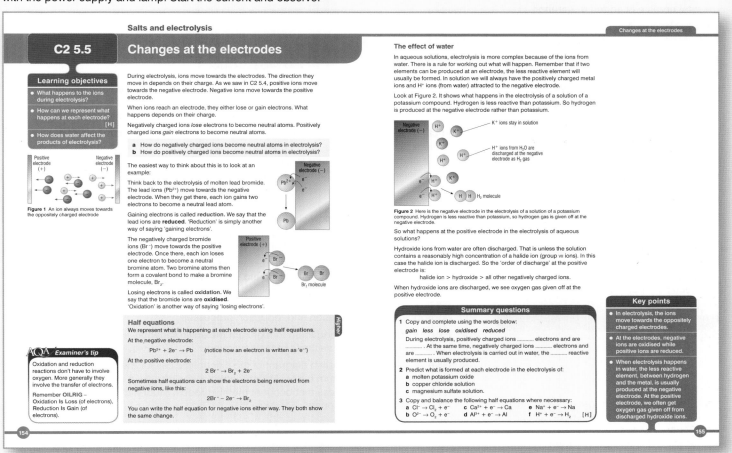

Further teaching suggestions

Writing half-equations

- Higher Tier students could be asked to write the following symbol equation and half equations for the electrolysis of a concentrated solution of iron(III) chloride:
  $2FeCl_3(aq) \rightarrow [2Fe(s)] + [3Cl_2(g)]$
  Positive electrode: $[2Cl^-(aq) \rightarrow Cl_2(g) + 2e^-]$
  Negative electrode: $[Fe^{3+}(aq) + 3e^- \rightarrow Fe(s)]$

Electrolysis circus

- Students could be encouraged to electrolyse a circus of different solutions and record their observations in a table. They could electrolyse solutions of other halides, e.g. sodium chloride, zinc bromide and zinc iodide. The experiments are all similar to the one with copper chloride solution, as detailed in 'Practical support' in C2 5.4 'Electrolysis'.
  They could then write word equations for the reactions. Higher Tier students could write half equations and balanced

symbol equations for the reactions. You may wish to use conductivity sensors to monitor changes in conductivity.

Positive and negative

- Ask students to copy the key points and to write any word that has a positive charge in red (e.g. oxidation, positive,) and any with a negative charge in blue.

Moving ions

- You may wish to demonstrate the movement of ions to each electrode by demonstrating by the electrolysis of a crystal of $KMnO_4$ on filter paper dampened with sodium chloride solution, or the electrolysis of $CuCrO_4$ in a saturated urea solution using a U-tube. Another example of the electrolysis of copper chromate, can be found in CLEAPSS PS67-13. It is possible for students to complete this experiment.

Summary answers

1 gain, reduced, lose, oxidised, less

2 a potassium at −, oxygen at +
  b copper at −, chlorine at +
  c hydrogen at −, oxygen at +

3 a $2Cl^- \rightarrow Cl_2 + 2e^-$
  b $2O^{2-} \rightarrow O_2 + 4e^-$
  c $Ca^{2+} + 2e^- \rightarrow Ca$
  d $Al^{3+} + 3e^- \rightarrow Al$
  e $Na^+ + e^- \rightarrow Na$
  f $2H^+ + 2e^- \rightarrow H_2$

C2 5.6 The extraction of aluminium

Learning objectives

Students should learn:

- how aluminium is extracted from aluminium oxide
- why cryolite is added to the melt
- what happens at each electrode in the process.

Learning outcomes

Most students should be able to:

- recall the products of the electrolysis of aluminium oxide
- explain why cryolite is added to the melt
- label a simple diagram of the electrolytic cell used for the extraction of aluminium
- explain how the products form at each electrode.

Some students should also be able to:

- generate half equations for the electrolysis of aluminium oxide. [HT only]

Support

- Encourage students to ensure that they know the main processes involved in extracting aluminium [mine aluminium ore, purify into aluminium oxide, electrolyse to make aluminium at the negative electrode]. Give the students these statements and allow them to flesh them out as a spider diagram.

Extend

- Ask students to explain why the carbon positive electrodes need to be replaced frequently [oxygen gas produced at the electrode immediately reacts with the carbon]. Students could represent this process as a balanced symbol equation, including state symbols [$C(s) + O_2(g) \rightarrow CO_2(g)$]. Ask students to suggest why inert electrodes such as platinum are not used [expense].

AQA Specification link-up: Chemistry C2.7

- Aluminium is manufactured by the electrolysis of a molten mixture of aluminium oxide and cryolite. Aluminium forms at the negative electrode and oxygen at the positive electrode. The positive electrode is made of carbon, which reacts with the oxygen to produce carbon dioxide. [C2.7.1 h)]

Lesson structure

Starters

Uses – Ask students to reflect back on their work in C1 3.4 'Aluminium and titanium', and to recall a use of aluminium and the property that makes this material fit for its purpose [e.g. aeroplane fuselage as its alloys have a low density and are strong]. *(5 minutes)*

Predict – Ask students to work in pairs to predict the products of electrolysis of molten aluminium oxide and write a word equation for this process. Support students by giving them the names of the reactant and products. Higher Tier students could also complete half-equations to show the formation of the products. *(10 minutes)*

Main

- Students could make a flow chart to explain how aluminium ore is mined and then the metal extracted and finally used. Support students by giving them the stages in the wrong order. They could then cut and stick to make their flow chart.
- Students should ensure that they include the name of the raw materials [bauxite, cryolite], conditions [electrolytic cell] and how energy consumption is reduced [addition of cryolite to reduce the melting point and recycling of the carbon electrodes]. Students should also include any relevant equations and where appropriate, detail oxidation and reduction processes.
- Extend students by asking them to highlight the environmental, social and economic impacts of the different sections of the flow chart.
- Give students an unlabelled diagram of the electrolytic cell for the extraction of aluminium from aluminium oxide. Ask students to label the main parts of the diagram and to explain the process that occur at the electrodes. Students should include equations where appropriate.

Plenaries

Key points – Ask students to write questions that could be answered by each of the key points. Support students by supplying them with a selection of questions. They have to choose the one that matches each key point. Extend students by asking them to form the question and then rewrite the key point to include the formula, half equations or symbol equations as appropriate. *(5 minutes)*

Flow chart summary – Ask students to summarise the extraction of aluminium from bauxite, including any equations in a flow chart. Support students by making this a 'cut-and-stick' exercise. Extend students by encouraging them to include symbol equations in their flow chart. They could also write all reduction processes in blue and oxidation processes in red. *(10 minutes)*

Further teaching suggestions

Handling samples
- You may have samples of cryolite, aluminium oxide, bauxite and aluminium that students could handle and observe. Students could create a table to detail their observations.

Video
- The RSC Industrial reactions have a video on aluminium extraction that you could play to students.

Cartoon strip
- Ask students to draw a cartoon strip using particles to demonstrate what happens at the electrodes. You could

support the students by supplying the images or the words for them to complete the cartoon strip.

Animation
- Show an animation of what happens at each electrode in terms of the ions, electrons and atoms. Ask students to work in small groups and to create a 'voice-over' for the animation. Animations are freely available on the internet. Use a search engine.

Salts and electrolysis

C2 5.6 The extraction of aluminium

The extraction of aluminium

Learning objectives
- How is aluminium obtained from aluminium oxide?
- Why is cryolite used in the process?
- What happens at each electrode in the process?

You already know that aluminium is a very important metal. The uses of the metal or its alloys include:
- pans
- overhead power cables
- aeroplanes
- cooking foil
- drink cans
- window and patio door frames
- bicycle frames and car bodies.

a Why is aluminium used to make overhead power cables?

Aluminium is quite a reactive metal. It is less reactive than magnesium but more reactive than zinc or iron. Carbon is not reactive enough to use in its extraction so we must use electrolysis. The compound electrolysed is aluminium oxide, Al_2O_3.

We get aluminium oxide from bauxite ore. The ore is mined by open cast mining. Bauxite contains mainly aluminium oxide. However, it is mixed with other rocky impurities. So the first step is to separate aluminium oxide from the ore. The impurities contain a lot of iron(III) oxide. This colours the waste solution from the separation process rusty brown. The solution has to be stored in large lagoons.

Figure 1 Aluminium alloys have a low density but are very strong

Extracting metals from ores

BAUXITE
Purified ↓ (aluminium oxide is separated from the ore)

ALUMINIUM OXIDE
Extracted ↓ (by electrolysis)

ALUMINIUM METAL

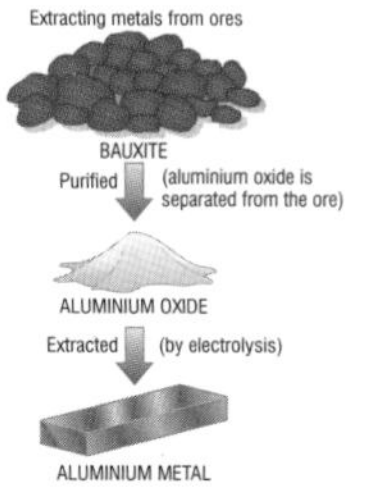

Figure 2 Extracting aluminium from its ore. This process requires a lot of energy. The purification stage makes aluminium hydroxide. This is separated from the impurities but then must be heated to turn it back to pure aluminium oxide. Then even more energy is needed melting and electrolysing the oxide.

Electrolysis of aluminium oxide

To electrolyse the aluminium oxide we must first melt it. This enables the ions to move to the electrodes.

Unfortunately aluminium oxide has a very high melting point. It melts at 2050°C. However, chemists have found a way of saving at least some energy. This is done by mixing the aluminium oxide with molten cryolite. Cryolite is another ionic compound. The molten mixture can be electrolysed at about 850°C. The electrical energy transferred to the electrolysis cells keeps the mixture molten.

b Why must aluminium oxide be molten for electrolysis to take place?

The overall reaction in the electrolysis cell is:

aluminium oxide $\xrightarrow{\text{electrolysis}}$ aluminium + oxygen

$$2Al_2O_3(l) \longrightarrow 4Al(l) + 3O_2(g)$$

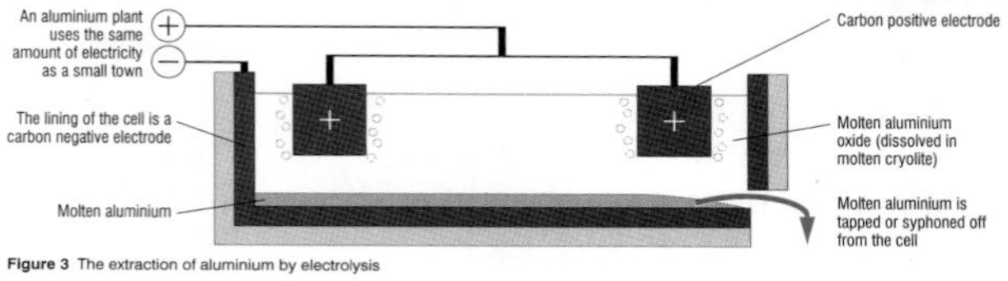

Figure 3 The extraction of aluminium by electrolysis

At the negative (–) electrode:

Each aluminium ion (Al^{3+}) gains 3 electrons. The ions turn into aluminium atoms. We say that the Al^{3+} ions are reduced to form Al atoms.

The aluminium metal formed is molten at the temperature of the cell and collects at the bottom. It is siphoned or tapped off.

At the positive (+) electrode:

Each oxide ion (O^{2-}) loses 2 electrons. The ions turn into oxygen atoms. We say that the O^{2-} ions are oxidised to form oxygen atoms. These bond in pairs to form molecules of oxygen gas (O_2).

The oxygen reacts with the hot, positive carbon electrodes, making carbon dioxide gas. So the positive electrodes gradually burn away. They need to be replaced in the cells regularly.

c Are the oxide ions reduced or oxidised in the electrolysis of molten aluminium oxide?

Summary questions

1 Copy and complete using the words below:
positive oxygen extraction carbon cryolite negative energy
In the .... of aluminium, aluminium oxide is dissolved in molten .... in order to use less .... to melt it. The aluminium metal is collected at the .... electrode in the cells, while oxygen is formed at the .... electrode. The electrodes used are made of .... The positive electrodes burn away as they react with .... and form carbon dioxide gas.

2 **a** Explain which ions are oxidised and which ions are reduced in the electrolysis of molten aluminium oxide.
  b Why are the positive electrodes replaced regularly in the industrial electrolysis of aluminium oxide? Include a word equation.

3 Write half equations for the changes at each electrode in the electrolysis of molten aluminium oxide. [H]

Key points

- Aluminium oxide is electrolysed in the manufacture of aluminium metal.
- The aluminium oxide is mixed with molten cryolite to lower its melting point.
- Aluminium forms at the negative electrode and oxygen at the positive electrode.
- The positive carbon electrodes are replaced regularly as they gradually burn away.

Answers to in-text questions

a Aluminium is a good conductor of electricity and has a low density.

b Its ions must be free to move to the electrodes.

c Oxidised (ions lose electrons to become neutral atoms).

Summary answers

1 extraction, cryolite, energy, negative, positive, carbon, oxygen

2 **a** Aluminium ions (Al^{3+}) are reduced (electrons gained); oxide ions (O^{2-}) are oxidised (electrons lost).
  b The carbon in the positive electrodes reacts with oxygen produced to give off carbon dioxide gas, burning the electrodes away:
  carbon + oxygen → carbon dioxide

3 At negative electrode: $Al^{3+} + 3e^- \rightarrow Al$;
  At positive electrode: $2O^{2-} \rightarrow O_2 + 4e^-$

C2 5.7

Electrolysis of brine

Learning objectives

Students should learn that:

- the products of the electrolysis of brine
- how the products are used.

Learning outcomes

Most students should be able to:

- state the products of the electrolysis of brine
- describe how brine can be electrolysed
- list some uses of the products of the electrolysis of brine.

Some students should also be able to:

- generate half equations for the electrolysis of brine. [HT only]

Support

- Students may need support to understand why there are three different products from the electrolysis of brine. You may wish to ask them again to list all of the particles present in the electrolyte [H^+, OH^-, Na^+, Cl^- and H_2O]. State that hydrogen is given off at the negative electrode and ask a volunteer to come to the board and rub out the ion that would make hydrogen. Then repeat this for chlorine. Ask students what are left [OH^-, Na^+ and H_2O]. Ask students what would be left if the water was removed [NaOH or sodium hydroxide]. You could ask students to suggest how the water could be removed [evaporation].

Extend

- Extend students by asking them to research the Solvay process, which uses sodium chloride. Students could research the industrial production of sodium carbonate and sodium hydrogencarbonate using this method.

AQA Specification link-up: Chemistry C2.7

- The electrolysis of sodium chloride solution produces hydrogen and chlorine. Sodium hydroxide solution is also produced. These are important reagents for the chemical industry, e.g. sodium hydroxide for the production of soap and chlorine for the production of bleach and plastics. [C2.7.1 i)]

Lesson structure

Starters

Spot the odd one out – Show students a picture of a bar of soap, rayon, paper, a bottle marked brine and a bottle of detergent. Ask students to suggest the odd one out [brine as all the others are products made using sodium hydroxide]. *(5 minutes)*

Predict – Ask students to work in pairs to predict the products of electrolysis of molten sodium chloride and a solution of sodium chloride. Support students by giving them a list of the particles present in each of the electrolytes. Higher Tier students could also complete half equations to show the formation of the products. *(10 minutes)*

Main

- Students can complete their own electrolysis of sodium chloride. They could record their observations on a diagram of the apparatus. They could also annotate the formation of the products and detail their uses.
- Show students different popular science publications, from *New Scientist* to *Horrible Science*. Ask the students to write a magazine article for a popular science magazine to explain the importance of the chloro-alkali industry (search for 'electrolysis of salt' or 'chlor-alkali').
- Students could use desktop publishing packages to produce their article. They could be encouraged to use photographs of the industrial processes using the internet, or they could use a digital camera to take images in the lab to be used in their article.

Plenaries

Uses – Give the students separate cards with the words 'hydrogen', 'chlorine' and 'sodium hydroxide' printed on them. Read out the following uses of the products of electrolysis of sodium chloride solution, then students hold up the card that shows which product is used for that specific use:

- Margarine [hydrogen]
- PVC [chlorine]
- Bleach [sodium hydroxide, chlorine]
- Soap [sodium hydroxide]
- Paper [chlorine, sodium hydroxide]
- Rayon fibres [sodium hydroxide]
- Detergents [sodium hydroxide, chlorine]
- Purification of aluminium ore [sodium hydroxide]
- Hydrochloric acid manufacture [chlorine, hydrogen] *(5 minutes)*

Demonstration – Show the electrolysis of sodium chloride solution in a Petri dish. This could be completed on an overhead projector and projected on to a whiteboard. The colours of the universal indicator solution can be clearly seen. Take care not to spill solution into the projector. Ask the students to explain their observations. Support students by giving them statements that they can use to label directly the image that is being projected. Extend students by encouraging them to write half equations next to each electrode. *(10 minutes)*

Answers to in-text questions

a Chlorine, hydrogen, sodium hydroxide solution.

b Water treatment, making bleach, making plastics (PVC).

c For example, making margarine.

d Making soap and paper, making bleach (with chlorine).

Practical support

Electrolysing brine in the lab

Equipment and materials required

Beaker or electrolysis cell, saturated sodium chloride solution, two carbon electrodes, two crocodile clips, two wires, low-voltage power supply (0–12 V), litmus paper, water, two test tubes, splint, matches, gloves, eye protection (chemical splashproof).

Details

Half-fill the beaker with the sodium chloride solution and submerge one end of the carbon electrodes. Using the wires and crocodile clips, connect to the power supply. Wearing gloves, fill the test tube with the solution and hold, inverted with the neck in the solution over the negative electrode (the carbon electrode attached to the black terminal of the power supply). Put on eye protection and start the electrolysis. Once the test tube is full of gas, put a gloved finger over the end of the tube to seal it, and remove it from the water. Test the gas with a lighted splint (a pop should be heard). While the gas is being collected, test the gas at the positive electrode by holding a damp piece of litmus paper over the electrode and observe.

Safety: This practical produces chlorine gas (CLEAPSS Hazcard 22A – toxic, could irritate asthmatics) and should only be completed in a well-ventilated area. The equipment should be switched off when the products have been tested. The solution produces sodium hydroxide and this is why gloves should be worn to collect the gas by displacement.

Salts and electrolysis

C2 5.7 Electrolysis of brine

Learning objectives
- What is produced when we electrolyse brine?
- How do we use these products?

The electrolysis of **brine** (concentrated sodium chloride solution) is a very important industrial process. When we pass an electric current through brine we get three products:
- chlorine gas is produced at the positive electrode
- hydrogen gas is produced at the negative electrode
- sodium hydroxide solution is also formed.

We can summarise the electrolysis of brine as:

sodium chloride solution $\xrightarrow{\text{electrolysis}}$ hydrogen + chlorine + sodium hydroxide solution

a What are the three products made when we electrolyse brine?

At the positive electrode (+):
The negative chloride ions (Cl⁻) are attracted to the positive electrode. When they get there, they each lose one electron. The chloride ions are oxidised, as they lose electrons. The chlorine atoms bond together in pairs and are given off as chlorine gas (Cl₂).

At the negative electrode (–):
There are H⁺ ions in brine, formed when water breaks down:

$$H_2O \rightarrow H^+ + OH^-$$

These positive hydrogen ions are attracted to the negative electrode. The sodium ions (Na⁺) are also attracted to the same electrode. But remember in C2 5.5, we saw what happens when two ions are attracted to an electrode. It is the less reactive element that gets discharged. In this case, hydrogen ions are discharged and sodium ions stay in solution.

When the H⁺ ions get to the negative electrode, they each gain one electron. The hydrogen ions are reduced, as they each gain an electron. The hydrogen atoms formed bond together in pairs and are given off as hydrogen gas (H₂).

The remaining solution:
You can test the solution around the negative electrode with indicator. It shows that the solution is alkaline. This is because we can think of brine as containing aqueous ions of Na⁺ and Cl⁻ (from salt) and H⁺ and OH⁻ (from water). The Cl⁻ and H⁺ ions are removed during electrolysis. So this leaves a solution containing Na⁺ and OH⁻ ions, i.e. a solution of sodium hydroxide.

Look at the way we can electrolyse brine in industry in Figure 1.

Practical

Electrolysing brine in the lab

Turn off the electricity once the tubes are nearly full of gas to avoid inhaling chlorine gas (toxic).
- How can you positively test for the gases collected?

Test the solution near the negative electrode with universal indicator solution.
- What does the indicator tell us?

Safety: Wear eye protection. Do not smell the gas.

🔗 links
For information about what happens when two ions are attracted to an electrode, see C2 5.2 Making salts from metals or bases.

Figure 1 In industry, brine can be electrolysed in a cell in which the two electrodes are separated by a porous membrane. This is called a diaphragm cell.

Half equations for the electrolysis of brine
The half equations for what happens in the electrolysis of brine are:

At the positive electrode (+):

$$2Cl^-(aq) \rightarrow Cl_2(g) + 2e^-$$

[remember that this can also be written as: $2Cl^-(aq) - 2e^- \rightarrow Cl_2(g)$]

At the negative electrode (–):

$$2H^+(aq) + 2e^- \rightarrow H_2(g)$$

Using chlorine

We can react chlorine with the sodium hydroxide produced in the electrolysis of brine. This makes a solution of **bleach**. Bleach is very good at killing bacteria.

Chlorine is also important in making many other disinfectants, as well as plastics such as PVC.

b What is chlorine used for?

Using hydrogen

The hydrogen that we make by electrolysing brine is particularly pure. This makes it very useful in the food industry. We make margarine by reacting hydrogen with vegetable oils.

c What is hydrogen used for?

Using sodium hydroxide

The sodium hydroxide from the electrolysis of brine is used to make soap and paper. It is also used to make bleach (see above).

d What is sodium hydroxide used for?

📝 Did you know ...?
Smelly drains, dustbins and other 'pongs' in hot summer weather result in people using far more bleach in summer than in winter.

Figure 2 The chlorine made when we electrolyse brine is used to kill bacteria in drinking water, and also in swimming pools

Summary questions

1 Copy and complete using the words below:
   hydrogen bleach hydroxide chlorine
   When we pass an electric current through brine we can collect _____ gas at the positive electrode, and _____ gas at the negative electrode. Sodium _____ solution is formed in the cell. Two of these products are also used to make _____.

2 We can electrolyse *molten* sodium chloride. Compare the products formed with those from the electrolysis of sodium chloride solution. What are the differences?

3 For the electrolysis of brine, write half equations, including state symbols, for the reactions **a** at the positive electrode and **b** at the negative electrode.   [H]

Key points
- When we electrolyse brine we get three products – chlorine gas, hydrogen gas and sodium hydroxide solution (an alkali).
- Chlorine is used to make bleach, which kills bacteria, and to make plastics.
- Hydrogen is used to make margarine.
- Sodium hydroxide is used to make bleach, paper and soap.

Further teaching suggestions

Video
- Show students the industrial electrolysis of brine using a video, e.g. RSC Industrial Chemistry.

Internet search
- Electrolysis of brine occurs in two main ways: membrane cell and mercury cathode cell. Students could research these methods using the internet.

Displaying data
- Ask the students to find out the different uses of chlorine in the UK, represented as percentages. Then ask the students to display the information as a pie chart. Support some students by giving them the data, then they could plot a bar chart.

Diagram annotation
- Give students a diagram of the electrolysis of brine. They should then annotate their diagram so that it contains all the information from the key points.

Summary answers

1 chlorine, hydrogen, hydroxide, bleach

2 With molten sodium chloride we would get sodium metal produced at the negative electrode and chlorine gas produced at the positive electrode. With sodium chloride solution we get hydrogen gas given off. With sodium chloride solution we also get a solution of sodium hydroxide formed in the electrolysis cell but not with molten sodium chloride.

3 a $2Cl^-(aq) \rightarrow Cl_2(g) + 2e^-$ or $2Cl^-(aq) - 2e^- \rightarrow Cl_2(g)$
   b $2H^+(aq) + 2e^- \rightarrow H_2(g)$

C2 5.8

Electroplating

Learning objectives

Students should learn:

- the reasons for electroplating objects
- how a metal object is electroplated.

Learning outcomes

Most students should be able to:

- state a definition of electroplating
- give reasons why we electroplate some objects
- explain the process of electroplating.

Some students should also be able to:

- construct the half equations for the electroplating of an object. [HT only]

Answers to in-text questions

a Chromium, tin, gold, silver (copper, nickel).

b At the positive electrode (atoms lose electrons).

c Nickel ions (Ni^{2+}).

Support

- Some students may have difficulty selecting the important information to include on a diagram. You could give these students the labels to cut and stick on to their diagram of the electrolysis of copper.

Extend

- Students could suggest an experimental set-up for electroplating with precious metals as used by the jewellery industry. Students could write a half equation for each electrode. Encourage students to use secondary sources such as search engines on the internet to find out how electroplating is actually done in the industrial manufacture of jewellery.

AQA Specification link-up: Chemistry C2.7

- Electrolysis is used to electroplate objects. This may be for a variety of reasons and includes copper plating and silver plating. [C2.7.1 d)]
- Explain and evaluate processes that use the principles described in this unit, including the use of electroplating. [C2.7]

Lesson structure

Starters

Show and tell – Give students some examples of items that have been electroplated and where the top surface has been worn away, e.g. a silver-coated copper ring, cutlery, belt buckles. Then ask the students to suggest what has happened. [They have been made from one metal and coated in another.] *(5 minutes)*

Complete the sentences – Ask students to complete the following sentences about what happens to metal ions in electroplating:

If a [positive] electrode is made from nickel, the nickel [atoms] can lose two electrons to become nickel [ions]. These nickel ions then go into the electrolyte. This process is called [oxidation].

If a [negative] electrode attracts nickel ions from the electrolyte, the nickel [ions] gain two electrons from the negative electrode and become nickel [atoms]. This process is called [reduction].

Support students by giving them the missing words. Extend students by asking them to write two half equations, including state symbols to summarise the prose. *(10 minutes)*

Main

- Supply students with the parts of a diagram of the electroplating of a spoon. They should assemble the full diagram from the pieces and then label the image, including an explanation of why electroplating is done.

- Students can complete their own electroplating of copper. Allowing the set-up to run for a long time at low current will give the best results. Once the practical is up and running, it is often useful for students to work in pairs to make observations and comments together. Students could be given an A4 sheet of paper that has been split into six equal sections. They could draw a pictorial flow chart with labelled diagrams to record their method and observations as the electrolysis continues. The students should explain what they see at each electrode (including half equations if they are Higher Tier students).

- Encourage students to draw how electroplating happens in a cartoon-strip style. To guide students, ask them to use the key words, e.g. electrolysis, electrode, electron, at least once. More artistic students may wish to personify the ions and electrons to make the cartoon more amusing.

- The electroplating practical provides a good opportunity to develop investigative aspects of Controlled Assessment (AS4.1.1). For example, students could investigate the factors that might affect the rate of electroplating.

Plenaries

I went to the shops ... – Sit the students in a circle, the first student says 'I went to the shops to buy ...' (insert an electroplated object here). The next student repeats the first and adds another electroplated item to the list. This continues around the circle. *(5 minutes)*

AfL (Assessment for Learning) – Lay the cartoons or observation flow charts on the side bench of the room, with an A4 sheet of paper at one side. Ask each student to study some of the work and comment on the science content, by noting his or her thoughts on the paper. Support students by giving them a marking scheme with statements that they need to look for in the work. Extend students by asking them to suggest how the work could be improved. The owners of the work could then make the suggested changes for homework before handing their materials in for assessment by the teacher. *(10 minutes)*

Practical support

Nickel plating copper metal

Equipment and materials required

A 250 cm³ beaker, nickel sulfate solution (dissolve 5 g of nickel ammonium sulfate in 100 cm³ of water), wax in a 100 cm³ beaker held in a water bath set at 80 °C, low voltage power supply (0–12 V), two wires, two crocodile clips, copper foil strips cut small enough to fit into the beaker, nickel electrode, mounted needle, sandpaper, eye protection.

Details

Wear eye protection throughout this practical. Using sandpaper, clean the surface of the copper foil. Dip the copper foil into the molten wax and allow it to dry. Scratch a design into the wax using the mounted needle. Half-fill the beaker with nickel sulfate solution. Add the nickel electrode and connect to the positive terminal of the power supply using the wires and crocodile clips. Add the wax-coated copper foil and connect to the negative terminal. Ensure that one end of each electrode is submerged in the solution, while the other is out of it. The slower the rate of deposition, the better the nickel will adhere to the copper. Turn off the power supply and remove the copper foil. Rinse off the nickel sulfate solution and remove the excess wax.

Safety: CLEAPSS Hazcard 65B Nickel sulfate – harmful. Hot wax can cause burns.

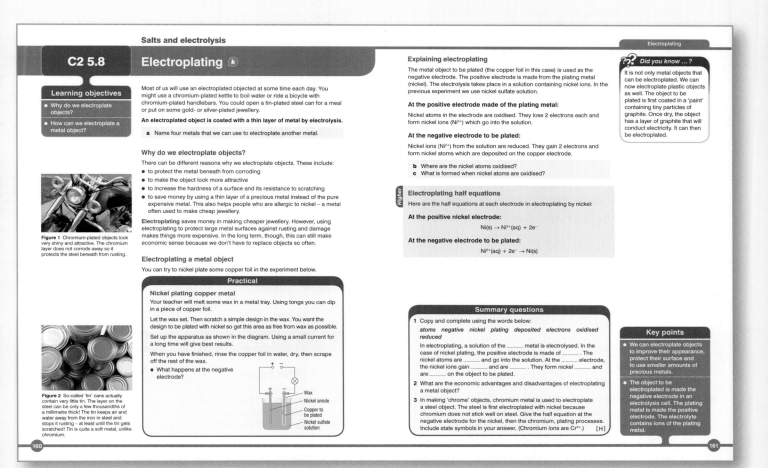

Salts and electrolysis

C2 5.8   Electroplating (k)

Learning objectives

- Why do we electroplate objects?
- How can we electroplate a metal object?

Most of us will use an electroplated objected at some time each day. You might use a chromium-plated kettle to boil water or ride a bicycle with chromium-plated handlebars. You could open a tin-plated steel can for a meal or put on some gold- or silver-plated jewellery.

An electroplated object is coated with a thin layer of metal by electrolysis.

a Name four metals that we can use to electroplate another metal.

Why do we electroplate objects?

There can be different reasons why we electroplate objects. These include:

- to protect the metal beneath from corroding
- to make the object look more attractive
- to increase the hardness of a surface and its resistance to scratching
- to save money by using a thin layer of a precious metal instead of the pure expensive metal. This also helps people who are allergic to nickel – a metal often used to make cheap jewellery.

Electroplating saves money in making cheaper jewellery. However, using electroplating to protect large metal surfaces against rusting and damage makes things more expensive. In the long term, though, this can still make economic sense because we don't have to replace objects so often.

Figure 1 Chromium-plated objects look very shiny and attractive. The chromium layer does not corrode away so it protects the steel beneath from rusting.

Electroplating a metal object

You can try to nickel plate some copper foil in the experiment below.

Practical

Nickel plating copper metal

Your teacher will melt some wax in a metal tray. Using tongs you can dip in a piece of copper foil.

Let the wax set. Then scratch a simple design in the wax. You want the design to be plated with nickel so get this area as free from wax as possible.

Set up the apparatus as shown in the diagram. Using a small current for a long time will give best results.

When you have finished, rinse the copper foil in water, dry, then scrape off the rest of the wax.

- What happens at the negative electrode?

Wax
Nickel anode
Copper to be plated
Nickel sulfate solution

Figure 2 So-called 'tin' cans actually contain very little tin. The layer on the steel can be only a few thousandths of a millimetre thick! The tin keeps air and water away from the iron in steel and stops it rusting – at least until the tin gets scratched! Tin is quite a soft metal, unlike chromium.

Explaining electroplating

The metal object to be plated (the copper foil in this case) is used as the negative electrode. The positive electrode is made from the plating metal (nickel). The electrolysis takes place in a solution containing nickel ions. In the previous experiment we use nickel sulfate solution.

At the positive electrode made of the plating metal:

Nickel atoms in the electrode are oxidised. They lose 2 electrons each and form nickel ions (Ni^{2+}) which go into the solution.

At the negative electrode to be plated:

Nickel ions (Ni^{2+}) from the solution are reduced. They gain 2 electrons and form nickel atoms which are deposited on the copper electrode.

b Where are the nickel atoms oxidised?
c What is formed when nickel atoms are oxidised?

Electroplating half equations

Here are the half equations at each electrode in electroplating by nickel:

At the positive nickel electrode:

$$Ni(s) \rightarrow Ni^{2+}(aq) + 2e^-$$

At the negative electrode to be plated:

$$Ni^{2+}(aq) + 2e^- \rightarrow Ni(s)$$

?? Did you know …?

It is not only metal objects that can be electroplated. We can now electroplate plastic objects as well. The object to be plated is first coated in a 'paint' containing tiny particles of graphite. Once dry, the object has a layer of graphite that will conduct electricity. It can then be electroplated.

Summary questions

1 Copy and complete using the words below:

atoms negative nickel plating deposited electrons oxidised reduced

In electroplating, a solution of the .... metal is electrolysed. In the case of nickel plating, the positive electrode is made of .... The nickel atoms are .... and go into the solution. At the .... electrode, the nickel ions gain .... and are .... They form nickel .... and are .... on the object to be plated.

2 What are the economic advantages and disadvantages of electroplating a metal object?

3 In making 'chrome' objects, chromium metal is used to electroplate a steel object. The steel is first electroplated with nickel because chromium does not stick well on steel. Give the half equation at the negative electrode for the nickel, then the chromium, plating processes. Include state symbols in your answer, (Chromium ions are Cr^{3+}.) [H]

Key points

- We can electroplate objects to improve their appearance, protect their surface and to use smaller amounts of precious metals.
- The object to be electroplated is made the negative electrode in an electrolysis cell. The plating metal is made the positive electrode. The electrolyte contains ions of the plating metal.

160   161

Further teaching suggestions

Electroplating research

- Students could research into the use of electrolysis to plate other metals (electroplating) or for colouring aluminium by anodising.

Advert

- Students could be asked to imagine that they work in the marketing department of an industrial electroplating firm. They have been asked to make radio adverts to see their services. Students could record their adverts as MP3 files and the best ones could be uploaded on to the school website to showcase exemplar work.

Summary answers

1 plating, nickel, oxidised, negative, electrons, reduced, atoms, deposited

2 The plating process itself will cost money in terms of energy and chemicals. However, in jewellery this will still make it cheaper than an object made of a pure precious metal. Plating metals to protect them from corrosion or damage again costs money but the object will need replacing less frequently.

3 $Ni^{2+}(aq) + 2e^- \rightarrow Ni(s)$ then $Cr^{3+}(aq) + 3e^- \rightarrow Cr(s)$

Summary answers

1 a i zinc oxide/zinc hydroxide

 ii zinc oxide + sulfuric acid → zinc sulfate + water

 or

 zinc hydroxide + sulfuric acid → zinc sulfate + water

 b Add zinc oxide/zinc hydroxide to the acid. Warm the mixture and stir. Filter to remove the excess zinc oxide/zinc hydroxide from the zinc sulfate solution. Heat the solution in an evaporating basin on a water bath until the point of crystallisation. Then leave the liquid for a few days to allow the rest of the water to evaporate off and the crystals to form.

2 a $2KOH(aq) + H_2SO_4(aq) \rightarrow K_2SO_4(aq) + 2H_2O(l)$

 b $ZnO(s) + 2HNO_3(aq) \rightarrow Zn(NO_3)_2(aq) + H_2O(l)$

 c $Ca(s) + 2HCl(aq) \rightarrow CaCl_2(aq) + H_2(g)$

 d $Ba(NO_3)_2(aq) + Na_2SO_4(aq) \rightarrow BaSO_4(s) + 2NaNO_3(aq)$

3 a B

 b A

 c B

 d A

 e B

 f A

4 Negative electrode: sodium, calcium, zinc, aluminium. Positive electrode: iodide, fluoride, oxide, bromide.

5 **A** chlorine gas, **B** hydrogen gas, **C** sodium hydroxide solution

6 a $2H_2O \rightarrow 2H_2 + O_2$

 b Negative electrode (−): $2H^+ + 2e^- \rightarrow H_2$
 Positive electrode (+): $4OH^- \rightarrow O_2 + 2H_2O + 4e^-$

 c 1 mole.

 d The power supply.

7 a $K^+ + e^- \rightarrow K$

 b $Ba^{2+} + 2e^- \rightarrow Ba$

 c $2I^- \rightarrow I_2 + 2e^-$

 d $2O_2^- \rightarrow O_2 + 4e$

8 Description should include the object to be plated as the negative electrode in a solution containing metal ions (e.g. $CuSO_4$ solution for copper plating). To keep the concentration of metal ions in solution constant, a positive electrode made of the metal to be plated should be used. Half equation: $Cu^{2+} + 2e^- \rightarrow Cu$

Kerboodle resources

Resources available for this chapter on Kerboodle are:

● Chapter map: Salts and electrolysis
● Practical: Making salts from solutions (C2 5.3)
● Support: Making salts (C2 5.3)
● Animation: Electrolysis (C2 5.4)
● Bump up your grade: Explaining electrolysis (C2 5.4)
● Extension: Explaining electrolysis (C2 5.4)
● Webquest: Extracting aluminium (C2 5.6)
● How Science Works: Wouldn't give a nickel for the whole process (C2 5.8)
● Interactive activity: Salts and electrolysis
● Revision podcast: Electrolysis of brine
● Test yourself: Salts and electrolysis
● On your marks: Salts and electrolysis
● Examination-style questions: Salts and electrolysis
● Answers to examination-style questions: Salts and electrolysis

---

Summary questions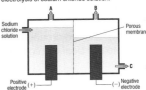

1 Zinc sulfate crystals can be made from an insoluble base and sulfuric acid.

 a i Name the insoluble base that can be used to make zinc sulfate.

 ii Write a word equation to show the reaction.

 b Describe how you could make crystals of zinc sulfate from the reaction in **a ii**.

2 Write balanced symbol equations, including state symbols, to describe the reactions below. (Each reaction forms a salt.)

 a Potassium hydroxide (an alkali) and sulfuric acid.

 b Zinc oxide (an insoluble base) and nitric acid.

 c Calcium metal and hydrochloric acid.

 d Barium nitrate and sodium sulfate (this reaction produces an insoluble salt – Hint: all sodium salts are soluble). [H]

3 Select A or B to describe correctly what happens at the positive electrode (+) and negative electrode (−) in electrolysis for **a** to **f**.

 A Positive electrode

 B Negative electrode

 a Positive ions move towards this.

 b Negative ions move towards this.

 c Reduction happens here.

 d Oxidation happens here.

 e Connected to the negative terminal of the power supply.

 f Connected to the positive terminal of the power supply.

4 Make a table to show which of the following ions would move towards the positive electrode and which towards the negative electrode during electrolysis. (You may need to use a copy of the periodic table to help you.)

 sodium   iodide   calcium   fluoride
 oxide   zinc   aluminium   bromide

5 The diagram shows an industrial process used for the electrolysis of sodium chloride solution.

 Identify the products **A**, **B** and **C** on the diagram using substances from the list.

 chlorine gas   oxygen gas   hydrogen gas
 sodium hydroxide solution   sodium metal

6 Water can be split into hydrogen and oxygen using electrolysis. The word equation for this reaction is:

 water → hydrogen + oxygen

 a Write a balanced symbol equation for this reaction using the correct chemical symbols.

 b Write half equations to show what happens at the positive and negative electrodes.

 c When some water is electrolysed it produces 2 mole of hydrogen. How much oxygen is produced?

 d Where does the energy needed to split water into hydrogen and oxygen come from during electrolysis

7 Copy and complete the following half equations:

 a $K^+ \rightarrow K$

 b $Ba^{2+} \rightarrow Ba$

 c $I^- \rightarrow I_2$

 d $O^{2-} \rightarrow O_2$

8 Electrolysis can be used to produce a thin layer of metal on the surface of a metal object. Using words an diagrams, describe how you would cover a small piece of steel with copper. Make sure that you write down the half equation that describes what happens at the surfa of the steel.

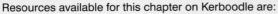

AQA Practical suggestions

Practicals	AQA	k	📖	⚙
The preparation of soluble salts.	✓		✓	
The preparation of insoluble salts.	✓		✓	
The electrolysis of molten lead bromide or zinc chloride.	✓		✓	
Investigation of the electrolysis of any solutions of a soluble ionic compound, e.g. copper chloride, sodium chloride, zinc bromide, zinc iodide.	✓		✓	
A demonstration of the Hoffman voltameter.	✓		✓	
The electroplating of copper foil with nickel in a nickel sulfate solution.	✓		✓	✓
The movement of ions, e.g. by the electrolysis of a crystal of $KMnO_4$ on filter paper dampened with sodium chloride solution, or the electrolysis of $CuCrO_4$ in a saturated urea solution using a U-tube.	✓		✓	
Using conductivity sensors to monitor conductivity and changes in conductivity.	✓		✓	

QA Examination-style questions

Hydrogen chloride gas reacts with water to make hydrochloric acid. The equation for the reaction is:

$HCl(g) \rightarrow H^+(aq) + Cl^-(aq)$

a Which of the following shows that an acid has been made?

A An aqueous solution has been made.

B Hydrogen ions have been made.

C Chloride ions have been made. (1)

b Choose a number from the list for the pH of hydrochloric acid.

1 7 12 (1)

c Hydrochloric acid reacts with sodium hydroxide solution to produce a salt and water.

i Choose a word from the list that describes sodium hydroxide. (1)

alcohol alkali insoluble

ii Choose a word from the list to complete the sentence.

The reaction between hydrochloric acid and sodium hydroxide is an example of .... (1)

combustion neutralisation oxidation

iii Name the salt made when hydrochloric acid reacts with sodium hydroxide. (1)

Lead chloride is a white insoluble salt. It can be made by mixing lead nitrate solution with sodium chloride solution. Both of these solutions are colourless.

a What would you *see* when lead nitrate solution is mixed with sodium chloride solution? (1)

b Write a word equation for the reaction. (2)

c A mining company produces wastewater that contains dissolved lead ions. Suggest how the company could treat the wastewater to reduce the concentration of lead ions. (2)

In this question you will be assessed on using good English, organising information clearly and using specialist terms where appropriate.

Copper(II) oxide is an insoluble base.

Describe how you could make crystals of copper(II) sulfate from copper(II) oxide. (6)

4 The diagram shows a nickel spoon being coated with silver.

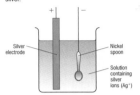

a Explain why silver ions in the solution move towards the spoon. (2)

b Use words from the list to complete the sentence.

gaining losing sharing electron neutron proton

When silver ions reach the spoon they change into silver atoms by .... an .... (2)

c Suggest one reason why spoons made from nickel are coated with silver. (1)

AQA, 2002

5 Magnesium is manufactured by the electrolysis of molten magnesium chloride. The container is made of steel, which is the negative electrode. Carbon (graphite) is used for the positive electrode.

a Steel and carbon (graphite) both conduct electricity.

i Suggest one other reason why the negative electrode is made of steel. (1)

ii Suggest one other reason why the positive electrode is made of carbon (graphite). (1)

b Magnesium chloride melts at 950 °C. It is mixed with sodium and calcium chloride so that it can be electrolysed at 750 °C.

i Suggest one way this benefits the manufacturer. (1)

ii Suggest one way this benefits the environment. (1)

c Complete and balance the equations for the reactions at the electrodes.

i At the negative electrode: $Mg^{2+} + e^- \rightarrow Mg$ (1)

ii At the positive electrode: $Cl^- \rightarrow Cl_2 + e^-$ [H] (1)

163

copper(II) sulfate. The spelling, punctuation and grammar are very weak. The answer is poorly organised with almost no specialist terms and/or their use demonstrating a general lack of understanding of their meaning. *(1–2 marks)*

No relevant content. *(0 marks)*

Examples of chemistry points made in the response:

- Use dilute sulfuric acid.
- Place acid in a beaker.
- Warm the acid.
- Add copper(II) oxide.
- In small amounts.
- Until in excess or there is no further reaction.
- Filter (to remove excess copper(II) oxide).
- Heat filtrate/solution to evaporate some water.
- Allow solution to cool and crystallise or allow to evaporate slowly at room temperature.
- Remove/filter crystals from remaining solution.

4 a Ions can move in solution, silver ions are positive and are attracted to the negatively charged spoon. *(2 marks)*

b gaining, electron *(2 marks)*

c Any sensible suggestion – e.g. better appearance; less toxic; less likely to corrode; less expensive than solid silver. *(1 mark)*

5 a i Sensible suggestion – e.g. high melting point; strong; can be shaped; holds (hot) liquid, does not react with liquid (magnesium chloride/magnesium); low cost, at high temperature carbon electrode would burn with oxygen from the air to produce carbon dioxide. *(1 mark)*

ii Sensible suggestion – e.g. does not react with chlorine; high melting point; low cost (but do not accept if low cost already allowed in **i**). *(1 mark)*

b i Less heat/energy needed or lower cost of energy *(accept less heat lost)*. *(1 mark)*

ii Less fossil fuel burned (for heat/energy) so less pollution; less global warming; resources conserved; less mining (must be linked) or less thermal; heat pollution. *(1 mark)*

c i $Mg^{2+} + 2e^- \rightarrow Mg$ *(1 mark)*

ii $Cl^- \rightarrow Cl_2 + 2e^-$ *(1 mark)*

AQA Examination-style answers

1 a B *(1 mark)*

b 1 *(1 mark)*

c i alkali *(1 mark)*

ii neutralisation *(1 mark)*

iii sodium chloride *(1 mark)*

2 a A white precipitate or a white solid. *(1 mark)*

b lead nitrate + sodium chloride → lead chloride + sodium nitrate *(reactants for one mark, products for one mark)* *(2 marks)*

c Add sodium chloride or any other soluble salt that will give a precipitate with lead ions or a named alkali; allow to settle or filter. *(2 marks)*

3 There is a clear and detailed scientific description of how to prepare copper(II) sulfate solution from copper(II) oxide and dilute sulfuric acid and how to obtain crystals from the solution. The answer shows almost faultless spelling, punctuation and grammar. It is coherent and in an organised, logical sequence. It contains a range of appropriate and relevant specialist terms used accurately. *(5–6 marks)*

There is a scientific description of the preparation of copper(II) sulfate. There are some errors in spelling, punctuation and grammar. The answer has some structure and organisation. The use of specialist terms has been attempted but not always accurately. *(3–4 marks)*

There is a brief description of the reaction of copper(II) oxide with an acid or of crystallisation of a solution of

AQA Examination-style answers

1 a CaF_2 *(1 mark)*

b calcium ion with 2,8,8 electrons on three circles square bracket with 2+ charge outside top right chloride ion with 2,8,8 electrons on three circles square bracket with − charge outside top right *(4 marks)*

c The (electrostatic) forces/bonds between oppositely charged ions are strong, and there are many bonds/ forces or it has a giant structure/lattice, and so a large amount of energy is needed to break the bonds so that ions can move freely. *(3 marks)*

2 a 183.5 or 184 *(2 marks)*
(if answer incorrect, correct working 63.5 or 64 + 56 + 32 × 2 gains one mark).

b 34.6 or 34.8 or 34.78 *(2 marks)*
(if answer incorrect (63.5 or 64 × 100) ÷ (183.5 or 184) gains one mark).

c Any **one** from: contains a higher percentage *(accept greater amount or more)* of copper; contains no iron or fewer impurities. *(1 mark)*

d i Diagram showing any **three** from: spoon as negative electrode; pure copper as positive electrode; in (beaker/container) copper(II) sulfate solution; power supply or battery or cell symbol or electrodes labelled + and −. *(3 marks)*

ii Copper ions are positively charged and so are attracted to or move to the negative electrode, where they gain electrons or are reduced, forming copper atoms which are deposited on the spoon. *(3 marks)*

3 a There is a clear, logical and detailed scientific description of how to do paper chromatography. The answer shows almost faultless spelling, punctuation and grammar. It is coherent and in an organised, logical sequence. It contains a range of appropriate and relevant specialist terms used accurately. *(5–6 marks)*

There is a scientific description of how to do paper chromatography. There are some errors in spelling, punctuation and grammar. The answer has some structure and organisation. The use of specialist terms has been attempted, but not always accurately. *(3–4 marks)*

There is a brief description of how to do paper chromatography with. The spelling, punctuation and grammar are very weak. The answer is poorly organised with almost no specialist terms and/or their use demonstrating a general lack of understanding of their meaning. *(1–2 marks)*

No relevant content. *(0 marks)*

Examples of chemistry points made in the response:
- Draw a pencil line on paper (close to bottom).
- Mark/label starting points (in pencil).
- Put spots of colours/samples onto starting points.
- Put paper into solvent/water.
- Solvent/water below (pencil) line/spots.
- Use cover/lid on beaker/container.
- Allow solvent to run to (near to) top of paper.
- Remove from solvent/allow paper to dry.
- Any other technical detail, e.g. use capillary tube for sample spots.

b Any **three** from: drink contains two colours; one colour in drink is C2; one colour in drink is unknown *(allow not permitted)*; drink does not contain C1 and/or C3. *(3 marks)*

c i To separate the (flavour) compounds *(allow to show how many flavours/compounds there are)*. *(1 mark)*

Examination-style questions

1 Calcium chloride is an ionic compound.
Use a table showing the charges on ions to help you answer this question.
   a Which of these is the formula of calcium chloride?
      CaF   Ca₂F   CaF₂   Ca₂F₂   (1)
   b A sodium ion can be represented in the following way:

      Draw diagrams like this to show the ions in calcium chloride.   (4)
   c Calcium chloride is a crystalline solid with a high melting point.
      Explain why calcium chloride has these properties.   (3)

2 A company extracts copper from an ore that contains the mineral chalcopyrite, CuFeS₂.
   a Calculate the relative formula mass (M_r) of CuFeS₂. *(Relative atomic masses (A_r): Cu = 63.5; Fe = 56; S = 32)*   (2)
   b What is the percentage by mass of copper in chalcopyrite?   (2)
   c Suggest one reason why the company might prefer to use an ore containing the mineral chalcocite, Cu₂S.   (1)
   d The company uses the copper it produces to restore items made of copper. It electroplates the copper items with a new coating of copper. Pure copper is used as the positive electrode and the copper item is the negative electrode. The electrolyte is a solution containing copper(II) sulfate.
      i Draw a diagram showing how you could electroplate a copper spoon in the laboratory.   (3)
      ii Explain how copper is deposited onto the spoon by electrolysis.   (3)

3 A blackcurrant-flavoured drink was analysed for artificial colours and flavours. A scientist used paper chromatography to identify the artificial colours in the drink. The result of the chromatography is shown in the diagram.

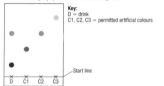

   Key:
   D = drink
   C1, C2, C3 = permitted artificial colours

   a *In this question you will be assessed on using good English, organising information clearly and using specialist terms where appropriate.*
      Describe how the chromatography was done to produce this result.   (6)
   b What conclusions can you make about the colours in the drink?   (3)
   c To identify the flavour compounds in the drink the scientist put a sample of the drink into a gas chromatography column linked to a mass spectrometer. The output of the column showed five main peaks.
      i What was the purpose of the gas chromatography column?   (1)
      ii What was the purpose of the mass spectrometer?   (1)

AQA *Examiner's tip*
The AQA data sheet that you will have in the exam has a table showing the charges on some common ions.

AQA *Examiner's tip*
Do not be put off by unusual formulae that you may not have seen before (**Q2** and **Q4**). Some questions are testing your ability to apply what you know in new situations.

AQA *Examiner's tip*
Q3 a i requires a description in a logical order so that someone else could do the experiment. Think about your answer before writing. Make a brief list of the key steps and number them in the correct sequence. Read them through in your head to check the order. Then write your answer. Cross out any notes that you do not want to be marked.

---

ii To identify the compounds *(allow to find the M_r or relative masses of the compounds)*. *(1 mark)*

4 a 2.61 (g) *(2 marks)*
If the answer is incorrect then correct working, e.g. 2/138 or (180/138) × 2 or 1 g → 180/138 gains one mark.

b 42.1 (per cent) *(2 marks)*
If answer incorrect then or (1.1/ecf from a) × 100 correctly evaluated gains two marks, or correct working, e.g. (1.1/2.61) × 100 gains one mark.

c Any **one** from: errors in weighing; some (of the aspirin) lost; not all of the reactant may have been converted to product or reaction didn't go to completion; the reaction is reversible; side reactions; reactants impure; not heated for long enough; not hot enough for reaction to take place. *(1 mark)*

d

C	H	O	
$\dfrac{75.7}{12}$	$\dfrac{8.80}{1}$	$\dfrac{15.5}{16}$	divide per cent by M_r
= 6.308 or 6.31	= 8.80	= 0.969 or 0.97	proportions
6.501 or 6.51 or 6.5	9.08 or 9.1 or 9	1	divide by 0.969 or 0.97
or 13	18	2	

empirical formula = $C_{13}H_{18}O_2$ *(4 marks)*
(correct answer with no working gains only 1 mark)

5 a Diamond is very hard because it has a giant (covalent) structure/lattice, in which each carbon atom forms four (covalent) bonds, and so there are many strong

End of unit questions

4 A student carried out an experiment to make aspirin. The method is given below.
1. Weigh 2.00 g of salicylic acid.
2. Add 4 cm³ of ethanoic anhydride (an excess).
3. Add 5 drops of concentrated sulfuric acid.
4. Warm the mixture for 15 minutes.
5. Add ice cold water to remove the excess ethanoic anhydride.
6. Cool the mixture until a precipitate of aspirin is formed.
7. Collect the precipitate and wash it with cold water.
8. The precipitate of aspirin is dried and weighed.

a The equation for this reaction is:

$$C_7H_6O_3 + C_4H_6O_3 \rightarrow C_9H_8O_4 + CH_3COOH$$

salicylic acid   aspirin

The relative formula mass (M_r) of salicylic acid, $C_7H_6O_3$, is 138.

The relative formula mass (M_r) of aspirin, $C_9H_8O_4$, is 180.

Calculate the maximum mass of aspirin that could be made from 2.00 g of salicylic acid. (2)

b The student made 1.10 g of aspirin from 2.00 g of salicylic acid.

Calculate the percentage yield of aspirin for this experiment. (2)

c Suggest **one** possible reason why this method does not give the maximum amount of aspirin. (1)

d The student made another compound with properties similar to aspirin. The student sent this compound to a laboratory for analysis. The analysis showed that the compound contained 75.7% C, 8.80% H and 15.5% O.

Calculate the empirical formula of this compound. You must show all of your working to gain full marks. (4)

[H]

5 The element carbon has several forms.

a Diamond is one form of carbon. Explain, in terms of structure and bonding, why diamond is very hard. (3)

b *In this question you will be assessed on using good English, organising information clearly and using specialist terms where appropriate.*

Another form of carbon is graphite. Graphite is used for the contacts in electric motors because it conducts electricity and is soft and slippery. Explain, in terms of structure and bonding, why graphite has these properties. (6)

c Carbon can also form fullerenes. The first fullerene to be discovered has a structure that contains 60 carbon atoms. Other fullerenes contain a few hundred atoms.

i What is the basic unit of the structure of fullerenes? (1)

ii Give two reasons why there has been much research interest in the fullerenes since their discovery in 1985. (2)

[H]

AQA *Examiner's tip*

Always show your working when you do a calculation. If you make a mistake calculating the final answer you may still gain some marks if you show that you know how to do the calculation.

AQA *Examiner's tip*

Q5 b requires you to describe the structure and bonding in graphite and use this to explain the properties given in the question. You need to link the properties clearly to particular points in your description. Before writing your answer, briefly list the key points that you know about the structure and bonding in graphite and then link these to the properties. Then write your answer in a logical order, giving as much detail as you can.

165

- Electrons delocalised **or** electrons free.
- Electrons carry the charge/current.
- Giant structure/lattice.
- Covalent (bonds).
- Strong bonds **or** a lot of energy needed to break bonds.
- Diagrams could be used: to show layered structure, to show that each carbon is bonded to three other carbon atoms, to show giant structure (at least three rings required).

c **i** Hexagons of carbon atoms or rings of six carbon atoms. *(1 mark)*

ii Any **two** correct reasons, e.g. they have special properties as they are nanoparticles; can form nanotubes; can be used for drug delivery; as catalysts; as lubricants; for reinforcing materials; or any other specific correct use. *(2 marks)*

Bump up your grades

Examiners are expected to challenge candidates at all levels with open questions requiring prose answers. Responses to these questions should be clearly and logically written using correct scientific terms. You should encourage your students to plan their answers before writing, using space on the question paper for notes.

Bump up your grades

Encourage your students to show their working when attempting calculations. Some students seem reluctant to do this, but it may gain them marks if they make an arithmetical error.

(covalent) bonds to break. (Covalent must be mentioned at least once for full marks.) *(3 marks)*

b There is a clear, logical and detailed scientific description of the structure and bonding in graphite correctly explaining both of the properties. The answer shows almost faultless spelling, punctuation and grammar. It is coherent and in an organised, logical sequence. It contains a range of appropriate and relevant specialist terms used accurately. *(5–6 marks)*

There is a scientific description of the structure and bonding in graphite and some explanation of at least one the properties. There are some errors in spelling, punctuation and grammar. The answer has some structure and organisation. The use of specialist terms has been attempted, but not always accurately. *(3–4 marks)*

There is a brief description of the structure and bonding in graphite and an attempt at an explanation of one the properties. The spelling, punctuation and grammar are very weak. The answer is poorly organised with almost no specialist terms and/or their use demonstrating a general lack of understanding of their meaning. *(1–2 marks)*

No relevant content. *(0 marks)*

Examples of chemistry points made in the response:
- Each carbon/atom joined/bonded to three other carbon/atoms.
  or Each carbon forms three bonds.
- In layers.
- Only weak forces (of attraction)/bonds between layers.
- Layers/atoms can slide over each other.
- One electron on each carbon is not used for bonding.

P2 1.1

Distance–time graphs

Learning objectives

Students should learn:

- how to interpret the gradient of a distance–time graph
- how to calculate the speed of an object using the speed formula
- how to use a distance–time graph to compare the speeds of different objects.

Learning outcomes

Most students should be able to:

- state that the gradient of a distance–time graph represents the speed
- use the speed formula to calculate the average speed of an object.

Some students should also be able to:

- rearrange and use the speed formula
- compare the speed of different objects using the gradient of a distance–time graph.

Answers to in-text questions

a The gradient would have been less steep.

b 30 m/s

c 500 s

d 13.3 m/s

Support

- Construct graphs one section at a time so that the students can fully understand one part of the graph before moving on to the next part of the motion. Build up the complexity of the graphs as the lessons in this section of the course continue.

Extend

- Using the details from the train timetable (see 'Further teaching suggestions' for 'Calculating speeds'), the students can plot graphs to compare the speeds of local trains and express trains.

- The gradient of a distance–time graph represents speed. *[P2.1.2 b)]*

Lesson structure

Starters

Understanding graphs – Show the students slides of a range of graphs showing the relationship between two variables and ask them to describe what is happening. Use this activity to support students and ensure that they understand the key terms used in describing a graph (the axes and gradient). You can extend students by giving more complex examples leading to ideas such as an increase in rate (changes of gradient). *(5 minutes)*

Speedy start – Give the students a set of cards showing different moving objects and ask them to put them in order from fastest to slowest. Add some data on the objects so that the students can actually work out the speed of the objects using the speed formula. Examples could be a worm (0.5 cm/s), human walking (0.5 m/s), bicycle (5 m/s), car (20 m/s), passenger jet (200 m/s), and missile (1 km/s). *(10 minutes)*

Main

- Some students have difficulty understanding what you mean by the term 'object' and you will have to exemplify this idea by talking about cars, trains or runners. Students can also have difficulty with the whole idea of a 'time axis'. You might like to show time as moving on by revealing the graph from left to right, and discussing what is happening to the distance the object has moved over each second.

- There are quite a few who fail to understand that the horizontal portions of the graph show that the object is stationary. Emphasise that the distance isn't changing, even though time is; 'the object hasn't got any further away during this second so it must be still'. You should use additional simple graphs to discuss the motion of several objects until you are sure that the students can identify when the objects are moving fastest.

- The students should be familiar with the speed equation, but it may have been some time since they used it in KS3. A few practice questions should remind them of the basic idea. Be very cautious of students using inappropriate units for speed such as 'mph' or even 'm/s' (metres per second). If students find 'per' difficult, then just use 'each'.

- To extend students, you can get them to read information off the graphs to calculate speed, although this is covered in detail in a later lesson at an appropriate level. They should be able to calculate the overall average speed and the speed during individual phases of the motion.

- You should also extend students by discussing displacement instead of distance, or you could leave this until you are discussing velocity in the next topic.

- The practical activity is a good way to round off the lesson, and it can be as brief as 10 minutes long if bicycles are not involved.

Plenaries

Record breakers – The students should analyse data about the 100 m sprint records (or other records such as swimming). They can try to find out if there appears to be a continuous improvement in running speeds or if there are leaps where the records change suddenly. They can also discuss the precision of the records and link this to improvements in timing technology. *(5 minutes)*

A driving story – Give the students a paragraph describing the motion of a car through a town, including moving at different speeds and stopping at traffic lights, etc. Ask them to sketch a graph of the described motion. Students can be supported by giving them the graph and asking for them to generate the story or extended by providing numerical information that has to be plotted accurately. *(10 minutes)*

Practical support

Be a distance recorder!

Measuring speed is a simple activity and livens up what can be a fairly dry start to the 'Motion' chapter.

Equipment and materials required

For each group: stopwatch, metre wheel. Clipboards and marker cones are also useful.

Details

The students should measure out distances first and then time each other walking, running, hopping or riding over these fixed distances. An outdoor netball court, or similar, can provide a set of straight and curved lines for the students to follow. You may like to see if the students travel faster along the straight edges or if they follow the curves on the court. If you intend to use bicycles, then a lot more space will be needed and the students must wear the appropriate safety gear. Check with the PE department to see if they have cones to mark out the distances and if they mind bicycles on their running tracks or shoes on their indoor courts!

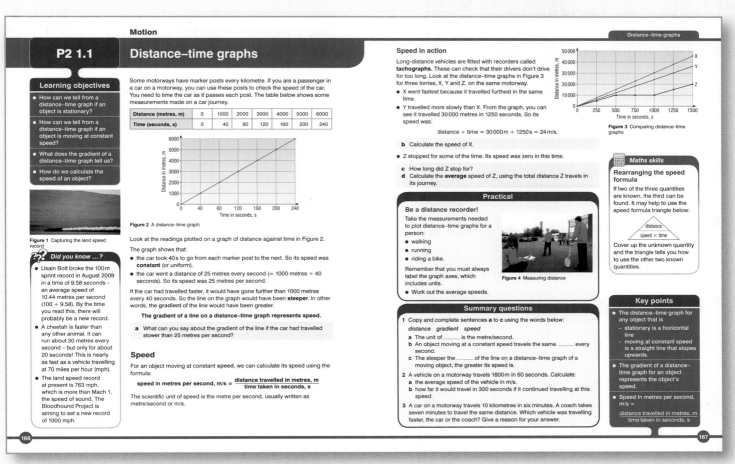

Motion

P2 1.1 — Distance–time graphs

Learning objectives

- How can we tell from a distance–time graph if an object is stationary?
- How can we tell from a distance–time graph if an object is moving at constant speed?
- What does the gradient of a distance–time graph tell us?
- How do we calculate the speed of an object?

Figure 1 Capturing the land speed record

Did you know ...?

- Usain Bolt broke the 100 m sprint record in August 2009 in a time of 9.58 seconds – an average speed of 10.44 metres per second (100 ÷ 9.58). By the time you read this, there will probably be a new record.
- A cheetah is faster than any other animal. It can run about 30 metres every second – but only for about 20 seconds! This is nearly as fast as a vehicle travelling at 70 miles per hour (mph).
- The land speed record at present is 763 mph, which is more than Mach 1, the speed of sound. The Bloodhound Project is aiming to set a new record of 1000 mph.

Some motorways have marker posts every kilometre. If you are a passenger in a car on a motorway, you can use these posts to check the speed of the car. You need to time the car as it passes each post. The table below shows some measurements made on a car journey.

Distance (metres, m)	0	1000	2000	3000	4000	5000	6000
Time (seconds, s)	0	40	80	120	160	200	240

Figure 2 A distance–time graph

Look at the readings plotted on a graph of distance against time in Figure 2. The graph shows that:

- the car took 40 s to go from each marker post to the next. So its speed was **constant** (or uniform).
- the car went a distance of 25 metres every second (= 1000 metres ÷ 40 seconds). So its speed was 25 metres per second.

If the car had travelled faster, it would have gone further than 1000 metres every 40 seconds. So the line on the graph would have been **steeper**. In other words, the **gradient** of the line would have been greater.

The gradient of a line on a distance–time graph represents speed.

a What can you say about the gradient of the line if the car had travelled slower than 25 metres per second?

Speed

For an object moving at constant speed, we can calculate its speed using the formula:

$$\text{speed in metres per second, m/s} = \frac{\text{distance travelled in metres, m}}{\text{time taken in seconds, s}}$$

The scientific unit of speed is the metre per second, usually written as metre/second or m/s.

Speed in action

Long-distance vehicles are fitted with recorders called **tachographs**. These can check that their drivers don't drive for too long. Look at the distance–time graphs in Figure 3 for three lorries, X, Y and Z, on the same motorway.

- X went fastest because it travelled furthest in the same time.
- Y travelled more slowly than X. From the graph, you can see it travelled 30 000 metres in 1250 seconds. So its speed was:

distance ÷ time = 30 000 m ÷ 1250 s = 24 m/s.

b Calculate the speed of X.

- Z stopped for some of the time. Its speed was zero in this time.

c How long did Z stop for?
d Calculate the **average** speed of Z, using the total distance Z travels in its journey.

Figure 3 Comparing distance–time graphs

Practical

Be a distance recorder!
Take the measurements needed to plot distance–time graphs for a person:

- walking
- running
- riding a bike.

Remember that you must always label the graph axes, which includes units.

- Work out the average speeds.

Figure 4 Measuring distance

Maths skills

Rearranging the speed formula

If two of the three quantities are known, the third can be found. It may help to use the speed formula triangle below:

distance / speed × time

Cover up the unknown quantity and the triangle shows you how to use the other two known quantities.

Summary questions

1 Copy and complete sentences **a** to **c** using the words below:
distance gradient speed
a The unit of .... is the metre/second.
b An object moving at a constant speed travels the same .... every second.
c The steeper the .... of the line on a distance–time graph of a moving object, the greater its speed is.

2 A vehicle on a motorway travels 1800 m in 60 seconds. Calculate:
a the average speed of the vehicle in m/s.
b how far it would travel in 300 seconds if it continued travelling at this speed.

3 A car on a motorway travels 10 kilometres in six minutes. A coach takes seven minutes to travel the same distance. Which vehicle was travelling faster, the car or the coach? Give a reason for your answer.

Key points

- The distance–time graph for any object that is
  - stationary is a horizontal line
  - moving at constant speed is a straight line that slopes upwards.
- The gradient of a distance–time graph for an object represents the object's speed.
- Speed in metres per second, m/s = distance travelled in metres, m / time taken in seconds, s

---

Further teaching suggestions

Detailed speed measurements

- To make more detailed measurements of the speed of an object, a distance sensor can be used.

Equipment and materials required

- Distance sensor, data logger and a simple moving object.

Details

- The distance sensor should be mounted in a fixed position and the object moves in front of it while the data logger records. You can use this to measure your distance in front of the meter while you walk back and forth at different speeds. The students can then analyse the graphs and see if they can describe the motion from them.

A need for speed

- The students could find out about how the land speed record has changed over the past 150 years (from trains to rocket cars). They could plot a graph of the record speed against the year and see if they can extrapolate to find what the record will be in 50 years' time. A similar activity can be carried out for the air and water speed records.

Calculating speeds

- Provide the students with a graph and ask them to describe the motion of the object. Students who complete this quickly should also calculate the speed of the object during each stage of the motion. Alternately, ask the students to get a bus or train timetable and a map. They should use the information in these to work out the average speed of the trains or buses between different locations.

Summary answers

1 a speed   b distance   c gradient

2 a 30 m/s   b 9000 m

3 The car travels faster because it takes less time to travel the same distance as the coach.

P2 1.2

Velocity and acceleration

Learning objectives

Students should learn:

- that velocity is the speed in a particular direction
- that acceleration is the rate of change of velocity.

Learning outcomes

Most students should be able to:

- explain the difference between the velocity of an object and the speed
- calculate the acceleration of an object using the acceleration equation.

Some students should also be able to:

- rearrange and use the acceleration equation.

Support

- The difference between speed–time and distance–time graphs should be reinforced. You might want to use different colour sets to plot the graphs to make them visually different.

Extend

- Extend students by asking them to look into the details of the concepts of displacement and velocity. Ask: 'What is the average speed of a Formula One car over one whole lap? What is the average velocity for the complete lap?' The students could draw a diagram to explain the difference.

Specification link-up: Physics P2.1

- The velocity of an object is its speed in a given direction. *[P2.1.2 d)]*
- The acceleration of an object is given by the equation: $a = \dfrac{v - u}{t}$. *[P2.1.2 e)]*

Controlled Assessment: AS4.3 Collect primary and secondary data. *[AS4.3.2 d)]*

Lesson structure

Starters

Getting nowhere fast – A racing driver completes a full circuit of a 3 km racetrack in 90 seconds. Ask: 'What is his average speed? Why isn't he 3 km away from where he started?' Demonstrate this idea to explain the difference between distance travelled and displacement. Lead on to a discussion about objects that are moving but do not get further away from the origin as they are following closed paths. *(5 minutes)*

Treasure island – Give the students a scaled map with a starting point, hidden treasure, protractor and a ruler. At first, only give them the times they have to walk for, then the speeds they must go at, and finally the matching directions. See which group can find the treasure first. This shows how important direction is when describing movement. Support students by starting with very simple examples. Extend students by asking them to produce a set of instructions to get to a treasure chest while avoiding a set of obstacles such as the 'pit of peril'. *(10 minutes)*

Main

- Talking about fairground rides or roundabouts helps to get across the idea that you can be moving at a constant speed but be feeling a force. You can link this experience into the idea that unbalanced forces cause acceleration, see later topics.

- Some students will not be clear about the difference between speed and velocity, and a few examples are needed. These can include simply walking around the room and describing your velocity as you go in one direction or another.

- You might like to discuss a collision between two cars travelling at 45 and 50 km/h. If they collide while travelling in opposite directions the impact will be devastating, because the relative velocity is 95 km/h. If they collide when they are travelling in the same direction only a 'nudge' will be felt, because their relative velocity is only 5 km/h. Clearly, the direction is very important. Check that all of the students can give an example of a velocity.

- Velocity–time graphs look similar enough to distance–time graphs to cause a great deal of confusion for students. Because they have just learned that the horizontal region on a distance–time graph shows that the object is stationary, they will probably feel that this is true for the velocity–time graph too. Time should be taken to explain that the object is moving at a steady velocity.

- As usual, some students will take the calculations in their stride while you may need to provide extra support for others. When using v and u as symbols in equations, be very careful that the students are discriminating between them clearly.

- Many students are unclear on the units for acceleration (m/s²) and ask what the 'squared bit' is. If they are mathematically strong, you might like to show where the unit comes from, using the equation, but otherwise they should not worry about it. Always check that they are applying the unit correctly.

- There may be some confusion with the terms 'acceleration', 'deceleration' and 'negative acceleration', especially if you consider objects that move backwards as well as forwards. To extend students, you can show a graph of the motion of an object moving forwards then backwards, and describe the acceleration in detail.

Plenaries

Comparing graphs – Ask the students to make a comparison of what a distance–time graph and a velocity–time graph show. They should produce a chart/diagram that could be used to show another group of students the similarities and differences, highlighting the distinctions between what the gradients of these graphs represent. *(5 minutes)*

Accelerated learning – The students should try a few additional acceleration questions. They might be supported using simple structured questions, or extended by asking for calculations involving the rearrangement of the basic acceleration equation. *(10 minutes)*

Further teaching suggestions

Acceleration, power and mass in vehicles

- The students could find out about what makes a vehicle good at accelerating. By finding out the power output (bhp or kW) and mass of some vehicles (include motorcycles), they could investigate if there is a relationship between mass, power and acceleration. They could explain how well the data fits any pattern.

ICT link-up

- Distance sensors need to be used to measure velocity and changes in velocity accurately. Motion can also be monitored with video equipment and frame by frame playback. (This relates to How Science Works: making measurements.)

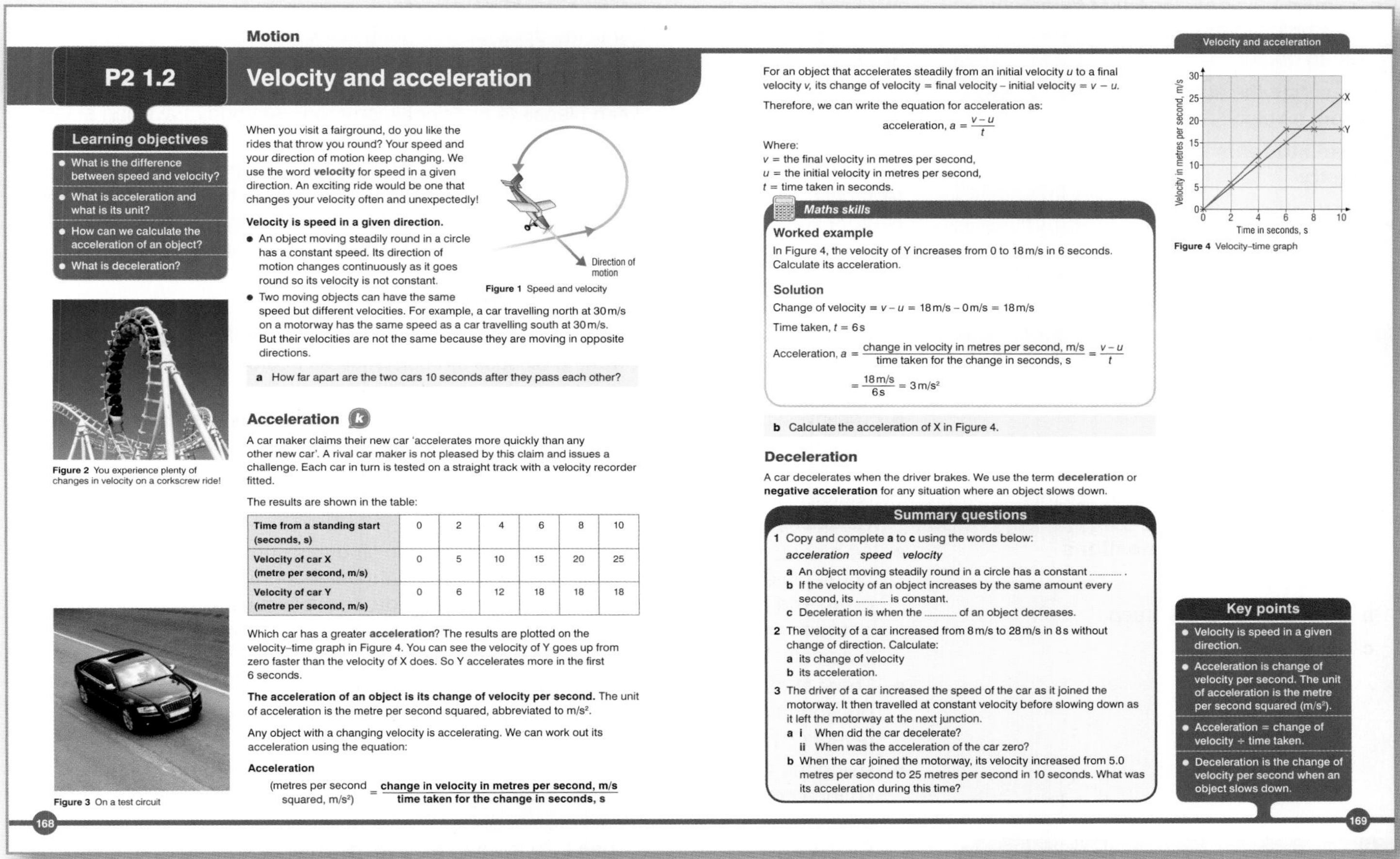

Motion

P2 1.2 Velocity and acceleration

Learning objectives

- What is the difference between speed and velocity?
- What is acceleration and what is its unit?
- How can we calculate the acceleration of an object?
- What is deceleration?

Figure 2 You experience plenty of changes in velocity on a corkscrew ride!

When you visit a fairground, do you like the rides that throw you round? Your speed and your direction of motion keep changing. We use the word **velocity** for speed in a given direction. An exciting ride would be one that changes your velocity often and unexpectedly!

Velocity is speed in a given direction.

- An object moving steadily round in a circle has a constant speed. Its direction of motion changes continuously as it goes round so its velocity is not constant.
- Two moving objects can have the same speed but different velocities. For example, a car travelling north at 30 m/s on a motorway has the same speed as a car travelling south at 30 m/s. But their velocities are not the same because they are moving in opposite directions.

Figure 1 Speed and velocity
Direction of motion

a How far apart are the two cars 10 seconds after they pass each other?

Acceleration

A car maker claims their new car 'accelerates more quickly than any other new car'. A rival car maker is not pleased by this claim and issues a challenge. Each car in turn is tested on a straight track with a velocity recorder fitted.

The results are shown in the table:

Time from a standing start (seconds, s)	0	2	4	6	8	10
Velocity of car X (metre per second, m/s)	0	5	10	15	20	25
Velocity of car Y (metre per second, m/s)	0	6	12	18	18	18

Which car has a greater **acceleration**? The results are plotted on the velocity–time graph in Figure 4. You can see the velocity of Y goes up from zero faster than the velocity of X does. So Y accelerates more in the first 6 seconds.

The acceleration of an object is its change of velocity per second. The unit of acceleration is the metre per second squared, abbreviated to m/s².

Any object with a changing velocity is accelerating. We can work out its acceleration using the equation:

Acceleration
(metres per second squared, m/s²) = change in velocity in metres per second, m/s / time taken for the change in seconds, s

Figure 3 On a test circuit

For an object that accelerates steadily from an initial velocity u to a final velocity v, its change of velocity = final velocity − initial velocity = $v - u$.

Therefore, we can write the equation for acceleration as:

$$\text{acceleration, } a = \frac{v - u}{t}$$

Where:
v = the final velocity in metres per second,
u = the initial velocity in metres per second,
t = time taken in seconds.

Maths skills

Worked example

In Figure 4, the velocity of Y increases from 0 to 18 m/s in 6 seconds. Calculate its acceleration.

Solution

Change of velocity = $v - u$ = 18 m/s − 0 m/s = 18 m/s

Time taken, t = 6 s

Acceleration, $a = \dfrac{\text{change in velocity in metres per second, m/s}}{\text{time taken for the change in seconds, s}} = \dfrac{v - u}{t}$

$= \dfrac{18 \text{ m/s}}{6 \text{ s}} = 3 \text{ m/s}^2$

b Calculate the acceleration of X in Figure 4.

Deceleration

A car decelerates when the driver brakes. We use the term **deceleration** or **negative acceleration** for any situation where an object slows down.

Figure 4 Velocity–time graph

Summary questions

1 Copy and complete **a** to **c** using the words below:
   acceleration   speed   velocity
   a An object moving steadily round in a circle has a constant ....
   b If the velocity of an object increases by the same amount every second, its .... is constant.
   c Deceleration is when the .... of an object decreases.

2 The velocity of a car increased from 8 m/s to 28 m/s in 8 s without change of direction. Calculate:
   a its change of velocity
   b its acceleration.

3 The driver of a car increased the speed of the car as it joined the motorway. It then travelled at constant velocity before slowing down as it left the motorway at the next junction.
   a i When did the car decelerate?
      ii When was the acceleration of the car zero?
   b When the car joined the motorway, its velocity increased from 5.0 metres per second to 25 metres per second in 10 seconds. What was its acceleration during this time?

Key points

- Velocity is speed in a given direction.
- Acceleration is change of velocity per second. The unit of acceleration is the metre per second squared (m/s²).
- Acceleration = change of velocity ÷ time taken.
- Deceleration is the change of velocity per second when an object slows down.

168

169

Answers to in-text questions

a 600 m

b 2.5 m/s²

Summary answers

1 **a** speed
  b acceleration
  c velocity

2 **a** 20 m/s
  b 2.5 m/s²

3 **a i** The car decelerated as it left the motorway.
     ii The acceleration of the car was zero when it was travelling on the motorway at constant velocity.
  b 2.0 m/s²

P2 1.3

More about velocity–time graphs

AQA
Specification link-up: Physics P2.1
- The gradient of a velocity–time graph represents acceleration. *[P2.1.2 f)]*
- Calculation of the acceleration of an object from the gradient of a velocity–time graph. *[P2.1.2 g)]* **[HT only]**
- Calculation of the distance travelled by an object from a velocity–time graph. *[P2.1.2 h)]* **[HT only]**

  Controlled Assessment: AS4.3 Collect primary and secondary data. *[AS4.3.2 a)]*; AS4.5 Analyse and interpret primary and secondary data. *[AS4.5.3 a)]*

Learning objectives

Students should learn:
- how to interpret the gradient of a velocity–time graph
- how to calculate the distance travelled by an object from the area under a velocity–time graph. **[HT only]**

Learning outcomes

Most students should be able to:
- explain how data-logging equipment can be used to measure the velocity of an object
- describe the acceleration of an object from a velocity–time graph.

Some students should also be able to:
- use velocity–time graphs to compare accelerations
- use velocity–time graphs to compare distance travelled. **[HT only]**

Lesson structure

Starters

Late again? – Give the students the distance from their last class to the laboratory and ask them to work out their speed on the journey to you, using the time it took them to arrive. You can provide some example distances from other likely rooms if they have no idea about how far it is between places (surprisingly common). Anybody travelling at less than 1 m/s clearly isn't keen enough! *(5 minutes)*

Finding areas – Get the students to calculate the total area of a shape made up of rectangles and triangles. Students can be extended by asking them to find the total areas of more complex graphs, while others can be supported by providing graphs in which the shape has already been broken down into basic rectangles and triangles. *(10 minutes)*

Main

- Demonstrate the results produced for test A in the Student Book. If you do not get a straight line, you might want to discuss air resistance as a force opposing the movement of the trolley.
- The investigation into the motion of an object is a good one if you have sufficient equipment. Alternatives using light gates do not give a simple comparison of the accelerations, but you may be able to demonstrate that the velocity has increased. (This relates to: How Science Works: types of variable; fair testing; relationships between variables.)
- As before, time should be taken to ensure that the students understand what the gradients of the different graphs mean. They should be encouraged to break the graph down and just look at one section at a time, in order to explain what is happening between these sections. Real motion may not produce straight lines and simple gradients, but these are the best to use in examples for now.
- There should be no difficulty explaining that braking will reduce the velocity of the car, but you might like to ask what braking would look like on the graph if the car was in reverse. The change can confuse some students.
- Using the area under the graph to find the distance travelled is commonly forgotten, so try a couple of examples and refer back to it in later lessons. When calculating the area, ensure that the students are not giving their answers as 'distance = 15 cm², or similar. This can happen when they 'count boxes' or do their calculations based on the area being measured in centimetres. Make sure that they are reading the distances and times off the graph, not the actual dimensions of the shapes. **[HT only]**
- Finally, you could show what would happen if the deceleration took longer, by superimposing the new gradient over the old one and showing that the area is greater.

Answers to in-text questions

a Less steep.
b It would not be as steep.
c Greater.

Support

- Focus on the basics of measuring the area, reminding the students of the calculations needed to find the area of the triangular parts. Watch out for students reading incorrect values from the graphs; instead of reading the changes they can often just read the higher value.

Extend

- The students should look at the effect of aerodynamics on motion; it is air resistance that makes the motion of objects much more complex. They should find out about how these effects are investigated.

Plenaries

Busy teacher – Wear a pedometer throughout the lesson, calculate your average step distance and then ask the students to work out how far you have moved and your average speed. A typical example stride distance is 0.5 m with somewhere between 400 and 600 paces per lesson, giving a distance of 200 to 300 m in 1 h. The students could estimate their average daily speed too. *(5 minutes)*

Comparing graphs – Ask the students to describe the differences in the movement of three cars as shown on the same velocity–time graph. You can also use distance–time graphs. These comparisons should cover the speeds at different times and even the acceleration of the cars over periods by comparing the gradients. Support students by taking them through the examples step by step. Students can be extended by asking them to read data from the graphs (such as starting speed and final speed) and attempt to calculate the acceleration. *(10 minutes)*

Practical support

Investigating acceleration

Dynamics trolleys are an excellent way of studying motion, but class sets are very expensive. If none are available, then fairly large toy cars can be used for the basic experiments. Velocity sensors are also expensive and you may need to modify this experiment into a demonstration.

Equipment and materials required
Dynamics trolley, adjustable slope, protractor and data-logging equipment including a velocity sensor.

Details
Set up the equipment so that the angle of the ramp can be adjusted and easily measured. Make sure that the sensor is pointing along the path of the slope as otherwise the velocity will not be measured accurately. The students activate the sensor and then release the trolley.

Repeating this for a range of slope angles should give the result that the steeper the slope the greater the acceleration.

Alternative equipment

Light gates
As an alternative to a velocity sensor, a set of light gates can be used in experiments. This involves mounting a card of known length on top of the trolley, so that it interrupts the beam and the sensor measures the time for this to take place. This data can be used to determine the velocity; some software will do this for you directly. To determine acceleration, you can use a slotted card that interrupts the beam twice. This allows you to determine acceleration by looking at the speed at which the trolley was travelling when it first interrupted the beam and the speed the second time. Several sets of light gates can be used to measure the velocity at different stages of the motion.

Distance sensors
These use ultrasound or infrared to measure the distance to an object. Some software will convert these distance values into speed values and plot the required graphs.

Safety: Make sure trolley does not shoot off the end of the runway. Protect feet and bench.

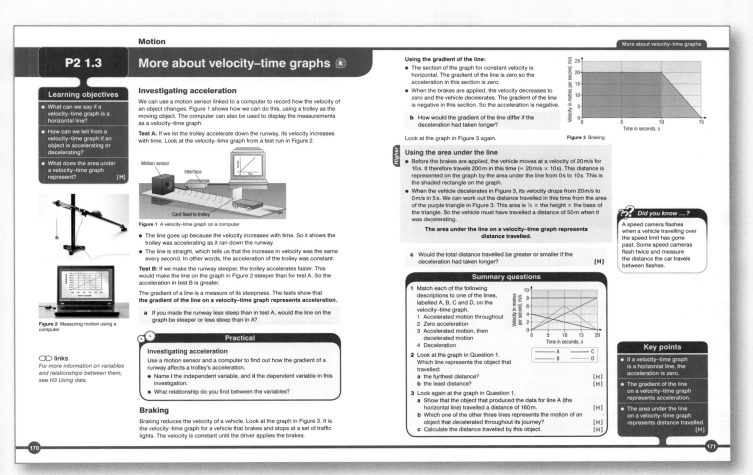

Further teaching suggestions

Calculating distance
- The students could calculate the distance travelled by an object using a velocity–time graph. **[HT only]**

ICT link-up
- Using route planner software, the students can find the distances between points on their journey to school or other locations. They can time themselves travelling between these points and work out their average speed. Sharing this information will allow them to compare different modes of transport.

Summary answers

1 1 B   2 A   3 D   4 C

2 a A
   b C

3 a 8 m/s (velocity) × 20 s (time) = 160 m (distance)
   b C
   c 40 m

P2 1.4

Using graphs

Learning objectives

Students should learn:

- how to calculate the speed from a distance–time graph [HT only]
- how to calculate the distance travelled from a velocity–time graph [HT only]
- how to calculate the acceleration of an object from a velocity–time graph. [HT only]

Learning outcomes

Most students should be able to:

- calculate the gradient of a distance–time graph and relate this to the speed of an object [HT only]
- calculate the gradient of a velocity–time graph and hence the acceleration [HT only]
- find the area under a velocity–time graph for constant velocity and use this to calculate the distance travelled by an object [HT only]
- find the area under a velocity–time graph for constant acceleration and use this to calculate the distance travelled by an object. [HT only]

Support

- Although the content of this lesson is Higher Tier, not all students working on this topic will be mathematically strong. Some will need support with any form of rearrangement of the equations. Use additional worked examples for finding acceleration and distance travelled.

Extend

- Students can be challenged with more complex examples of motion calculations including ones requiring rearrangement of the basic equations. They could also look at more realistic motion graphs involving non-constant acceleration, and discuss what the shapes in these graphs indicate. Although they do not need to be able to describe or explain graphs like this, it can be useful to push them beyond the limits of the specification to enhance their understanding and analytical skills.

AQA Specification link-up: Physics P2.1

- Calculation of the speed of an object from the gradient of a distance–time graph. *[P2.1.2 c)]* **[HT only]**
- The gradient of a velocity–time graph represents acceleration. *[P2.1.2 f)]*
- Calculation of the acceleration of an object from the gradient of a velocity–time graph. *[P2.1.2 g)]* **[HT only]**
- Calculation of the distance travelled by an object from a velocity–time graph. *[P2.1.2 h)]* **[HT only]**
- Interpret data from tables and graphs relating to speed, velocity and acceleration. *[P2.1]*

Lesson structure

Starters

Graph matching – The students have to match the description of the movement of objects with graphs of distance–time and velocity–time. Provide three different descriptions of journeys and three graphs that represent the movement for the students to match them with. The descriptions can contain numerical values such as 10 m/s so that the students can find this value from one of the graphs. *(5 minutes)*

Plot – Give the students a set of velocity–time data for a moving object, and ask them to plot a graph of displacement–time. Check the graphs for accuracy of plotting and clear labelling of the axes. You can make this more challenging by asking the students to plot several graphs on to the same axes, leading to a discussion about why you would want all of the data on one set of axes (ease of comparison). Students can be supported by providing partially completed graphs to add points to. *(10 minutes)*

Main

- This topic is for Higher Tier students only.
- As 'gradient' is the correct term, it should be encouraged; if the students are used to 'slope', then gently correct them through the lesson to help them change their ways. They need to know that the examination questions will always be using the term gradient.
- With a bit of practice, students should have no difficulty determining gradients. Watch out for students reading off the total distance and total time instead of the change in distance and change in time.
- Get the students to describe what is happening to the speed of a range of objects. You might like to show graphs, followed by video clips of objects doing what was shown in the graph, e.g. cars accelerating from 0–100 km/h or balls bouncing, etc. (Search an internet video hosting site). Some unusual, and funny, changes in motion can make the lesson livelier.
- When you move on to velocity–time graphs, yet again emphasise that these show something different than the speed-time ones. Hopefully, the students will never get the two types of graph confused after your constant reminders. The students should be reading the changes in velocity and time from the graphs, but some may make the same mistakes as mentioned previously.
- After numerous examples, the students should have a firm grip. Additional homework questions should be used to consolidate their learning.

Plenaries

Dynamic definitions – The students should provide detailed definitions of speed, velocity, distance, displacement and acceleration, including how they are represented on graphs. This should form a one page summary of all of the material from this set of four lessons. Support students by giving them definitions to match up with the key terms. *(5 minutes)*

Stretch – Take the opportunity to stretch the students' skills by giving a challenging set of questions involving several levels of complexity. Look for them to change units, identify and read values off a graph, and rearrange the acceleration equation. All of these things may be needed by Higher Tier candidates so push them to their limits. *(10 minutes)*

Further teaching suggestions

The students should have found the distance travelled by an object from a velocity–time graph in the last topic, so challenge them with more difficult graphs of motion.

You may want to see if they can find the distance travelled when the acceleration is not uniform. This would involve square-counting techniques (see 'Counting squares' below).

For additional challenge, look into graphs showing the object moving back towards the origin. You could try some velocity–time graphs in which the velocity becomes negative, and see if the students can calculate the distance the object ends up from the origin.

Graph work

- Follow-up work can be set on analysing or plotting a range of graphs of motion.

ICT link-up

- Simulation software can be used to investigate motion and to plot graphs of the behaviour. These can be either quite simple or rather complex, so you should be able to find something suitable for all ranges of ability.

Counting squares

- One common technique for working out the area under a line on a graph is to count the squares on the graph paper. Anything less than half a square doesn't count, and anything more than half a square counts as a complete square. This works reasonably well for simple graphs including those with straight gradients. You could discuss how to improve the accuracy of the method by using smaller and smaller squares on the graph paper. Make sure that the students know the distance each square of the graph paper represents.

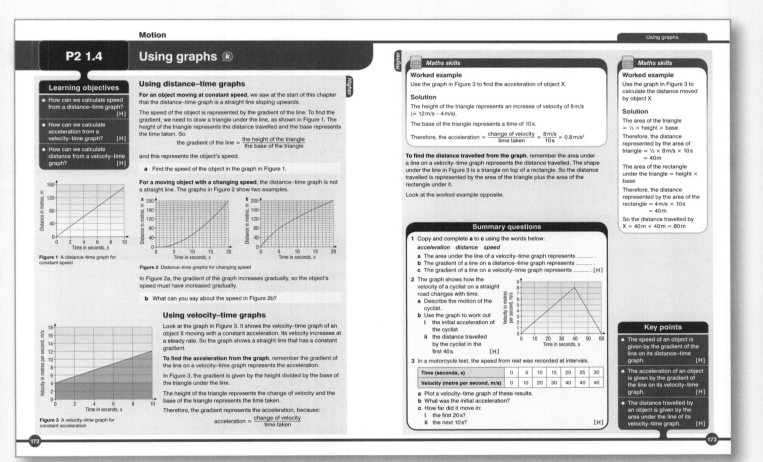

Answers to in-text questions

a 15 m/s.

b The speed decreased gradually and became constant.

Summary answers

1 **a** distance
   b speed
   c acceleration

2 **a** The cyclist accelerates with a constant acceleration for 40 s, and then decelerates to a standstill in 20 s.
   b i 0.2 m/s^2
   ii 160 m

3 **a** Student's graph, accurately drawn.
   b 2 m/s^2
   c i 400 m
   ii 400 m

Summary answers

1 a i Start the stopwatch when the car passes the marker and stop it when the car has completed 10 laps.

ii Take the car off the track and bend the tape measure round the track along the path the car takes. Use the tape measure to measure the distance of one lap. Multiply this distance by 10 to get the distance for 10 laps.

b 1.2 m/s

2 a 700 m

b 40 s

3 a A to B

b i 2000 m, 100 s

ii 20 m/s

4 a i 20 m/s

ii 2.5 m/s^2

b −1.2 m/s^2

5 a 3.0 m/s^2

b 2400 m

6 a

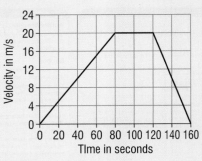

b 0.25 m/s^2, 0, −0.50 m/s^2

c 2000 m

d 2000 m (distance)/160 s (time) = 12.5 m/s (average speed)

7 a

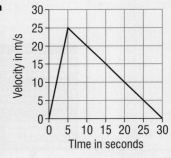

b 25 m/s (velocity)/5 s (time) = 5.0 m/s^2 (acceleration)

c −25 m/s (velocity)/25 s (time) = −1.0 m/s^2 (deceleration)

d 62.5 m + 312.5 m = 375 m

Summary questions

1 A model car travels round a circular track at constant speed.

a If you were given a stopwatch, a marker, and a tape measure, how would you measure:

i the time taken by the car to travel 10 laps

ii the distance the car travels in 10 laps.

b If the car travels 36 metres in 30 seconds, calculate its speed.

2 A train travels at a constant speed of 35 m/s. Calculate:

a how far it travels in 20 s

b how long it takes to travel a distance of 1400 m.

3 The figure shows the distance–time graph for a car on a motorway.

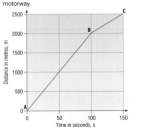

a Which part of the journey was faster, A to B or B to C?

b i How far did the car travel from A to B and how long did it take?

ii Calculate the speed of the car between A and B.

4 a A car took 8 s to increase its velocity from 8 m/s to 28 m/s. Calculate:

i its change of velocity

ii its acceleration.

b A vehicle travelling at a velocity of 24 m/s slowed down and stopped in 20 s. Calculate its deceleration.

5 The figure shows the velocity–time graph of a passenger jet before it took off.

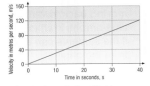

a Calculate the acceleration of the jet.

b Calculate the distance it travelled before it took off.

6 The table below shows how the velocity of a train changes as it travelled from one station to the next.

Time (seconds)	0	20	40	60	80	100	120	140
Velocity (m/s)	0	5	10	15	20	20	20	10

a Plot a velocity–time graph using this data.

b Calculate the acceleration in each of the three parts of the journey.

c Calculate the total distance travelled by the train.

d Show that the average speed for the train's journey was 12.5 m/s.

7 A motorcyclist started from rest and accelerated steadily to 25 m/s in 5 seconds then slowed down steadily to a halt 30 seconds after she started.

a Draw a velocity–time graph for this journey.

b Show that the acceleration of the motorcyclist in the first 5 seconds was 5.0 m/s^2.

c Calculate the deceleration of the motorcyclist in the last 25 seconds.

d Use your graph to show that the total distance travelled by the motorcyclist was 375 metres.

Kerboodle resources

Resources available for this chapter on Kerboodle are:

- Chapter map: Motion
- Extension: Distance–time gradient calculations (P2 1.1)
- Support: What is my distance–time graph? (P2 1.1)
- Bump up your grade: What is my distance–time graph? (P2 1.1)
- How science works: Acceleration of a trolley (P2 1.2)
- Bump up your grade: Velocity–time graph: Using motion graphs to show how fast things move (P2 1.3)
- Extension: Velocity–time gradient calculations (P2 1.3)
- Interactive activity: Speed, velocity and acceleration on graphs
- Revision podcast: Velocity and acceleration
- Test yourself: Motion
- On your marks: Motion
- Examination-style questions: Motion
- Answers to examination-style questions: Motion

AQA Examination-style questions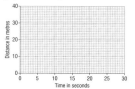

The table gives values of distance and time for a child travelling along a straight track competing in an egg and spoon race.

Time (seconds)	0	5	10	15	20	25
Distance (metres)	0	8	20	20	24	40

a Copy the graph axes below on to graph paper. Plot a graph of distance against time for the child. (3)

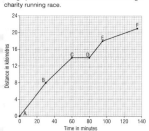

b Name the dependent variable shown on the graph. (1)
c What type of variable is this? (1)
d Use your graph to estimate the distance travelled in 22 seconds. (1)
e Use your graph to estimate the time taken for the child to travel 15 metres. (1)
f Describe the motion of the child between 10 seconds and 15 seconds.
Give a reason for your answer. (2)

The graph shows how far a runner travels during a charity running race.

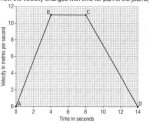

a What was the distance of the race? (1)
b How long did it take the runner to complete the race? (1)
c For how long did the runner rest during the race? (1)
d Between which two points was the runner moving the fastest?
Give a reason for your answer. (2)
e Between which two points did the runner travel at the same speed as they did between A and B? (1)
f Calculate the speed of the runner between B and C in metres per second.
Write down the equation you use. Show clearly how you work out your answer. (3)

3 A cyclist is travelling along a straight road. The graph shows how the velocity changes with time for part of the journey.

a Explain how the acceleration can be found from a velocity–time graph. (1)
b Copy and complete the following sentences using the list of words and phrases below. Each one can be used once, more than once or not at all.
is stationary   travels at a constant speed
accelerates   decelerates
  i Between A and B the cyclist .... (1)
  ii Between B and C the cyclist .... (1)
  iii Between C and D the cyclist .... (1)
c i Use the graph to find the maximum speed of the cyclist. (2)
  ii Use the graph to calculate the distance travelled in metres between 4 and 8 seconds. Show clearly how you work out your answer. (2)
  iii Use the graph to calculate the total distance travelled in metres.
  Show clearly how you work out your answer. [H] (6)

175

AQA Examination-style answers

1 a
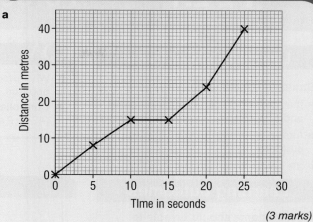

(3 marks)

b distance *(1 mark)*
c continuous *(1 mark)*
d 30 to 31 metres *(1 mark)*
e 7.5 to 8.5 seconds *(1 mark)*
f stationary; no change in distance/gradient is zero
  (2 marks)

2 a 21 km *(1 mark)*
b 135 minutes (2 hours 15 minutes) *(1 mark)*
c 20 minutes *(1 mark)*
d A to B or D to E; steepest gradient *(2 marks)*
e D to E *(1 mark)*
f speed = gradient = $\dfrac{(14\,000 - 8000)}{(30 \times 60)}$
$= \dfrac{6000}{1800}$
$= 3.3\,\text{m/s}$ *(3 marks)*

3 a gradient = acceleration *(1 mark)*
b i Between A and B the cyclist **accelerates** *(1 mark)*
  ii Between B and C the cyclist **travels at a constant speed** *(1 mark)*
  iii Between C and D the cyclist **decelerates** *(1 mark)*
c i 11 m/s *(1 mark)*
  ii $(8 - 4) \times 11 = 44\,\text{m}$ *(2 marks)*
  iii $\dfrac{44}{2} + \dfrac{44 + (6 \times 11)}{2} = 99\,\text{m}$ *(3 marks)*

AQA Examiner's tip

These questions cover most of the skills needed to answer questions on motion graphs. Candidates may have to plot a graph from a table of data and will need plenty of practice. Only Higher Tier candidates will need to find the gradient of a distance–time or a velocity–time graph, or find the area of a velocity–time graph. However, the Foundation Tier will need to know what the respective gradients represent without calculating them. They could also be asked to calculate the acceleration using the equation if they are given the initial and the final velocity.

AQA Examiner's tip

It is very common for students to get confused between distance–time and velocity–time graphs. It is therefore a good exercise to get pupils to sketch both types of graph for several made up journeys that involve acceleration, deceleration and constant velocity. These graphs can be sketched with the same time axis to enable a comparison. This will help to highlight the difference between sloping sections and horizontal sections for each type of graph.

P2 2.1

Forces between objects

Learning objectives

Students should learn:

- that forces between objects are equal and opposite
- friction is a contact force between surfaces
- the unit of force is the newton (N).

Learning outcomes

Most students should be able to:

- state the unit of force and that forces occur in equal and opposite pairs
- describe how frictional forces act between objects.

Some students should also be able to:

- explain examples of equal and opposite forces acting when two objects interact.

Answers to in-text questions

a 50 N upwards.

b 200 N.

c The wheels slip on the ground.

Support

- Start with some simple reminders of forces and force diagrams. Provide some diagrams with some of the forces already marked on with indications of their direction and magnitude and ask the students to complete them.

Extend

- Ask: 'What is the ideal launch angle of a projectile? Can you discover the ideal angle to fire a projectile and make it travel the furthest distance?' They need to design a launch system to make this investigation work. Alternatively you can look at the forces required to drag objects; when the objects are accelerating, the force is larger than that at constant speed. The students can look into why this happens and perhaps the relationship force = mass × acceleration.

AQA Specification link-up: Physics P2.1

- Whenever two objects interact, the forces they exert on each other are equal and opposite. *[P2.1.1 a)]*
  Controlled Assessment: AS4.3 Collect primary and secondary data. *[AS4.3.2 a) b) c) d) e) f)]*

Lesson structure

Starters

It's a drag – Show a video clip of a drag racer (do an online video search for 'drag racer') deploying parachutes to assist in braking. Ask the students to explain how the parachutes help to slow it down. Try and draw out the key concepts of forces and friction. You can also check that the students use force arrows appropriately. *(5 minutes)*

Picture the force – Show a set of diagrams of objects standing still or in motion and ask the students to mark on all of the forces. Check that the students are using 'force arrows' and that they are marked clearly onto the point at which the force acts. *(10 minutes)*

Main

- Some of the material here checks the students' understanding of basic forces; they need to be encouraged to draw clear diagrams of the forces acting on objects. Look for force arrows in the right directions and see if the students draw them of differing lengths and are trying to represent the magnitude.

- It will help if the students have a clear understanding of what a one newton force feels like, so pass around a 100 g mass so they can get a feel for it. You could also give examples of very large forces (e.g. the force between the Sun and Earth) and very small forces (e.g. the force of attraction between adjacent students) to show the vast range of forces scientists deal with.

- The idea of equal and opposite forces needs to be reinforced with plenty of examples. Show a range of objects in equilibrium such as a boat, see-saw, car rolling, and identify the pairs of forces on diagrams. (Search for pictures online.)

- The car stuck in mud situation is one where the forces do not appear to be equal and opposite. The force in the rope is clear (you can show this with a model) but this is not the only force at work. To analyse the situation more fully would require including the frictional forces and the forces exerted by the tractor on the Earth. As the car and tractor accelerate, the Earth is accelerated in the opposite direction by a tiny amount.

- You can demonstrate equal and opposite forces using skates (see 'Practical support') or by dragging objects along the floor with a string with newtonmeters at each end. It can be difficult to read moving newtonmeters, but the students will get the hang of it with practice. (This relates to 'How Science Works: making measurements, repeatability and reproducibility'.)

- When discussing the operation of wheels, you might like to go through some of the stages of the force being transferred to the wheel from the engine; especially with those interested in automotive engineering.

- To round off, you could show a car trying to accelerate too rapidly and skidding; this provides a visual answer to in-text question **c**. (Search for 'racing' or 'car skid' at a video hosting site.)

Plenaries

Pulling power – Support students understanding of balanced forces by giving the students cards describing ten (or more) players and ask them to assign them to two tug-of-war teams, so that the teams are balanced. There may be several solutions. Have players with force strengths of 50 N, 100 N, 150 N, 200 N, 250 N, 300 N, 350 N, 400 N, 450 N, 500 N. You can use more complicated numbers if you want to extend some students more. *(5 minutes)*

The force is strong in which one? – Give the students a set of cards showing the size of the forces between objects (e.g. force on a person due to the gravity of Earth, force produced by a tug of war team) and a description of the objects and ask them to match up the cards. *(10 minutes)*

Practical support

Action and reaction

Equipment and materials required

Two sets of roller skates or skateboards, full sets of safety equipment (helmet, pads, etc.) a connecting rope, two newtonmeters.

Details

The students should firstly demonstrate the effect of pushing each other. If student A pushes student B forwards gently, then student A should move backwards. If the students are roughly the same size and the skates are similar, then you could show that they both move the same distance before friction stops them. One student can then try to pull the other with a rope; they should both move closer. Measuring the forces to show that they are identical in size is trickier; the rope becomes slack. You might want to pull a skater around instead and take force measurements at both ends of the rope.

Safety: Make sure there is enough room for students to move around safely.

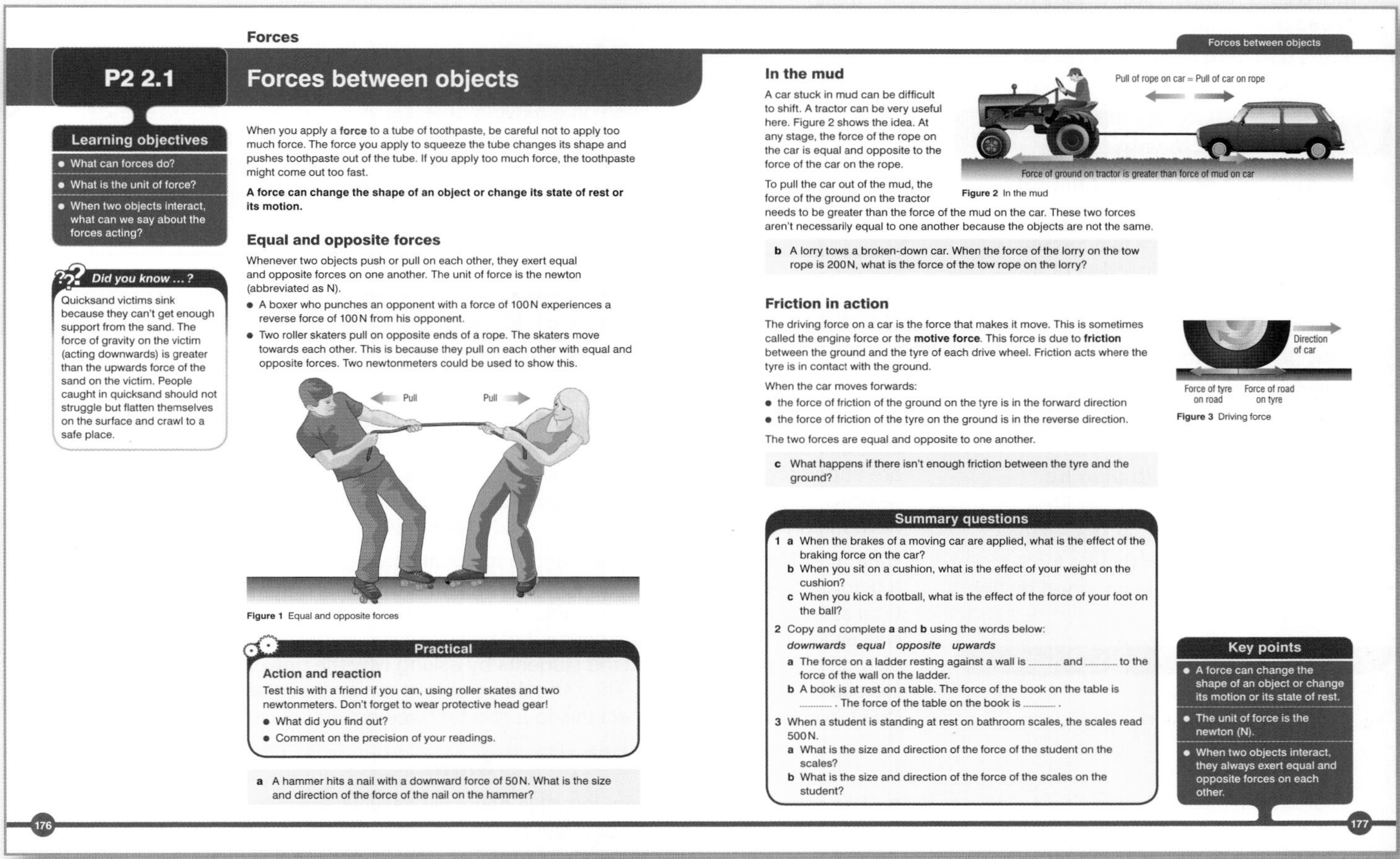

Forces

P2 2.1 — Forces between objects

Forces between objects

Learning objectives

- What can forces do?
- What is the unit of force?
- When two objects interact, what can we say about the forces acting?

When you apply a **force** to a tube of toothpaste, be careful not to apply too much force. The force you apply to squeeze the tube changes its shape and pushes toothpaste out of the tube. If you apply too much force, the toothpaste might come out too fast.

A force can change the shape of an object or change its state of rest or its motion.

Equal and opposite forces

Whenever two objects push or pull on each other, they exert equal and opposite forces on one another. The unit of force is the newton (abbreviated as N).

- A boxer who punches an opponent with a force of 100 N experiences a reverse force of 100 N from his opponent.
- Two roller skaters pull on opposite ends of a rope. The skaters move towards each other. This is because they pull on each other with equal and opposite forces. Two newtonmeters could be used to show this.

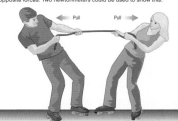

Figure 1 Equal and opposite forces

Did you know ... ?

Quicksand victims sink because they can't get enough support from the sand. The force of gravity on the victim (acting downwards) is greater than the upwards force of the sand on the victim. People caught in quicksand should not struggle but flatten themselves on the surface and crawl to a safe place.

Practical

Action and reaction

Test this with a friend if you can, using roller skates and two newtonmeters. Don't forget to wear protective head gear!

- What did you find out?
- Comment on the precision of your readings.

a A hammer hits a nail with a downward force of 50 N. What is the size and direction of the force of the nail on the hammer?

In the mud

A car stuck in mud can be difficult to shift. A tractor can be very useful here. Figure 2 shows the idea. At any stage, the force of the rope on the car is equal and opposite to the force of the car on the rope.

To pull the car out of the mud, the force of the ground on the tractor needs to be greater than the force of the mud on the car. These two forces aren't necessarily equal to one another because the objects are not the same.

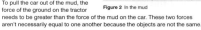

Pull of rope on car = Pull of car on rope

Force of ground on tractor is greater than force of mud on car

Figure 2 In the mud

b A lorry tows a broken-down car. When the force of the lorry on the tow rope is 200 N, what is the force of the tow rope on the lorry?

Friction in action

The driving force on a car is the force that makes it move. This is sometimes called the engine force or the **motive force**. This force is due to **friction** between the ground and the tyre of each drive wheel. Friction acts where the tyre is in contact with the ground.

When the car moves forwards:

- the force of friction of the ground on the tyre is in the forward direction
- the force of friction of the tyre on the ground is in the reverse direction.

The two forces are equal and opposite to one another.

Direction of car

Force of tyre on road   Force of road on tyre

Figure 3 Driving force

c What happens if there isn't enough friction between the tyre and the ground?

Summary questions

1 **a** When the brakes of a moving car are applied, what is the effect of the braking force on the car?
  b When you sit on a cushion, what is the effect of your weight on the cushion?
  c When you kick a football, what is the effect of the force of your foot on the ball?

2 Copy and complete **a** and **b** using the words below:
  downwards equal opposite upwards
  a The force on a ladder resting against a wall is .... and .... to the force of the wall on the ladder.
  b A book is at rest on a table. The force of the book on the table is .... The force of the table on the book is ....

3 When a student is standing at rest on bathroom scales, the scales read 500 N.
  a What is the size and direction of the force of the student on the scales?
  b What is the size and direction of the force of the scales on the student?

Key points

- A force can change the shape of an object or change its motion or its state of rest.
- The unit of force is the newton (N).
- When two objects interact, they always exert equal and opposite forces on each other.

Further teaching suggestions

Investigating quicksand

- Slowly adding water to a bowl of cornstarch will produce a substance similar to quicksand. It's a bit hit and miss to get the consistency just right. When it is stirred gently, it will flow, but when it is hit, it will become solid. You could try to float objects on top of the mixture and see if vibrations (produced by a signal generator and loudspeaker) will cause them to sink. You could also measure the size of the force needed to pull out objects slowly or quickly.

Equipment and materials required

- Cornstarch (cornflour), 250 cm^3 beaker, signal generator, loudspeaker.

Applying forces

- Have the students describe how forces are used in various simple devices such as doors, tin openers, bicycles, etc.

Did you know ... ?

Quicksand

On average, quicksand is actually denser than the human body, so it is difficult to sink in it further than your chest even if you panic. Survival guides suggest the following method of escape. Stay calm; if you don't struggle you *will* float. Slowly adjust your position so you are lying on your back and then wiggle your legs gently in a circular motion. You will crawl towards the edge. Don't get your friends to pull you out vertically; this apparently takes a very large force. It may be possible to investigate this with a cornflour-based practical.

Summary answers

1 **a** It slows the car down.
  b It squashes the cushion.
  c It squashes the ball for a short time and makes it move.

2 **a** equal, opposite
  b downwards, upwards

3 **a** 500 N downwards.
  b 500 N upwards.

P2 2.2

Resultant force

AQA Specification link-up: Physics P2.1

- A number of forces acting at a point may be replaced by a single force that has the same effect on the motion as the original forces all acting together. This single force is called the resultant force. [P2.1.1 b)]
- A resultant force acting on an object may cause a change in its state of rest or motion. [P2.1.1 c)]
- If the resultant force acting on a stationary object is:
  – zero, the object will remain stationary
  – not zero, the object will accelerate in the direction of the resultant force. [P2.1.1 d)]
- If the resultant force acting on a moving object is:
  – zero, the object will continue to move at the same speed and in the same direction
  – not zero, the object will accelerate in the direction of the resultant force. [P2.1.1 e)]

  Controlled Assessment: AS4.5 Analyse and interpret primary and secondary data. [AS4.5.3 a)]

Lesson structure

Starters

Mad maths – Before stating to look at forces, you can provide some additional support for students with their mathematical skills. Give the students several addition sums that include negative numbers to check their understanding. Link this to the idea that forces are added together but ones in opposite directions are treated as negative. The students need to be able to add together accurately. The sizes of forces are often measured in kilo-newton so you might like to have the students handle larger numbers too. (5 minutes)

Balanced forces – Show the students a toy boat floating on water and ask them to draw a diagram of all of the forces on the boat. Add small masses, one at a time, until the boat sinks. Ask them to draw a diagram showing the forces at the time when the boat was sinking. This leads to the concept of balanced and unbalanced forces, but you can also discuss density. Extend the students by asking why the upward thrust of the water increases as the load does. They should be able to make observations that the boat is lower in the water and connect this to a greater force acting upwards. (10 minutes)

Main

- The calculation of resultant forces is generally easy when limited to one direction. The students must take care about the directions of the forces as some can get confused and simply add all of the numbers together. This is more likely when there are more than two forces. It is best to get the students to add all of the forces in one direction, then all of the forces in the other direction and then subtract these totals.

- It is well worth making the hovercraft (described in the 'Practical support'), but remember that the glue will take some time to cool so do this bit early in the lesson and give it 30 minutes to set thoroughly.

- Demonstrating a linear air track is a good way of showing motion without friction, and it can help the students get to grips with the idea that objects only slow down because of the friction.

- If you have footage of a jet plane taking off, use it to discuss the forces involved. If it is of an aircraft carrier launch system, you can point out the extra force applied by the steam catapult and ask why this is necessary. (Search for 'jet plane' at an internet video hosting site). The heavily loaded fighter planes often seem to dip as they leave the short runway as they are still not travelling quite fast enough to give sufficient uplift.

- An aeroplane cruising is a good example of balanced forces. The students can draw a diagram and discuss the sensations they feel when they are in a plane like this. Because the forces are balanced, the students should feel no acceleration. If they close their eyes they would not be able to tell they were moving at all. Make sure that you explain that the engines need to be generating a force as there is a substantial amount of air resistance.

- When discussing braking, be careful that the students do not think that the force applied to the pedal is the actual braking force applied to the wheels. If this were the case, then a car would take a lot longer to stop.

- If the glue is set, then this is a good time to go back to the hovercraft. The hovercrafts should glide well on flat desks. Get the students to explain why they float; include a diagram.

Plenaries

Hovercraft tests – The hovercraft should be finished so you can have a range of simple competitions. Which travels furthest from the starting point, which stays hovering for longest, which can move a 50 g mass, and so on? *(5 minutes)*

An uphill struggle – Challenge students to come up with some explanations about forces and link the ideas to energy transfer. Example questions could include: 'Why is it harder to push a car uphill rather than on a flat road?' [You have to overcome friction and part of the weight of the object, you are also increasing its potential energy] and 'Is it easier to drag a piano up a ramp rather than upstairs? Why?' [You have to lift the object up each step so overcoming its weight]. How can an aeroplane maintain speed if the engines are turned off [Some of the potential energy is transferred to kinetic as the plane reduces its height]. *(10 minutes)*

Practical support

Investigating forces

Hovercrafts are fun to make. There are various designs but this one uses an old CD.

Equipment and materials required

Balloons and balloon pump, old CD, thick paper, 'sports bottle' top and glue gun.

Details

Glue the sports bottle top on to the centre of the CD with the glue gun so that it covers the hole, making sure that the seal around the edge is good. Let this cool for at least 10 minutes. Blow up the balloon and carefully pull the end over the bottle top so that the air will be released through the base of the CD. The CD will act like a hovercraft. It is vastly improved by fixing a cylinder of paper around the top edge of the CD so that it holds the balloon vertically and stops it dragging on the desk. You should be able to blow up the balloon while it is still attached to the CD. Searching the internet will yield a range of designs and pictures to help with this activity.

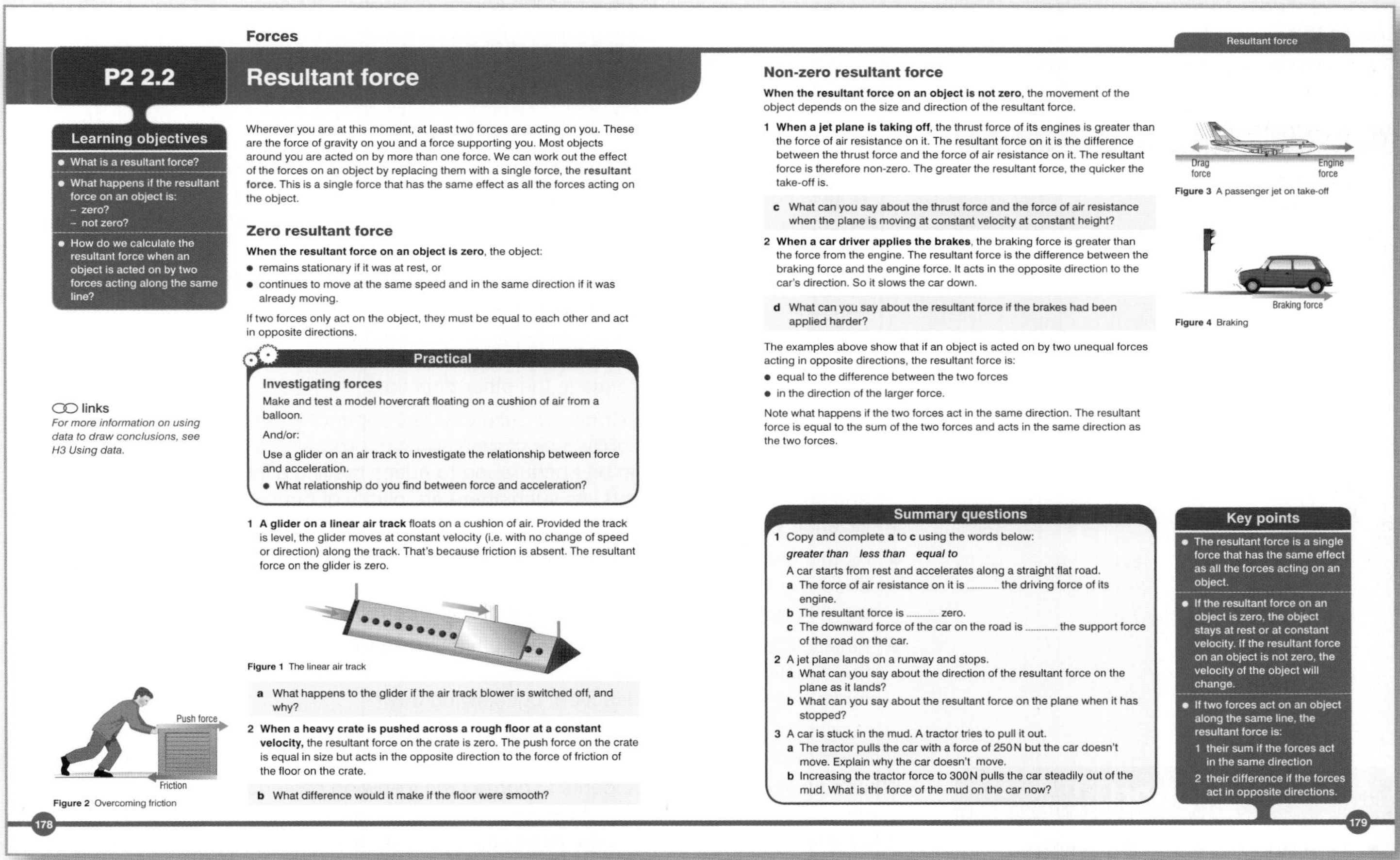

Forces

P2 2.2

Resultant force

Learning objectives

- What is a resultant force?
- What happens if the resultant force on an object is:
  - zero?
  - not zero?
- How do we calculate the resultant force when an object is acted on by two forces acting along the same line?

Wherever you are at this moment, at least two forces are acting on you. These are the force of gravity on you and a force supporting you. Most objects around you are acted on by more than one force. We can work out the effect of the forces on an object by replacing them with a single force, the **resultant force**. This is a single force that has the same effect as all the forces acting on the object.

Zero resultant force

When the resultant force on an object is zero, the object:

- remains stationary if it was at rest, or
- continues to move at the same speed and in the same direction if it was already moving.

If two forces only act on the object, they must be equal to each other and act in opposite directions.

links
For more information on using data to draw conclusions, see H3 Using data.

Practical

Investigating forces

Make and test a model hovercraft floating on a cushion of air from a balloon.

And/or:

Use a glider on an air track to investigate the relationship between force and acceleration.

- What relationship do you find between force and acceleration?

1 **A glider on a linear air track** floats on a cushion of air. Provided the track is level, the glider moves at constant velocity (i.e. with no change of speed or direction) along the track. That's because friction is absent. The resultant force on the glider is zero.

Figure 1 The linear air track

a What happens to the glider if the air track blower is switched off, and why?

2 **When a heavy crate is pushed across a rough floor at a constant velocity**, the resultant force on the crate is zero. The push force on the crate is equal in size but acts in the opposite direction to the force of friction of the floor on the crate.

Figure 2 Overcoming friction

b What difference would it make if the floor were smooth?

Non-zero resultant force

When the resultant force on an object is not zero, the movement of the object depends on the size and direction of the resultant force.

1 **When a jet plane is taking off**, the thrust force of its engines is greater than the force of air resistance on it. The resultant force on it is the difference between the thrust force and the force of air resistance on it. The resultant force is therefore non-zero. The greater the resultant force, the quicker the take-off is.

c What can you say about the thrust force and the force of air resistance when the plane is moving at constant velocity at constant height?

2 **When a car driver applies the brakes**, the braking force is greater than the force from the engine. The resultant force is the difference between the braking force and the engine force. It acts in the opposite direction to the car's direction. So it slows the car down.

d What can you say about the resultant force if the brakes had been applied harder?

Figure 3 A passenger jet on take-off

Figure 4 Braking

The examples above show that if an object is acted on by two unequal forces acting in opposite directions, the resultant force is:

- equal to the difference between the two forces
- in the direction of the larger force.

Note what happens if the two forces act in the same direction. The resultant force is equal to the sum of the two forces and acts in the same direction as the two forces.

Summary questions

1 Copy and complete **a** to **c** using the words below:

greater than   less than   equal to

A car starts from rest and accelerates along a straight flat road.

a The force of air resistance on it is .... the driving force of its engine.

b The resultant force is .... zero.

c The downward force of the car on the road is .... the support force of the road on the car.

2 A jet plane lands on a runway and stops.

a What can you say about the direction of the resultant force on the plane as it lands?

b What can you say about the resultant force on the plane when it has stopped?

3 A car is stuck in the mud. A tractor tries to pull it out.

a The tractor pulls the car with a force of 250 N but the car doesn't move. Explain why the car doesn't move.

b Increasing the tractor force to 300 N pulls the car steadily out of the mud. What is the force of the mud on the car now?

Key points

- The resultant force is a single force that has the same effect as all the forces acting on an object.
- If the resultant force on an object is zero, the object stays at rest or at constant velocity. If the resultant force on an object is not zero, the velocity of the object will change.
- If two forces act on an object along the same line, the resultant force is:
  1 their sum if the forces act in the same direction
  2 their difference if the forces act in opposite directions.

Answers to in-text questions

a It stops because friction between the glider and the track is no longer zero.

b The crate would slide across the floor after being given a brief push.

c They are equal and opposite to each other.

d The resultant force would have been greater.

Summary answers

1 **a** less than   **b** greater than   **c** equal to

2 **a** It acts in the opposite direction to the direction in which the plane moves.

  b It is zero.

3 **a** The tractor force is less than or equal to the force of the mud on the car so the car remains stationary.

  b The force of the mud on the car is now 300 N.

P2 2.3

Force and acceleration

Learning objectives

Students should learn:

- the relationship between the resultant force on an object and its acceleration
- how to use the equation $F = ma$ to determine the acceleration of an object.

Learning outcomes

Most students should be able to:

- calculate the force required to produce a given acceleration of an object of known mass
- state that objects of larger mass require greater forces to produce a given acceleration
- determine the direction of the acceleration on an object.

Some students should also be able to:

- rearrange and use the equation $F = ma$.

Specification link-up: Physics P2.1

- The acceleration of an object is determined by the resultant force acting on the object and the mass of the object. $a = \dfrac{F}{m}$ or $F = m \times a$ [P2.1.2 a)]

Controlled Assessment: AS4.4 Select and process primary and secondary data. [AS4.4.2 b)]; AS4.5 Analyse and interpret primary and secondary data. [AS4.5.3 a)]

Lesson structure

Starters

Accelerator – Ask: 'What does the accelerator in a car do? How do you think it works?' Use this question to link back to energy, fuels and forces. [The pedal causes more fuel to be fed to the engine; this is burnt releasing energy at a greater rate; the energy generates a force – by exerting a pressure in the cylinder – and this force is transferred by a mechanical system to the wheels.] You should be able to find an animation of the process with a simple internet search. With some students you might like to move on to a discussion about the advantages of maintaining a constant speed instead of accelerating and braking between junctions. Significantly less energy is wasted. *(5 minutes)*

Lift off – Show the students footage of a chemical rocket launch and ask them to describe as much of what is happening as possible using accurate scientific language. The students should be able to describe the energy changes happening and then link to the ideas of this change, producing forces. You can support some students by providing a list of key words that must be incorporated into their descriptions including: fuel, combustion, thrust, kinetic energy, potential energy. *(10 minutes)*

Main

- A DVD showing a snooker match is a very useful resource. You can use it to discuss what is happening to the balls during impact and their movement across the green baize. Remind the students that there are frictional forces at work which is one of the reasons the balls slow.

- Pause the play and discuss the forces at work at each stage. With a data projector you can even draw force arrows over the action on your whiteboard. Show clips where the balls are moving in opposite directions and hit each other causing them to recoil. This can be used to illustrate forces in the opposite direction to motion, causing objects to decelerate or even accelerate in the other direction.

- The experiments can be simple or quite detailed depending on the time you have available. They produce quite a bit of data and can produce an excellent analysis task. The students should be encouraged to notice the limitations of the experiments and suggest improvements. As such, there are plenty of opportunities to cover 'How Science Works' concepts.

- As this is another fairly mathematically intensive topic, you will have to spend time on checking the students' ability to use the equation. As usual, encourage students to use a rigorous layout to increase the chances of a correct answer.

- Finally, watch out for students thinking that a moving object will always be moving in the direction of the resultant force. They need to understand that the object could be moving in the opposite direction, but slowing down.

Answers to in-text questions

a 640 N

b 4.0 m/s²

Plenaries

What's wrong? – Ask the students to correct the following sentence that describes a common misconception: 'Objects always move in the direction of the resultant force.' [Students need to understand the forces will cause an acceleration that will speed up or slow down the object but this does not mean that it will instantly move in the direction of the force.] *(5 minutes)*

I'm snookered – The students must draw a series of diagrams showing the forces involved in getting out of a 'snooker', where the object ball, the blue, is behind the pink. They draw each of the stages of the movements, showing the forces as the ball is first hit and the collisions with the cushions. Obviously you can differentiate this task by having some simple and some complex situations. With some students you might want to make sure that the angles are accurately plotted. You might be able to use a snooker or pool simulation game to describe the effects too; these are more interactive and more fun for the students. *(10 minutes)*

Support

- Give students plenty of examples for the calculations to provide extra support.

Extend

- See the more detailed acceleration investigation in the 'Further teaching suggestions' box. 'Why doesn't the snooker table move when a ball hits the cushion?'

Practical support

Investigating force and acceleration

This is a simple experiment, except for keeping the force constant; the alternative (see 'Further teaching suggestions') is more accurate but needs more equipment.

Equipment and materials required

For each group: dynamics trolley, string, masses (similar to trolley mass), stopwatch and possibly motion sensor or light gates.

Details

The students pull the trolley along attempting to use a constant force by watching the newtonmeter. They should pull the trolley along a track of known distance, so that they can compare the acceleration easily. If insufficient trolleys are available to double up, then just let the students add masses roughly equivalent to that of the trolley.

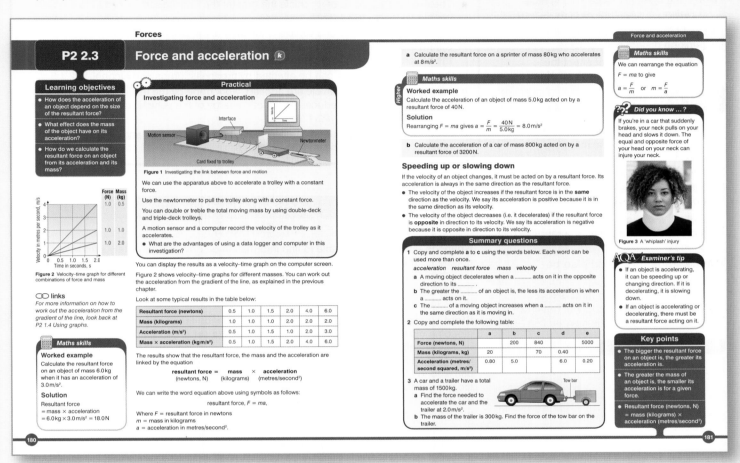

Forces

Force and acceleration

P2 2.3 — Force and acceleration ⓚ

Learning objectives

- How does the acceleration of an object depend on the size of the resultant force?
- What effect does the mass of the object have on its acceleration?
- How do we calculate the resultant force on an object from its acceleration and its mass?

Figure 2 Velocity–time graph for different combinations of force and mass

Force (N)	Mass (kg)
1.0	0.5
1.0	1.0
1.0	2.0

links

For more information on how to work out the acceleration from the gradient of the line, look back at P2 1.4 Using graphs.

Maths skills

Worked example

Calculate the resultant force on an object of mass 6.0 kg when it has an acceleration of 3.0 m/s².

Solution

Resultant force
= mass × acceleration
= 6.0 kg × 3.0 m/s² = 18.0 N

Practical

Investigating force and acceleration

Interface
Motion sensor
Newtonmeter
Card fixed to trolley

Figure 1 Investigating the link between force and motion

We can use the apparatus above to accelerate a trolley with a constant force.

Use the newtonmeter to pull the trolley along with a constant force.

You can double or treble the total moving mass by using double-deck and triple-deck trolleys.

A motion sensor and a computer record the velocity of the trolley as it accelerates.

- What are the advantages of using a data logger and computer in this investigation?

You can display the results as a velocity–time graph on the computer screen.

Figure 2 shows velocity–time graphs for different masses. You can work out the acceleration from the gradient of the line, as explained in the previous chapter.

Look at some typical results in the table below:

Resultant force (newtons)	0.5	1.0	1.5	2.0	4.0	6.0
Mass (kilograms)	1.0	1.0	1.0	2.0	2.0	2.0
Acceleration (m/s²)	0.5	1.0	1.5	1.0	2.0	3.0
Mass × acceleration (kg m/s²)	0.5	1.0	1.5	2.0	4.0	6.0

The results show that the resultant force, the mass and the acceleration are linked by the equation

resultant force = mass × acceleration
(newtons, N) (kilograms) (metres/second²)

We can write the word equation above using symbols as follows:

resultant force, $F = ma$,

Where F = resultant force in newtons
m = mass in kilograms
a = acceleration in metres/second².

a Calculate the resultant force on a sprinter of mass 80 kg who accelerates at 8 m/s².

Maths skills

Worked example

Calculate the acceleration of an object of mass 5.0 kg acted on by a resultant force of 40 N.

Solution

Rearranging $F = ma$ gives $a = \dfrac{F}{m} = \dfrac{40\,N}{5.0\,kg} = 8.0\,m/s^2$

b Calculate the acceleration of a car of mass 800 kg acted on by a resultant force of 3200 N.

Speeding up or slowing down

If the velocity of an object changes, it must be acted on by a resultant force. Its acceleration is always in the same direction as the resultant force.

- The velocity of the object increases if the resultant force is in the **same** direction as the velocity. We say its acceleration is positive because it is in the same direction as its velocity.
- The velocity of the object decreases (i.e. it decelerates) if the resultant force is **opposite** in direction to its velocity. We say its acceleration is negative because it is opposite in direction to its velocity.

Summary questions

1 Copy and complete **a** to **c** using the words below. Each word can be used more than once.

acceleration   resultant force   mass   velocity

a A moving object decelerates when a .... acts on it in the opposite direction to its ....

b The greater the .... of an object is, the less its acceleration is when a .... acts on it.

c The .... of a moving object increases when a .... acts on it in the same direction as it is moving in.

2 Copy and complete the following table:

	a	b	c	d	e
Force (newtons, N)		200	840		5000
Mass (kilograms, kg)	20		70	0.40	
Acceleration (metres/second squared, m/s²)	0.80	5.0		6.0	0.20

3 A car and a trailer have a total mass of 1500 kg.

a Find the force needed to accelerate the car and the trailer at 2.0 m/s².

b The mass of the trailer is 300 kg. Find the force of the tow bar on the trailer.

Tow bar

Maths skills

We can rearrange the equation
$F = ma$ to give
$$a = \frac{F}{m} \quad \text{or} \quad m = \frac{F}{a}$$

?? Did you know …?

If you're in a car that suddenly brakes, your neck pulls on your head and slows it down. The equal and opposite force of your head on your neck can injure your neck.

Figure 3 A 'whiplash' injury

AQA Examiner's tip

- If an object is accelerating, it can be speeding up or changing direction. If it is decelerating, it is slowing down.
- If an object is accelerating or decelerating, there must be a resultant force acting on it.

Key points

- The bigger the resultant force on an object is, the greater its acceleration is.
- The greater the mass of an object is, the smaller its acceleration is for a given force.
- Resultant force (newtons, N) = mass (kilograms) × acceleration (metres/second²)

Further teaching suggestions

ICT link-up

- A range of good simulations of force experiments are available.

More investigating force and acceleration

- In this experiment, the students can discover the effect of different forces on acceleration or the effect of the objects mass.

Equipment and materials required

For each group: dynamics trolley (or similar), string, pulley, clamp, 10 × 20 g masses and mass holder, stopwatch and possibly motion sensor or light gates.

Details

The students mount the pulley over the end of the desks. One end of the string is attached to the mass holder (which hangs down) and the other to the trolley. The mass is released and falls to the floor pulling the trolley with a constant force. With larger masses, you will need to protect the floor and students' feet.

The movement of the trolley can be monitored by a motion sensor, or the time it takes to move between two marked points can be recorded. The students can load the mass holder with different masses to increase the force on the trolley in order to investigate the effect of the size of the force on the acceleration. (This relates to: 'How Science Works': relationships between variables.) Some may even look into the effect of the mass of the trolley by loading it up with increasing mass and accelerating it with a fixed force. By analysing graphs and discovering that a is proportional to F and a is also inversely proportional to m, some students should be able to link the concepts together to reach $F = ma$.

Summary answers

1 a resultant force, velocity
b mass, resultant force
c acceleration, resultant force

2 a 16 N
b 40 kg
c 12 m/s²
d 2.4 N
e 25 000 kg

3 a 3000 N
b 600 N

P2 2.4

On the road

AQA Specification link-up: Physics P2.1

Learning objectives

Students should learn:

- that the resultant force on a vehicle travelling at constant velocity is zero
- about the factors that affect the thinking distance of vehicles
- about the factors that affect the braking distance of moving vehicles.

Learning outcomes

Most students should be able to:

- use a chart to find the stopping distance, the braking distance and the thinking distance at a given speed
- list and describe the factors that affect the stopping distance of a vehicle
- explain which are the most important factors for cars moving at a range of speeds.

Some students should also be able to:

- differentiate between factors that affect the thinking distance, braking distance or both distances.

Support

- Allow the students to use an experiment template with clear instructions and a results table during the practical task.

Extend

- Concentrate on the links between forces, acceleration and mass using $F = ma$ calculations. You can challenge some students to tackle realistic-sized objects (cars of mass 1000 kg) and accelerations. Discuss the idea that the fast-moving cars have large amounts of kinetic energy.

Specification link-up: Physics P2.1

- When a vehicle travels at a steady speed the resistive forces balance the driving force. *[P2.1.3 a)]*
- The greater the speed of a vehicle the greater the braking force needed to stop it in a certain distance. *[P2.1.3 b)]*
- The stopping distance of a vehicle is the sum of the distance the vehicle travels during the driver's reaction time (thinking distance) and the distance it travels under the braking force (braking distance). *[P2.1.3 c)]*
- A driver's reaction time can be affected by tiredness, drugs and alcohol. *[P2.1.3 d)]*
- When the brakes of a vehicle are applied, work done by the friction force between the brakes and the wheel reduces the kinetic energy of the vehicle and the temperature of the brakes increase. *[P2.1.3 e)]*
- A vehicle's braking distance can be affected by adverse road and weather conditions and poor condition of the vehicle. *[P2.1.3 f)]*

Lesson structure

Starters

Chances – You should be able to find information on government safety sites about car collisions. You can extend this to cover bicycle crashes and simple accidents in the home. Link these results to the idea of speed restrictions in your area, especially around primary schools. Overall, students should realise that greater speed significantly increases the injury. *(5 minutes)*

Stop! – To support students in understanding the wide range of factors that can affect the stopping distance of cars, ask the students to sort a set of cards about things which may or may not affect stopping distances. Correct ones can include the physical properties of the car, the tyres, the driver and weather conditions along with a lot of incorrect ones. You can extend students by asking them to discuss and describe how the factor affects the stopping distance and construct well-formed descriptions like 'The greater the mass of a car, the more kinetic energy it will have when moving at a fixed speed. This means that a more massive car will be more difficult to stop.' *(10 minutes)*

Main

- Video clips of vehicles braking and skidding make this topic more visually stimulating. (Search for videos of crash tests at an internet video site.)
- When discussing reaction times, you could try a simple experiment in concentration. At the beginning of the lesson give the students an unusual key word that won't usually crop up in the lesson ('banana') and ask them to put their hands up as quickly as possible whenever they hear it. Early in the lesson they will be quite quick but later, as their concentration flags, they will struggle. If you are using a digital projector, slip in a banana slide somewhere in the lesson and see how the students react; are they faster at reacting to visual stimuli?
- You could ask the students to evaluate the data used to produce the stopping distance chart. It is based on an alert driver, driving a medium-sized car, but it does not take into account the improved braking systems of modern cars and the increase in the size (mass) of the average car. This can lead to a discussion of whether large cars are safer or more dangerous to passengers and pedestrians.
- The students should understand the factors affecting overall stopping distance, but they need to be clear which affects the thinking distance and which affects the braking distance. You can link these concepts with $F = ma$ from the previous topic and again with kinetic energy in previous lessons. Note that the speed of the car affects thinking and braking distance, so it is usually the most important factor overall.
- Testing reaction time rounds the lesson off well, you can try the simple version or driving simulation software.

Plenaries

Expect the unexpected – Use the unusual key word one more time as the students are packing away. Reaction times will be dramatically reduced as they are paying attention to other things. *(5 minutes)*

I said stop! – Using the cards from the Starter, students have to separate those that were correct into ones that affect thinking distance and ones that affect braking distance. This task should solidify their understanding of the two phases of stopping. Ask: 'Do some factors affect both?' [e.g. speed] Students could put them in order of importance for a car travelling at 30 mph. Push the students further by showing them a detailed graph of stopping distances for different speeds; this should have the braking distance and thinking distances separate. Ask the students to describe the relationships. *(10 minutes)*

Practical support

Reaction times

This is a fairly simple activity only requiring a stopwatch with separate start and lap-time buttons.

Equipment and materials required

Stopwatches.

Details

The students can try the simple activity and see the wide range of response times. They should appreciate that the times improve with practice and when they are fully concentrating on the clock. In a real car situation, the driver would not be able to focus on one simple task, so the times would be significantly greater.

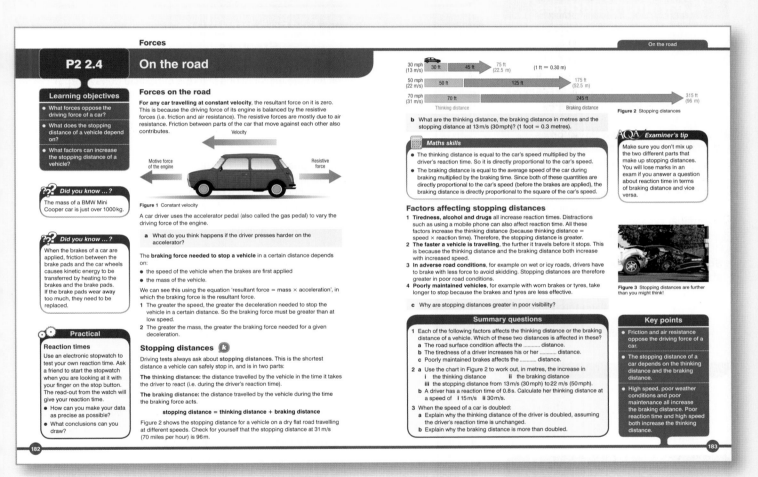

Answers to in-text questions

a The car speeds up.

b 9 m, 13.5 m, 22.5 m.

c The reaction time of the driver is longer because the road ahead is more difficult to see.

Summary answers

1. **a** braking **b** thinking **c** braking
2. **a** **i** 6 m **ii** 24 m **iii** 30 m
   b **i** 12 m **ii** 24 m
3. **a** The thinking distance is equal to the speed of the car multiplied by the driver's reaction time. So if the speed is doubled, the thinking distance is doubled.
   b The braking distance is equal to the average speed of the car during braking multiplied by the time taken for the brakes to stop the car. If the speed is doubled, the average speed is doubled and the time taken is increased, so the braking distance more than doubles. The time taken actually doubles as well, so the braking distance becomes four times greater.

P2 2.5

Falling objects

AQA

Specification link-up: Physics P2.1

- The faster an object moves through a fluid the greater the frictional force that acts on it. [P2.1.4 a)]
- An object falling through a fluid will initially accelerate due to the force of gravity. Eventually the resultant force will be zero and the object will move at its terminal velocity (steady speed). [P2.1.4 b)]
- Draw and interpret velocity–time graphs for objects that reach terminal velocity, including a consideration of the forces acting on the object. [P2.1.4 c)]
- Calculate the weight of an object using the force exerted on it by a gravitational force:
  $W = m \times g$ [P2.1.4 d)]

  Controlled Assessment: AS4.1 Plan practical ways to develop and test candidates' own scientific ideas. [AS4.1.1 a) b) c)]

Learning objectives

Students should learn:

- the difference between mass and weight
- the mass of the object is a constant value whereas the weight depends on the strength of the gravitational field it is in
- why an object falling through a fluid accelerates until it reaches its terminal velocity.

Learning outcomes

Most students should be able to:

- explain the difference between mass and weight
- calculate the weight of an object of a given mass
- describe the forces acting on an object falling through a fluid such as air or water, and how these forces affect the acceleration of the object
- describe how the velocity of an object released from rest in a fluid changes as it falls
- explain why an object reaches a terminal velocity and describe some of the factors that determine this velocity.

Some students should also be able to:

- explain the motion of an object released from rest falling through a fluid including how the acceleration decreases and becomes zero at terminal velocity.

Lesson structure

Starters

Fluid facts – Support students by giving them cards with information (including diagrams) about the physical properties and the explanations in terms of particle behaviour for solids, liquids and gases and ask them to match them up. This should help them revise the states of matter and the particle theory in particular. *(5 minutes)*

Air resistance – What causes air or water resistance? The students need to use their understanding of particles and forces to give a description. They should sketch the movement of objects and label the forces on them and then try to show the particles being pushed out of the way and pushing back. Extend the students by trying to draw out the idea that moving faster through a fluid will require a greater force as more particles will need to be pushed out of the way each second. They may also be able to explain that the particles will need to be pushed 'harder' to get them out of the way faster. *(10 minutes)*

Main

- Video clips of falling objects are ideal for this topic, in particular clips of parachutists or bird flight. (Search for video clips at an internet video hosting site.)
- Weight and mass are commonly confused. Let the students handle a 1 kg mass and emphasise that the '1 kg' is the material in the block and this will not change just because you take it to the Moon. It has weight because it is attracted towards the Earth. Weigh the mass and explain that the weight is the force that is pulling it towards the centre of the Earth. If there were less gravity, then this force would be less.
- There are a couple of phrases used to describe 'the strength of gravity' and these are sometimes interchanged. Try to stick to 'gravitational field strength' and explain that there is a 'field' around the Earth where its gravity affects other objects. The students should accept this field idea after discussing the effect of a magnetic field.
- Remind students that all liquids and gases are fluids, so all motion we see on the Earth is motion through fluids.
- Air resistance is easy to show by throwing around bits of paper of various sizes, some scrunched, some not.
- When discussing terminal velocity, point out that this depends on the shape, or aerodynamics, of the object falling. A skydiver can adjust his shape and change speeds. Also point out that with the parachute opens, there is still a terminal velocity but this is much less than the one without the parachute opened.

Support

- Allow the students to use an experiment template with clear instructions and a results table during the practical task. They then concentrate on reaching a conclusion and explain it in terms of the forces acting on the parachute.

Extend

- Ask the students about objects falling on other planets and moons. Show them footage of a coin experiment on the Moon; does it fall faster than on the Earth? Ask the students to describe the motion in detail.

Plenaries

Top speed – Show the students a list of top speeds for cars along with some other information such as engine power and a photograph. They can discuss why the cars have a maximum speed [there is a limit to the size of the force the engine can produce to overcome air resistance]. They should also realise that doubling the engine power does not double the terminal velocity [top speed]. *(5 minutes)*

Falling forces – The students should draw a comic strip with stick figures showing the forces at various stages of a parachute jump. This should summarise the concepts and demonstrate the changing size of the forces. You can support students by providing the images in the correct order and label them. Extend students by asking them to draw the force arrows to scale (they should have some appreciation of their own weight). *(10 minutes)*

Practical support

Investigating falling

This investigation can be trickier than it sounds, mainly because many objects don't fall straight down. Parachutes are particularly tricky as they take some time to unfurl, so you might want to miss them out if you don't have a suitable location.

Parachutes

For each group (parachutes): small mass (20 g), string or cotton, scissors, approximately 15 cm by 15 cm square of cloth.
Give the students a few minutes to make a parachute. The higher the parachutes are dropped from, the more effective they are, so find somewhere with sufficient height; a wide stairwell can be good if proper supervision can be arranged. It is just possible to notice the effect if you drop objects when standing on the desk, but great care must be taken. (This relates to 'How Science Works': designing investigations.) It would be safer to pick one responsible student to do this rather than the whole class.

Other objects

For each group: paper and a paper clip to make spinners or small paper cones, bun cases (or muffin cases).

The students drop the objects from a fixed height as with the parachutes; this does not need to be as high. The results will vary quite a bit as there will be timing errors and some variation due to draughts, so use the opportunity to discuss the importance of repeating and finding an average value. You could also use this as an open-ended planning exercise.

Feather and coin

You can demonstrate the effect of air resistance on falling objects with this traditional demonstration.

Equipment and materials required

Vacuum pump, sturdy acrylic tube containing a feather and metal coin, sealed and connected to the pump.

Details

With air in the tube you should be able to show that the coin falls faster than the feather as students would expect. Remove as much air as possible and the two objects fall at the same rate.

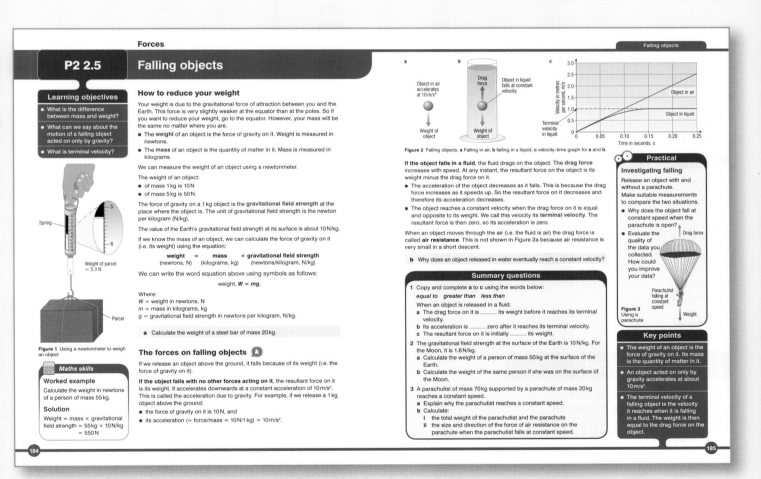

Figure 2 Falling objects. a Falling in air, b falling in a liquid, c velocity–time graph for a and b.

Answers to in-text questions

a 200 N

b The drag force on it increases (as its velocity increases) until it is equal and opposite to its weight. The resultant force on it is then zero and its acceleration is zero.

Summary answers

1 a less than   b equal to   c equal to
2 a 500 N   b 80 N
3 a As the parachutist falls, the drag force increases, so the resultant force decreases. The resultant force is zero when the drag force becomes equal and opposite to the weight of the parachutist and the parachute. The speed is then constant.
  b i 900 N   ii 900 N upwards

P2 2.6

Stretching and squashing

Learning objectives

Students should learn:

- that the extension of an object is the change in length due to a force being applied
- the extension of a spring is proportional to the force applied to it up to the spring's limit of proportionality
- the spring constant is the force per unit extension needed to extend the spring.

Learning outcomes

Most students should be able to:

- describe how a spring extends in terms of the force acting on it and 'Hooke's law'
- calculate the force required to extend a spring of known spring constant.

Some students should also be able to:

- use the spring constant and load to calculate the extension of a spring.

Answers to in-text questions

a An overloaded plastic shopping bag usually gives way at the handles first.

b 2.5 N

Support

- Provide a clear results table demonstrating how to calculate the extension of the objects for the experiment. This will let the students concentrate on the plotting and analysis of the graph.

Extend

- Challenge the students to investigate the stretching of elastic as described in 'Practical support'. They should calculate the cross-sectional area and see if it is related to the extension. After this they can look into the reasons why materials stretch and return to their original shape by considering the forces between the particles on the material.

Specification link-up: Physics P2.1

- A force acting on an object may cause a change in shape of the object. [P2.1.5 a)]
- A force applied to an elastic object such as a spring will result in the object stretching and storing elastic potential energy. [P2.1.5 b)]
- For an object that is able to recover its original shape, elastic potential energy is stored in the object when work is done on the object to change its shape. [P2.1.5 c)]
- The extension of an elastic object is directly proportional to the force applied, provided that the limit of proportionality is not exceeded:
  $F = k \times e$ [P2.1.5 d)]

Controlled Assessment: AS4.5 Analyse and interpret primary and secondary data. [AS4.5.3 a)]

Lesson structure

Starters

Distortion – Get the students to list the basic things that forces can do (cause acceleration, change the shape of the object). They can draw diagrams showing forces acting on objects that cause these things to happen. Concentrate on the forces in the diagrams that cause objects to compress or stretch, and use these to discuss if these changes are permanent or can be reversed. You can then show the behaviour of elastic material compared to the behaviour of material that is not elastic (e.g. plastic). (5 minutes)

In proportion – In this lesson the students will be finding a relationship that is proportional, so start the lesson by asking the students to compare some graphs and the relationship between them. Use their descriptions to come up with the idea of proportionality. This can be quite difficult for some students, so support them with a simple graph such as one showing the amount of money earned compared to hours worked. They should be able to see the relationship that if paid at an hourly rate then the money you earn is proportional to the length of time you work. Extend students by discussing the gradient of graphs and what it means in particular examples. (10 minutes)

Main

- Demonstrate elastic behaviour and the property of returning to its original dimensions. You can show other objects that return to their original shapes and explain that the term 'elastic' in science has a specific meaning. Check that the students also understand the term 'deforming'.

- You can now demonstrate the extension of a spring and show the students how to make measurements. Take time to explain the problems with measuring the length (where do you measure from and to) and show the basic process. The students can then try out the experiment and record the results clearly including the calculation of extension as shown in the Student Book. For some students, you might like to try the elastic band version of the experiment as described in the 'Practical support'. The term 'directly proportional' can be confusing to the students; explain what it means using a graph. (How Science Works: relationships between variables.) You could also use this as a planning exercise.

- Now link back to the idea of elastic energy and the transfers involved when loading and unloading the spring.

- The 'Hooke's law' definition is very important; the trickiest part is the idea of the limit of proportionality. If some of your students have overloaded the spring, you can show this point on graphs of their data. If not, then you can overload the spring yourself and show this proportionality limit or the elastic limit.

- The spring constant can be explained by showing the students a range of springs, some stiffer than others.

- Finally, the students can investigate the energy stored by testing out some catapults as described in the 'Practical support' section.

Plenaries

Graphical analysis – Give the students a graph showing the extension of different springs and ask them to describe the differences. They should look at the limit of proportionality and the spring constants. To extend students and check their graph plotting skills, you could just provide the raw data and ask the students to plot the graphs. Expect all of the students to use the correct terms in their descriptions. (5 minutes)

Cushions – The students can design basic impact protection systems using springs and other elastic materials. These could be for vehicles or personal protection. You can then demonstrate the effects springs can have using dynamics trolleys. *(10 minutes)*

Practical support

Stretch tests

This investigation can be used to verify Hooke's law for a spring or to look at how other materials extend.

Equipment and materials required

For each group: set of masses and holder (50 g), retort stand, clamp, spring, rulers (you will likely need 30 cm, 50 cm and 1 m), G-clamp (to hold the retort stand on the bench if needed).

Details

The students could plan their investigation after setting up the equipment as shown in Figure 1 from the Student Book. They need to measure the initial length of the spring and record this. They can then load the spring by placing 50 g masses on it and record the new length leading to the extension. The results should indicate the relationship for Hooke's law.

You can extend the practical by investigating the stretching of elastic. Elastic bands are fine to use but you should try fishing pole elastic. You can easily get this from a fishing supplier. It comes in a range of diameters (each of a different colour) so you can actually investigate the relationship between cross-sectional area and the way the elastic stretches. Other materials such as strips of plastic can also be investigated.

Catapult

The students can build catapults to investigate the energy that can be stored in them.

Equipment and materials required

Elastic bands (or fishing pole elastic), wooden stakes, rulers and tape measure, small projectiles.

Details

Students should construct a simple catapult from a piece of elastic (bands or similar) and the wooden stakes. They can then stretch the elastic by measured distances and fire projectile to find the distance the projectile travels. This leads to a discussion about the amount of energy stored in the bands and how it is transferred into kinetic energy as the band contracts. You can then try different thicknesses of bands to see if more energy is stored when they are stretched by the same length.

Safety: Ensure students behave responsibly and do not stand in firing line of the projectiles.

Forces

P2 2.6 Stretching and squashing

Learning objectives

- How do we measure the extension of an object when it is stretched?
- How does the extension of a spring vary with the force applied to it?
- What is the spring constant of a spring?

Did you know ...?

Rubber and other soft materials such as flowers dipped in liquid nitrogen become as brittle as glass. Such frozen materials shatter when struck with a hammer or explode when hit with a projectile.

Figure 2 A flower dipped in nitrogen and then smashed

Squash players know that hitting a squash ball changes the ball's shape briefly. A squash ball is **elastic** because it regains its original shape. A rubber band is also elastic as it regains its original length after it is stretched and then released. Rubber is an example of an elastic material.

An elastic object regains its original shape when the forces deforming it are removed.

Practical

Stretch tests

We can investigate how easily a material stretches by hanging weights from it, as shown in Figure 1.

- The strip of material to be tested is clamped at its upper end. A weight hanger is attached to the material to keep it straight.
- The length of the strip is measured using a metre ruler. This is its original length.
- The weight hung from the material is increased by adding weights one at a time. The strip stretches each time more weight is hung from it.
- The length of the strip is measured each time a weight is added. The total weight added and the total length of the strip are recorded in a table.

Figure 1 Investigating stretching

The increase of length from the original is called the **extension**. This is calculated each time a weight is added and recorded, as shown in Table 1.

The extension of the strip of material at any stage = its length at the stage – its original length

The measurements may be plotted on a graph of extension on the vertical axis against weight on the horizontal axis. Figure 3 shows the results for strips of different materials and a steel spring plotted on the same axes.

- The steel spring gives a straight line through the origin. This shows that the extension of the steel spring is **directly proportional** to the weight hung on it. For example, doubling the weight from 2.0 N to 4.0 N doubles the extension of the spring.
- The rubber band does not give a straight line. When the weight on the rubber band is doubled from 2.0 N to 4.0 N, the extension more than doubles.
- The polythene strip does not give a straight line either. As the weight is increased from zero, the polythene strip stretches very little at first then it 'gives' and stretches easily.

a Which part of a plastic shopping bag 'gives' if you overload the bag?

Table 1 Weight versus length measurements for a rubber strip

Weight (N)	Length (mm)	Extension (mm)
0	120	0
1.0	152	32
2.0	190	70
3.0	250	
4.0		

Elastic energy

When an elastic object is stretched, elastic potential energy is stored in the object. This is because work is done on the object by the stretching force.

When the stretching force is removed, the elastic energy stored in the object is released. Some of this energy may be transferred into kinetic energy of the object or may make its atoms vibrate more so it becomes warmer.

Hooke's law

In the tests above, the extension of a steel spring is directly proportional to the force applied to it. We can use the graph to predict what the extension would be for any given force. But if the force is too large, the spring stretches more than predicted. This is because the spring has been stretched beyond its **limit of proportionality**.

The extension of a spring is directly proportional to the force applied, provided its limit of proportionality is not exceeded.

The above statement is known as Hooke's law. If the extension of any stretched object or material is directly proportional to the stretching force, we say it obeys Hooke's law.

1 The lines on the graph in Figure 3 show that rubber and polythene have a low limit of proportionality. Beyond this limit, they do not obey Hooke's law. A steel spring has a much higher limit of proportionality.

2 Hooke's law may be written as an equation:

Force applied = **spring constant** × **extension**
(in newtons, N) (in newtons per metre, N/m) (in metres, m)

The **spring constant** is equal to the force per unit extension needed to extend the spring, assuming its limit of proportionality is not reached. The stiffer a spring is, the greater its spring constant is.

b A spring has a spring constant of 25 N/m. How much force is needed to make the spring extend by 0.10 m?

Figure 3 Extension versus weight for different materials

Maths skills

We can write the word equation for Hooke's law using symbols as follows:

$$F = k \times e,$$

Where:

F = force in newtons, N
k = the spring constant in newtons per metre, N/m
e = extension in metres, m.

Summary questions

1 Copy and complete **a** to **c** using the words below.

elastic limit extension length

a When a steel spring is stretched, its .... is increased.
b When a strip of polythene is stretched beyond its .... , its length is permanently increased.
c When rubber is stretched and unstretched, its .... afterwards is zero.

2 What is meant by:
a the limit of proportionality of a spring?
b the spring constant of a spring?

3 **a** In Figure 3, when the weight is 4.0 N, what is the extension of:
   i the spring **ii** the rubber band **iii** the polythene strip?
b **i** What is the extension of the spring when the weight is 3.0 N?
   ii Calculate the spring constant of the spring.

Key points

- The extension is the difference between the length of the spring and its original length.
- The extension of a spring is directly proportional to the force applied to it, provided the limit of proportionality is not exceeded.
- The spring constant of a spring is the force per unit extension needed to stretch it.

Summary answers

1 **a** length
b elastic limit
c extension

2 **a** The limit of proportionality of a spring is the point at which the extension is no longer directly proportional to the force applied when the spring is stretched.

b The spring constant of a spring is the force per unit extension needed to stretch the spring, assuming its limit of proportionality is not exceeded.

3 **a** **i** 80 mm **ii** 52 mm **iii** 12 mm
b **i** 60 mm **ii** 0.05 N/mm

P2 2.7
Force and speed issues

Learning objectives

Students should learn:

- that fuel use can be reduced by a range of measures including reducing average speed
- that an average speed camera calculates the average speed of a vehicle using timing and distance information
- how to judge the effectiveness of anti-skid surfaces.

Learning outcomes

Most students should be able to:

- discuss a range of speed and travel-related issues linking their discussions to scientific knowledge and understanding.

Answers to in-text questions

a The engine force is greater than the air resistance.

b Students' discussion.

Support

- Provide some templates or fact sheets for all of the debates and discussions. Assign individual research roles to the students and give them time to prepare their arguments.

Extend

- Students could find out how much a human life is worth in monetary terms. Risk assessors look into various safety measures and decide if the cost is worth the benefit. Billions of pounds are spent on safety features every year; however, many billions more could be spent but are not because the benefits are not significant enough. It should be possible for the students to find out information about this idea and to see if all industries put the same value on a single life.

AQA Specification link-up: Physics P2.1

- The greater the speed of a vehicle the greater the braking force needed to stop it in a certain distance. [P2.1.3 b)]
- The stopping distance of a vehicle is the sum of the distance the vehicle travels during the driver's reaction time (thinking distance) and the distance it travels under the braking force (braking distance). [P2.1.3 c)]
- When the brakes of a vehicle are applied, work done by the friction force between the brakes and the wheel reduces the kinetic energy of the vehicle and the temperature of the brakes increase. [P2.1.3 e)]
- A vehicle's braking distance can be affected by adverse road and weather conditions and poor condition of the vehicle. [P2.1.3 f)]
- Evaluate the effects of alcohol and drugs on stopping distances. [P2.1]
- Evaluate how the shape and power of a vehicle can be altered to increase the vehicle's top speed. [P2.1]

Lesson structure

Starters

The Tufty Club – Show a few road safety films, these can be current ones and a few historical examples (Green cross code, Clunk-click, Tufty, and so on). Discuss how some of these advertisements have changed over time to make them appeal to each new generation. Have they become too scary? *(5 minutes)*

Transport survey – The students survey themselves to try to find out the total number of kilometres they travel by foot, car, bus and so on during a week. To support students, you should provide a worksheet for this so that the calculations are relatively simple. You could also provide them with some example data to use instead. Students can be extended further by asking them to find the total distances travelled and even average distances per student per year. You can then discuss the results and see if the students are willing to make changes to their travel arrangements. *(10 minutes)*

Main

- This lesson is based around a range of speed-related issues and leads to discussions or debates between the students. You can choose to focus on one or two of the issues or go through them all. You can assign different discussion topics to different groups.

- Students could test different shapes of deflectors, including a V-shaped deflector with the 'V' horizontal then vertical, and a curved deflector with sloped sides. A curved deflector fitted to the lorry trailer is sometimes referred to as a 'nose cone' deflector. About half the fuel consumption of a fast-moving HGV is used to overcome air resistance. Friction and tyre resistance (referred to as 'rolling resistance') accounts for the other half. Average fuel usage for a lorry in the United Kingdom is about 3 litres per kilometre. A 20% reduction in the force of air resistance would therefore reduce fuel consumption by about 0.3 litres per kilometre. Measurements by transport engineers have shown that a wind deflector like the one shown in P2 2.7 could reduce fuel usage by about 0.3 litres per kilometre and a nose cone deflector could reduce fuel usage by about 0.5 litres per kilometre. Students could be asked to use the current price of diesel to work out the annual saving of a wind deflector on a lorry that travels 100 000 km per year – a very significant figure!

- If you are discussing speed limits and choose not to use the Starter, you can look at some safety footage during the lesson. With some extra time, you can actually record radio or even TV adverts.

- Speed cameras are meant to save lives but some people regard them as revenue sources. Discuss the statistics but include some recent revenue information to present the other side of the argument. You should be able to find recent data using the internet.

- The students can discuss anti-skid surfaces. They can request a new surface to be laid outside the school in a letter to the council. Any letter about anti-skid surfaces should contain the scientific arguments about how the material works and economic arguments about how it will save money in the long run. You might also want to discuss other traffic-calming measures such as speed bumps.

Plenaries

Safety signage – You could use a slideshow of the symbols drivers are meant to recognise and see how many of them the students know. An automatic slideshow can be set up showing the symbols for a few seconds each and you could see which student identifies the most. *(5 minutes)*

Positive solutions – The students have looked at a range of issues and now should make firm decisions on them. Set up a vote on any issue you have discussed. To support students, you may have to provide a range of options if the students have difficulty selecting items to vote on. To extend students further, you may want to ask them to produce more formal recommendations about what action to take instead of a simple yes or no vote. *(10 minutes)*

Did you know … ?

Columbus's journey took 43 days and so his effective velocity was around 6.7 km/h. This isn't fast, but he did not go in a straight line. The Apollo 11 crew travelled at an average speed of nearly 4000 km/h. Accelerating at 2 m/s² for a year is not very realistic and a huge amount of fuel would be required. As an alternative, a 'light sail' could give accelerations of 0.5 mm/s² which could get you to Pluto in around 5 years.

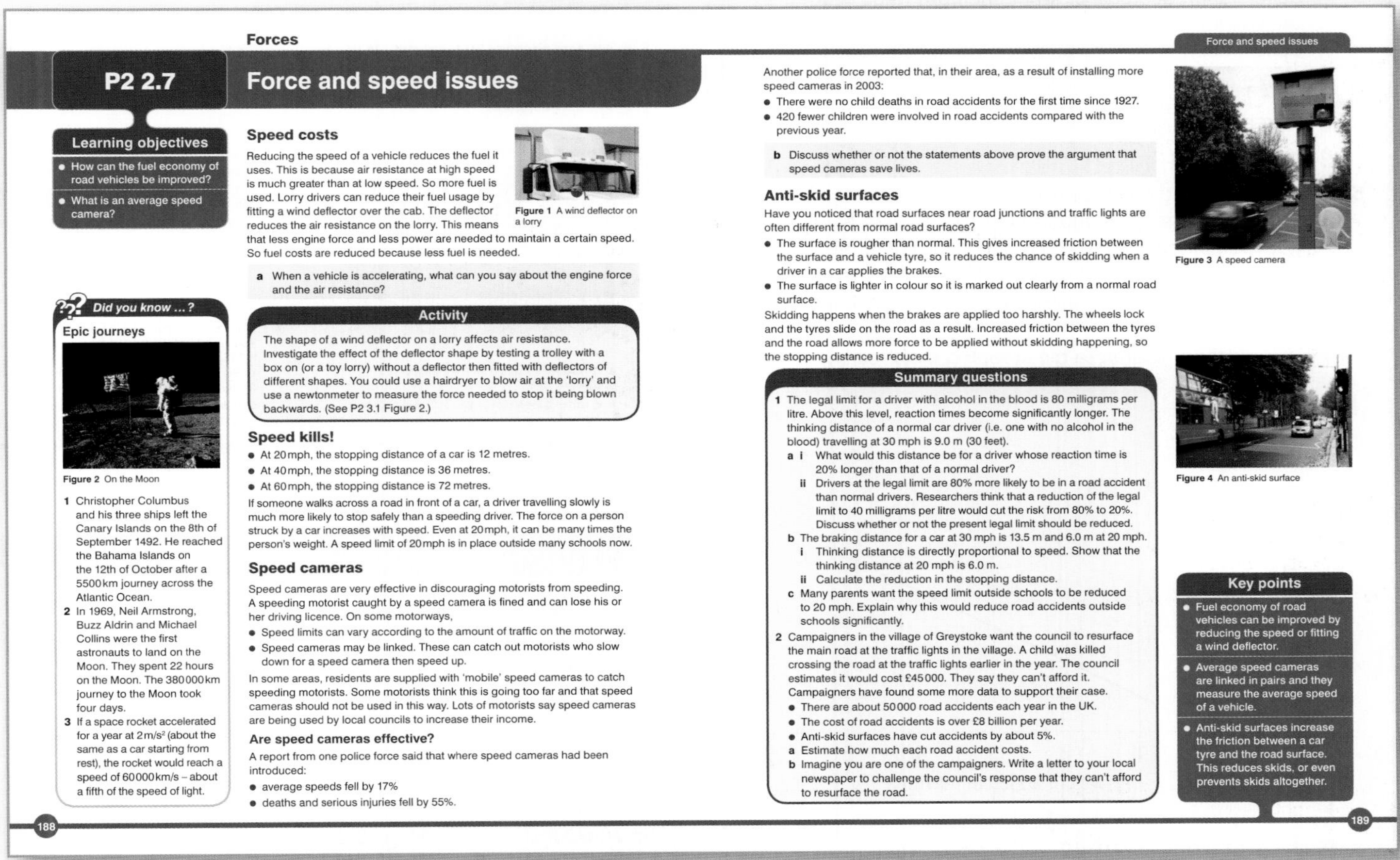

Forces

Force and speed issues

P2 2.7 Force and speed issues

Learning objectives

- How can the fuel economy of road vehicles be improved?
- What is an average speed camera?

Did you know … ?

Epic journeys

Figure 2 On the Moon

1 Christopher Columbus and his three ships left the Canary Islands on the 8th of September 1492. He reached the Bahama Islands on the 12th of October after a 5500 km journey across the Atlantic Ocean.
2 In 1969, Neil Armstrong, Buzz Aldrin and Michael Collins were the first astronauts to land on the Moon. They spent 22 hours on the Moon. The 380 000 km journey to the Moon took four days.
3 If a space rocket accelerated for a year at 2 m/s² (about the same as a car starting from rest), the rocket would reach a speed of 60 000 km/s – about a fifth of the speed of light.

Speed costs

Reducing the speed of a vehicle reduces the fuel it uses. This is because air resistance at high speed is much greater than at low speed. So more fuel is used. Lorry drivers can reduce their fuel usage by fitting a wind deflector over the cab. The deflector reduces the air resistance on the lorry. This means that less engine force and less power are needed to maintain a certain speed. So fuel costs are reduced because less fuel is needed.

Figure 1 A wind deflector on a lorry

a When a vehicle is accelerating, what can you say about the engine force and the air resistance?

Activity

The shape of a wind deflector on a lorry affects air resistance. Investigate the effect of the deflector shape by testing a trolley with a box on (or a toy lorry) without a deflector then fitted with deflectors of different shapes. You could use a hairdryer to blow air at the 'lorry' and use a newtonmeter to measure the force needed to stop it being blown backwards. (See P2 3.1 Figure 2.)

Speed kills!

- At 20 mph, the stopping distance of a car is 12 metres.
- At 40 mph, the stopping distance is 36 metres.
- At 60 mph, the stopping distance is 72 metres.

If someone walks across a road in front of a car, a driver travelling slowly is much more likely to stop safely than a speeding driver. The force on a person struck by a car increases with speed. Even at 20 mph, it can be many times the person's weight. A speed limit of 20 mph is in place outside many schools now.

Speed cameras

Speed cameras are very effective in discouraging motorists from speeding. A speeding motorist caught by a speed camera is fined and can lose his or her driving licence. On some motorways,

- Speed limits can vary according to the amount of traffic on the motorway.
- Speed cameras may be linked. These can catch out motorists who slow down for a speed camera then speed up.

In some areas, residents are supplied with 'mobile' speed cameras to catch speeding motorists. Some motorists think this is going too far and that speed cameras should not be used in this way. Lots of motorists say speed cameras are being used by local councils to increase their income.

Are speed cameras effective?

A report from one police force said that where speed cameras had been introduced:

- average speeds fell by 17%
- deaths and serious injuries fell by 55%.

Another police force reported that, in their area, as a result of installing more speed cameras in 2003:

- There were no child deaths in road accidents for the first time since 1927.
- 420 fewer children were involved in road accidents compared with the previous year.

b Discuss whether or not the statements above prove the argument that speed cameras save lives.

Anti-skid surfaces

Have you noticed that road surfaces near road junctions and traffic lights are often different from normal road surfaces?

- The surface is rougher than normal. This gives increased friction between the surface and a vehicle tyre, so it reduces the chance of skidding when a driver in a car applies the brakes.
- The surface is lighter in colour so it is marked out clearly from a normal road surface.

Skidding happens when the brakes are applied too harshly. The wheels lock and the tyres slide on the road as a result. Increased friction between the tyres and the road allows more force to be applied without skidding happening, so the stopping distance is reduced.

Figure 3 A speed camera

Figure 4 An anti-skid surface

Summary questions

1 The legal limit for a driver with alcohol in the blood is 80 milligrams per litre. Above this level, reaction times become significantly longer. The thinking distance of a normal car driver (i.e. one with no alcohol in the blood) travelling at 30 mph is 9.0 m (30 feet).
   a i What would this distance be for a driver whose reaction time is 20% longer than that of a normal driver?
     ii Drivers at the legal limit are 80% more likely to be in a road accident than normal drivers. Researchers think that a reduction of the legal limit to 40 milligrams per litre would cut the risk from 80% to 20%. Discuss whether or not the present legal limit should be reduced.
   b The braking distance for a car at 30 mph is 13.5 m and 6.0 m at 20 mph.
     i Thinking distance is directly proportional to speed. Show that the thinking distance at 20 mph is 6.0 m.
     ii Calculate the reduction in the stopping distance.
   c Many parents want the speed limit outside schools to be reduced to 20 mph. Explain why this would reduce road accidents outside schools significantly.
2 Campaigners in the village of Greystoke want the council to resurface the main road at the traffic lights in the village. A child was killed crossing the road at the traffic lights earlier in the year. The council estimates it would cost £45 000. They say they can't afford it. Campaigners have found some more data to support their case.
   - There are about 50 000 road accidents each year in the UK.
   - The cost of road accidents is over £8 billion per year.
   - Anti-skid surfaces have cut accidents by about 5%.
   a Estimate how much each road accident costs.
   b Imagine you are one of the campaigners. Write a letter to your local newspaper to challenge the council's response that they can't afford to resurface the road.

Key points

- Fuel economy of road vehicles can be improved by reducing the speed or fitting a wind deflector.
- Average speed cameras are linked in pairs and they measure the average speed of a vehicle.
- Anti-skid surfaces increase the friction between a car tyre and the road surface. This reduces skids, or even prevents skids altogether.

188

189

Summary answers

1 a i 10.8 m (= 9.0 m + 20% of 9.0 m)
   ii The research evidence needs to be confirmed by other researchers. If confirmed, many people would argue for a reduction on the grounds that a risk that is 80% greater than 'normal' would be unacceptable in many other situations where the public are involved. In addition, if the limit were to be reduced, the number of other road casualties caused by drivers would be reduced.
  b i Thinking distance = speed × reaction time. A reduction of speed from 30 mph to 20 mph would therefore reduce the normal thinking distance of 9 m at 30 mph by a third which is a reduction of 3.0 metres.

     ii In addition to the 3.0 m reduction of thinking distance, the braking distance would be reduced by 7.5 m. Therefore the stopping distance would be reduced by 10.5 m (from 22.5 m to 12 metres).
   c Anyone stepping in front of a car within its stopping distance would be hit by the car. So a reduction of more than 10 metres in the stopping distance would greatly reduce the number of road accidents to children and adults crossing a road or stepping into a road unexpectedly.

2 a £160 000
  b Students' letters

Summary answers

1 a i in the opposite direction to
  ii in the same direction as
 b i Away from the door
  ii Away from the door

2 a i 1.6 N/kg
  ii 1000 N
 b i 8 m/s², 640 N
  ii −0.4 m/s², 28 000 N

3 a The acceleration of X is constant and equal to 10 m/s².
 b The object accelerates at first. The drag force on it increases with speed, so the resultant force on it and its acceleration decreases. When the drag force is equal to the weight of the object, the resultant force is zero. The acceleration is then zero, so the velocity is constant.

4 a decreasing
 b increasing
 c terminal

5 a i The braking distance is increased because friction between the tyres and the road is reduced by the driver, otherwise the car would skid. Therefore the stopping distance is increased.
  ii The reaction time is increased, so the distance travelled in this time (the thinking distance) is increased. Therefore the stopping distance is increased.
 b i 12.6 m
  ii 3.4 m

6 a 79, 121, 160, 201, 239
 b

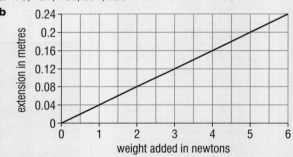

 c 280 mm
 d i 0.025 N/mm or 25 N/m
  ii 3.5 N

7 a i 225 N
  ii 450 N
 b The cyclist exerts a constant force driving her forward. Crouching reduces the force of air resistance (the drag force). The drag force increases with speed. So the cyclist can get to a higher speed before the drag force becomes equal to the driving force.

Summary questions

1 A student is pushing a box across a rough floor. Friction acts between the box and the floor.
 a Copy and complete sentences **i** and **ii** using the words below:

in the same direction as   in the opposite direction to

   i The force of friction of the box on the floor is .... the force of friction of the floor on the box.
   ii The force of the student on the box is .... the force of friction of the box on the floor.
 b The student is pushing the box towards a door. Which direction, towards the door or away from the door, is:
   i the force of the box on the student?
   ii the force of friction of the student on the floor?

2 a The weight of an object of mass 100 kg on the Moon is 160 N.
   i Calculate the gravitational field strength on the Moon.
   ii Calculate the weight of the object on the Earth's surface.
     The gravitational field strength near the Earth's surface is 10 N/kg.
 b Calculate the acceleration and the resultant force in each of the following situations.
   i A sprinter of mass 80 kg accelerates from rest to a speed of 9.6 m/s in 1.2 s.
   ii A train of mass 70 000 kg decelerates from a velocity of 16 m/s to a standstill in 40 s without change of direction.

3 The figure shows the velocity–time graphs for a metal object X dropped in air and a similar object Y dropped in a tank of water.

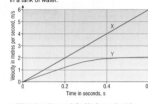

 a What does the graph for X tell you about its acceleration?
 b In terms of the forces acting on Y, explain why it reached a constant velocity.

4 Copy and complete **a** to **c** using the words below:
decreasing   increasing   terminal
 a When the resultant force on an object is not zero a .... acts in the opposite direction to the object's veloci[ty] its velocity is ....
 b When an object falls in a fluid and the drag force [is] is less than its weight, its velocity is ....
 c When the drag force on an object falling in a fluid is equal to its weight, the object moves at its .... velocity.

5 a Explain why the stopping distance of a car is increased if:
   i the road is wet instead of dry
   ii the driver is tired instead of alert.
 b A driver travelling at 18 m/s takes 0.7 s to react whe[n] a dog walks into the road 40 m ahead. The braking distance for the car at this speed is 24 m.
   i Calculate the distance travelled by the car in th[e] time it takes the driver to react.
   ii How far in front of the dog does the car stop?

6 In a Hooke's law test on a spring, the following result[s] were obtained.

Weight (N)	Length (mm)	Extension (m[m])
0	245	0
1.0	285	40
2.0	324	
3.0	366	
4.0	405	
5.0	446	
6.0	484	

 a Copy and complete the third column of the table.
 b Plot a graph of the extension on the vertical axis against the weight on the horizontal axis.
 c If a weight of 7.0 N is suspended on the spring, wh[at] would be the extension of the spring?
 d i Calculate the spring constant of the spring.
  ii An object suspended on the spring gives an extension of 140 mm. Calculate the weight of th[e] object.

7 a A racing cyclist accelerates at 5 m/s² when she sta[rts] from rest. The total mass of the cyclist and her bic[ycle] is 45 kg. Calculate:
   i the resultant force that produces this accelerat[ion]
   ii the total weight of the cyclist and the bicycle.
 b Explain why she can reach a higher speed by crouching than by staying upright.

Kerboodle resources

Resources available for this chapter on Kerboodle are:
- Chapter map: Forces
- Support: Resultant forces (P2 2.2)
- Extension: Making sense of resultant forces (P2 2.2)
- Bump up your grade: What is the resultant force? (P2 2.2)
- Maths skills: Force, mass and acceleration (P2 2.3)
- Practical: Does the force on a trolley affect acceleration? (P2 2.3)
- WebQuest: Safe driving (P2 2.4 & 2.7)
- Extension: Finding the stopping distance of a vehicle (P2 2.4)
- How Science Works: Reaction time challenge (P2 2.4)
- Support: Stop that bike! (P2 2.4)
- Animation: Skydiver (P2 2.5)
- Support: Let's hope that chute opens! (P2 2.5)
- Extension: Weight and mass – planets apart! (P2 2.5)
- Practical: Terminal velocity of a ball in a liquid (P2 2.5)
- Data handling skills: Investigating Hooke's law using springs (P2 2.6)
- Support: Stretching your grades! (P2 2.6)
- Practical: Does a stretched spring obey Hooke's law? (P2 2.6)
- Interactive activity: Stopping distances and motive forces
- Revision podcast: Forces
- Test yourself: Forces
- On your marks: Forces
- Examination-style questions: Forces
- Answers to examination-style questions: Forces

AQA Examination-style questions

a The tractor is pulling a trailer. The force acting on the trailer is labelled A, and the force acting on the tractor is labelled B.

Copy and complete the following sentences using the list of words and phrases below. Each one can be used once, more than once or not at all.

A and B are the same   A is greater than B
B is greater than A

i If the tractor and trailer are accelerating .... (1)
ii If the tractor and trailer are moving at a constant speed .... (1)

b The driving force from the tractor is 12 000 N and the total resistive forces are 10 000 N.
  i Calculate the resultant force. (2)
  ii Calculate the acceleration of the tractor and trailer. Mass of the tractor and trailer = 2300 kg Write down the equation you use. Show clearly how you work out your answer and give the unit. (2)

2 A car is travelling at 30 m/s when the vehicle in front suddenly stops. The car travels 19 m before the driver applies the brake.
  a What is the name given to this distance? (1)
  b Calculate the reaction time of the driver. Write down the equation you use. Show clearly how you work out your answer. (2)
  c The driver applies the brakes and stops 6 seconds later. Calculate the deceleration of the car. Write down the equation you use. Show clearly how you work out your answer. (2)
  d The braking distance is 81 m. What is the total stopping distance in metres? (1)
  e Give two factors that would increase reaction time. (2)

3 The diagram shows the forces acting on a dragster just before it reaches its top speed. The resistive forces are represented by arrow **X**. The driving force is shown by arrow **Y**.

a What is the main type of resistive force acting on the dragster? (1)
b If the driving force remains the same, what will happen to force X?
Give a reason for your answer. (2)
c The dragster slows down by applying its brakes and using a parachute. The velocity–time graph shows the motion of the dragster from a stationary start until it stops.
Explain, in terms of energy changes, the shape of the graph when the brakes are applied. (3)

4 A student carries out an experiment to find if extension is proportional to the force applied for an elastic hair bobble. She measures the extension with one and then two 0.1 kg masses. She holds the bobble with one hand and the ruler in the other.

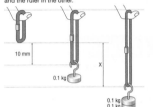

10 mm

X

0.1 kg

0.1 kg
0.1 kg

a If the extension is proportional to the force applied, what value should the student expect to obtain for distance X? (1)
b Give the name of the form of energy stored in the stretched hair bobble. (1)
c Calculate the weight of one of the 0.1 kg masses. (g = 10 N/kg) (2)
d *In this question you will be assessed on using good English, organising information clearly and using specialist terms where appropriate.*
The student is unable to draw a valid conclusion because she has not carried out the investigation with sufficient precision. Describe the improvements she could make in order to carry out the investigation more precisely and gain sufficient data to draw a valid conclusion. (6)

191

AQA Examination-style answers

1 a i If the tractor and trailer are accelerating **A is greater than B**. *(1 mark)*
  ii If the tractor and trailer are moving at a constant speed **A and B are the same** *(1 mark)*
b i $12\,000 - 10\,000 = 2000\,N$ *(1 mark)*
  ii $a = \dfrac{F}{m} = 2000/2300 = 0.87\,m/s^2$ *(3 marks)*

2 a Thinking distance *(1 mark)*
  b time = distance/speed = 19/30 = 0.63 s *(2 marks)*
  c $-5\,m/s^2$ *(2 marks)*
  d 100 m *(1 mark)*
  e Any two relevant factors, for example, consuming alcohol/drugs/medicine/fatigue/old age/illness *(2 marks)*

3 a Air resistance/drag *(1 mark)*
  b Increase (until it equals the driving force); air resistance increases with speed *(2 marks)*
  c Work done by friction force/friction between the brakes and the wheel;
  reduces kinetic energy; temperature of brakes increases and the dragster slows to a stop *(3 marks)*

4 a 20 mm *(1 mark)*
  b elastic potential energy *(1 mark)*
  c $W = m \times g = 0.1 \times 10 = 1\,N$ *(2 marks)*
  d Marks awarded for this answer will be determined by the Quality of Written Communication (QWC) as well as the standard of the scientific response.

There is a clear, balanced and detailed description of the improvements she could make in order to carry out the investigation more precisely and gain sufficient data to draw a valid conclusion. The answer shows almost faultless spelling, punctuation and grammar. It is coherent and in an organised, logical sequence. It contains a range of appropriate or relevant specialist terms used accurately. *(5–6 marks)*

There is a description of a range of the ways in which improvements could be made in order to carry out the investigation more precisely and gain sufficient data to draw a valid conclusion. There are some errors in spelling, punctuation and grammar. The answer has some structure and organisation. The use of specialist terms has been attempted, but not always accurately. *(3–4 marks)*

There is a brief description of at least two ways in which improvements could be made in order to carry out the investigation more precisely and gain sufficient data to draw a valid conclusion, which has little clarity and detail. The spelling, punctuation and grammar are very weak. The answer is poorly organised with almost no specialist terms and/or their use demonstrating a general lack of understanding of their meaning. *(1–2 marks)*

No relevant content. *(0 marks)*

Examples of physics points made in the response:
- use a boss/clamp/stand
- ruler in fixed position
- method to reduce parallax, e.g. use a set square
- repeats measurements
- use a larger range of masses
- and smaller intervals.

AQA Practical suggestions

Practicals	AQA	(k)	📖	⚙
Dropping a penny and a feather in a vacuum and through the air to show the effect of air resistance.	✓		✓	
Plan and carry out an investigation into 'Hooke's law'.	✓	✓	✓	
Catapult practicals to compare stored energy.	✓		✓	
Measurement of acceleration of trolleys using known forces and masses.	✓	✓	✓	✓
Timing objects falling through a liquid, e.g. wallpaper paste or glycerine, using light gates or stop clocks.	✓	✓		
Plan and carry out an investigation to measure the effects of air resistance on parachutes, paper spinners, cones or bun cases.	✓		✓	
Measuring reaction time with and without distractions, e.g. iPod 'off' and then 'on'.	✓	✓	✓	✓

P2 3.1

Energy and work

Learning objectives

Students should learn:

- that the term 'work' means the amount of energy transferred to an object
- that when a force is used to move an object, work is done against friction and this is transferred as heat.

Learning outcomes

Most students should be able to:

- state that the 'work done' is the amount of energy transferred
- calculate the work done when a force moves an object through a distance.

Some students should also be able to:

- perform calculations including the rearrangement of the work done equation.

Answers to in-text questions

a Energy transferred to the surroundings by heating and as sound.

b 80 000 J

c Friction between the box and the surface is greater with the rubber bands in place. More force is needed to overcome the frictional force.

Support

- Before you start the topic, refresh the students' knowledge by providing a partially completed mind map that they can complete. This should cover the key points they would have learned in the earlier topic.

Extend

- You could extend students by asking them to look into the more formal definition of work done. This is 'that the work done is equal to the force required multiplied by the distance travelled **in the direction** of the force'. This can lead to analysis of an object moving up slopes, where the direction travelled and direction of the force are not the same.

AQA Specification link-up: Physics P2.2

- When a force causes an object to move through a distance work is done. *[P2.2.1 a)]*
- Work done, force and distance are related by the equation:
    $W = F \times d$. *[P2.2.1 b)]*
- Energy is transferred when work is done. *[P2.2.1 c)]*
- Work done against frictional forces. *[P2.2.1 d)]*
    Controlled Assessment: AS4.3 Collect primary and secondary data. *[AS4.3.2 c) d) e)]*

Lesson structure

Starters

Hard at work – Give the students a list of activities involving the use of forces and ask them to put them in order of the amount of energy transferred. They should identify that the energy transferred depends on the size of the force used and the distance moved. A simple example would be pushing a block across a desk by 1 m and then 2 m, followed by pushing a much larger block 1 m and then 3 m. *(5 minutes)*

Energy transfer – The students should draw energy transfer diagrams for a range of machines and identify useful energy output. They should reinforce the ideas of describing energy and energy transfer including concepts such as the conservation of energy and amounts of energy wasted through this process. To support students, you can provide partially completed diagrams and word lists of the 'forms' of energy, so that they are using the correct terms. To extend the students, concepts such as efficiency can be revised so that the students can calculate the amounts of wasted energy. *(10 minutes)*

Main

- The term 'work done' has a very particular meaning in physics and the students will have to accept that it does not mean the same as its everyday usage. Two main types of work can be done: work done against a force (as covered in this topic) and work done in heating. The examples when people are holding up a heavy object (but are doing no mechanical work) should be discussed in terms of energy being transferred to heat by the muscles.

- The calculation is relatively straightforward, but check that the students are confident with it and that they remember to use the correct units. Try a few examples with large or small transfers to reinforce the use of kilojoules (or megajoules).

- In the main practical activity, the students should quickly realise the limitations of data collected; it is not easy to measure the amount of useful work done and very difficult to even estimate how much energy is being wasted. If the meter is not horizontal, then the force also acts at an angle to the movement. This gives the opportunity to teach students the 'How Science Works' concepts of resolution, precision and accuracy.

- The heating effect due to friction should be demonstrated in some way, even if it is simple hand rubbing. You may be able to find footage of Formula One cars braking, where the brake discs literally glow red-hot. This can lead to a discussion about how frictional forces can be reduced.

Plenaries

All work – Give the students some scenarios and let them decide if mechanical work is being done. They must explain why work is being done or not. Include scenarios where there is no movement (pushing against a brick wall) and ones where there is movement (pushing a car). Discuss the idea that energy might be being transferred but as there is no movement, there is no effective work done. Is writing in a book doing work? *(5 minutes)*

Demonstrating friction – The students design their own demonstration to show that doing work against friction has a heating effect. This should be aimed at primary school children so should only involve equipment readily available to them. Support can be provided by giving the students some suggested materials and diagrams while extension opportunities can include asking the students to show that it is possible to start a fire with sufficient frictional forces. *(10 minutes)*

Practical support

Doing work

In this task, the students measure the work done in moving an object across a surface.

Equipment and materials required
Range of Newton meters, box or metal block that can be dragged, string, metre rule and some elastic bands.

Details
The task is straightforward; the students simply drag the box with or without elastic bands. A measured distance of a metre is the simplest, and provides an easy calculation. The bands will increase the frictional forces so more work will be done. The quality of the

results will depend on the students moving the object at a steady speed, so that a constant force is used. Check that they can easily read the newtonmeters during the experiment. This experiment should reveal the value of repeat measurements. Remind students that precision can be judged by the range in a set of repeat measurements and that resolution is the smallest detectable change that can be measured by a particular instrument.

The work can be extended by moving an object up slopes; this will link to gravitational potential energy in later lessons.

You might like to link to power, getting the students to measure the time it takes to do the task and sort out the power output, using the equation power = work done divided by time. If the students move the object faster, does the force change?

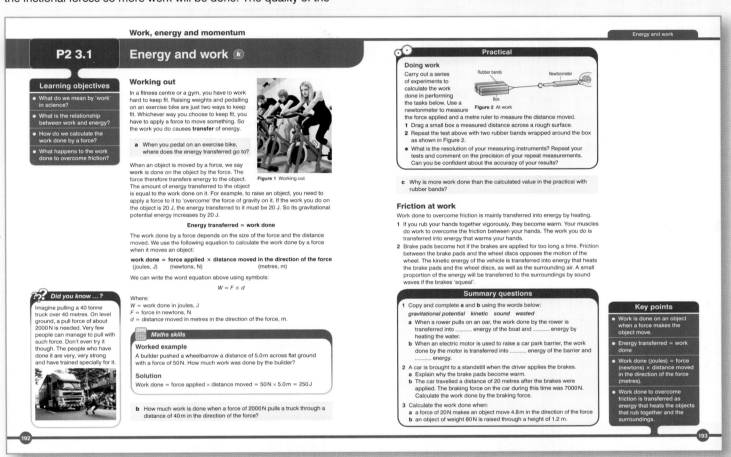

P2 3.1 — Work, energy and momentum

Energy and work (k)

Learning objectives
- What do we mean by 'work' in science?
- What is the relationship between work and energy?
- How do we calculate the work done by a force?
- What happens to the work done to overcome friction?

Working out
In a fitness centre or a gym, you have to work hard to keep fit. Raising weights and pedalling on an exercise bike are just two ways to keep fit. Whichever way you choose to keep fit, you have to apply a force to move something. So the work you do causes **transfer** of energy.

a When you pedal on an exercise bike, where does the energy transferred go to?

When an object is moved by a force, we say **work** is done on the object by the force. The force therefore transfers energy to the object. The amount of energy transferred to the object is equal to the work done on it. For example, to raise an object, you need to apply a force to it to 'overcome' the force of gravity on it. If the work you do on the object is 20 J, the energy transferred to it must be 20 J. So its gravitational potential energy increases by 20 J.

Energy transferred = work done

The work done by a force depends on the size of the force and the distance moved. We use the following equation to calculate the work done by a force when it moves an object:

work done = force applied × distance moved in the direction of the force
(joules, J)   (newtons, N)   (metres, m)

We can write the word equation above using symbols:

$$W = F \times d$$

Where:
W = work done in joules, J
F = force in newtons, N
d = distance moved in metres in the direction of the force, m.

Figure 1 Working out

Did you know ...?
Imagine pulling a 40 tonne truck over 40 metres. On level ground, a pull force of about 2000 N is needed. Very few people can manage to pull with such force. Don't even try it though. The people who have done it are very, very strong and have trained specially for it.

Maths skills

Worked example
A builder pushed a wheelbarrow a distance of 5.0 m across flat ground with a force of 50 N. How much work was done by the builder?

Solution
Work done = force applied × distance moved = 50 N × 5.0 m = 250 J

b How much work is done when a force of 2000 N pulls a truck through a distance of 40 m in the direction of the force?

Practical

Doing work
Carry out a series of experiments to calculate the work done in performing the tasks below. Use a newtonmeter to measure the force applied and a metre ruler to measure the distance moved.
1 Drag a small box a measured distance across a rough surface.
2 Repeat the test above with two rubber bands wrapped around the box as shown in Figure 2.
● What is the resolution of your measuring instruments? Repeat your tests and comment on the precision of your repeat measurements. Can you be confident about the accuracy of your results?

Figure 2 At work — Rubber bands, Box, Newtonmeter

c Why is more work done than the calculated value in the practical with rubber bands?

Friction at work
Work done to overcome friction is mainly transferred into energy by heating.
1 If you rub your hands together vigorously, they become warm. Your muscles do work to overcome the friction between your hands. The work you do is transferred into energy that warms your hands.
2 Brake pads become hot if the brakes are applied for too long a time. Friction between the brake pads and the wheel discs opposes the motion of the wheel. The kinetic energy of the vehicle is transferred into energy that heats the brake pads and the wheel discs, as well as the surrounding air. A small proportion of the energy will be transferred to the surroundings by sound waves if the brakes 'squeal'.

Summary questions
1 Copy and complete **a** and **b** using the words below:
gravitational potential   kinetic   sound   wasted
a When a rower pulls on an oar, the work done by the rower is transferred into .... energy of the boat and .... energy by heating the water.
b When an electric motor is used to raise a car park barrier, the work done by the motor is transferred into .... energy of the barrier and .... energy.
2 A car is brought to a standstill when the driver applies the brakes.
a Explain why the brake pads become warm.
b The car travelled a distance of 20 metres after the brakes were applied. The braking force on the car during this time was 7000 N. Calculate the work done by the braking force.
3 Calculate the work done when:
a a force of 20 N makes an object move 4.8 m in the direction of the force
b an object of weight 80 N is raised through a height of 1.2 m.

Key points
- Work is done on an object when a force makes the object move.
- Energy transferred = work done
- Work done (joules) = force (newtons) × distance moved in the direction of the force (metres).
- Work done to overcome friction is transferred as energy that heats the objects that rub together and the surroundings.

Further teaching suggestions

Work done against friction
- To show that the work done against frictional force causes heating. You can use a bicycle.

Equipment and materials required
A bicycle that will stand upside down, gloves.

Details
Turn the bicycle upside down and get the wheel spinning by turning the pedal by hand. Don't go too fast because you now need to stop the wheel by slowing it down with the palm of your gloved hand against the tyre. Once you

know the right speed to cause a noticeable heating effect but no hand damage, you can get a volunteer to have a go. As an alternative, you could lift the rear wheel and drive it very quickly before applying the brakes gently. Repeat this until the smell of burning rubber is obvious.

Spy plane
- The frictional forces on rapidly moving objects are very high. The SR-71 'Blackbird' spy plane used to leak quite a bit of fuel when on the ground, but when it was at full speed it became hotter and the metal expanded and sealed up the gaps. Ask: 'What colour was the plane and why?'

Summary answers

1 **a** kinetic, wasted   **b** gravitational potential, sound
2 **a** Friction between the brake pads and the wheel discs make the pads and the discs hot because they slide against each other until the car stops.
   b 140 000 J
3 **a** 96 J
   b 96 J

P2 3.2

Gravitational potential energy

Students should learn:

- that the gravitational potential energy of an object depends on its weight and height
- how to calculate gravitational potential energy from the appropriate equation.

Learning outcomes

Most students should be able to:

- state that the gravitational potential energy of an object depends on its weight and height above 'ground'
- calculate changes in gravitational potential energy.

Some students should also be able to:

- perform calculations including the rearrangement of the gravitational potential energy equation.

Support

- There are a couple of calculations in this topic that students might need extra support with. As usual, plenty of examples and templates showing how to lay out the calculations would be of great benefit.

Extend

- Students should consider why we measure changes in gravitational potential energy instead of amounts of gravitational potential energy. This is because of the difficulty in defining a place where the gravitational potential energy would be zero. For most purposes we would consider the ground level to have no gravitational potential but what about when objects fall down mines? The students could look into where the place at which an object would have zero gravitational potential energy actually is.

AQA Specification link-up: Physics P2.2

- Power is the work done or energy transferred in a given time.

$$P = \frac{E}{t} \ [P2.2.1 \ e)]$$

- Gravitational potential energy is the energy that an object has by virtue of its position in a gravitational field.

$$E_p = m \times g \times h \ [P2.2.1 \ f)]$$

Lesson structure

Starters

Lifting work – Remind the students of the idea of work being done by a force when an object moves a distance. Demonstrate lifting things from the floor to a desk and ask them to explain where the energy 'used' has gone. Some should realise that the objects have gained gravitational potential energy. Now ask them to explain what factors affect the amount of energy; they should be able to identify the height and weight. You can move on to ask about what affects the weight (mass and the strength of gravity). *(5 minutes)*

Power recap – The students have studied power in the first section of the course (P1 3.2) and will need to use the equation again here. Ask them to define or explain what power is and then calculate the power of some simple mechanical systems. Students can be supported by calculation frames and the use of straightforward questions while others can be pushed further by asking questions that require rearrangement of the equations and the use of more 'difficult' numbers (kilojoules, megajoules, etc.). *(10 minutes)*

Main

- Start with some form of demonstration of lifting either by you or a video clip of something extraordinary being lifted. This should lead to the idea that energy is required to move the object and link this concept back to the equation for work done from the last lesson. In lifting, work is being done because a force is being used to move an object through a distance. You can identify the distance the object is lifted and then ask about the force that was required. It should be clear that the force is actually the weight of the object. In this way you can lead the students to discover the equation itself using the idea of conservation of energy: the energy you use to lift the object is stored in the object.

- You can now talk about the object moving through heights and the changes in energy that are occurring. Use props, for example, have a set of 1 kg masses (weighing 10 N each), move them up and down to different heights and get the students to explain how much energy is being transferred. Move two or three masses at a time until the simple calculation comes naturally.

- Introduce the symbol E_p (for gravitational potential energy) as quickly as you can, so the students start using it and save time. Let them try a couple of calculations with more difficult numbers to get used to it.

- You can now move on to the second form of the equation (where weight is replaced with mass × gravitational field strength). The idea is just that the weight of an object is the product of the mass and gravitational field strength, so you can replace weight to give this new equation but some students can struggle with this simple substitution. It is worth spending some time with the units here as there are four of them to get to grips with.

- After the maths, the practical task is short but it will give the students something physical to do. You can get some to walk up a flight of stairs if no boxes are suitable.

Plenaries

How high – Finish with a calculation that looks at something big that travels quite high. A jumbo jet is about 400 000 kg with a cruising altitude of 10 700 m. The E_p is 41 986 800 000 J (~42 GJ). All students should be capable of handling larger numbers although they may need support as this figure is larger than most calculators can display in 'normal' notation. *(5 minutes)*

A hard day – The students can estimate the energy they expend by climbing stairs when moving between lessons during a typical day by estimating the height changes and their weight. They can work out how much energy they would need if they were to climb to the top of a tall tower (Burj Khalifa in the United Arab Emirates is 800 m). To support students, provide some suitable estimates of the numbers; they may have a mass of 50 kg giving an approximate weight of 500 N and travel upwards through 15 m each day. This gives a total work done of 7.5 kJ. To extend students, have them consider walking; when a step is taken the centre of gravity of your body rises slightly (you may be able to find a video clip demonstrating this). This means that work is being done during each step. Ask them to estimate the energy transfer for a day. If needed, provide some suitable estimates such as: if they take 5000 steps each day (while their centre of gravity is raised by 5 cm) each step and the person weighs 600 N, this would be 150 kJ. *(10 minutes)*

Practical support

Stepping up

Any tasks preformed should be relatively simple and non-strenuous. Make sure that the students have no medical conditions that could be triggered by the activities.

Equipment and materials required

Scales that measure weight in newtons, objects to step on to. The objects should be robust enough to pose no significant hazards; you might just want to use steps or your PE department may still have a few benches that are appropriate.

Details

The practical should only take a few minutes. Some students may be sensitive about their weight but you could ask them to move objects onto shelves or up some stairs as an alternative task.

Work, energy and momentum

P2 3.2

Gravitational potential energy

Learning objectives

- What does the gravitational potential energy of an object depend on?
- What happens to the gravitational potential energy of an object when it moves up or down?
- How can we calculate the change of gravitational potential energy of an object when it moves up or down?

Maths skills

Worked example

A student of weight 300 N climbs on a platform which is 1.2 m higher than the floor. Calculate the increase of her gravitational potential energy.

Solution

Increase of GPE = 300 N × 1.2 m
 = 360 J

Note: We often use the abbreviation 'GPE' or E_p for gravitational potential energy.

Did you know ... ?

You use energy when you hold an object stationary in your outstretched hand. The biceps muscle of your arm is in a state of contraction. Energy must be supplied to keep the muscles contracted. No work is done on the object because it doesn't move. The energy supplied heats the muscles and is transferred by heating to the surroundings.

Gravitational potential energy transfers

Every time you lift an object up, you do some work. Some of your muscles transfer chemical energy from your muscles into **gravitational potential energy** of the object.

Gravitational potential energy is energy stored in an object because of its position in the Earth's gravitational field.

The force you need to lift an object steadily is equal and opposite to the force of gravity on the object. Therefore, the upward force you need to apply to it is equal to its weight. For example, a force of 80 N is needed to lift a box of weight 80 N.

GPE gain = 2 J
GPE gain = 2 J
GPE gain = 1 J
1 m   1 m   2 m
1 N   1 N   1 N
Figure 1 Using joules

- When an object is moved up, its gravitational potential energy increases. The increase of its gravitational potential energy is equal to the work done on it by the lifting force.
- When an object moves down, its gravitational potential energy decreases. The decrease of its gravitational potential energy is equal to the work done by the force of gravity acting on it.

The work done when an object moves up or down depends on:
1 how far it is moved vertically (its change of height)
2 its weight.

Using the formula $W = F × d$ (work done = force applied × distance moved in the direction of the force), we can therefore say:

the change of its gravitational = its weight × its change of height
potential energy (in joules)   (in newtons)   (in metres)

a Read the 'Did you know?' box. What happens to the energy supplied to the muscles to keep them contracted?

Gravitational potential energy and mass

Astronauts on the Moon can lift objects much more easily than they can on the Earth. This is because, at their surfaces, the gravitational field strength of the Moon is only about a sixth of the Earth's gravitational field strength.

In P2 2.5, 'Falling objects', we saw that the weight of an object in newtons is equal to its mass × the gravitational field strength.

Therefore, when an object is lifted or lowered, because its change of gravitational potential energy is equal to its weight × its change of height:

change of gravitational = mass × gravitational field × change of height
potential energy (in J)   (in kg)   strength (in N/kg)   (in metres)

We can write the word equation on the previous page using symbols:
$$E_p = m × g × h$$
Where:
E_p = change of GPE in joules, J
m = mass in kilograms, kg
g = gravitational field strength in newtons per kilogram, N/kg
h = change in height in metres, m.

Maths skills

Worked example

A 2.0 kg object is raised through a height of 0.4 m. Calculate the gain of gravitational potential energy of the object. The gravitational field strength of the Earth at its surface is 10 N/kg.

Solution

Gain of GPE = mass × gravitational field strength × height gain
 = 2.0 kg × 10 N/kg × 0.4 m
 = 8.0 J

Power and energy

Power is the rate of transfer of energy. If energy E (in joules) is transferred in time t (in seconds):

$$\text{power, } P \text{ (in watts)} = \frac{E}{t}$$

b A weightlifter raises a 20 kg metal bar through a height of 1.5 m.
  i Calculate the gain of gravitational potential energy. The gravitational field strength of the Earth at its surface is 10 N/kg.
  ii The bar is raised by the weightlifter in 0.5 seconds. Calculate the power of the weightlifter.

Summary questions

1 Copy and complete a to c using the words below. Each word can be used more than once.

decreases increases stays the same

a When a ball falls, its gravitational potential energy ....
b When a car travels along a level road, the gravitational potential energy of the car ....
c When a child on a swing moves from one extreme to the opposite extreme, her gravitational potential energy .... then ....

2 A student of weight 450 N steps on a box of height 0.20 m.
a Calculate the gain of gravitational potential energy of the student.
b Calculate the work done by the student if she steps on and off the box 50 times.

3 a A weightlifter raises a steel bar of mass 25 kg through a height of 1.2 m. Calculate the change of gravitational potential energy of the bar. The gravitational field strength at the surface of the Earth is 10 N/kg.
b The weightlifter then drops the bar and it falls vertically to the ground. Assume air resistance is negligible. What is the change of its gravitational potential energy in this fall?

Activity

Stepping up

Measure your mass in kilograms using floor scales.

Step on and off a sturdy box or low platform.

Measure the height of the box.

- Use the formula change of GPE = $m × g × h$ where g = 10 N/kg to calculate how much potential energy you gained when you stepped on the box.

Key points

- The gravitational potential energy of an object depends on its weight and how far it moves vertically.
- The gravitational potential energy of an object increases when the object goes up and decreases when the object goes down.
- The change of gravitational potential energy of an object is equal to its mass × the gravitational field strength × its change of height.

194 / 195

Further teaching suggestions

- These are important calculations and homework should be used to reinforce the work done in the lesson.

Answers to in-text questions

a It heats the muscles then is transferred by heating directly (or indirectly via the blood system) from the muscles to the surroundings.

b i 300 J   ii 600 W

Summary answers

1 a decreases
  b stays the same
  c decreases, increases

2 a 90 J
  b 4500 J

3 a an increase of 300 J
  b a decrease of 300 J

P2 3.3

Kinetic energy

AQA Specification link-up: Physics P2.2

Learning objectives

Students should learn:

- that kinetic energy is the energy a moving object has
- that the kinetic energy of an object increases when the object is travelling faster or is more massive
- how to calculate the kinetic energy of a moving object
- that elastic potential energy is energy stored in an object when work is done to change the shape of the object.

Learning outcomes

Most students should be able to:

- explain how the kinetic energy of an object depends on the speed and mass of the object
- perform calculations using the kinetic energy equation
- describe situations where elastic potential energy is stored.

Some students should also be able to:

- perform calculations using the kinetic energy equation including those that involve rearrangement of the equation.

- A force applied to an elastic object such as a spring will result in the object stretching and storing elastic potential energy. *[P2.1.5b)]*
- For an object that is able to recover its original shape, elastic potential energy is stored in the object when work is done on the object to change its shape. *[P2.1.5c)]*
- The kinetic energy of an object depends on its mass and its speed:
  $E_k = \frac{1}{2} \times m \times v^2$ *[P2.2.1 g)]*
- Evaluate the benefits of different types of braking system, such as regenerative braking. *[P2.2]*

  Controlled Assessment: AS4.3 Collect primary and secondary data. *[AS4.3.2 c) d) e)]*; AS4.5 Analyse and interpret primary and secondary data. *[AS4.5.3 a)]*

Lesson structure

Starters

Mass and velocity – Using mini-whiteboards, the students must give accurate definitions of mass and velocity. Ask: 'What are the units of each?' make sure that the students are comfortable with kilograms (show them one) and metres per second (walk at 1 m/s). In addition, check the way they are writing the units; are they using m/s or m s^{-1}? *(5 minutes)*

Kinetic cards – Give the students a set of cards with pictures of various moving objects. Each card shows the mass and the velocity; the students have to put them into order from least kinetic energy to most. Possible cards include a marble (0.01 kg, 5 m/s), tennis ball (0.2 kg, 25 m/s), bullet (0.02 kg, 200 m/s), car (750 kg, 20 m/s), and train (100 000 kg, 15 m/s). Support the students by identifying the factors that affect kinetic energy beforehand through discussion. Extend students by showing them the kinetic energy of an object of mass 10 kg moving at 2 m/s and then the effect of doubling the mass and then the velocity. Can they identify which factors are most significant? *(10 minutes)*

Main

- The students should remember that moving objects have energy and this is called 'kinetic energy'. Some will still be using the term 'movement energy', but it is time to leave this behind and get them to use the correct term as 'movement energy' will not be credited on the exam. Be tough on this point as it's an easy way to lose a mark even though the student understands the ideas involved.
- The 'Investigating kinetic energy' 'Practical support' works well with light gates. If you don't have them, then the modified version is a reasonable alternative. There are a few sources of error in the results and this would be a good opportunity to look into the nature of taking measurements ('How Science Works') and how repeating readings can improve the quality of the data. You could have a set of results in a spreadsheet table so that you can show the relationship graphically, or let the students enter data as they go along. (This relates to 'How Science Works': relationships between variables.)
- Clearly, many students will not come up with the relationship themselves, although most will see that the relationship is not a simple linear one. It is more important to show that the data fits a pattern that we already know.
- Some of the students will have a problem with the '$\{\frac{1}{2}\}$' in the kinetic energy equation and ask you: 'half of what?' This is tricky to explain without going into the derivation, so tell the students that they will find out if they go on to study A-level physics. The kinetic energy equation is the most difficult equation that students need to rearrange, and you should lead them through this carefully.
- The elastic potential energy ideas are a bit simpler, but the students will need to be able to give a reasonable definition like the one in the Student Book. This should be easier when linked back to the lesson on stretching (P2 2.6 'Stretching and squashing'). Making elastic band toys is a good endpoint and shows another important energy transfer. The models can also be tested by applying concepts from 'How Science Works' in another lesson.

Support

- This is the most difficult calculation the students will attempt in the course. Take extra care with the equation going through each stage in a very formal way. Even if the students don't fully understand the maths, a methodical technique will always lead them to the correct answer.

Extend

- Challenge students to build their own elastic-powered vehicles and hold a competition on whose can go the furthest. The vehicles should all have identical elastic bands and could be cars, boats or aeroplanes. The results can lead to a discussion about which of the modes of transport is the most efficient. You might want to consider transfers involving kinetic energy and E_p; these can be quite demanding.

Plenaries

Higher/lower – Go through a series of objects with different masses and velocities and ask the students to say (or calculate) if the kinetic energy is higher or lower than the previous one. You can use some of the values from the Starter activity or throw in some gravitational potential energy calculations too. *(5 minutes)*

Kinetic cards revisited – Try the same activity as in the Starter, but the students now have to calculate the energy to check their order. Use this task to make sure that the students are treating the calculations correctly. To support the students' calculation, frames can be provided for some of the cards. To extend, you can provide some additional cards that show the mass and kinetic energy and request that the students find the velocity.
(10 minutes)

Practical support

Investigating kinetic energy

This experiment can be demonstrated with a ball and motion sensor or with a dynamics trolley and light gates.

Equipment and materials required (ball)
A ramp (or drainpipe), tennis ball, velocity or distance sensor, balance to measure mass of object.

Details
If you don't have a velocity sensor, then the software may be able to convert the distance measurements into speed measurements. Some velocity sensors have two parts; one of which needs to be mounted on the moving object. Clearly a ball won't do, so a trolley can be used.

Equipment and materials required (trolley)
Long ramp, dynamics trolley, card of known length, light gate, balance to measure mass of object.

Details
Mount the card on the trolley so that it interrupts the light gate when it passes through. Position the trolley at various measured heights on the track so that it rolls down the track and its speed is measured at the bottom. The ramp works well at an angle of around 30°.

Alternative equipment
It is possible to measure the speed of the object by letting it pass through a measured distance and timing it with a stopwatch. For this, you will need to ensure that the object isn't travelling very fast, so shallow launch angles will be needed.

Safety: Protect bench and feet from falling trolleys.

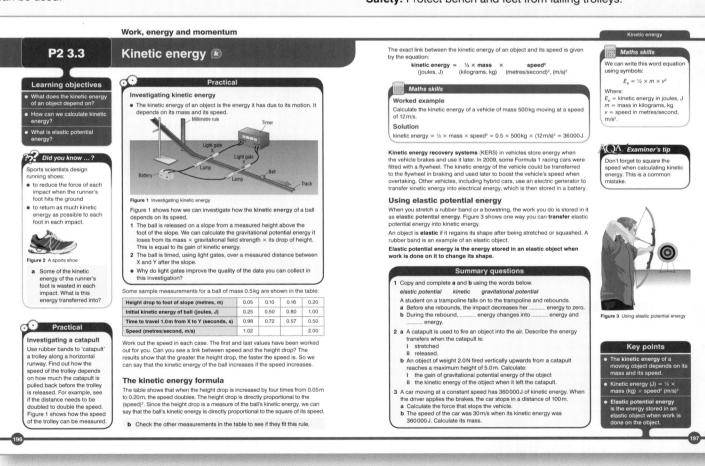

Summary answers

1 a kinetic
  b elastic potential, kinetic, gravitational potential
2 a i Chemical energy in the muscles is transferred into elastic energy of the bow and energy due to heating in the muscles.
    ii Elastic potential energy of the bow is transferred into kinetic energy and gravitational potential energy of the arrow.
  b i 10 J ii 10 J
3 a 3600 N   b 800 kg

P2 3.4 | Momentum

AQA Specification link-up: Physics P2.2

- Momentum is a property of moving objects
  $p = m \times v$ [P2.2.2 a)]
- In a closed system, the total momentum before an event is equal to the total momentum after the event. This is called conservation of momentum. [P2.2.2 b)]

Learning objectives

Students should learn:
- that the momentum of an object is the product of the mass and velocity of the object
- that the unit of momentum is the kilogram metre/second (kg m/s)
- that momentum is conserved in any collision provided no external forces act on the colliding objects.

Learning outcomes

Most students should be able to:
- calculate the momentum of an object of known mass and velocity
- state that momentum is conserved in any collision in a closed system (one where no external forces act on the colliding bodies).

Some students should also be able to:
- apply and rearrange the appropriate equations to two bodies that collide in a straight line.

Answers to in-text questions
- **a** 240 kg m/s
- **b** 0.48 m/s

Support

- Students might have difficulty remembering the mass of an object is not the same as the weight. Use props to remind the students of the difference; the mass is the amount of matter in the object.

Extend

- Who came up with the ideas about forces and momentum? What is inertia? The students can look up and explain Newton's laws of motion. Ask why conservation of momentum is considered a very important part of physics.

Lesson structure

Starters

Trying to stop – The students should explain why it takes an oil tanker several kilometres to stop, but a bicycle can stop in only a few metres. You can point out that they may be travelling at the same speed and this will lead to the conclusion that it is something to do with the mass (size). Discuss if this is always the case; larger objects are more difficult to stop. *(5 minutes)*

Stopping power – Give the students a set of cards with various sports balls on them. Ask the students to put them in order of difficulty to stop, and then explain what properties make the balls more difficult. They should be able to links the 'stopability' to the speed and mass of the balls. To make the activity more stimulating borrow a real set of balls so that the students can compare them. They should realise that even though a table tennis ball can travel as fast as a cricket ball, it isn't going to be as hard to stop. *(10 minutes)*

Main

- It is best to begin with a discussion about trying to stop something moving or start something off. Trains are a good example of something with a large mass that can travel quickly. The students can find out how long it takes a train to get up to speed and how long it takes it to stop, even in an emergency.

- The students are looking at basic 'closed systems' where there are no external forces applied to the objects. In reality, there are frictional forces acting, so the situation can be more complicated and it can be hard to see where the momentum 'goes' when the objects stop. This is generally to the Earth, but the effect on such a large object is not noticeable.

- The demonstration will take a little time to explain, but should give good results. Any discrepancies should be accounted for using the idea that external forces (frictional) have changed the momentum. Conservation of momentum is a **fundamental** concept in physics; just as important as conservation of energy.

- You could talk about the famous 'everybody in China jumping at the same time' idea. It is a scientific myth that this would cause an earthquake or even change the orbit of the Earth. This would actually have no real effect on the Earth at all as the mass of all of the people combined is tiny when compared to the mass of the Earth.

- The shunting effect can be demonstrated by a Newton's cradle. This can be improvised from a set of ping-pong balls on wire, or similar, if a real one is not available. You could always resort to a video clip if you can't get one to work.

- The calculation is a multi-stage one and this type of calculation often confuses students. Make sure students have plenty of practice calculating the momentum of objects before they try to work out velocities after collisions. To extend students, you can look at collisions where both of the trolleys are moving before the collision or collisions where the trolleys 'bounce off' and end up travelling in opposite directions.

Plenaries

The skate escape – Two people are trapped on a **perfectly** friction-free circular surface just out of reach of each other. They are both 10 m from the edge and all that they have to help them escape is a tennis ball. Ask: 'How do they both escape?' [All they need to do is throw something from one to the other, this will give them momentum in opposite directions and they will slowly drift to the sides. If they repeatedly throw the ball to each other they will speed up.] *(5 minutes)*

Impossibly super – In several films, superheroes stop cars or trains by standing in front of them and letting them crash into them. The cars stop dead and the costumed hero doesn't move an inch. Ask: 'What's wrong with the science here?' The students should come up with an explanation using the conservation of momentum. Students can be supported by watching the clip; pause it before the collision and ask them what is going to happen and to compare it with what would happen in reality. Extend students by having them perform a calculation of the collision. They should note that a superhero of mass 100 kg attempting to stop a train of mass 100 000 kg travelling at 50 m/s will have very little effect. They can then consider what forces would do to the system (do they think that the friction of the feet on the ground would make any significant difference?) *(10 minutes)*

Practical support

Investigating collisions

This activity can be carried out with dynamics trolleys or a linear air track. Two light gates are required.

Equipment and materials required

Two or three dynamics trolleys or gliders on a linear air track, card of known length, two light gates.

Details

Mount the card on the first trolley so that it passes through a light gate before the collision. The trolleys can be made to stick together using velcro or a pin and bit of cork. After the collision, they should pass through the second light gate to measure the new velocity. Keep the light gates close to the collision point, so that the trolleys do not slow down too much. If the trolleys have the same mass then the velocity should simply halve after the collision. If frictional forces are affecting the result, it is possible to tilt the track slightly, so that the frictional force is balanced by a small component of the weight of the trolleys. It is important to try this if a detailed investigation is taking place.

Safety: Protect feet and bench from falling trolleys.

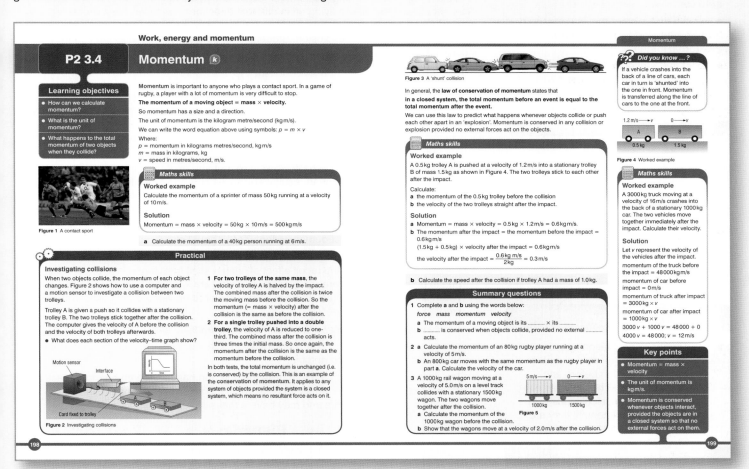

Work, energy and momentum

P2 3.4 — **Momentum** (k)

Learning objectives

* How can we calculate momentum?
* What is the unit of momentum?
* What happens to the total momentum of two objects when they collide?

Momentum is important to anyone who plays a contact sport. In a game of rugby, a player with a lot of momentum is very difficult to stop.

The momentum of a moving object = mass × velocity.

So momentum has a size and a direction.

The unit of momentum is the kilogram metre/second (kg m/s).

We can write the word equation above using symbols: $p = m \times v$

Where:

p = momentum in kilograms metres/second, kg m/s

m = mass in kilograms, kg

v = speed in metres/second, m/s.

Figure 1 A contact sport

Maths skills

Worked example

Calculate the momentum of a sprinter of mass 50 kg running at a velocity of 10 m/s.

Solution

Momentum = mass × velocity = 50 kg × 10 m/s = 500 kg m/s

a Calculate the momentum of a 40 kg person running at 6 m/s.

Practical

Investigating collisions

When two objects collide, the momentum of each object changes. Figure 2 shows how to use a computer and a motion sensor to investigate a collision between two trolleys.

Trolley A is given a push so it collides with a stationary trolley B. The two trolleys stick together after the collision. The computer gives the velocity of A before the collision and the velocity of both trolleys afterwards.

* What does each section of the velocity–time graph show?

Figure 2 Investigating collisions

1 For two trolleys of the same mass, the velocity of trolley A is halved by the impact. The combined mass after the collision is twice the moving mass before the collision. So the momentum (= mass × velocity) after the collision is the same as before the collision.

2 For a single trolley pushed into a double trolley, the velocity of A is reduced to one-third. The combined mass after the collision is three times the initial mass. So once again, the momentum after the collision is the same as the momentum before the collision.

In both tests, the total momentum is unchanged (i.e. is conserved) by the collision. This is an example of the conservation of momentum. It applies to any system of objects provided the system is a closed system, which means no resultant force acts on it.

Figure 3 A 'shunt' collision

In general, the **law of conservation of momentum** states that **in a closed system, the total momentum before an event is equal to the total momentum after the event.**

We can use this law to predict what happens whenever objects collide or push each other apart in an 'explosion'. Momentum is conserved in any collision or explosion provided no external forces act on the objects.

Maths skills

Worked example

A 0.5 kg trolley A is pushed at a velocity of 1.2 m/s into a stationary trolley B of mass 1.5 kg as shown in Figure 4. The two trolleys stick to each other after the impact.

Calculate:

a the momentum of the 0.5 kg trolley before the collision

b the velocity of the two trolleys straight after the impact.

Solution

a Momentum = mass × velocity = 0.5 kg × 1.2 m/s = 0.6 kg m/s.

b The momentum after the impact = the momentum before the impact = 0.6 kg m/s

(1.5 kg + 0.5 kg) × velocity after the impact = 0.6 kg m/s

the velocity after the impact = $\frac{0.6\,kg\,m/s}{2\,kg}$ = 0.3 m/s

b Calculate the speed after the collision if trolley A had a mass of 1.0 kg.

Summary questions

1 Complete a and b using the words below:

force mass momentum velocity

a The momentum of a moving object is its .... × its ....

b .... is conserved when objects collide, provided no external .... acts.

2 a Calculate the momentum of an 80 kg rugby player running at a velocity of 5 m/s.

b An 800 kg car moves with the same momentum as the rugby player in part a. Calculate the velocity of the car.

3 A 1000 kg rail wagon moving at a velocity of 5.0 m/s on a level track collides with a stationary 1500 kg wagon. The two wagons move together after the collision.

a Calculate the momentum of the 1000 kg wagon before the collision.

b Show that the wagons move at a velocity of 2.0 m/s after the collision.

Figure 5

Did you know ... ?

If a vehicle crashes into the back of a line of cars, each car in turn is 'shunted' into the one in front. Momentum is transferred along the line of cars to the one at the front.

Figure 4 Worked example

Maths skills

Worked example

A 3000 kg truck moving at a velocity of 16 m/s crashes into the back of a stationary 1000 kg car. The two vehicles move together immediately after the impact. Calculate their velocity.

Solution

Let v represent the velocity of the vehicles after the impact.

momentum of the truck before the impact = 48000 kg m/s

momentum of car before impact = 0 m/s

momentum of truck after impact = 3000 kg × v

momentum of car after impact = 1000 kg × v

$3000\,v + 1000\,v = 48000 + 0$

$4000\,v = 48000$; $v = 12$ m/s

Key points

* Momentum = mass × velocity
* The unit of momentum is kg m/s.
* Momentum is conserved whenever objects interact, provided the objects are in a closed system so that no external forces act on them.

198 / 199

Further teaching suggestions

ICT link-up

* Detailed models are available to simulate these collisions. These can be used as a demonstration for individual student use. Snooker or pool games can also be used. There are several commercial and free simulations available ranging widely in their complexity.

Summary answers

1 a mass, velocity   b momentum, force

2 a 400 kg m/s   b 0.5 m/s

3 a 5000 kg m/s

b Total momentum after collision = (1000 kg + 1500 kg) × v = 2500 v, where v is the final velocity to be calculated. Using conservation of momentum, 2500 v = 5000. Therefore v = 5000 ÷ 2500 = 2 m/s.

P2 3.5

Explosions

Specification link-up: Physics P2.2

- Momentum is a property of moving objects

  $p = m \times v$ [P2.2.2 a)]

- In a closed system, the total momentum before an event is equal to the total momentum after the event. This is called conservation of momentum. [P2.2.2 b)]

  Controlled Assessment: AS4.5 Analyse and interpret primary and secondary data. [AS4.5.2 a) b)]

Learning objectives

Students should learn:

- that momentum has size and direction, and the direction of travel is important in collisions
- that there is no change in momentum in an explosion (momentum is always conserved).

Learning outcomes

Most students should be able to:

- state that the total momentum before and after an explosion is the same, provided no external forces act
- describe how the launching of a bullet causes recoil.

Some students should also be able to:

- explain that momentum is conserved in all interactions that do not include external forces
- apply the conservation of momentum to perform calculations where an explosion occurs causing two objects to recoil from each other.

Lesson structure

Starters

Jumping frogs – Position a few spring-loaded jumping frog toys on the desk and set them off. The students have to explain the energy transfers before they all go off. They need to mention elastic potential, kinetic, gravitational potential and sound. They should also account for where the energy finally ends up. *(5 minutes)*

Slow motion – Show a video of a simple explosion frame-by-frame and ask the students to explain what is happening. (Search for 'explosion' at an internet video hosting site.) They should see the pieces flying off in different directions; some will have greater speed than others. Support students by providing key words or a set of cartoon diagrams showing the stages of the explosion. Students can be extended by insisting that they incorporate the idea of conservation of momentum into their descriptions. *(10 minutes)*

Main

- Students may only think of explosions as chemical explosions instead of simple spring ones. Talk about an explosion being caused when some kind of stored energy (chemical or elastic) is suddenly transferred into kinetic. You can show a few basic chemical explosions and point out that too much is going on to explain clearly, so you are going to stick with some simple ones during the lesson.

- The explosion experiment usually works well, but you might want to repeat it a couple of times and analyse the mean results. This gives an opportunity for the students to consider the errors inherent in these measurements and why repeat readings are so important. This is an excellent opportunity to explore concepts in 'How Science Works'.

- Show the students some footage of crash-test dummies. Search an internet video hosting site for 'crash-test dummy video'. They should clearly see the area of impact in a collision.

- A good way of showing the recoil effect of firing a shell from a gun is to show a field gun in operation. These are really quite large and are knocked backwards significantly. When firing a '21-gun salute', there is little backwards movement because no shell is fired.

- The calculation can be very difficult for many students, so lead them through it carefully.

- You can discuss the energy transfers involved with the damping spring and perhaps link this to the suspension on cars.

- The students should be made to realise that the gun has to have much more mass that the projectile, otherwise it would recoil at very high velocities. A modern shell is fired at velocities of up to 1000 m/s and may have a mass of 100 kg.

Plenaries

It's against the frog – Have a set of quick questions handy and use the jumping frogs again. A student has the time it takes for the frog to go off in which to answer a question. Play this as a knockout game with teams if needed. You can differentiate by setting different levels of question to provide support or extension material. *(5 minutes)*

Boating – Discuss what happens when somebody steps on to a boat but falls in the water because the boat moves away. (There are plenty of video clips showing this effect.) Ask the students to explain what happened, perhaps with diagrams. They should understand that the person is actually pushing the boat away; when they move left, the boat will always be forced to the right as a consequence of the conservation of momentum. The effect is clearly greatest when the mass of the boat is similar to the mass of the person. *(10 minutes)*

Support

- Momentum conservation questions are best posed as a set of diagrams showing the situation before and after the collisions. The students can be led through the calculations with a calculation template until they are more comfortable with the technique.

Extend

- Ask: 'Why doesn't momentum change?' The students could try to link the idea of conservation of momentum to equal and opposite forces. Ask: 'What exactly is a force? What is the scientific definition?' Mathematically skilled students could look at collisions in two dimensions and calculate the resulting velocities.

Practical support

Investigating a controlled explosion

This demonstration can be used to show that momentum is conserved in explosions.

Equipment and materials required
Four dynamics trolleys, two light gates or velocity sensors or wooden blocks.

Details
This experiment can be carried out with wooden blocks as shown in the Student Book or with light gates or velocity sensors to measure the speed. If the sensors are used, then use cards as in previous experiments to interrupt light beams. The momentum of the objects can be calculated using the equation.

You should make sure that the sensors are positioned close to the explosion point, so that not too much energy is lost due to friction. The same kind of experiment can be carried out with a linear air track.

Safety: Protect feet and bench from falling trolleys.

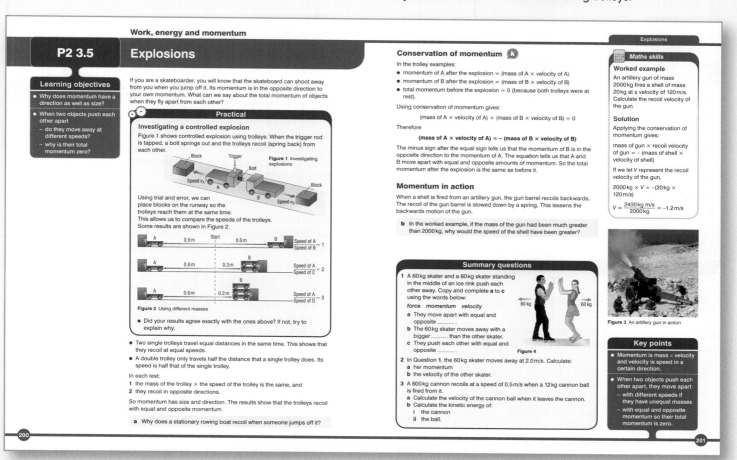

Work, energy and momentum

P2 3.5 Explosions

Learning objectives
- Why does momentum have a direction as well as size?
- When two objects push each other apart
  - do they move away at different speeds?
  - why is their total momentum zero?

If you are a skateboarder, you will know that the skateboard can shoot away from you when you jump off it. Its momentum is in the opposite direction to your own momentum. What can we say about the total momentum of objects when they fly apart from each other?

Practical
Investigating a controlled explosion
Figure 1 shows controlled explosion using trolleys. When the trigger rod is tapped, a bolt springs out and the trolleys recoil (spring back) from each other.

Figure 1 Investigating explosions

Using trial and error, we can place blocks on the runway so the trolleys reach them at the same time. This allows us to compare the speeds of the trolleys. Some results are shown in Figure 2.

$$\frac{\text{Speed of A}}{\text{Speed of B}} = 1$$
$$\frac{\text{Speed of A}}{\text{Speed of C}} = 2$$
$$\frac{\text{Speed of A}}{\text{Speed of D}} = 3$$

Figure 2 Using different masses

- Did your results agree exactly with the ones above? If not, try to explain why.

- Two single trolleys travel equal distances in the same time. This shows that they recoil at equal speeds.
- A double trolley only travels half the distance that a single trolley does. Its speed is half that of the single trolley.

In each test:
1 the mass of the trolley × the speed of the trolley is the same, and
2 they recoil in opposite directions.

So momentum has size and direction. The results show that the trolleys recoil with equal and opposite momentum.

a Why does a stationary rowing boat recoil when someone jumps off it?

Conservation of momentum
In the trolley examples:
- momentum of A after the explosion = (mass of A × velocity of A)
- momentum of B after the explosion = (mass of B × velocity of B)
- total momentum before the explosion = 0 (because both trolleys were at rest).

Using conservation of momentum gives:

(mass of A × velocity of A) + (mass of B × velocity of B) = 0

Therefore

(mass of A × velocity of A) = − (mass of B × velocity of B)

The minus sign after the equal sign tells us that the momentum of B is in the opposite direction to the momentum of A. The equation tells us that A and B move apart with equal and opposite amounts of momentum. So the total momentum after the explosion is the same as before it.

Momentum in action
When a shell is fired from an artillery gun, the gun barrel recoils backwards. The recoil of the gun barrel is slowed down by a spring. This lessens the backwards motion of the gun.

b In the worked example, if the mass of the gun had been much greater than 2000 kg, why would the speed of the shell have been greater?

Summary questions
1 A 60 kg skater and a 80 kg skater standing in the middle of an ice rink push each other away. Copy and complete a to c using the words below:
force momentum velocity
   a They move apart with equal and opposite ....
   b The 60 kg skater moves away with a bigger .... than the other skater.
   c They push each other with equal and opposite ....

Figure 4

2 In Question 1, the 60 kg skater moves away at 2.0 m/s. Calculate:
   a her momentum
   b the velocity of the other skater.

3 A 600 kg cannon recoils at a speed of 0.5 m/s when a 12 kg cannon ball is fired from it.
   a Calculate the velocity of the cannon ball when it leaves the cannon.
   b Calculate the kinetic energy of:
     i the cannon
     ii the ball.

Maths skills
Worked example
An artillery gun of mass 2000 kg fires a shell of mass 20 kg at a velocity of 120 m/s. Calculate the recoil velocity of the gun.

Solution
Applying the conservation of momentum gives:

mass of gun × recoil velocity of gun = − (mass of shell × velocity of shell)

If we let V represent the recoil velocity of the gun,

2000 kg × V = −(20 kg × 120 m/s)

$V = \frac{2400\,\text{kg m/s}}{2000\,\text{kg}} = -1.2\,\text{m/s}$

Figure 3 An artillery gun in action

Key points
- Momentum is mass × velocity and velocity is speed in a certain direction.
- When two objects push each other apart, they move apart:
  - with different speeds if they have unequal masses
  - with equal and opposite momentum so their total momentum is zero.

Further teaching suggestions

Crash-test dummies
- If you have a few old toys you can improvise crash-test dummies. These can lead to a discussion about the limitations of the model. Ask: 'How close are the crash-test dummies to people?' Use a full-sized skeleton to discuss the joints a more realistic dummy should have, and point out the weak spots in impact such as the neck. You can discuss why the dummies are simplified; only certain data is needed to estimate the effect on humans. The extra data generated by a more realistic dummy would not be useful. It would cause more difficulties in the study and would make the dummies even more expensive than they already are.

Answers to in-text questions
a The boat has equal and opposite momentum to the jumper after the jump, so it moves in the opposite direction to the jumper.

b The gun would recoil much less, so more of the energy released would have been transferred into kinetic energy of the shell.

Summary answers

1 a momentum
   b velocity
   c force

2 a 120 kg m/s
   b 1.5 m/s

3 a 25 m/s
   b i 75 J
      ii 3750 J

P2 3.6 | Impact forces

Learning objectives

Students should learn:

- how the force during an impact will depend on the change in momentum and the time over which the impact takes place
- that forces are equal and opposite during impacts.

Learning outcomes

Most students should be able to:

- state that a resultant force will change the momentum of an object
- describe the factors that affect the size of a force in an impact.

Some students should also be able to:

- calculate the force produced in a collision using the equations:
$$a = \frac{v - u}{t} \text{ and } F = ma$$

Answers to in-text questions

a If a child falls off the swing, the impact force is lessened because the rubber mat increases the duration of the impact.

b The wearer's kinetic energy is reduced over a greater distance if a seat belt is worn. (Or the wearer's momentum is reduced over a longer time if a seat belt is worn.)

c 1800 N

Support

- This can be a challenging set of calculations as there are two separate stages needed to determine the forces. Provide a set of layout templates to guide the students through the calculations until they get into the habit of laying out their work correctly. Check that the students are calculating the deceleration correctly before moving on to the calculation of the force.

Extend

- There is plenty of scope for looking at the impact forces calculations in more depth and in more complex situations. You can look at collisions between two moving cars, in opposite or the same directions linking this into the safety features designed for these situations described in the next lesson.

AQA Specification link-up: Physics P2.1, P2.2

- The acceleration of an object is determined by the resultant force acting on the object and the mass of the object.
$$a = \frac{F}{m} \text{ or } F = m \times a \text{ [P2.1.2 a)]}$$
- The acceleration of an object is given by the equation:
$$a = \frac{v - u}{t} \text{ [P2.1.2 e)]}$$
- Evaluate the benefits of air bags, crumple zones, seat belts and side impact bars in cars. [P2.2]

Lesson structure

Starters

Skids – Why does a car take longer to stop in wet weather? Show students some pictures of cars stopping suddenly and discuss the sizes of the forces. What reduces the forces and why does this mean that the car takes a greater distance to stop? Extend students by asking them to provide equations for acceleration and then for an equation linking force and acceleration, link these to change of momentum. Extra support can be provided by revising the ideas of friction as a force beforehand. *(5 minutes)*

Sudden impact – Arrange some bathroom tiles on the floor (inside a tray and wear safety glasses). Drop some objects onto the tiles to see if they break. These can include heavy but soft objects and a hammer. Ask the students to explain why the tiles break or why they do not. *(10 minutes)*

Main

- Calculating the forces involved in collisions requires the use of two equations and so is quite a tricky concept, and some students will struggle with the mathematics. A good starting point is to show a video clip of crash testing. (Search the internet for a 'crash testing' video); there are a few available. You should emphasise the large amount of energy that is transferred during the collision and ask the students where they think it is transferred to.

- The 'Investigating impacts' practical clearly shows that the forces involved in impact are reduced by using a material that distorts. These plastic materials absorb some of the energy of the impact. You might like to show what happens if a spring (an elastic material) is used instead.

- A key element to understanding the impacts and forces involved is that the size of the force can be reduced by extending the time of the impact. Discuss how materials that can compress (foam, crumple zones and so on) mean that the impact is taking place over a significantly longer time so the forces acting can be much smaller. This is why 'padding' can make impact less painful or damaging.

- The calculations will take a bit of explaining and the students will most likely need to go through the ideas a couple of times. Use plenty of examples including ones involving the trolleys or toys that you have been using. Impact times tend to be very short, so you may like to start with longer-lasting collisions before moving on to the bullet example.

- After the maths, either demonstrate the egg-throwing or let the students have a go at the egg-hurling competition (see 'Further reading suggestions').

Plenaries

Bouncy castles – Small children often cry when they fall over, but not on bouncy castles. The students should draw a diagram showing why not. Check that they are identifying the forces and the timings involved. *(5 minutes)*

'Owwzatt!' – How should cricketers catch fast-moving cricket balls? The students should write out instructions explaining the science behind their ideas. This should include the reasons why gloves are used to 'cushion' the catch. Students can extend their explanations by explaining the hand motion of the fielders when they catch the ball (show some video footage). The fielders move their hands in the direction the ball is travelling. Again this increases the impact time (and reduces the chances of the ball bouncing off their hands). Support can be provided by demonstrating the actions and properties of the ball and glove in the laboratory. Borrow some props from the PE department if they have them. *(10 minutes)*

Practical support

Investigating impacts

The impacts can be investigated on a simple or more detailed level depending on time available.

Equipment and materials required

Dynamics trolley, plasticine, motion sensor, launch ramp.

Details

You can compare the two impacts just by observing them or by monitoring the movement with a distance sensor. The trolleys should be launched from the same height on the ramp; firstly onto the brick directly and then with a round blob of plasticine. With the motion sensor, you can then compare the two impacts, and you should be able to show that the second impact took place over a longer time. The first impact should make a nice thud, and this helps you to discuss what happened to the kinetic energy.

Safety: Protect feet and bench from falling bricks and trolleys. Wear eye protection.

Work, energy and momentum

Impact forces

P2 3.6 Impact forces

Learning objectives

- When vehicles collide, what does the force of the impact depend on?
- How does the impact force depend on the impact time?
- What can we say about the impact forces and the total momentum when two vehicles collide?

Figure 2 A crash test. Car makers test the design of a crumple zone by driving a remote control car into a brick wall.

Figure 3 Impact force

Did you know ...?

Scientists at Oxford University have developed new lightweight material for bullet-proof vests. The material is so strong and elastic that bullets bounce off it.

Crumple zones at the front end and rear end of a car are designed to lessen the force of an impact. The force changes the momentum of the car.

- In a front-end impact, the momentum of the car is reduced.
- In a rear-end impact (where a vehicle is struck from behind by another vehicle), the momentum of the car is increased.

In both cases the effect of a crumple zone is to increase the impact time and so lessen the impact force.

Practical

Investigating impacts

We can test an impact using a trolley and a brick, as shown in Figure 1. When the trolley hits the brick, the plasticine flattens on impact, making the impact time longer. This is the key factor that reduces the impact force.

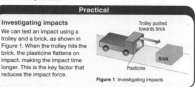

Figure 1 Investigating impacts

a Why is rubber matting under a child's swing a good idea?

Impact time

Let's see why making the impact time longer reduces the impact force.

Suppose a moving trolley hits another object and stops. The impact force on the trolley acts for a certain time (the impact time) and causes it to stop. A soft pad on the front of the trolley would increase the impact time and would allow the trolley to travel further before it stops. The momentum of the trolley would be lost over a longer time and its kinetic energy would be transferred over a greater distance.

1 The kinetic energy of the trolley is transferred to the pad as work done by the impact force in squashing the pad.
2 Since work done = force × distance, the impact force is therefore reduced because the distance is increased.

The longer the impact time is, the more the impact force is reduced.

If we know the impact time, we can calculate the impact force as follows:

- From P2 1.2, since acceleration = change of velocity ÷ time taken, we can work out the deceleration by dividing the change of velocity by the impact time.
- From P2 2.3, since force = mass × acceleration, we can now calculate the impact force by multiplying the mass of the trolley by the deceleration.

The above method shows how much the impact force can be reduced by increasing the impact time. Car safety features such as crumple zones and side bars increase the impact time and so reduce the impact force.

b In a car crash, why does wearing a car seat belt reduce the impact force on the wearer?

Maths skills

Worked example

A bullet of mass 0.004 kg moving at a velocity of 90 m/s is stopped by a bulletproof vest in 0.0003 s.

Calculate **a** the deceleration and **b** the impact force.

Solution

a Initial velocity of bullet = 90 m/s
Final velocity of bullet = 0
Change of velocity = final velocity − initial velocity
= 0 − 90 m/s = −90 m/s
(where the minus sign tells us the change of velocity is a decrease)
$$\text{Deceleration} = \frac{\text{change of velocity}}{\text{impact time}} = \frac{-90 \text{ m/s}}{0.0003 \text{ s}} = -300000 \text{ m/s}^2$$

b Using 'force = mass × acceleration', impact force = 0.004 kg × −300000 m/s² = −1200 N

c Calculate the impact force if the impact time had been 0.0002 s.

Two-vehicle collisions

When two vehicles collide, they exert equal and opposite impact forces on each other at the same time. The change of momentum of one vehicle is therefore equal and opposite to the change of momentum of the other vehicle. The total momentum of the two vehicles is the same after the impact as it was before the impact, so momentum is conserved – assuming no external forces act.

For example, suppose a fast-moving truck runs into the back of a stationary car. The impact decelerates the truck and accelerates the car. Assuming the truck's mass is greater than the mass of the car, the truck loses momentum and the car gains momentum.

Summary questions

1 Copy and complete **a** to **c** using the words below:

equal   greater   smaller

a The greater the mass of a moving object is the _____ the force needed to stop it in a certain time.
b When two objects collide, they exert _____ forces on each other.
c When two vehicles collide, the vehicle with the _____ mass has a greater change of velocity.

2 **a** An 800 kg car travelling at 30 m/s is stopped safely when the brakes are applied. What deceleration and braking force is required to stop it in **i** 6.0 s? **ii** 30 s?
b If the vehicle in part **a** had been stopped in a collision lasting less than a second, explain why the force on it would have been much greater.

3 A 2000 kg van moving at a velocity of 12 m/s crashes into the back of a stationary truck of mass 10000 kg. Immediately after the impact, the two vehicles move together.
a Show that the velocity of the van and the truck immediately after the impact was 2 m/s.
b The impact lasted for 0.3 seconds. Calculate the **i** deceleration of the van **ii** force of the impact on the van.

Did you know ...?

We sometimes express the effect of an impact on an object or person as a force to weight ratio. We call this the **g-force**. For example, a g-force of 2g means the force on an object is twice its weight. You would experience a g-force of:

- about 3–4 g on a fairground ride that whirls you round
- about 10 g in a low-speed car crash
- more than 50 g in a high-speed car crash. You would be lucky to survive!

Key points

- When vehicles collide, the force of the impact depends on mass, change of velocity, and the duration of the impact.
- The longer the impact time is, the more the impact force is reduced.
- When two vehicles collide,
  - they exert equal and opposite forces on each other
  - their total momentum is unchanged.

202 | 203

Further teaching suggestions

Egg hurling

- The students can be provided with some simple equipment; cardboard tubes, sponge tape, etc. Ask the students to design egg safety capsules. You can then see which work by dropping eggs or throwing them. If there is no time in the lesson, the students could construct their egg safety capsule at home for testing next lesson.

Summary answers

1 **a** greater
  b equal
  c smaller

2 **a** **i** 5.0 m/s², 4000 N
  ii 1 m/s², 800 N
  b The deceleration is greater because the impact time is shorter and the change of velocity is the same. The impact force is equal to the mass × the deceleration, so the impact force is greater.

3 **a** Initial momentum = 24 000 kg m/s;
  $$\text{velocity after impact} = \frac{\text{momentum}}{\text{mass}} = \frac{24\,000}{12\,000} = 2 \text{ m/s}.$$
  b **i** 33 m/s²
  ii 330 000 N

P2 3.7

Car safety

Learning objectives

Students should learn:
- that seat belts and air bags reduce the force of an impact by extending the duration of the impact
- that energy can be absorbed by distorting material during impacts
- that detailed calculation of damage can be used to assess the speed of a collision.

Learning outcomes

Most students should be able to:
- describe the safety features of a modern car and their effects
- describe how a safety feature works in relation to reducing the forces of impacts by extending the duration of the impact
- describe how road traffic accidents can be investigated using the evidence from the scene.

Answers to in-text questions

a The wearer would not be stopped until his or her head hit the windscreen.

b The seat belt would go across the body above the chest. The child might slip through the seat belt in an accident.

Support

- Students should relate well to demonstrations and videos before constructing their own devices to crash together. Lego constructions can work well.

Extend

- There is plenty of scope here to look at the details of collisions. You may like to see if the students can design a crumple zone for the trolley out of paper or aluminium foil. Give each student a small amount of sticky tape and a single sheet of A4 paper, and ask them to try to make a crumple zone that they can attach to the front of a trolley to absorb the kinetic energy. The trolley can be rolled from a fixed height on a ramp to make the test fair, and the collisions observed or even measured with a motion sensor. This should give an indication of the effectiveness.

AQA Specification link-up: Physics P2.1, P2.2

- The acceleration of an object is determined by the resultant force acting on the object and the mass of the object. [P2.1.2 a)]
- Evaluate the benefits of air bags, crumple zones, seat belts and side impact bars in cars. [P2.2]
- Evaluate the benefits of different types of braking system, such as regenerative braking. [P2.2]

Lesson structure

Starters

Crash flashback – Give the students a momentum problem to solve to refresh the ideas from the last topic. Include cars or other large things as the objects involved in the collision. You can differentiate by providing a straightforward calculation to support some students while also providing a more complex situation requiring rearrangement of the basic equation to extend others. *(5 minutes)*

Crumpled cars – Show the students selected photographs of crashed cars (search the internet for images) and ask them to describe the damage they see. They should notice the crumpling effect; especially at the front or rear of the car, but may not realise that this is a deliberate design. Point this out to them and ask them to think of reasons why a designer would deliberately want this effect. Give them clues by linking back to plastic and elastic materials. The key is to understand that forces have been used to stop the car and the kinetic energy of the car has partly gone into distorting the car's shape. *(10 minutes)*

Main

- The students need to understand that a fast-moving car will have a great deal of kinetic energy and to stop, this energy needs to be transferred. This is done when a force acts on the car so a rapid change in kinetic energy is accompanied by very large forces causing very large accelerations. It is the large forces that have to be handled as they cause the damage to the car and passengers. The reduction of the forces is generally achieved by making the impacts last longer.

- The pressures involved in collisions can also be reduced by making the forces act over a wider area, (hence the wide seatbelts and large airbags).

- You might be able to find a seatbelt from a scrap car so that you can explain why it is not totally rigid and is so wide. If not, you will have to settle for photographs. Video clips of crash tests can be easily found and these show the behaviour of a body and seatbelt in a car crash. You can also find examples of the dummies not wearing a seatbelt.

- Similarly, you can find slow motion footage of the effect of air bags in crashes. Emphasise the effect of increasing the collision time and spreading the force over a much larger area of the body. The impact time can be increased tenfold and the area of impact by a similar amount, reducing the pressure on the body one hundred times.

- You can discuss the idea of child safety seats. If you (or another member of staff) have one, you can look at the side impact padding and the extensive belting to secure the child. Seats facing backwards are safer that those facing forwards, so should passenger seats on cars, buses and trains be facing backwards?

- If you have access to computers, the students can find out about the improved safety features of cars and complete a summary of the costs and benefits. If not then a range of brochures are usually available from the dealers.

Plenaries

Best car – Give the students pictures and information about cars through the ages and get them to identify the innovations that have taken place. They can produce a timeline showing the changes. You can also include information about changes to maximum speeds and road types like the introduction of motorways. You can support some students by providing a blank timeline and some articles (to find information from) to add to the timeline. To extend other students, you might ask them to continue at home and evaluate the origin and success of a particular new safety idea (for example who invented airbags and how successful have they been?). *(5 minutes)*

Hard sell – The students must produce an advertisement for the expensive safety features in a new car. This could be hard hitting or more subtle in its persuasiveness. Most safety features started off as expensive accessories but as their benefits were proven, they became required by law. *(10 minutes)*

Practical support

Investigating impacts

The impacts can be investigated on a simple or more detailed level depending on time available.

Equipment and materials required

Dynamics trolley, plasticine, motion sensor, launch ramp.

Details

You can compare the two impacts just by observing them or by monitoring the movement with a distance sensor. The trolleys should be launched from the same height on the ramp; firstly onto the brick directly and then with a round blob of plasticine. With the motion sensor, you can then compare the two impacts, and you should be able to show that the second impact took place over a longer time. The first impact should make a nice thud, and this helps you to discuss what happened to the kinetic energy.

You may like to see if the students can design a crumple zone for the trolley out of paper. Give each student a small amount of sticky tape and a single sheet of A4 paper, and ask them to try to make a crumple zone that they can attach to the front of a trolley to absorb the kinetic energy. The trolley can be rolled from a fixed height on a ramp to make the test fair, and the collisions observed or even measured with a motion sensor. This should give an indication of the effectiveness.

Safety: Protect feet and bench from falling trolleys and bricks. Wear eye protection.

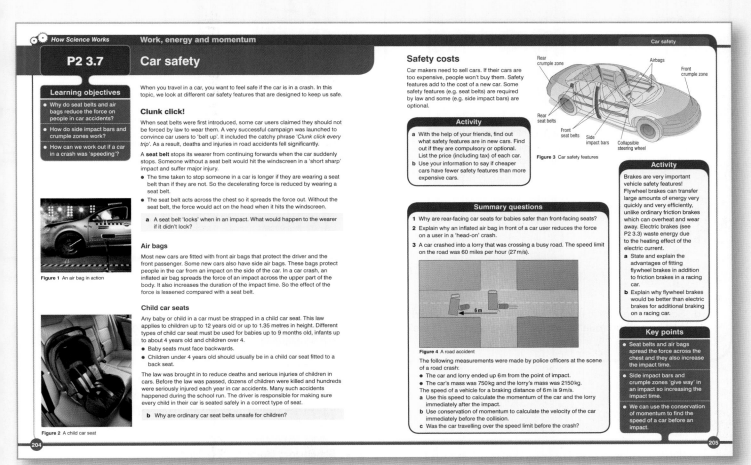

How Science Works — Work, energy and momentum

P2 3.7 — Car safety

Learning objectives
- Why do seat belts and air bags reduce the force on people in car accidents?
- How do side impact bars and crumple zones work?
- How can we work out if a car in a crash was 'speeding'?

When you travel in a car, you want to feel safe if the car is in a crash. In this topic, we look at different car safety features that are designed to keep us safe.

Clunk click!
When seat belts were first introduced, some car users claimed they should not be forced by law to wear them. A very successful campaign was launched to convince car users to 'belt up'. It included the catchy phrase 'Clunk click every trip'. As a result, deaths and injuries in road accidents fell significantly.

A **seat belt** stops its wearer from continuing forwards when the car suddenly stops. Someone without a seat belt would hit the windscreen in a 'short sharp' impact and suffer major injury.

- The time taken to stop someone in a car is longer if they are wearing a seat belt than if they are not. So the decelerating force is reduced by wearing a seat belt.
- The seat belt acts across the chest so it spreads the force out. Without the seat belt, the force would act on the head when it hits the windscreen.

a A seat belt 'locks' when in an impact. What would happen to the wearer if it didn't lock?

Air bags
Most new cars are fitted with front air bags that protect the driver and the front passenger. Some new cars also have side air bags. These bags protect people in the car from an impact on the side of the car. In a car crash, an inflated air bag spreads the force of an impact across the upper part of the body. It also increases the duration of the impact time. So the effect of the force is lessened compared with a seat belt.

Child car seats
Any baby or child in a car must be strapped in a child car seat. This law applies to children up to 12 years old or up to 1.35 metres in height. Different types of child car seat must be used for babies up to 9 months old, infants up to about 4 years old and children over 4.
- Baby seats must face backwards.
- Children under 4 years old should usually be in a child car seat fitted to a back seat.

The law was brought in to reduce deaths and serious injuries of children in cars. Before the law was passed, dozens of children were killed and hundreds were seriously injured each year in car accidents. Many such accidents happened during the school run. The driver is responsible for making sure every child in their car is seated safely in a correct type of seat.

b Why are ordinary car seat belts unsafe for children?

Figure 1 An air bag in action

Figure 2 A child car seat

Safety costs
Car makers need to sell cars. If their cars are too expensive, people won't buy them. Safety features add to the cost of a new car. Some safety features (e.g. seat belts) are required by law and some (e.g. side impact bars) are optional.

Activity
a With the help of your friends, find out what safety features are in new cars. Find out if they are compulsory or optional. List the price (including tax) of each car.
b Use your information to say if cheaper cars have fewer safety features than more expensive cars.

Figure 3 Car safety features

Summary questions
1 Why are rear-facing car seats for babies safer than front-facing seats?
2 Explain why an inflated air bag in front of a car user reduces the force on a user in a 'head-on' crash.
3 A car crashed into a lorry that was crossing a busy road. The speed limit on the road was 60 miles per hour (27 m/s).

Figure 4 A road accident

The following measurements were made by police officers at the scene of a road crash:
- The car and lorry ended up 6 m from the point of impact.
- The car's mass was 750 kg and the lorry's mass was 2150 kg.
The speed of a vehicle for a braking distance of 6 m is 9 m/s.
a Use this speed to calculate the momentum of the car and the lorry immediately after the impact.
b Use conservation of momentum to calculate the velocity of the car immediately before the collision.
c Was the car travelling over the speed limit before the crash?

Activity
Brakes are very important vehicle safety features! Flywheel brakes can transfer large amounts of energy very quickly and very efficiently, unlike ordinary friction brakes which can overheat and wear away. Electric brakes (see P2 3.3) waste energy due to the heating effect of the electric current.
a State and explain the advantages of fitting flywheel brakes in addition to friction brakes in a racing car.
b Explain why flywheel brakes would be better than electric brakes for additional braking on a racing car.

Key points
- Seat belts and air bags spread the force across the chest and they also increase the impact time.
- Side impact bars and crumple zones 'give way' in an impact so increasing the impact time.
- We can use the conservation of momentum to find the speed of a car before an impact.

Activity answers

Braking systems

a Advantages:
- Less fuel is used because kinetic energy is stored in the flywheel when the brakes are applied and returned to the vehicle when it accelerates.
- The initial acceleration at the start is greater because the engine and the flywheel can both be used to accelerate the vehicle.
- Energy can be transferred rapidly and efficiently to and from the flywheel when the vehicle slows down at a bend and speeds up on leaving the bend.
- Less energy is wasted as the flywheel brake does not heat up like the ordinary friction brake.

b Electric brakes would waste more energy. Also, the wires carrying the electric current might overheat.

Summary answers

1 In an accident where the car suddenly stopped, the child would press against the back of the car seat. This would prevent the child from being thrown forwards.

2 The air bag increases the time taken to stop the person it acts on. This reduces the force of the impact. Also, the force is spread out across the chest by the air bag, so its effect is lessened again.

3 a 26 100 kg m/s
  b 35 m/s
  c yes

Summary answers

1 a i equal to
   ii less than

  b i 180 J
    ii 11 N × 20 m = 220 N m = 220 J
    iii Friction between the trolley and the slope causes some of the energy from the student to be transferred to the surroundings by braking.

2 a $\dfrac{700\,kg \times (20\,m/s)}{2} = 140\,000\,J$

  b 1750 N

3 a 12 kg m/s

  b 6 m/s

4 Initial velocity $u = 4\,m/s$, final velocity $v = 0$ (because the crash stops the car), time taken $t = 1.8\,s$.
Acceleration, $a = (v - u) \div t = (0 - 4) \div 1.8 = 2.2\,m/s^2$

5 a i elastic potential energy
   ii kinetic energy

  b i 3.0 J
    ii Some of the kinetic energy of the stone was transferred to the surroundings by air resistance; the stone was still moving horizontally at maximum height, so it still had kinetic energy due to this movement.

6 a i 3600 kg m/s
   ii 1200 kg m/s

  b i 2400 kg m/s
    ii 3.0 m/s

  c i 5400 J
    ii 600 J
    iii 3600 J

  d Some of the kinetic energy was transferred into sound and by heating (due to friction) to the wagons and the surroundings.

Summary questions

1 a Copy and complete i and ii using the words below. Each term can be used once, twice or not at all.
   equal to   **greater than**   **less than**
   When a braking force acts on a vehicle and slows it down,
   i the work done by the force is .... the energy transferred from the object
   ii the kinetic energy after the brakes have been applied is .... the kinetic energy before they were applied.

  b A student pushes a trolley of weight 150 N up a slope of length 20 m. The slope is 1.2 m high.

   i Calculate the gravitational potential energy gained by the trolley.
   ii The student pushed the trolley up the slope with a force of 11 N. Show that the work done by the student was 220 J.
   iii Give one reason why all the work done by the student was not transferred to the trolley as gravitational potential energy.

2 A 700 kg car moving at 20 m/s is stopped in a distance of 80 m when the brakes are applied.
  a Show that the kinetic energy of the car at 20 m/s is 140 000 J.
  b Calculate the braking force on the car.

3 A student of mass 40 kg standing at rest on a skateboard of mass 2.0 kg jumps off the skateboard at a speed of 0.30 m/s. Calculate:
  a the momentum of the student
  b the recoil velocity of the skateboard.

4 A car bumper is designed not to bend in impacts at less than 4 m/s. It was fitted to a car of mass 900 kg and tested by driving the car into a wall at 4 m/s. The time of impact was measured and found to be 1.8 s.
Show that the deceleration of the car was 2.2 m/s².

5 a Copy and complete i and ii using the words below. Each term can be used once, twice or not at all.
   elastic potential energy   **kinetic energy**
   gravitational potential energy
   An object is catapulted from a catapult.
   i .... is stored in the catapult when it is stretche[d]
   ii The object has .... when it leaves the catapul[t]

  b A stone of mass 0.015 kg is catapulted into the air a[nd] it reaches a height of 20 m before it descends and h[its] the ground some distance away.
   i Calculate the increase of gravitational potential energy of the stone when it reached its maximu[m] height (g = 10 N/kg).
   ii State two reasons why the catapult stored more energy than that calculated in part b i?

6 A 1200 kg rail wagon moving at a velocity of 3.0 m/s on[ ] a level track collides with a stationary wagon of mass 800 kg. The 1200 kg truck is slowed down to a velocity[ ] 1.0 m/s as a result of the collision.

  a Calculate the momentum of the 1200 kg wagon
   i before the collision
   ii after the collision.
  b Calculate
   i the momentum, and
   ii the velocity of the 800 kg wagon after the collisio[n]
  c Calculate the kinetic energy of:
   i the 1200 kg wagon before the collision
   ii the 1200 kg wagon after the collision
   iii the 800 kg wagon after the collision.
  d Give a reason why the total kinetic energy after the collision is not equal to the total kinetic energy befo[re] the collision.

Kerboodle resources

Resources available for this chapter on Kerboodle are:

- Chapter map: Work, energy and momentum
- Bump up your grade: Meteor fall (P2 3.1)
- Interactive activity: Calculating kinetic energy (P2 3.3)
- Practical: Finding the elastic energy of springs (P2 3.3)
- Video: Momentum in sports (3.4)
- Simulation: Momentum (P2 3.4)
- Bump up your grade: Momentum calculations – understanding conservation of momentum (P2 3.4)
- How Science Works: Momentum in action (P2 3.4)
- Bump up your grade: What a bang! (P2 3.5)
- Revision podcast: Kinetic energy and momentum (P2s 3.7 & 3.8)
- Test yourself: Work, energy and momentum
- On your marks: Work, energy and momentum
- Examination-style questions: Work, energy and momentum
- Answers to examination-style questions: Work, energy and momentum

Examination-style questions

a Copy and complete the following sentences using the list of words and phrases below. Each one can be used once.

kinetic energy   work   power
gravitational potential energy

i Energy is transferred when .... is done. (1)
ii .... is the energy that an object has by virtue of its position in a gravitational field. (1)
iii The .... of an object depends on its mass and speed. (1)
iv .... is the energy transferred in a given time. (1)

b Explain why a meteorite 'burns up' as it enters the Earth's atmosphere. Use ideas about work and energy. (3)

The diagram shows three cars, **A**, **B** and **C**, travelling along a straight, level road.

A   Speed
40 m/s

650 kg

B   18 m/s

1250 kg

C   15 m/s

1500 kg

a Calculate the momentum of each of the vehicles and explain which one has the greatest momentum. Write down the equation you use. Show clearly how you work out your answer and give the unit. (3)

b Car **C**, travelling at 15 m/s, crashes into the back of car **A** when car **A** is stationary. The cars move together after the collision.
i Calculate the total momentum of the cars just after the collision. (1)
ii Calculate the speed of the two cars just after the collision. (2)

c Explain, using ideas about momentum changes, how the crumple zone at the front of car **C** may reduce the chance of injury to the occupants during the collision. (3)

3 When ploughing a field a horse and plough move 170 m and the horse pulls with a force of 800 N.

a Calculate the work done by the horse.
Write down the equation you use. Show clearly how you work out your answer and give the unit. (3)

b **i** The horse takes 3 minutes to plough 170 m. Calculate the power of the horse.
Write down the equation you use. Show clearly how you work out your answer and give the unit. (3)
ii Calculate the kinetic energy of the horse.
Write down the equation you use. Show clearly how you work out your answer and give the unit.
Mass of horse = 950 kg (3)

c Explain why the horse has to do more work if the field slopes uphill than it would do on level ground. (2)

4 The picture shows a catapult.

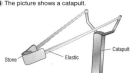

Stone   Elastic   Catapult

When a force is applied to the stone, work is done in stretching the elastic and the stone moves backwards.

a Calculate the work done if the average force applied to the stone is 20 N. The force moves it backwards 0.15 m. Write down the equation you use. Show clearly how you work out your answer and give the unit. (3)

b Calculate the maximum speed of the stone after the catapult is released. The mass of the stone is 0.049 kg. Assume all the work done is transferred to the stone as kinetic energy when the catapult is released. Write down the equation you use. Show clearly how you work out your answer and give the unit. (3)

207

Examination-style answers

1 a
i Energy is transferred when **work** is done. *(1 mark)*
ii **Gravitational potential energy** is the energy that an object has by virtue of its position in a gravitational field. *(1 mark)*
iii The **kinetic energy** of an object depends on its mass and speed. *(1 mark)*
iv **Power** is the energy transferred in a given time. *(1 mark)*

b work is done on the meteorite; energy transferred by heating; kinetic energy transferred by heating *(3 marks)*

2 a $p = m \times v$
A: $= 650 \times 40 = 26\,000$ kg m/s
B: $= 1250 \times 18 = 22\,500$ kg m/s
C: $= 1500 \times 15 = 22\,500$ kg m/s
A is greatest because although it has the smallest mass, it has a much larger velocity. *(3 marks)*

b **i** $22\,500$ kg m/s *(1 mark)*
ii $(1500 + 650) \times v = 22\,500$
$v = 22\,500/2150 = 10.5$ m/s *(2 marks)*

c The crumple zone causes the change in momentum to happen over a longer time;
This means the maximum force on the occupants is reduced;
This reduces chance of injury. *(3 marks)*

3 a $WD = F \times d = 800 \times 170$
$= 136\,000$ J *(3 marks)*

b **i** $P = \dfrac{E}{t} = (800 \times 170)/180$
$= 756$ W *(3 marks)*
ii $E_k = \frac{1}{2} \times m \times v^2 = \frac{1}{2} \times 950 \times (170/180)^2$
$= 424$ J *(3 marks)*

c work done against gravitational force; when an object is raised vertically *(2 marks)*

4 a $W = F \times d = 20 \times 0.15$
$= 3.0$ J *(3 marks)*

b $E_k = \frac{1}{2} \times m \times v^2$
$3 = 0.5 \times 0.049 \times v^2$
$v^2 = 122$
$v = 11$ m/s *(3 marks)*

Practical suggestions

Practicals	AQA	k	📖	⚙
Investigating the transfer of E_p to E_k by dropping a card through a light gate.	✓		✓	
Plan and carry out an investigation to measure velocity using trolleys and ramps.	✓		✓	
Running upstairs and calculating work done and power, lifting weights to measure power.	✓		✓	
A motor lifting a load to show how power changes with load.	✓		✓	
Stretching different materials before using as catapults to show the different amounts of energy transferred, indicated by speed reached by the object or distance travelled.	✓	✓		

Examiner's tip

Question 2 shows that the greatest momentum can be possessed by the least massive vehicle if it is travelling sufficiently fast. Students may enjoy a practical illustration of this idea: 'The momentum challenge'. This involves pupils sprinting (in a suitable area) and then multiplying their velocity by their mass. The class results can be displayed in a bar chart. The fastest runner is often not the winner.

Examiner's tip

Calculations based on conservation of momentum for collisions and explosions need to be practised by Higher Tier and Foundation Tier students alike. Question 2 can be repeated for different combinations of cars colliding. Some students could be extended by investigating collisions where both cars are initially moving. The students can assume that each car's clutch is disengaged and the brakes are not applied.

P2 4.1

Electrical charges

AQA

Specification link-up: Physics P2.3

- When certain insulating materials are rubbed against each other, they become electrically charged. Negatively charged electrons are rubbed off one material and onto the other. *[P2.3.1 a)]*
- The material that gains electrons becomes negatively charged. The material that loses electrons is left with an equal positive charge. *[P2.3.1 b)]*
- When two electrically charged objects are brought together they exert a force on each other. *[P2.3.1 c)]*
- Two objects that carry the same type of charge repel. Two objects that carry different types of charge attract. *[P2.3.1 d)]*

Learning objectives

Students should learn:

- that when insulating materials are rubbed together, charge can be transferred from one to the other
- that objects become electrically charged when electrons move from one material to the other
- that when charged objects are brought together, like charges repel and unlike charges attract.

Learning outcomes

Most students should be able to:

- state that there are two types of electrical charge and that electrons carry a negative charge whereas protons carry a positive charge
- draw diagrams showing how charge can be transferred from one object to another indicating the fact that charges are equal and opposite
- describe the forces that act between charged objects.

Some students should also be able to:

- provide a detailed description of the transfer of charge in terms of electron movement.

Support

- The concepts discussed here are best shown through a range of demonstrations, each one supported by clear diagrams showing the charge on the objects. You can provide diagrams without the charges shown and ask students to add this feature after each demonstration.

Extend

- Ask: 'Is it actually friction that charges up objects?' Apparently objects of different materials can become charged up just by being left in contact with each other, and rubbing objects together just increases the area of contact. The students can find out about this explanation.

Lesson structure

Starters

Laws of attraction – Give the students a set of three cards with pictures of bar magnets on them and ask them to arrange them so that they all attract each other or all repel each other. Use real magnets to check the answers. Students should come up with some kind of triangular arrangement. *(5 minutes)*

Invisible force fields – Give the students two bar magnets and ask them to balance them so that the end of one is floating above the end of the other. Ask: 'Can they balance two magnets above one another?' Demonstrate magnet rings on a pole if you have them and ask the students to explain what is happening. You should reach the idea that there are invisible, non-contact forces. Students needing support should be able to draw diagrams demonstrating the effects. Extend students by asking them to state what factors affect the size of the forces and to consider gravitational forces too. Compare these with the electric force later in the lessons and discuss the factors that affect the size of this force. *(10 minutes)*

Main

- Start by demonstrating the balloon-sticking effect; it should be fairly easy to get the balloon to stick to a wall or to your own body. You may also be able to show that two charged balloons repel each other. You can discuss the static build up on a TV screen by talking about the amount of dust that builds up on it.

- The use of a 'Van de Graaff' generator is fairly essential. Students tend to get excited and some volunteer to receive a shock. Try some of the demonstrations in 'Practical support'. Make sure that you do not shock any students who have medical problems.

- The students should be familiar with the structure of the atom by now and you should be able to go through this part quickly. Highlight the idea of an ion; this will be used in later explanation around resistance.

- Emphasis needs to be placed on the idea that it is only the electrons that are free to move. When electrons leave an object, it becomes positively charged and when they enter a neutral object it becomes negatively charged. Some students struggle with the idea that adding electrons makes something negative. They need to grasp that the electron has a negative charge and so if you have more electrons, you have more negative charge.

- To demonstrate the effect that charged objects have on each other, the students can carry out the simple practical activity, 'The force between two charged objects' from the Student Book. They should have no trouble finding that like charges repel and opposites attract.

- At the end, the students should be able to tell you the simple attraction/repulsion rules.

Plenaries

Static force – Support students by giving them a set of diagrams with charged objects on them, two or more on each card, and ask them to draw force arrows. Some students can be extended by asking them to try to draw the direction of the resultant force. *(5 minutes)*

Forever amber – The students should write a brief newspaper report for the ancient Greek newspaper νΣ⟨, Σιδησ∑∫ʃ announcing the discovery and properties of static electricity. It was first discovered using amber or 'electrum' as they called it. This could be extended as homework in which the ancient Greeks might like to speculate about future uses of this mysterious 'electricity'. *(10 minutes)*

Practical support

The 'Van de Graaff' generator

This is an impressive and fun piece of equipment that can be used to demonstrate many of the aspects of static electricity. It is not just for giving shocks!

Equipment and materials needed

A 'Van de Graaff' generator (VDG) and accessory kit. (See CLEAPSS Handbook, Section 12.9).

Details

- A VDG is a very temperamental device. Some days it will work very well but on others you will barely get a crackle. Dry days are best, and it is advisable to polish the dome to make it shiny. Keep computers (and mobile phones) away from the VDG.
- It is traditional to start by showing the sparks that the VDG can produce. Connect the discharging wand (or discharging dome) to earth and switch on the generator. Give the dome a couple of minutes to build up charge while you explain what the VDG is doing. Bring the wand close to the dome and with luck you will get reasonably big sparks.
- Hair standing on end can be demonstrated easily, and works best if the student stands on an insulating box. Make sure that the dome is discharged before the student steps off the insulator. If you don't want to use a student, then you may have a hair

sample that can be attached to the top of the dome or use a set of polystyrene balls in a container.
- Other demonstrations can include bringing a fluorescent tube close to the dome or demonstrating a current as a flow of charge.

Safety: Make sure students do not have any heart conditions.

The force between two charged objects

With this simple experiment, the students should be able to find that there are two types of charge and investigate how they affect each other.

Equipment and materials needed

For each group: retort stand with boss and clamp, cotton, two perspex rods, two polythene rods and a dry cloth.

Details

The students first need to make a 'hammock' from the cotton to be able to suspend one of the rods from the retort stand; they might find this easier if they use some light card as a base. They then rub one of the rods vigorously with the dry cloth and place it in the hammock. Next, they rub one of the other rods and bring it close to the suspended one and note the interaction; the suspended rod should rotate towards or away. They continue this procedure for all of the combinations of rods. If there seems to be little movement, it is probably because the cloth is not dry enough.

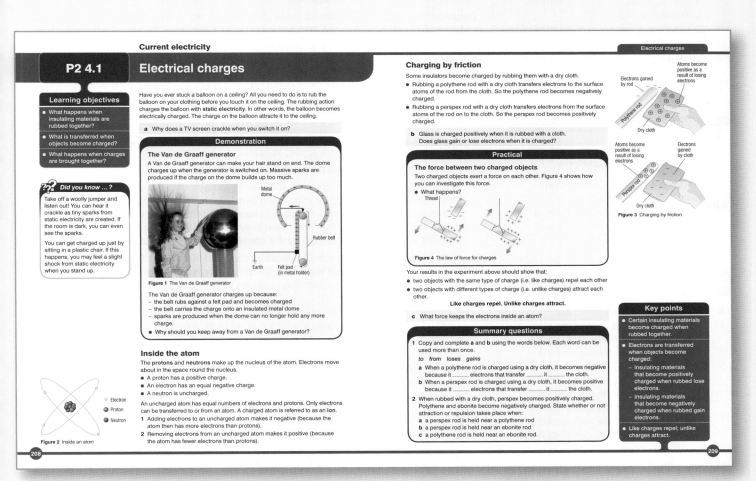

Answers to in-text questions

a Static electricity builds up on the screen.

b Glass loses electrons when it is charged.

c The electron is negative. The nucleus is positive. There is a force of (electrostatic) attraction between them.

Summary answers

1 a gains, to, from
   b loses, from, to

2 a attraction
   b attraction
   c repulsion

P2 4.2

Electric circuits

AQA Specification link-up: Physics P2.3

- Electrical charges can move easily through some substances, e.g. metals. *[P2.3.1 e)]*
- Electric current is a flow of electric charge. The size of the electric current is the rate of flow of electric charge. The size of the current is given by the equation:
  $$I = \frac{Q}{t}[P2.3.2\ a)]$$
- Circuit diagrams using standard symbols. The following standard symbols should be known: *(See Student Book pages 210 and 215 for symbols).* *[P2.3.2 c)]*

Learning objectives

Students should learn:

- that electrical circuits are drawn using standard symbols
- the difference between a cell and a battery
- the size of an electric current is measured in amperes using an ammeter
- the symbols used to represent common circuit components.

Learning outcomes

Most students should be able to:

- recognise and draw the circuit symbols for a cell, a battery, a switch, an indicator, a resistor, a variable resistor, a diode, a fuse, a voltmeter, an ammeter and an LED
- describe the function of each of the above components
- state the difference between a cell and a battery
- draw circuit diagrams using the above symbols.

Answers to in-text questions

a So current passes through it and through the torch bulb.
b A battery formed from two cells, a switch and a heater.
c No.

Support

- Some students have particular difficulties with connecting up electronic circuits correctly because they cannot match the neat circuit diagrams with the jumble of wires they are given. You can support students by using fixed boards, such as the Locktronic ones. It is a good idea to write the names of the component on them until the students can match the symbol and name correctly.

Extend

- For the circuit-building exercise, extend students by asking them to look at the currents through the different branches of the circuit and find any relationships. They could even look into the potential differences and see if they can come up with the relationship before you discuss it in future lessons.

Lesson structure

Starters

It's symbolic – Show a set of slides/diagrams to the students containing common symbols and ask them to say what they mean. Use road signs, hazard symbols, washing symbols, etc. This should help them to understand that symbols are a simple way of representing information clearly. You can use symbols used in countries where the language is very different. *(5 minutes)*

Describe the circuit – Give the students diagrams of two circuits containing cells, switches and bulbs, one series and one parallel, and ask them to describe them both in a paragraph. The student can demonstrate their understanding of circuit symbols this way and you can check their prior knowledge of concepts such as current, voltage, series and parallel. Support students by providing simple circuits with the minimal number of components. Students can be extended by asking them to draw a circuit when given a description of it. *(10 minutes)*

Main

- The students should be familiar with the basic ideas of circuits and circuit symbols from KS3. You can use this topic to check the students' circuit-building skills, so that you can be sure that they can carry out the investigations later.

- Start by showing the components and asking 'Do symbols have to look like what they represent?' When introducing each symbol, show the students a real device represented by that symbol. You could show them that there are several physically-different looking devices that match each symbol. For example, there are a range of different ammeters represented by the same symbol and a wide range of resistors.

- Most students cope well with the basic symbols for bulbs, switches and batteries. You may find that they struggle more with the various types of resistors because they are so similar. The best way to describe resistors is to discuss what is added to the basic resistor symbol.
  - The variable resistor has an arrow through it showing that you can adjust it.
  - The LDR has arrows going towards it representing light.
  - The fuse has a thin line representing the thin wire that runs inside it.

- Point out the difference between a cell and a battery. Many students still do not understand that a battery is a series of cells. It helps to physically show a 1.5 V cell and then put two or more together to produce a battery. You can point out that the word 'battery' means 'a collection put close together' as in 'battery hens' and a 'battery of guns'.

- The concept of current needs to be covered in some detail. The students need to work with the formal definition shown in the book; it's a bit like measuring the rate of flow of water in a pipe; the water current would be the mass of water passing each second. Simulation software really helps students to visualise the charges moving through the wire, discuss the charge moving around the circuit from positive to negative carrying energy with it. You will explain this energy transfer in more detail in future lessons.

- With the remaining time, you should let the students build a couple of circuits. Those in the 'Circuit tests' practical support are fine, or you could extend students further (see 'Extend' idea).

Plenaries

Current calculations – The students have a few calculations based on the equation to perform. You can extend the students by asking them to perform a calculation based on rearrangements of the equation and using unusual quantities (a time of 1 hour and a current of 40 mA when recharging a mobile phone for example). Support can be provided by sticking to relatively simple quantities and calculations requiring no rearrangement. *(5 minutes)*

Symbol domino loop – Give the students a set of cards showing circuit symbols and descriptions of their functions. Each card would have a symbol and a description that matches the symbol on a different card but when they are placed together correctly, the whole set would make a complete loop. Can the students name them all? *(10 minutes)*

Practical support

Circuit tests

This is a simple introduction to building circuits allowing the students to refresh their skills.

Equipment and materials needed

Cells (1.5 V), torch bulb (1.5 V), leads, diode, variable resistor.

Details

The students set up a simple circuit with the variable resistor and the bulb. They should find that the variable resistor can be used to alter the brightness of the bulb and be told that this is due to the current being changed. The students then include a diode in the circuit. They should then reverse the diode. This will show that the diode only allows the current in one direction.

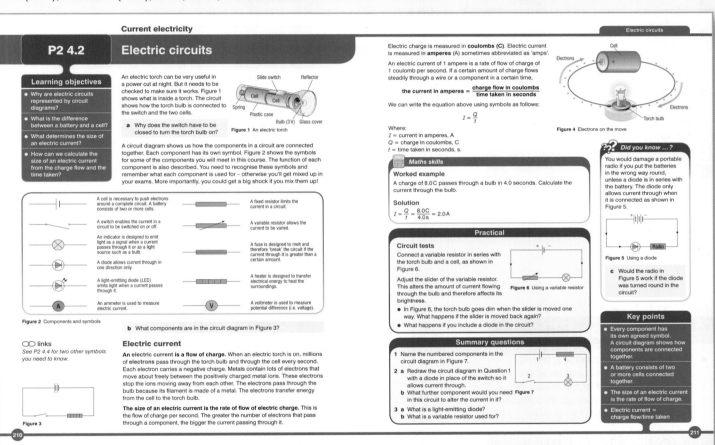

Further teaching suggestions

Circuit building

● This is more of a support activity to help students remember how to build basic circuits.

Equipment and materials required

Battery pack (3 V), three torch bulbs (3 V), leads, ammeter.

Details

Ask the students to set up a simple series circuit with two bulbs, and then a parallel one with a bulb on each branch. Can they make a parallel circuit with one bulb on one branch and two on the other? What can they say about the brightness of the bulbs? They should draw circuit diagrams of all these circuits before they construct them.

Summary answers

1 cell, switch, indicator, fuse

2 a [circuit diagram]   b A variable resistor.

3 a A light-emitting diode is a diode that emits light when current passes through it.

b A variable resistor is used to change the current in a circuit.

P2 4.3 Resistance

AQA

Learning objectives

Students should learn:

- how to use an ammeter and voltmeter
- how to measure the resistance of a component
- that a wire at a constant temperature obeys Ohm's law
- that the resistance of a metal wire does not depend on the direction of the current.

Learning outcomes

Most students should be able to:

- measure the resistance of a resistor using an ammeter and voltmeter
- calculate the resistance of a device from the current through it and the potential difference across it
- state Ohm's law for a metal wire.

Some students should also be able to:

- perform calculations that involve rearrangement of the resistance equation.

Answers to in-text questions

a $8.0\,\Omega$

b $10\,\Omega$

Support

- For resistance calculations, provide the students with a question sheet that has templates for the layout for equations, so that they go through the process step-by-step.

Extend

- The current–potential difference graphs shown in the Student Book all show constant resistance and no error in the measurements as the gradients are perfectly straight lines. Show the students some graphs produced from real measurements (containing some degree of error in readings) and discuss how the students would determine the resistance in this case. A gradient is often used to find resistance so they may like to calculate this after determining a best fit.

Specification link-up: Physics P2.3

- The potential difference (voltage) between two points in an electric circuit is the work done (energy transferred) per coulomb of charge that passes between the points:
  $$V = \frac{W}{Q} \text{ [P2.3.2 b)]}$$
- Current–potential difference graphs are used to show how the current through a component varies with the potential difference across it. *[P2.3.2 d)]*
- The current–potential difference graphs for a resistor at constant temperature ... . *[P2.3.2 e)]*
- The resistance of a component can be found by measuring the current through, and potential difference across, the component. *[P2.3.2 f)]*
- The current through a resistor (at a constant temperature) is directly proportional to the potential difference across the resistor. *[P2.3.2 g)]*
- Calculate current, potential difference or resistance using the equation: $V = I \times R$. *[P2.3.2 h)]*

Controlled Assessment: AS4.5 Analyse and interpret primary and secondary data. *[AS4.5.3 a)]*

Lesson structure

Starters

Resistors – Show the students the circuit symbols for all of the different types of resistor and ask them to describe the similarities in the symbols. Ask: 'What do they think the other parts of the symbols mean?' This is a simple recap. *(5 minutes)*

Reading the meter – Show the students some pictures of analogue meters and ask them to read off the value shown. Use a variety of different scales for the meters. Some students may need to be supported when trying to read digital scales; for example 0.21 is often read as 'nought point twenty one' or even just 'twenty one', so go through some examples of this. To extend students, you can ask them to design suitable scales (by making choices of suitable ranges and precision) for displaying sets of values clearly. For example, what set of scales could be used to display 0.55, 0.78 and 0.49 mV most clearly. *(10 minutes)*

Main

- It is very important that the students understand how to use an ammeter and voltmeter, and they have a good opportunity to do that in this lesson. Currents through components are often less than 1 ampere, so the students will have to get used to using 'milliamperes' (most people just use 'milliamps') in a lot of their work. The terms potential difference and voltage are often used interchangeably, try to enforce the use of potential difference (pd) as this will be used in examination questions.

- When a charge is moved through a potential difference, energy is transferred and so work is done. This is slightly similar to a force doing work when it moves an object. For some students, the equation defining potential difference will make more sense if it is stated as $W = VQ$ (work done = charge × pd moved through). In the end, some students may not be able to grasp exactly what pd is; this can be OK as long as they can use the equation.

- A simple analogy explaining resistance is a student moving along a packed corridor with his eyes closed. Other students in the corridor will get in the way, resisting his progress. If all of the other students are moving about a lot, the resistance will be higher – a bit like the wire heating up. During the movement, the electrons will lose energy as they collide with the ions in the metal. Link this idea to earlier energy transformation work. It is always important to check that the students do not think that electrons are used up as they move. They just lose (transfer) energy. Some computer simulations of electron movement show that the electrons are losing energy as they move through the potential difference. These are very useful.

- The students may be more comfortable just using word equations but they have to be able to recognise the symbols, so give them some questions that use them; they are quicker to write anyway.

- The practical activity in the Student Book is a good way of checking the students' skills in using the meters and using the equation. It will also give opportunities for students to manipulate variables, and discuss the 'directly proportional' relationship between variables (this relates to 'How Science Works').

Plenaries

An electron's tale – Students write a paragraph about the journey of an electron around a circuit containing a bulb and resistor. They should write about the energy changes that are going on in the circuit. A good description should also reference the collisions that take place. *(5 minutes)*

Reinforced resistance – The students have met two calculations in the lesson and plenty of reinforcement is required to ensure that they use the equations correctly. Give some additional ones, differentiating as appropriate. Students can be further extended by looking at combining the equations (or using one after another) to solve more complex problems. *(10 minutes)*

Practical support

Investigating the resistance of a wire

The students can investigate if the resistance of a wire depends on the current flowing through it. Constantan wires work well, as these do not change resistance as much when they heat up. It is also advisable to use battery packs or power packs with lockable voltage outputs, as the wires can heat up and cause burns if high currents are used.

Equipment and materials required

For each group: a power supply or battery pack, connecting leads, switch, crocodile clips, variable resistor, length of wire (30–50 cm), heatproof mat, ammeter and voltmeter.

Details

The students connect up the circuit with the variable resistor and test wire in series. The ammeter is also placed in series and the voltmeter in parallel across the test wire. Some students will struggle to set this up, so check the circuits before they are switched on. Using the variable resistor, the students can control the current through the test wire and measure both the current and the potential difference. In general, they should find that the resistance stays constant unless the wire heats up too much. The experiment shouldn't get too hot if low pd's are used, but use a heatproof mat anyway.

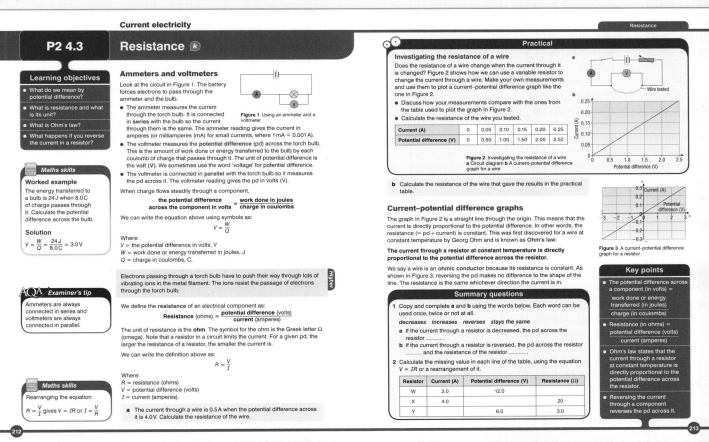

Further teaching suggestions

ICT link-up

- If you get different groups to investigate the current–potential different characteristics of different lengths (or diameters) of wire, then the data can be collected in a spreadsheet. This can be used to calculate the mean resistance of the wire from the data, and then to check for a relationship between the length (or diameter) and the resistance by quickly plotting a graph.

Summary answers

1 **a** decreases
   b reverses, stays the same
2 W: $6.0\,\Omega$; X: $80\,V$; Y: $2.0\,A$

P2 4.4

More current–potential difference graphs

AQA

Specification link-up: Physics P2.3

- Current–potential difference graphs are used to show how the current through a component varies with the potential difference across it. *[P2.3.2 d)]*
- The resistance of a filament bulb increases as the temperature of the filament increases … . *[P2.3.2 m)]*
- The current through a diode flows in one direction only. The diode has a very high resistance in the reverse direction … . *[P2.3.2 n)]*
- An LED emits light when a current flows through it in the forward direction. *[P2.3.2 o)]*
- The resistance of a light-dependent resistor (LDR) decreases as light intensity increases. *[P2.3.2 p)]*
- The resistance of a thermistor decreases as the temperature increases. *[P2.3.3 q)]*
- Apply the principles of basic electrical circuits to practical situations. *[P2.3]*

  Controlled Assessment: AS4.5 Analyse and interpret primary and secondary data. *[AS4.5.3 a)]*

Learning objectives

Students should learn that:
- that the resistance of a filament bulb increases as the temperature rises
- how the resistance of a diode depends on the pd applied across it
- how the resistance of a thermistor decreases when its temperature increases
- how the resistance of an LDR decreases when the light level increases.

Learning outcomes

Most students should be able to:
- draw current–pd graphs for a resistor, a filament bulb and a diode
- describe how the resistance of a filament bulb changes depending on the current through it
- describe how the resistance of a diode depends on which way round it is connected in a circuit
- describe how the resistance of a thermistor and light-dependent resistor (LDR) depend on the temperature and light level, respectively.

Some students should also be able to:
- explain the changes that take place in a series circuit including a thermistor or a LDR when the temperature or the light level changes
- explain resistance change in terms of ions and electrons. **[HT only]**

Support

- Using data logging equipment is a very good way of collecting data for current–potential difference graphs. Once set up, the students just have to adjust the variable resistor, press the space bar to take readings and then repeat until all the data is collected. The graphs can be displayed in seconds.

Extend

- Students could be asked to read values accurately off graphs and use these values in further calculations. For example, the students can read the resistance of a thermistor at a certain temperature and then calculate what current would pass through it at certain potential differences. They could see if the operation of a thermistor is independent of the pd across it.

Lesson structure

Starters

Three switches – Ask: 'You are outside a room with three switches that control three light bulbs inside the room; one switch for each light. How can you work out which switch controls which light if you are only allowed to open the door and go into the room once?' This is a test of deduction (quite an old one at that); it involves leaving one switch on, one off and turning one on for a minute then off again before entering the room. *(5 minutes)*

Pop! – Set up a circuit with a filament bulb that will have too high a current. Switch it on when the room is silent (so that they can hear the 'tink' sound) and ask the students to explain what happened. Their descriptions should mention the heating effect causing the wire to melt. If they don't, then demonstrate again by slowly increasing the current so that the students can appreciate the wire getting hotter and hotter. To support students, you may need to provide a brief recap of the effect of high resistance. Extend students by asking for a description in terms of electrons and ions and then ask what happens to the ions as the wire heats up and what this would do to the resistance. *(10 minutes)*

Main

- Start this topic with a reminder of the practical work from last lesson. Demonstrate how to build a circuit component-by-component in a logical way so that the students will follow this technique.
- The initial practical activities can take up a lot of time if the students wish to take plenty of measurements. You may like to let some groups do one of the experiments while the rest do the other, and then get them to share the results.
- The results should show that the filament bulb does not have a straight line on its current–potential difference graph. This is because it is heating up and the resistance is increasing, the greater the current in the wire. Link this back to the students' ideas about what happens to a metal when it gets hotter. The ions are vibrating more and the electrons are having more collisions with them. This increases the resistance. Higher Tier candidates should be able to explain this point in examinations.
- A diode is a more complex device. It behaves in a non-ohmic way. The reasons for its behaviour are beyond KS4. Some students will have heard of light-emitting diodes and think that all diodes give out light. You could demonstrate one of these in a circuit, showing that it only lights up if it is placed in the circuit the right way. The arrow on the symbol shows the direction of the current.
- As with the initial practical task, you might like to set different groups different tasks for the thermistor and LDR. They can then share the results with the other groups. These two devices can be investigated to focus on one of the many of the investigative aspects of 'How Science Works'.

Plenaries

Inside the black box – An electrical component has been placed inside a black box with only the two connections visible. The students should design an experiment to find out what it is. Support candidates by giving them some suggested equipment that includes a voltmeter and ammeter. *(5 minutes)*

Electrical evaluation – The students should evaluate the results of their experiments by comparing sets of data collected by different groups. This will allow them to assess the reliability of their techniques and suggest some improvements. Extend students by asking them to calculate values such as the resistance of the thermistor at a certain temperature; they should be able to suggest that collecting more data over a narrow range around this temperature may lead to a more reliable and precise result. For additional support you should demonstrate how to read values of the graph to determine the resistance. *(10 minutes)*

Practical support

Investigating different components

The students can investigate how the resistance of a filament bulb and a diode change when the potential difference across them is changed.

Equipment and materials required
For each group: a power supply or battery pack, connecting leads, variable resistor, ammeter, voltmeter, filament bulb, fixed resistor and diode.

Details
The students connect up the circuit with the component under test in series with the variable resistor. The ammeter is also placed in series and the voltmeter is placed in parallel with the test component. Using the variable resistor, the students change the pd across the component and record the current and pd. From the results, the students produce a current–potential difference graph. They should also try the circuit with the current flowing in the opposite direction, to show that this does not affect the bulb, but is very important for the diode.

Thermistors and light-dependent resistors (LDRs)
The students can investigate an LDR by finding out how its resistance is related to the distance it is from a bright light. Sensitive thermistors can have a significant change in resistance from just placing them between finger and thumb to warm them up. With low voltage electrical supplies, it is possible to set up circuits in which a thermistor can be attached by crocodile clips and placed in a beaker of hot water (from a kettle) and the resistance can be measured as the water cools.

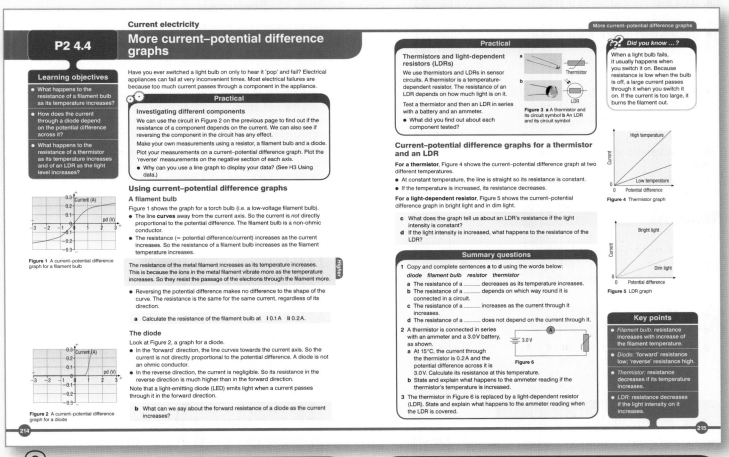

More current–potential difference graphs

?? Did you know … ?

The longest lasting light bulb has been on for more than 110 years. It is in a fire station in Livermore, USA, and was installed in 1901. It is never off, except in power cuts and when it was moved to the new fire station. You might like to check if it is still going!

Answers to in-text questions

a i 5 Ω   **ii** 10 Ω
b It decreases.
c The resistance is constant.
d The resistance decreases.

Summary answers

1 a thermistor
  b diode
  c filament bulb
  d resistor

2 a 15 Ω
  b The ammeter reading increases because the resistance of the thermistor decreases.

3 When the LDR is covered, its resistance increases. The current decreases because the resistance of the LDR increases and the pd across the LDR is still 3.0 V.

P2 4.5

Series circuits

Learning objectives

Students should learn that:

- in a series circuit the same current passes through all components
- the pd of the voltage supply is shared across the components in a series circuit
- cells in series add their potentials to give the total voltage
- the total resistance in a series circuit is the sum of the component resistances.

Learning outcomes

Most students should be able to:

- state that the current through components in series is the same
- find the total potential difference across several components in series, given the potential difference across each component
- find the total potential difference of a group of cells connected in series
- calculate the total resistance in a series circuit.

Some students should also be able to:

- analyse a series circuit to find the current and pd across components.

Answers to in-text questions

a 0.12 A
b 0.4 V
c 1.1 V
d 5 Ω

Support

- Provide the students with a printed set of circuit rules containing the ones from this topic and the next, to help them remember them all.

Extend

- There are a set of rules about the current and potentials in a circuit called Kirchhoff's laws. These are basically an electrical statement of the laws of conservation of energy, and the students should be able to find out what they are.

AQA Specification link-up: Physics P2.3

- The potential difference provided by cells connected in series is the sum of the potential difference of each cell (depending on the direction in which they are connected). [P2.3.2 j)]
- For components connected in series:
  - the total resistance is the sum of the resistance of each component
  - there is the same current through each component
  - the total potential difference of the supply is shared between the components. [P2.3.2 k)]
- Apply the principles of basic electrical circuits to practical situations. [P2.3]
  Controlled Assessment: AS4.5 Analyse and interpret primary and secondary data. [AS4.5.2 a) b)]

Lesson structure

Starters

Duff battery – Ask the students to correct this information: 'A chemical reaction in a battery makes electrons. These move quickly around a circuit and go through the components until there are no electrons left. The battery "runs out" when there are no chemicals left in it to make electrons from.' [e.g. 'A chemical reaction in the battery provides electrons with energy. These electrons move slowly around the circuit and push other electrons through it. As the electrons move through the components of the circuit, they lose energy until they reach the cell again when they have transferred all of the energy they were provided with. The battery "runs out" when all of the chemicals in it have reacted together and it cannot provide the electrons with any more energy.'] *(5 minutes)*

One way only – Ask: 'In what situation are we allowed only one way through something?' Let the students think for a few moments. Ask: 'If there is only one way to go on a tour, do the same number of people come out as go in?' Link the idea to the conservation of a property such as the cars on a motorway. To extend students, ask them to think about what happens if the pathway gets narrower. For extra suppor,t use animation of flow to show that the same number of objects must leave as enter. *(10 minutes)*

Main

- When discussing series and parallel circuits, many teachers use the analogy of a central heating system with the water representing the electrons, a pump representing the battery, etc. There are limitations with this concept, but it can help some students. The students need to be reminded that the current is the rate of **flow** of electrons. The larger the current, the more electrons are passing a point each second. The electrons cannot be destroyed and they do not escape from the circuit.

- As noted in the practical, there can be some minor errors produced by the meters so you will have to explain them to the students. This is a useful opportunity to consider 'How Science Works': variation in data and sources of error.

- Simulation software can be used to show the measurement of the pd across many bulbs connected in series. It is also easy to add more cells to show that the total pd drop across the components always matches the pd of the battery.

- Many students will simply accept that the total resistance of a set of components in series is just the same as the individual resistances without the need for calculations. Test their understanding by showing them a set of resistors in series, and asking for the total resistance. Students should have no problems with this.

- You might like to show some more difficult resistors such as 1.5 MΩ or 33 mΩ to get the students used to them. They should see that the physical size of a resistor is not always an indication of how much resistance it represents.

Plenaries

Controlling current – Give the students a set of cards representing cells (1.5 V) and resistors (1 Ω, 2 Ω, 5 Ω, etc.) and ask them to put some of them together to produce a current of 1 A, then a current of 0.5 A. There should be a number of ways to do this. You can extend the students by providing more difficult values to use or a situation where they must use a LED or select a suitable thermistor using its resistance characteristics. Support can be provided by giving only simple possibilities. *(5 minutes)*

Circuit rules – The students should start making a list of circuit rules that help them work out the currents, potential differences and resistances in series and parallel circuits. *(10 minutes)*

Practical support

Investigating potential differences in a series circuit

This experiment helps to verify the rule about potential differences in series circuits.

Equipment and materials required
For each group: a power supply or battery pack (1.5 V), connecting leads, variable resistor, 1.5 V bulb and three voltmeters.

Details
The students connect up a bulb and variable resistor in series. Connect up one voltmeter across the bulb (with voltage, V_1) and one across the variable resistor (with voltage, V_2). When the circuit is switched on, the students should find that $V_1 + V_2 = V_{tot}$ when the variable resistor is set to any position. You may find that the voltmeters don't quite show this, and so it is a good time to discuss errors and limitations of the equipment (this relates to 'How Science Works'). In the discussion, students could observe the circuit again with a third voltmeter connected across the cell. This should demonstrate that the cell pd is always shared between the bulb and the variable resistor, even if the cell pd changes.

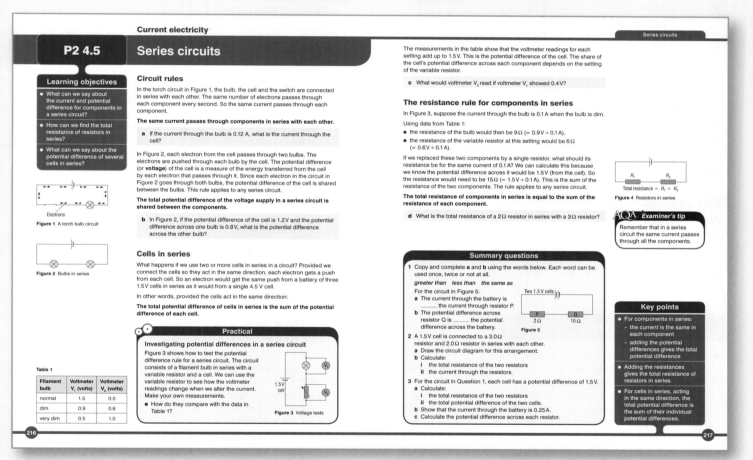

Further teaching suggestions

ICT link-up
● If at all possible, show a simulation of electron movement through the circuit to show that the electrons pass all the way around the circuit and are not used up. The simulation should also have some way of showing that the electrons are transferring energy as they go.

Missing values
● Give the students some series circuit diagrams with missing pd's, currents or resistances. Ask them to find the missing values. This should test their knowledge of the current–pd–resistance relationship and the total resistance rule.

Summary answers

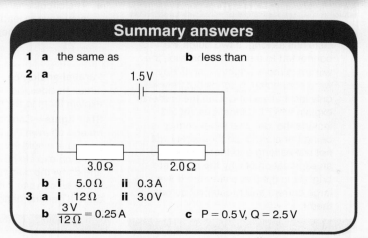

P2 4.6

Parallel circuits

- The current through a component depends on its resistance. The greater the resistance, the smaller the current for a given potential difference across the component. *[P2.3.2 i)]*
- For components connected in parallel:
  - the potential difference across each component is the same
  - the total current through the whole circuit is the sum of the currents through the separate components. *[P2.3.2 l)]*
- Apply the principles of basic electrical circuits to practical situations. *[P2.3]*
  Controlled Assessment: AS4.5 Analyse and interpret primary and secondary data. *[AS4.5.2 a) b)]*

Learning objectives

Students should learn:

- that the potential difference across components in parallel is the same
- that the total current in a parallel circuit is the sum of the currents in the individual branches.

Learning outcomes

Most students should be able to:

- recognise components in parallel with each other
- calculate the current in a branch of a parallel circuit, given the total current and the current in the other branches
- identify, for resistors of known resistance in parallel, which resistor has the most current passing through it and which has the least.

Some students should also be able to:

- analyse parallel circuits to find the current through branches and the potential difference across components.

Lesson structure

Starters

Circuit jumble – Show the students a diagram of a parallel circuit with three branches and several components on each branch. The wires and components are jumbled up and the students have to redraw the circuit properly. This should be a clear diagram with no gaps in the connections. *(5 minutes)*

The river – Show the students a picture of a river that branches and rejoins. Ask them to explain what happens to the current in the river before, during and after the split. Support students by showing clips of the flow or demonstrating the same idea with pipes (transparent ones work best). They should realise that the current divides and then rejoins, meaning that the total current is unchanged after the merger. Less obvious is that fact that each kilogram of water that went down one branch has travelled by the same distance **downhill** as each kilogram that went the other way. This concept is similar to the ideas of pd and energy transfer in different branches of a circuit. Students can be extended by asking them to identify the limitations of this model of current and pd at the end of the lesson. *(10 minutes)*

Main

- The initial investigation is straightforward and the students should be able to find the rule easily. A discussion of errors involved in the ammeter readings helps to get across concepts involving single measurements from 'How Science Works'.
- A simulation can be used if there are not enough ammeters, but you should show the results in a real circuit too.
- Spend a bit of time explaining that at the junction of a branch some of the electrons go one way, whereas the rest go the other way, but they all come from and go back to the battery.
- The bypass idea helps some students realise that because there are more paths for the current, a larger current can flow.
- The second simple circuit should confirm that the potential difference is the same across both of the resistors. If the resistors are the same size, then the currents should also be the same through each branch. To extend students, ask them to investigate a circuit that has two resistors on one branch and one on the other. Ask: 'Does the potential difference across the first branch match that across the second?'
- The circuit analysis will show if the students have got a firm grip of the equations. You may have to lead them through the analysis one step at a time. Try a couple more circuits if time permits.

Support

- There are some more tricky circuits here and the students may need a step-by-step guide to assemble them: 'connect the positive end of the battery to the ammeter', etc. You might also think about attaching labels A_1, A_2 to the ammeters to reduce confusion.

Extend

- The light that shines twice as bright lasts half as long. If two bulbs are connected to a battery in parallel, they will shine more brightly than if they were connected in series but they will only last half as long. Can the students explain why? Explanations should include the idea that more energy is being transferred, so the battery will not last as long and there should be an explanation of why the bulbs are brighter in the first place (there is a large current and greater pd across them).

Plenaries

Parallel analogies – Can the students come up with any more analogies for a parallel circuit besides the ones from the 'Did you know' box in the Student Book? They should explain them to each other to decide which is best. *(5 minutes)*

Stair lights – Can the students design a simple circuit that can be used to turn the lights on and off from the top and bottom of a set of stairs? If time permits, they could build one. This would involve a pair of switches; one at the bottom of the stairs. The students can then explain how the lights operate. For support you can demonstrate the circuit and show the diagram asking the students to explain how it operates. For extension the students can see if it is possible to control a circuit like this from three or more switches; is there a general pattern to the design? *(10 minutes)*

Practical support

Investigating parallel circuits

This experiment shows that that the current is divided through parallel branches.

Equipment and materials required

For each group: a power supply or battery pack (1.5 V), connecting leads, variable resistor, two 1.5 V bulbs and three ammeters.

Details

The students set up the circuit with two parallel branches, each with an ammeter. The third ammeter is placed in series with the power supply or battery to measure total current, and the variable resistor is used in series with the battery to control the current. The readings from the two ammeters on the branches (A_2 and A_3) should be equal to the total current from the battery (A_1). As in the experiment from the last lesson, there can be inaccuracies in the readings so go

through the results with the students and discuss the reasons for these errors (this relates to 'How Science Works').

Potential difference in a parallel circuit

This is another simple circuit used to verify that the potential difference across parallel components is the same.

Equipment and materials required

For each group: a power supply or battery pack (1.5 V), connecting leads, a 2 Ω resistor and a 5 Ω resistor, a variable resistor, and two voltmeters.

Details

The students connect up the circuit as shown and measure the pd across the two resistors. This should be the same. To show that this fact does not change, replace one of the resistors with a variable one and alter its resistance.

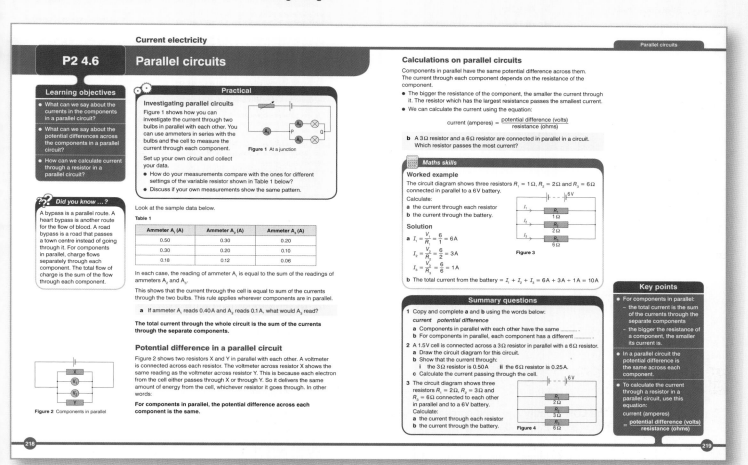

Current electricity

P2 4.6   Parallel circuits

Learning objectives

- What can we say about the currents in the components in a parallel circuit?
- What can we say about the potential differences across the components in a parallel circuit?
- How can we calculate current through a resistor in a parallel circuit?

Did you know ...?

A bypass is a parallel route. A heart bypass is another route for the flow of blood. A road bypass is a road that passes a town centre instead of going through it. For components in parallel, charge flows separately through each component. The total flow of charge is the sum of the flow through each component.

Practical

Investigating parallel circuits

Figure 1 shows how you can investigate the current through two bulbs in parallel with each other. You can use ammeters in series with the bulbs and the cell to measure the current through each component.

Figure 1 At a junction

Set up your own circuit and collect your data.

- How do your measurements compare with the ones for different settings of the variable resistor shown in Table 1 below?
- Discuss if your own measurements show the same pattern.

Look at the sample data below.

Table 1

Ammeter A_1 (A)	Ammeter A_2 (A)	Ammeter A_3 (A)
0.50	0.30	0.20
0.30	0.20	0.10
0.18	0.12	0.06

In each case, the reading of ammeter A_1 is equal to the sum of the readings of ammeters A_2 and A_3.

This shows that the current through the cell is equal to sum of the currents through the two bulbs. This rule applies wherever components are in parallel.

a If ammeter A_1 reads 0.40 A and A_2 reads 0.1 A, what would A_3 read?

The total current through the whole circuit is the sum of the currents through the separate components.

Potential difference in a parallel circuit

Figure 2 shows two resistors X and Y in parallel with each other. A voltmeter is connected across each resistor. The voltmeter across resistor X shows the same reading as the voltmeter across resistor Y. This is because each electron from the cell either passes through X or through Y. So it delivers the same amount of energy from the cell, whichever resistor it goes through. In other words:

For components in parallel, the potential difference across each component is the same.

Figure 2 Components in parallel

Calculations on parallel circuits

Components in parallel have the same potential difference across them. The current through each component depends on the resistance of the component.

- The bigger the resistance of the component, the smaller the current through it. The resistor which has the largest resistance passes the smallest current.
- We can calculate the current using the equation:

$$\text{current (amperes)} = \frac{\text{potential difference (volts)}}{\text{resistance (ohms)}}$$

b A 3 Ω resistor and a 6 Ω resistor are connected in parallel in a circuit. Which resistor passes the most current?

Maths skills

Worked example

The circuit diagram shows three resistors $R_1 = 1\,\Omega$, $R_2 = 2\,\Omega$ and $R_3 = 6\,\Omega$ connected in parallel to a 6 V battery.
Calculate:
a the current through each resistor
b the current through the battery.

Solution

a $I_1 = \dfrac{V_1}{R_1} = \dfrac{6}{1} = 6\,\text{A}$

$I_2 = \dfrac{V_2}{R_2} = \dfrac{6}{2} = 3\,\text{A}$

$I_3 = \dfrac{V_3}{R_3} = \dfrac{6}{6} = 1\,\text{A}$

Figure 3

b The total current from the battery = $I_1 + I_2 + I_3$ = 6 A + 3 A + 1 A = 10 A

Summary questions

1 Copy and complete **a** and **b** using the words below:
current   potential difference
   a Components in parallel with each other have the same _____ .
   b For components in parallel, each component has a different _____ .

2 A 1.5 V cell is connected across a 3 Ω resistor in parallel with a 6 Ω resistor.
   a Draw the circuit diagram for this circuit.
   b Show that the current through:
      i the 3 Ω resistor is 0.50 A   **ii** the 6 Ω resistor is 0.25 A.
   c Calculate the current passing through the cell.

3 The circuit diagram shows three resistors $R_1 = 2\,\Omega$, $R_2 = 3\,\Omega$ and $R_3 = 6\,\Omega$ connected to each other in parallel and to a 6 V battery.
Calculate:
   a the current through each resistor
   b the current through the battery.   **Figure 4**

Key points

- For components in parallel:
  – the total current is the sum of the currents through the separate components
  – the bigger the resistance of a component, the smaller its current is.
- In a parallel circuit the potential difference is the same across each component.
- To calculate the current through a resistor in a parallel circuit, use this equation:
  current (amperes)
  $= \dfrac{\text{potential difference (volts)}}{\text{resistance (ohms)}}$

218   219

Further teaching suggestions

ICT link-up

- A range of software is available to simulate circuit construction and measure current and potential differences. This can be much easier to use than assembling larger parallel circuits with a number of voltmeters and ammeters.

Analysing circuits

- Give the students some series and parallel circuits to analyse. They should find the missing currents, potential differences and resistances.

Answers to in-text questions

a 0.30 A

b The 3 Ω resistor.

Summary answers

1 **a** potential difference
  b current

2 **a**

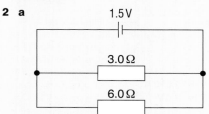

1.5 V

3.0 Ω

6.0 Ω

  b **i** current = 1.5 V/3 Ω = 0.50 A
      ii current = 1.5 V/6 Ω = 0.25 A
  c cell current = 0.5 + 0.25 = 0.75 A

3 **a** R_1: 3 A; R_2: 2 A; R_3: 1 A
  b 6 A

Summary answers

1 a

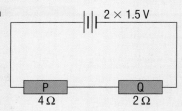

b

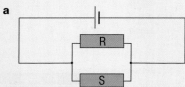

2 a filament bulb   **b** resistor

  c thermistor   **d** diode

3 a

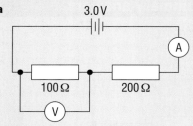

2 × 1.5 V

P   4 Ω   Q   2 Ω

  b **i** 3.0 V

     ii 6 Ω

    iii 0.5 A

    iv P: 2.0 V; Q: 1.0 V

4 a

R

S

  b **i** 1.0 A

     ii 0.5 A

    iii 1.5 A

5 a different from

  b equal to

6 a **i** 2.0 V

    ii pd across the LDR = battery pd − pd across the 200 Ω resistor = 3.0 − 2.0 = 1.0 V

  b The resistance of the LDR increases when it is covered, so the total resistance of the circuit increases. Therefore, the current decreases, so the ammeter reading decreases.

7 a

3.0 V

A

100 Ω   200 Ω

V

  b **i** 300 Ω   **ii** 0.010 A

    iii 1.0 V   **iv** 2.0 V

8 a **i** The battery pd of 3.0 V is shared between the LED and the resistor. Since the potential difference across the LED is 0.6 V when it emits light, the potential difference across the resistor is 3.0 − 0.6 = 2.4 V.

    ii 0.024 A

Current electricity: P2 4.1–P2 4.6

Summary questions

1 Sketch a circuit diagram to show:

  a a torch bulb, a cell and a diode connected in series so that the torch bulb is on

  b a variable resistor, two cells in series and a torch bulb whose brightness can be varied by adjusting the variable resistor.

2 Match each component in the list to each statement **a** to **d** that describes it.

  diode filament bulb resistor thermistor

  a Its resistance increases if the current through it increases.

  b The current through it is proportional to the potential difference across it.

  c Its resistance decreases if its temperature is increased.

  d Its resistance depends on which way round it is connected in a circuit.

3 a Sketch a circuit diagram to show two resistors P and Q connected in series to a battery of two cells in series with each other.

  b In the circuit in part **a**, resistor P has a resistance of 4 Ω, resistor Q has a resistance of 2 Ω and each cell has a potential difference of 1.5 V. Calculate:

    i the total potential difference of the two cells

    ii the total resistance of the two resistors

    iii the current in the circuit

    iv the potential difference across each resistor.

4 a Sketch a circuit diagram to show two resistors R and S in parallel with each other connected to a single cell.

  b In the circuit in part **a**, resistor R has a resistance of 2 Ω, resistor S has a resistance of 4 Ω and the cell has a potential difference of 2 V. Calculate:

    i the current through resistor R

    ii the current through resistor S

    iii the current through the cell in the circuit.

5 Copy and complete **a** and **b** using the phrases below. Each option can be used once, twice or not at all.

  different from equal to

  a For two components X and Y in series, the potential difference across X is usually .... the potential difference across Y.

  b For two components X and Y in parallel, the potential difference across X is .... the potential difference across Y.

6 Figure 1 shows a light-dependent resistor is series w 200 Ω resistor, a 3.0 V battery and an ammeter.

3.0 V

LDR   200 Ω

Figure 1

  a With the LDR in daylight, the ammeter reads 0.010

    i Calculate the potential difference across the 20 resistor when the current through it is 0.010 A.

    ii Show that the potential difference across the L is 1.0 V when the ammeter reads 0.010 A.

  b If the LDR is then covered, explain whether the ammeter reading increases or decreases or stays same.

7 In Figure 1 in Question 6, the LDR is replaced by a 10 resistor and a voltmeter connected in parallel with th resistor.

  a Draw the circuit diagram for this circuit.

  b Calculate:

    i the total resistance of the two resistors in the ci

    ii the current through the ammeter

    iii the voltmeter reading

    iv the potential difference across the 200 Ω resistc

8 Figure 2 shows a light-emitting diode (LED) in series a resistor and a 3.0 V battery.

3.0 V

LED   1000 Ω

Figure 2

  a The LED in the circuit emits light. The potential difference across it when it emits light is 0.6 V.

    i Explain why the potential difference across the 1000 Ω resistor is 2.4 V.

    ii Calculate the current in the circuit.

  b If the LED in the circuit is reversed, what would be current in the circuit? Give a reason for your answe

9 State and explain how the resistance of a filament bulb changes when the current through the filament i increased.

---

  b The current would be (almost) zero as the 'reverse' resistance of the LED is very high. The total resistance of the LED and the resistor would therefore be much greater than it was when the LED was in its 'forward' direction so the current would be much less than 0.024 A.

9 The resistance increases when the current is increased. This is because the increase of current makes the bulb hotter. As a result, the metal ions of the filament vibrate more, so they resist the passage of electrons through the filament more.

Kerboodle resources

Resources available for this chapter on Kerboodle are:

- Chapter map: Current electricity
- Maths skills: Potential difference, current and resistance (P2 4.3)
- How Science Works: What's the potential (P2 4.3)
- Practical: Resistance in a wire (P2 4.3)
- Interactive activity: Circuit symbols and resistance
- Revision podcast: Series and parallel circuits
- Test yourself: Current electricity
- On your marks: Current electricity
- Examination-style questions: Current electricity
- Answers to examination-style questions: Current electricity

Examination-style questions

A plastic rod is rubbed with a dry cloth.

a Explain how the rod becomes negatively charged. (3)

b What charge is left on the cloth? (1)

c What happens if the negatively charged rod is brought close to another negatively charged rod? (1)

a Copy and complete the table of circuit symbols and their names. (5)

Circuit symbol	Name
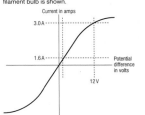 V	i
ii	ammeter
iii	
iv	LDR
v	

b Copy and complete the following sentences using the list of words and phrases below. Each word can be used once, more than once or not at all.

energy transferred   charge   resistance   voltage

Electric current is a flow of ....

The potential difference between two points in a circuit is the .... per unit of .... that passes between the points.

The greater the .... the lower the current for a given potential difference. (4)

Complete the following calculations. Write down the equation you use. Show clearly how you work out your answer and give the unit.

a i Calculate the potential difference between A and B. (1)

ii The potential difference across the 15 Ω resistor is 5 V. Calculate the potential difference across the 12 Ω resistor. (1)

b i Calculate the combined resistance of the 12 Ω and the 15 Ω resistors in series. (1)

ii Calculate the current that flows through the circuit at X. (2)

iii Calculate the current flowing through the circuit at Y. (1)

c Calculate the resistance of the resistor labelled R. (2)

d Calculate the charge that flows through resistor R in 2 minutes. (3)

e Calculate the work done (energy transferred) by the cell if the total charge that has flowed through it is 3000 C. (2)

4 a Sketch and label a graph of current against potential difference for a diode. (3)

b The graph of current against potential difference for a filament bulb is shown.

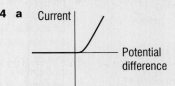

i Calculate the potential difference when the resistance of the filament bulb is 2 Ω when the current is 1.6 A. Write down the equation you use. Show clearly how you work out your answer and give the unit. (2)

ii Calculate the resistance at a potential difference of 12 V. Write down the equation you use. Show clearly how you work out your answer and give the unit. (3)

c *In this question you will be assessed on using good English, organising information clearly and using specialist terms where appropriate.*

Explain the change in resistance of the filament bulb in terms of ions and electrons. [H] (6)

Examination-style answers

1 a electrons move from cloth to rod; electrons have negative charge *(3 marks)*

b positive *(1 mark)*

c repels *(1 mark)*

2 a i voltmeter *(1 mark)*

ii (A) *(1 mark)*

iii variable resistor *(1 mark)*

iv *(1 mark)*

v battery/power supply *(1 mark)*

b Electric current is a flow of **charge**. The potential difference between two points in a circuit is the **energy transferred** per unit of **charge** that passes between the points.

The greater the **resistance** the lower the current for a given potential difference. *(4 marks)*

3 a i 9 V *(1 mark)*

ii 4 V *(1 mark)*

b i 27 Ω *(1 mark)*

ii $I = \dfrac{V}{R} = 9/27 = 0.33\,A$ *(2 marks)*

iii $0.33 + 0.5 = 0.83\,A$ *(1 mark)*

c $I = \dfrac{V}{R} = 9/0.5 = 18\,\Omega$ *(2 marks)*

d $Q = I \times t = 0.5 \times 120 = 60\,C$ *(3 marks)*

e $W = V \times Q = 9 \times 3000 = 27\,000\,J$ *(2 marks)*

4 a

Current | Potential difference

(3 marks)

b i $V = I \times R = 1.6 \times 2 = 3.2\,V$ *(2 marks)*

ii $R = \dfrac{V}{I} = 12/3 = 4\,\Omega$ *(3 marks)*

c There is a clear, balanced and detailed description of how the change in resistance of the filament bulb occurs. The answer shows almost faultless spelling, punctuation and grammar. It is coherent and in an organised, logical sequence. It contains a range of appropriate or relevant specialist terms used accurately. *(5–6 marks)*

There is a description of a range of the ways in which the change in resistance of the filament bulb occurs. There are some errors in spelling, punctuation and grammar. The answer has some structure and organisation. The use of specialist terms has been attempted, but not always accurately. *(3–4 marks)*

There is a brief description of at least two ways in which the change in resistance of the filament bulb occurs, which has little clarity and detail. The spelling, punctuation and grammar are very weak. The answer is poorly organised with almost no specialist terms and/or their use demonstrating a general lack of understanding of their meaning. *(1–2 marks)*

No relevant content. *(0 marks)*

Examples of physics points made in the response:

- as the voltage increases, the current increases
- this increases the collisions
- between electrons and ions
- the ions vibrate with a greater amplitude
- and this increases the temperature
- and the resistance.

Practical suggestions

Practicals	AQA	k	📖	⚙
Using filament bulbs and resistors to investigate potential difference/current characteristics.	✓	✓	✓	✓
Investigating potential difference/current characteristics for LDRs and thermistors.	✓		✓	
Setting up series and parallel circuits to investigate current and potential difference.	✓		✓	
Plan and carry out an investigation to find the relationship between the resistance of thermistors and their temperatures.	✓			
Investigating the change of resistance of LDRs with light intensity.	✓		✓	

P2 5.1

Alternating current

AQA Specification link-up: Physics P2.4

- Cells and batteries supply current that always passes in the same direction. This is called direct current (dc). *[P2.4.1 a)]*
- An alternating current (ac) is one that is constantly changing direction. *[P2.4.1 b)]*
- Mains electricity is an ac supply. In the UK it has a frequency of 50 cycles per second (50 hertz) and is about 230 V. *[P2.4.1 c)]*

Learning objectives

Students should learn:

- that direct current involves the flow of electrons in one direction and can be provided by cells or batteries
- that alternating current involves the rapid change in direction of the current
- that UK mains electricity is alternating current with a frequency of 50 Hz
- to use oscilloscope traces to compare (ac) and (dc) supplies.

Learning outcomes

Most students should be able to:

- distinguish between alternating and direct current
- state the frequency of UK mains electricity
- describe how the potential of the live wires varies with each cycle
- use oscilloscope traces to compare direct and alternating potential differences and measure the peak voltage of an ac source.

Some students should also be able to:

- measure the period and frequency of an ac source using an oscilloscope or diagrams of oscilloscope traces. [HT only]

Support

- Provide a diagram comparing an (ac) source to a (dc) source and ask the students to mark on the amplitude (voltage) and the period of the waveforms. You will most likely need a classroom assistant or technician to demonstrate the oscilloscope to small groups at a time.

Extend

- Ask: 'Why is our mains electricity frequency 50 Hz?' 'What is the physical reason for this and is it the same in all countries?' 'How was this frequency and voltage decided on and why?' They should find out information about the speed of rotation of the generators and the decisions made.

Lesson structure

Starters

Wave forms – Show the students a wave diagram (e.g. picture from the Student Book) and ask them to discuss it. They should recognise the sine wave shape and perhaps the wavelength (or period) and amplitude. *(5 minutes)*

Mains facts – Ask the students some true/false questions about mains electricity to see what they already know. These should include some basic questions that have already been covered [A dc conventional current travels from positive to negative, the current through series circuits is the same in each component] and some testing of their mains knowledge (Mains voltage is 240 V [false], the three pins in a mains plug are positive, negative and neutral [false]). You can differentiate to support or extend by selecting appropriately challenging questions. *(10 minutes)*

Main

- Many of the students will have been wondering what the other two outputs on a power supply are for. Show them that a bulb will light up from a dc source and also from the ac source. The dc outputs are colour coded for positive and negative, but the ac ones are not: ask the students why they think this is.

- In a dc circuit the electrons eventually make it around the complete circuit. In an ac circuit they just oscillate back and forth a few centimetres. Describe this to the students pointing out that the electrons are still transferring energy. Make sure that the students know that mains electricity supply is 230 V ac at 50 Hz. This is frequently asked for in examination papers. Don't use these high voltages in demonstrations.

- Some students may know that fluorescent lamps in some buildings flicker or buzz. Let them hear a 50 Hz signal using a signal generator and loudspeaker, and they will probably recognise the noise.

- The oscilloscope is a complex device, but the students only need to know about the time base and the Y-gain. (See 'Practical support'.) Higher Tier students will need to be able to take measurements from CRO traces. Make sure that they are only using the controls that they need. You can explain what some of the other buttons do, but make sure that the students know that they only have to be able to read the traces.

- If you have a computer-based oscilloscope, it is much better to use this for demonstrations rather than a small CRO. Connect it up to a signal generator or ac power supply to show the traces. The whole class should be able to see it at once if you use a data projector too. Most of them allow you to capture ('freeze') the signal and this makes measurement easier.

Plenaries

ac/dc? – Give the students a set of electrical appliances and ask them to stack them in two piles: ac operation and dc operation. If you want to extend the students, you can ask 'What about appliances such as laptops that have transformers and rectifiers to convert?' You can then discuss what the connecting box does. *(5 minutes)*

Traces – Show the students a series of oscilloscope traces and ask them to say if the peak pd is higher or lower, and the frequency higher or lower, than the previous one. They could read off the time period and the voltage from the traces. Extend students by asking them to read exact values of peak pd and time period from the traces; they should then calculate the frequency (make sure that different diagrams have different time bases). For support, you should use a single time-base setting for most of the diagrams. *(10 minutes)*

Practical support

The oscilloscope

Oscilloscopes can be fiddly to use and are expensive, but they are essential to understanding alternating current. If not enough equipment is available, let the students use what there is, one group at a time.

Equipment and materials needed

Per group: cathode ray oscilloscope, low voltage ac source, battery and leads.

Details

The greatest problem the students will have with this experiment is setting the time base and volts per centimetre (Y-gain) dials on the CRO. If these are incorrectly set, then the students will not get a useful trace. To make things easier for them, put small blobs of paint on the scale around the dials showing the correct setting to show a 2 V, 50 Hz trace clearly. This will be a common function, so don't worry too much about defacing the scopes. If you want to show what would happen to the trace if the frequency of the pd is changed, you can set up a signal generator instead of the ac source.

Mains electricity

P2 5.1   Alternating current 🄚

Learning objectives

- What is meant by direct current and alternating current?
- What do we mean by the peak voltage of an alternating potential difference?
- What do we mean by the live wire and the neutral wire of a mains circuit?
- How do we use an oscilloscope to measure the frequency of an alternating current? [H]

Figure 1 Mains voltage v. time

The battery in a torch makes the current to go round the circuit in one direction only. We say the current in the circuit is a **direct current (dc)** because it is in one direction only.

When you switch a light on at home, you use **alternating current (ac)** because mains electricity is an ac supply. An alternating current repeatedly reverses its direction. It flows one way then the opposite way in successive cycles. Its frequency is the number of cycles it passes through each second.

In the UK, the mains frequency is 50 cycles per second (or 50 Hz). A light bulb works just as well at this frequency as it would with a direct current.

a   Why would a much lower frequency than 50 Hz be unsuitable for a light bulb?

Mains circuits

Every mains circuit has a **live wire** and a **neutral wire**. The current through a mains appliance alternates. That's because the mains supply provides an alternating potential difference between the two wires.

The neutral wire is **earthed** at the local substation. The potential difference between the live wire and 'earth' is usually referred to as the 'potential' or voltage of the live wire. The live wire is dangerous because its voltage repeatedly changes from + to – and back every cycle. It reaches over 300 V in each direction, as shown in Figure 1.

Practical

The oscilloscope

We use an oscilloscope to show how an alternating potential difference (pd) changes with time.

1   Connect a signal generator to an oscilloscope, as shown in Figure 2.
- The trace on the oscilloscope screen shows electrical waves. They are caused by the potential difference increasing and decreasing continuously.
- The highest potential difference is reached at each peak. The peak potential difference or the **peak voltage** is the difference in volts between the peak and the middle level of the waves. Increasing the pd of the ac supply makes the waves on the screen taller.
- Increasing the frequency of the ac supply increases the number of cycles you see on the screen. So the waves on the screen get squashed together.
- How would the trace change if the pd of the ac supply were reduced?

2   Connect a battery to the oscilloscope. You should see a flat line at a constant potential difference.
- What difference is made by reversing the battery?

Figure 2 Using an oscilloscope

Measuring an alternating potential difference

We can use an **oscilloscope** to measure the peak potential difference and the frequency of a low voltage ac supply. For example, in Figure 2:
- the peak voltage is 2.1 V if the peaks are 8.4 cm above the troughs. Each peak is 4.2 cm above the middle which is at zero pd. The Y-gain control at 0.5 V/cm tells us each centimetre of height is due to a potential difference of 0.5 V. So the peak potential difference is 2.1 V (= 0.5 V/cm × 4.2 cm).

Higher

- the frequency is 12.5 Hz if each cycle on the screen is 8 cm across. The time base control at 10 milliseconds per centimetre (ms/cm) tells us each centimetre across the screen is a time interval of 10 ms. So the time taken for one cycle is 80 ms (= 10 ms/cm × 8 cm). The frequency is therefore 12.5 Hz (= 1/80 ms or 1/0.08 s).

Note: the frequency of ac supply = $\dfrac{1}{\text{the time for one cycle}}$

More about mains circuits

Look at Figure 1 again. It shows how the potential of the live wire varies with time.
- The live wire alternates between +325 V and –325 V. In terms of electrical power, this is equivalent to a direct voltage of 230 V. So we say the voltage of the mains is 230 V.

Higher

Each cycle in Figure 1 takes 0.02 second. The frequency of the mains supply (the number of cycles per second) is therefore 50 Hz (= $\dfrac{1}{0.02 \text{ seconds}}$)

b   What is the maximum potential difference between the live wire and the neutral wire in Figure 1?

Summary questions

1   Choose the correct potential difference from the list for each appliance a to d.

   1.5 V   12 V   230 V   325 V

   a   a car battery   c   a torch cell
   b   the mains voltage   d   the maximum potential of the live wire.

2   In Figure 2, how would the trace on the screen change if the frequency of the ac supply was:
   a   increased   b   reduced?

3   In Figure 2, what is the frequency if one cycle measures 4 cm across the screen for the same time base setting?   [H]

4   a   How does an alternating current differ from a direct current?
    b   Figure 4 shows a diode and a resistor in series with each other connected to an ac supply. Explain why the current in the circuit is a direct current not an alternating current.

Figure 4

⁇? Did you know …?

Breakdown vans usually carry a 'fast charger' to recharge a 'flat' car battery as quickly as possible. A flat battery needs a 12 V battery charger to charge it. An ordinary battery charger converts ac from the mains to 12 V dc but it can take hours to recharge a flat battery.

Figure 3 A battery charger

Key points

- Direct current is in one direction only. Alternating current repeatedly reverses its direction.
- The peak voltage of an alternating potential difference is the maximum voltage measured from zero volts.
- A mains circuit has a live wire that is alternately positive and negative every cycle and a neutral wire at zero volts.
- To measure the frequency of an a.c. supply, we measure the time period of the waves then use the formula: frequency = $\dfrac{1}{\text{time taken for 1 cycle}}$ [H]

⁇? Did you know …?

A rapid car battery recharge can produce currents of over 100 A for short periods. At 12 V, this means that it is transferring 1200 J each second. For comparison, a normal AA battery operates at 1.5 V and produces a current of only 100 mA, so transfers 0.15 J each second.

Further teaching suggestions

ICT link-up

- There are excellent computer-based oscilloscopes that can display traces (e.g. picoscope). These are very useful for demonstrations, because the display can be projected so that everybody can see it at once. It is still worth showing the students an old-fashioned one too. Simulations are also available online; search the web for 'oscilloscope' simulation.

Answers to in-text questions

a   The bulb would flicker continuously.

b   325 V

Summary answers

1   a   12 V
    b   230 V
    c   1.5 V
    d   325 V

2   The number of cycles on the screen would:
    a   increase
    b   decrease

3   25 Hz

4   a   A direct current in a circuit is in one direction only; an alternating current repeatedly reverses its direction.
    b   The diode only allows current through when the polarity of the ac supply is such that the diode conducts. This happens every other half-cycle when the polarity of the supply is such that diode is 'forward-biased' (i.e. in its 'forward' direction relative to the ac supply).

P2 5.2 Cables and plugs

Learning objectives

Students should learn:

- that mains plugs and sockets are made from robust insulating materials
- that mains cables are made from copper conductive wires insulated by flexible plastic
- the names and colours of the wires in a three-pin plug
- the structure of a mains three-pin plug and the functions of the live wire, the neutral wire and the earth wire.

Learning outcomes

Most students should be able to:

- describe the design and function of a three-pin mains plug, including the materials and the colours of the wires
- explain why it is important that appliances are double-insulated
- explain why it is necessary to connect some appliances to the earth via the earth wire
- explain, in terms of safety, why the fuse in the plug of an appliance and the switch of an appliance are on the live side of the appliance.

Some students should also be able to:

- explain in detail the choice of materials used for the mains parts of a three-pin mains plug.

Answers to in-text questions

a So each one can be switched on or off without affecting the others.
b Brass is harder than copper or zinc.
c The live wire could be exposed where the cable is worn away or damaged.
d The green and yellow wire.

Support

- Provide the students with a large diagram of plug wiring. They should then label the parts, colour the wires and describe the materials used for each part.

Extend

- Get the students to write a 'How to wire a plug' guide as found in some DIY stores. The guide should contain idiot-proof step-by-step instructions of what equipment you need and what you should do.

Specification link-up: Physics P2.4

- Most electrical appliances are connected to the mains using cable and a three-pin plug. *[P2.4.1 d)]*
- The structure of electrical cable. *[P2.4.1 e)]*
- The structure and wiring of a three-pin plug. *[P2.4.1 f)]*
- Understand the principles of safe practice and recognise dangerous practice in the use of mains electricity. *[P2.4]*
- Evaluate and explain the need to use different cables for different appliances. *[P2.4]*

Lesson structure

Starters

Mystery object – Put a mains plug in a bag and ask one student to describe it to the rest of the class, but only using shape and texture. This can be made more difficult by using a continental plug. They should describe the materials used and the shape; later this leads to reasons for these design features. *(5 minutes)*

Material sorting – Give each group of students a bag containing a range of materials and ask them to sort the materials in any way they wish. They must explain how they sorted them to other groups in terms of the properties. To support students, you can give them a list of properties to use during the sorting process. Extend the students by selecting materials that require additional discussion and ask them to define what they mean by the category they have chosen. You should make sure that you ask them to sort information into groups including conductors, insulators, hard and flexible, as these are good ways of describing why particular materials are chosen for plugs and cables. *(10 minutes)*

Main

- Only use appliances that have been safety-checked for this lesson!
- If you have a metal electric heater, then use it to introduce the idea of earthing an appliance. Discuss the materials used in a plug and cable by actually showing them. If you have very old appliances you might like to show how these have improved over the years. The students need to be able to explain why each material has been chosen.
- Emphasise the importance of the insulating properties of plastic and how this is linked to the idea of double insulation. You should be able to show a few appliances with the appropriate symbol on.
- The colour coding is usually well understood, but some students will know the black and red wires used in mains circuits in houses – this can lead to some confusion. (All new wiring now uses the new colours.)
- The students need to know that the diameter of the wires in the plug is important as thicker wires can carry a larger current without overheating. Link this back to their knowledge of resistance; thicker wires have lower resistance and so heat up less for the same current.
- Show the students some badly wired plugs. This works best if the plugs are real, but use diagrams if necessary. Make sure these can not be plugged in by using a plug-wiring board. Some of the faults should be hard to spot. One commonly missed mistake is the cable grip gripping the wires instead of the larger cable.
- You may have plugs for different countries, electrical systems or adapters for them. Showing them to students will emphasise that each country has its own designs for plugs.
- A tip for wiring a plug is: When looking down on to a plug as it is being wired the **BR**own wire connects to the **B**ottom **R**ight, the **BL**ue wire connects to the **B**ottom **L**eft. The other wire goes to the other pin!

Plenaries

Materials summary – The students should make a table listing the parts of a plug and cable, the materials used and the reasons for those choices. This should be centred on ideas about good conductors and insulators along with flexibility or rigidity. *(5 minutes)*

Wonky wiring – Show the students incorrectly wired plugs and ask them to describe the problems. You can also include some cartoons of bad habits in wiring including too many plugs in one socket, wires taped together, leads trailing across the floor and water near electrical appliances. Students can be supported by asking them to match known problems with particular pictures of plugs. Some can be extended by showing appliances with multiple problems. *(10 minutes)*

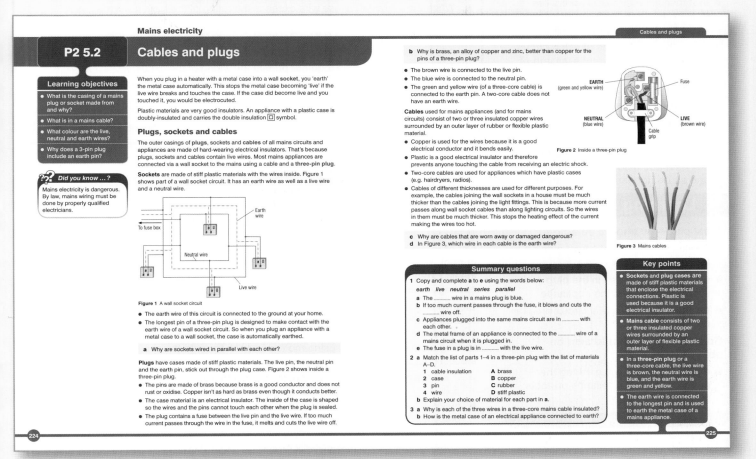

Mains electricity

Cables and plugs

P2 5.2 Cables and plugs

Learning objectives
- What is the casing of a mains plug or socket made from and why?
- What is in a mains cable?
- What colour are the live, neutral and earth wires?
- Why does a 3-pin plug include an earth pin?

Did you know …?
Mains electricity is dangerous. By law, mains wiring must be done by properly qualified electricians.

When you plug in a heater with a metal case into a wall **socket**, you 'earth' the metal case automatically. This stops the metal case becoming 'live' if the live wire breaks and touches the case. If the case did become live and you touched it, you would be electrocuted.

Plastic materials are very good insulators. An appliance with a plastic case is doubly-insulated and carries the double insulation ▢ symbol.

Plugs, sockets and cables

The outer casings of **plugs**, sockets and **cables** of all mains circuits and appliances are made of hard-wearing electrical insulators. That's because plugs, sockets and cables contain live wires. Most mains appliances are connected via a wall socket to the mains using a cable and a **three-pin plug**.

Sockets are made of stiff plastic materials with the wires inside. Figure 1 shows part of a wall socket circuit. It has an earth wire as well as a live wire and a neutral wire.

Figure 1 A wall socket circuit
(To fuse box, Earth wire, Neutral wire, Live wire)

- The earth wire of this circuit is connected to the ground at your home.
- The longest pin of a three-pin plug is designed to make contact with the earth wire of a wall socket circuit. So when you plug an appliance with a metal case to a wall socket, the case is automatically earthed.

a Why are sockets wired in parallel with each other?

Plugs have cases made of stiff plastic materials. The live pin, the neutral pin and the earth pin, stick out through the plug case. Figure 2 shows inside a three-pin plug.

- The pins are made of brass because brass is a good conductor and does not rust or oxidise. Copper isn't as hard as brass even though it conducts better.
- The case material is an electrical insulator. The inside of the case is shaped so the wires and the pins cannot touch each other when the plug is sealed.
- The plug contains a fuse between the live pin and the live wire. If too much current passes through the wire in the fuse, it melts and cuts the live wire off.

b Why is brass, an alloy of copper and zinc, better than copper for the pins of a three-pin plug?

- The brown wire is connected to the live pin.
- The blue wire is connected to the neutral pin.
- The green and yellow wire (of a three-core cable) is connected to the earth pin. A two-core cable does not have an earth wire.

Cables used for mains appliances (and for mains circuits) consist of two or three insulated copper wires surrounded by an outer layer of rubber or flexible plastic material.

- Copper is used for the wires because it is a good electrical conductor and it bends easily.
- Plastic is a good electrical insulator and therefore prevents anyone touching the cable from receiving an electric shock.
- Two-core cables are used for appliances which have plastic cases (e.g. hairdryers, radios).
- Cables of different thicknesses are used for different purposes. For example, the cables joining the wall sockets in a house must be much thicker than the cables joining the light fittings. This is because more current passes along wall socket cables than along lighting circuits. So the wires in them must be much thicker. This stops the heating effect of the current making the wires too hot.

c Why are cables that are worn away or damaged dangerous?
d In Figure 3, which wire in each cable is the earth wire?

Figure 2 Inside a three-pin plug
(EARTH (green and yellow wire), Fuse, NEUTRAL (blue wire), LIVE (brown wire), Cable grip)

Figure 3 Mains cables

Summary questions

1 Copy and complete **a** to **e** using the words below:
earth live neutral series parallel
a The .... wire in a mains plug is blue.
b If too much current passes through the fuse, it blows and cuts the .... wire off.
c Appliances plugged into the same mains circuit are in .... with each other.
d The metal frame of an appliance is connected to the .... wire of a mains circuit when it is plugged in.
e The fuse in a plug is in .... with the live wire.

2 a Match the list of parts 1–4 in a three-pin plug with the list of materials A–D.
1 cable insulation	A brass
2 case	B copper
3 pin	C rubber
4 wire	D stiff plastic
b Explain your choice of material for each part in a.

3 a Why is each of the three wires in a three-core mains cable insulated?
b How is the metal case of an electrical appliance connected to earth?

Key points
- Sockets and plug cases are made of stiff plastic materials that enclose the electrical connections. Plastic is used because it is a good electrical insulator.
- Mains cable consists of two or three insulated copper wires surrounded by an outer layer of flexible plastic material.
- In a three-pin plug or a three-core cable, the live wire is brown, the neutral wire is blue, and the earth wire is green and yellow.
- The earth wire is connected to the longest pin and is used to earth the metal case of a mains appliance.

Further teaching suggestions

Plug wiring board
- If you have concerns about the safety of plug wiring in your laboratory, then you can pass around a plug board for the students to see faulty wiring.

Equipment and materials required
A plank of wood with six incorrectly wired plugs mounted on it.

Details
All that is involved is mounting six plugs onto a board with the pins sticking through it, so that they cannot be plugged in. Drill or chisel out the board, stick the cases down with strong glue and wire up the six plugs in incorrect ways so that the students can try to explain what has been done wrong. You might like to glue the pins into the wood to make sure that they don't fall out. Here are some examples of problems: wires stripped all the way back to the cable grip so that they short, live and neutral wire swapped, wires not tightened at the pins, fuse replaced with metal pin or similar, cable gripping wires not cable, cracked case (glue it down, then whack it with a screwdriver). If you have a bigger board then add others.

Summary answers

1 a neutral   b live   c parallel
d earth   e series

2 a 1 **C**; 2 **D**; 3 **A**; 4 **B**
b 1 Rubber is flexible and is an insulator.
2 Stiff plastic is an insulator, it doesn't wear and it can't be squashed.
3 Brass is a good conductor and doesn't deteriorate.
4 Copper is an excellent conductor and copper wires bend easily.

3 a The three wires must be insulated from each other otherwise there would be a dangerously large current in the cable due to the very low resistance between the live wire and the other wires where they touch.
b The earth wire of the cable is connected to a terminal fixed to the metal case. The other end of the earth wire is connected to the earth pin in the three-pin plug attached to the cable. When the plug is connected to a three-pin wall socket, the metal case is therefore connected via the earth wire to the ground.

P2 5.3

Fuses

AQA / Specification link-up: Physics P2.4

- If an electrical fault causes too great a current, the circuit is disconnected by a fuse or a circuit breaker in the live wire. [P2.4.1 g)]
- When the current in a fuse wire exceeds the rating of the fuse, it will melt, breaking the circuit. [P2.4.1 h)]
- Some circuits are protected by Residual Current Circuit Breakers (RCCBs). [P2.4.1 i)]
- Appliances with metal cases are usually earthed. [P2.4.1 j)]
- The earth wire and fuse together protect the wiring of the circuit. [P2.4.1 k)]
- Understand the principles of safe practice and recognise dangerous practice in the use of mains electricity. [P2.4]
- Compare the uses of fuses and circuit breakers. [P2.4]
- Evaluate and explain the need to use different cables for different appliances. [P2.4]

Learning objectives

Students should learn:

- that fuses and circuit breakers are devices that cut off electrical circuits when too large a current flows
- about the advantages of using circuit breakers to cut off circuits instead of fuses
- how to choose the correct rating of fuse for an appliance
- why it is important that appliances are earthed
- that double insulated appliances have a shell made of insulating materials and so do not need to be earthed.

Learning outcomes

Most students should be able to:

- explain how and why a fuse cuts off an electrical circuit
- explain why the fuse in the plug of an appliance protects the appliance
- list the advantages of a circuit breaker over a fuse.

Some students should also be able to:

- explain in detail why earthing the metal case of an appliance protects the user.

Answers to in-text questions

a The fuse wire would melt.

b The mains voltage is across less resistance because only part of the element is between the live and the neutral wire and so the current is bigger.

c The fault has not been put right so consult an electrician.

Support

- For the 'Electromagnets' Starter, give the students a set of cards to put in order.

Extend

- The students can look at the internal action of a circuit breaker and explain how it works in terms of electromagnetism. You should be able to find some suitable diagrams or animations to help the discussion along.

Lesson structure

Starters

Heating effect – Ask: 'Why do wires get hot when a current passes through them?' The students should explain the effect in terms of electron collisions with ions in the wire. Check that the students know that the wire is full of free electrons even when there is no current. To support students, you can show an animation of the effect to revise the key ideas. Extend students by asking them to describe all of the factors they think will cause heating in the wires and why they think this is. *(5 minutes)*

Electromagnets – Demonstrate an electromagnetic switch or relay and get the students to draw a flow chart of what is happening. This should describe electrical currents and the magnetic field and the effect of the field on other objects. You could expand this by looking at an electric bell causing motion and link this into the circuit breaker idea later in the lesson. *(10 minutes)*

Main

- Fuses are a bit dull without demonstrations, so try to fit in a few of the ones in the practical. If you are showing a fuse melting, use one with a glass casing, so that the students can see the wire becoming hot and then melting. This will disappoint some students who think a fuse actually explodes in some way.
- Many students will think that the fuse is a device that protects the user of an appliance. It is important to point out that the fuse really prevents an appliance from catching fire through overheating. Emphasise that it only takes a small current to kill and a 3.5 A appliance with a 5 A fuse in it can provide a current of 1.5 A without troubling the fuse.
- Earthing confuses some, but just point out that the basic idea is to provide an easy path for the current to take if there is a fault. Usually, if the appliance is earthed, then a large current would flow if the live wire touched the case and the fuse should melt and cut off the appliance. This is the common reason why an appliance keeps melting fuses. If the students see this happen, they should realise that the live wire is disconnected.
- Even if the fuse does not melt (usually because of putting 13 A fuses in everything), the earth wire provides a low resistance path for the current and the user would not be electrocuted by touching the case.
- You can demonstrate the use of circuit-breakers as outlined in the 'Further teaching suggestions' box. The students should realise the advantages fairly quickly. If you want to go into extra detail, then you can show a large model circuit-breaker. They should be able to link the idea of a current creating a magnetic field and pulling open a switch, therefore cutting off the current.
- Finally the students can look at a RCCB. They should note that no earth wire is needed. If there is a difference in the current between the live and neutral wire, there must be a current leak indicating a fault in the appliance.

Plenaries

Mains safety – The students produce a jingle, catchphrase or slogan to encourage people to use mains electricity safely. It should cover the dangers but also remind people that electricity is perfectly safe when used correctly. *(5 minutes)*

Dump your fuses – The students can produce an outline of an advertisement from a company that manufactures circuit-breakers and is trying to convince householders to swap their fuse boxes for breaker boxes. They should concentrate on the advantages of using a circuit-breaker in comparison with a fuse. Students can be extended by insisting that a full explanation of how a circuit-breaker works is included. Others can be supported by asking them to complete a simple comparison instead. *(10 minutes)*

Practical support

Demonstrating fuses

This is a simple demonstration to show that 1 A fuses melt before they allow excess current through them, then 3 A and so on.

Equipment and materials required

Power supply, leads, crocodile clips, fuses (1 A, 3 A, 5 A).

Details

You can show the students the differences between fuses, by showing them the fuse wire that is found in them. Connect up some 1 A, 3 A and 5 A fuse wire together in series with an ammeter and variable resistor, and pass an increasing current through it to show that the 1 A fuse wire melts first. You should reconnect the circuit (without the 1 A fuse) and increase the current again until the 3 A fuse melts, and finish with the 5 A melting. Discuss the thickness of the wires; the greater the diameter the greater the current required to melt the fuse wire. Hopefully this will be when a current of 1 A passes through it, but just how accurately is fuse wire manufactured? This would give a good opportunity to discuss aspects of 'How Science Works' on making measurements.

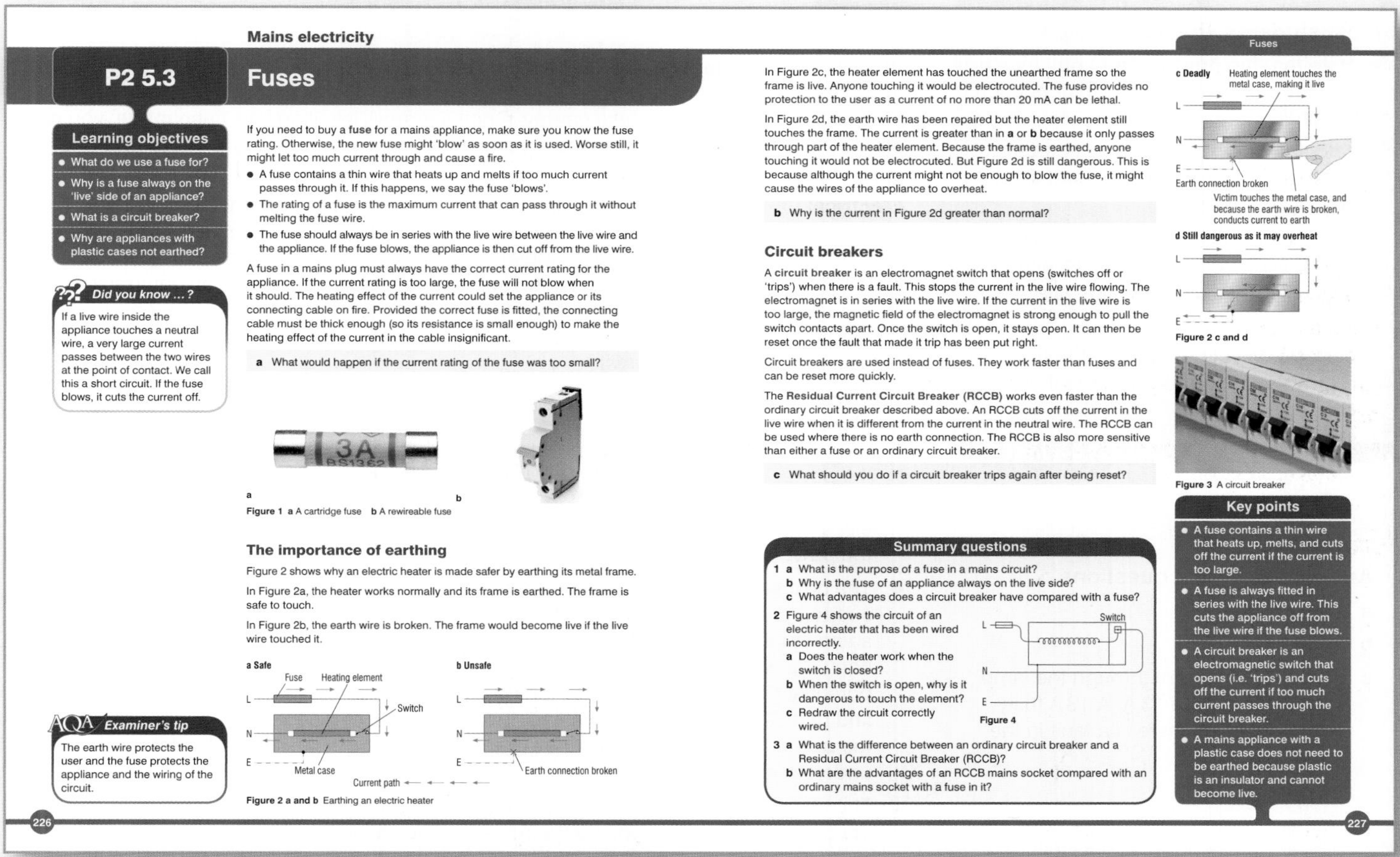

Mains electricity

P2 5.3 — Fuses

Learning objectives

- What do we use a fuse for?
- Why is a fuse always on the 'live' side of an appliance?
- What is a circuit breaker?
- Why are appliances with plastic cases not earthed?

Did you know …?

If a live wire inside the appliance touches a neutral wire, a very large current passes between the two wires at the point of contact. We call this a short circuit. If the fuse blows, it cuts the current off.

If you need to buy a fuse for a mains appliance, make sure you know the fuse rating. Otherwise, the new fuse might 'blow' as soon as it is used. Worse still, it might let too much current through and cause a fire.

- A fuse contains a thin wire that heats up and melts if too much current passes through it. If this happens, we say the fuse 'blows'.
- The rating of a fuse is the maximum current that can pass through it without melting the fuse wire.
- The fuse should always be in series with the live wire between the live wire and the appliance. If the fuse blows, the appliance is then cut off from the live wire.

A fuse in a mains plug must always have the correct current rating for the appliance. If the current rating is too large, the fuse will not blow when it should. The heating effect of the current could set the appliance or its connecting cable on fire. Provided the correct fuse is fitted, the connecting cable must be thick enough (so its resistance is small enough) to make the heating effect of the current in the cable insignificant.

a What would happen if the current rating of the fuse was too small?

Figure 1 **a** A cartridge fuse **b** A rewireable fuse

The importance of earthing

Figure 2 shows why an electric heater is made safer by earthing its metal frame.

In Figure 2a, the heater works normally and its frame is earthed. The frame is safe to touch.

In Figure 2b, the earth wire is broken. The frame would become live if the live wire touched it.

a Safe — Fuse, Heating element, Switch, L, N, E, Metal case, Current path

b Unsafe — Earth connection broken

Figure 2 a and b Earthing an electric heater

AQA Examiner's tip

The earth wire protects the user and the fuse protects the appliance and the wiring of the circuit.

In Figure 2c, the heater element has touched the unearthed frame so the frame is live. Anyone touching it would be electrocuted. The fuse provides no protection to the user as a current of no more than 20 mA can be lethal.

In Figure 2d, the earth wire has been repaired but the heater element still touches the frame. The current is greater than in **a** or **b** because it only passes through part of the heater element. Because the frame is earthed, anyone touching it would not be electrocuted. But Figure 2d is still dangerous. This is because although the current might not be enough to blow the fuse, it might cause the wires of the appliance to overheat.

b Why is the current in Figure 2d greater than normal?

Circuit breakers

A circuit breaker is an electromagnet switch that opens (switches off or 'trips') when there is a fault. This stops the current in the live wire flowing. The electromagnet is in series with the live wire. If the current in the live wire is too large, the magnetic field of the electromagnet is strong enough to pull the switch contacts apart. Once the switch is open, it stays open. It can then be reset once the fault that made it trip has been put right.

Circuit breakers are used instead of fuses. They work faster than fuses and can be reset more quickly.

The Residual Current Circuit Breaker (RCCB) works even faster than the ordinary circuit breaker described above. An RCCB cuts off the current in the live wire when it is different from the current in the neutral wire. The RCCB can be used where there is no earth connection. The RCCB is also more sensitive than either a fuse or an ordinary circuit breaker.

c What should you do if a circuit breaker trips again after being reset?

c Deadly — Heating element touches the metal case, making it live. Earth connection broken. Victim touches the metal case, and because the earth wire is broken, conducts current to earth

d Still dangerous as it may overheat

Figure 2 c and d

Figure 3 A circuit breaker

Summary questions

1 **a** What is the purpose of a fuse in a mains circuit?
  b Why is the fuse of an appliance always on the live side?
  c What advantages does a circuit breaker have compared with a fuse?

2 Figure 4 shows the circuit of an electric heater that has been wired incorrectly.
  a Does the heater work when the switch is closed?
  b When the switch is open, why is it dangerous to touch the element?
  c Redraw the circuit correctly wired.

Figure 4

3 **a** What is the difference between an ordinary circuit breaker and a Residual Current Circuit Breaker (RCCB)?
  b What are the advantages of an RCCB mains socket compared with an ordinary mains socket with a fuse in it?

Key points

- A fuse contains a thin wire that heats up, melts, and cuts off the current if the current is too large.
- A fuse is always fitted in series with the live wire. This cuts the appliance off from the live wire if the fuse blows.
- A circuit breaker is an electromagnetic switch that opens (i.e. 'trips') and cuts off the current if too much current passes through the circuit breaker.
- A mains appliance with a plastic case does not need to be earthed because plastic is an insulator and cannot become live.

Summary answers

1 **a** A fuse protects an appliance or a circuit.
  b So it cuts off the live wire if too much current passes through it.
  c It is faster than a fuse and doesn't need to be replaced after it 'trips'.

2 **a** Yes.
  b The element is live.
  c

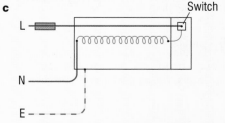

Switch

3 **a** An ordinary circuit-breaker switches the current in the live wire off if the current is greater than a certain value. An RCCB switches the current in the live wire if the current in the live wire and the neutral wire differ.
  b An RCCB cuts off the current in the live wire faster than a fuse does. Also, an RCCB is more sensitive than a fuse.

P2 5.4

Electrical power and potential difference

Learning objectives

Students should learn that:

- that the power of an electrical appliance is the rate at which it transfers energy
- how to calculate the electrical power of an appliance using the current and potential difference
- how to select an appropriate fuse for an electrical appliance.

Learning outcomes

Most students should be able to:

- state that the power of an appliance is the amount of energy it transfers each second
- calculate the power of an electrical appliance from the current and the potential difference
- find the fuse required for an appliance based on its electrical power rating.

Some students should also be able to:

- perform calculations involving the rearrangement of the electrical power equation.

Answers to in-text questions

a   About 1 W

b   1150 W

c   The normal current through the lamp is much less than 13 A. A 13 A fuse may not blow if there is a fault in the lamp.

Support

- The calculations here can be very confusing to some students, and they should be provided with a template to encourage them to lay them out correctly.

Extend

- Can the students produce a comparison between electrical potential difference and gravitational potential difference? This is a tricky task, but one that can cement understanding of what a potential difference represents.

AQA   Specification link-up: Physics P2.4

- The rate at which energy is transferred by an appliance is called the power.

$$P = \frac{E}{t} \qquad [P2.4.2 \text{ b})]$$

- Power, potential difference and current are related by the equation:

$$P = I \times V \ [P2.4.2 \text{ c})]$$

Controlled Assessment: AS4.3 Collect primary and secondary data. [AS4.3.2 a) b) c) d) e) f)]; AS4.2 Assess and manage risks when carrying out practical work. [AS4.2.1 a) b)]

Lesson structure

Starters

Power – Can the students give a scientific definition of the word power? Can they remember any equations? You could even set them a mechanical power question involving gravitational or kinetic energy. Once a formal definition had been made, you can ask how this could be connected to electrical energy where no force is apparently causing anything to move. *(5 minutes)*

Electrical units – The students match up electrical quantities, with their definitions, abbreviations and units. Include current (I, ampere), voltage (V, volts), resistance (Ω, ohms), power (P, watts), energy (E, joule). Can they provide any definitions for these units? To extend the students, ask them to describe how these factors are interrelated by giving equations or describing the links in sentences. Students can be supported by forming the activity as a jigsaw puzzle that can be assembled to produce a complete table of the information. *(10 minutes)*

Main

- Start with a brief recap about power; the students should remember how to calculate the power of a mechanical device. Point out that if energy is being transferred by a device, then some form of work must be being done, so there is a power output. With electricity, there is no force or distance moved, so there must be another way of finding the power output.

- The next section involves a derivation of an equation; you will have to provide extra support and spend a little more time demonstrating what to do with the equations for some students. Take some time to go through what each of the phrases means and to come up with the final equation; some students will find this difficult. The definition of potential difference as 'electrical energy per unit charge' is one that many students will find particularly hard to understand. In the end, most students will happily accept that the power is the current times the potential difference, even if they don't thoroughly understand why.

- The calculations are not difficult but the students should have quite a bit of practice. Get them to work out the power of several appliances before moving on to rearrangement. Sometimes examiners ask the students to work out the power of a mains appliance without giving the voltage. Students are expected to remember that mains voltage is 230 V.

- The practical task serves as reinforcement in the use of the calculation of current and power.

- Show the students real fuses and point out that they are all the same physical size, so it is easy to select the wrong one without thinking. They might like to see the 30 A fuses used for cookers. Ask: 'Why are these physically larger?' and link back to the diameter of the wire needed for a larger current.

- When choosing a fuse, always choose one that is slightly higher than the operating current, otherwise it will melt during normal operation. For example, if the appliance needs exactly 3 A, then a 5 A fuse should be used.

Plenaries

Electrical error – 'I'm sick of all my stuff fusing; I'm going to put a 13 A fuse in all of my things, so that they'll all keep working.' Ask: 'Is this a good plan or not?' Discuss the hazards associated with doing this. *(5 minutes)*

Match the fuse – The students need to find the correct fuse for an electrical appliance after being told the power rating. This involves calculating the current and then choosing the fuse that is slightly higher. Use 3 A, 5 A, 13 A and 30 A fuses. To extend, you can ask the students to select fuses for circuits where there are several appliances connected (e.g. a four-socket extension). For additional support, you can turn this activity into a simple matching one with only one fuse suitable for each appliance. *(10 minutes)*

Practical support

Comparing electrical power

The students can measure the electrical power of a range of 12 V appliances and make a comparison using a joulemeter or an ammeter and voltmeter combination. There are a wide range of 12 V appliances available designed to fit into a car electrical socket or for camping, and these can easily be adapted for the practical. Search online for '12 V appliance' and you will find some suggestions.

You may want the students to assess the risk of the experiment ('How Science Works') and discuss why you are using 12 V appliances instead of the cheaper mains ones.

Equipment and materials required

Per group: power supply (12 V), joulemeter (or ammeter and voltmeter combination), leads and a few appliances that operate at 12 V. The appliances could be a lamp, clocks, a small heater, and so on.

Details

The students can connect up the power supply to the appliance along with the joulemeter and determine the electrical power by measuring the energy transfer over a minute. Alternatively, they can connect the ammeter in series and voltmeter in parallel and determine the power rating using the electrical equation power = current × potential difference. Different groups can compare their results to establish if there is any variation.

P2 5.4

Electrical power and potential difference

Learning objectives

- What is the relationship between power and energy?
- How can we calculate electrical power and what is its unit?
- How can we calculate the correct current for a fuse?

?? Did you know ... ?

A surgeon fitting an artificial heart in a patient needs to make sure the battery will last a long time. Even so, the battery may have to be replaced every few years.

When you use an electrical appliance, it transfers electrical energy into other forms of energy. The **power** of the appliance, in watts, is the energy it transfers, in joules per second. We can show this as the following equation:

$$\text{Power (watts, W)} = \frac{\text{energy transferred (joules, J)}}{\text{time (seconds, s)}}$$

We can write the equation for the power of an appliance as:

$$P = \frac{E}{t}$$

Where:
P = power in watts, W
E = energy transferred in joules, J
t = time taken in seconds, s.

Maths skills

Worked example

A light bulb transfers 30 000 J of electrical energy when it is on for 300 s. Calculate its power.

Solution

$$\text{Power} = \frac{\text{energy transferred}}{\text{time}} = \frac{30\,000\,J}{300\,s} = 100\,W$$

a The human heart transfers about 30 000 J of energy in about 8 hours. Calculate an estimate of the power of the human heart.

Calculating power

Millions of electrons pass through the circuit of an artificial heart every second. Each electron transfers a small amount of energy to it from the battery. So the total energy transferred to it each second is large enough to enable the appliance to work.

For any electrical appliance:
- the current through it is the charge that flows through it each second
- the potential difference across it is the energy transferred to the appliance by each coulomb of charge that passes through it
- the power supplied to it is the energy transferred to it each second. This is the electrical energy it transfers every second.

Therefore:
the energy transfer to the appliance each second = the charge flow per second × the energy transfer per unit charge.

In other words:

$$\underset{\text{(watts, W)}}{\text{power supplied}} = \underset{\text{(amperes, A)}}{\text{current}} \times \underset{\text{(volts, V)}}{\text{potential difference}}$$

Figure 1 An artificial heart

The equation can be written as:

$$P = I \times V$$

Where:
P = electrical power in watts, W
I = current in amperes, A
V = potential difference in volts, V.

For example, the power supplied to:
- a 4 A, 12 V electric motor is 48 W (= 4 A × 12 V)
- a 0.1 A, 3 V torch lamp is 0.3 W (= 0.1 A × 3.0 V).

b Calculate the power supplied to a 5 A, 230 V electric heater.

Rearranging the equation $P = I \times V$ gives:

$$\text{potential difference, } V = \frac{P}{I} \text{ or}$$

$$\text{current, } I = \frac{P}{V}$$

Choosing a fuse

Domestic appliances are often fitted with a 3 A, 5 A or 13 A fuse. If you don't know which one to use for an appliance, you can work it out. You use the power rating of the appliance and its potential difference (voltage). The next time you change a fuse, do a quick calculation to make sure its rating is correct for the appliance (see the worked example opposite).

c Why would a 13 A fuse be unsuitable for a 230 V, 100 W table lamp?

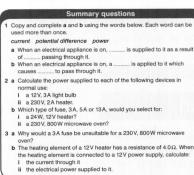

Figure 2 Changing a fuse

Maths skills

Worked example

a Calculate the normal current through a 500 W, 230 V heater.
b Which fuse, 3 A, 5 A or 13 A, would you use for the appliance?

Solution

a Current = $\frac{500\,W}{230\,V}$ = 2.2 A

b You would use a 3 A fuse.

Summary questions

1 Copy and complete **a** and **b** using the words below. Each word can be used more than once.

current   potential difference   power

a When an electrical appliance is on, ... is supplied to it as a result of .... passing through it.

b When an electrical appliance is on, a .... is applied to it which causes .... to pass through it.

2 **a** Calculate the power supplied to each of the following devices in normal use:
  i a 12 V, 3 A light bulb
  ii a 230 V, 2 A heater.

  b Which type of fuse, 3 A, 5 A or 13 A, would you select for:
  i a 24 W, 12 V heater?
  ii a 230 V, 800 W microwave oven?

3 **a** Why would a 3 A fuse be unsuitable for a 230 V, 800 W microwave oven?

  b The heating element of a 12 V heater has a resistance of 4.0 Ω. When the heating element is connected to a 12 V power supply, calculate:
  i the current through it
  ii the electrical power supplied to it.

Key points

- The power supplied to a device is the energy transferred to it each second.
- Electrical power supplied (watts)
  = current (amperes) × potential difference (volts)
- Correct rating (in amperes) for a fuse:
  = $\frac{\text{electrical power (watts)}}{\text{potential difference (volts)}}$

Further teaching suggestions

Enlightenment

- This is a simple way to show that the higher the power rating of an appliance, the more energy it transfers.

  #### Equipment and materials required

  Three identical lamps except that one has a 40 W bulb, the others have 60 W and 100 W. As with all mains appliances, these should have passed safety tests.

  #### Details

  Just plug all of the lamps in and turn them on. The students should easily see the difference in brightness and relate this to the amount of energy being transferred. Explain that all are operating at 230 V; the students should then calculate the current in each lamp. [0.17 A, 0.26 A, 0.43 A] Ask: 'What fuse should each of the lamps have?'

Summary answers

1 **a** power, current
  b potential difference, current

2 **a** i 36 W   ii 460 W
  b i 3 A   ii 5 A

3 **a** The current supplied to the microwave oven
  = 800 W/230 V = 3.5 A. A 3 A fuse would blow when the oven is switched on (at full power).
  b i 3.0 A   ii 36 W

P2 5.5

Electrical energy and charge

Learning objectives

Students should learn:

- that an electric current is a flow of charge; in metal wires this charge is carried by electrons
- that the unit of charge is the coulomb where one ampere represents a flow of charge of one coulomb per second **[HT only]**
- that charge transferred is current × time, that potential difference is energy transferred per unit charge **[HT only]**
- that a resistor transfers electrical energy by heating to the surroundings.

Learning outcomes

Most students should be able to:

- state that an electrical current is a flow of charge
- describe how a resistor transfers electrical energy by heating to the surroundings.

Some students should also be able to:

- calculate the energy transferred using the pd and the charge transferred **[HT only]**
- perform calculations involving rearrangement of the charge = current × time equation and the potential difference = energy transferred per unit charge equation. **[HT only]**

Support

- Use calculation templates to help the students through the equations and to make sure that they are laying out their calculations clearly.

Extend

- Ask: 'How many electrons are passing each second at a point, if there is a current of 1 A and each electron carries a charge of 1.6×10^{-19} C?' [The students should be able to figure out that 1 C of charge passes each second, so the number of electrons is given by 1 C/1.6×10^{-19} C which is 6.25×10^{18} electrons. This shows just how small the charge on a single electron is.] These numbers are impossible for a calculator to handle without using scientific notation, so it is a good opportunity to improve these skills.

AQA / Specification link-up: Physics P2.3, P2.4

- Electric current is a flow of electric charge. The size of the electric current is the rate of flow of electric charge. The size of the current is given by the equation:
  $$I = \frac{Q}{t} \text{ [P2.3.2 a)]}$$
- When an electrical charge flows through a resistor, the resistor gets hot. *[P2.4.2 a)]*
- Energy transferred, potential difference and charge are related by the equation:
  $$E = V \times Q \text{ [P2.4.2 d)] } \textbf{[HT only]}$$

Lesson structure

Starters

Stuck for words? – Pair up the students and give one of them cards with electrical words including charge, current, pd, power, resistance, etc. Ask them to mime the words to the other students. This is remarkable difficult as they are quite abstract ideas but it can lead to students using their imagination of what the words mean. *(5 minutes)*

Electrical energy transfer – How many electrical appliances can the students draw energy transfer diagrams for? Provide some example appliances if you can. The students could even estimate the electrical efficiency of the appliances once they are clear about which form of energy is useful. Differentiate by providing some simple appliances (and possible starting points for the diagrams) to give extra support while asking about more challenging appliances to extend the students. *(10 minutes)*

Main

- This is another fairly mathematically intense topic with two important equations; keep the emphasis on the electrons carrying charge from place to place and in doing so, carrying energy. Much of the spread is only needed for students taking the Higher Tier examination.
- The first equation comes from the definition of current and charge. The size of the electric current is just how much charge passes each second (just as the size of a water current is how many litres of water pass each second). Use water flowing down a tube into a big measuring cylinder if you want a visual illustration.
- Many students struggle to remember the unit coulomb, so say it a lot. Some students are more apt with the word equations than the symbols, so give them plenty of practice using the symbol form, since this will be needed in the exam. Students should learn to use $Q = It$.
- The second part of the spread contains material for Higher Tier students only.
- The derivation of the energy-transferred equation will again be confusing for some. For these students, just concentrate on the end equation. Using the equation is fairly straightforward after a few examples. Check that the students are using the correct units. With so many equations, it it is easy for them to pick the wrong one. A reference wall display is very handy.
- There may be situations on higher level examination papers where the students are expected to combine the equations, so give these students some examples; e.g. 'How much energy is transferred when a current of 2 A passes through a potential difference of 4 V for 1 minute'? [480 J]
- The last section deals with energy transfer. You should go through the description of the energy being provided to the electrons, then carried by them and transferred to the bulb and resistor, carefully. The students should be picturing electrons as energy carriers by now, and then thinking of a coulomb as the charge carried by a big bunch of electrons. Remember that there is conservation of energy; the electrons can only release the amount of energy they have been provided with in the battery.
- Try more examples of this, making sure that the students are picking up the idea that **each** coulomb of charge (bunch of electrons) is getting the same number of joules as the battery potential difference. It's actually the changes in the electric field that the charge produces that transfers the energy, but the students need not worry about this.

Plenaries

Electrical spelling – Hold a spelling competition about electrical words using mini-whiteboards. If a student gets a word wrong, they get knocked out. Start with simple words like charge and then get more difficult. The last one in wins the competition. 'Coulomb' eliminates a fair few! *(5 minutes)*

Electric crossword – The students have nearly finished this look into current and mains electricity, so let them have a go at a crossword with answers based on this (and the previous) chapter. It's easy to give differentiated clues to cover a range of abilities for support and extension. For example 'the rate of flow of charge, and 'the movement of charge through a wire' are both clues to 'electric current'. *(10 minutes)*

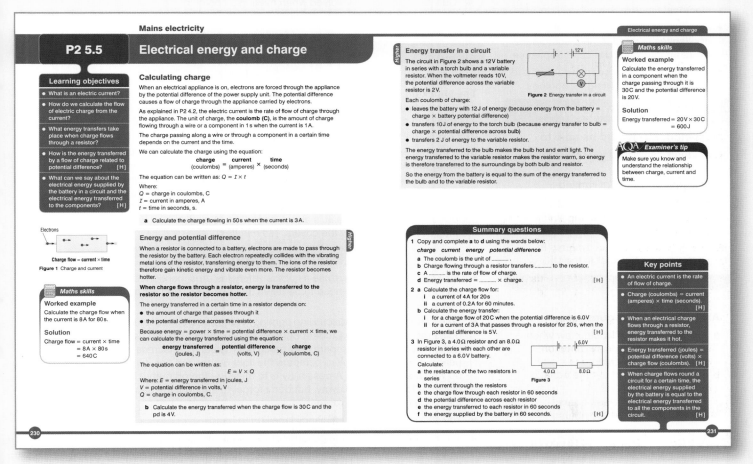

Further teaching suggestions

Map it out

● The students should produce a summary or mind map of the information about current electricity, mains electricity and electrical energy calculations. This has been quite a lot of information, so encourage the use of small diagrams on the map to enhance the readability. For example, a little diagram of where to place a voltmeter in a circuit should be present. Mind mapping only really works if the students review and refine the map **regularly**. You might want them to do this at home and check the improved version after a week.

Calculations

● Use this opportunity to give the students some additional calculations to check their understanding and ability.

Summary answers

1 a charge
   b energy
   c current
   d potential difference

2 a i 80 C
      ii 720 C
    b i 120 J
      ii 300 J

3 a 12.0 Ω
    b 0.50 A
    c 30 C
    d 4 Ω: 2.0 V; 8.0 Ω: 4.0 V
    e 4 Ω: 60 J (= 30 C × 2.0 V); 8.0 Ω: 120 J (= 30 C × 4.0 V)
    f 180 J

Answers to in-text questions

a 150 C

b 120 J

P2 5.6

Electrical issues

Learning objectives

Students should learn:

- that electrical faults can lead to electrocution or fires and even small currents through the body are potentially lethal
- how to recognise and prevent electrical faults
- how the efficiency of electrical appliances is rated to help customers make an informed choice of appliance
- why energy efficiency is important and the advances in lighting technology.

Learning outcomes

Most students should be able to:

- recognise a wide range of electrical hazards
- describe the range of lighting available and compare its efficiency
- describe how the efficiency of an electrical appliance is shown
- compare the electrical systems in other countries to that in the UK.

Answers to in-text questions

a
  i The new fuse would blow when the appliance is switched on.
  ii A three-core cable.
b
  i 30
  ii 11
  iii Number of kilowatt hours
     = 0.1 kW × 30 000 hours
     = 3000 kW h
     Cost = 3000 kW h × 10 p/kW h
     = £300
  iv £172 (= £234 saving on electricity costs − £62 extra 'capital' cost).

Support

- This lesson is far easier to understand if you have props, so seek out some adaptors, efficiency-rating cards and different light bulbs. You could get students to bring in some ones they have used on holiday.

Extend

- Students could find out about the wiring of ring mains in houses. They should find the specification of the wires needed, colours, fuses used and so on. They can present this information to the rest of the class.

AQA Specification link-up: Physics P2.3, P2.4

- Apply the principles of basic electrical circuits to practical situations. *[P2.3]*
- Evaluate the use of different forms of lighting, in terms of cost and energy efficiency. *[P2.3]*
- Understand the principles of safe practice and recognise dangerous practice in the use of mains electricity. *[P2.4]*
- Evaluate and explain the need to use different cables for different appliances. *[P2.4]*
- Consider the factors involved when making a choice of electrical appliances. *[P2.4]*

Lesson structure

Starters

The shocking truth – There are a number of electrical-safety videos that can be found, many to do with railways. Show the students one (have a good look first to see it is suitable) and discuss what happens. There are several thousands of electrical injuries every year many from DIY work. *(5 minutes)*

Spot the hazards – The hazard-spotting task is a good way to start the lesson. Most students should be able to spot the hazards in Shockem Hall. You should ask them to explain how they could be fixed too. The students could then perform a safely check of the laboratory and other classrooms they visit during the school day. Students can be extended by asking them to design an appropriate checklist for room inspections or supported by providing one. It is also a good time to explain why not to stick pencils into the plug socket or unscrew the covers. *(10 minutes)*

Main

- Take the opportunity to revise all of the safety features mentioned in the previous lessons and how these need to be taken into account when wiring appliances and mains circuits.

- When you move on to discussing lighting, you can demonstrate each of the three bulbs mentioned in the Student Book in a mains socket. If you have a mains-rated joule meter you can compare how much energy each consumes within a 1 minute period. It is more difficult to compare the light output, but see if the students can come up with a suitable idea. A possibility is to measure the pd output from a solar panel placed a fixed distance away, but don't forget to subtract the background reading from the ambient light in the room.

- You should have some efficiency labelling to hand.

- It took a lot of effort for the government to regulate electrical work in the same way as gas has been regulated for many years. The students can discuss why this was necessary (there were lots of fires or accidents). Many 'DIYers' were unhappy at the decision. What would happen if the homeowner did their own work and sold the house only to have it burn down due to a fault? Will the law make it too expensive to do simple jobs in the home?

- You should be able to find a range of adapters (or photographs of them) for different purposes to show the students. Spanish mains supply is 220 V and 50 Hz, so most appliances will work but kettles will take a little longer to boil. You can ask the student why this is [power = current × voltage]. The sockets only have two holes for pins but can have an earth connection at the edge.

- You can also discuss the electrical systems in the USA. Here the frequency of the mains is 60 Hz and the voltage is 110 V. Larger currents are needed to provide the same power as UK systems. This would require thicker wires to achieve the same level of safety.

Plenaries

Overall efficiency – Buildings are rated for their overall efficiency and so your school building may have such a report. Show the students the report and overall rating and discuss it. What could be done to improve the rating? *(5 minutes)*

Setting standards – There are a range of electrical standards around the World but which is best? The students can compare the systems in terms of pd, frequency and design of cables and sockets, and make a decision about which would be best as a 'World standard'. Extend the students by asking them to define what 'best' means; i.e. let them set the criteria. To support others, you can make the task more of a comparison and then have a discussion about which pd is best or plug design is safest. The students can expand on this task as homework through independent research. *(10 minutes)*

 How Science Works | **Mains electricity**

P2 5.6   Electrical issues

Learning objectives

- Why are electrical faults dangerous?
- How can we prevent electrical faults?
- When choosing an electrical appliance, what factors in addition to cost should we consider?
- How do different forms of lighting compare in terms of cost and energy efficiency?

Activity

Spot the hazards!

How many electrical faults and hazards can you find in Shockem Hall? See how many you can spot in the main hall.

Figure 1 Shockem Hall

Did you know ... ?

What kills you – current or voltage? Mains electricity is dangerous. A current of no more than about 0.03 A through your body would give you a severe shock and might even kill you. Your body has a resistance of about 1000 Ω including contact resistance at the skin. If your hands get wet, your resistance is even lower.

An electrical fault is dangerous. It could give someone a nasty shock or even electrocute them, resulting in death. Also, a fault can cause a fire. This happens when too much current passes through a wire or an appliance and heats it up.

Fault prevention

Electrical faults can happen if sockets, plugs, cables or appliances are damaged. Users need to check for loose fittings, cracked plugs and sockets and worn cables. Any such damaged items need to be repaired or replaced by a qualified electrician.

- If a fuse blows or a circuit breaker trips when a mains appliance is in use, switch the appliance off. Then don't use it until it has been checked by a qualified electrician.
- If an appliance (or its cable or plug or socket) overheats and/or you get a distinctive burning smell from it, switch it off. Again, don't use it until it has been checked.

Too many appliances connected to a socket may cause the socket to overheat. If this happens, switch the appliances and the socket off and disconnect the appliances from the socket.

Smoke alarms and infrared sensors connected to an alarm system are activated if a fire breaks out. An electrical fault could cause an appliance or a cable to become hot and could set fire to curtains or other material in a room. Smoke alarms and sensors should be checked regularly to make sure they work properly.

An electrician selecting a cable for an appliance needs to use:

- a two-core cable if the appliance is 'double-insulated' and no earth wire is needed
- a three-core cable if an earth wire is needed because the appliance has a metal case
- a cable with conductors of suitable thickness so the heating effect of the current in the cable is insignificant.

> **a**   **i**   If a mains appliance suddenly stops working, why is it a mistake to replace the fuse straightaway?
>   **ii**   Should the cable of an electric iron be a two-core or a three-core cable?

New bulbs for old

When choosing an electrical appliance, most people compare several different appliances. The cost of the appliance is just one factor that may need to be considered. Other factors might include the power of the appliance and its efficiency.

If you want to replace a bulb, a visit to an electrical shop can present you with a bewildering range of bulbs.

A **filament bulb** is very inefficient. The energy from the hot bulb gradually makes the plastic parts of the bulb socket brittle and they crack.

Low energy bulbs are much more efficient so they don't become hot like filament bulbs do. Different types of low energy bulb are now available:

- **Low-energy compact fluorescent bulbs (CFLs)** are now used for room lighting instead of filament bulbs.
- **Low-energy light-emitting diodes (LEDs)** used for spotlights are usually referred to as high-power LEDs. They operate at low voltage and low power. They are much more efficient than filament bulbs or halogen bulbs and they last much longer.

This table gives more information about these different bulbs.

Type	Power	Efficiency	Lifetime in hours	Cost of bulb	Typical use
Filament bulb	100 W	20%	1000	50p	room lighting
Halogen bulb	100 W	25%	2500	£2.00	spotlight
Low-energy compact fluorescent bulb (CFL)	25 W	80%	15000	£2.50	room lighting
Low-energy light-emitting diode (LED)	2 W	90%	30000	£7.00	spotlight

> **b**   A householder wants to replace a 100 W room light with a row of low-energy LEDs with the same light output. Use the information in the table above to answer the following questions.
>   **i**   How many times would the filament bulb need to be replaced in the lifetime of an LED?
>   **ii**   How many LEDs would be needed to give the same light output as a 100 W filament bulb?
>   **iii**   The householder reckons the cost of the electricity for each LED at 10p per kWh over its lifetime of 30 000 hours would be £6. Show that the cost of the electricity for a 100 W bulb over this time would be £300.
>   **iv**   Use your answers above to calculate how much the householder would save by replacing the filament bulb with LEDs.

Summary questions

1 An 'RCCB' socket should be used for mains appliances such as lawnmowers where there is a possible hazard when the appliance is used. Such a socket contains a residual current circuit breaker instead of a fuse. This type of circuit breaker switches the current off if the live current and the neutral current differ by more than 30 mA. This can happen, for example, if the blades of a lawnmower cut into the cable.

Create a table to show a possible 'electrical' hazard for each of these appliances: lawnmower, electric drill, electric saw, hairdryer, vacuum cleaner. The first entry has been done for you.

Appliance	Hazard
Lawnmower	The blades might cut the cable.

Did you know ... ?

All new appliances like washing machines and freezers sold in the EU are labelled clearly with an efficiency rating. The rating is from A (very efficient) to G (lowest efficiency). Light bulbs are also labelled in this way on the packaging.

Figure 2 Efficiency measures

Key points

- Electrical faults are dangerous because they can cause electric shocks and fires.
- Never touch a mains appliance (or plug or socket) with wet hands. Never touch a bare wire or a terminal at a potential of more than 30 V.
- Check cables, plugs and sockets for damage regularly. Check smoke alarms and infrared sensors regularly.
- When choosing an electrical appliance, the power and efficiency rating of the appliance need to be considered.
- Filament bulbs and halogen bulbs are much less efficient than low energy bulbs.

Further teaching suggestions

Investigating lighting efficiency

- You can turn the activity of assessing different lighting types into a full investigation. The students would need to plan ways to measure the energy input to the lamp and some form of measurement of the brightness of the bulb. Leave this relativity open for the students to plan. Include cost implications of each type of lighting.

Make your own test

- The students can devise their own test questions and compile an examination for each other. You can set the criteria such as number of questions and time it takes to complete and then the students make a set of questions in teams. The students can sit the best test next lesson.

Electricians

- Students interested in becoming electricians can find out about the training and qualifications.

Mind maps

- Mind mapping only really works if the students review and refine the map regularly; get them to do this with their previous map.

ICT link-up

- There are plenty of opportunities here for ICT-based research. As usual, a list of suitable websites should be provided along with some form of research template.

Summary answers

1 An example of each possible electrical hazard is given in the table.

Appliance	Hazard
Electric drill	The drill might 'hit' a live wire in a cable in the wall.
Electric saw	The saw might cut the cable (or cut a limb).
Hairdryer	Anyone with wet hands using a hairdryer would be at risk.
Vacuum cleaner	The vacuum cleaner might run over and damage its cable.

Summary answers

1 a i The neutral wire.
ii The live wire.

b i The waves on the screen would be taller.
ii There would be more waves on the screen.

2 a live, neutral

b i neutral
ii live
iii earth

3 a i parallel
ii series, live

b i A fuse has a wire that melts if too much current passes through it. A circuit breaker has a switch that is pulled open if too much current passes through it.
ii A circuit breaker is faster. Also a circuit breaker does not need to be replaced, but a fuse does.

4 a i 10.8 A
ii 13 A

b 920 W

5 a

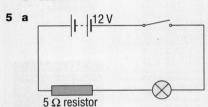

5 Ω resistor

b i 432 J
ii 108 J
iii 324 J

c i 30 Ω
ii $I = V/R = 12/30 = 0.4$ A
iii battery = 4.8 W, 5 Ω resistor = 0.8 W, 25 Ω resistor = 4.0 W

6 a i 2.5 A
ii 2.4 Ω

b The current through the lamp is less at 3 V than at 6 V, so the lamp filament is not as hot. Therefore, its resistance is less.

7 a i 3.0 A
ii 600 C

b i Energy = power × time
= 36 W × 200 s = 7200 J
ii 12 J/C

8 a 28.7 A

b i D, because the maximum safe current through D is greater than the current that would pass through it when the oven operates at full power. So D would not overheat. E would not overheat either but it would be more expensive than D.
ii Cables A, B and C would overheat as their maximum safe current is less than the current that would pass through them when the oven is at full power. The overheated cable might cause a fire. Also, the cable insulation could melt and cause a short-circuit that may start a fire.

Summary questions 🅚

1 a In a mains circuit, which wire:
i is earthed at the local sub-station
ii alternates in potential?

b An oscilloscope is used to display the potential difference of an alternating voltage supply unit. How would the trace change if:
i the pd is increased
ii the frequency is increased?

2 Copy and complete **a** and **b** using the words below. Each word can be used more than once.

earth   live   neutral

a When a mains appliance is switched on, current passes through it via the .... wire and the .... wire.

b In a mains circuit:
i the .... wire is blue
ii the .... wire is brown
iii the .... wire is green and yellow.

3 a Copy and complete the following sentences:
i Wall sockets are connected in .... with each other.
ii A fuse in a mains plug is in .... with the appliance and cuts off the .... wire if too much current passes through the appliance.

b i What is the main difference between a fuse and a circuit breaker?
ii Give two reasons why a circuit breaker is safer than a fuse.

4 a i Calculate the current in a 230 V, 2.5 kW electric kettle.
ii Which fuse, 3 A, 5 A or 13 A, would you fit in the kettle plug?

b Calculate the power supplied to a 230 V electric toaster when the current through it is 4.0 A.

5 A 5 Ω resistor is in series with a bulb, a switch and a 12 V battery.
a Draw the circuit diagram.
b When the switch is closed for 60 seconds, a direct current of 0.6 A passes through the resistor. Calculate:
i the energy supplied by the battery
ii the energy transferred to the resistor
iii the energy transferred to the bulb.   [H]
c The bulb is replaced by a 25 Ω resistor.
i Calculate the total resistance of the two resistors.
ii Show that a current of 0.4 A passes through the battery.

iii Calculate the power supplied by the battery and the power delivered to each resistor.

6 When a 6 V bulb operates normally, the electrical power supplied to it is 15 W.
a Calculate:
i the current through the bulb when it operates normally
ii the resistance of the bulb when it operates normally.
b If the bulb is connected to a 3 V battery, state and explain why its resistance is less than at 6 V.

7 A 12 V 36 W bulb is connected to a 12 V supply.
a Calculate:
i the current through the bulb.
ii the charge flow through the bulb in 200 s.
b i Show that 7200 J of electrical energy is delivered to the bulb in 200 s.
ii Calculate the energy delivered to the bulb by each coulomb of charge that passes through it.

8 An electrician has the job of connecting a 6.6 kW electric oven to the 230 V mains supply in a house.
a Calculate the current needed to supply 6.6 kW of electrical power at 230 V.
b The table below shows the maximum current that can pass safely through five different mains cables. For each cable the cross-sectional area (csa) of each conductor is given in square millimetres (mm²).

	Cross-sectional area of conductor (mm²)	Maximum safe current (A)
A	1.0	14
B	1.5	18
C	2.5	28
D	4.0	36
E	6.0	46

i To connect the oven to the mains supply, which cable should the electrician choose? Give a reason for your answer.
ii State and explain what would happen if she chose a cable with thinner conductors?

Kerboodle resources 🅚

Resources available for this chapter on Kerboodle are:
- Chapter map: Mains electricity
- Practical: ac/dc display (P2 5.1)
- How Science Works: Are you energy smart? (P2 5.4)
- WebQuest: Light bulbs (P2 5.6)
- Interactive activity: Electrical power
- Revision podcast: Electric charge and electric power
- Test yourself: Mains electricity
- On your marks: Mains electricity
- Examination-style questions: Mains electricity
- Answers to examination-style questions: Mains electricity

AQA Examiner's tip

It is important in Question 1 that candidates describe the fault fully and explain the possible consequences in sufficient detail, i.e. 'It's dangerous' is not enough. Encourage answers more along the lines of: 'The knife may touch the live wires in the toaster, the knife conducts electricity, and therefore the person may get electrocuted'.

AQA Examiner's tip

In Question 3 candidates are expected to recall that UK mains voltage is about 230 V. Look out for questions where this voltage is not given but the value is needed for the calculation.

Examination-style questions

The pictures show situations in which electricity is not being used safely.

For each picture **a**, **b** and **c**, explain how electricity is not being used safely.

a

(2)

b

(2)

c

(2)

d The colour of the earth wire in a plug is .... (1)

e The pins of the plug are made of brass because it is a good .... (1)

f The voltage on the neutral wire is about .... V. (1)

g RCCB stands for .... (1)

Most domestic appliances are connected to the 230 V mains supply with a 3-pin plug containing a fuse. 3 A, 5 A and 13 A fuses are available.

a A bulb for a desk lamp has a normal current of 0.26 A.
　i Which of the three fuses should be used? (1)
　ii Calculate the power of the lamp. (2)
　iii Calculate how many coulombs of charge pass through the lamp if it is left on for 1 hour. [H] (3)

b i Calculate the current passing through a 1.15 kW electric fan heater. (2)
　ii Which fuse should be used in the plug for this heater? (1)

c Calculate how much electrical energy is transferred when the fan heater is left on for 30 minutes. Write down the equation you use. Show clearly how you work out your answer and give the unit. (3)

d *In this question you will be assessed on using good English, organising information clearly and using specialist terms where appropriate.*

　The heater is made of metal and has an earth wire connected to it. Explain how the fuse and earth wire together protect the wiring of the circuit. (6)

3 A kettle is connected to the UK mains supply and boiled. An energy monitoring device measures that 420 000 J has been transferred to the kettle in the time it takes to boil.

a Calculate how much charge has flowed through the kettle. Write down the equation you use. Show clearly how you work out your answer and give the unit. [H] (3)

b The power of the kettle is 2.2 kW. How long did the kettle take to boil? (3)

4 An oscilloscope is connected to a power supply. The trace is shown on a centimetre grid.

a Explain how you know that it is an ac supply being measured. (1)

b Give the peak voltage if each division on the *y*-axis is 2 V/cm. (1)

c Each *x*-axis division is 0.01 s/cm.
　i Calculate the time period of the supply. (1)
　ii Calculate the frequency of the supply. [H] (2)

d Describe the position and appearance of the trace on the screen if the supply was switched to 6 V dc. (2)

235

Examination-style answers

1 a Too many plugs in one socket. The current may be too large in the socket and cause a fire. *(2 marks)*

b The cable has been repaired with tape. This tape could come off and leave a bare live wire. *(2 marks)*

c A knife is being pushed into the toaster. The knife may touch the live heating element inside the toaster and the person could be electrocuted. *(2 marks)*

d green and yellow *(1 mark)*

e electrical conductor *(1 mark)*

f 0 volts *(1 mark)*

g Residual Current Circuit Breaker *(1 mark)*

2 a **i** 3 A *(1 mark)*
　ii $P = I \times V = 0.26 \times 230$
　　　　$= 59.8$ W *(2 marks)*
　iii $Q = I \times t = 0.26 \times 3600 = 936$ C *(3 marks)*

b **i** $I = \dfrac{P}{V} = 1150/230 = 5$ A *(2 marks)*
　ii 13 A *(1 mark)*

c $E = P \times t = 1150 \times 30 \times 60$
　　　$= 2.1$ MJ *(3 marks)*

d There is a clear, balanced and detailed description of how the fuse and earth wire together protect the wiring of the circuit. The answer shows almost faultless spelling, punctuation and grammar. It is coherent and in an organised, logical sequence. It contains a range of appropriate or relevant specialist terms used accurately. *(5–6 marks)*

There is a description of how the fuse and earth wire together protect the wiring of the circuit. There are some errors in spelling, punctuation and grammar. The answer has some structure and organisation. The use of specialist terms has been attempted, but not always accurately. *(3–4 marks)*

There is a brief description of how the fuse and earth wire together protect the wiring of the circuit, which has little clarity and detail. The spelling, punctuation and grammar are very weak. The answer is poorly organised with almost no specialist terms and/or their use demonstrating a general lack of understanding of their meaning. *(1–2 marks)*

No relevant content. *(0 marks)*

Examples of physics points made in the response:
- a fault may cause the live wire to touch the metal casing
- the metal casing is connected to the earth wire
- a large current will flow through the live wire to earth
- due to the low resistance of the earth wire
- the large current will blow the fuse which is in the live wire
- this disconnects the circuit
- which prevents the circuit being damaged by the large current.

3 a $Q = \dfrac{E}{V} = 420\,000/230 = 1826$ C *(3 marks)*

b $t = \dfrac{E}{P} = 420\,000/2\,200$
　　　$= 191$ seconds *(3 marks)*

4 a The trace goes above and below the central line (positive and negative). *(1 mark)*

b 4 V or 4.1 V *(1 mark)*

c **i** 0.04 seconds *(1 mark)*
　ii Frequency $= \dfrac{I}{t} = 1/0.04 = 25$ Hz *(2 marks)*

d A horizontal line on the third division below the centre. *(2 marks)*

Practical suggestions

Practicals	AQA	k	📖	⚙
Measuring oscilloscope traces.	✓	✓	✓	
Demonstrating the action of fuse wires.	✓		✓	
Using fluctuations in light intensity measurements from filament bulbs to determine the frequency of ac.	✓			
Measuring the power of 12 V appliances by measuring energy transferred (using a joulemeter or ammeter and voltmeter) in a set time.	✓		✓	

Examiner's tip

Question 4 illustrates an oscilloscope trace of an ac supply. Note that ac and dc wave forms can easily be displayed on an oscilloscope as a demonstration. There are many 'PC oscilloscopes' on the market that are more compact than a cathode ray oscilloscope (CRO) and relatively inexpensive. To demonstrate a 'traditional' CRO, a flexible camera attached to a projector can be employed with great effect.

P2 6.1

Observing nuclear radiation

Learning objectives

Students should learn:

- that unstable nuclei decay and emit invisible radiation when the structure of the nucleus changes to become more stable
- that this radiation can be detected in a number of ways including by a GM tube
- that background radiation is present everywhere due to cosmic rays and decay of unstable isotopes in rocks (among other sources).

Learning outcomes

Most students should be able to:

- draw a diagram illustrating the structure of an atom (nuclear model)
- state what we mean by a 'radioactive' substance and describe the types of radiation emitted from these substances
- describe the origins of background radiation.

Some students should also be able to:

- explain how radioactive materials were discovered.

Answers to in-text questions

- **a** No, the salts give out radiation all the time.
- **b** Yes.
- **c** Because it is emitted from the nucleus of an atom.

Support

- Building atoms and nuclei is a really good way of cementing the idea of the particles that make up the nucleus. Have some circular component cut out in advance. If you want to go further, you can use polystyrene balls stuck together with cocktail sticks or use marbles held together with modelling clay.

Extend

- Introduce nuclear notation and the formal definitions of atomic number, mass number and focus on the layout. The students should be shown some recently discovered elements and find out how there are produced. They can also look into the discovery of radiation a little more.

AQA Specification link-up: Physics P2.5

- The basic structure of an atom is a small central nucleus composed of protons and neutrons surrounded by electrons. *[P2.5.1 a)]*
- Some substances give out radiation from the nuclei of their atoms all the time, whatever is done to them. These substances are said to be radioactive. *[P2.5.2 a)]*
- The origins of background radiation. *[P2.5.2 b)]*

Lesson structure

Starters

'Lookie likey' – What does an atom look like? Ask the students to draw and label one before showing them our current (nuclear) model. Does an atom really *look* like this? Show the students some caricatures of famous people to see if these capture the 'essence' of the person. Use this to point out that sometimes images are not realistic but they capture the important information, just like the pictures of atoms and nuclei used throughout this chapter. *(5 minutes)*

Atom models – Ask students to draw some simple atomic models. You can support the students by giving them a set of cut-out protons, neutrons and electrons to use. Give them some specifications like carbon: 6 protons, 6 neutrons and 6 electrons to see if they arrange the particles correctly. Extend students by asking them to present a range of atoms and insisting that they use the correct electron configurations (providing the rules if needed). Ask students to note any of the properties of the components that they already know. *(10 minutes)*

Main

- Before carrying out any demonstrations involving radioactive material, make certain that you are familiar with local handling rules. (See 'Practical support'.)
- Start by checking knowledge of atomic structure, protons, neutrons and electrons, as this is essential in discussing isotopes later. You can then discuss the history of the discovery of radioactivity. You should point out that although the initial discovery was accidental; the investigation into the cause was a thorough scientific one. Marie Curie died aged 67 partly because of her work. Similar things happened with early researchers into X-rays. This shows that even scientists underestimated the hazards of their research.
- Show the presence of radiation due to the sources by using a GM tube or spark detector. (See 'Practical support'.) If you have a video camera and projector, you may want to use it to show the detail of the experiment without getting the students too close.
- Emphasise that nuclear radiation is caused by changes in the nucleus. You might ask the students to draw a nucleus and describe the parts. If you do this, it is worth reminding them that the nucleus is really spherical; not just a disc. Show a model made of marbles stuck together; if one falls off, then attribute it to nuclear decay.
- Demonstrate background radiation by letting the Geiger counter run without any sources present. Explain that it is normal for there to be a low level of radiation, this is 'background radiation', and go through some of the sources. Explain that the contributions vary from place to place depending on things like the rock type (e.g. fresh igneous rocks are more active than sandstone).
- Some students may like to know more about why the nucleus decays. The reason for the nucleus changing is linked to energy. The nucleus changes so that it has less energy; the parts that make it up have become more tightly bound; this is yet another example of energy spreading out.

Plenaries

Murder mystery – The body of a press photographer has been found in a sealed room, and all of the film in her camera has gone black even though it hasn't been used. Write a letter to the police explaining what you think happened and how you know. [Hopefully students will come up with the idea that they have been blasted by a large amount of ionising radiation.] *(5 minutes)*

Comparing locations – Provide the students with some data about the sources of background radiation in different locations. They must produce a pie chart of this information and compare the risks in each of the locations. To support students, you can provide pie chart drawing apparatus (percentage wheels). To extend students, you can provide extra information including the actual values (instead of percentages) and ask them to calculate percentages from the source information. *(10 minutes)*

Practical support

Using a GM tube and ratemeter

The usual way of showing the presence of ionising radiation is by using a Geiger–Müller tube and ratemeter. This has the advantage that the count rate is proportional to the activity, and some of the students will be familiar with the device from films and television. Many modern devices have the counter and tube components combined and so are simpler to use.

Equipment and materials needed

Geiger–Müller tube, ratemeter (and possibly high voltage power supply), large plastic tray, tongs, radioactive sources, laboratory coat.

Details

The operating voltage of the GM tube is usually 400 V and this is usually provided by the ratemeter, but you may need an external supply for tubes that connect to computers. Check with the manual. Position the detector in the tray and switch it on. Bring the sources close to the tube window (and above the tray) and the ratemeter should count. If you can find a ratemeter that clicks, the demonstration is a lot more fun.

If you do not want the student to get too close to the sources, then you could connect a small video camera to a data projector to show the demonstrations more clearly.

Radioactivity

P2 6.1 — Observing nuclear radiation

Learning objectives

- What is a radioactive substance?
- What types of radiation are given out from a radioactive substance?
- When does a radioactive source give out radiation (radioactive decay)?
- Where does background radiation come from?

A key discovery

Figure 1 Becquerel's key

If your photos showed a mysterious image, what would you think? In 1896, the French physicist, **Henri Becquerel**, discovered the image of a key on a film he developed. He remembered the film had been in a drawer under a key. On top of that there had been a packet of uranium salts. The uranium salts must have sent out some form of radiation that passed through paper (the film wrapper) but not through metal (the key).

Marie Curie

Becquerel asked a young research worker, **Marie Curie**, to investigate. She found that the salts gave out radiation all the time. It happened no matter what was done to them. She used the word **radioactivity** to describe this strange new property of uranium.

She and her husband, Pierre, did more research into this new branch of science. They discovered new radioactive elements. They named one of the elements **polonium**, after Marie's native country, Poland.

a You can stop a lamp giving out light by switching it off. Is it possible to stop uranium giving out radiation?

Becquerel and the Curies were awarded the Nobel Prize for the discovery of radioactivity. When Pierre died in a road accident, Marie went on with their work. She was awarded a second Nobel Prize in 1911 for the discovery of polonium and radium. She died in 1934 from leukaemia, a disease of the blood cells. It was probably caused by the radiation from the radioactive materials she worked with.

Figure 2 Marie Curie 1867–1934

Practical

Investigating radioactivity

We can use a **Geiger counter** to detect radioactivity. Look at Figure 3. The counter clicks each time a particle of radiation from a radioactive substance enters the Geiger tube.

Figure 3 Using a Geiger counter

What stops the radiation? Ernest Rutherford carried out tests to answer this question about a century ago. He put different materials between the radioactive substance and a detector.

He discovered two types of radiation:

- One type (**alpha radiation**, symbol α) was stopped by paper.
- The other type (**beta radiation**, symbol β) went through the paper.

Scientists later discovered a third type, **gamma radiation** (symbol γ), even more penetrating than beta radiation.

b Can gamma radiation go through paper?

A radioactive puzzle

Why are some substances radioactive? Every atom has a nucleus made up of protons and neutrons. Electrons move about in energy levels (or shells) surrounding the nucleus.

Most atoms each have a stable nucleus that doesn't change. But the atoms of a radioactive substance each have a nucleus that is unstable. An unstable nucleus becomes stable by emitting alpha, beta or gamma radiation. We say an unstable nucleus **decays** when it emits radiation.

We can't tell when an unstable nucleus will decay. It is a **random** event that happens without anything being done to the nucleus.

c Why is the radiation from a radioactive substance sometimes called 'nuclear radiation'?

The origins of background radiation

A Geiger counter clicks even when it is not near a radioactive source. This effect is due to **background radiation**. This is radiation from radioactive substances:

- in the environment (e.g. in the air or the ground or in building materials), or
- from space (cosmic rays), or
- from devices such as X-ray tubes.

Some of these radioactive substances are present because of nuclear weapons testing and nuclear power stations. But most of it is from naturally occurring substances in the Earth. For example, radon gas is radioactive and is a product of the decay of uranium found in the rocks in certain areas.

Summary questions

1 Copy and complete **a** and **b** using the words below. Each word can be used more than once.

   protons   neutrons   nucleus   radiation

   a The .... of an atom is made up of .... and ....
   b When an unstable .... decays, it emits ....

2 **a** The radiation from a radioactive source is stopped by paper. What type of radiation does the source emit?
   b The radiation from a different source goes through paper. What can you say about this radiation?

3 **a** Explain why some substances are radioactive.
   b State two sources of background radioactivity.

Unstable nucleus

Electrons in orbit around the nucleus

Particle emitted by the nucleus

Figure 4 Radioactive decay

Figure 5 The origins of background radiation

- Nuclear weapons 0.2%
- Air travel 0.2%
- Food and drink 11.5%
- Cosmic 10%
- Nuclear reactors 0.1%
- Ground 14%
- Medical 14%
- Air (radon) 50%

Key points

- A radioactive substance contains unstable nuclei that become stable by emitting radiation.
- There are three main types of radiation from radioactive substances – alpha, beta and gamma radiation.
- Radioactive decay is a random event – we cannot predict or influence when it will happen.
- Background radiation is from radioactive substances in the environment or from space or from devices such as X-ray machines.

Further teaching suggestions

ICT link-up

- The students cannot handle radioactive material, but simulations allow them to explore ideas safely. These are an excellent way to visualise the behaviour of the particles and waves and to study absorption. They can also demonstrate the half-life of materials, a process that is too difficult to show with real substances in class. However, it is best to use these simulations alongside real apparatus if possible, to show that the models are linked to physical reality.

Summary answers

1 **a** nucleus, protons, neutrons
  b nucleus, radiation

2 **a** alpha radiation
  b This radiation is either beta or gamma radiation.

3 **a** Because they have an unstable nucleus that can become more stable by emitting radiation.
  b Any two from radioactive isotopes in the air, the ground or in building materials; X-ray machines; cosmic radiation.

P2 6.2

The discovery of the nucleus

Learning objectives

Students should learn:

- that alpha-scattering experiments led Rutherford to deduce the nuclear model of the atom
- that the nuclear model of the atom was accepted because it could explain alpha scattering much better than the previous models could
- that this led to the replacement of the 'plum pudding' model of the atom by the nuclear model.

Learning outcomes

Most students should be able to:

- describe the Rutherford scattering experiment and the evidence it produced
- explain how this evidence leads to the nuclear model of the atom
- describe the 'plum pudding' model and explain why this model proved to be inadequate.

Some students should also be able to:

- draw and explain in detail the paths of alpha particles scattered by a nucleus.

Answers to in-text questions

a It had hit something much heavier.

b Rutherford's model would have been incorrect.

Support

- Provide a diagram of the experiment including the paths taken by the alpha particles so that the students can add the conclusions to the evidence presented.

Extend

- Ask: 'How was the neutron discovered?' Because it has no electrical charge, it is much more difficult to detect than the electron or proton. The students should find out who discovered it and how. Point out that the neutron was referred to in science books before its actual discovery – scientists were so convinced of its existence.

AQA / Specification link-up: Physics P2.5

- The basic structure of an atom is a small central nucleus composed of protons and neutrons surrounded by electrons. *[P2.5.1 a)]*
- Explain how results from the Rutherford and Marsden scattering experiments led to the 'plum pudding' model being replaced by the nuclear model. *[P2.5]*

Lesson structure

Starters

What's in the tin? – Peel the label off a tin of sponge pudding. Show the unmarked tin to the students and ask them to describe ways they could find out about what's inside without opening it. [They should consider X-rays, weighing and measuring it to find the density. They might even suggest drilling and sampling.] Discuss how sometimes, scientists have to investigate things that cannot be simply observed; they need to use techniques beyond what we can see. *(5 minutes)*

Believe it or not? – What does it take to change the students' minds about something? How much evidence would be needed to convince them that NASA has really sent men to the Moon? Discuss how difficult it is to change people's strongly held beliefs and point out that scientists are the same; they won't want to change ideas that they have been working with for many years. To support students give them a set of cards showing possible evidence and have them prioritise them (e.g. photographs, testimony, rock samples, radio communications). To extend the students you can have them come up with counter arguments to the evidence. *(10 minutes)*

Main

- This topic is all about a famous experiment and it should be built up as such. Through hard work and brilliant ideas, our idea of 'what an atom is' was developed. You might want to establish the context; electrons (cathode rays) had not long been discovered and Rutherford had discovered that one element could change into another when it emitted an 'alpha particle'.
- The actual experiment took weeks in a very dark laboratory where Geiger or Marsden had to count tiny flashes of light through a microscope. Each flash was one alpha particle hitting the fluorescent screen. If you have electron tubes, you can show a little bit of what this would be like (see 'Further teaching suggestions' box).
- The most important result of the experiment was the few particles that bounced back. These showed that there was something massive at the centre of the atom. One possible analogy would be to spread a large sheet of paper out vertically and behind it fix a small metal disc held firmly by a stand. If you threw darts at it, most would go straight through but one in a thousand may hit the metal disc and bounce back.
- It will be impossibly difficult for the students to imagine the size of an atom and then the relative size of the nucleus. You might like to point out that 99.99% of the chair they are sitting on is just empty space; then again so is 99.99% of their bodies!
- The problem with plum puddings is that nobody eats them any more, so many students don't understand what you are referring to (a Christmas pudding is a good substitute). Try illustrating with a real plum pudding. They are cheap and you can always eat it afterwards.
- This whole topic links in neatly with 'How Science Works' and the section on 'Observation as a stimulus to investigation'. This relates to how data and observations from testing a prediction can either support or refute existing theories and models.

Plenaries

It's not like a solar system – Some people think of an atom as being a bit like a solar system. The students should make a list of similarities but, more importantly, the differences. [The nucleus is not much like a star, it is made up of different bits (protons and neutrons) and the electrons don't actually orbit in ellipses]. *(5 minutes)*

I don't believe it – Can the students write a letter to an unconvinced scientist who wants to hold on to the plum pudding model? This will help them reinforce their understanding by explaining the concepts to others. They need to include all of the evidence and then the explanations that are used. Differentiate by asking for different levels of detail for different students or by providing some sample phrases describing pieces of evidence that must be included. *(10 minutes)*

Practical support

Lucky strike

This practical really needs no additional explanation. A more advanced version is outlined in the 'Further teaching suggestions' box.

Hot cross buns

A hot cross bun can be used to give an impression of the 'plum pudding' model for students who are not familiar with a plum pudding. The currants represent the electrons spread throughout the positive dough. The big cross is a handy reminder of the fact the bun is positive.

Radioactivity

The discovery of the nucleus

P2 6.2 — The discovery of the nucleus

Learning objectives

- How was the nuclear model of the atom established?
- Why was the plum pudding model of the atom rejected?
- Why was the nuclear model accepted?

?? Did you know ...?

Ernest Rutherford was awarded the Nobel Prize in 1908 for his discoveries on radioactivity. His famous discovery of the nucleus was made in 1913. He was knighted in 1914 and made a member of the House of Lords in 1931. He hoped that no one would discover how to release energy from the nucleus until people learned to live at peace with their neighbours. He died in 1937 before the discovery of nuclear fission.

Figure 2 Ernest Rutherford

Practical

Lucky strike!
Fix a small metal disc about 2 cm thick at the centre of a table. Hide the disc under a cardboard disc about 20 cm in diameter. See if you can hit the metal disc with a rolling marble.

Ernest Rutherford made many important discoveries about radioactivity. He discovered that alpha and beta radiation consists of different types of particles. He realised alpha (α) particles could be used to probe the atom. He asked two of his research workers, Hans Geiger and Ernest Marsden, to investigate. They used a thin metal foil to scatter a beam of alpha particles. Figure 1 shows the arrangement they used.

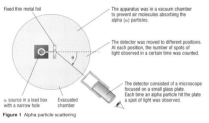

Fixed thin metal foil

The apparatus was in a vacuum chamber to prevent air molecules absorbing the alpha (α) particles.

The detector was moved to different positions. At each position, the number of spots of light observed in a certain time was counted.

The detector consisted of a microscope focused on a small glass plate. Each time an alpha particle hit the plate a spot of light was observed.

α source in a lead box with a narrow hole

Evacuated chamber

Figure 1 Alpha particle scattering

They measured the number of alpha particles deflected per second through different angles. The results showed that:

- most of the alpha particles passed straight through the metal foil
- the number of alpha particles deflected per minute decreased as the angle of deflection increased
- about 1 in 10000 alpha particles were deflected by more than 90°.

a If you kicked a football at an empty goal and the ball bounced back at you, what would you conclude?

Rutherford was astonished by the results. He said it was like firing 'naval shells' at tissue paper and discovering the occasional shell rebounds. He knew that α particles are positively charged. He deduced from the results that there is a nucleus at the centre of every atom that is:

- positively charged because it repels α particles (remember that like charges repel and unlike charges attract)
- much smaller than the atom because most α particles pass through without deflection
- where most of the mass of the atom is located.

Using this model, Rutherford worked out the proportion of α particles that would be deflected for a given angle. He found an exact agreement with Geiger and Marsden's measurements. He used his theory to estimate the diameter of the nucleus. He found it was about 100000 times smaller than the atom.

Rutherford's nuclear model of the atom was quickly accepted because:

- It agreed exactly with the measurements Geiger and Marsden made in their experiments.
- It explains radioactivity in terms of changes that happen to an unstable nucleus when it emits radiation.
- It predicted the existence of the neutron, which was later discovered.

b What difference would it have made if Geiger and Marsden's measurements had not fitted Rutherford's nuclear model?

Goodbye to the plum pudding model!

Before the nucleus was discovered in 1914, scientists didn't know what the structure of the atom was. They did know atoms contained electrons and they knew these are tiny negatively charged particles. But they didn't know how the positive charge was arranged in an atom, although there were different models in circulation. Some scientists thought the atom was like a 'plum pudding' with:

- the positively charged matter in the atom evenly spread about (as in a pudding), and
- electrons buried inside (like plums in the pudding).

Rutherford's discovery meant farewell to the 'plum pudding' atom.

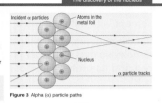

Incident α particles — Atoms in the metal foil

Nucleus

α particle tracks

Figure 3 Alpha (α) particle paths

Sphere of positive charge

Electrons

Figure 4 The plum pudding atom

?? Did you know ...?

Almost all the mass of an atom is in its nucleus. The density of the nucleus is about a thousand million million times the density of water. A matchbox full of nuclear matter would weigh about a million million tonnes!

Summary questions

1 Copy and complete **a** to **c** using the words below:
   charge   diameter   mass
   a A nucleus has the same type of .... as an alpha particle.
   b A nucleus has a much smaller .... than the atom.
   c Most of the .... of the atom is in the nucleus.

2 **a** Figure 5 shows four possible paths, labelled A, B, C and D, of an alpha particle deflected by a nucleus. Which path would the alpha particle travel along?
   b Explain why each of the other paths in part **a** is not possible.

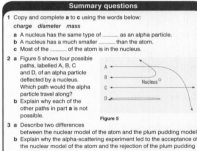

   Figure 5

3 **a** Describe two differences between the nuclear model of the atom and the plum pudding model.
   b Explain why the alpha-scattering experiment led to the acceptance of the nuclear model of the atom and the rejection of the plum pudding model.

Key points

- Rutherford used the measurements from alpha-scattering experiments to prove that an atom has a small positively charged central nucleus where most of the mass of the atom is located.
- The plum pudding model could not explain why some alpha particles were scattered through large angles.
- The nuclear model of the atom correctly explained why the alpha particles are scattered and why some are scattered through large angles.

238 / 239

Further teaching suggestions

A scattering experiment

- It is possible to model the scattering experiment of Rutherford using a hidden cone and marbles. The marbles are rolled at the cone and scatter in directions similar to those in the original experiment. You should find a kit available in a good science equipment catalogue. This is really only suitable for small groups though. More useful animations can be found at various websites on the internet.

Electron tubes

- These are generally only used at A-level, but you could use them here to extend the students.

   Details
   Use the manual for the tube to set it up. It will require an extremely high-tension power supply and some proper connecting leads. These shouldn't be able to provide a dangerous current but take care with any high voltages. With the tube you should be able to show the phosphorescence effect of a charged particle and some magnetic deflection if you wish.

?? Did you know ...?

There are objects made up of purely nuclear material. A neutron star is made up of neutrons packed together as tightly as the protons and neutrons in a nucleus.

Summary answers

1 **a** charge   **b** diameter   **c** mass

2 **a** Path B.
   b A is wrong because it is attracted by the nucleus;
      C is wrong because it is unaffected by the nucleus;
      D is wrong because it is repelled by the nucleus through too great an angle.

3 **a** Any two of the following three points:
   1 In the nuclear model, all the positive charge is concentrated in a nucleus that is much smaller than the atom. In the 'plum pudding' atom, the positive charge is spread out throughout the atom.
   2 In the nuclear model, most of the mass of the atom is concentrated in the nucleus. In the 'plum pudding' atom, most of the mass is spread out throughout the atom.
   3 In the nuclear model, most of the atom is empty space. In the 'plum pudding' model, there is no empty space in the atom.
   b The nuclear model explains why some of the alpha particles are scattered through large angles. According to the 'plum pudding' model, such large-angle scattering should not be observed.

P2 6.3 Nuclear reactions

AQA Specification link-up: Physics P2.5

- The relative masses and relative electric charges of protons, neutrons and electrons. [P2.5.1 b)]
- In an atom the number of electrons is equal to the number of protons in the nucleus. The atom has no overall electrical charge. [P2.5.1 c)]
- Atoms may lose or gain electrons to form charged particles called ions. [P2.5.1 d)]
- The atoms of an element always have the same number of protons, but have a different number of neutrons for each isotope. The total number of protons in an atom is called its atomic number. The total number of protons and neutrons in an atom is called its mass number. [P2.5.1 e)]
- Identification of an alpha particle as 2 neutrons and 2 protons, the same as a helium nucleus, a beta particle as an electron from the nucleus and gamma radiation as electromagnetic radiation. [P2.5.2 c)]
- Nuclear equations to show single alpha and beta decay. [P2.5.2 d)] [HT only]

Learning objectives

Students should learn:

- that isotopes are atoms of the same element with different mass numbers
- that when a nucleus emits an alpha particle, its mass number is reduced by 4 and its proton number is reduced by 2
- that when a nucleus decays by beta emission, its mass number stays the same but its proton number increases by 1.

Learning outcomes

Most students should be able to:

- state the relative charge and mass of the constituents of an atom
- state how many protons and neutrons are in a nucleus, given its mass number and its atomic number
- describe what happens to an isotope when it undergoes alpha or beta decay.

Some students should also be able to:

- write nuclear equations to represent alpha or beta decay given appropriate data. [HT only]

Answers to in-text questions

a $92 \, p$, $143 \, n$

b $^{228}_{90}\text{Th} = 90 \, p + 138 \, n$
   $^{224}_{88}\text{Ra} = 88 \, p + 136 \, n$

c $^{40}_{19}\text{K} = 19 \, p + 21 \, n$; $^{40}_{20}\text{Ca} = 20 \, p + 20 \, n$

Support

- Support students by providing a list of the terms and symbols used in this topic, along with diagrams representing the basic decays for them to label.

Extend

- Alchemists dreamed for thousands of years that lead could be transformed into gold. With nuclear physics, this can now actually be achieved. The students should find out who has done this and why the market has not been flooded with this artificial gold.

Lesson structure

Starters

Fact or fiction – The students use red, amber and green cards to decide if a series of statements about radioactivity are false, they don't know, or true. These can include things like: radioactive materials glow [mostly false], radioactive material are all metals [false], there is no safe dose of nuclear radiation [true], radioactivity is artificial [false] and so on. *(5 minutes)*

Chemical change – Give the students a demonstration of a chemical reaction (magnesium + oxygen → magnesium oxide, or magnesium + hydrochloric acid → magnesium chloride + hydrogen. Ask the students to describe what is happening in terms of particles and see if they understand basic conservation of particles in this experiment. Use the idea later to help discuss conservation of protons and neutrons in nuclear decay. Support students by providing them with simple atom diagrams showing the process and ask them to describe the making or breaking of bonds. To extend the students, you should require descriptions of energy changes. *(10 minutes)*

Main

- There is quite a lot of information in this spread and students are likely to become confused if they move too quickly through it. The main source of confusion is often with the large number of scientific terms.
- Start with a reminder of the structure of an atom, but do not dwell on it too long because this will be the fifth or sixth time the students have been through it. There are alternative terms for the number of protons and total number of nucleons (proton number and nucleon number) but the AQA specifications sticks to 'atomic number' and 'mass number' and so should you. Watch out for students getting confused about finding the number of neutrons. Some think that there is *always* the same number of neutrons as protons (as there often are in smaller atoms of elements).
- Some students find it very difficult to write out the superscript and subscripts on the isotopes in the correct positions. Try to encourage them to be precise and write out plenty of examples. It may be difficult to write these on an interactive whiteboard too.
- Higher Tier students need to be able to understand the format of decay equations so that they can find the missing values when needed. Give them a few extra ones with missing numbers.
- You will find animations of nuclear decays helpful, as the students can see the alpha or beta particle leave the nucleus and how it is changed by the process. Somebody might ask where the electron comes from in beta decay. They may think that a neutron is an electron and a proton stuck together, and it just splits; you should point out that this is not the case but you won't be explaining it until the students opt for advanced-level physics.
- Gamma ray emission is really just the release of excess energy by the nucleus after another form of decay leaves it with a bit too much energy. As there are no particles emitted and there is no change to the nucleus.

Plenaries

Name that isotope – Provide the students with a table describing different isotopes with gaps in and ask them to complete the table. They need to fill in missing details such as element name, proton number, mass number and number of electrons using the information provided. They will need a periodic table to help. *(5 minutes)*

Definitions – The students must give accurate definitions of the terms: 'proton, neutron, electron, ion, mass number, atomic number, alpha particle, beta particle and gamma ray.' These should be linked to the learning that has taken place already in this chapter. Select the best and use these definitions on a wall display to remind the students. To support students, you can make this activity a simple phrase or card-matching task. To extend students, you can insist on illustrations demonstrating the ideas. *(10 minutes)*

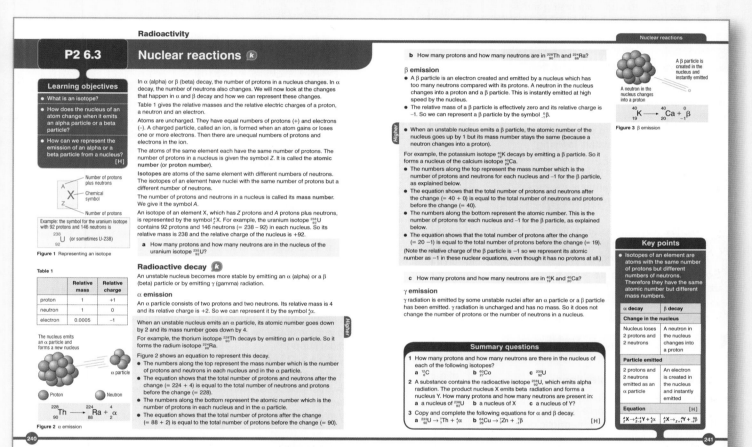

Radioactivity

P2 6.3 Nuclear reactions

Learning objectives
- What is an isotope?
- How does the nucleus of an atom change when it emits an alpha particle or a beta particle?
- How can we represent the emission of an alpha or a beta particle from a nucleus? [H]

Figure 1 Representing an isotope

In α (alpha) or β (beta) decay, the number of protons in a nucleus changes. In α decay, the number of neutrons also changes. We will now look at the changes that happen in α and β decay and how we can represent these changes.

Table 1 gives the relative masses and the relative electric charges of a proton, a neutron and an electron.

Atoms are uncharged. They have equal numbers of protons (+) and electrons (–). A charged particle, called an ion, is formed when an atom gains or loses one or more electrons. Then there are unequal numbers of protons and electrons in the ion.

The atoms of the same element each have the same number of protons. The number of protons in a nucleus is given the symbol Z. It is called the **atomic number (or proton number)**.

Isotopes are atoms of the same element with different numbers of neutrons. The isotopes of an element have nuclei with the same number of protons but a different number of neutrons.

The number of protons and neutrons in a nucleus is called its **mass number**. We give it the symbol A.

An isotope of an element X, which has Z protons and A protons plus neutrons, is represented by the symbol ^A_ZX. For example, the uranium isotope $^{238}_{92}$U contains 92 protons and 146 neutrons (= 238 – 92) in each nucleus. So its relative mass is 238 and the relative electric charge of the nucleus is +92.

a How many protons and how many neutrons are in the nucleus of the uranium isotope $^{235}_{92}$U?

Radioactive decay

An unstable nucleus becomes more stable by emitting an α (alpha) or a β (beta) particle or by emitting γ (gamma) radiation.

α emission

An α particle consists of two protons and two neutrons. Its relative mass is 4 and its relative charge is +2. So we can represent it by the symbol $^4_2\alpha$.

When an unstable nucleus emits an α particle, its atomic number goes down by 2 and its mass number goes down by 4.

For example, the thorium isotope $^{228}_{90}$Th decays by emitting an α particle. So it forms the radium isotope $^{224}_{88}$Ra.

Figure 2 shows an equation to represent this decay.
- The numbers along the top represent the mass number which is the number of protons and neutrons in each nucleus and in the α particle.
- The equation shows that the total number of protons and neutrons after the change (= 224 + 4) is equal to the total number of neutrons and protons before the change (= 228).
- The numbers along the bottom represent the atomic number which is the number of protons in each nucleus and in the α particle.
- The equation shows that the total number of protons after the change (= 88 + 2) is equal to the total number of protons before the change (= 90).

Table 1

	Relative mass	Relative charge
proton	1	+1
neutron	1	0
electron	0.0005	–1

The nucleus emits an α particle and forms a new nucleus

$^{228}_{90}$Th → $^{224}_{88}$Ra + $^4_2\alpha$

Figure 2 α emission

b How many protons and how many neutrons are in $^{228}_{90}$Th and $^{224}_{88}$Ra?

β emission

- A β particle is an electron created and emitted by a nucleus which has too many neutrons compared with its protons. A neutron in the nucleus changes into a proton and a β particle. This is instantly emitted at high speed by the nucleus.
- The relative mass of a β particle is effectively zero and its relative charge is –1. So we can represent a β particle by the symbol $^0_{-1}\beta$.
- When an unstable nucleus emits a β particle, the atomic number of the nucleus goes up by 1 but its mass number stays the same (because a neutron changes into a proton).

For example, the potassium isotope $^{40}_{19}$K decays by emitting a β particle. So it forms a nucleus of the calcium isotope $^{40}_{20}$Ca.
- The numbers along the top represent the mass number which is the number of protons and neutrons for each nucleus and –1 for the β particle, as explained below.
- The equation shows that the total number of protons and neutrons after the change (= 40 + 0) is equal to the total number of neutrons and protons before the change (= 40).
- The numbers along the bottom represent the atomic number. This is the number of protons for each nucleus and –1 for the β particle, as explained below.
- The equation shows that the total number of protons after the change (= 20 –1) is equal to the total number of protons before the change (= 19). (Note the relative charge of the β particle is –1 so we represent its atomic number as –1 in these nuclear equations, even though it has no protons at all.)

A β particle is created in the nucleus and instantly emitted

A neutron in the nucleus changes into a proton

$^{40}_{19}$K → $^{40}_{20}$Ca + $^0_{-1}\beta$

Figure 3 β emission

c How many protons and how many neutrons are in $^{40}_{19}$K and $^{40}_{20}$Ca?

γ emission

γ radiation is emitted by some unstable nuclei after an α particle or a β particle has been emitted. γ radiation is uncharged and has no mass. So it does not change the number of protons or the number of neutrons in a nucleus.

Summary questions

1 How many protons and how many neutrons are there in the nucleus of each of the following isotopes?
   a $^{12}_6$C   b $^{60}_{27}$Co   c $^{235}_{92}$U

2 A substance contains the radioactive isotope $^{238}_{92}$U, which emits alpha radiation. The product nucleus X emits beta radiation and forms a nucleus Y. How many protons and how many neutrons are present in:
   a a nucleus of $^{238}_{92}$U   b a nucleus of X   c a nucleus of Y?

3 Copy and complete the following equations for α and β decay.
   a $^{235}_{92}$U → $^{?}_{?}$Th + $^4_2\alpha$ b $^{64}_{29}$Cu → $^{?}_{?}$Zn + $^0_{-1}\beta$ [H]

Key points
- Isotopes of an element are atoms with the same number of protons but different numbers of neutrons. Therefore they have the same atomic number but different mass numbers.

α decay	β decay
Change in the nucleus	
Nucleus loses 2 protons and 2 neutrons	A neutron in the nucleus changes into a proton
Particle emitted	
2 protons and 2 neutrons emitted as an α particle	An electron is created in the nucleus and instantly emitted
Equation	[H]
$^A_ZX \rightarrow ^{A-4}_{Z-2}Y + ^4_2\alpha$	$^A_ZX \rightarrow ^A_{Z+1}Y + ^0_{-1}\beta$

Further teaching suggestions

Nuclear reactions
- Give the students some additional questions on the constituents of different isotopes, and ask them to determine what new isotopes are formed following certain decays. You might like to stretch some students by giving them some decay sequences. The students will need a periodic table.

Summary answers

1 a $6p + 6n$
   b $27p + 33n$
   c $92p + 143n$

2 a $92p + 146n$
   b $90p + 144n$
   c $91p + 143n$

3 a $^{235}_{92}U \rightarrow ^{231}_{90}Th + ^4_2\alpha$
   b $^{64}_{29}Cu \rightarrow ^{64}_{30}Zn + ^0_{-1}\beta$

P2 6.4

More about alpha, beta and gamma radiation

Learning objectives

Students should learn that:

- that the different radiations have different penetrating powers
- the range in air is different for each type of radiation and that they are affected differently by electric and magnetic fields
- that nuclear radiation is ionising and this damages living cells causing cancer or cell death.

Learning outcomes

Most students should be able to:

- describe the penetrating powers of the three radiations
- describe the range in air of each type of radiation, their relative ionising power and how they are affected in a magnetic or electric field
- evaluate which radiation is the most hazardous inside and outside of the human body
- describe ways of reducing the hazards presented when handling radioactive substances.

Some students should also be able to:

- explain in detail why radiation is dangerous in terms of damage to cells.

Answers to in-text questions

a To stop the radiation, so it can't affect objects or people nearby.
b It is not deflected by a magnetic or an electric field.
c To keep the source out of range.

Support

- Ask students to complete just one gap in a nuclear equation with all other data provided.

Extend

- Where do the beta particles come from? The beta particles are high-energy electrons that come from the nucleus, but there are no electrons in the nucleus! The students need to find an explanation of what is happening in the nucleus that is producing these electrons. This might have been asked about in a prior lesson. Students could also research particle accelerators such as the Large Hadron Collider.

AQA / Specification link-up: Physics P2.5

- Identification of an alpha particle as 2 neutrons and 2 protons, the same as a helium nucleus, a beta particle as an electron from the nucleus and gamma radiation as electromagnetic radiation. [P2.5.2 c)]
- Properties of the alpha, beta and gamma radiations limited to their relative ionising power, their penetration through materials and their range in air. [P2.5.2 e)]
- Alpha and beta radiations are deflected by both electric and magnetic fields but gamma radiation is not. [P2.5.2 f)]
- The uses of and the dangers associated with each type of nuclear radiation. [P2.5.2 g)]
  Controlled Assessment: AS4.2 Assess and manage risks when carrying out practical work. [AS4.2.1 a) b)]

Lesson structure

Starters

It's all Greek to me – Scientists use a lot of symbols in their work. Discuss the reasons that scientists use symbols for elements, equations, the names of things, etc. Reasons include internationalisation, simplicity, clarity, brevity. To demonstrate this, ask the students to write out '7 − 3 = 4' in words and then show a longer equation. You might ask the students to list all of the symbols that they know the meaning of; they know more than they think. *(5 minutes)*

Magnetism – The students should be familiar with magnetic fields. Ask them to show their knowledge in a diagram/mind map/spider diagram. They should include the shape of simple fields and the effect that magnetism has on certain materials. You can support students by providing a set of 'facts' cards and asking them to sort them into true of false (or an interactive quiz). To extend students you should require appropriate force diagrams and information about the strength of the field reducing with distance. *(10 minutes)*

Main

- A simulated experiment allows students to test what different types of radiation can penetrate. You may also demonstrate the penetrating powers of radiations with the method set out in 'Practical support'.
- The difference between alpha and beta particles and the electromagnetic wave nature of gamma should be emphasised. Gamma radiation causes no change in the structure of the nucleus; it is really the nucleus releasing some excess energy it didn't lose in a previous decay. The lack of charge on the gamma rays accounts for their higher penetrating power; they interact with matter a lot less than alpha or beta.
- A strong magnet can be used to deflect alpha and beta particles away from the detector but you will find it hard to show which way they have deflected so settle for the count rate being reduced and let the students imagine the particles being deflected by the magnetic field and not reaching the detector. You can't really show the acceleration caused by an electric field but you could extend some students by making links to particle accelerators.
- The students may not have encountered the idea of ionisation before. It is important that they grasp the concept of the radioactive particle stripping away electrons from atoms and causing unwanted chemical reaction in cells. The main danger is that the cell will be damaged and reproduce out of control. Explain that this becomes more likely the larger the dose of radiation, but that it is possible for a single damaged cell to cause cancer, so there is no minimum safe limit to radiation. We should therefore try to limit our exposure by keeping sources safely away from our bodies.
- Spark detectors are simple and it is well worth showing the effect if you have one. Discuss the safety precautions while using it, focusing on the harmful ionisation that would happen to your cells if you were too close. The alpha source should produce a lot more sparks so you can say it is highly ionising.
- Both of the following plenaries are useful for assessing risk in 'How Science Works'.

Plenaries

Local rules – The students should make a plan for a poster or booklet explaining how your radioactive sources should be stored and handled. Remind them of the precautions when you demonstrate the radiation but it is up to the students to explain why these precautions are needed. They should link all of the measures to harm reduction. They can then produce this booklet as homework. *(5 minutes)*

Protect and survive – What if one of the radioactive sources was dropped and lost? How would it be found and what precautions would need to be taken during the search? You should be able to find what really should be done in CLEAPSS resources. Show some footage of radiological protection officers suited up and wandering around with Geiger counters; this would be over the top for a dropped source. Differentiate the sources of information you provide to the students: to extend them you can provide the full guidance and ask them to explain why each measure is needed; to support students you should provide only the key recommendations and discuss why these are required. *(10 minutes)*

Practical support

Penetrating power

The techniques used on the previous spread can be expanded to show the penetrating power of the three radiations. (Teacher demonstration only.)

Equipment and materials required

Geiger–Müller tube, ratemeter (and possibly high voltage power supply), large plastic tray, tongs, radioactive sources, set of absorbers (paper, card, plastic, aluminium of various thicknesses and lead plates).

Details

Set the equipment up in the tray, as before, but add a mount to position a source in place. Between the source holder and detector, position a holder to hold the absorbers. Make sure that the detector is less than 10 cm from the source holder or the alpha particles will not reach. Turn on the detector and then mount an alpha emitter in the holder and note the count rate. This function can be performed by most meters, but you may have to count for 20 seconds if not. Position a paper absorber between the source and detector and note the count rate. Test the beta source with paper, plastic and then aluminium plates. Test the gamma with aluminium and then various thicknesses of lead.

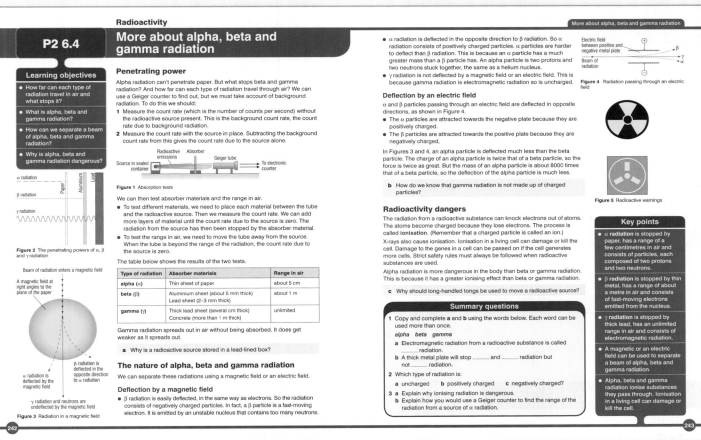

Further teaching suggestions

More detectors

- There are other ways of detecting and analysing ionising radiation, including cloud and bubble chambers and photographic films. The students could find out about these devices and why they are used. Which of the devices reveals most about the radiation and in what circumstances are they used?

Summary answers

1. **a** gamma
   b alpha, beta, (alpha and beta in either order) gamma
2. **a** gamma   **b** alpha   **c** beta
3. **a** Radiation can knock electrons from atoms. This ionisation damages the genes in a cell which can be passed on if the cell generates more cells.
   b Using long-handled tongs to hold the source above the spark counter, move the source gradually downwards towards the spark counter. When the spark counter begins to spark, fix the position of the source, switch off the power supply and measure the distance between source and the spark counter. This is the range of the α-radiation.

P2 6.5

Half-life

AQA
Specification link-up: Physics P2.5

- The half-life of a radioactive isotope is the average time it takes for the number of nuclei of the isotope in a sample to halve, or the time it takes for the count rate from a sample containing the isotope to fall to half its initial level. *[P2.5.2 h)]*

Controlled Assessment: AS4.5 Analyse and interpret primary and secondary data. *[AS4.5.2 a) b)], [AS4.5.3 a)], [AS4.5.4 a)]*

Learning objectives

Students should learn:

- that the activity of a radioactive source decreases with time because the number of parent atoms is decreasing
- that the half-life of a source is a measure of the average time it takes for the activity of a source to reach half of its initial value.

Learning outcomes

Most students should be able to:

- define the term half-life in relation to the activity of a radioactive source
- determine the half-life of a source from a graph or table of data.

Answers to in-text questions

a 75 cpm
b 6.5 hours

Support

- Students should be provided with a results table with one set of results already filled in to help explain the idea. Make sure students are removing 'dead' dice and only rolling the 'survivors' after each round.

Extend

- Collect the whole class data together to find a total for each round. This will give a smoother graph. You can then use a spreadsheet to plot the graphs and also find the number of dice decaying after each roll. This will reveal the decrease in the count rate over time.

Lesson structure

Starters

An exponential decay puzzle – A farmer has a warehouse with two million corn cobs in it. Every day he sells exactly half of his remaining stock. How long before he has sold every last **nugget** (not cob) of corn? The students should realise that this takes quite a while with the amount remaining just halving each day (1 000 000, 500 000, 250 000, 125 000 and so on) and then the nuggets on the last cob takes a few more weeks to get rid of. You can use a calculator and just keep dividing by two to see how many steps this would take. *(5 minutes)*

An exponential growth puzzle – A philosopher places a grain of rice on the first square of a chess board, two on the next, four on the next and so on. How many go on the last (sixty-fourth) square? The pattern goes 1, 2, 4, 8, 16, 32, 64, 128 for the first row.

[By the end, there would be 9 223 372 036 854 775 808 (2^{63}) on the last square]. Extend students by showing a graph of a function like this and ask the students to describe the key features; they should identify the 'accelerating' rate clearly. To support students you might want to limit the calculation to the first two rows and then show the graph to see what happens next. *(10 minutes)*

Main

- Isotopes can be hard to discuss in isolation. It is easier to use the term isotopes (plural) and make a comparison, for example 'carbon has three isotopes C-12, C-13 and C-14, which are all carbon because they have six protons (and electrons), but they have different numbers of neutrons'. It's much harder to get the idea across if you talk about 'an isotope'.

- The students should be familiar with the structure of the atoms and should quickly recall that the number of neutrons in the atoms of a particular element may vary. Try to get across the idea of activity early. The more active an isotope the more rapid the decay. 'Parent' and 'daughter' are important terms also. You could show a nuclear decay equation to get these terms across.

- The rolling dice decay model is an enjoyable experiment, but it can be time-consuming. To improve the average values, the groups can share data and this will lead to a more accurate half-life. At the start and end of the experiment, make sure that the students understand that the dice represented nuclei and removing them represented decay. They should have a reasonable understanding that the pattern is the same each time, even though we do not know exactly which of the dice decays each time. If you feel like being a bit 'all knowing', seal the answer [4.16 rolls] in an envelope in advance and stick it to the board in plain sight. Then 'reveal' it at the end, which allows you to discuss the fact that we can accurately model random behaviour using mathematics.

- The experiment lends itself well to the ideas of repeating to improve reliability, but can also be used to explain that statistics work best on very large samples, so the more dice the better the fit. (This relates to ideas of reliability of data in 'How Science Works'.) There is also opportunity to develop or assess graph-plotting skills along with drawing lines of best fit. (This relates to the skills of presenting data in 'How Science Works'.)

- You can discuss what happens to the 'count rate' after each roll. The number of dice eliminated in each round represents this and this rate should decrease as the number of surviving dice falls. This gives the students a decent understanding of why the count rate falls as time goes on.

Plenaries

Activity and decay – Show the students a graph with three decay curves on them. Can they identify which has the longest half-life and which is the most active source? [They should identify the relationship that the longer the half-life, the less active the material is for the same initial quantity]. *(5 minutes)*

Coin toss – If I have 120 coins and toss them all, removing all of the heads after each toss, how many tosses until I should only have 15 left? [This would be three half-lives so three tosses]. You could show this for real with a tray of pennies and compare the real result with the theoretical one. To extend the students, they should be asked to discuss why the real results can diverge from theoretical models. How could the simulation become more like the mathematical model? They should realise that the smaller the number of particles (coins) in the simulations, the more likely divergence is. You can give additional support by allowing the students to try smaller numbers of coins and make predictions about the decay patterns. *(10 minutes)*

Practical support

Radioactive dice

This is a simple model of the randomness of radioactive decay and how to find the half-life.

Equipment and materials required

For each group: a set of 59 identical six-sided cubes and one cube of a different colour. The dice should have a dot on one face only. (You can use more or less dice depending on how many you have, but 60 works well.)

Details

The students roll the full set of dice, and after each roll, they remove the dice that landed showing a spot. They record the number of dice

'surviving' and then roll only these dice, and so on. They continue this process of elimination for 20 rolls, or until no dice survives.

During this, they should also note down when the special dice lands spot up causing it to be removed. If time permits, they repeat this process and calculate an average number of dice remaining after each roll. Plotting a graph of the number of dice remaining (*y*-axis) against roll number (*x*-axis) reveals that the dice behave like decaying atoms and a half-life can be calculated; this should be 4.16 rolls. The single dice should show that the process is random; it is impossible to predict when any individual dice will be eliminated. For some groups, it will be removed after the first roll and for others it will survive until the end.

Radioactivity

P2 6.5   Half-life

Learning objectives
- What do we mean by the 'half-life' of a radioactive source?
- What do we mean by the activity of a radioactive source?
- What happens to the activity of a radioactive isotope as it decays?

Every atom of an element always has the same number of protons in its nucleus. However, the number of neutrons in the nucleus can differ. Each type of atom is called an isotope. (So isotopes of an element contain the same number of protons but different numbers of neutrons.)

The **activity** of a radioactive isotope is the number of atoms that decay per second. As the nucleus of each unstable atom (the 'parent' atom) decays, the number of parent atoms goes down. Therefore the activity of the sample decreases.

We can use a Geiger counter to monitor the activity of a radioactive sample. We need to measure the **count rate** due to the sample. This is the number of counts per second (or per minute). The graph below shows how the count rate of a sample decreases.

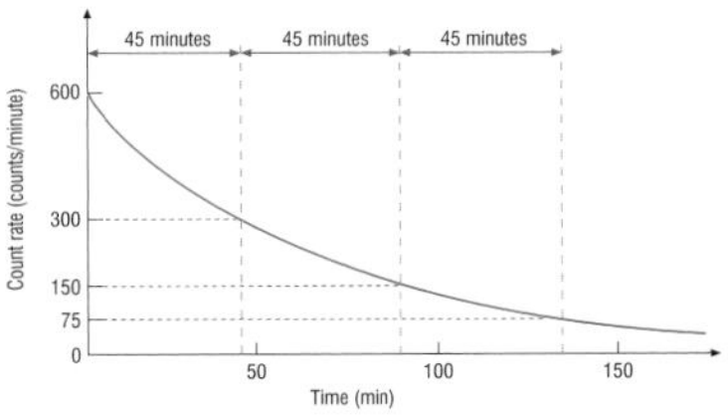

Figure 1 Radioactive decay: a graph of count rate against time

The graph shows that the count rate decreases with time. The count rate falls from:

- 600 counts per minute (c.p.m.) to 300 c.p.m. in the first 45 minutes
- 300 counts per minute (c.p.m.) to 150 c.p.m. in the next 45 minutes.

The average time taken for the count rate (and therefore the number of parent atoms) to fall by half is always the same. This time is called the **half-life**. The half-life shown on the graph is 45 minutes.

a What will the count rate be after 135 minutes from the start?

The half-life of a radioactive isotope is the average time it takes:
- for the number of nuclei of the isotope in a sample (and therefore the mass of parent atoms) to halve
- for the count rate the isotope in a sample to fall to half its initial value.

?? Did you know ...?

Some radioactive isotopes have half-lives of a fraction of a second, whereas others have half-lives of more than a billion years. The nitrogen isotope N-12 has a half-life of 0.0125 seconds. The uranium isotope U-238 has a half-life of 4.5 billion years.

The random nature of radioactive decay

Radioactive decay is a random process. We can't predict *when* an individual atom will suddenly decay. But we *can* predict how many atoms will decay in a certain time – because there are so many of them. This is a bit like throwing dice. You can't predict what number you will get with a single throw. But if you threw 1000 dice, you would expect one-sixth to come up with a particular number.

Suppose we start with 1000 unstable atoms. Look at the graph on the right:

If 10% decay every hour, then:
- 100 atoms will decay in the first hour, leaving 900
- 90 atoms (= 10% of 900) will decay in the second hour, leaving 810.

The table below shows what you get if you continue the calculations. The results are plotted as a graph in Figure 2.

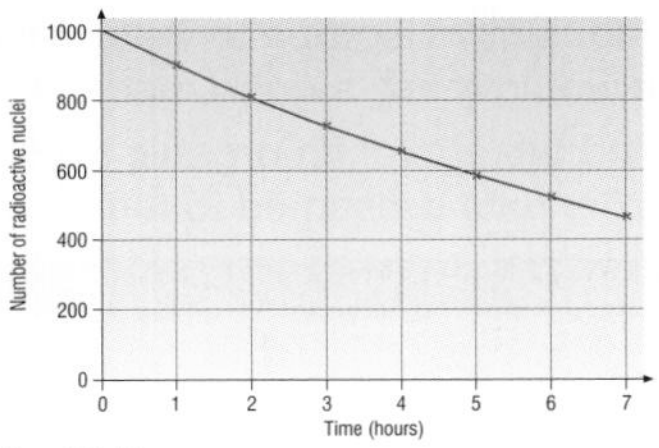

Figure 2 Half-life

Time from start (hours)	0	1	2	3	4	5	6	7
No. of unstable atoms present	1000	900	810	729	656	590	530	477
No. of unstable atoms that decay in the next hour	100	90	81	73	66	59	53	48

b Use the graph in Figure 2 to work out the half-life of this radioactive isotope.

?? Did you know ...?

Next time you help someone choose numbers for the lottery, think about whether this is something you can predict. The balls come out of the machine at random; is there any way of predicting what they will be?

Summary questions

1 Copy and complete **a** and **b** using the words below. Each word can be used more than once.

    half-life   stable   unstable

  a In a radioactive substance, ... atoms decay and become ....
  b The .... of a radioactive isotope is the time taken for the number of .... atoms to decrease to half.

2 A radioactive isotope has a half-life of 15 hours. A sealed tube contains 8 milligrams of this isotope. What mass of the isotope is in the tube:
  a 15 hours later?
  b 45 hours later?

3 A sample of a radioactive isotope contains 320 million atoms of the isotope. How many atoms of the isotope are present after:
  a one half-life
  b five half-lives?

Key points
- The half-life of a radioactive isotope is the average time it takes for the number of nuclei of the isotope in a sample to halve.
- The activity of a radioactive source is the number of nuclei that decay per second.
- The number of atoms of a radioactive isotope and the activity both decrease by half every half-life.

Further teaching suggestions

Roll the dice
- Starting with the basic six-sided dice experiment, the students could investigate what would happen if a different set of dice were used. Dice with 4, 8, 10, 12 and 20 sides are available from gaming shops, and will produce similar exponential decay curves but with different half-lives.

Summary answers

1 **a** unstable, stable   **b** half-life, unstable

2 **a** 4 milligrams   **b** 1 milligram

3 **a** 160 million atoms   **b** 10 million atoms

P2 6.6 Radioactivity at work

Learning objectives

Students should learn:

- that radioactive sources have a number of uses including thickness measurement, medical tracing and determining the age of materials
- how to select an appropriate radioactive source for a particular use given data.

Learning outcomes

Most students should be able to:

- describe how a beta source can be used to measure the thickness of a material like aluminium foil
- describe how radioactive traces are used in medical analysis
- describe how radioactive isotopes can be used to determine the age of a rock or organic material.

Some students should also be able to:

- evaluate the properties of a radioactive isotope to determine why it would make a good medical tracer
- find the age of an organic sample from data presented to them.

Answers to in-text questions

a The detector reading increases and the pressure from the rollers is decreased.

b Alpha (α) radiation would be stopped by the foil.

c B because radioactive iodine did not leave the kidney.

d It was formed recently (in geological terms).

Support

- Provide a partially completed flow chart for the operation of the foil press. You can also use a diagram for the students to label up the action of a tracer (or have them draw a cartoon illustrating the process).

Extend

- Very large numbers of radioactive particles are produced in nuclear reactors. How are these particles contained, and are there any that escape into the environment? The students may find out about neutrons and neutrinos.

AQA — Specification link-up: Physics P2.5

- The uses of and the dangers associated with each type of nuclear radiation. [P2.5.2 g)]
- Evaluate the appropriateness of radioactive sources for particular uses, including as tracers, in terms of the type(s) of radiation emitted and their half-lives. [P2.5]

Lesson structure

Starters

All around the body – Show a video clip of a radioactive tracer being injected into a patient (including all of the safety precautions if possible) and the resulting tracer footage. Discuss how the students think that the images have been made until they come up with the idea that the radiation passes out of the body and is detected. You can contrast this idea with X-rays later. *(5 minutes)*

Just how thick? – Ask the students to measure the thickness of a sheet of paper. Can they find out if all of the sheets are the same thickness? How? Give them some basic equipment to try this out (rulers, callipers, perhaps a micrometer) and then discuss how they think that manufacturers can get the right thickness each time. Extend students by asking them to consider the errors in these types of measurements and how these can be reduced. Support can be provided by giving some exact instructions to see if students can reach a consensus about the thickness. *(10 minutes)*

Main

- Using radioactivity to determine the thickness of a material is a fairly straightforward idea; you can link it to the idea of light being absorbed by paper. How many sheets of white paper will stop all light passing through it? The function of the foil press can best be shown as a flow chart with terms like: 'Is too much radiation getting through?' and 'Open up rollers a bit.' Demonstrate that the thicker a material is, the less beta radiation passes through. This could be a quick demonstration as described in 'Practical support', or you could look into it in more depth.

- When discussing radioactive tracers, you should be able to find a video clip of a tracer being used in the body to find a blood vessel blockage. (For example, search a video or image bank for 'radioactive tracer'.) The students should be made aware that the tracer must be picked for the job based on a range of factors, including the type of radiation it emits (gamma), the half-life, and its biochemical properties, i.e. will it build up in the organ we want it to? There are isotopes suitable for a wide range of medical studies, some of which are artificially generated in nuclear reactors. You may want to talk about tracers being used to find gas leaks and monitor the path of underground rivers. These too are carefully chosen so that they decay away quite quickly.

- Carbon dating is only useful over a certain range of times and the materials must be organic. The limit is about 50 000 years, which is good enough for all recorded human history. The technique also needs to be calibrated against objects of known ages; ancient trees are handy for this. Ask the students how we know the age of these trees. Some Egyptian artefacts are also used as we are fairly certain of their actual age due to good record-keeping.

- Uranium dating is generally used to date rocks and is part of the evidence for the Earth being 4.5 billion years old. There are some assumptions that are made with dating processes and you may wish to discuss these with the students. Do the levels of carbon-14 remain constant in the atmosphere? Is there any other way of lead being produced in rocks?

Plenaries

Careful! You can have your eye out with that! – An archaeologist claims to have found the arrow that killed King Harold in 1066. Can the students explain how a scientist would try to check this claim? This should link into carbon dating of the material revealing it is about 1000 years old. *(5 minutes)*

Radioactivity's great – Radioactivity usually gets a fairly bad press; the students should produce a simple poster expounding the virtues of radioactive material. This can cover all of the useful things that radiation can be used for. To provide support, you can provide some extra information on medical treatment to complement the diagnosis, and on nuclear power and its advantages then the students can prioritise and assemble it. To extend the students, you should ask them to target the poster at a specific group of people and give suitable explanations of key phrases. *(10 minutes)*

Practical support

Demonstrating absorption

See local rules for handling radioactive sources.

It is possible to show how radioactivity can be used to measure the thickness of materials. (Teacher demonstration only.)

Equipment and materials required
G–M tube and rate meter, set of aluminium absorbers, beta source, tongs.

Details

Mount the G–M tube and absorber holder in line with the source holder. Position the source carefully and record the count rate (or take a count over 30 seconds). Test the aluminium absorbers one at a time, noting the decreasing count rate as the thickness of the aluminium increases.

You may wish to get the students to plot a graph of count rate against absorber thickness to determine how much aluminium is required to reduce the count to half of the original value. This half-value thickness is an important concept for absorption of gamma rays at A-level.

Radioactivity

P2 6.6 — Radioactivity at work

Learning objectives
- How do we choose a radioactive isotope for a particular job?
- How can we use radioactivity for monitoring?
- What are radioactive tracers?
- What is radioactive dating?

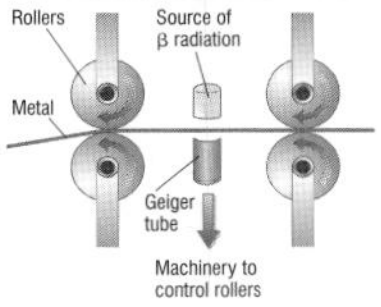

Radioactivity has many uses. For each use, we need a radioactive isotope that emits a certain type of radiation and has a suitable half-life.

Automatic thickness monitoring

This is used when making metal foil.

Look at Figure 1. The radioactive source emits β radiation. The amount of radiation passing through the foil depends on the thickness of the foil. A detector on the other side of the metal foil measures the amount of radiation passing through it.

- If the thickness of the foil increases too much, the detector reading drops.
- The detector sends a signal to the rollers to increase the pressure on the metal sheet.

This makes the foil thinner again.

a What happens if the thickness of the foil decreases too much?
b Why is alpha radiation not used here?

Radioactive tracers 🔑

These are used to trace the flow of a substance through a system. For example, doctors use radioactive iodine to find out if a patient's kidney is blocked.

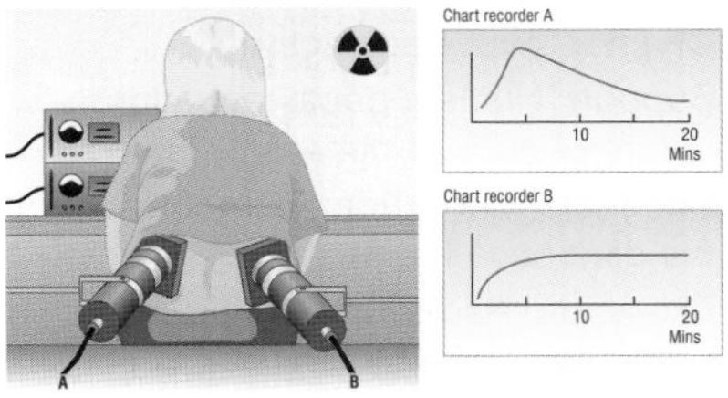

Figure 1 Thickness monitoring using a radioactive source

Figure 2 Using a tracer to monitor a patient's kidneys

Before the test, the patient drinks water containing a tiny amount of the radioactive substance. A detector is then placed against each kidney. Each detector is connected to a chart recorder.

- The radioactive substance flows in and out of a normal kidney. So the detector reading goes up then down.
- For a blocked kidney, the reading goes up and stays up. This is because the radioactive substance goes into the kidney but doesn't flow out again.

Radioactive iodine is used for this test because:

- Its half-life is 8 days, so it lasts long enough for the test to be done but decays almost completely after a few weeks.
- It emits gamma radiation, so it can be detected outside the body.
- It decays into a stable product.

c In Figure 2, which kidney is blocked, A or B?

Radioactive dating

This is used to find the age of ancient material. We can use:

- **Carbon dating** – this is used to find the age of ancient wood and other organic material. Living wood contains a tiny proportion of radioactive carbon. This has a half-life of 5600 years. When a tree dies, it no longer absorbs any carbon. So the amount of radioactive carbon in it decreases. To find the age of a sample, we need to measure the count rate from the wood. This is compared with the count rate from the same mass of living wood. For example, suppose the count rate in a sample of wood is half the count rate of an equal mass of living wood. Then the sample must be 5600 years old.
- **Uranium dating** – this is used to find the age of igneous rocks. These rocks contain radioactive uranium, which has a half-life of 4500 million years. Each uranium atom decays into an atom of lead. We can work out the age of a sample by measuring the number of atoms of uranium and lead. For example, if a sample contains 1 atom of lead for every atom of the uranium, the age of the sample must be 4500 million years. This is because there must have **originally** been 2 atoms of uranium for each atom of uranium now present.

d What could you say about an igneous rock with uranium but no lead in it?

Did you know ... ?

Smoke alarms save lives. A radioactive source inside the alarm sends out alpha particles into a gap in a circuit in the alarm. The alpha particles ionise the air in the gap so it conducts a current across the gap. The current across the gap drops and the alarm sounds. The battery in a smoke alarm needs to be checked regularly – to make sure it is still working!

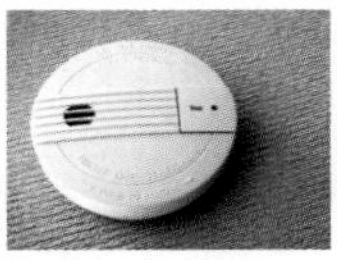

Figure 3 A smoke alarm

Summary questions

1 Copy and complete **a** to **c** using the words below. Each word can be used more than once.

alpha   beta   gamma

a In the continuous production of thin metal sheets, a source of .... radiation should be used to monitor the thickness of the sheets.
b A radioactive tracer given to a hospital patient needs to emit .... or .... radiation.
c The radioactive source used to trace a leak in an underground pipeline should be a source of .... radiation.

2 a Explain why γ radiation is not suitable for monitoring the thickness of metal foil.
b When a radioactive tracer is used, why is it best to use a radioactive isotope that decays into a stable isotope?

3 a What are the ideal properties of a radioactive isotope used as a medical tracer?
b A sample of old wood was carbon dated and found to have 25% of the count rate measured in an equal mass of living wood. The half-life of the radioactive carbon is 5600 years. How old is the sample of wood?

Key points

- The use we can make of a radioactive isotope depends on:
  a its half-life
  b the type of radiation it gives out.
- For monitoring, the isotope should have a long half-life.
- Radioactive tracers should be β or γ emitters that last long enough to monitor but not too long.
- For radioactive dating of a sample, we need a radioactive isotope that is present in the sample which has a half-life about the same as the age of the sample.

Further teaching suggestions

ICT link-up
- A simulation of the absorption of beta particles by various materials is available. The students can find out for themselves how the particles are absorbed by different materials by searching for 'radioactivity absorption simulation' on the internet.

You're history
- Ask the students to come up with some more historical artefacts that could be radiocarbon dated. Make sure they understand that only materials with carbon can be tested by this method.

Summary answers

1 a beta.
  b beta, gamma (beta and gamma in either order)
  c beta

2 a γ-radiation would hardly be absorbed by the foil as it would all pass straight through the foil.
  b A stable isotope in the body (or elsewhere) would not be dangerous whereas an unstable isotope would be harmful as it is radioactive.

3 a It needs to be detectable outside the body, (non-toxic), have a short half-life (1–24 hours) and decay into a stable product.
  b 11 200 years old.

Summary answers

1 a **i** $6p + 8n$
　　ii $90p + 138n$

　b **i** $7p + 7n$
　　ii $^{14}_{7}N$

　c **i** $88p + 136n$
　　ii $^{224}_{88}Ra$

2 a gamma

　b alpha

　c beta

　d beta

　e alpha

　f gamma

3 1B, 2D, 3A, 4C

4 a Graph

　b 1 h 40 min

5 a 2

　b 11 200 years

6 a Background radioactivity.

　b 356 cpm

　c Beta radiation, because it penetrates thin foil and is stopped by an aluminium plate. Alpha radiation would be stopped by the foil. Gamma radiation would pass through the foil and the plate.

7 a They are positively charged so they are repelled by the nucleus because it is also positively charged.

　b It doesn't approach the nucleus as closely as A does, so the force on it is less.

　c The nucleus is very small in size compared to the atom, so most α particles don't pass near enough to the nucleus to be affected by it.

AQA Examiner's tip

Question 1 is a good test of the students' understanding of atomic structure and the meanings of 'ion' and 'isotope'.

AQA Examiner's tip

Foundation Tier candidates must know that alpha and beta are deflected in opposite directions both in magnetic fields and in electric fields. Only the Higher Tier students need to be able to explain why this is so in terms of the charge and the mass of the particles.

Summary questions 🄚

1 a How many protons and how many neutrons are in a nucleus of each of the following isotopes?
　i $^{14}_{6}C$
　ii $^{228}_{90}Th$

　b $^{14}_{6}C$ emits a β particle and becomes an isotope of nitrogen (N).
　i How many protons and how many neutrons are in this nitrogen isotope?
　ii Write down the symbol for this isotope.

　c $^{228}_{90}Th$ emits an α particle and becomes an isotope of radium (Ra).
　i How many protons and how many neutrons are in this isotope of radium?
　ii Write down the symbol for this isotope.

2 Which type of radiation, alpha, beta or gamma:
　a can pass through lead?
　b travels no further than about 10 cm in air?
　c is stopped by an aluminium metal plate but not by paper?
　d consists of electrons?
　e consists of helium nuclei?
　f is uncharged?

3 The table below gives information about four radioactive isotopes A, B, C and D.

Isotope	Type of radiation emitted	Half-life
A californium-241	alpha	4 minutes
B cobalt-60	gamma	5 years
C hydrogen-3	beta	12 years
D strontium-90	beta	28 years

Match each statement 1 to 4 with A, B, C or D.
1 the isotope that gives off radiation with an unlimited range
2 the isotope that has the longest half-life
3 the isotope that decays the fastest
4 the isotope with the smallest mass of each atom.

4 The following measurements were made of the count rate due to a radioactive source.

Time (hours)	0	0.5	1.0	1.5	2.0	2.5
Count rate due to the source (counts per minute)	510	414	337	276	227	188

　a Plot a graph of the count rate (on the vertical axis) against time.
　b Use your graph to find the half-life of the source.

5 In a carbon dating experiment of ancient wood, a sam of the wood gave a count rate of 0.4 counts per minut The same mass of living wood gave a count rate of 1. counts per minute.
　a How many half-lives did the count rate take to decrease from 1.6 to 0.4 counts per minute?
　b The half-life of the radioactive carbon in the wood i 5600 years. What is the age of the sample?

6 In an investigation to find out what type of radiation was emitted from a given source, the following measurements were made with a Geiger counter.

Source	Average count rate (in counts per minut
No source present	29
Source at 20 mm from tube with no absorber between	385
Source at 20 mm from tube with a sheet of metal foil between	384
Source at 20 mm from tube with a 10 mm thick aluminium plate between	32

　a What caused the count rate when no source was present?
　b What was the count rate due to the source with no absorbers present?
　c What type of radiation was emitted by the source? Explain how you arrive at your answer.

7 Figure 1 shows the path of two α particles labelled A and B that are deflected by the nucleus of an atom.
　a Why are they deflected by the nucleus?
　b Why is B deflected less than A?
　c Why do most α particles directed at a thin metal foil pass straight through it?

Figure 1

248

Kerboodle resources 🄚

Resources available for this chapter on Kerboodle are:
- Chapter map: Radioactivity
- Support: Nuclear decay equations – understanding the nature of nuclear decays (P2 6.3)
- Bump up your grade: Elements, isotopes and ions – what's the difference? (6.3)
- Extension: Radiation hunt (P2 6.4)
- How Science Works: Radiation in action (P2 6.6)
- WebQuest: Radioactive tracers (P2 6.6)
- Interactive activity: Half-life and the uses of radioactivity
- Revision podcast: Radioactivity
- Test yourself: Radioactivity
- On your marks: Radioactivity
- Examination-style questions: Radioactivity
- Answers to examination-style questions: Radioactivity

Examination-style questions

Diagrams **A** and **B** show two atoms of carbon.

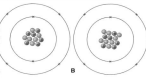

A   **B**

a Copy and complete the following sentences using the list of words and phrases below. Each one can be used once, more than once or not at all.

electrons positive isotopes nuclear plum pudding negative nucleus ions neutrons

Particles shown by the symbol **x** in the diagram are called .... They orbit the .... of an atom. This is made up of protons and .... Protons have a .... charge. This diagram shows the .... model of the atom which replaced the .... model. (6)

b Explain how a carbon **ion** would be different from atom **A**. (1)

c Give the mass number of atom **A**. (1)

d Give the atomic number of atom **A**. (1)

e Compare atom **B** with atom **A**. (3)

2 A geologist wishes to know what types of radiation are emitted by three radioactive rock samples. Different absorbers are placed between each sample and a detector. The counts per second are shown in the table.

Absorber	Counts per second		
	Sample 1	Sample 2	Sample 3
1 cm of air	140	80	120
paper	90	50	70
3 mm of aluminium	30	49	0
1 cm of lead	0	1	0

For each sample state which of the three types of radiation (alpha, beta, gamma) are emitted. A rock may emit more than one type. (3)

b Describe the nature of an alpha particle. (2)

c List the three types of nuclear radiation in order of their relative ionising power from the least ionising to the most ionising. (3)

d The source of radiation shown below emits alpha, beta and gamma. When the radiation travels through air in an electric field between two plates, the three types of radiation behave differently.

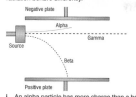

i An alpha particle has more charge than a beta particle. Explain why the beta particle is deflected more by the electric field and in the opposite direction. [H] (3)

ii Explain why the gamma radiation is not affected by the electric field. (1)

iii Explain why the alpha particle does not reach the plate. (2)

3 Technetium-99 is a gamma-emitting radioisotope used as a tracer inside the body in order to diagnose problems with various organs. Cobalt-60 is a gamma emitter used for radiotherapy where the source is used outside the body to kill cancer cells on the inside.

	Half-life	Radiation	Relative ionising power
technetium-99	6.0 hours	gamma	1
cobalt-60	5.3 years	gamma	10

a Technetium-99 emits a gamma ray and then decays to an isotope of ruthenium (Ru) by beta decay. Balance the nuclear equation by giving the appropriate atomic numbers and mass numbers.

$$^{99}_{43}\text{Tc} \rightarrow {}^{(i)}_{(ii)}\text{Ru} + {}^{(iii)}_{(iv)}\beta$$ [H] (4)

b *In this question you will be assessed on using good English, organising information clearly and using specialist terms where appropriate.*

Explain why cobalt-60 is not used as a medical tracer in humans and why technetium-99 is used for this purpose. (6)

Practical suggestions

Practicals	AQA	k	📖	⚙
Using hot-cross buns to show the 'plum pudding' model.	✓		✓	
Using dice to demonstrate probabilities involved in half-life.	✓		✓	
Using Geiger counters to measure the penetration and range in air of the radiation from different sources.	✓		✓	

AQA Examination-style answers

1 a Particles shown by the symbol **x** in the diagram are called **electrons**. They orbit the **nucleus** of an atom. This is made up of protons and **neutrons**. Protons have a **positive** charge. This diagram shows the **nuclear** model of the atom which replaced the **plum pudding** model. *(6 marks)*

b more (or less) electrons *(1 mark)*

c 12 *(1 mark)*

d 6 *(1 mark)*

e same number of protons (it is also carbon); same number of electrons;
2 more neutrons (carbon-14, a different isotope of carbon) *(3 marks)*

2 a Sample 1: alpha, beta and gamma
Sample 2: alpha and gamma
Sample 3: alpha and beta *(3 marks)*

b Two protons and two neutrons; helium nucleus *(2 marks)*

c Gamma, beta, alpha *(3 marks)*

d i Alpha particle has positive charge, beta particle has negative charge. Positive plate further away so beta more deflected. *(4 marks)*

ii Gamma particles have no charge *(1 mark)*

iii Absorbed by air particles *(1 mark)*

3 a i 99 *(1 mark)*

ii 44 *(1 mark)*

iii 0 *(1 mark)*

iv −1 *(1 mark)*

b There is a clear, balanced and detailed description of the reasons why cobalt-60 is not used as a medical tracer in humans and why technetium-99 is used. The answer shows almost faultless spelling, punctuation and grammar. It is coherent and in an organised, logical sequence. It contains a range of appropriate or relevant specialist terms used accurately. *(5–6 marks)*

There is a description of a range of the main reasons why cobalt-60 is not used as a medical tracer in humans and why technetium-99 is. There are some errors in spelling, punctuation and grammar. The answer has some structure and organisation. The use of specialist terms has been attempted, but not always accurately. *(3–4 marks)*

There is a brief description of at least one reason why cobalt-60 is not used as a medical tracer in humans or why technetium-99 is, which has little clarity and detail. The spelling, punctuation and grammar are very weak. The answer is poorly organised with almost no specialist terms and/or their use demonstrating a general lack of understanding of their meaning. *(1–2 marks)*

No relevant content. *(0 marks)*

Examples of physics points made in the response:

- half-life (of cobalt) is longer than necessary
- and could cause harm long after diagnosis
- ionising power of cobalt is much higher
- and could damage cells unnecessarily.
- half-life of technetium-99 is short enough to limit harm/risk
- but long enough to allow detection (before the count rate falls significantly)
- the low ionising power reduces harm/risk to a minimum.

P2 7.1

Nuclear fission

AQA

Specification link-up: Physics P2.6

- There are two fissionable substances in common use in nuclear reactors: uranium-235 and plutonium-239. *[P2.6.1 a)]*
- Nuclear fission is the splitting of an atomic nucleus. *[P2.6.1 b)]*
- For fission to occur the uranium-235 or plutonium-239 nucleus must first absorb a neutron. *[P2.6.1 c)]*
- The nucleus undergoing fission splits into two smaller nuclei and two or three neutrons and energy is released. *[P2.6.1 d)]*
- The neutrons may go on to start a chain reaction. *[P2.6.1 e)]*
- Compare the uses of nuclear fusion and nuclear fission. *[P2.6]*

Learning objectives

Students should learn:

- that uranium and plutonium isotopes are used in nuclear fission reactors as fuel
- that nuclear fission is the splitting of large nuclei into small ones; a process that releases energy
- how a fission reactor operates.

Learning outcomes

Most students should be able to:

- state the isotopes used as fuel in nuclear fission reactors
- describe what happens in a fission event
- sketch a labelled diagram to show how a chain reaction may occur.

Some students should also be able to:

- explain in detail how a chain reaction in a nuclear reactor can take place.

Lesson structure

Starters

Protection from radiation – Can the students describe the penetrating powers of the three radiations and explain how we can be protected from them? This leads on to a discussion about the shielding of the nuclear reactor later in the lesson. *(5 minutes)*

Power station basics – The students should draw a quick diagram showing how a fossil fuel power station operate. They need to remember the furnace, boiler, turbines and generator and perhaps the transformers including what each part does. Many of the components are the same as those in a nuclear power station. To support students, provide a diagram and ask them to describe the processes that take place at each stage. To further extend students, ask them to draw a Sankey energy transfer diagram indicating the approximate energy losses at each stage. *(10 minutes)*

Main

- You can show an example of a chain reaction with dominoes, see 'Practical support'.
- In a nuclear chain reaction, the released neutrons are important as these are the cause of further fissions, so emphasise them in any diagram or animation.
- In a nuclear reactor core, it is important to keep the reaction critical; that is at a steady rate (not getting faster or slower).The reactor can become 'super critical' if the nuclear reaction is accelerating (an increasing number of fissions per second), the reactor will heat up rapidly but not like a nuclear explosion. More likely the reaction becomes 'sub-critical' where the reaction rate decreases and the reactor will cool.
- You need to clearly distinguish between the parts of the nuclear reactor as students often get them backwards or their properties mixed up. Good **moderators** slow down the fast neutrons without absorbing them. If the moderator absorbs too many neutrons, then the chain reaction cannot continue. In some reactors, graphite is used instead of water. The **control rods** have to be good at absorbing neutrons. When they are inserted, the number of available neutrons is decreased and the reaction becomes sub-critical, cooling the core down. Cadmium and boron are common materials for this job. In an emergency, the rods are dropped completely into the core, rapidly reducing the reaction to almost zero. The reactor still produces some heat through natural (non-induced) decay of the radioactive materials. This means that it still has to be cooled or it will meltdown. The **coolant** may be water, heavy water or some more exotic material such as liquid sodium. It has to be able to rapidly carry energy from the core (so has a high specific heat capacity), but in carrying out its function, it becomes radioactive.
- The core itself is very heavily shielded by concrete, steel and some lead, so only a few gamma rays can escape. It is quite possible to walk on top of a nuclear reactor core safely.

Support

- Give the students a large diagram of the reactor, so that they can label the parts and write their notes around it.

Extend

- The students can find out about the choice of materials used for the moderator, control rods and coolant in different types of reactor. You can then discuss the properties of these materials that make them the best choice for the job.

Plenaries

The China syndrome – If a nuclear core melts down, it gets so hot that it can melt the rock beneath it and start sinking into the Earth. If an American reactor melts down, ask 'What's to stop it melting all the way through to China?' Hopefully, students will realise that if it reaches the centre of the Earth it would have gone as far 'down' as possible and it would be travelling upwards to reach China. *(5 minutes)*

Chain reaction – The students should be asked to develop an idea to show a chain reaction. To support students you could ask them to set up dominoes to demonstrate the idea if you didn't do this yourself; the teams with the most wins. It's possible to arrange sensible students into a suitable configuration too. To extend the students, you can ask them to calculate how many nuclei would be splitting after five stages if each split realises an average of 2.5 neutrons. *(10 minutes)*

Practical support

Domino theory

A chain reaction can be demonstrated using dominos. Set up a simple chain where one domino knocks over another; this represents a critical reaction where the rate stays constant. To show an increasing reaction, you simply set the dominoes up so that one knocks over two, two knock over three, and so on.

Energy from the nucleus

P2 7.1 Nuclear fission

Learning objectives

- What is nuclear fission?
- Which radioactive isotopes undergo fission?
- What is a chain reaction?
- How is a chain reaction in a nuclear reactor controlled?

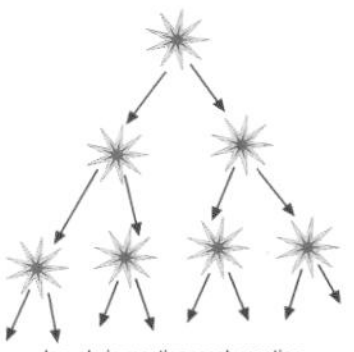

In a chain reaction, each reaction causes more reactions which cause more reactions, etc. etc.

Figure 1 A chain reaction

Did you know ...?

A nuclear bomb is two lumps of pure uranium-235 or plutonium-239. Each lump can't produce a chain reaction because it loses too many fission neutrons. But if you bring the two together ...!

Chain reactions

Energy is released in a nuclear reactor as a result of **nuclear fission**. In this process, the nucleus of an atom of a fissionable substance splits into two smaller 'fragment' nuclei. This event can cause other fissionable nuclei to split. This then produces a **chain reaction** of fission events.

Fission neutrons

When a nucleus undergoes fission, it releases:

- two or three neutrons (referred to as 'fission' neutrons) at high speeds
- energy, in the form of radiation, plus kinetic energy of the fission neutrons and the fragment nuclei.

The fission neutrons may cause further fission resulting in a chain reaction. In a **nuclear fission reactor**, on average, exactly one fission neutron from each fission event goes on to produce further fission. This ensures energy is released at a steady rate in the reactor.

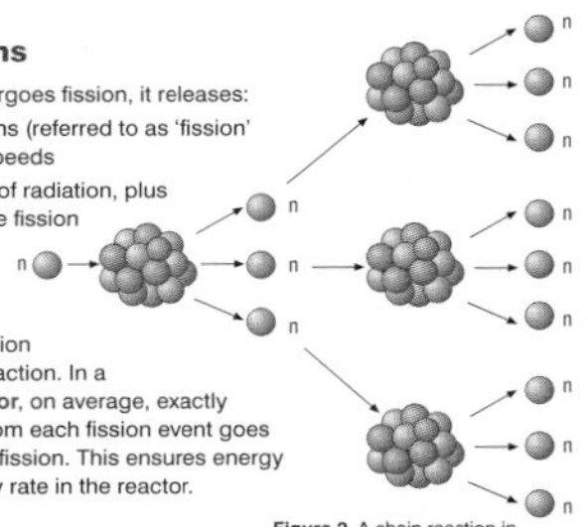

Figure 2 A chain reaction in a nuclear reactor

a What would happen if, on average, more than one fission neutron per event went on to produce further fission?

Fissionable isotopes

The fuel in a nuclear reactor must contain fissionable isotopes.

- Most reactors at the present time are designed to use 'enriched uranium' as the fuel. This consists mostly of the non-fissionable uranium isotope $^{238}_{92}U$ (U-238) and about 2–3% of the uranium isotope $^{235}_{92}U$ (U-235) which is fissionable. In comparison, natural uranium is more than 99% U-238.
- The U-238 nuclei in a nuclear reactor do not undergo fission but they change into other heavy nuclei, including plutonium-239 (the isotope $^{239}_{94}Pu$). This isotope is fissionable. It can be used in a different type of reactor but not in a uranium reactor.

Inside a nuclear reactor

A nuclear reactor consists of uranium fuel rods spaced evenly in the reactor core. Figure 3 shows a cross-section of a pressurised water reactor (PWR).

- The reactor core contains the fuel rods, control rods and water at high pressure. The fission neutrons are slowed down by collisions with the atoms in the water molecules. This is necessary as fast neutrons do not cause further fission of U-235. We say the water acts as a **moderator** because it slows down the fission neutrons.

- Control rods in the core absorb surplus neutrons. This keeps the chain reaction under control. The depth of the rods in the core is adjusted to maintain a steady chain reaction.
- The water acts as a **coolant**. Its molecules gain kinetic energy from the neutrons and the fuel rods. The water is pumped through the core. Then it goes through sealed pipes to and from a heat exchanger outside the core. The water transfers energy for heating to the heat exchanger from the core.
- The reactor core is made of thick steel to withstand the very high temperature and pressure in the core. The core is enclosed by thick concrete walls. These absorb radiation that escapes through the walls of the steel vessel.

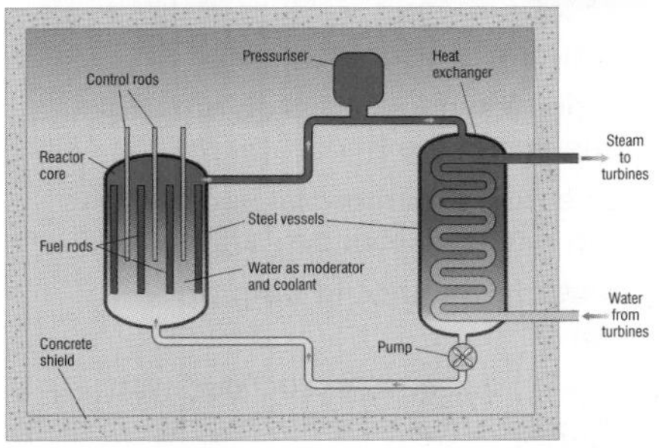

Figure 3 A nuclear reactor

b What would happen if the control rods were removed from the core?

Examiner's tip

During nuclear fission a large nucleus breaks up into two smaller nuclei. Make sure you know how to spell 'fission' – with two s's.

Summary questions

1 Copy and complete **a** and **b** using the words below. Each word can be used more than once.

nucleus uranium-235 uranium-238 plutonium-239

a Nuclear fission happens when a .... of .... or .... splits.
b A nucleus of .... in a nuclear reactor changes without fission into a nucleus of ....

2 Put the statements A to D in the list below into the correct sequence to describe a steady chain reaction in a nuclear reactor.
A A U-235 nucleus splits
B a neutron hits a U-235 nucleus
C neutrons are released
D energy is released

3 Look at the chain reaction shown in Figure 4.
a i Which of the nuclei A to F have been hit by a neutron?
ii What has happened to these nuclei?
iii Which two of the other nuclei A to F could undergo fission from a fission neutron shown?
b State one process that could happen to a fission neutron that does not produce further fission.

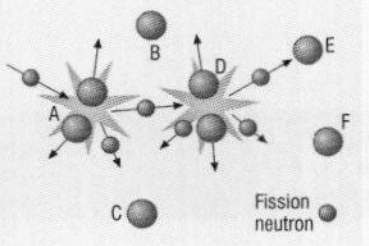

Figure 4

Key points

- Nuclear fission is the splitting of a nucleus into two approximately equal fragments and the release of two or three neutrons.
- Nuclear fission occurs when a neutron hits a uranium-235 nucleus or a plutonium-239 nucleus and the nucleus splits.
- A chain reaction occurs in a nuclear reactor when each fission event causes further fission events.
- In a nuclear reactor, control rods absorb fission neutrons to ensure that, on average, only one neutron per fission goes on to produce further fission.

Further teaching suggestions

Chain reactions

- Animations and simulations showing chain reactions are available in commercial software. There are also some simple animations available freely on the internet. Search for 'chain reaction simulation'.

Shut down the reactor!

- The emergency shutting down of a reactor is called 'scramming'. Where does this term come from? There are a couple of possibilities.

Answers to in-text questions

a The chain reaction would go out of control and the reactor would overheat and possibly explode.
b The chain reaction would go out of control and the reactor would overheat and possibly explode.

Summary answers

1 **a** nucleus, uranium-235, plutonium-239
   b uranium-238, plutonium-239

2 1**A**, 2**D**, 3**C**, 4**B**, 5**A**

3 **a** i A and D
   ii They have undergone fission and released neutrons and energy.
   iii C and E
   b One process only: Each such neutron could escape from the reactor core or be absorbed by a uranium-238 nucleus without fission or be absorbed by a nucleus of the control rod.

P2 7.2

Nuclear fusion

Learning objectives

Students should learn:

- that the Sun releases energy due to nuclear fusion of hydrogen isotopes
- that nuclear fusion is the joining of two small nuclei and this process releases energy
- that nuclear fusion reactors are difficult to build mainly due to the difficulty of reaching sufficiently high temperatures and pressures.

Learning outcomes

Most students should be able to:

- describe the nuclear fusion process happening in the Sun
- outline how experimental nuclear fusion reactors work on Earth.

Some students should also be able to:

- evaluate the issues associated with nuclear fusion reactors.

Support

- It is best if the students can physically model the fusion process as described in the main part of the lesson. You can use different-coloured marbles as protons and neutrons; the student can build heavy hydrogen from two protons (one changes into a neutron), then follow through the remaining steps to give helium.

Extend

- Ask: 'What's so special about iron?' The students can find out more details about nuclear energy release by researching binding energy. It is this energy that is released by fusion and fission processes when the nucleons rearrange. If they go on to look at stars and supernovae, they will discover the importance of iron in these explosions. Alternatively, students could find out about the claims made by Pons and Fleischmann in the late 1980s regarding 'cold fusion'.

AQA **Specification link-up: Physics P2.6**

- Nuclear fusion is the joining of two atomic nuclei to form a larger one. [P2.6.2 a)]
- Nuclear fusion is the process by which energy is released in stars. [P2.6.2 b)]
- Compare the uses of nuclear fusion and nuclear fission. [P2.6]

Lesson structure

Starters

A Sun myth – The Sun has a lot of mythology based on it and a lot of religions had a 'sun god'. What stories do the students know? Where do the students think the Sun's energy comes from? Can they remember some of the properties and behaviour of stars? *(5 minutes)*

Star one – Ask: 'Where does the Sun get its energy?' The students brainstorm their ideas and then discuss possible problems with them. They will probably know that the Sun contains flammable hydrogen but there is not enough oxygen to let it actually burn. To extend the students, you can discuss how even great scientists, such as Lord Kelvin, struggled to explain the energy source of the Sun until radioactivity and the structure of the atom was discovered. To support students, you should provide some possible suggestions and ask the students to come up with answers as to why these are not realistic proposals. *(10 minutes)*

Main

- Students may confuse the words 'fission' and 'fusion' in general conversation, but should be able to remember the difference when writing answers. Make them think of 'fusing together'.

- The reactions in the Sun are hugely powerful. Its power output is around 4×10^{26} watts. The students might like to imagine how many light bulbs' worth that represents. The tiny fraction of this that reaches Earth provides all of the energy for plants and food chains.

- If you like, you can model the reaction process in the Sun with marbles or with molecular-modelling kits; build the starting nuclei and then forcing the components together during the fusion.

- The overall process shown is four protons (hydrogen nuclei) converting into one helium nucleus, and so the Sun is generally said to be converting hydrogen into helium. This means that the percentages of hydrogen and helium are slowly changing. The reactions also produce a lot of positrons and neutrinos. The main difficulty to overcome is the fact that the protons strongly repel each other. In the Sun, the gravitational forces are strong enough to keep the very high temperature protons close enough together so that they will collide and fuse. It is this process that is proving very difficult to replicate on Earth.

- Some of the students will have heard the term 'plasma' before, and when you tell them that it is at a temperature of several thousand degrees, they will assume it has a lot of energy and will be very dangerous. The plasma is actually of very low density and so hasn't got that much energy.

- When discussing the promising future of fusion-produced energy, remind the students that we have been working on the project for a long time and it has proved very difficult to achieve. There is a lot of work yet to be done and opportunities for great scientists to make a difference.

- Fusion-reactor research continues with the construction of the latest testing facility in France. This International Thermonuclear Experimental Reactor (ITER) may actually be able to sustain a reaction long enough for it to be useful. It will cost over 10 billion euros though.

- There are possible hazards associated with a fusion reactor: free neutrons are produced and could be absorbed by the materials in the reactor. This would produce dangerous radioactive isotopes. However, there would be much less radiation released than in the nuclear fission reaction and so it would be easier to deal with this nuclear waste.

Plenaries

A bright future – A company claims to have developed a working nuclear fusion plant and wants to build one in the local area. Do the students object or rejoice? They should have a quick discussion and vote. *(5 minutes)*

Compare and contrast – The students should make a poster, comparing and contrasting the processes of nuclear fission and nuclear fusion. They need to discuss what happens to the protons and neutrons in each and why energy is released by both processes. They could outline why one is easier to achieve than the other. To support students, provide the information for the students to sort and perhaps assign teams, so that they can concentrate on one poster or the other. To extend the task, the students could be asked to incorporate the ideas of fuel source and how to deal with waste. *(10 minutes)*

Energy from the nucleus

Nuclear fusion

P2 7.2 Nuclear fusion Ⓚ

Learning objectives
- What is nuclear fusion?
- How can nuclei be made to fuse together?
- Where does the Sun's energy come from?
- Why is it difficult to make a nuclear fusion reactor?

Imagine if we could get energy from water. Stars release energy as a result of fusing small nuclei such as hydrogen to form larger nuclei. Water contains lots of hydrogen atoms. A glass of water could provide the same amount of energy as a tanker full of petrol. But only if we could make a fusion reactor here on Earth.

Fusion reactions

Two small nuclei release energy when they are fused together to form a single larger nucleus. This process is called **nuclear fusion**. It releases energy only if the relative mass of the nucleus formed is no more than about 55 (about the same as an iron nucleus). Energy must be supplied to create bigger nuclei.

Figure 1 A nuclear fusion reaction

The Sun is about 75 per cent hydrogen and 25 per cent helium. The core is so hot that it consists of a 'plasma' of bare nuclei with no electrons. These nuclei move about and fuse together when they collide. When they fuse, they release energy. Figure 2 shows how protons fuse together to form a $^4_2$He nucleus. Energy is released at each stage.

Figure 2 Fusion reactions in the Sun
● Proton ● Neutron

- When two protons (i.e. hydrogen nuclei) fuse, they form a 'heavy hydrogen' nucleus, $^2_1$H. Other particles are created and emitted at the same time.
- Two more protons collide separately with two $^2_1$H nuclei and turn them into heavier nuclei.
- The two heavier nuclei collide to form the helium nucleus $^4_2$He.
- The energy released at each stage is carried away as kinetic energy of the product nucleus and other particles emitted.

a Look at Figure 2 and work out what is formed when a proton collides with a $^2_1$H nucleus.

Fusion reactors

There are enormous technical difficulties with making fusion a useful source of energy. The plasma of light nuclei must be heated to very high temperatures before the nuclei will fuse. This is because two nuclei approaching each other will repel each other due to their positive charges. If the nuclei are moving fast enough, they can overcome the force of repulsion and fuse together.

In a fusion reactor:
- the plasma is heated by passing a very large electric current through it
- the plasma is contained by a magnetic field so it doesn't touch the reactor walls. If it did, it would go cold and fusion would stop.

Scientists have been working on these problems since the 1950s. A successful fusion reactor would release more energy than it uses to heat the plasma. At the present time, scientists working on experimental fusion reactors are able to do this by fusing heavy hydrogen nuclei to form helium nuclei – but only for a few minutes!

b Why is a fusion reactor unlikely to explode?

Figure 3 An experimental fusion reactor

A promising future Ⓚ

Practical fusion reactors could meet all our energy needs.

- The fuel for fusion reactors is readily available as heavy hydrogen and is naturally present in sea water.
- The reaction product, helium, is a non-radioactive inert gas, so is harmless.
- The energy released could be used to generate electricity.

In comparison, fission reactors mostly use uranium, which is only found in certain parts of the world. Also, they produce nuclear waste that has to be stored securely for many years. However, fission reactors have been in operation for over 50 years, unlike fusion reactors, which are still under development.

Summary questions

1 Copy and complete **a** and **b** using the words below:
large small stable
   a When two .... nuclei moving at high speed collide, they form a .... nucleus.
   b Energy is released in nuclear fusion if the product nucleus is not as .... as an iron nucleus.
2 **a** Why does the plasma of light nuclei in a fusion reactor need to be very hot?
   b Why would a fusion reactor that needs more energy than it produces not be much use?
3 **a** How many protons and how many neutrons are present in a $^3_2$H nucleus?
   b Copy and complete the equation below to show the reaction that takes place when two $^2_1$H nuclei fuse together to form a helium nucleus.
   $^2_1$H + $^2_1$H → ^{4}He   [H]

Key points
- Nuclear fusion is the process of forcing two nuclei close enough together so they form a single larger nucleus.
- Nuclear fusion can be brought about by making two light nuclei collide at very high speed.
- Energy is released when two light nuclei are fused together. Nuclear fusion in the Sun's core releases energy.
- A fusion reactor needs to be at a very high temperature before nuclear fusion can take place. The nuclei to be fused are difficult to contain.

252

253

Further teaching suggestions

Fusion update
- The latest state of nuclear fusion research is available online. The students should be able to find news articles about the new and previous research centres. (Search for 'nuclear fusion breakthrough'.)

Explaining the Sun
- You can find a paper by Lord Kelvin here http://zapatopi. net/kelvin and some other suggested processes with an internet search.

Fission versus fusion
- The poster comparing the two types of nuclear power could be a homework task, as could research into the latest developments.

Answers to in-text questions

a $^3_2$He nucleus.

b If it goes out of control, the plasma would touch the walls and go cold.

Summary answers

1 **a** small, large
   b stable

2 **a** So the nuclei have enough kinetic energy to overcome the force of repulsion between them and fuse.
   b The energy output would be less than the energy input, so it would not produce any energy overall.

3 **a** 1 proton and 1 neutron
   b $^2_1$H + $^2_1$H → $^4_2$He

P2 7.3

Nuclear issues

Learning objectives

Students should learn:

- how nuclear waste is treated and stored
- about the hazards associated with radon gas
- how to assess the safety of nuclear reactors.

Learning outcomes

Most students should be able to:

- discuss a range of nuclear issues balancing points of view appropriately
- balance the advantages and risks of using nuclear material in medicine.

Some students should also be able to:

- present arguments about nuclear issues from a wide range of viewpoints.

Answers to in-text questions

a Natural radioactivity in the air.

b Nuclear power.

c
  i It needs to be stored securely because it is hazardous and would be a danger to people and animals if it escaped.

  ii It needs to be stored for a long time because it contains radioactive isotopes with long half-lives.

d The α-radiation from the source will be absorbed by the surrounding tissues and it could damage or kill cells in the body or cause cancer.

Support

- Provide some extra fact sheets for the topics you want to discuss and assign clear roles to each of the students.

Extend

- Students can find out the current state of the nuclear building programme in the UK. They could see how far decommissioning and construction programmes have got and if any new reactors are due to be commissioned in their area. Will the new power stations meet the increasing demand for electricity?

AQA Specification link-up: Physics P2.5, P2.6

- Evaluate the effect of occupation and/or location on the level of background radiation and radiation dose. *[P2.5]*
- Evaluate the possible hazards associated with the use of different types of nuclear radiation. *[P2.5]*
- Evaluate measures that can be taken to reduce exposure to nuclear radiations. *[P2.5]*
- Compare the uses of nuclear fusion and nuclear fission. *[P2.6]*

Lesson structure

Starters

An empty pie – Show the students a pie chart with all of the sources of background radiation and their contribution to an average dose removed. Ask the students to guess what each slice of the pie represents and then compare with the real figures. Figures vary from place to place but a typical example is: radon gas 50%, food and drink 12%, cosmic rays 10%, buildings and ground 14%, medical 12%, nuclear fallout 0.4%, air travel 0.4%, nuclear waste 0.1%. *(5 minutes)*

Risk awareness – All activities have some associated risk but we must balance this against the benefits. Discuss some activities with the students such as driving, crossing a road, walking to school, and ask the students to assess how risky they think these things are. To provide support you could find some accident statistics (from www.hse.gov.uk – Search for 'statistics') and various other government sites) and make a card sort game in which the students rank the risks of different tasks. For extension, you should compare the actual risks with the perceived risk and discuss why people are prepared to take part in risky activities while being afraid of some that are actually surprisingly safe. *(10 minutes)*

Main

- There are a wide range of issues to discuss here. You may want to select just a couple or take an extra lesson to cover all of them.
- To add an element of practical work you can measure the background count during the lesson. The data collected can be used to discuss variation (show data you have collected over the previous periods).
- Radon gas causes around 2500 deaths per year, so it is a significant cause of lung cancer. You could show maps of where the effect is greatest (Cornwall for example). Further information can be found from the Health Protection Agency (www.hpa.gov.uk).
- When discussing the medical use of radioactive materials, you should make sure that you discuss the benefits of using ionising radiation along with the health risks. This in itself can fill a substantial amount of time.
- Extensive details of the storage and handling of nuclear waste can be found on the internet from sites like BNFL and Greenpeace. This should supply you with enough information to have a debate or discussion about the topic.
- You can also find similar points to discuss about Chernobyl. There are plenty of photographs of the abandoned towns and maps of the fallout moving across Europe that you can use.
- You should remind students of the safety precautions when handling the sources.
- The use of nuclear bombs on Japan at the end of World War II is obviously a contentious issue. Show a video of a nuclear weapon exploding and then discuss these kinds of issue:
  - The lack of warning or demonstration to Japan – the first bomb was dropped without any form of warning. This was to prevent the remaining Japanese forces from trying to intercept the mission. After this, bombers dropped leaflets on Japanese cities to say that more bombs would come if there was no surrender. Three days later the warning was fulfilled on Nagasaki.
  - Were the Americans demonstrating their technology to the Russians to warn them not to invade the rest of Europe?

Plenaries

Working in the nuclear industry – Discuss the advantages and disadvantages of working in the nuclear industry. This can include the health risks, the medical benefits, employment prospects, economic prospects, and so on. *(5 minutes)*

Where's the waste? – Provide the students with a map of the World and ask them to decide where the UK's nuclear waste should be stored. They need to provide explanations about why it is safe and how to transport the waste to this location safely. Extend students by asking them to develop the criteria needed to store the waste safely for extended periods (geological stability, low population density, etc.) You can produce these types of criteria to support students. *(10 minutes)*

How Science Works | **Energy from the nucleus** | Nuclear issues

P2 7.3 Nuclear issues

Learning objectives
- What is radon gas and why is it dangerous?
- How safe are nuclear reactors?
- What happens to nuclear waste?

links
For more information on ionising radiation, look back at P2 6.4 More about alpha, beta and gamma radiation.

Did you know …?
Nuclear waste
Used fuel rods are very hot and very radioactive.
- After removal from a reactor, they are stored in large tanks of water for up to a year. The water cools the rods down.
- Remote-control machines are then used to open the fuel rods. The unused uranium and plutonium are removed chemically from the used fuel. These are stored in sealed containers so they can be used again.
- The remaining material contains many radioactive isotopes with long half-lives. This radioactive waste must be stored in secure conditions for many years.

Figure 2 Storage of nuclear waste

Radioactivity all around us
When we use a Geiger counter, it clicks even without a radioactive source near it. This is due to background **radiation**. Radioactive substances are found naturally all around us.

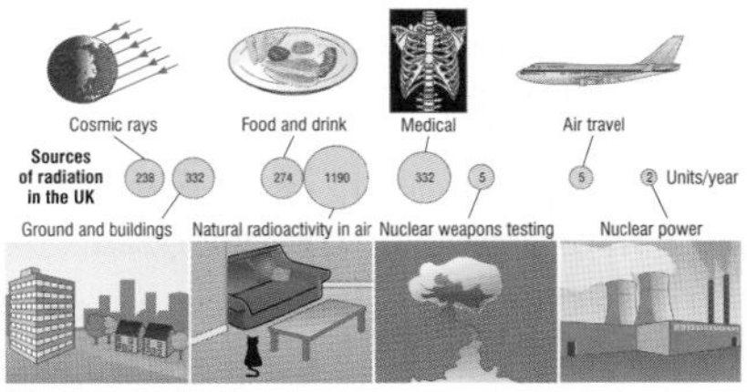

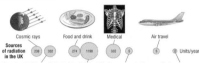

Cosmic rays   Food and drink   Medical   Air travel

Sources of radiation in the UK   238 332   274 1190   332   5   9   Units/year

Ground and buildings   Natural radioactivity in air   Nuclear weapons testing   Nuclear power

Figure 1 Radioactivity

Figure 1 shows the sources of background radiation. As explained in P2 6.4, the radiation from radioactive substances is hazardous, as it ionises substances it passes through. The numbers in Figure 1 tell you the **radiation dose** or how much radiation each person gets in a year from each source.
- Medical sources include X-rays as well as radioactive substances, as X-rays have an ionising effect. People who work in jobs that involve the use of ionising radiation have to wear personal radiation monitors to ensure they are not exposed to too much ionising radiation.
- Background radiation in the air is due mostly to radon gas that seeps through the ground from radioactive substances in rocks deep underground. Radon gas emits alpha particles so it is a health hazard if it is breathed in. It can seep into homes and other buildings in certain locations. In homes and buildings where people are present for long periods, methods need to be taken to reduce exposure to radon gas. For example, pipes under the building can be installed and fitted with a suction pump to draw the gas out of the ground before it seeps into the building.

a What is the biggest source of background radioactivity?
b Which source in the chart contributes least to background radioactivity?

Chernobyl
In 1986, a nuclear reactor in Ukraine exploded. Emergency workers and scientists struggled for days to contain the fire. A cloud of radioactive material from the fire drifted over many parts of Europe, including Britain. More than 100000 people were evacuated from Chernobyl and the surrounding area. Over 30 people died in the accident. Many more have developed leukaemia or cancer since then. It was and remains (up to now) the world's worst nuclear accident.

Could it happen again?
- Most nuclear reactors are of a different design.
- The Chernobyl accident did not have a high-speed shutdown system like most reactors have.
- The operators at Chernobyl ignored safety instructions.
- There are thousands of nuclear reactors in the world. They have been working safely for many years.

Radioactive risks
The effect on living cells of radiation from radioactive substances depends on:
- the type and the amount of radiation received (the dose)
- whether the source of the radiation is inside or outside the body
- how long the living cells are exposed to the radiation.

	Alpha radiation	Beta radiation	Gamma radiation
source inside the body	**very dangerous** – affects all the surrounding tissue	**dangerous** – reaches cells throughout the body	
source outside the body	**some danger** – absorbed by skin; damages skin cells		

- The larger the dose of radiation someone gets, the greater the risk of cancer. High doses kill living cells.
- The smaller the dose, the less the risk – but it is never zero. So there is a very low level of risk to each and every one of us because of background radioactivity.

Workers who are at risk from ionising radiations cut down their exposure to the radiation by:
- keeping as far as possible from the source of radiation, using special handling tools with long handles
- spending as little time as possible in 'at-risk' areas
- shielding themselves from the radiation by staying behind thick concrete barriers and/or using thick lead plates.

c Why does radioactive waste need to be stored **i** securely **ii** for many years?
d Why is a source of alpha radiation very dangerous inside the body but not outside it?

Summary questions
1 In some locations, the biggest radiation hazard comes from radon gas which seeps up through the ground and into buildings. The dangers of radon gas can be minimised by building new houses that are slightly raised on brick pillars and modifying existing houses. Radon gas is an α-emitting isotope.
   a Why is radon gas dangerous in a house?
   b Describe one way of making an existing house safe from radon gas.

2 Should the UK government replace our existing nuclear reactors with new reactors, either fission or fusion or both? Answer this question by discussing the benefits and drawbacks of new fission and fusion reactors.

Figure 3 Chernobyl

Did you know …?
New improved nuclear reactors
Most of the world's nuclear reactors in use now will need to be replaced in the next 20 years. New improved 'third generation' nuclear reactors will replace them. The new types of reactors have:
- a standard design to cut down costs and construction time
- a longer operating life – typically 60 years
- more safety features, such as convection of outside air through cooling panels along the reactor walls
- much less effect on the environment.

Key points
- Radon gas is an α-emitting isotope that seeps into houses in certain areas through the ground.
- There are thousands of fission reactors safely in use in the world. None of them are of the same type as the Chernobyl reactors that exploded.
- Nuclear waste is stored in safe and secure conditions for many years after unused uranium and plutonium (to be used in the future) is removed from it.

Further teaching suggestions

Research topics
- There is a lot of scope for extra research about most of the topics. The students can produce quite extensive reports, so fix clear limits on any research projects you set. This can be a good way of stimulating interest for students who want to study physics beyond GCSE level.

New reactions
- You can discuss improved reactors, the students will have to bear in mind the strong opposition. The students should be better informed than members of the general public about the technology, so what do they think? No matter how many safety features are employed, there is always a small risk. However, the damage from a coal power station may be even larger over its lifetime. The contribution to global warming could be far more serious in the long run.

Summary answers

1 **a** Radon gas in a house may be more concentrated than outdoors and people in the house would breathe it in. The lungs would be exposed to α-radiation from radon gas atoms that enter the lungs. The α-particles from the radon atoms in the lungs would be absorbed by lung tissues. Their ionising effect in the tissue cells would damage or kill the cells or cause cancer.
  b Install pipes under the house and connect them to a suction pump to draw radon gases out of the ground before it seeps into the house. The top of the outlet pipe from the pump would need to be high up outside the house.

2 Benefits to building either type of reactor should include no greenhouse gas emissions, reliable and secure electricity supplies, and large-scale generation from small sites compared with renewable supplies that would take up much larger areas, etc. Drawbacks should include long-term storage of nuclear waste, possible escape of radioactive substances into the environment, impracticality of fusion reactors, etc.

P2 7.4

The early universe

AQA
Specification link-up: Physics P2.6

- Stars form when enough dust and gas from space is pulled together by gravitational attraction. Smaller masses may also form and be attracted by a larger mass to become planets. [P2.6.2 c)]

Learning objectives

Students should learn:

- that a galaxy is a collection of millions or billions of stars bound together by gravitational attraction
- that the structure of the early universe is vastly different to that which we see today
- that stars are formed by the action of gravitational forces of gas clouds.

Learning outcomes

Most students should be able to:

- describe the structure of a galaxy
- describe how the universe changed after the Big Bang and how gravitational forces brought matter together to form structures like galaxies and stars.

Some students should also be able to:

- explain why stars stay in a galaxy and why there are vast spaces between galaxies.

Support

- The concepts covered here are fairly difficult to comprehend for many students. There are a good range of videos from a range of sources including the internet that cover them well, so make use of these to support the topic.

Extend

- Students can look at a few examples of fusion reactions that take place in stars to enhance their understanding of the fusion processes. These can include (H-2 + H-3 → He-4 + n); the formation of helium from hydrogen, He-3 + He-4 → Li-7 + γ; which occurs at the surface of the Sun in solar flares. They should consider the changes that occur to nucleons in some of these reactions.

Lesson structure

Starters

From the beginning – The students draw a simple cartoon showing what they know about the beginning of the universe. This could include information about the Big Bang, how stars operate and the structure of the solar system. This may help identify some significant misconceptions. (5 minutes)

Galaxies – Show the students some images of galaxies and ask them to describe their shapes. How do they think that these were formed? You can show video clips of galaxy formation along with the diagrams. These reveal possible reasons why we have a lot of spiral shapes; collisions between galaxies tend to cause this. Students can decide if a range of 'facts' about galaxies are true or false. These could include the names of ours, the number of stars in a typical galaxy, the distances and so on. You can differentiate the questions to provide extra support or extension where needed. (10 minutes)

Main

- This is a bit of a 'story' topic where you have to convey a sense of wonder at the scale of the universe and its age. Computer animations of the interaction of galaxies will be very helpful with this topic.

- Hopefully, the students will remember the lesson on the Big Bang in P1. Get them to give their own descriptions of this, mentioning the creation of space, matter, energy and time. They should also know that the universe expanded rapidly and is still expanding, so discuss the evidence we have for this: background radiation and red shift.

- It can be hard to get across the sheer scale of the universe, the number of stars in each galaxy and the number of galaxies. The words 'billions of billions' tend to wash over the students. Try to get across the size as best you can.

- The Dark Age of the universe just means that no visible light was produced. Get the students to connect this with the lack of stars. Make sure that the students understand the reasons why matter did not come together in large quantities before the formation of neutral atoms, i.e. repulsion by the protons. Once there were neutral atoms. They did not repel each other, so could be forced closer together to form molecules.

- The lumpiness of the universe is a direct result of early fluctuations in the structure. You might want to show them the famous COBE picture of the early unevenness in the universe. This is easily found along with discussion articles on the internet. It was this tiny amount of variation that leads to the structures we see today.

- At the end, it is important to remind the students of the processes that are releasing energy in the stars. They will cover this in a bit more depth in lesson P2 7.5 'The life history of a star'.

Plenaries

Sizes and distances – Can the students put a set of cards in order of how large the objects are and then arrange them in order of how far away from us they are? Use cards with asteroid, Moon, planets, black hole, our Sun, solar system, galaxy and the universe on them. They can then match up some example distances. This can lead to a discussion about whether all stars are the same size. (5 minutes)

A better picture – To demonstrate developments in astronomy and in the telescope in particular, you can show students a range of images linking telescopes to the images that they are able to produce. This can include some historical telescopes and some of the more modern ones. To extend students you can discuss some of the images produced by X-ray or radio telescopes and how these have been converted into images we can see. For support you could ask the students to match images with the telescopes that produce them. (10 minutes)

Further teaching suggestions

Galaxy formation
- Use the internet to search for animations of galaxy formation and you should come up with some impressive computer-generated imagery. You should also find with some free-to-use presentations.

Other galaxies
- The students should find out about a galaxy other than our own. Ask: 'What is its name, how big is it, how far away and where in the sky can it be found?' A picture is compulsory.

??? Did you know ... ?

Look out at the universe and remember that most of it is missing. Astronomers can measure the mass of galaxies but the number of stars in them is not enough to account for all of it. There are a few theories about where this mass is, including brown dwarfs, neutrinos and super-heavy particles (WIMPS). Some students might like to find out more about this missing mass.

How Science Works — Energy from the nucleus

P2 7.4 — The early universe

Learning objectives
- What is a galaxy?
- What was the universe like in the billions of years before stars and galaxies were formed?
- What is the force responsible for the formation of stars and galaxies?

The Big Bang that created the universe was about 13 thousand million (13 billion) years ago. Space, time and radiation were created in the Big Bang. At first, the universe was a hot glowing ball of radiation and matter. As it expanded, its temperature fell. Now the universe is cold and dark, except for hot spots we call stars.

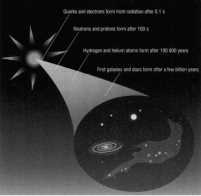

Quarks and electrons form from radiation after 0.1 s

Neutrons and protons form after 100 s

Hydrogen and helium atoms form after 100 000 years

First galaxies and stars form after a few billion years

Figure 1 Timeline for the universe

??? Did you know ... ?

In the Cold War, US satellites detected bursts of gamma radiation from space. At first, the US military thought nuclear weapons were being tested in space by Russia. Then astronomers found the bursts were from violent events long ago in distant galaxies – maybe stars being sucked into black holes!

Figure 2 Andromeda – the nearest big galaxy to the Milky Way

The stars we see in the night sky are all in the Milky Way galaxy, our home galaxy. The Sun is just one of billions of stars in the Milky Way galaxy. Using powerful telescopes, we can see many more stars in the Milky Way galaxy. We can also see individual stars in other galaxies.

We now know there are billions of galaxies in the universe. There is vast empty space between them. Light from the furthest galaxies that we can see has taken billions of years to reach us.

a Why do powerful telescopes give us a picture of the universe long ago?

The Dark Age of the universe

As the universe expanded, it became transparent as radiation passed through the empty space between its atoms. The background microwave radiation that causes the spots on an untuned television was released at this stage. The Dark Age of the universe had begun!

For the next few billion years, the universe was a completely dark, patchy, expanding cloud of hydrogen and helium. Then the stars and galaxies formed and lit up the universe!

b How long, to the nearest billion years, has background microwave radiation been travelling for?

The force of gravity takes over

Uncharged atoms don't repel each other. But they can attract each other. During the Dark Age of the universe, the force of gravitational attraction was at work without any opposition from repulsive forces.

As the universe continued to expand, it became more patchy as the denser parts attracted nearby matter. Gravity pulled more matter into the denser parts and turned them into gigantic clumps.

Eventually, the force of gravity turned the clumps into galaxies and stars. A few billion years after the Big Bang, the Dark Age came to an end, as the stars lit up the universe.

c Why would the force of gravity between two helium nuclei be unable to pull the nuclei together?

Figure 3 Arno Allan Penzias and Robert Woodrow Wilson standing on the radio antenna that unexpectedly discovered the universe's microwave background radiation

Figure 4 The force of gravity takes over

Summary questions

1 Copy and complete **a** to **c** using the words below:
attracted   cooled   expanded   formed
   a As the universe ...., it ....
   b Uncharged atoms .... each other.
   c Galaxies and stars .... from uncharged atoms.

2 a i Why can't we take a photo of the Milky Way galaxy from outside?
     ii Why can't we take photos of a distant galaxy at different stages in its formation?
   b i Why do the stars in a galaxy not drift away from each other?
     ii Why are there vast spaces between the galaxies?

3 Put these events in the correct sequence with the earliest event first.
   1 Cosmic background radiation was released.
   2 Hydrogen nuclei were first fused to form helium nuclei.
   3 The Big Bang took place.
   4 Neutrons and protons formed.

Key points
- A galaxy is a collection of billions of stars held together by their own gravity.
- Before galaxies and stars formed, the universe was a dark patchy cloud of hydrogen and helium.
- The force of gravity pulled matter into galaxies and stars.

Answers to in-text questions

a When we use a powerful telescope to see a distant galaxy, we are seeing the galaxy as it was billions of years ago because the light from it has taken billions of years to reach us.

b About 13 billion years.

c They are both positively charged, so they repel each other. The force of repulsion is much greater than the force of gravity between them.

Summary answers

1 a expanded, cooled
   b attracted
   c formed

2 a i We could not send a probe far enough.
     ii Galaxies take millions of years to form; we couldn't wait that long.
   b i Gravitational forces hold the stars in their positions.
     ii The universe has expanded leaving these vast spaces.

3 3, 4, 1, 2

P2 7.5 The life history of a star

AQA
Specification link-up: Physics P2.6

- Stars form when enough dust and gas from space is pulled together by gravitational attraction. Smaller masses may also form and be attracted by a larger mass to become planets. [P2.6.2 c)]
- During the 'main sequence' period of its life cycle a star is stable because the forces within it are balanced. [P2.6.2 d)]
- A star goes through a life cycle. This life cycle is determined by the size of the star ... . [P2.6.2 e)]

Learning objectives

Students should learn:

- that the Sun is a typical small star and how it developed into its current 'main sequence' state
- that the Sun will continue to develop, passing through a red giant and white dwarf stage before reaching the end of its energy-producing life
- that bigger stars can explode in a supernova and produce exotic objects like neutron stars or black holes.

Learning outcomes

Most students should be able to:

- describe the stages in the complete life cycle of a typical star such as the Sun
- outline the stages that larger stars can go through in producing neutron stars and black holes.

Some students should also be able to:

- describe what a black hole is and what its main property is.

Answers to in-text questions

a The energy to heat the star comes from the potential energy of gas and dust, which decreases as the gas and dust gathers and forms a protostar.

b The outward pressure of radiation from its core stops it collapsing.

c Gravity.

d Gravity.

Support

- Give the students a set of diagrams to cut out and paste in order. They should add information to these during the lesson.

Extend

- The life cycle of a star can be described through a diagram known as the 'Hertzsprung–Russell' diagram. The students should find out what this is and how the life of the Sun would be represented on it. They can compare the positions of red giants, white dwarfs and some supergiants. Give them some examples of each.

Lesson structure

Starters

The seven ages of man – Can the students come up with a list of words used to describe the stages of human development and ageing? [Shakespeare had infant, whining schoolboy, lover, soldier, justice, old age and finally a second childhood (senility), but these are hardly scientific.] *(5 minutes)*

The celestial sphere – Show the students some photographs of the night sky pointing out a large range of stars. Ask the student to find a pattern in the stars and come up with a legend of how it got there. You can show them some of the traditional constellations and tell them the accompanying tale if you know it. Extend students by asking them to consider what the constellations would look like from a different perspective. They should understand that constellations are not really any particular shape and the interpretation of the positions of stars is very different now than it was thousands of years ago. For support, you can provide some constellations with the appropriate images to start off the discussions. *(10 minutes)*

Main

- The constituents that combine to make a star are mostly hydrogen gas. During the collapse, the material heats up by frictional processes and begins to radiate infrared radiation so astronomers are hoping to detect this to confirm the formation process. This is very difficult because the protostar would still have a lot of gas and dust surrounding it (a Bok globule). Stars are formed in groups as the different parts of the original nebula collapse. One of these is in the heart of the Orion nebula; you could show pictures of stellar nurseries.

- The star is properly 'born' when nuclear fusion starts in the core. It is worth quickly going through the basic fusion process again, emphasising the fact that new elements are being made. This will be covered again in more depth in the next lesson.

- Use the term 'equilibrium' when describing the two processes involved in maintaining the star, so that the students link this ideas across all of the work on forces. The star remains on the main sequence for most of its life although the larger the star is, the quicker it 'burns out'.

- Make sure that you emphasise the longevity of the stars. Although they are consuming tens of millions of tonnes of hydrogen each second, it will still take them billions of years to get through a few per cent of the original material.

- The description of the change into a red giant should be accompanied by an animation. You should be able to find one showing the expansion of our Sun swallowing up Mercury and (possibly) Venus. The star may oscillate in size as it moves on to different fusion processes in the core.

- The white dwarf phase produces an object of massive density. Beware: the students may still be thinking that the object is 'gas' so it is light. The density is actually many times that of the normal matter we find on Earth. White dwarves would take hundreds of billions of years to cool into black dwarfs so there aren't any about yet. Ask the students why this is. [The universe just isn't old enough yet.]

- You can do a comparison of the radii, surface temperatures and density of the Sun, a red giant, a white dwarf and a black dwarf.

- Big stars are much more fun. You should be able to find animations of supernova explosions on the internet to support the discussions. Neutron stars and black holes sound strange and exciting so use the opportunity to encourage the students to find out more about them.

- The students should be left with the idea that the processes involved take billions of years and that our Sun has plenty of life left in it yet, so there is no need to worry.

Plenaries

SDRAWKCAB – The students should draw a flow chart of the life cycle of a star, but make it backwards. They need to decide whether to start from a black hole or a black dwarf. *(5 minutes)*

Sequence sort – Give the students a set of cards describing the *processes* that are happening in the life cycle of stars (but not the name of the stages) and ask them to sort them into order. For example: 'the star is expanding and its surface is cooling' [red giant] and 'the surface temperature is at its highest' [white dwarf]. To extend students, you can add details of nuclear fusion for them to sort and describe. To provide additional support, you can simply ask the students to sort the names of the stellar life stages into a diagram and then add some of the process on top of this. *(10 minutes)*

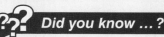

Did you know ...?

Before nuclear fusion was discovered and recognised as the process that releases energy in the Sun, scientists had worked out the age of the Sun to be a maximum of 10 million years old because they thought it was burning and releasing energy from chemical reactions.

Energy from the nucleus

The life history of a star

P2 7.5   The life history of a star

Learning objectives
- What is a protostar?
- What are the stages in the life of a star?
- What will eventually happen to the Sun?
- What is a supernova?

The birth of a star
Stars form out of clouds of dust and gas.

- The particles in the clouds are pulled together by their own gravitational attraction. The clouds merge together. They become more and more concentrated to form a **protostar**, the name for a star to be.
- As a protostar becomes denser, it gets hotter. If it becomes hot enough, the nuclei of hydrogen atoms and other light elements fuse together. Energy is released in this fusion so the core gets hotter and brighter and starts to shine. A star is born!
- Objects may form that are too small to become stars. Such objects may be attracted by a protostar to become **planets**.

a Where does the energy to heat a protostar come from?

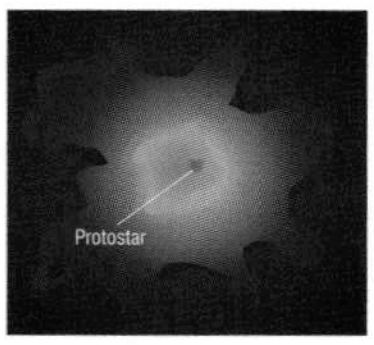

Shining stars
Stars like the Sun radiate energy because of hydrogen fusion in the core. They are called **main sequence stars** because this is the main stage in the life of a star. It can maintain its energy output for millions of years until the star runs out of hydrogen nuclei to fuse together.

- Energy released in the core keeps the core hot so the process of fusion continues. Radiation flows out steadily from the core in all directions.
- The star is stable because the forces within it are balanced. The force of gravity that makes a star contract is balanced by the outward force of the radiation from its core. These forces stay in balance until most of the hydrogen nuclei in the core have been fused together.

b Why doesn't the Sun collapse under its own gravity?

Figure 1 Star birth

Protostar

Did you know ...?
- The Sun is about 5000 million years old and will probably continue to shine for another 5000 million years.
- The Sun will turn into a red giant bigger than the orbit of Mercury. By then, the human race will probably have long passed into history. But will intelligent life still exist?

The end of a star
When a star runs out of hydrogen nuclei to fuse together, it reaches the end of its main sequence stage and it swells out.

Stars about the same size as the Sun (or smaller) swell out, cool down and turn red.

- The star is now a **red giant**. At this stage, helium and other light elements in its core fuse to form heavier elements.
- When there are no more light elements in its core, fusion stops and no more radiation is released. Due to its own gravity, the star collapses in on itself. As it collapses, it heats up and turns from red to yellow to white. It becomes a **white dwarf**. This is a hot, dense white star much smaller in diameter than it was. Stars like the Sun then fade out, go cold and become **black dwarfs**.

Stars much bigger than the Sun end their lives much more dramatically.

- Such a star swells out to become a red **supergiant** which then collapses.
- In the collapse, the matter surrounding the star's core compresses the core more and more. Then the compression suddenly reverses in a cataclysmic explosion known as a **supernova**. Such an event can outshine an entire galaxy for several weeks.

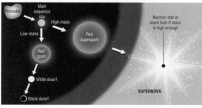

Figure 2 The life cycle of a star

c What force causes a red giant to collapse?

What remains after a supernova occurs?
The explosion compresses the core of the star into a **neutron star**. This is an extremely dense object composed only of neutrons. If the star is massive enough, it becomes a **black hole** instead of a neutron star. The gravitational field of a black hole is so strong that nothing can escape from it. Not even light, or any other form of electromagnetic radiation, can escape.

d What force causes matter to be dragged into a black hole?

Figure 3 M87 is a galaxy that spins so fast at its centre that it is thought to contain a black hole with a billion times more mass than the Sun

Summary questions
1 **a** The list below shows some of the stages in the life of a star like the Sun. Put the stages in the correct sequence.
 A main sequence
 B protostar
 C red giant
 D white dwarf
 b **i** Which stage in the above list is the Sun at now?
 ii What will happen to the Sun after it has gone through the above stages?

2 **a** Copy and complete **i** and **ii** using the words below. Each word can be used more than once.
 collapse expand explode
 i The Sun will eventually .... then ....
 ii A red supergiant will .... then ....
 b **i** What is the main condition needed for a supergiant to form a black hole?
 ii Why is it not possible for light to escape from a black hole?

3 **a** **i** What force makes a red supergiant collapse?
 ii What force prevents a main sequence star from collapsing?
 b Why does a white dwarf eventually become a black dwarf?

Key points
- A protostar is a gas and dust cloud in space that can go on to form a star.

Low mass star:
Protostar → main sequence star → red giant → white dwarf → black dwarf

High mass star:
Protostar → main sequence star → red supergiant → supernova → neutron star → black hole if sufficient mass

- The Sun will eventually become a black dwarf.
- A supernova is the explosion of a supergiant after it collapses.

258

259

Further teaching suggestions

Stellar research
- Give the students a stellar object each to research (or pair them up), to make a wall display about the life cycle of stars. They will need access to the internet and various drawing tools.

 The students should find examples and details about a range of objects associated with the life cycle of stars. Some suitable objects to find out about are: our Sun (Sol), stellar nurseries, protostars, giant molecular clouds, neutron stars, black holes, pulsars, white dwarfs, black dwarfs, red giants, blue giants and planetary nebulae.

ICT link-up
- Search the internet for 'life cycle of stars' or 'life cycle of stars video'. These are much better at showing the processes than diagrams, so try to use one.

The life of our solar system
- The students could write a story, or draw a comic strip, about an ageless observer that watches the life of our solar system from beginning to end.

Summary answers

1 **a** B, A, C, D
 b **i** A
 ii It will fade out and go cold.

2 **a** **i** expand, collapse
 ii explode, collapse
 b **i** The neutron star must have sufficient mass.
 ii The gravitational field is so strong that nothing can escape from it.

3 **a** **i** The force of attraction due to its gravity acting on its own mass.
 ii The force of the radiation flowing outwards to its surface from its core.
 b A white dwarf cools down and when it no longer emits light, it has become a black dwarf because it can no longer be seen.

P2 7.6 How the chemical elements formed

AQA Specification link-up: Physics P2.6

- Fusion processes in stars produce all of the naturally occurring elements. These elements may be distributed throughout the universe by the explosion of a massive star (supernova) at the end of its life. [P2.6.2 f)]

Learning objectives

Students should learn:

- that elements as heavy as iron are formed in nuclear fusion processes in stars
- that heavier elements are formed in supernova explosions
- that the material produced in stars can be spread out in explosions and can end up in new solar systems.

Learning outcomes

Most students should be able to:

- state that elements as heavy as iron are formed by nuclear fusion processes
- describe a supernova event and how such events can lead to the formation of new stars.

Some students should also be able to:

- explain why the Earth contains elements heavier than iron as well as lighter elements.

Answers to in-text questions

a In a supernova explosion.

b Its half-life is very short compared with the age of the Sun. Any plutonium formed when the Sun formed would have decayed long ago.

c Carbon atoms are in all the molecules that make up living objects.

Support

- The students can concentrate on the requirements that would be needed for life similar to ours. Once they have decided on what was needed, they can design a possible rival species to us.

Extend

- There are smaller explosions involving stars called 'simple novas'. Can the students find an explanation of what causes these? They should find connections between red giants and their companion white dwarfs.

Lesson structure

Starters

Star stuff – 'We are all made of stars.' What do the students think this means; is it a scientific statement? You could play the song of the same title (by Moby) while the students think about their answers. *(5 minutes)*

Building blocks – How many separate elements can the students name? You could play the famous periodic table elements song by Tom Lehrer (search for 'elements song' and you will find a number of versions). Ask: 'What is the meaning of the word 'element'?' Show them a graph or chart showing the proportion of these elements found throughout the universe; this should be dominated by hydrogen and helium with trace amounts of everything else. Use this to start the discussion about where the other elements come from. To extend the students, you can ask them to present the information in an appropriate manner (pie chart or bar chart). For additional support, consider revising the nature of elements using prompts such as Lego blocks; you can create a 'wall' with blocks showing the percentages of hydrogen, carbon and other elements using three different colour blocks. *(10 minutes)*

Main

- Start by again reminding the students about nuclear fusion processes, but expand on these ideas leading to the manufacture of heavier nuclei such as carbon. Some of the students should remember that there is a limit to this process: iron nuclei. This is because it takes more energy to produce heavier nuclei than would be given out. Ask the students where they think that the extra energy required comes from; they could come up with the idea that the supernova explosion provides it.

- This can lead on to a discussion of the energy output from a supernova, which is something like 10^{46} joules. The power output of the Sun is 10^{28} watts, so it would take about 32 billion years to release this amount of energy. Hopefully this will give the students some impression of the scale of the explosion.

- You should be able to find an animation showing the formation of the solar system. You can discuss that fact that some of this material had been manufactured in other stars and some has even come from supernovas.

- When discussing heavy elements, you can use the opportunity to show a nuclear equation for revision. Bombardment of nitrogen by neutrons to form carbon-14 is an important process. ($n + N-14 \rightarrow C-14 + H-1$). For a heavy metal example, use ($U-238 + n \rightarrow U-239 + \gamma$).

- Some of the students may know that, in addition to the original quantity of lead when the Earth formed, some lead has been formed from the nuclear decay of heavier elements.

- If you have time, you can have a talk about the idea of extraterrestrial life which most students are very interested in. It goes beyond the specification, but it is worth discussing. Some students will have strong opinions about this as they will have been exposed to a lot of 'facts' from various sources. It is worth getting the latest details on the search for life on Mars to have a discussion with the students. (See 'Activity and extension ideas.') In addition, you can discuss the techniques needed to spot planets in other solar systems. This is a rapidly developing field with none known until 1989. Detection of planets around the size of the Earth is the next big step in this project.

Plenaries

We come in peace – Students have to send a message to a potential alien civilisation as a radio signal. They have a limited number of words for their message – what will it be? To extend students, you might ask them to decode an alien message as shown in the 'hidden message' suggestion although this will take a little longer. *(5 minutes)*

Star jewellery – Students could make an advert for a piece of finely crafted 'star stuff'; made in the heart of a supernova and costing a mere £20 000. It is only made of copper though! *(10 minutes)*

Further teaching suggestions

Students may be interested in the search for extraterrestrial life and, although it is not required by the specification, they might like to try some of these activities.

Mars

- Mars is the most studied planet in the solar system besides the Earth. It has huge mythological and scientific importance. If evidence of life can be found so close to us, it would mean that the likelihood of life outside the solar system would be very high. The students can look in detail at the history of Mars and its exploration. Highlights include the 'canals' and volcanoes on Mars, the Viking and Pathfinder probes and the proposed manned exploration later in the twenty-first century. They can look into some of the less scientific ideas too, including the invasion from *War of the Worlds* and the many faces and pyramids that 'prove' that there is life.

Hidden message

- To show how difficult it is to find a message in random background noise, try this task.

Details

Create a 12 by 12 table in a word processor and fill in the cells with the symbols ':' and 'X', so that they create a shape; a smiley face works well. Get the word processor to convert the table into text and delete any line breaks, to end up with a long sequence of ':'s and 'X's. Without telling the students about the size of the grid, see if they can find out what the symbol is. A smaller starting grid will make this easier.

Space exploration

- Use an astronomy CD or internet searches to help students find out about exploration of the solar system and Mars, in particular. Search the internet for 'exploration solar system Mars' and see www.nasa.com.

Energy from the nucleus

P2 7.6 How the chemical elements formed

Learning objectives

- What chemical elements are formed inside stars?
- What chemical elements are formed in supernovas?
- Why does the Earth contain heavy elements?

The birthplace of the chemical elements

- Light elements are formed as a result of fusion in stars.

Stars like the Sun fuse hydrogen nuclei (i.e. protons) into helium and similar small nuclei, including carbon. When it becomes a red giant, it fuses helium and the other small nuclei into larger nuclei.

Nuclei larger than iron cannot be formed by this process because too much energy is needed.

- Heavy elements are formed when a massive star collapses then explodes as a supernova.

The enormous force of the collapse fuses small nuclei into nuclei larger than iron. The explosion scatters the star into space.

The debris from a supernova contains all the known elements from the lightest to the heaviest. Eventually, new stars form as gravity pulls the debris together.

Planets form from debris surrounding a new star. As a result, such planets will be composed of all the known elements too.

a Lead (Pb) is much heavier than iron (Fe). How did the lead we use form?

Did you know …?

The Crab Nebula is the remnants of a supernova explosion that was observed in the 11th century. In 1987, a star in the southern hemisphere exploded and became the biggest supernova to be seen for four centuries. Astronomers realised that it was Sandaluk ll, a star in the Andromeda galaxy millions of light years from Earth.

If a star near the Sun exploded, the Earth would probably be blasted out of its orbit. We would see the explosion before the shock wave hit us.

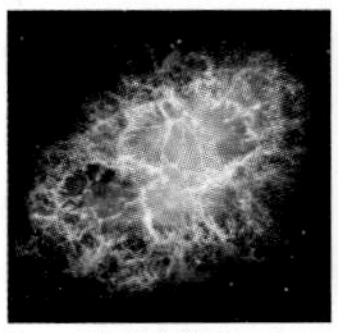

Figure 1 The Crab Nebula

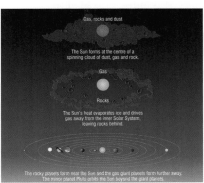

Gas, rocks and dust

The Sun forms at the centre of a spinning cloud of dust, gas and rock.

Gas

Rocks

The Sun's heat evaporates ice and drives gas away from the inner Solar System, leaving rocks behind.

The rocky planets form near the Sun and the gas giant planets form further away. The minor planet Pluto orbits the Sun beyond the giant planets.

Figure 2 Formation of the Solar System

Did you know …?

Molecules of carbon-based chemicals are present in space. Life on Earth probably developed from chemicals reacting in lightning storms. So are we looking for any scientific evidence about life on other planets, either in our own Solar System or around other stars?

- **Space probes sent to Mars** have tested the atmosphere, rocks and soil on Mars looking for microbes or chemicals that might indicate life was once present on Mars. Water is necessary for life. Astronomers now have strong evidence of the presence of 'underground' water breaking through to the surface of Mars.
- **The search for extra-terrestrial intelligence**, known as **SETI**, has gone on for more than 40 years using radio telescopes. Signals from space would indicate the existence of living beings with technologies at least as advanced as our own. No signals have been detected – yet!

Figure 3 The NASA Exploration Rovers looked for signs of life on Mars

Planet Earth

The heaviest known natural element is uranium. It has a half-life of 4500 million years. The presence of uranium in the Earth is evidence that the Solar System must have formed from the remnants of a supernova.

Elements such as plutonium are heavier than uranium. Scientists can make these elements by bombarding heavy elements like uranium with high-speed neutrons. They would have been present in the debris which formed the Solar System. Elements heavier than uranium formed then have long since decayed.

b Plutonium-239 has a half-life of about 24 000 years. Why is it not found naturally like uranium?
c Why is carbon an important element?

Summary questions

1 Match each statement below with an element in the list.
helium hydrogen iron uranium
a Helium nuclei are formed when nuclei of this element are fused.
b This element is formed in a supernova explosion.
c Stars form nuclei of these two elements (and others not listed) by fusing smaller nuclei.
d The early universe mostly consisted of this element.

2 Copy and complete **a** to **c** using the words below. Each word can be used more than once.
galaxy planets stars supernova
a Fusion inside .... creates light elements. Fusion in a .... creates heavy elements.
b A .... scatters the elements throughout a ....
c .... and planets formed from the debris of a .... contain all the known elements.

3 Uranium-238 is a radioactive isotope found naturally in the Earth. It has a half-life of about 4500 million years. It was formed from lighter elements.
a i What is the name of the physical process in which this isotope is formed?
ii What is the name for the astronomical event in which the above process takes place?
b Why has all the uranium in the Earth not decayed by now?

Key points

- Elements as heavy as iron are formed inside stars as a result of nuclear fusion.
- Elements heavier than iron are formed in supernovas as well as light elements.
- The Sun and the rest of the Solar System were formed from the debris of a supernova.

Did you know …?

You can find a before and after picture of Sanduleak (SN1987A) easily on the internet. You should also find images of the object taken by the Hubble Space Telescope several years later, showing the material thrown off by the explosion in a set of rings. The reason for the ring formation is still under investigation.

Summary answers

1 a hydrogen
b uranium
c helium, iron
d hydrogen

2 a stars, supernova
b supernova, galaxy
c stars, supernova

3 a i nuclear fusion
ii a supernova event
b The Sun and the rest of the solar system formed from the debris of a supernova. Much of the uranium-238 formed from the debris of the supernova still exists because it has a half-life which is comparable with the age of the Earth.

Summary answers

1 a i stays the same
ii decreases
iii increases

b i The reactor would overheat and the materials in it might melt. In the meltdown, the reactor pressure might be high enough to cause an explosion releasing radioactive material into the atmosphere.
ii The excess neutrons would be absorbed and the reaction would slow down releasing less energy.

2 a i The process where two small nuclei fuse together to form a single larger nucleus.
ii Because they are both positively charged.
iii To overcome the force of repulsion between them due to their charge.

b The plasma needs to be very hot. The plasma is difficult to control.

3 a i fusion
ii fission
iii fission

b The fuel is readily available. The products of fusion are not radioactive.

4 a i nuclear fusion
ii hydrogen

b The Sun will cool down and swell out to become a red giant.

5 a planet
b galaxy
c stars
d stars, galaxy

6 a gravity
b The core doesn't become hot enough to fuse hydrogen nuclei.
c Fusion.

7 a A, C, B, D, E.
b i It will fade out.
ii It will explode as a supernova, leaving a neutron star at its core. If the mass of the neutron star is large enough, it will be a black hole.

8 a i A large star that explodes.
ii A star that becomes a supernova suddenly becomes much brighter, then it fades. A star like the Sun has a constant brightness.

b i A massive object which nothing can escape from.
ii They would be pulled in by the force of gravity and then disappear.

9 a i helium
ii helium

b i lead, uranium
ii Heavy elements can only have formed in a supernova. The presence of heavy elements in the Earth tells us that the solar system formed from the debris of a supernova.

Summary questions 🄚

1 a Copy and complete **i** to **iii** using the words below:
decreases   increases   stays the same
When energy is released at a steady rate in a nuclear reactor,
i the number of fission events each second in the core ....
ii the amount of uranium-235 in the core ....
iii the number of radioactive isotopes in the fuel rods ....

b Explain what would happen in a nuclear reactor if:
i the coolant fluid leaked out of the core
ii the control rods were pushed further into the reactor core.

2 a i What do we mean by nuclear fusion?
ii Why do two nuclei repel each other when they get close?
iii Why do they need to collide at high speed in order to fuse together?

b Give two reasons why nuclear fusion is difficult to achieve in a reactor.

3 a Copy and complete **i** to **iii** using the words below. Each word can be used more than once.
fission   fusion
i In a .... reactor, two small nuclei join together and release energy.
ii In a .... reactor, a large nucleus splits and releases energy.
iii The fuel in a .... reactor contains uranium-235.

b State two advantages that nuclear fusion reactors would have in comparison with nuclear fission reactors.

4 a i What physical process causes energy to be released in the Sun?
ii Which element is used in the physical process named in part **i** to release energy in the Sun?

b How will the Sun change in the next stage of its life cycle when it has used up all the element named in part **a ii**?

5 Copy and complete **a** to **d** using the words below. Each word can be used more than once.
galaxy   planet   stars
a A .... isn't big enough to be a star.
b The Sun is inside a ....
c .... became hot after they formed from matter pulled together by the force of gravity.
d The force of gravity keeps .... together inside a ....

6 a What force pulls dust and gas in space?
b Why do large planets like Jupiter not produce their own light?
c What is the name for the type of reaction that releas[e] energy in the core of the Sun?

7 a The stages in the development of the Sun are liste[d] below. Put the stages in the correct sequence.
A   dust and gas
B   present stage
C   protostar
D   red giant
E   white dwarf

b i After the white dwarf stage, what will happen to [the] Sun?
ii What will happen to a star that has much more mass than the Sun?

8 a i What is a supernova?
ii How could we tell the difference between a supernova and a distant star like the Sun at present?

b i What is a black hole?
ii What would happen to stars and planets near a black hole?

9 a i Which element as well as hydrogen is formed in [the] early universe?
ii Which of the two elements is formed from the o[ther] one in a star?

b i Which two of the elements listed below is no[t] formed in a star that gives out radiation at a stea[dy] rate?
carbon   iron   lead   uranium
ii How do we know that the Sun formed from the debris of a supernova?

Kerboodle resources 🄚

Resources available for this chapter on Kerboodle are:
- Chapter map: Energy from the nucleus
- Animation: A chain reaction (P2 7.1)
- How Science Works: A domino chain (P2 7.1)
- Viewpoint: Is fusion the energy source of the future? (P2 7.2)
- Viewpoint: Where should we store nuclear waste? (P2 7.3)
- Animation: The life cycle of a star (P2 7.5)
- Interactive activity: The life cycles of different types of star
- Revision podcast: Energy from the nucleus
- Test yourself: Energy from the nucleus
- On your marks: Energy from the nucleus
- Examination-style questions: Energy from the nucleus
- Answers to examination-style questions: Energy from the nucleus

---

AQA Examiner's tip

Students often get fission and fusion mixed up due to the similarity of the words. Remind students that a fissure is a split and fusing together is joining up.

AQA Examination-style questions

1 a Copy and complete the following diagram to show how a chain reaction may occur inside a nuclear fuel rod containing many uranium-235 nuclei. (3)

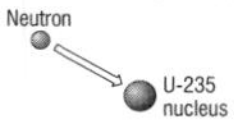

b Name the other fissionable substance that is used in some nuclear reactors. (1)

c The passages below reflect some of the conflicting opinions about nuclear power.

> Nuclear power is a low-emission source of energy and is the only readily available, large-scale alternative to fossil fuels for a continuous, reliable supply of electricity. The waste from nuclear power occupies a tiny volume and can be safely returned to the Earth for underground storage.

> A new generation of nuclear power stations will only reduce our emissions by four per cent by 2024: far too little, far too late, to stop global warming. They will create tens of thousands of tonnes of the most hazardous radioactive waste, which remains dangerous for up to a million years.

i What are the 'emissions' that both sources refer to? (1)

ii Why can nuclear waste remain dangerous for millions of years? (2)

iii Give one advantage and one disadvantage of the storage of nuclear waste underground. (2)

iv Explain why it would not be possible to replace fossil fuels with wind power alone. (1)

d For over 50 years scientists have been experimenting with fusion reactors with the aim of eventually generating electricity. The latest research project, called ITER, is scheduled to start operating in France in 2018 and is a collaboration between many countries.

i State two of the potential benefits of fusion power. (2)

ii Why are some people opposed to the research into fusion power? (2)

2 a Copy and complete the following sentences using the list of words and phrases below. Each one can be used once, more than once or not at all.

split fusion join a larger one fission two smaller nuclei

The Sun's energy is produced by nuclear ....
This is where atomic nuclei .... to form .... (3)

b Which element was the first to form in the universe? (1)

c The red super giant star Betelgeuse is likely to explode as a supernova and then form a neutron star. The red supergiant VV Cephei is likely to explode as a supernova and become a black hole. What causes the fate of these two stars to be different? (2)

d Which type of star produces all the elements up to iron? (1)

e The diagram shows the forces acting within a star. The grey arrows show the outward force created by radiation. Star A is stable but in star B the outward force has become less.

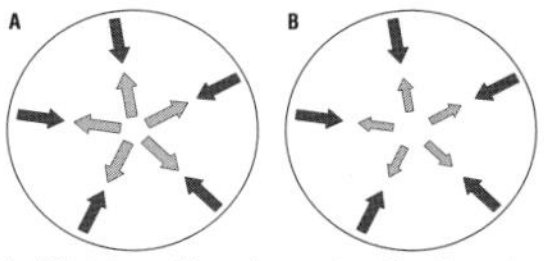

i What type of force is counteracting the outward force from radiation? (1)

ii What is about to happen to star B? (1)

iii Suggest why the force from radiation may suddenly decrease. (2)

3 *In this question you will be assessed on using good English, organising information clearly and using specialist terms where appropriate.*

Explain how the solar system formed and why there were elements heavier than iron present when it formed. (6)

263

AQA Practical suggestions

Practicals	AQA	k		
Using domino tracks for fission/chain reactions.	✓	✓	✓	✓

AQA Examination-style answers

1 a

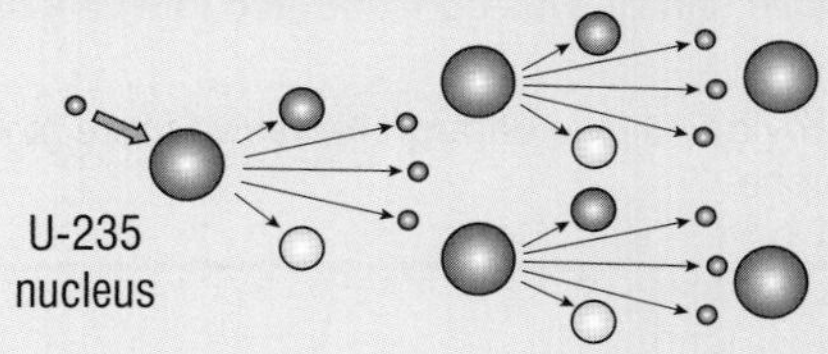

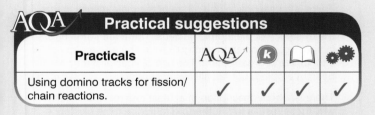

(3 marks)

b Plutonium-239 (Pu-239) *(1 mark)*

c **i** Carbon dioxide *(1 mark)*

ii It can have a very long half-life. *(1 mark)*

iii One advantage from: land not used; no visual pollution; rocks shield surface from radiation; security
One disadvantage from: more difficult to monitor or repair containers; expensive *(2 marks)*

iv Any suitable explanation, for example: not all countries have enough wind; wind doesn't blow all the time; not enough suitable sites for wind farms. *(2 marks)*

d **i** Any **two** benefits from the following: safer than nuclear fission; accidents that release large amounts of radioactive substances are not possible; large amounts of power could be generated to meet increasing world demand; no greenhouse gases; very little waste; fuel is abundant. *(2 marks)*

ii Any **two** of the following objections: expensive to research and develop; a working power station may be 20 to 50 years away; investment into renewables or making current methods safer and cleaner may be a better solution. *(2 marks)*

2 a The Sun's energy is produced by nuclear **fusion**. This is where atomic nuclei **join** to form **a larger one**. *(3 marks)*

b hydrogen *(1 mark)*

c VV Cephei has a greater mass than Betelgeuse.
So the gravitational force on VV Cephei is larger (and the star continues to collapse). *(2 marks)*

d A main sequence star/a star during its stable period. *(1 mark)*

e **i** gravitational force *(1 mark*

ii Star **B** is about to collapse. *(1 mark*

iii Fusion stops, or is reduced, as the fuel (e.g. hydrogen) is used up. *(2 marks)*

3 There is a clear, balanced and detailed description of the formation of the solar system and why it contains elements heavier than iron. The answer shows almost faultless spelling, punctuation and grammar. It is coherent and in an organised, logical sequence. It contains a range of appropriate or relevant specialist terms used accurately. *(5–6 marks)*

There is a description of the formation of the solar system and possibly why it contains elements heavier than iron. There are some errors in spelling, punctuation and grammar. The answer has some structure and organisation. The use of specialist terms has been attempted, but not always accurately. *(3–4 marks)*

There is a brief description of either the formation of the solar system or why it contains elements heavier than iron. There is little clarity and detail. The spelling, punctuation and grammar are very weak. The answer is poorly organised with almost no specialist terms and/or their use demonstrating a general lack of understanding of their meaning. *(1–2 marks)*

No relevant content. *(0 marks)*

Examples of physics points made in the response:

- the Sun/solar system formed when enough dust
- and enough gas
- were pulled together by gravitational attraction
- smaller masses/planets also formed due to gravitational attraction
- and were attracted to the larger mass/Sun
- elements heavier than iron are formed in supernovae
- the Sun/solar system is formed from gas/dust from supernovae
- the Sun is a second-generation star.

AQA Examination-style answers

1 a $a = \dfrac{v-u}{t} = 0.3/0.6$
$= 0.5 \, \text{m/s}^2$ (allow negative sign) *(2 marks)*

b In a closed system, the total momentum before an event is equal to the total momentum after the event. *(2 marks)*

c $m_1 \times v_1 = m_2 \times v_2$
$0.15 \times -0.3 = 0.0045 \times v_2$
$v_2 = 0.045/0.0045$
$= 10 \, \text{m/s}$ *(3 marks)*

d $E_k = \frac{1}{2} \times m \times v^2 = \frac{1}{2} \times 0.15 \times 0.3^2$
$= 0.00675 \, \text{J}$ *(2 marks)*

e i $k = \dfrac{F}{e}$
$= 23/0.02$
$= 1150 \, \text{N/m}$ *(3 marks)*

ii elastic potential energy to kinetic energy and to sound/heating of surroundings;
loss of GPE of ball *(2 marks)*

2 a Adding a component in parallel will reduce the original resistance because there is an additional path for the current. *(2 marks)*

b 4 V *(1 mark)*

c i $I = \dfrac{V}{R}$
$= 8/18 = 0.44 \, \text{A}$ *(1 mark)*

ii $0.44/2 = 0.22 \, \text{A}$ *(2 marks)*

d i Less bright
Resistance between B and C increases so resistance of circuit increases
So current fails *(3 marks)*

ii $18 + 18 = 36 \, \Omega$ *(1 mark)*

iii $I = \dfrac{V}{R} = 12/36$
$= 0.33 \, \text{A}$ *(2 marks)*

iv $P = I \times V = 0.333 \times 12$
$= 4 \, \text{W}$ *(2 marks)*

e $t = \dfrac{Q}{I}$
$= 500/0.333 = 1500 \, \text{s}$ *(2 marks)*

3 a i the isotope can be split by the absorption of a neutron. *(2 marks)*

ii Every 24 200 years, the number of nuclei (the count rate) would half. *(2 marks)*

iii halve 0.8 kg three times to get 0.1 kg (3 half-lives)
after 3 half-lives, 0.7 kg of U-235 is present
$3 \times 24\,200 = 72\,600$ years *(3 marks)*

iv No effect *(1 mark)*

b In supernovae large stars explode at the end of their lives. This causes fusion of lighter elements into heavier elements such as uranium. *(3 marks)*

c Any one of the following sources of background radiation: cosmic rays/plants/air/building materials/food *(1 mark)*

d $^{239}_{94}Pu \rightarrow {}^{235}_{92}U + {}^{4}_{2}\alpha$ (or He) *(6 marks)*

e protostar, main sequence star, red giant, white dwarf, black dwarf *(5 marks)*

4 There is a clear, balanced and detailed description of the main results of this experiment and why these results led Rutherford to suggest the existence of the atomic nucleus. The answer shows almost faultless spelling, punctuation and grammar. It is coherent and in an organised, logical sequence. It contains a range of appropriate or relevant specialist terms used accurately. *(5–6 marks)*

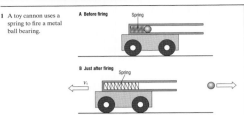
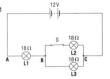
There is a description of a range of the main results of this experiment and why these results led Rutherford to suggest the existence of the atomic nucleus. There are some errors in spelling, punctuation and grammar. The answer has some structure and organisation. The use of specialist terms has been attempted, but not always accurately. *(3–4 marks)*

There is a brief description of at least one result or reason why these results led Rutherford to suggest the existence of the atomic nucleus, which has little clarity and detail. The spelling, punctuation and grammar are very weak. The answer is poorly organised with almost no specialist terms and/or their use demonstrating a general lack of understanding of their meaning. *(1–2 marks)*

No relevant content. *(0 marks)*

Examples of physics points made in the response:

- only a small number of alpha particles were deflected by a large angle
- so they must have encountered something very small
- most alpha particles travelled through gold atoms unaffected
- so most of the atom is empty space
- if all the positive charge was concentrated in a very small region
- this would provide a large enough repulsive force to deflect the alpha.

3 Plutonium-239 has a half-life of 24 200 years and decays into uranium-235 with a half-life of 703 million years. These substances are both *fissionable*.

a i Explain what is meant by *fissionable*. (2)

ii What is meant by 'a half-life of 24 200 years'? (2)

iii A sample of plutonium-239 of mass 0.8 kg is being stored. How many years will pass before the sample contains 0.7 kg of uranium-235? Show clearly how you work out your answer. (3)

iv If the sample were kept at a higher temperature and pressure, what effect would this have on your answer to part **a iii**? (1)

b Explain how a small amount of uranium-235 is found in the Earth's crust in rocks such as granite, when hardly any plutonium is found occurring naturally and nearly all of it is formed in nuclear reactors. (3)

c Name one other natural source of background radiation that we are constantly exposed to, apart from rocks. (1)

d Plutonium (Pu) has 94 protons. Copy and complete the following decay equation to show how it decays into uranium-235. [H] (6)

$$^{239}_{\square}Pu \rightarrow {}^{\square}_{\square}U + {}^{\square}_{\square}\square$$

e List the stages below in the correct order to describe the life cycle of a star that is about the same size as the Sun. One of the stages is not part of the life cycle of this type of star. (5)

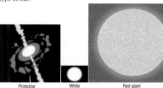

Protostar   White dwarf   Red giant

Black dwarf   Main sequence star   Supernova

4 *In this question you will be assessed on using good English, organising information clearly and using specialist terms where appropriate.*

In 1911 Ernest Rutherford published a scientific paper in which he suggested the existence of a very small region at the centre of every atom where most of the charge and mass is concentrated. Rutherford was interpreting the results of an experiment carried out by his research workers Geiger and Marsden in 1909.

Outline the main results of this experiment and explain why these results led Rutherford to suggest the existence of the atomic nucleus. (6)

AQA Examiner's tip

Tricky calculations involving half-life start to become quite straightforward when you have practised a few.

When completing any decay equation, the atomic numbers on the right must add to give the atomic number on the left. The same rule applies to the mass numbers.

AQA Examiner's tip

A question that requires an extended written answer will have 6 marks available and the quality of your written English will influence your mark. Once you have written your answer, read the question again, before reading your answer through to check that all parts of the question have been answered.

Don't just know the results of the Rutherford and Marsden scattering experiments, know why these results were so important.

Bump up your grades

P2 requires students to carry out more calculations than P1. Therefore, students who are weaker at calculations may struggle in places unless they are given plenty of practice. However, as for P1, Foundation Tier students will only have to learn to use the formulae as given in the specification, without having to rearrange. These students may benefit from working through a page of calculations on each equation that they encounter. Group work may help initially, but this must be followed up by individual work to simulate exam conditions.

Bump up your grades

There are plenty of learning aids to help students study and revise, including the Student Book, the Revision Guide and Kerboodle resources from Nelson Thornes. However, the AQA specification should not be overlooked as an essential 'tick list' for students.

AQA Examiner's comments

Higher Tier students should understand that velocity is a vector. A velocity to the right is usually treated as positive and a velocity to the left as negative. The toy cannon in Question 1, together with the cannon ball, has a momentum of zero before firing and will therefore have a collective momentum of zero afterwards. There is a great deal of footage on the internet showing various types of cannon firing where the recoil can be seen.

AQA Examiner's comments

Question 2 tests the students' understanding and application of circuit rules. Students should understand how adding or taking away components in parallel affects the resistance, even though they will not have to use the parallel resistor formula. Any number of analogies can help here. For instance, opening or closing turnstiles at a football ground, traffic or water circuits.

H1   How science works for us

Learning objectives

Students should learn:

- the importance of continuous and categoric variables
- what is meant by 'valid evidence'
- the difference between repeatability and reproducibility
- to look for links between the independent and dependent variables, and how good observations can be used to make hypotheses
- how hypotheses can generate predictions that can be tested
- how to reduce risks in hazardous situations.

Learning outcomes

Students should be able to:

- recognise measurements as continuous, or categoric
- suggest how an investigation might demonstrate its validity
- distinguish between repeatability and reproducibility
- state whether variables are linked, and if so, in what way
- state that observation can generate hypotheses
- recall that hypotheses can generate predictions and investigations
- identify potential hazards and take action to minimise risk.

AQA / Specification link-up: Controlled Assessment

Develop hypotheses and plan practical ways to test them, by:

- being able to develop a hypothesis *[AS4.1.1 a)]*
- being able to test their hypotheses. *[AS4.1.1 b)]*

Assess and manage risks when carrying out practical work, by:

- identifying some possible hazards in practical situations *[AS4.2.1 a)]*
- suggesting ways of managing risks. *[AS4.2.1 b)]*

Make observations, by:

- carrying out practical work and research, and using data collected to develop hypotheses. *[AS4.3.1 a)]*

Demonstrate an understanding of the need to acquire high quality data, by:

- appreciating that, unless certain variables are controlled, the results may not be valid *[AS4.3.2 a)]*
- identifying when repeats are needed in order to improve reproducibility. *[AS4.3.2 b)]*

Chapter structure

How Science Works is treated here as an appendix to the Additional Science units. It is not intended that the 'thinking behind the doing' is taught here as a separate set of lessons. It is of course an integral part of the way students will learn about science and these skills must be nurtured throughout the course. It is anticipated that sections of this appendix will be taught as the opportunity presents itself during the teaching programme.

Activity

Finding out what they know

Students should appreciate the 'thinking behind the doing' which was developed during Science A units. It would be useful to illustrate this by a simple demonstration (e.g. calcium carbonate into hydrochloric acid, catalase used to decompose hydrogen peroxide; or terminal velocity of a body falling through a liquid) and posing questions that build into a flow diagram of the way science progresses from observations to hypotheses, predictions, investigations, conclusions and evaluations that relate to the original hypothesis. This could lead into recap questions to ascertain each individual student's progress.

The recap questions should identify each individual student's gaps in understanding. Therefore, it is best carried out as an assessment. It might be appropriate to allow students to apply each of these terms to the particular example demonstrated to them.

Revealing to the students that they are using scientific methods to solve problems during their everyday life can make their work in science more relevant.

Other situations could illustrate the importance of scientific research to everyday life and should be discussed in groups or as a class.

For example:
- the discovery of penicillin as an antibiotic
- the discovery of microwaves
- the discovery of polythene.

Extend students by asking them to discuss what Isaac Newton meant by 'If I have seen further it is by standing on the shoulders of giants', a description used by many subsequent scientists including Stephen Hawking.

Activity notes

Emphasise the importance of recognising the difference between myth or hearsay and science. Collect newspaper articles and news items from the television to illustrate good and poor uses of science. There are some excellent television programmes illustrating good and poor science. Have a competition for who can bring in the poorest example of science used to sell products – shampoo adverts are a very good starter!

Thinking scientifically

Deciding on what to measure

The demonstration could be chosen from the biology, chemistry or physics section of this book could be developed to test a prediction. Choose an example that could include different types of variable so that their relative merits can be discussed, e.g. lumps of limestone versus mass of limestone or celery used as a source of catalase on hydrogen peroxide; or time taken for different objects to fall through oil.

Create a table for the results. Consider the use of preliminary work, controls, precision and what to do with anomalies.

Checking for misconceptions

Some common misconceptions that can be dealt with here and throughout the course are:

- **The purpose of controls** – some students believe that it is about making accurate measurements of the independent variable.
- **The purpose of preliminary work** – some believe that it is the first set of results.
- **That the table of results is constructed after the practical work** – students should be encouraged to produce the table before carrying out their work and complete it during their work.
- **That precision is the number of places of decimals they can write down.**
- **That anomalies are identified after the analysis** – they should preferably be identified during the practical work or at the latest before any calculation of a mean.
- Students often automatically extrapolate the graph to its origin.

Starting an investigation

Observation

Use a simple investigation, such as the falling helicopter, split dandelion stems in different salt solutions or calcium dropped into water. Encourage students to make suggestions for any theory that they could use to help to explain their observations.

What is a hypothesis?

Each student could construct a hypothesis to suggest an explanation for their observation.

Starting to design a valid investigation

The hypothesis is put into terms that can be used as a prediction. Remember that for Additional Science, students will be required to make their own predictions, unlike Science A, where they will be given a prediction.

Dependent, independent and control variables are identified. It would be useful here to illustrate chance or association links which could masquerade as causal relationships, e.g. the number of schools and the number of pubs in different sized towns.

Making your investigation repeatable, reproducible and valid

Students could be asked to design an investigation for homework and then pass this to a friend for criticism. This should be constructive and based on the need for validity, reproducibility and repeatability.

Making your investigation safe

Teachers must of course carry out a risk assessment of each investigation. Students will be required to make their own assessment by identifying potential hazards and saying how they will minimise the risk.

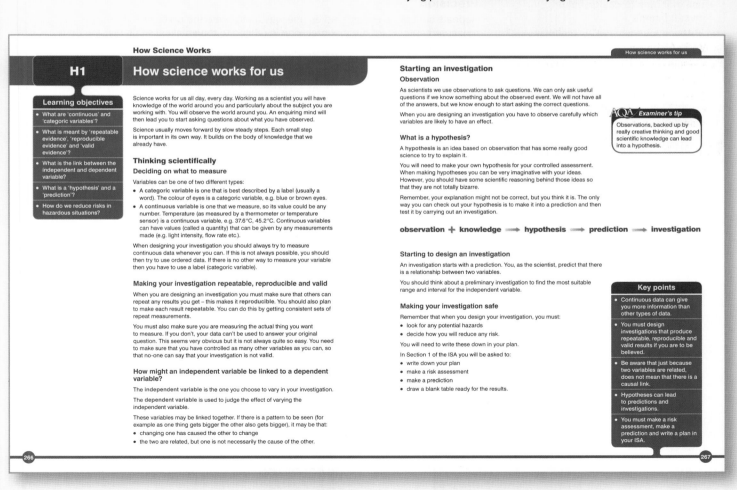

H2

The investigation

Learning objectives

Students should learn:

- how to design a fair test
- how to set up a survey, a control group or control experiment
- how to choose the best values for the variables
- how to decide on a suitable range and suitable intervals
- how to ensure accuracy and precision
- that instruments vary in their accuracy and resolution
- that human error can affect results, and what to do with anomalies.

Learning outcomes

Students should be able to:

- design a fair test that will yield valid and repeatable results
- design a survey, fair test and understand the use of control variables and control groups
- use trial runs to design valid investigations
- differentiate between results that vary and anomalies
- explain that instruments vary in their accuracy and resolution
- explain that anomalies should be discarded or repeated before calculationg a mean.

Specification link-up: Controlled Assessment

Demonstrate an understanding of the need to acquire high quality data, by:

- recognising the value of further readings to establish repeatability and accuracy [AS4.3.2 c)]
- considering the resolution of the measuring device. (output) [AS4.3.2 d)]
- considering the precision of the measured data where precision is indicated by the degree of scatter from the mean. [AS4.3.2 e)]

Fair testing

Students should now be able to describe how at least one control variable can be carried out, for example for the falling helicopter.

Choosing values of a variable

Constructing a table with units and suggestions for the range of the independent variable should now be possible.

Designing an investigation

Accuracy

Consideration should now be given as to how the independent variable can be used with accuracy and how the dependent variable can be measured accurately. Stress that an accurate measurement is one near the true value.

Precision

Repeats should be considered as one way to illustrate the precision of a set of measurements. Point out that precision is related to the smallest scale division on a measuring instrument.

Making measurements

Using instruments

It might be useful at this stage to set up a circus of instruments. This could be presented as a way of identifying the uses of the instruments, in terms of their accuracy and precision. Consideration should be given as to how easy they are to use and the likelihood of generating systematic or random errors.

Instruments could include: different thermometers, digital and analogue ammeters and voltmeters, measuring cylinders, gas syringes, burettes, pipettes, stopwatches, timing gates, various data logging devices, etc.

Resolution is the smallest change in the quantity being measured (input) of a measuring instrument that gives a perceptible change in the indication.

Errors

Students should be given practice in identifying and distinguishing between random errors and systematic errors. They could be shown a graph of, say, current against voltage where the points are well scattered away from the line of best fit (random errors). The line of best fit should be drawn so that there is still a current when the voltage is zero (systematic error).

Anomalies

Sets of data could be given which illustrate clear anomalies and show the normal variation to be expected. Students should be asked to judge anomalies in the context in which they are presented and not as a strict routine. For example, a range of 10% in the oxygen collected in a photosynthesis investigation is less significant than a 10% range in a resistance investigation, using a multimeter to measure resistance. For this reason it would be useful to present data with which students are familiar. Graphs could be drawn to discover less obvious anomalies.

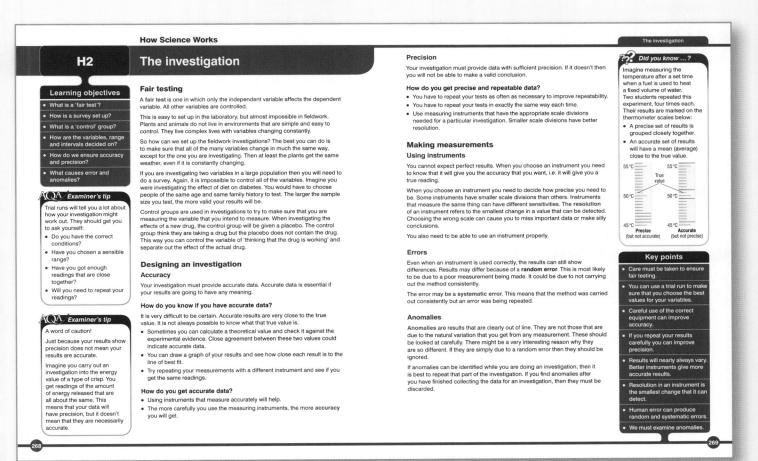

How Science Works

The investigation

H2 — The investigation

Learning objectives
- What is a 'fair test'?
- How is a survey set up?
- What is a 'control' group?
- How are the variables, range and intervals decided on?
- How do we ensure accuracy and precision?
- What causes error and anomalies?

AQA Examiner's tip

Trial runs will tell you a lot about how your investigation might work out. They should get you to ask yourself:
- Do you have the correct conditions?
- Have you chosen a sensible range?
- Have you got enough readings that are close together?
- Will you need to repeat your readings?

AQA Examiner's tip

A word of caution!

Just because your results show precision does not mean your results are accurate.

Imagine you carry out an investigation into the energy value of a type of crisp. You get readings of the amount of energy released that are all about the same. This means that your data will have precision, but it doesn't mean that they are necessarily accurate.

Fair testing

A **fair test** is one in which only the independent variable affects the dependent variable. All other variables are controlled.

This is easy to set up in the laboratory, but almost impossible in fieldwork. Plants and animals do not live in environments that are simple and easy to control. They live complex lives with variables changing constantly.

So how can we set up the fieldwork investigations? The best you can do is to make sure that all of the many variables change in much the same way, except for the one you are investigating. Then at least the plants get the same weather, even if it is constantly changing.

If you are investigating two variables in a large population then you will need to do a survey. Again, it is impossible to control all of the variables. Imagine you were investigating the effect of diet on diabetes. You would have to choose people of the same age and same family history to test. The larger the sample size you test, the more valid your results will be.

Control groups are used in investigations to try to make sure that you are measuring the variable that you intend to measure. When investigating the effects of a new drug, the control group will be given a placebo. The control group think they are taking a drug but the placebo does not contain the drug. This way you can control the variable of 'thinking that the drug is working' and separate out the effect of the actual drug.

Designing an investigation
Accuracy

Your investigation must provide accurate data. Accurate data is essential if your results are going to have any meaning.

How do you know if you have accurate data?

It is very difficult to be certain. Accurate results are very close to the true value. It is not always possible to know what true value is.
- Sometimes you can calculate a theoretical value and check it against the experimental evidence. Close agreement between these two values could indicate accurate data.
- You can draw a graph of your results and see how close each result is to the line of best fit.
- Try repeating your measurements with a different instrument and see if you get the same readings.

How do you get accurate data?
- Using instruments that measure accurately will help.
- The more carefully you use the measuring instruments, the more **accuracy** you will get.

Precision

Your investigation must provide data with sufficient precision. If it doesn't then you will not be able to make a valid conclusion.

How do you get precise and repeatable data?
- You have to repeat your tests as often as necessary to improve repeatability.
- You have to repeat your tests in exactly the same way each time.
- Use measuring instruments that have the appropriate scale divisions needed for a particular investigation. Smaller scale divisions have better resolution.

Making measurements
Using instruments

You cannot expect perfect results. When you choose an instrument you need to know that it will give you the accuracy that you want, i.e. it will give you a true reading.

When you choose an instrument you need to decide how precise you need to be. Some instruments have smaller scale divisions than others. Instruments that measure the same thing can have different sensitivities. The **resolution** of an instrument refers to the smallest change in a value that can be detected. Choosing the wrong scale can cause you to miss important data or make silly conclusions.

You also need to be able to use an instrument properly.

Errors

Even when an instrument is used correctly, the results can still show differences. Results may differ because of a **random error**. This is most likely to be due to a poor measurement being made. It could be due to not carrying out the method consistently.

The error may be a **systematic error**. This means that the method was carried out consistently but an error was being repeated.

Anomalies

Anomalies are results that are clearly out of line. They are not those that are due to the natural variation that you get from any measurement. These should be looked at carefully. There might be a very interesting reason why they are so different. If they are simply due to a random error then they should be ignored.

If anomalies can be identified while you are doing an investigation, then it is best to repeat that part of the investigation. If you find anomalies after you have finished collecting the data for an investigation, then they must be discarded.

Did you know …?

Imagine measuring the temperature after a set time when a fuel is used to heat a fixed volume of water. Two students repeated this experiment, four times each. Their results are marked on the thermometer scales below:
- A precise set of results is grouped closely together.
- An accurate set of results will have a mean (average) close to the true value.

Precise (but not accurate) — Accurate (but not precise)

Key points
- Care must be taken to ensure fair testing.
- You can use a trial run to make sure that you choose the best values for your variables.
- Careful use of the correct equipment can improve accuracy.
- If you repeat your results carefully you can improve precision.
- Results will nearly always vary. Better instruments give more accurate results.
- Resolution in an instrument is the smallest change that it can detect.
- Human error can produce random and systematic errors.
- We must examine anomalies.

268

269

H3

Using data

Presenting data

Tables

Students could be given data in a very poor state of presentation and asked to organise them into a table.

The range of the data

They should identify the range of the independent and dependent variables.

The mean of the data

They should calculate the mean.

Bar charts and line graphs

Decide on the style of presentation of the results. Perhaps using a spreadsheet to illustrate the many different ways for presentation and deciding on the best form.

Using data to draw conclusions

Identifying patterns and relationships

A range of graphs or data for graphs could be given to groups of students. Depending on their ability to use graphs, they could be presented with simple or complex relationships to identify. For example, data relating resistance to current or rate of photosynthesis in relation to light, with a limiting factor of carbon dioxide, or neutralisation of an acid and an alkali.

Drawing conclusions

The group, working together, should produce a considered conclusion that takes into account all of the other possible interpretations of that data.

Evaluation

Students could be asked to draw conclusions about the graphs. They could then be asked questions by other students to establish their justifications for their conclusions. Questions should be phrased to determine the validity, repeatability and reproducibility of the data.

How Science Works

H3 | Using data

Learning objectives

- What is meant by the 'range' and the 'mean' of a set of data?
- How should data be displayed?
- Which charts and graphs are best to identify patterns in data?
- How are relationships within data identified?
- How do scientists draw valid conclusions from relationships?
- How do I evaluate the reproducibility of an investigation?

Presenting data

Tables

Tables are really good for getting your results down quickly and clearly. You should design your table before you start your investigation.

The range of the data

Pick out the maximum and the minimum values and you have the range. You should always quote these two numbers when asked for a range. For example, the range is between ... (the lowest value) and ... (the highest value) and don't forget to include the units!

The mean of the data

Add up all of the measurements and divide by how many there are.

Bar charts

If you have a categoric independent variable and a continuous dependent variable then you should use a bar chart.

Line graphs

If you have a continuous independent and a continuous dependent variable then use a line graph.

Scatter grams

These are used in much the same way as a line graph, but you might not expect to be able to draw such a clear line of best fit. For example, if you want to see if lung capacity is related to how long people can hold their breath, you might draw a scatter gram of your results.

Using data to draw conclusions

Identifying patterns and relationships

Now you have a bar chart or a graph of your results you can begin looking for patterns in your results. You must have an open mind at this point.

Firstly, there could still be some anomalous results. You might not have picked these out earlier. How do you spot an anomaly? It must be a significant distance away from the pattern, not just within normal variation.

A line of best fit will help to identify any anomalies at this stage. Ask yourself – do the anomalies represent something important or were they just a mistake?

Secondly, remember a line of best fit can be a straight line or it can be a curve – you have to decide from your results.

The line of best fit will also lead you into thinking what the relationship is between your two variables. You need to consider whether your graph shows a linear relationship. This simply means can you be confident about drawing a straight line of best fit on your graph? If the answer is yes, then is this line positive or negative?

A directly proportional relationship is shown by a positive straight line that goes through the origin (0, 0).

Your results might also show a curved line of best fit. These can be predictable, complex or very complex!

Drawing conclusions

Your graphs are designed to show the relationship between your two chosen variables. You need to consider what that relationship means for your conclusion. You must also take into account the repeatability and the validity of the data you are considering.

You will continue to have an open mind about your conclusion.

You will have made a prediction. This could be supported by your results, it might not be supported, or it could be partly supported. It might suggest some other hypothesis to you.

You must be willing to think carefully about your results. Remember it is quite rare for a set of results to completely support a prediction and be completely repeatable.

Look for possible links between variables. It may be that:

- Changing one has caused the other to change.
- The two are related, but one is not necessarily the cause of the other.

You must decide which is the most likely. Remember a positive relationship does not always mean a causal link between the two variables.

Your conclusion must go no further than the evidence that you have. Any patterns you spot are only strictly valid in the range of values you tested. Further tests are needed to check whether the pattern continues beyond this range.

The purpose of the prediction was to test a hypothesis. The hypothesis can:

- be supported,
- be refuted, or
- lead to another hypothesis.

You have to decide which it is on the evidence available.

Evaluation

If you are still uncertain about a conclusion, it might be down to the repeatability and the validity of the results. You could check these by:

- looking for other similar work on the Internet or from others in your class,
- getting somebody else to redo your investigation,
- trying an alternative method to see if you get the same results.

AQA Examiner's tip

Poor science can often happen if a wrong decision is made here. Newspapers have said that living near electricity sub-stations can cause cancer. All that scientists would say is that there is possibly an association. Getting the correct conclusion is very important.

Key points

- The range states the maximum and the minimum value.
- The mean is the sum of the values divided by how many values there are.
- Tables are best used during an investigation to record results.
- Bar charts are used when you have a categoric independent variable and a continuous dependent variable.
- Line graphs are used to display data that are continuous.
- Drawing lines of best fit help us to study the relationship between variables. The possible relationships are linear, positive and negative; directly proportional; predictable and complex curves.
- Conclusions must go no further than the data available.
- The repeatability, reproducibility and validity of data can be checked by looking at other similar work done by others, perhaps on the internet. It can also be checked by using a different method or by others checking your method.

H4

Scientific evidence and society

Learning objectives

Students should learn:

- that science must be presented in a way that takes into account the repeatability, reproducibility and the validity of the evidence
- that science should be presented without bias from the experimenter
- that evidence must be checked to appreciate whether there is any political influence
- that the status of the experimenter can influence the weight attached to a scientific report.

Learning outcomes

Students should be able to:

- make judgements about the repeatability, reproducibility and the validity of scientific evidence
- identify when scientific evidence might have been influenced by bias or political influence
- judge scientific evidence on its merits, taking into account the weight given to it by the status of the experimenter.

AQA / Specification link-up: How Science Works

Distinguish between a fact and an opinion, by:

- recognising that an opinion might be influenced by factors other than scientific fact [AS4.5.1 a)]
- identifying scientific evidence that supports an opinion. [AS4.5.1 b)]

Scientific evidence and society

Students should be given a topic to research. They should gather some relevant data. They should be asked to present a case for or against supporting the data. They could be asked to present it to the class, using as many of the key points in the Student Book as possible. They could role-play a scientist or a politician.

For example:

- Data relating the incidence of thyroid cancer in children exposed to radiation at Chernobyl in 1986 as compared to those not exposed.
- The effectiveness of biological detergents.
- Efficient production of a meat product.
- The safety of background radiation.

The limitations of science

Examples could be given of the following issues:

- We are still finding out about things and developing our scientific knowledge (e.g. the use of the hadron collider).
- There are some questions that we cannot yet answer, maybe because we do not have enough repeatable, reproducible and valid evidence (e.g. are mobile phones completely safe to use?).
- There are some questions that science cannot answer at all (e.g. why was the universe created?).

How Science Works

H4   Scientific evidence and society

- Is science always presented in a way that takes into account the repeatability, reproducibility and the validity of the evidence?
- What is 'bias'?
- Why is it important to think about who is providing scientific evidence?
- What are the limitations of science?

Scientific evidence and society

Now you have reached a conclusion about a piece of scientific research, what comes next? If it is pure research then your fellow scientists will want to look at it very carefully. If it affects the lives of ordinary people then society will also want to examine it closely.

You can help your cause by giving a balanced account of what you have found out. It is much the same as any argument you might have. If you make ridiculous claims then nobody will believe anything you have to say.

Figure 1 Some scientists are paid by companies to do research

Figure 2 Be careful in reaching judgements, think about who is presenting the scientific evidence

Be open and honest. If you only tell part of the story then someone will want to know why! Equally, if somebody is only telling you part of the truth you cannot be confident with anything they say.

You must be on the lookout for people who might be biased when representing scientific evidence. Some scientists are paid by companies to do research. When you are told that a certain product is harmless, check out who is telling you this.

?? Did you know ... ?

A scientist who rejected the idea of a causal link between smoking and lung cancer was later found to be being paid by a tobacco company.

AQA Examiner's tip

If you are asked about bias in scientific evidence, there are two types:
- The measuring instruments may have introduced a bias because they were not calibrated correctly.
- The scientists themselves may have a biased opinion (e.g. if they are paid by a company to promote their product).

We also have to be very careful in reaching judgements according to who is presenting scientific evidence to us. An example could be when the evidence comes with some political significance. If the evidence might provoke public or political problems then it might be played down. Equally others might want to exaggerate the findings. They might make more of the results than the evidence suggests.

The status of the experimenter may place more, or less, weight on evidence.

The limitations of science

Science can help us in many ways but it cannot supply all the answers. We are still finding out about things and developing our scientific knowledge. For example, the Hubble telescope has helped us to revise our ideas about the beginnings of the universe.

Figure 3 The Hubble space telescope can look deep into space and tell us things about the Universe's beginning from the formations of early galaxies

There are some questions that we cannot answer, maybe because we do not have enough reproducible, repeatable and valid evidence. For example, research into the causes of cancer still needs much work to be done to provide data.

There are some questions that science cannot answer at all. These tend to be questions where beliefs, opinions and ethics are important. For example, science can suggest what the universe was like when it was first formed, but cannot answer the question of why it was formed.

Key points

- Scientific evidence must be presented in a balanced way that points out clearly how repeatable, reproducible and valid the evidence is.
- The evidence must not contain any bias from the experimenter.
- The evidence must be checked to appreciate if there has been any political influence.
- The status of the experimenter can influence the weight placed on the evidence.
- Scientific knowledge can be used to develop technologies.
- People can exploit scientific and technological developments to suit their own purposes.
- The uses of science and technology can raise ethical, social, economic and environmental issues.
- These issues are decided upon by individuals and by society.
- There are many questions left for science to answer.
- Science cannot answer questions that start with 'Should we ...?'